BJ
464
.446
1996

THEOLOGICAL PERSPECTIVES ON CHRISTIAN FORMATION

a reader on theology and Christian education

COLORADO CHRISTIAN UNIVERSITY
LIBRARY
180 S. GARRISON
LAKEWOOD, COLORADO 80226

THEOLOGICAL PERSPECTIVES ON CHRISTIAN FORMATION

a reader on theology and Christian education

edited by

Jeff Astley
Director
North of England Institute for Christian Education,
Durham, England

Leslie J Francis
D J James Professor of Pastoral Theology
Trinity College, Carmarthen
and the University of Wales, Lampeter

and

Colin Crowder
Lecturer in Theology
University of Durham, England

Gracewing.

W. B. Eerdmans Publishing Company
Grand Rapids, Michigan

First published in 1996
jointly by

Gracewing
Fowler Wright Books
2 Southern Avenue   &
Leominster
Herefordshire HR6 0QF

Wm B Eerdmans Publishing Co
225 Jefferson Ave SE
Grand Rapids
Michigan 49505
USA

All rights reserved. No part of this publication may be reproduced, stored in a retrieval system, or transmitted in any form, or by any means, electronic, mechanical, photocopying, recording, or otherwise, without the written permission of the publisher.

Compilation and editorial material © Jeff Astley, Leslie J Francis and Colin Crowder
Copyright for individual chapters resides with the authors.

The right of the editors and the contributors to be identified as the authors of this work has been asserted in accordance with the Copyright, Designs and Patents Act, 1988

UK ISBN 0 85244 288 2   US ISBN 08028 0777 1

Typesetting by
Action Typesetting Ltd, Gloucester, GL1 1SP

Printed by
The Cromwell Press, Broughton Gifford, Wiltshire, SN12 8PH

Contents

Preface

Jeff Astley, Leslie J Francis and Colin Crowder

Theological Perspectives on Christian Formation: a reader on theology and Christian education is the second volume of a trilogy of readers designed to explore key issues in Christian education. Its companion volume, *Critical Perspectives on Christian Education: a reader on the aims, principles and philosophy of Christian education* was published in 1994 (Gracewing Fowler Wright Books, ISBN 0 85244 254 8), and has been well received by reviewers and readers. A volume illustrating *Psychological Perspectives on Christian Education* is in preparation. These three volumes are offered to promote research and reflection on the theory and practice of Christian education.

The editors believe that the debate about Christian education is best advanced in an interdisciplinary, international and ecumenical context. In particular we have become increasingly aware of the important contribution being made to the field of Christian education during the past two decades through seminal articles published in scholarly journals in the USA, Canada, Australia and Europe, as well as within the UK. Our aim in this trilogy of readers is to re-publish collections of these articles and thereby to make them more readily accessible to a wider readership. In so doing we hope both to advance the quality of scholarly debate about Christian education and to promote good practice and practical application.

The task of editing this reader has been appropriately located mainly within the North of England Institute for Christian Education in Durham, and the Centre for Theology and Education at Trinity College in Carmarthen. Both institutions are church foundations, concerned to undertake research in and promote the development of Christian education.

There is a vast literature on the interrelationship between theological reflection and Christian education. The editors have therefore needed to be highly selective not only about the articles themselves, but also with regard to the range of theological approaches and foundations surveyed and the particular contexts of Christian and theological education considered. Inevitably many excellent papers have been omitted and several significant areas ignored.

In this reader, as in the last, we have been assisted in our editorial task by an international group of scholars who have nominated journal articles from the past twenty-five years or so that they regard as being worthy of consideration. Our thanks are due particularly to: George Brown Jr (Holland, Michigan, USA), Gloria Durka (New York, USA), Edward Farley (Nashville, Tennessee, USA), John M Hull (Birmingham, England), Leon McKenzie (Indianapolis, USA), Allen J Moore (Claremont, California, USA), Mary Elizabeth Moore (Claremont, California, USA), Gabriel Moran (New York, USA), Karl Ernst Nipkow (Tübingen, Germany), Graham Rossiter (Strathfield, New South Wales, Australia), Elmer J Thiessen (Medicine Hat, Alberta, Canada), Michael Warren (Jamaica, New York, USA), Derek Webster (Hull, England), and John H Westerhoff III (Atlanta, Georgia, USA).

We are most grateful to these colleagues for helping us to overcome the inevitable limitations of our own interests, sympathies and knowledge, although the final responsibility for the editorial selection again remains our own. A select bibliography of articles on the theology of Christian education, drawing on these nominations and our own surveys of the literature, is included at the end of this volume.

We also wish to record our thanks to those who helped in the processes of collating resources, compiling materials, checking references, copy-editing text, word processing, and seeking permissions, especially Diane Drayson, Paul Fletcher, Michael Fraser, Dorothy Greenwell and Anne Rees.

Finally, we are again truly delighted that so many internationally renowned authors and publishers have been willing to join us in creating this reader, which is now published to mark the fifteenth anniversary of the foundation of the North of England Institute for Christian Education.

Jeff Astley
Leslie J Francis
Colin Crowder
October 1996

Foreword

Stephen W Sykes

This book will provide the reader with both a comprehensive map of how contemporary Christian theologians approach the tasks of Christian education, and also skilfully selected excursions into the complex terrain. A moment's thought reveals that there are a variety of ways of shaping, or of coming to apprehend the shape of, the subject-matter. What does it mean to be a Christian? What is the Christian's relationship with the church? What is salvation and sanctification? How does one 'grow up into Christ'? A seminary syllabus, a church education programme, a parish study group, or even a course of sermons will presuppose answers to some or all of these basic questions. To be conscious of the issues, and aware of alternative approaches, is a better state to be in than to be at the mercy of unexamined presuppositions.

To be sure there is a robust tradition of Christian education that relies on a combination of piety and common-sense. Augustine's delightful instructions to Deogratias, a deacon of Carthage, on how to prevent catechumens from yawning, looking at their watches, or even falling off their chairs, contains still-applicable hints on teaching technique (*The First Catechetical Instruction*, translated by J P Christopher, *Ancient Christian Writers II*, London, Longmans, 1946). But even at this date, it is apparent that deeper issues are at stake. Augustine's book involves the identification of the central theme of all Christian education, the love of God; it also contains a first delineation of his philosophy of history and teaching on the two cities. At once we see how the processes and procedures of Christian education challenge the teacher to the articulation of an explicit standpoint.

The modern debate about Christian education is intense and many-sided. The skilled editors of this collection have taken very great care to ensure the representation of a variety of points of view, to which they have provided in their initial overview a lucid introduction. Christian educators cannot fail to profit from this helpful book. All teachers, or would-be-teachers should themselves be learners; so that, as Augustine said, learners 'speak in us what they hear, while we, after a fashion, learn in them what we teach'.

Stephen Ely
Bishop's House
Ely
October 1996

Theological perspectives on Christian education: an overview

Jeff Astley and Colin Crowder

Introduction

This overview offers a general introduction to some key aspects of the interrelationship between theological reflection and the theory and practice of Christian education.[1] References to sections and articles in the reader are indicated in brackets.

The nature of Christian education

First we attempt some definition of the term 'Christian education' and the related terms 'spiritual formation', 'theological education' and 'religious education'. 'Christian education' may be defined in a variety of ways (see article 1.1).[2] The phrase is often used quite generally to refer to those processes by which people learn to become Christian and to be more Christian, through their learning Christian beliefs, attitudes, values, emotions and dispositions to engage in Christian actions and to be open to Christian experiences. This learning-change is usually intentionally facilitated by a teacher or educator (see article 1.4). *Christian formation* or *nurture* (see sections 7 and 8) may properly be complemented by another dimension of Christian education: the development in the learners of a critical analysis and evaluation of the church's worldview in the light of their own experience and understanding. This is sometimes described as *Christian criticism* or *critical Christian education*.[3] It often takes the form of a 'rational' or philosophical critique, and is construed in this way in much of the literature on 'theological education' (see below and section 9). But many Christian educationalists advocate a more moral, social and political critique, aligning themselves with liberation educators and liberation and feminist theologians (see sections 5 and 6). This understanding connects with another usage of the phrase 'Christian education', as designating a Christian philosophy, or critique, of general education (compare article 6.2).

'*Spiritual formation*' may be understood as one dimension of religious formation. Spirituality has been defined quite generally in terms of 'those attitudes, beliefs and practices which animate people's lives and help them to reach out towards super-sensible realities'.[4] Many would claim that the fostering of Christian spiritual growth, that is the formation of the Christian learner in the attitudes, values, dispositions, beliefs and other dimensions of Christian spirituality, 'cannot but be a constant concern of Christian educators'.[5] Certainly,

Christianity is a religion that offers to people a set of symbols and stories which affect them. It introduces them to, and 'imposes' on them, certain spiritual values, which they experience as salvific; for it is in commitment to the values of Christian spirituality that a new life is engendered that is seen by the believer both as intrinsically valuable and (therefore?) as salvation. To be Christian, it may be argued, is to have this life; and if Christianity is to be learned in any full sense, this is what must primarily be learned. Spiritual formation and transformation is considered in this reader (in sections 7 and 8) in two rather different contexts: Christian worship and ministerial education.

Although some commentators use the phrase *'theological education'* as synonymous with Christian education, it should properly be reserved for those elements within Christian education that form people in, and enable them to reflect on, Christian beliefs. Christian theology is essentially the coherent, systematic and self-critical articulation of Christian beliefs, whose cognitive content and method (skills and processes), and indeed affective attitudes (dispositions, values and virtues), are learned through theological education (see article 1.3).

However, theological education is a term that is frequently used more narrowly to refer to the theological education of adults in higher education (whether religiously-sponsored or secular) and, in particular, the education and professional training of Christian ministers in seminaries and theological colleges or on ordination courses.[6] (Sections 8, 9 and 10 of this volume draw heavily on the literature generated with reference to these contexts.) But many aspects of this discussion have a relevance that goes beyond the limited concerns of ministerial or theological education.

'Religious education' is a problematic term for two reasons. The first reason is that religious education is routinely used in the United States and elsewhere as synonymous with – or as including – religious formation, and in a Christian context as equivalent to the broad understanding of 'Christian education'. This is made explicit when the phrase 'Christian religious education' is adopted. The second reason is that in Britain and other countries where education about or in religion is accepted as a proper part of the curriculum of publicly-funded schools and colleges, religious education ('RE') is usually reserved for *that* activity. A distinction is then commonly made between (i) a 'non-confessional' (that is, non-formative and non-evangelistic) religious education, whose primary task is educating students about religious traditions ('religious studies'),[7] and (ii) confessional religious nurture, formation or catechesis. Readers need to be aware of these different usages of the term 'religious education' in discussions arising out of different contexts.

The theology of Christian education

In addition to debates about the place of theological beliefs, skills and attitudes in the teaching of the Christian religion, and reflections on the nature and problems of academic and/or 'professional' theological education, this book also includes material that may be described as contributing to the 'theology of Christian education'. There is a considerable literature in Christian education[8] and theological education[9] that is relevant here. This theological reflection on the aims, principles, content, processes, theories, models, problems or practices of Christian education will vary with the type of theology adopted, in terms of particular theological approach, method, emphases and foundations (compare sections 2 to 6).

Among the issues with which a theology of Christian education must deal is the question of the nature of Christianity. This is a theological question, rather than a question that can be answered by the descriptive disciplines of religious studies or the social sciences (including education). Insofar as Christian education theory and practice is concerned with substantive content, it must be concerned with the answer to this normative question.[10]

But some issues are broader than this and lead to questions about the theoretical basis for Christian education. As David Heywood has put it:[11]

> Christian education is a religious undertaking, and as such needs to be informed by theology. Christian education is a form of education, which has its own body of theory, in which the social sciences play a major role. In Christian education, the practices of education and theology meet. Yet what is to be the relationship between them? Is Christian education simply a particular variety of education, or is it a branch of practical or pastoral theology? Which is to be the dominant or foundational 'macrotheory' for Christian education, theology or the social sciences?

The spectrum of possible positions here is wide, from those who would argue for a Christian education primarily construed as a theological discipline (compare article 1.3),[12] to those who reject entirely such a 'theological approach' in favour of one which is determined by the understanding of religion and learning offered by the social sciences (compare article 1.4).[13] Members of the latter group often disavow the claim that they are engaged in a 'theology of Christian education' at all, although their approach has implications for the doctrines of God and of humanity, and our theology of God's relationship to the world.

Theological resources

Differing perspectives on Christian education are shaped, in part, by the kinds of explicit and implicit appeals that they make to the foundations of Christian theology. To understand Christian education, therefore, it is essential to attend to the ways in which educational theory and practice are related, as they often are in the literature, to the bible and to the church.

However, the relation between these theological foundations and the Christian educational thinking that appeals to them is far from straightforward. The recovery of biblical models of education, for example, is complicated by a variety of factors. One of these is that biblical perspectives on education, even when they can be reconstructed, may resist systematisation – in fact, this may well be the whole theological point (see article 2.3). The recovery of traditional Christian educational theories and practices involves parallel difficulties. In both cases, moreover, judgements concerning the authority of the past are bound up with judgements concerning the present: they presuppose some kind of ecclesiology, a vision of what the church is now (see section 3). This means that Christian education must attend to the question of hermeneutics – the theory of the interpretation of texts – and, in particular, to the significance and function of our prior understanding of the subject-matter in question in shaping the results of our reading. Therefore the horizons of our world, of our own experience, are far more significant than the idea of appealing to the theological foundations might at first appear to suggest.

A corollary of this conclusion, perhaps, is that the critical distinction in Christian education is not so much a narrowly confessional one, between a Protestant theological 'style', emphasising the bible, and a Catholic one, emphasising the church, as a distinction between a more conservative approach and a more liberal one, with the latter placing more *explicit* emphasis upon experience. Two ways in which this distinction manifests itself in Christian educational thinking are outlined in the next section of this overview. Important though the distinction is, however, it can help to reinforce the idea that fidelity to the tradition and commitment to the contemporary context are forces essentially opposed to one another, and therefore that the church can only solve 'the crisis of relevance' by precipitating 'the crisis of identity', and can only solve 'the crisis of identity' by precipitating 'the crisis of relevance'.[14]

Several contemporary theological approaches can be interpreted as attempts to move beyond the antithesis between conservative and liberal methodologies. Postliberal theology, for example (see section 4), questions the liberal stress upon experience and the contemporary context, but distinguishes its own understanding of the bible and the church from that of the traditional conservatives. The theologies of liberation, including feminist theology (see sections 5 and 6), which are scarcely theologically conservative, emphasise experience and the contemporary context but reject the idea of a *universal* experience of the modern world. For all the differences between these theological approaches, they both employ sophisticated hermeneutical strategies, and in doing so offer Christian education new ways of understanding its relation to its own theological foundations.

Theological issues

We turn now to reflect on just two of the many specific theological issues that arise within Christian education discussion: the way in which one thinks of God's role in the enterprise in relation to the role of human activity;[15] and the relative value of didactic and experiential models for Christian education in the context of a doctrine of revelation. In each case we will attempt a picture of two extreme options that may be adopted on the topic, and offer a modest proposal for avoiding such polarisation by means of a mediating position.

Many evangelists and Christian educators hold an interventionist view of God's activity. This allows them to affirm not only God's immanent 'presence' through the natural laws of individual and social psychology whereby people learn Christian beliefs and ways, but also particular interventions over, above and beyond these processes. Such a view can lead to the position that the transcendent God is the main Christian teacher and all that human beings can do is to prepare the ground and hope (and pray) for God's unpredictable action. James Michael Lee has disparaged these attempts at what he describes as a 'blow theory' of Christian learning, arguing that the assertion that 'the Holy Spirit blows where it wills' provides us with no explanation, predictions or guidance about either our activity or that of the Spirit (see article 1.4).[16]

Non-interventionism is an ugly name for a popular theological position that denies, or is very sceptical of, all claims about God's anomalous activity within creation.[17] Advocates of this view, if they wish to be consistent, will want to study very seriously the empirical evidence about the natural laws by which people learn, so as to discover how God has so structured the world that people may learn to be Christian. Those who defend such a viewpoint, however, sometimes leave themselves open to the criticism that they encourage a view of Christian education as behavioural manipulation.[18] Denying God the freedom, or claiming that God has denied himself the freedom, to operate other than through natural laws, does not exempt Christian educators from taking account of the unpredictable element of freedom in the learner. This may make the practice of Christian education, and indeed any education, less clear-cut than it first appears. Yet the more traditional 'transcendist' or interventionist approach, while it is certainly more orthodox in refusing to limit *a priori* the activity of God, tends to place its own limits on the human contribution to the processes of Christian education, by undervaluing the role of the teacher.[19] What is the point of *our* working at Christian education, if God's activity is the only activity that counts?

In such discussions about the nature and relative contribution of divine and human activity in Christian education, however, it is important not to polarise the debate. Various mediating positions may plausibly be developed that allow the theological axiom ('God is at work here') without denying either the real responsibility that lies within human action or the contributions of the social scientist to an understanding of the processes of religious learning. Thus one tentative proposal offering a way forward for the interventionist would be to describe our human activity as being *sometimes* a necessary condition for Christian learning; whereas God's (particular) activity is *always* a necessary condition and may sometimes be sufficient to produce Christian learning on its own. But some attempt must still be made to give an account of the link or hinge between the human educator's ('horizontal') work and God's ('vertical') activity.

Moving to our second theological issue, God's revelation, we may note that many theological approaches to Christian education display a highly transmissive view, on which the content of the primordial Christian revelation is handed on from one generation to the next by the teachers of the Christian tradition. This tradition is treated as constituting God's saving Word to humanity, and is often understood in propositional form.[20] Other accounts of Christian education have viewed the role of the bible and the church's tradition rather differently (compare article 2.3). For some, the transmission of the content of the primordial revelation has an instrumental function, serving as a means of precipitating a contemporary personal encounter with God. This revelation may be historically secondary in time but it is of primary significance in the life of the Christian learner.[21] Such accounts give rise to, and need to be informed by, discussions within theology about the use of scripture in Christian believing[22] and the form and content of divine revelation.[23]

Theological liberals are often on the verge of designating as a 'revelation' any learning experience that makes people more humane or gives them a greater insight into reality. They tend to treat all such events as much more significant to the learner, because they actually happen *to* him or her, than the classical Christian revelation that catalyses them. This position, which places most emphasis on what God is revealing in my life now, is often described as an *experiential approach* to Christian education, and fits in well with those parts of Christian education that involve education in personal relationships and other life-skills. It encourages reflection on personal experience and its significance, and focuses attention on the methods of Christian learning rather than its subject-matter content. It thus stands in clear contrast to more conservative, *didactic approaches* to Christian education that understand it in terms of handing on the content of revelation for its own sake.

Again a middle way may be discerned. Increasingly, Christian education has attempted to combine both styles of education by adopting a 'faith translation' or 'interpretation' approach[24] which places great stress on an interpretative dialogue or dialectic between the learners' present experience, insights, needs and concerns and 'The Faith'. Thus Thomas Groome's influential work[25] outlines a method of 'shared praxis' (group reflection on action) in which the learning group (i) critically reflects on its own 'story and vision' (the origins and consequences of its present action); (ii) is presented with the Story and Vision of the Christian community; and (iii) is encouraged to ask 'What does the Community Story say to (affirm, deny, push beyond) our stories and what do our stories say to (affirm, deny, call beyond) the Community Story?'[26] This method at least recognises that all Christian education is a two way process in which the tradition not only challenges our own understanding and experience, but is criticised by them.[27] Even biblical and traditional fundamentalists actually educate like this, for what they pass on to the next generation is the result of their own selective and filtering dialectic. Groome's 'present dialectical hermeneutic' gives every generation the freedom to utilise the past for itself, both by allowing the Christian tradition to work its power on their lives and by testing it against their own experiences. Arguably this may result in a 'contemporary revelation' forged in the crucible of tradition and experience and capable of sustaining the church and moving it on, a learning outcome that many would claim as the main justification for engaging in Christian education at all.

Christian education in context

At the beginning of this overview we noted that 'Christian education' may be defined in a variety of ways. The semantic complexity of the term is the product of several factors, inevitably, but perhaps the most important of these is the way in which the meaning of the term can shift as different educational contexts are considered. In fact it is not only different understandings of Christian education that are contextually determined in this way, but also different approaches to the practices by which Christian educational aims are realised, and different accounts of the theological and pedagogical problems that face Christian educators today.

This reader reflects the contextual factor in a variety of ways. The thesis that the church is the fundamental context for Christian education is not in itself controversial, and it might even be argued that the life of the church simply *is* Christian education (see article 3.1). Ecclesiological reflection upon Christian education, however, is always in danger of a kind of abstraction and idealisation which must be corrected by attention to the life of the churches, as communities with a range of functions and activities. Reflecting upon Christian education in this context and, in particular, in relation to worship, involves paying special attention to the formative aspects of Christian education (see section 7). In the context of ministerial education, in the seminary or the university Divinity School, the critical aspects of Christian education necessarily have a higher profile, and as a result the centrality of spiritual formation in the educational process can no longer be taken for granted (see sections 8 and 9). Finally, in the context of the university as such, where – in practice – the formative is completely eclipsed by the critical, the Christian education debate is transformed into a debate about the place of theological enquiry in the study of religion (see section 10).

There is, however, a 'family resemblance' between all these different understandings and expressions of Christian education. In the articles reproduced below, we trust that readers will experience something of this unity, as well as noting the diversity, of Christian education.

Notes

1. Compare also Jeff Astley, 'On learning religion: some theological issues in Christian education', *The Modern Churchman*, 29, 1987, pp. 26–34, on which some sections of this overview are based, with permission.

2. See also Jeff Astley and David Day, 'The contours of Christian education', in Jeff Astley and David Day (eds), *The Contours of Christian Education*, Great Wakering, McCrimmons, 1992, chapter 1, and Kevin Nichols, 'The logical geography of catechesis', in *ibid.*, chapter 4.

3. See Jeff Astley, *The Philosophy of Christian Religious Education*, Birmingham, Alabama, Religious Education Press; London, SPCK, 1994, chapter 5, and Basil Mitchell, *Faith and Criticism*, Oxford, Oxford University Press, 1994, *passim*.

4. Gordon Wakefield, 'Spirituality', in Alan Richardson and John Bowden (eds), *A New Dictionary of Christian Theology*, London, SCM, 1983, p. 549.

5. David Lonsdale, 'Fostering spiritual growth', in Jill Robson and David Lonsdale (eds), *Can Spirituality Be Taught?*, London, ACATE, no date, p. 79.

6. See the literature cited in note 9 below.

7. See, for example, Ninian Smart, *Secular Education and the Logic of Religion*, London, Faber and Faber, 1968; Schools Council, *Religious Education in Secondary Schools*, London, Evans/Methuen, 1971; Michael Grimmitt, *What Can I do in RE?*, Great Wakering, Mayhew-McCrimmon, 1973, chapter 3; Peter Gardner, 'Religious education: in defence of non-commitment', *Journal of Philosophy of Education*, 14, 1980, pp. 157–168. It should be noted that 'school RE' is often said to have additional aims, including one or more of the following: critical reflection on religious traditions; the formation of moral attitudes such as tolerance; the exploration and development of the learner's own world-view, experiences or sensitivity. See, for example, Bishop of Durham's Commission on Religious Education in Schools, *The Fourth R*, London, National Society/SPCK, 1970, chapter 4; Schools Council Project on Religious Education in Primary Schools, *Discovering an Approach*, London, Macmillan, 1977, chapters 6 and 7; Michael Grimmitt, *Religious Education and Human Development*, Great Wakering, McCrimmons, 1987, chapter 6.

8. See, for example, Sara Little, 'Theology and religious education', in Marvin J Taylor (ed.), *Foundations for Christian Education in an Era of Change*, Nashville, Tennessee, Abingdon, 1976, chapter 3; John H Westerhoff III (ed.), *Who are We? The quest for a religious education*, Birmingham, Alabama, Religious Education Press, 1978; Norma H Thompson (ed.), *Religious Education and Theology*, Birmingham, Alabama, Religious Education Press, 1982; John L Elias, *Studies in Theology and Education*, Malabar, Florida, Krieger, 1986, chapter 3; Jack L Seymour and Donald E Miller (eds), *Theological Approaches to Christian Education*, Nashville, Tennessee, Abingdon, 1990; Peter Jarvis and Nicholas Walters (eds), *Adult Education and Theological Interpretations*, Malabar, Florida, Krieger, 1993; and Randolph Crump Miller (ed.), *Theologies of Religious Education*, Birmingham, Alabama, Religious Education Press, 1995. On the dialogue between Christian education and practical or pastoral theology, compare James W Fowler, 'Practical theology and the shaping of Christian lives', in Don S Browning (ed.), *Practical Theology*, San Francisco, Harper and Row, 1983, pp. 148–166 and 'Practical theology and theological education: some models and questions', *Theology Today*, 42, 1985, pp. 43–58; Don S Browning, 'Practical theology and religious education', in Lewis S Mudge and James N Poling (eds), *Formation and reflection: the promise of practical theology*, Philadelphia, Fortress, 1987, chapter 5; Don S Browning, 'Religious education as growth in practical theological reflection and action', in Mary C Boys (ed.), *Education for Citizenship and Discipleship*, New York, Pilgrim, 1989, pp. 133–162; and Don S Browning, *A Fundamental Practical Theology*, Minneapolis,

Minnesota, Fortress, 1991, *passim*. On the place of Christian education in theological education more generally, see David C Hester, 'Christian education in a theological curriculum', *Religious Education*, 87, 1992, pp. 337–350, and Ronald H Cram, 'Christian education in theological education', *Religious Education*, 87, 1992, pp. 331–336. On the dialogue between Christian theology and school-based religious education (as in a British context), see Leslie J Francis and Adrian Thatcher (eds), *Christian Perspectives for Education: a reader in the theology of education*, Leominster, Fowler Wright, 1990, and Jeff Astley and Leslie J Francis (eds), *Christian Theology and Religious Education: connections and contradictions*, London, SPCK, 1996.

9. In addition to the literature cited in the introductions to sections 1, 8, 9 and 10 of this reader, see also Edward Farley, 'The reform of theological education as a theological task', *Theological Education*, 17, 1981, pp. 93–117; Joseph C Hough and John B Cobb, *Christian Identity and Theological Education*, Chico, California, Scholars Press, 1985; Joseph D Ban, 'Christological foundations of theological education', *Ministerial Formation*, 34, 1986, pp. 12–24; Edward Farley and Barbara G Wheeler (eds), *Shifting Boundaries: contextual approaches to the structure of theological education*, Louisville, Kentucky, Westminster/John Knox Press, 1991; David H Kelsey, *To Understand God Truly: what's theological about a theological school*, Louisville, Kentucky, Westminster/John Knox Press, 1992, and *Between Athens and Berlin: the theological education debate*, Grand Rapids, Michigan, Eerdmans, 1993. On pastoral or ministerial education more specifically, see Allen J Moore, 'Pastoral teaching: a revisionist view', *Quarterly Review*, 3, 1983, pp. 63–76; Joseph C Hough, 'The education of practical theologians', *Theological Education*, 20, 1984, pp. 55–84; Paul H Ballard (ed.), *The Foundations of Pastoral Studies in Practical Theology*, Cardiff, University College, 1986; Don S Browning, David Pok and Ian Evinson (eds), *The Education of the Practical Theologian*, Atlanta, Georgia, Scholars Press, 1989. Literature on theological education that illustrates a more British context includes: Stephen G Mackie, *Patterns of Ministry: theological education in a changing world*, London, Collins, 1969; Donald Mackinnon, 'Theology as a discipline of a modern university', in Teodor Shanin (ed.), *The Rules of the Game*, London, Tavistock, 1972; Stephen W Sykes, 'Theological study: the nineteenth century and after', in Brian Hebblethwaite and Stewart R Sutherland (eds), *The Philosophical Frontiers of Christian Theology*, Cambridge, Cambridge University Press, 1982; Stephen W Sykes, 'The study of theology in university and school', in James Barnett (ed.), *Theology at 16+*, London, Epworth, 1984; and Rupert Hoare, 'Academic theology and ministerial training', in Peter Eaton (ed.), *The Trial of Faith: theology and the church today*, Worthing, Churchman, 1988. Compare also the following occasional papers and reports of the Church of England's Advisory Council for the Church's Ministry (London): *An Integrating Theology* (by Peter Baelz, 1983), *Experience and Authority* (1984), *Education for the Church's Ministry* (1987) and *Ordination and the Church's Ministry: a theological evaluation* (1990).

10. See Jeff Astley, *The Philosophy of Christian Religious Education*, op. cit., pp. 122–123, 133–135, and chapter 6 *passim*.

11. David Heywood, 'Theology or social science? The theoretical basis for Christian education', in Jeff Astley and David Day (eds), *The Contours of Christian Education*, op. cit., chapter 7 (quotation from p. 99). For Heywood's own perceptive analysis of the interaction between theology and the social sciences in Christian education theory, see his *Revelation and Christian Learning*, unpublished PhD dissertation, University of Durham, 1989.

12. See also, for example, Randolph Crump Miller, 'Theology and the future of religious education', *Religious Education*, 72, 1977, pp. 46–60 and *The Theory of Christian Education Practice*, Birmingham, Alabama, Religious Education Press, 1980; John H Westerhoff III, 'Christian education as a theological discipline', *St Luke's Journal of Theology*, 21, 1978, pp. 280–288.

13. In addition to James Michael Lee's works referred to in note 16 below, see also Leon McKenzie, *The Religious Education of Adults*, Birmingham, Alabama, Religious Education Press, 1982, chapter 1, and Harold William Burgess, *An Invitation to Religious Education*, Birmingham, Alabama, Religious Education Press, 1975, chapters 5 and 6.

14. Jürgen Moltmann, *The Crucified God*, ET London, SCM, 1974, chapter 1.

15. Compare also Jeff Astley, 'The idea of God, the reality of God, and religious education', *Theology*, 84, 1981, pp. 115–120. For some reflections on process theology and religious education relevant to this issue, see the literature cited in note 1 of the introduction to section 4 of the present book.

16. See also James Michael Lee, *The Flow of Religious Instruction*, Birmingham, Alabama, Religious Education Press, 1973, pp. 174–180, and *The Shape of Religious Instruction*, Birmingham, Alabama, Religious Education Press, 1971, chapter 9.

17. It is espoused by many liberal theologians. See, for example, Gordon D Kaufman, *God the Problem*, Cambridge, Massachusetts, Harvard University Press, 1972; John Hick, 'Prayer, providence and miracle', in Michael Goulder and John Hick, *Why Believe in God?*, London, SCM, 1983, chapter 4; and Maurice Wiles, *God's Action in the World*, London, SCM, 1986. For a critique, compare Keith Ward, *Divine Action*, London, Collins, 1990.

18. See Didier-Jacques Piveteau and J T Dillon, *Resurgence of Religious Instruction*, Birmingham, Alabama, Religious Education Press, 1977, pp. 148–149.

19. Harold William Burgess, *An Invitation to Religious Education*, op. cit., p. 113 and Ian P Knox, *Above or Within? The supernatural in religious education*, Birmingham, Alabama, Religious Education Press, 1976, *passim*.

20. As, for example, in Johannes Hofinger, *The Art of Teaching Christian Doctrine*, Notre Dame, Indiana; London, Sands, 1962, and *Our Message is Christ*, South Bend, Indiana, Fides, 1974. See also Josef A Jungmann, *Handing on the Faith*, New York, Herder and Herder, 1964.

21. James D Smart, *The Teaching Ministry of the Church*, Philadelphia, Westminster, 1954; Gabriel Moran, *God Still Speaks*, London, Burns and Oates, 1967; Randolph Crump Miller, *The Theory of Christian Education Practice*, op. cit.

22. See, for example, David H Kelsey, *The Uses of Scripture in Recent Theology*, London, SCM; Philadelphia, Fortress, 1975; Edward Farley and Peter C Hodgson, 'Scripture and tradition', in Peter C Hodgson and Robert H King (eds), *Christian Theology*, Philadelphia, Fortress, 1982; London, SPCK, 1983.

23. See, for example, Piet Schoonenberg, 'Revelation and experience', *Lumen Vitae*, 25, 1970, pp. 551–560; Avery Dulles, *Models of Revelation*, London, Gill and Macmillan, 1982; Paul Helm, *The Divine Revelation*, London, Marshall, Morgan and Scott, 1982; Richard Swinburne, *Revelation*, Oxford, Oxford University Press, 1992.

24. Compare Jack L Seymour and Carol A Wehrheim, 'Faith seeking understanding: interpretation as a task of Christian education', in J L Seymour and D E Miller (eds), *Contemporary Approaches to Christian Education*, op. cit. chapter 6, and Jeff Astley and Leslie J Francis (eds), *Critical Perspectives on Christian Education: a reader on the aims, principles and philosophy of Christian education*, Leominster, Gracewing, 1994, section 5.

25. See especially Thomas H Groome, *Christian Religious Education*, San Francisco, Harper and Row, 1980 and *Sharing Faith*, San Francisco, Harper Collins, 1991.

26. Thomas H Groome, 'Christian education for freedom: a "shared-praxis" approach', in Padraic O'Hare (ed.), *Foundations of Religious Education*, New York, Paulist, 1978, p. 30. Similar questions arise in the dialectic between the Christian Vision and the learners' own visions.

27. See also Jeff Astley, 'Tradition and experience: conservative and liberal models for Christian education', in Jeff Astley and David Day (eds), *The Contours of Christian Education*, op. cit., chapter 3 and 'Theology for the untheological? Theology, philosophy and the classroom', in Jeff Astley and Leslie J Francis (eds), *Christian Theology and Religious Education*, op. cit., chapter 4.

1. Theology and Christian education theory

In this section we bring together four articles that approach the relationship between Christian theology and the theory of Christian education in a variety of different ways.

Our first article sets the scene for this debate. Jack L Seymour's 'Contemporary approaches to Christian education' was first published in *The Chicago Theological Seminary Register*, 69, 1979, pp. 1–10. It offers a broad overview of six approaches to Christian education, namely religious instruction, socialisation/enculturation, developmental, liberation, 'educational system' and interpretation. Seymour contends that these approaches are not exclusive, and that useful insights may be derived from a dialogue between them.[1]

In the second article of this section, Karl Ernst Nipkow discusses the relationship between the churches, education and the Christian faith. He suggests a number of reasons why the churches have begun to pay more attention to educational questions, and analyses two patterns or theological paradigms for the dialogue between education and the Christian: the traditional Lutheran 'liberating differentiation' of the two realms of Law and Gospel and the 'deductive integration' that justifies educational statements directly by theological argument. Nipkow's third paradigm, that of 'self-critical interpretation', seeks to preserve the best elements of both and to supply their omissions. This last approach views theology as 'a partner of education' in a relationship of dialogue. 'Theological and educational concepts: problems of integration and differentiation' was first published in the *British Journal of Religious Education*, 1, 1978, pp. 3–13.

Edward Farley's account of the importance of education as 'ordered learning' in the life of the church is complemented by his analysis of the reasons why the vast majority of Christian believers 'remain largely unexposed to Christian learning'. The article offers an account of three themes that underlie this paradox: the professionalisation of theology with the concomitant shift in meaning of the term from a *habitus* of wisdom to a system of doctrines,[2] the inadequacy of the popular homiletic paradigm of Christian education and the broadening understanding of Christian education itself. Farley's article is entitled 'Can church education be theological education?', and was first published in *Theology Today*, 42, 1985, pp. 158-171.

A very different voice in the debate about the relationship between theology and Christian education is to be heard from James Michael Lee. In a trilogy of books,[3] Lee has detailed a 'social science approach' to the teaching of religion (which he terms 'religious instruction') and combatively distinguished it from any sort of theological approach. The article 'Religious education and theology' summarises his criticisms of theological approaches and develops his own position (see the *Overview*). It is an edited version of part of an essay entitled 'The authentic source of religious instruction', which was first published in Norma H Thompson (ed.), *Religious Education and Theology*, Birmingham, Alabama, Religious Education Press, 1982, pp. 100-197 (pp. 121–146, 165–172 and 174–177 are reprinted here).

Professor Jack L Seymour is Professor of Religious Education at Garrett Evangelical Theological Seminary, Evanston, Illinois, USA. Professor Karl Ernst Nipkow recently retired from the chair of religious pedagogy at the University of Tübingen, Germany. Professor Edward Farley is Professor of Theology at the Divinity School of Vanderbilt University, Nashville, Tennessee, USA. Professor James Michael Lee is Professor of Education at the University of Alabama in Birmingham, Alabama, USA.

Notes
1. See also Jack L Seymour and Donald E Miller (eds), *Contemporary Approaches to Christian Education*, Nashville, Tennessee, Abingdon, 1982, especially chapter 1.
2. Among Edward Farley's works, see particularly: *Ecclesial Reflection: an anatomy of theological method*, Philadelphia, Fortress, 1982; 'Theology and practice outside the clerical paradigm', in Don S Browning (ed.), *Practical Theology*, San Francisco, Harper and Row, 1983; *Theologia: the fragmentation and unity of theological education*, Philadelphia, Fortress, 1983; *The Fragility of Knowledge: theological education in the church and the university*, Philadelphia, Fortress, 1988; and 'The tragic dilemma of church education', in Parker J Palmer, Barbara G Wheeler and James W Fowler (eds), *Caring for the Commonweal: education for religious and public life*, Macon, Georgia, Mercer University Press, 1990, chapter 7.
3. James Michael Lee, *The Shape of Religious Instruction* (1971), *The Flow of Religious Instruction* (1973) and *The Content of Religious Instruction* (1985), all published by Religious Education Press, Birmingham, Alabama.

1.1 Contemporary approaches to Christian education

Jack L Seymour

Introduction

Over a century ago in April of 1872, delegates from twenty-two states, one territory and three foreign countries gathered in Indianapolis, Indiana for the Fifth National Sunday School Convention to address the issue of 'Sowing the Seed'. Sessions on the field, the seed, the sowers, the sowing and the harvest of Sunday school work were scheduled. This dynamic, organic image was used to describe the task of education in the church as sowing the seed of God's word into the fertile ground of the learner, and to identify the school of the church, the family, and the ministry of the sanctuary as the sowers who carefully nurtured and pruned the young plant with moral and spiritual guidance until a strong, mature Christian life could emerge.[1]

It has been a long time since such poetic imagery could capture the task of Christian education. In fact the key words used to describe the present situation of Christian education are confusion, loss of direction and frustration of purpose. Both Protestant and Catholic educators speak of a crisis of foundations in Christian education and call for a search for a new identity for the field.[2]

No longer can the unity of the evangelical empire of the nineteenth century, the optimism of Protestant liberalism, or the power of neo-orthodoxy provide a satisfactory base for Christian education. This age is one of theological confusion where religious leaders must search for adequate expressions of Christian faith and where traditional Christian institutions are questioned. Christian educators correspondingly need to search for adequate options for conducting their work in an age of theological pluralism.

Contemporary approaches to Christian education

Six distinct approaches in Christian education have emerged which hold promise of providing such a new foundation for the field. They are the religious instruction, socialisation/enculturation, developmental, liberation, educational system, and interpretation approaches.

The first, the **religious instruction** approach, is the most familiar, most closely mirroring ideals for present efforts to resource the church school, and is in continuity with the history of the Sunday school. James Michael Lee, a Catholic and Professor of Education at the University of Alabama-Birmingham, is one representative theorist.

He believes that 'religion teaching is basically no different from any other kind of teaching. Nor is the learning of religion basically different from any other kind of learning'.[3] Religious education, driver's education, sex education are all education; therefore, the task of the religious educator is to apply the best information in education to the teaching of Christian knowledge, understanding, beliefs, practices and lifestyle. Lee feels, as did many of the ancestors of the church school, that educational theory and methods need to be used fully and effectively in the church.

The key to the effectiveness of this proposal is the religion teacher who structures and controls the student's learning environment and attends to the student's needs and concerns in such a way as to enable the student to 'acquire behaviours which we may legitimately term "Christian"'.[4] While it is argued that both the formal school room and the informal setting, such as a campground, are laboratories for Christian learning where the same educational principles apply, this approach is most clearly adapted to formal school settings.

The religious instruction approach is helpful because it emphasises the importance of educational research for Christian education. It calls for a real professionalisation of Christian education demanding educational skill from teachers and pedagogical competence in curriculum development. For example, Lee says,[5]

> the religion teacher in the field not only ought to be adequately grounded in the science of religious instruction, but also must possess to a sufficiently high level the proficiency skills involved in facilitating religious behaviours in learners.

Nevertheless, past movements to enhance the educational effectiveness of church school work have not seemed to transcend the situation of volunteer structures and leaders. In fact, this approach tends to use secular education as definitive for Christian education, rather than as illustrative for it. While an approach to Christian education needs educational expertise, it also must clearly relate to the realities of church life and the nature of the church.

The second approach, **socialisation/enculturation**, has been heralded by John Westerhoff as a direct alternative to schooling-instruction which he feels has victimised religious education and imprisoned it to secular pedagogy.[6] Thinking to liberate the practice of Christian education, he defines Christian education as 'those deliberate, systematic and sustained efforts of the community of faith which enable persons and groups to evolve Christian lifestyles'.[7] From this definition, the key elements of his community of faith-enculturation paradigm for Christian education can be discerned.

First, the purpose of Christian education is to transmit the Christian faith and lifestyle. Too long, Westerhoff feels, has Christian education been merely concerned with knowledge such as the paths of Paul's missionary journeys, the numbers of Egyptian plagues, or the genealogy of Jesus. Christian education is rather to be concerned with conversion, with persons owning the Christian faith and seeking to fulfil its demands.

Second, such an agenda is only possible when a person experiences an 'intentional, covenanting, tradition-bearing faith community'.[8] Therefore the character of experience one has in the Christian community is most important for Christian education. Westerhoff feels that too often persons have experienced conflicting messages in experiences in the church. For example, a Sunday school may teach the doctrine of the priesthood of all believers, but a pastor and church official board who exclusively make all the decisions contradict that doctrine. Or a spoken commitment to Christian love may be contradicted by a church's closed attitude toward the mixed racial neighbourhood in which it is located. Consequently, church education must be broadened to include 'every aspect of the life of the church'.[9]

Finally, an educator must be deliberate about the various settings for education: the rites, rituals, myths, organisational patterns, activities, actions in the world.[10] The educator's task is to discover the settings within the community of believers which transmit the faith and intentionally use them to call persons to identify with the faith of the Christian community. The three central settings for this transmission are the rituals by which people are incorporated into the church and supported, the experiences persons have within the church, and the actions of the church into the world.

The identification of the many, previously ignored, ways in which faith has been learned in the church community is the strength of this position. While this awareness of the breadth of settings for education is not new, Westerhoff has expanded it and spoken it with such passion that persons have been forced to listen and to take it into account.

The next step in developing his approach is to provide clear tools for organising the interactions persons experience within the community, the worship programme, the fellowship life, the conduct of church business and the budget into a comprehensive programme of education which, parenthetically, realises the necessary role of the school in the church.

The awareness that faith is a constitutive part of human life which grows in a regular pattern is the contribution of the third approach, that of the **developmental** theorists of whom James Fowler of Emory University is representative.[11] While church educators have used developmental language for a long time, Fowler's work has added a theological dimension to psychological research and has described the pathways which persons follow in acquiring faith.

The approach describes the significant personal crises through which persons must pass in acquiring faith, the ways cultural and religious understandings are integrated into a personal perspective on reality, the relatedness of the growth of intelligence, the use of symbols and the building of human relationships, and the means one uses to tell the story of the personal faith journey.

The prime metaphor for the teaching/learning transaction is thus that of spiritual direction. Catholics have long been aware of the importance of spirituality for the Christian life and the necessity of spiritual direction. The great devotional classics of St Francis, of Ignatius Loyola and others have provided powerful models of spiritual guidance. In fact, the heritage of Protestant piety has also taken seriously the need for devotion. Yet, despite the old-time prayer meeting and Wesley's classes and band, Protestants have tended to see devotion as a private activity separated from their public profession of faith and their everyday lives in the world.

The developmental educator recalls that each Christian person has a religious vocation. The concern of spiritual guidance is therefore to appropriately expand the awareness of the person so that the power and will of God may direct and guide. Fowler has begun to present a description of the human side of this journey with the Transcendent, a description of how the faith is emotionally, intellectually and actively expressed and acquired. Spiritual formation needs to be reintegrated into church education.

The contribution of the developmental approach, therefore, is the identification of the particular ways that faith is interpreted at different stages of development and the key points at which faith can impact the lives of persons.

As the developmental approach is concerned about the personal pilgrimage, the fourth approach, the **liberation** approach, is concerned about the pilgrimage of the community of faith. Liberation educators begin with the biblical promise and vision of the kingdom of God – of the city of Shalom.

The mission of the church, issues of social responsibility and social justice, and of freedom and oppression thereby become primary concerns when building curricula or in defining methods. The goal is to enable the church and its members to be faithful to the calling of the kingdom of God; yet, they fear, too often the vision which motivates churches and their members is that of the secular world, rather than the kingdom of God. Persons get lost in the comforts of daily life and the busy-ness of church life, thereby forgetting the unjust distribution of resources and the inequality of life chances. Traditional Christian education is thought to be deficient because it tends to deal with individuals and with content which insulates from the harsh realities of the world.

One liberation educator, Malcolm Warford of Union Theological Seminary in New York, has defined the task of education as 'the continuing praxis of evoking the church's growth as a liberating community and encouraging the development of critical consciousness',[12] and sees their methods as enabling persons to analyse their everyday lives and that of the church, to reflect on their significant actions and commitments, and to define means of direct involvement in social and political structures, thereby transforming the world.

This approach to church education recalls the commitment to mission and to the kingdom which is at the centre of Christian faith and attempts to discover methods of action-reflection which enable the church to be faithful to this commitment.

The **educational system** approach, the fifth, locates the problem of current Christian education in the separation of the church school from the mission of the church and from the other goal-task areas of the church's life; therefore, education is prohibited from properly performing its function of enabling the mission of the church. The important church school questions of curriculum, classroom organisation, teacher training become self-enclosed when the relationship of formal church school education is not co-ordinated with the other education agencies in the church and when the responsibility of the education task in the life of the church remains unclear.

Robert Worley of McCormick Seminary summarises this approach in the following words:[13]

> The whole enterprise of church education has been tilted toward the Sunday school. This selective tilting or focusing of congregational resources to the church school has allowed educators and other church professionals to ignore the educational needs of the total congregation ... The educational tasks which are important for the congregation may be different from the educational tasks associated with the Sunday school. The Sunday school may be only one task area which is important in the congregation. It may suffer profoundly because the other educational tasks have been ignored or neglected ... The target is the congregation and the congregation has educational needs.

Church education is therefore to be the process of co-ordinating the educational settings (or configuration of settings) within the church community for the building of the faith. Basically educators are concerned with the progress of congregational development, of asking how a particular congregation may become more faithful to its mission. In seeking answers to this basic question, educators lead church members to assess personal and church needs, to learn an attitude of Christian discernment in attempting to understand the relationship of God's call to congregational and personal behaviour, and to define procedures to help the church respond to the twin responsibilities of nurture of its membership and of mission in the world. Church education is simultaneously intentional actions to transmit the faith and to build the faithing community.

This, systems educators say, is education in the fundamental sense of that term – helping a church engage in assessing the 'cultural patterns of people, examining and testing them as principles of faith',

	goals	*view of teacher*	Contemporary approaches	
			view of learner	*content*
religious instruction	transmission of Christian religion (understandings and practice)	teacher: a structurer of a learning environment	learner with developmental and personal needs and interests	Christian religion
socialisation/ enculturation	transmission of Christian lifestyles	priest for the community	person struggling to identify with the Christian community	Christian faith and lifestyle
spiritual development	enabling persons to grow in faith to spiritual maturity	spiritual guide or sponsor	person moving through stages of development to maturity	Christian faith
liberation	transformation of the church and persons for liberation and humanisation	colleague	both 'Christian' persons and groups	critical reflection on lifestyle in light of Christian faith
educational system	development of the congregation into a faithful Christian community	congregational developer or manager	congregation seeking to be faithful	means of embodying Christian faith and practice in congregation
interpretation	connecting Christian perspectives and practices to contemporary experience	guide	person seeking to interpret Christianity and experience	Christian story/vision and present experience

in struggling to interpret the word of God concretely, and in working to build a faithful church community.[14] Procedures of Christian discernment/interpretation and Christian leadership are the goals of this approach.

The final approach, the **interpretation** approach, is concerned primarily with how the Christian faith continues to make sense in the modern world. It recognises that Christian faith and Christian institutions are challenged by secularisation and its seemingly impervious faith in human intelligence, human power and human creativity. It also recognises that Christian education has had difficulty in enabling persons to unite their everyday experience with those they have in the to Christian education

settings for learning	*curriculum*	*contribution*	*problems*	*references*
primarily school settings	teacher structures the learning environment to enable the learner to acquire Christian religion	serious attention to the application of educational research to the church	expects a high level of professionalism that may not be present in church setting; biased toward more formal educational settings and the learning of content	James Michael Lee (see note 4)
community of faith	priest assesses enculturation points in the life of a Christian community and exposes 'catechumens' to them (for example, ritual, action, experience)	increases awareness of the community nature of the Christian church and its educational settings	difficulty of intentionally using enculturation structures; apparent assumption that a church community is faithful	John Westerhoff (see note 6)
person's total life	a spiritual guide nurtures a person through significant life crises to grow in faith	definition of the ways faith grown in children and adults	difficulty of assessing stages of development; over-emphasis on the individual	James Fowler (see note 11)
places where Christians involved in the world	colleague dialogues with persons about their everyday life in such a way as to bring to awareness structures of power, alternatives for society and actions for transformation	concern with the church's mission and involvement in issues of social justice and societal transformation	difficulty of dealing with power and change in the church; difficulty of linking present with faith tradition	Malcolm Warford (see note 12)
congregation's total life and ministries	congregational developer enables a church to assess its life and ministries, plan for change, define educational tasks and co-ordinate educational settings	definition of a means of co-ordinating the educational settings within the church	difficulty of co-ordinating a congregation's educational settings; lack of clarity as to how content of Christian faith is learned	Robert Worley (see note 13)
person's total life	guide helps persons analyse the meaning of experience in relation to the Christian story and vision	emphasis placed on discovering the relationships among Christian faith, God's present activity and contemporary experience	difficulty of linking present with faith tradition; difficulty of doing theological reflection on experience	Thomas Groome (see note 15)

church. It is too easy for persons to be Sunday Christians and everyday secularists.

Therefore, the concern of an interpretation educator is to help persons understand their daily experience and hopes in light of the story and vision which is available in Christian faith. Much attention is directed at assisting persons to come to awareness about the meaning they derive from daily experience and its meaning for understanding Christian faith.

One could call this approach theological reflection on experience, but while that name communicates the intent, it does give a false impression of rationalism. Songs, stories, rituals as well as concepts, become ways of unpacking daily experience and seeing it in relation to the Christian story.

Fr Thomas Groome of Boston College summarises this view:[15]

> We are a pilgrim people in whose present is embodied the past of our forefathers and foremothers and the seeds of our future ... The purpose of our education and the ministry of educators is to see to it that the past Story is critically remembered ... recreated and developed in and by present experiences, and the future Vision posed as the purpose and measure of our remembering and creating.

Many of our institutions are suffering from a crisis of meaning, and persons are searching for a foundation of meaning. The interpretation educators struggle to help persons re-mean their experience through a dialogue of Christian faith and contemporary experience, to find God in the world re-meaning it.

Sowing the seed into the 80s

The question now is where do we go from here? The solution for the future is not to take one of the contemporary approaches and remake education along its lines. In fact, the approaches are really not exclusive because each sees the others relating to it in important ways, although the emphases and nuances are very different. For example, the religious instruction approach uses developmental theory in planning curriculum to teach the Christian religion, and for its content is interested in teaching a liberating message and in interpreting the relationship of biblical faith to the modern world. The interpretation approach sees instruction, guidance, socialisation/enculturation, ritual as methods to use in its work of interpretation. The educational system view attempts to co-ordinate the settings described in the religious instruction and socialisation/enculturation views into a method which facilitates the mission of the church and interprets the linkage of biblical faith to present events.

While it is difficult to step outside one's preferred approach, and to see the contribution of the others, it is possible to list insights drawn from a dialogue of the approaches and the history of Christian education, thereby providing directions for the future. Today is a choice point in church education which needs to be taken very seriously.

First, one of the enduring tasks of the church school has been to seek to relate Christian faith to the contemporary spirit and experience. The Sunday school was called the expression of popular Protestantism for good reason. It has always been the place where Christian theology and tradition are interpreted directly to church persons. The evangelical theology of the late 1800s, the spirit of Protestant liberalism, the power of neo-orthodoxy, and the theological confusion of the late 1960s have all been represented in church school curriculum.

In an age with a crisis in meaning, which will continue to be true into the 1980s, the need is to work hard to assist persons to reflect on their experiences and understand them in light of the Christian story and vision. A demonstration of how theological reflection in fact occurs and a struggling to speak the plural theological currents of this time in language which communicates to persons where they live their everyday lives are essential. Educators need to become interpreters.

Second, more than this, ways of assisting persons in their spiritual pilgrimage must be developed. To be a Christian is to be engaged in a religious vocation. Neither can one engage in mission nor adequately express Christian faith unless one is daily open to the guidance of God. A new piety is needed and educators must be at the forefront helping persons reintegrate spirituality into daily living.

Third, in this world where economic and material resources are scarce, and world hunger and political injustice abound, the church and the church school can no longer afford to leave the question of the relation of the church school to mission unclear. A significant and pervading focus of the work of the church must be social justice and liberation.

Church education agencies must give more attention to helping churches understand the significant issues facing this day and acquire methods of action/reflection so as to enable churches for mission and social transformation.

Fourth, the concern for mission will lead directly to reassessing the role of the church school in the church. Rather than teaching individual persons, the prime goal of education will become assisting a church to develop into a 'covenanting, tradition-bearing, liberating, Christian community'. The task of individual growth and learning will only be effectively accomplished within a church which struggles to be Christian.

Therefore, education must concern itself with building a faithing community (congregational development) and enhancing the relationship of education settings within that community. The historic question of the relationship of the school of the church to a holistic programme of education must be solved. The value of the school as an agency in the church must be respected and developed, but the greater task is to understand how the school relates to a broader programme of church education which 'sows the seed', interprets concretely the biblical faith and extends the church's life in mission.

Within the history of the church school, just such an attempt at holistic church education uniting interpretation, spirituality and mission was at one time suggested. But at that choice point, in the late 1920s, and before the approach could be translated into practice, the concerns of educators for staffing and supplying curriculum for the church school, the Depression and the theological revolution of neo-orthodoxy redirected energies. Educational leaders had spoken about the ultimate Christian education objective as building a teaching church, but the same leaders spent their energies on other tasks.

In June of 1930 the International Council on Religious Education meeting in Toronto adopted the motto 'Every church a school in Christian living'. The motto reflected the commitment of the council to the vision of an educating church which reflected and taught in its total life 'the Christian way'. The educational leaders agreed that the goal of church education, to form Christian persons, would not be effectively accomplished until the spirit within congregation was renewed with a sense of mission and call.

But these same leaders chose a strategy to accomplish this end which defeated their purpose. They feared that it would be difficult to communicate this vision to pastors and churches, and out of fear settled for a 'proximate objective'. That proximate objective was the church school. They hoped that if the church school could become 'a school of Christian living maintained and administered by a church', that the broader vision of a teaching church could be realised at a later time.[16] The plan was to build onto the Sunday school the church school and eventually arrive at the school of Christian living.

The last fifty years have demonstrated that that plan was in error. There has been little movement beyond the proximate object. In fact, the vision had almost been forgotten until recently when educators were forcefully reminded of the communal nature of Christian faith and the importance of the mission of the community of faith for education. Today's task is to follow through on the vision of these ancestors – a vision which is rekindled in some of the contemporary approaches.

The educating church, the school of Christian living, must be built. Instead of losing Christian education in a proximate object, a full vision must be built. The school of Christian living is a task concerned with the development of the total ministry of the congregation, not a segmented 'educational' task concerned with one part of the church's life. In making plans for the 1980s, the points of emphasis will be very important. The vision of the learning church and of co-ordinating the ministry within the church to sow the seed of faith must be remembered. Issues of the relationship of mission, of congregational life and of reflecting theologically on experience must be addressed. The direction for church education in the 1980s is to become a pilgrim people on a journey toward God's world of Shalom. To seek to build a community which struggles to be faithful to the biblical vision of Shalom, to contemporary human expression and to the spirit of God acting in the present, is to seek to be the community of faith struggling to embody concretely God's will.[17]

Notes

1. *The Fifth National Sunday-School Convention, 1872*, New York, Aug. O Van Lennep, 1872.

2. Robert W Lynn, 'A little more "know-why", please', in John H Westerhoff III (ed.), *A Colloquy on Christian Education*, Philadelphia, Pilgrim Press, 1972, pp. 180–187; and Berard L Marthaler 'Towards a revisionist model in catechetics (reflections on David Tracy's *Blessed Rage for Order*)', *Living Light*, 13, 1976, pp. 458-469.

3. James Michael Lee, *The Flow of Religious Instruction: a social science approach*, Birmingham, Alabama, Religious Education Press, 1973, p. 269.
4. James Michael Lee, *The Shape of Religious Instruction: a social science approach*, Birmingham, Alabama, Religious Education Press, 1971, p. 74.
5. *Ibid.*, p. 51.
6. John H Westerhoff III, *Will Our Children Have Faith?* New York, Seabury Press, 1976.
7. John H Westerhoff III, 'Toward a definition of Christian education', in John H Westerhoff III (ed.), *A Colloquy on Christian Education*, Philadelphia, Pilgrim Press, 1972, pp. 60–70; here p. 63.
8. John H Westerhoff III, *Will Our Children Have Faith?* pp. 38–42 and 49–50.
9. John H Westerhoff III, 'Framing the future: church education in tomorrow', *The Quill*, 15, 1975, pp. 118–129.
10. John H Westerhoff III, 'A changing focus: toward an understanding of religious socialization', *Andover Newton Quarterly*, 14, 1973, pp. 118–129; here p. 129.
11. James W Fowler, 'Stages in faith: the structural/developmental approach', in Thomas C Hennessey (ed.), *Values and Moral Development*, New York, Paulist Press, 1976, pp. 173–211.
12. Malcolm Warford, *The Necessary Illusion: church culture and educational change*, Philadelphia, Pilgrim Press, 1976, p. 54.
13. Robert C Worley, 'Church education as an organizational phenomenon', in Marvin Taylor (ed.), *Foundations for Christian Education in an Era of Change*, Nashville, Abingdon Press, 1976, pp. 117–126; here p. 125.
14. William W Biddle and Loureide J Biddle, *The Community Development Process: the rediscovery of local initiative*, New York, Holt, Rinehart and Winston, 1965, pp. 243–244.
15. Thomas H Groome, 'Christian education: a task of present dialectical hermeneutics', *Living Light*, 14, 1977, pp. 408–423; here pp. 413 and 415.
16. E Morris Ferguson, *Historic Chapters in Christian Education in America: a brief history of the American Sunday school movement, and the rise of the modern church school*, New York, Fleming H Revell Co., 1935, pp. 172–173.
17. Sections of this article were delivered in an address to the Decision Point: Church School workshop sponsored by the United Methodist Board of Discipleship and held at Scarritt College, Nashville, Tennessee, May 17–19, 1978.

1.2 Theological and educational concepts: problems of integration and differentiation

Karl Ernst Nipkow

Historical background

In modern educational theory and in the associated fields of social sciences, Christian belief and theology play hardly any part. In publications dealing with school curriculum, religious instruction is at best touched marginally. Where in former educational concepts religion had held the central place, we now meet ideas like identity, self-determination, emancipation, creativity, communication, social learning and others.

The time has passed when the truly educated person was identical with the truly religious one. Beginning in the days of European Enlightenment, with some preceding movements in the Renaissance, the amalgamation of Christian, humanistic, idealistic and, above all, national ideas culminated in the nineteenth century, from then on forming an integrated concept that dominated the minds and influenced education, with some restorative come-backs after World War I, and even after the last war. Today, a naïve, simple continuation of a harmonised picture consisting of Jesus and Plato, Luther and Goethe is no longer viable.

And what about any other more modern alliances like those between Karl Barth and Sigmund Freud, Rudolf Bultmann and Karl Marx, Paul Tillich and Karl Popper? To mention these names means to highlight an extremely complex and controversial situation. These controversies can be perceived not only between theologians on the one hand and contemporary or past psychologists, sociologists and philosophers on the other, but also between the various positions themselves, on either side. All these names, and many others too, have been influential on general or religious education with the result that an extremely diversified variety of educational and theological schools have been left behind.

To sum up so far, one can state that first, the traditional forms of integrating Christianity, cultural life and national spirit as well as, correspondingly, religion, education and politics have dissolved. The times of *Kulturprotestantismus* belong to the past. Second, the present situation is pluralistic and heterogeneous, not only in general, but also among the theologians and educationists themselves. Our problem is not that of two clear-cut, homogeneous entities, such as theology here, theory of education there. Third, there is no dialogue between the two

camps in our country. Pedagogy has grown autonomous with no interest or only a marginal one in religion (cf. Nipkow, 1977a).

I do not include in this statement the lasting expectations of many
people towards the churches in their daily life, mainly gathering
around the critical stages in the life-cycle, such as the birth of children, confirmation, marriage and death. Nor do I refer to the
continuing, although mostly hidden, interests of the political powers
in appreciating religious belief and obedience as important factors of
inner appeasement and social control.

What counts here is that the *churches* have lost their position in the
main, official lines of modern educational developments. Their significance has not disappeared, but has been limited to that of particular
social groups among and aside others. The former officialness of their
influence has become private, having been transformed into an influence on matters of personal conviction. Like other organisations, the
Christian denominations today are selling their goods on the marketplace of a liberal, permissive and competitive society.

Under these historical conditions I am neither able nor allowed to
start the topic of the relationships between theology and education on
the side of the latter, saying that the educational sciences need or want
theology, that they have built bridges and developed theoretical
patterns for integration and so forth. All this would be wrong, resting
upon false assumptions. It is the churches that are interested in our
issue, and here we have to begin.

Why are the churches interested in educational questions?

The increased attention paid to educational questions by Christian
educators and, even more conspicuously, by quite a few church officials, is due to several reasons.

First, although most of the church leaders and theologians still
regard the proclamation of the gospel, worship, sacraments and the
spiritual renewal of the local congregation as the church's outstanding
obligatory mandates, they are realising the quantitative explosion of
education, not only in modern society, but also in their own house.
Beside the traditional forms of Christian education in the family, in
Sunday schools, day schools, confirmation classes and youth work,
the churches are shocked by the urgent problems in hundreds of
church-sponsored or church-affiliated schools concerning general
education or vocational training. Furthermore, new emphasis has been
given to adult education (parents' work, lay academies, etc.). In addition, new religious sub- and countercultures have come into existence,
for example, Jesus-people, Asiatic religious influences in marginal
groups (Schibilsky, 1976).

For centuries the issue of education was nothing else than the
narrow approach to catechetics. In the eras of the Reformation and
Protestant orthodoxy in Europe (sixteenth and seventeenth centuries)

and of Pietism and Enlightenment (seventeenth and eighteenth centuries), we merely find a slow development of some techniques of questioning, the so-called Socratic method, linked with a shift to 'natural' and 'Deist' theology being the most remarkable result.

In the nineteenth and early twentieth centuries the rudimentary forms of catechetics gradually became more sophisticated. In the era of liberal theology and *Kulturprotestantismus* the optimistic theological ideas on the religious and moral growth of the individual and on general cultural progress spawned an overwhelming number of educational ventures, but still they were mainly related to religious education in schools.

Barthian theology (Dialectical theology) was a great set-back to this development. The process of individual formation was looked upon as man's fatal attempt at self-edification and even self-redemption. Instead of trusting any longer in the power of (self-) education, now the believer was urged to rely on God's work only. 'The prayer for the Holy Spirit, who calls upon us to believe, is absolutely more important than any methodology' (Heckel, 1928, p. 29): this comment grew to be one of the new leading ideas, although Heckel himself would not have permitted such a neglect of educational methods as was thought to be justified by his statement.

The fact that educational theory in West Germany after the last war did not take much notice of theology (see above) can partly be explained as a complementary reaction to the defensive, indifferent and even hostile attitude of theology itself towards modern philosophies of education.

It is this former marginal attention on the part of the churches to education that has basically changed now. One reason is the mere fact of education's phenomenal expansion everywhere in the '50s and '60s of our century. This explosion of education as a part of the more frequently recognised explosions in knowledge, in technology, in population and in expectations forced itself on the churches' attention by 'the brute size of the phenomenon itself' (*Final Report of the Joint Study Commission on Education*, 1968, p. 6). 'Education has broken into fields where for long its approach was timid and slow' (*ibid.*). In particular it 'has broken out of the class-room' (p. 7).

Second, and even more important because it goes beyond a merely quantitative view, is the qualitative impact of education on church-membership. Church leaders, theologians, ministers and others are coming to understand teaching and learning as not something beside and separate from preaching, proclamation, worship, renewal, *diakonia*, etc., but as an inherent dimension of each of them.

People learn about the church and what it wants to communicate to them by all utterances of the church and how it communicates to them. Furthermore, growth in belief, understood as growing self-perception and personal theological clarity about Christian standards and views, is also dependent on the quality of learning provided in the churches.

In addition, and sociologically speaking, if nominal membership with little personal commitment is to change to acquired membership with high personal commitment, religious adherence to the church has to turn into a reflective one. This, too, cannot be achieved without a general promotion of the level of theological thinking.

The third reason why the issue of education has attracted new and major interest is due to the rather disquieting discovery, well proven by recent sociological research about the variables of church-membership (Hild, 1974; Matthes, 1975; similar results Schmidtchen, 1973), that prolonged and better schooling correlates to a more critical perception of, and to more urgent and progressive expectations of, church-members towards the church itself. Whereas the vast majority of members are rather content with the church as it is – they want and keep to 'the old church', only looking forward to some modest modernisation, not more – the groups of younger and more educated church-members differ significantly. If both variables (earlier age, better education) overlap, the critical distance from the church is greatest.

By these results the church in our country is thrust into a 'learning-dilemma'. On the one hand, as we have seen above in the second reason, it is by theological reflection and improved and prolonged education that the traditional, pre-critical and uncommitted ways of a more or less detached church-membership can be turned into an explicit and reflective engagement. The church's concern for education increases, therefore, and must increase. It is, however, the very nature of progressive education itself which, on the other hand, because of its inherent critical potentialities, threatens the church (as the data of research justify). Is education to be promoted or not? More or less 'conscientisation' (Freire, 1970), that is the question. Is it a question really? The number of people being exposed longer to the rational spirit of modern schooling together with 'life-long learning' (continuing education, recurrent education, in-service training, etc.) will surely and incontrovertibly grow. Therefore, the churches have necessarily to come to terms with education for both reasons given: because of its vital significance for the survival of the churches in a learning society and because of (and despite) its risky character (for more detailed analysis of this 'learning dilemma' cf. Nipkow, 1975, vol. 2, pp. 38–87).

A fourth reason is a very pragmatic one. Unfortunately, many are prone to reduce the whole issue to this point, to a technological use of education, applying educational, psychological and sociological findings to increasing efficiency only. It took a long time for the churches to learn that devising programmes and demanding the implementation of goals without any knowledge about changed conditions and appropriate methods is rather fruitless. Now many theologians and Christian educators try more or less to include empirical research in their deliberations. But the uncertainties about how to do so are great.

Fifth, theology is no empirical science, whereas most educationists regard their discipline as part of the social or behavioural sciences. Thus, one of the aspects of our problem is how to integrate different methodologies. As we see the methodology of behavioural sciences shaping the minds of educators more and more, theology feels obliged to test the effects of a rationalistic and technological approach.

The sixth and last factor by which the churches are prompted to re-define their relationship to education is the number of new and rival philosophies of education today, some leaning on psychoanalysis or on modern forms of humanitarianism (Erikson, Fromm, Rogers) while others follow Neo-Marxism (quite a few in the Third World and in Europe). The Protestant and Roman Catholic churches in the German Democratic Republic are confronted with a Marxist-Leninist ideology in society and education. So are many other churches in Eastern Europe. All over the world the Christian churches are challenged by rival or hostile ideological visions of human life. Furthermore, governments have discovered everywhere the eminent importance of education and schooling for national integration (Faure *et al.*, 1972), preferring for this purpose those ideologies which render the best service in adjusting the young generation.

In this first and smaller portion of my discussion, I have tried to show that our topic is not a purely academic one, nor can it be solved by retreat to academic paradigms. It has its 'seat in life'; it is brim-full of history, it exposes theology and education to a controversial situation; they them-selves are not well-defined and homogeneous entities, but are divided and pluralistic. Last but not least, our issue touches politics, for both sides are deeply involved in the conflict of interests in society. From all of this we may conclude that the problems of 'integration and differenti-ation' are more than merely those between theoretical theological and educational 'concepts'; they are those between church, state and society, too, since theories always mirror practice, the practice of real life. It is in this context that we have to analyse the answers.

Theological patterns of differentiation, integration, and interpretation

As far as I can see, theological answers have been developed up to now along the lines of three main patterns. Each of these has its strengths and weaknesses. The three frames of reference do not exclude one another. The third pattern will try to include the positive aspects of the two preced-ing ones, moulding them into a critical-hermeneutical approach that in my opinion is requisite for both theology and education in our times.

For reasons of space, the following analysis cannot be comprehen-sive. It must be limited to some major perspectives. Moreover, the three headings chosen for the three approaches are tentative and simplifying formulae, not comprising the total complexity.

Pattern one: liberating differentiation

It was an act of human liberation when Martin Luther declared that God justifies the believer simply on the basis of faith and on nothing else, not on anything which a person might attain of himself, either by moral accomplishment or intellectual achievement, not on anything which the church or the state might represent or demand as institutions, and not on anything which might be done by education. This healthy differentiation is expressed by the classical Lutheran theological doctrine of Law and Gospel which can be traced back to Paul. It frees man's mind from anxiously looking at worldly matters as if they were a condition of his justification. There is one thing only essentially needed, and that is belief (*fiducia*), confidence in God's reconciling love. What follows from this?

1. By this experience the Christian is set free to act within that 'realm of God' that has been called the worldly realm 'to the left'. Politics, ethics and education all belong to this side; they are of great importance, but not of ultimate importance.

When pondering on the relations between theology and education today, we should defend this fundamental liberating differentiation. Education in our day is a burden. For many it is a source of continuing frustration and even despair. For others it is a matter of far-reaching expectation and extreme hopes. From the Christian point of view, it is neither. Knowing the difference mentioned opens a way of sobriety in between, beyond the alternatives of pessimism or optimism, of resignation and unrealistic constructions. My first conclusion is, therefore, to look upon the relation between theology and education in an unconstrained attitude of personal relief.

Nowadays, people are living under heavy constraints, self-caused obligations, outer and inner pressures. It is this situation of social and individual coercive restrictions that I should like to call the 'Law' today, opposed to the 'Gospel'. The primary characteristic temptation of our era is not any religious burden as in the days of Jesus, or religious self-torment as with Martin Luther, but it is the achieving society with its relentless standards of competition, higher income, social prestige and hectic consumption. The differentiation between God's work and our work delivers from the Law's captivity those who accept this difference, who 'let it be done'. The educator could be delivered from perfectionist over-activity and over-anxiety, so that he will leave the impossible in order to tackle the possible.

The specific dimension of this approach is the personal one. The proper word of the church, that which expresses the very *proprium* of Christian belief, is the word of the Gospel, addressed to the person. The prime function of the church in the field of education is, therefore, not to devise educational programmes like other ideological educational systems, but to comfort and to encourage the educator himself by opening to him a totally new view upon the task of education as a whole (cf. Asheim 1961, pp. 179, 309).

2. But what about all the numerous practical and political aspects of education? It is wrong to say that the distinction between the two realms of God leaves the secular realm, and so education, to itself. It is God who sustains and helps man in his secular life, including education, by letting him find ways by virtue of his rational and ethical capacities.

It follows that education should be and can be principally governed by educational reason, by the rationale of secular sciences. Martin Luther himself frankly used the secular educational findings of his time, appreciating the new humanistic ideas as reasonable and helpful, nothing more and nothing less. If we apply this position to our situation, we might conclude that theology is principally free to deal with every philosophy of education and every specific result of empirical research. Let me give an example: I myself as a theologian draw much upon my work as an educationist without letting the theologian continuously intrude, since it is not necessary; many things can be solved by scientific analysis and scrutiny alone.

In a recent lecture on the concepts of 'meaningful learning' in general and religious education I tried to combine several lines of instructional concepts and learning theories, Ausubel's concept of 'meaningful receptive learning', Bruner's concept of learning 'by discovery', Wertheimer's and others' approach to 'productive thinking' and 'creative problem-solving', Rogers' ideas on 'personal significant learning', and even Freire's view of education as 'reflection-action-process' of 'conscientisation'. In order to evaluate these positions I generally do not need any theological categories; I use nontheological immanent standards. It is possible (and necessary) to criticise Ausubel by Bruner and vice versa, to add the dimension of 'personal meaning' to that of 'logical meaning' (Ausubel) by drawing upon Rogers, and to question individualistic biases with all of them by looking upon them with the more politically focusing eyes of Paulo Freire.

Following our first pattern, we conclude secondly that theology sets secular research free to relative autonomy. Thus, the freedom of theology to deal with the world and the freedom of the world from theology correspond. In this view, to make the Christian belief known to the world does not mean to Christianise politics, ethics, education, etc., since the Gospel is not something like a detailed Christian system of regulations. Certainly, the autonomy of the world (and of education) is only relative. There is no complete separation between the two 'realms'. We will see later on, and we have already pointed out, that from the side of the Gospel the Christians have to interfere and to appeal to the world. Nevertheless, one remarkable result remains: a detailed tutelage has to be abandoned. A clerical imperialistic dominance on the secular school has to be given up. Our Protestant churches in West Germany have done so, although hesitatingly. At one of the most famous synods after the last war, at Berlin-Weissensee (1958), the churches redefined their role as rendering 'a free service to a free school' (cf. Flitner, 1959).

I have added the word 'hesitatingly'. Why? The description of this first theological paradigm cannot be finished without remembering its well-known faults and grave failures in the past.

3. In a way, in the Lutheran theological tradition, the secular world has indeed been left to itself, particularly in the field of politics. The political institutions were on the whole either regarded as Christian authorities or at any rate as God's instruments in sustaining a fallen mankind, preserving them from greater chaos. Even if governments and their educational systems had to be questioned, it seemed better to support them by the church than to let the general political order be shattered by revolutionary ideas. It was not the left-wing groups of the Reformation that took the lead in the European Lutheran countries, but the conservative interpretations of Christian political ethics. Pious enthusiasm ('Pentecostalism') was considered a greater theological evil than the reproach of quietism. Thus, this first pattern used to endorse conservative educational concepts.

4. A related weakness was the preoccupation with individual piety and the lack of understanding of the rigid reality of institutions. A typical Lutheran Christian educator of this tradition is inclined to trust primarily in the renewing power of the mental and moral gifts of the individual. That the task of humanising an educational system might require a change of structures is of subordinate interest. This point leads to the last.

5. The struggle against a false mixture of 'Law' and 'Gospel' (the latter being God's word to man in the soteriological dimension and no instrument of ruling nations and educating them) has not prevented Lutherans from taking sides in education and in politics. But apart from doing so generally in a conservative way, as already mentioned above, the 'vicarious service' rendered to the world is mostly described in rather general, if not vague terms, as it is typically phrased in sentences like these of Siegfried Hebart (Wiencke, 1970, p. 23):

> The church must love, exhort, warn and counsel, help, watch, show pastoral concern, conduct a dialogue, and place its own insights and experience in the field of education at the disposal of all who are responsible for guiding and formulating educational policies.

The nature of a personal approach on the level of pastoral care is quite evident. Furthermore, it is characteristic that the details of education are left to the rational principles which govern it (*ibid.*). The challenge of education by theology is concentrated upon the one thing that counts, 'the radical question of what man is and what is his purpose' (*ibid.*). All these elements are reasonable and necessary as we have seen above. It is dissatisfying, however, that because of objections in principle to any further elaboration of educational categories and standards, named as 'Christian' ones, this Christian stance lacks concreteness. Certainly, there is much truth in the position proposed. Is education for love and peace a 'Christian' educational concept? Or what about education for social engagement, for ecological responsibility, etc.? The proponents of our first pattern would deny that these are specifically Christian. Therefore, we must turn to a second theological pattern to avoid the Christian vagueness of the first.

Pattern two: deductive integration

There are situations when not only individual Christians, but also the churches as collective bodies, are obliged to manifest their Christian identity as a whole, when, as it were, the existence of the church in the two realms of God comes together into one unshared confessing identity.

In this perspective a church body, a group of Christians, or an individual Christian educator advocates a specific educational issue, though of a thoroughly secular nature, in the name of Jesus Christ. There is no longer any differentiation between the proclamation of the Gospel on the one hand and worldly educational deliberations on the other. To be in favour of this or that political and educational concept and to be against another one is regarded as a part of the necessary, authentic act of proclamation, here and now, and is therefore included in it. You can also express this point from the other end. The appropriate witness to the living God requires this political or educational engagement, here and now, and nothing else.

From the last point of view this theological paradigm can be described as 'deductive': educational statements are straightforwardly derived from basic assumptions of belief. From the complementary point of view, mentioned before, you may call this procedure 'integrative', as secular standpoints are picked up and included in the theological view; educational positions are directly justified by theological arguments (not only by their own rationality as with pattern one). What is to be valued in this approach of 'deductive integration'? Where can we approve, where not?

1. The second pattern puts education under the close and direct appeal of a theological perspective, be this directness of approach expressed as affirmation or radical criticism.

As a first example of this, in a resolution of the Evangelical Church of Germany (Synod Frankfurt/M., 1971), we read a harsh attack upon a society and a schooling system that are one-sidedly bound to the standards of competitive achievement with relentless social selection. This criticism is justified as a compelling implication of the Christian conviction that God respects every person to the same degree regardless of any differences in intellectual achievement or social status (Kirchenkanzlei der Evangelischen Kirche in Deutschland, 1972).

As a second example, the motto 'Jesus Christ frees and unites' has been interpreted as being incompatible with alienating educational structures, as obliging Christians to vote for a liberating educational process (see Paton, 1976, pp. 86–93).

In all these cases Christians say 'no' or 'yes' as Christians, paying their witness in concrete educational decisions or in other decisions (political, economic, ethical), demonstrating by this theological direct-ness and secular concreteness two things: first, that the direct theological deduction shall express the lordship of Jesus Christ; second, that this 'lordship of Christ as king' is of absolute validity and significance everywhere. No part of human life is to be left to itself. The light of the gospel has to shine upon everything, and so upon education.

2. This theological approach refuses the opinion (pattern one) that the Gospel (as different from Law) is valid only in 'God's kingdom to the right' and, correspondingly, without direct implications for concrete directives in 'the kingdom to the left'. A separation of the two kingdoms (realms) is avoided; instead of this, the unity of God's sustaining and saving acts is expressed, the identity of God as the creator and the redeemer. The light of reconciliation falls upon all creation. Therefore, Christians have to say what the Gospel is good for, not only for the salvation of the inner person, but also for a fuller life of the whole person; not only for individual reconciliation with God, but also for peace between nations, classes and races, including the change of power structures. The report of the Nairobi assembly (Paton, 1976, p. 45) states:

> In confessing Christ and in being converted to his lordship, we experi-ence the freedom of the Holy Spirit and express the ultimate hope for the world. Through his true and faithful witness Jesus Christ has set us free from the slavery of sin to the glorious freedom of the Spirit. Within the vicious circle of sin, death and the devil are the vicious circles of hunger, oppression and violence. Likewise, liberation to justice, better community and human dignity on earth is within the great freedom of the Spirit, who is nothing less than the power of the new creation.
>
> We regret all divisions in thinking and practice between the personal and the corporate dimensions. 'The whole gospel for the whole person and the whole world' means that we cannot leave any area of human life and suffering without the witness of hope.

By this second paradigm, the character of the wholeness of God's gracious revelation, directed upon the whole life of man in all its dimensions, is expressed much more adequately.

In the recent discussion on religious education in our Protestant churches in West Germany, this approach which owes much to Barth and his different followers (above all Gollwitzer and Moltmann) has become widely influential. In a most conspicuous way the theology of the ecumenical movement and the World Council of Churches, particularly since the '60s (see Goodall, 1968), has been shaped by this 'Christ-centred' and 'society-orientated' approach. The 5th Assembly of the WCC at Nairobi (Paton, 1976) has renewed it ('Jesus Christ frees and unites'), although in some respects a noteworthy theological revision has taken place (see Nipkow, 1978).

To be more accurate in my survey I have to add that in the last decade this approach has also contributed considerably to the reshaping of the classical Lutheran pattern. Today, in many respects, both patterns are being integrated, the one drawing upon and correcting the other (see Wiencke, 1970).

This approach requires critical correction for several reasons.

3. Taking sides in politics and education in the theological directness which is characteristic of this approach – and it includes the declaring of very specific educational positions as being 'Christian' as well as excluding others – might be thoroughly adequate as authentic witness of an individual believer or of a group of committed Christians who have to go this way, or even a path of a revolutionary educational strategy, as they are confronted with brute oppression in their country. However, what if they force other Christians to see it the same way? What if official declarations of church authorities intrude upon all their members one particular educational interpretation of what the Gospel means? The reproach of the Gospel being transformed to a new Law is not very far off.

4. The following objection refers to the danger of a new usurpation of secular sciences. Although the true understanding of our second pattern requires us to distinguish most carefully between confessing Christ and propagating church politics, refusing the latter, it is difficult not to take the one for the other in reality. Direct theological deductions can arouse suspicion; they might easily block any further dialogue with educational and social scientists; they irritate already because of the mere language.

5. The last objection relates to the New Testament itself, questioning the possibility of drawing conclusions from the Gospel in such a concrete manner as it is assumed. The proponents of our second approach are used to refer to the Holy Spirit who 'will lead us into all truth'. 'Which are the concealed "auxiliary" hypotheses and interpretations, brought in "from the flank", that actually lead to the conclusions?' the opponents will legitimately retort.

Pattern three: (self-) critical interpretation

The last question has put us right in the middle of our final theological paradigm. The two preceding frames of reference are better known. This third is rather new. Its theological background cannot be highlighted by mentioning names of great theologians. Its intentions, however, can be briefly summarised: first, to preserve the positive aspects of the two approaches above, second, to add elements that are lacking.

1. We cannot drop the fundamental, liberating differentiation between Law and Gospel with its subsequent releasing of man to a free life in this world and a free application of secular educational knowledge (see above pattern one, 1 and 2), nor are we allowed to abandon the courage and directness of approaching the world by confessing Christ, by taking sides and by 'seeing education whole' (WCC, 1971): religious and general education, the individual and the group, personal growth and the transformation of structures (see above pattern two, 1 and 2).

By integrating both ways theology becomes a partner to education in a 'dialectic dialogue' which, by the way, ought to characterise practical Christian education too. What are its elements?

First, there is a basic openness to secular education, theoretically and practically, accompanied by a committed interest in communicating the Christian experience of God by distinct and concrete educational realisations, not by vague appeals.

Second is a fundamental care for theological clarity in order to avoid any unacceptable mixture of what is relevant to salvation and what is not, accompanied by the necessary and unavoidable responsibility in the world, even by getting involved in the very detailed complexity of educational and political issues.

Third is the conviction that the belief in Jesus Christ does not justify any theocratic thinking in education and politics, accompanied by the readiness to anticipate 'God's kingdom in daring acts', 'showing now something of the newness which Christ will complete' (Goodall, 1968, p. 5).

By this double-sided, dialectic approach, the theologian, when discussing with the educationist, will affirm here, contradict there. He will not defend a closed religious or educational system, and if his partner does so, he will deny the legitimation of it. He will instead co-operate in an attitude of certain uncertainties, trusting to new truth by learning from each other, yet also gratefully remembering the trustworthy truth that he has already experienced.

2. Why can we not end with this? What is lacking is best demonstrated by a brief exemplification. I take it from one of my own major fields of study.

In a discussion on moral development and the education of conscience, one theologian emphasises what he thinks to result from rational educational theory 'in the realm to the left'; he votes for an education that makes students feel deeply responsible for the given social order, sensitive to anything that might violate it. A second theologian opposes; he demands that the students' consciences be made sensitive to the oppression exercised by this same social order. He explicitly shows his support for the political opposition in his country. He justifies his stance by witnessing to the risen Lord, in the name of whom Christians, as he explains, have to advocate life against death, freedom against unfreedom. This, then, has presented the example, simplified for the purpose of showing the following open questions.

The first theologian thinks his educational view is free of a theological bias, since he explicitly refuses to derive it from the Gospel itself; he believes he follows reasonable educational reflection only. Actually, however, he interprets the issue of conscience from a concealed theological bias by shaping the relation of Law and Gospel in a specific way, stressing the importance of the Law more than that of the Gospel. Parallel to it, this theological bias induces him to favour conservative views of politics and education. It even may be that those secular views are the primary motives, shaping his theological ones.

The other theologian does not hide his direct theological deduction. His possible self-deception is that he overlooks, not his theological intentions which are explicitly conceded, but his concealed secular interpretations that have influenced his view, which may be any liberal or socialist traditions. The interdependence may run the same way as with his partner, either his secular interpretations operating as selective filters for his theology or vice versa.

To sum up so far, we see that neither approach sufficiently provides for the fact of intervening interpretations. There is no purely rational, 'worldly' approach in the realm to the left (pattern one), nor a purely theological deduction in the realm to the right (pattern two). Furthermore, there are always theological and non-theological interpretations operating by way of mutual influence. It is often extremely difficult, for one's own reflection and for others, to reveal true motives and leading ideas. Some pretend to be theological, although actually they are non-theological and vice versa. Let us call this the hermeneutical self-deception concerning hidden ideological backgrounds. We cannot completely represent our whole being in our consciousness (Apel, 1971, p. 38). Our 'hermeneutical experience' is 'ambiguous' (Bormann, 1971). Many things are operating through us, as it were, from behind our backs.

The character of the third pattern is now evident. We are forced to enter a very difficult and lengthy process of critical interpretation. Or more precisely, we have to acknowledge the fact that statements on education, made by theologians (and by educationists as well), are always human interpretations (even if they refer to 'revelation'), which by their nature are permanently subject to ideological self-deception. It follows that the characteristic function of our third approach is to interpret interpretations. This, however, requires much more than the usual business of hermeneutics (for example, [self-] understanding); it demands (self-) critical analysis of social and mental factors by which what cannot be 'understood' might be 'explained'.

It is obvious that this aspect of the third approach can be applied both to theological and educational concepts. Moreover, we have to see that such a 'hermeneutical-critical theory', as I should like to put it, is not primarily founded on theological insights. It was developed in the Federal Republic some years ago in the discussion about the methodology of social sciences, in the so-called *Positivismusstreit* (Adorno, Habermas *vs.* Popper, Albert) and in the subsequent discussion on the relation of hermeneutics and *Ideologiekritik* ('criticism of ideology', ideology=false consciousness) (cf. Apel, 1971). Some roots of the so-called 'critical theory' go back to Marxist criticism as far as structural economic biases and antagonisms are concerned.

Although this approach is not primarily based on theological assumptions, it should be theologically acceptable. This can be shown. Any questioning of pseudo-certainties contributes to openness; true theology, however, is a continuing critical endeavour to open man's search for truth to God's truth.

3. As a final step I should like to display the meaning of the phrase 'to interpret interpretations' from a specific angle. To do this we must move from the critical aspect of a 'critical-hermeneutical' approach to its hermeneutical aspect.

If we realise what is required to relate theological and educational concepts with regard to the example above, the origin and development of conscience, we hit upon many psychological, sociological, and anthropological findings: Freud's theory of the super-ego, Piaget's and Kohlberg's theories on the sequential stages of moral development, Kant's rationalistic idea of the conscience as an 'inner courtyard', Heidegger's existentialist view on conscience to be felt as a dark, prerational appeal, the Roman Catholic doctrine of synteresis, etc.

As to the educational aspect we meet a lot of additional results, more or less proved, for example, concerning the correlation of conscience to parental techniques of discipline ('power-assertive', 'conditional love', 'inductive', cf. Hoffman and Saltzstein, 1967), or concerning the development of 'empathy' as one precondition of 'consideration for others' (Flavell, 1966; Bork, 1973, etc.), or referring to the unconscious processes of 'identification' (Mitscherlich, 1963).

What I want to say is that all these different scientific concepts relate to man's pre-scientific experiences with conscience: Freud's observations and experiences which led to his construction of a 'super-ego' with its character of rigid, unconscious coercion were shaped by the authoritarianism of the nineteenth century. The view of conscience as experienced by others differs. Mitscherlich outlines the elements of a 'living, flexible' conscience, 'open to transformation' (1963). As human beings we are able to share these experiences; and as educators we are influenced by them. As Christians, however, we make experiences with our experiences (Jüngel, 1974, p. 122). By these double-sided experiences we should re-interpret our interpretations.

To interpret interpretations of life and of educational issues by relating to them (not intruding upon them) Christian experiences, seems to me one of the major future tasks as far as the dialogue of theology and education is concerned. The non-theological experiences and interpretations should not be left to themselves, accompanied with a general Christian warning or encouragement only (pattern one). Nor will a straightforward witness 'from above' be sufficient, even if it takes the shape of very practical and distinct positions (pattern two). In the one case we are running the risk of Lutheran quietism, in the other of theological 'short circuits'.

The third approach of (self-) critical hermeneutics, on the other hand, attempts to proclaim the gospel not by a one-way appeal, but by a dialogue. Dialogue requires a patient exchange of views and interpretations. The educational concepts of today – education in search for identity and self-reliance, or the struggle against alienation and oppression and for peace and social justice – call for theological interpretation. How is 'alienation' to be related to 'sin'; 'identity' to Christian 'confidence'; 'peace' to Christian 'reconciliation'; 'emancipation' to 'redemption' and so forth? By the exchange of interpretations both sides are touched, the classical theological symbols of Christian experience are also to be assessed and re-phrased.

As to conscience, Christians have their experiences with the haunted bad conscience as well as with the relieved. The first is usually interpreted in the perspective of the Law, the second in the light of the Gospel. However, looking upon Paul's records of the troubles he had with the Corinthians, we might learn that the Christian attitude should neither be the glorification of the scrupulous, bad conscience on behalf of the 'Law' (separated from Gospel), nor the haughty neglect of the 'weak' on behalf of a 'strong' conscience. For Paul, conscience always is the liberated conscience for others, bound in love (1 Corinthians 8 and 10, Romans 14). Thus, educational concepts of interpreting 'authority', 'obedience', 'self-determination' and 'consideration for others' are specifically re-interpreted.

Does the theological interpretation of non-theological interpretations result in a doubling of statements? Sometimes the conclusions drawn are very similar, since non-theological and theological criteria have a common history. In other cases the judgements differ remarkably; the radicalism of the Christian way of questioning (which must not be mistaken for a stubborn, dogmatic way) reveals boundaries and opens a new horizon (for a detailed analysis of the issue of conscience, see Nipkow, 1977b; for all three approaches and their application to religious education, see Nipkow, 1975).

What is the advantage of our third pattern? What are its deficiencies? One thing is unavoidable: mere theological interpretations do not solve educational problems as far as political power-structures or ideological conflicts of interest are concerned. Furthermore, the matter of interpretation by its very nature includes pluralistic divergencies, one of the most serious inner-theological controversies today being that between the proponents of a more conservative and a more liberating interpretation of the biblical truth.

On the other hand the third approach, by keeping the best of the two preceding patterns (1), by transforming theology into a self-critical theory (2), and by opening a room for mutual exchange of interpretations (3), changes traditional theology considerably. It becomes a partner of education that neither intrudes upon nor conceals its truth, but tries to make it understandable in a secular world.

References
Adorno, Theodor W, *et al.* (1969) *Der Positivismusstreit in der Deutschen Soziologie*, Neuwied, Berlin, Luchterhand.

Apel, Karl-Otto (1971) 'Scientistik, Hermeneutik, Ideologiekritik', in *Hermeneutik und Ideologiekritik,* mit Beiträgen von K O Apel, *et al.*, Frankfurt/M, Suhrkamp, pp. 7–44.

Asheim, Ivar (1961) *Glaube und Erziehung bei Luther,* Heidelberg, Quelle and Meyer, (Pädagogische Forschungen. Veröffentlichungen des Comenius-Instituts, Bd. 17).

Bork, Helene (1973) 'The development of empathy in Chinese and American children between three and six years of age: a cross-culture study', *Developmental Psychology,* 9, pp. 102-08.

Bormann, Claus von (1971) 'Die Zweideutigkeit der hermeneutischen Erfahrung', in K O Apel *et al., Hermeneutik und Ideologiekritik*, Frankfurt/M, Suhrkamp, pp. 83-119.

Faure, Edgar, *et al.* (1972) *Apprendre à être*, Paris, Libraire Fayard.

Final Report of the Joint Study Commission on Education (1964–1968) (1968) Geneva, WCC and WCCE.

Flavell, John H (1966) 'The development of the related forms of social cognition: role-making and verbal communication', in Aline H Kidd and Jeanne L Rivoire (eds), *Perceptual Development in Children,* New York, pp. 256-260.

Flitner, Andreas (1959) *Die Kirche vor den Aufgaben der Erziehung,* Heidelberg, Quelle and Meyer (Pädagogische Forschungen. Veröffentlichungen des Comenius-Instituts, Bd. 9), here Wort der Synode der EKD zur Schulfrage, pp. 19-21.

Freire, Paulo (1970) *Pedagogy of the Oppressed,* New York, Seabury.

Goodall, Norman (ed.) (1968) *The Uppsala Report 1968* (official report of the fourth assembly of the WCC), Geneva, WCC.

Heckel, Theodor (1928) *Zur Methodik des Evangelischen Religionsunterrichts,* München, Kaiser.

Hild, Helmut (Hg.) (1974) *Wie Stabil ist die Kirche?* Bestand und Erneuerung. Ergebnisse einer Meinungsbefragung, Gelnhausen, Berlin, Burckhardthaus.

Hoffman, M L and Saltzstein, H J (1967) 'Parental discipline and the child's moral development', *Journal of Personality and Social Psychology,* 5, pp. 45-57.

Jüngel, Eberhard (1974) 'Metaphorische Wahrheit. Erwägungen zur theologischen Relevanz der Metapher als Beitrag zur Hermeneutik einer narrativen Theologie', in Paul Ricoeur and Eberhard Jüngel, *Metapher: zur Hermeneutik religiöser Sprache*, München, Kaiser.

Kirchenkanzlei der Evangelischen Kirche in Deutschland (EKD) (Hg.) (1972) *Die Evangelische Kirche und die Bildungsplanung,* Eine Dokumentation, Gutersloh, Gerd Mohn, Heidelberg, Quelle and Meyer.

Matthes, Joachim (Hg.) (1975) *Erneuerung der Kirche.* Stabilität als Chance? Konsequenzen aus einer Umfrage, Gelnhausen, Berlin, Burckhardthaus.

Mitscherlich, Alexander (1963) *Auf dem Weg zur Vaterlosen Gesellschaft,* München, R Piper.

Nipkow, Karl Ernst (1975) *Grundfragen der Religionspädagogik*, Vol. 1: Gesellschaftliche Herausforderungen und theologische Ausgangspunkte, Vol. 2: Das pädagogische Handeln der Kirche, Gütersloh, Gerd Mohn (2nd edition, 1978).

Nipkow, Karl Ernst (1977a) 'Erziehung und Unterricht als Erschliessung von Sinn. Zum Gespräch zwischen Erziehungswissenschaft und Religionspädagogik in der Gegenwart', *Der Evangelische Erzieher,* 29, pp. 398–413.

Nipkow, Karl Ernst (1977b) 'Gott und Gewissen in der Erziehung', in Martin Hengel and Rudolf Reinhardt (Hg.), *Heute von Gott reden,* Mainz, Grünwald, München, Kaiser, pp. 83–113.

Nipkow, Karl Ernst (1978) 'Alienation, liberation, community: the educational policy of the

WCC before and after Nairobi', *The Ecumenical Review*, 30, pp. 139–154.

Paton, David M (ed.) (1976) *Breaking Barriers: Nairobi 1975* (official report of the fifth assembly of the WCC), London, SPCK.

Schibilsky, Michael (1976) *Religiöse Erfahrung und Interaktion*, Die Lebenswelt jugendlicher Randgruppen, Stuttgart, Berlin, Köln, Mainz, W Kohlhammer.

Schmidtchen, Gerhard (1973) *Gottesdienst in einer Rationalen Welt*, Stuttgart, Freiburg.

Wiencke, Gustav K (ed.) (1970) *Christian Education in a Secular Society*, Philadelphia, Fortress Press.

World Council of Churches (ed.) (1971) *Seeing Education Whole*, Geneva, WCC.

1.3 Can church education be theological education?

Edward Farley

Introduction

How is it that the Christian faith, committed as it is to relate faith to reality, world, knowledge and learning, continues to restrict this relating to its ordained leadership and to withhold it from the laity? Why is it that education in the congregation and for the believer at large is so conceived that it has little to do with the disciplines and rigours of ordered learning? Why is it that *theological* education, ongoing studies in disciplines and skills necessary for the understanding and interpretation of Scripture, doctrines, moral principles and policies, and areas of praxis, defines something needed by Christian clergy but never by Christian laity? In the face of the modern democratisation of education and learning, how is it that the church continues to settle for the pre-modern pattern of educated clergy and uneducated laity and for the almost uncrossable gulf between theological (clergy) education and church education? The persistence of this pattern is an anomaly in a religious tradition which repudiates obscurantist modes of faith and prizes learning. This article will explore both sides of this anomaly; that which impels Christian faith to take education (ordered learning) seriously, and the subterranean moves in the church's history which produced the restriction of ordered learning to clergy education.[1]

Faith, wisdom and ordered learning

Why is 'ordered learning' (education) an important undertaking in the Christian church? If we take this to be a *historical* question, we ask how does something born in the migrations of an ancient, nomadic and tribal people, and at the bloody scene of a crucified Jew and the fiery tongues of Pentecost, end up with classrooms, degrees, libraries, universities, Sunday schools and teaching elders? History provides a rather obvious answer, but we should not be too quick to embrace it. History says that education comes from the Greek side of our civilization's ancestry. Once the Christian movement became a permanent occupant of the ancient world and not just a temporary house guest, it took this Greek idea into itself. We can add to this historical explanation the sociological insight that any movement which is to survive over time must discover means of transmitting itself to future generations. Thus, we find teachers listed by Paul as embodying one of the gifts (charismata) which ordered the life of the church.

However, we need to resist explaining the presence of ordered learning in early Christianity by simply citing the hellenistic side of our heritage. Something like education had been going on in Israel and Judaism long before the Christian movement. The Septuagint used the Greek word *paideia* to translate the Hebrew word which meant to nurture, discipline, chasten. This discipline and nurture occurring in the Jewish family was the background for the Psalmist's description of God chastening or disciplining the people. When Judaism arose, developing a new institution of social survival and religious life in the diaspora, ordered learning as the study of Torah occurred with special teachers (rabbis) in a special place (the synagogue). The early Christian movement did not repudiate this tradition. It modelled its own congregations on the synagogue, proposed teachers for those congregations, and in one gospel applied the term 'rabbi' to Jesus himself. We conclude that the self-conscious transmission of the tradition by teachers is a deeper and older part of the Christian heritage than simply its roots in hellenistic culture.

Faith and reality

These observations of the continuity of early Christianity with its Jewish background account for the presence of ordered learning in Christianity only by means of historical influence and sociological utility. But education as a mere social necessity can be prompted by a movement's desire to perpetuate itself, and self-perpetuation can have the character of mere propaganda and ideology. We are, therefore, prompted to press our question in a different way. Is there something about the very nature of faith as an existence in the world before God which founds in the community of faith an inclination and seriousness about ordered learning? Two issues call for exploration at this point: faith and *reality* (truth), and faith and *theology*.

We are familiar with criticisms of religion as such and of Christian faith which argue that faith turns the human being away from reality. Faith, thus, is an opiate, a soporific. And there is plenty of documentation throughout the history of Christianity to support such an argument. Yet one of the recurring notions in the writings of Israel is the warning against deceit. 'Deceit' and 'deceive' do not name simply occasional and specific acts of trickery or telling lies, although these things are not excluded. These words describe, rather, a posture of the heart, something virtually synonymous with sin itself. In deceit, human beings are not just telling lies, but are themselves a kind of lie, a living deception. Another term found frequently in both Israel's writings and early Christian literature is the word 'truth'. Like the word deceit, truth does not name something trivial or occasional, whose opposite is an error or mistake. Truth too is a posture of the heart. It is something which comes from God who corrects deceit and redeems the heart. 'Send out thy light and thy truth. Let them lead us.'

And in Paul truth is both something that evil suppresses and that poses the issue of what is properly worshipped. A third term is 'wisdom', the central theme of Proverbs. Wisdom too is a matter of the heart, the very centre and depth of the human being. 'Teach me wisdom in my secret heart', says the Psalmist. Wisdom is constituted by awe, fear, knowledge of the Lord. Its opposite is not simply cleverness or the retention of information.

This language of deceit, truth and wisdom attests to something very central in faith as a mode of existence before God. The fundamental brokenness and alienation of the human being is a darkened posture of the heart and mind which orients the human being toward everything in the mode of deception and self-deception. Born from this darkened posture are trickery, lying, dishonesty, intellectual dishonesty and reality denial. Since these things attest the absence of the presence and grace of God, truth and wisdom are matters of redemption. With redemption comes a new posture of the heart, a wisdom founded in God, directed toward everything: to the other human being, nature, the self, the world in its perils and in its beauty. This is why faith has the opposite dynamics from an opiate. The corruption of the human being turns it away from reality, impels it to exploitative, oppressive, destructive relations with nature and other persons. All these acts are reality-indifferent and reality-destructive. If redemption liberates from these things, its effect is an opening up to reality, a seriousness about what is and what occurs, an interest in the autonomy, integrity, and even beauty of the world.

The second issue is the relation of faith and *theology*. Because of the unfortunate history and present connotations of the word theology, we are tempted to discuss this issue in other terms. However, the argument of this article is that the ordered learning (education) occurring in congregations should be theological education. Hence, faith's relation to theology is a central issue. What history has done to the word 'theology' is reduce its meaning to its objective referent (a system of doctrines, beliefs), and then narrow its locus to the specific school and scholarly enterprise which deals with doctrines. Given this objectification and professionalisation of the term, theology becomes the possession of schools and of a group of scholar-teachers in schools. These narrowings are now so stamped on the church and even the schools that the rescue of the word is highly unlikely. We can, however, attempt to recover the older meaning of theology for the purpose of understanding why ordered learning may be a concern intrinsic to faith itself. In this older sense, theology was not just the scholar's possession, the teacher's trade, but the wisdom proper to the life of the believer. This presupposed that faith (as a mode of existence before God) was not simply an emotion or feeling but included a kind of knowledge. Faith was a practical knowledge having the character of wisdom because it had to do with the believer's ways of existing in the world before God.

Because faith is a response to grace and redemption, thus grounded in the event and person of Jesus of Nazareth, the wisdom of faith has a certain natural structure. First, it has a ground or basis, something which evokes it, makes it possible. And this something is not simply grace in general, but grace as it has disposed history and a community. This is why one of the directions theology (wisdom) faces is toward its past heritage or tradition: the events, imagery, history through which grace is experienced. The believer's wisdom is, then, a perpetual appropriation and interpretation of this heritage. Second, wisdom is concerned with tradition neither simply in an antiquarian way nor in the idolatrous sense of absolutising tradition, but through its orientation toward truth and reality. Hence, faith's interpretation of the vast and complex Christian heritage or tradition is always critical, assessive, appropriative. It is never merely passive or reality-indifferent interpretation. Third, the believer's wisdom always occurs in the acual, contemporary setting of the believer's existence. Existing in that setting freely, responsibly, joyously, constitutes the situation of the believer. Hence, a third dimension of wisdom or theology is the interpretation of that setting in its various dimensions. This, too, is why faith's wisdom is not simply directed to the past. Tradition, truth and contemporaneity mark the ever-present aspects of theology or the believer's wisdom. Theology in this sense is a mark and task of faith as an existence in the world before God.

Faith and ordered learning

What do faith's orientation to reality (truth) and to theology (wisdom) have to do with ordered learning or education? Two extreme versions of faith's relation to learning need to be avoided. The one identifies faith with knowledge (*gnosis*); the other expels knowledge from faith altogether. A corrupted form of the Catholic version of the latter sees existence before God as a perpetual process of penance addressed to moral consciousness and action and assisted by the church's sacraments. A corrupted form of the Protestant version sees existence before God as a religio-moral piety taken more or less directly from the texts of Scripture interpreted in preaching. Insofar as both versions do expel knowledge and learning from faith, they presuppose that faith's wisdom can be formed in relation to the imagery and events of tradition, the issue of truth, and the press of the situation apart from the faithful person's own struggles, disciplines and insights. Thinking and insight are thus assigned to an elite leadership whose interpretations and cognitions occur above and on behalf of the believer. Insofar as the believer has insight or understanding, it is unrelated to knowledge and the sort of knowledge ordered learning addresses.

It goes without saying that anyone who participates in a living community is constantly formed by its inherited imagery and shaped by its normative events. We would not then dispute the valid point that the believer's wisdom is formed in deep social processes which are 'means of grace'; thus, proclamation, sacraments, intersubjective intentions and acts, liturgy, and the structures of ecclesial organisation and action.[2] But existence before God in the world is not simply an utterly spontaneous, pre-reflective matter. Human existence in the world, even in the mode of faith, is always a linguistic and interpretive existence. Uninterpreted responses are unassessing responses, and they turn the responder over to victimising causalities which exploit mere passivity and spontaneity. The refusal to assess a past heritage absolutises that heritage as something unhistorical and beyond corruption. The failure to interpret critically situations in the present makes the believer passively subject to them as if they were norms, untouchable powers. This is the primary reason why existence in the world before God requires a wisdom (theology) which is not merely spontaneous but is a self-conscious interpretive response. The complexity, power and corruptibility of reality itself sets this requirement.[3]

Reality does not mould itself to the wishfulness of human desire or the interiority of felt emotions. It places demands on human response and interpretation. Its complexity does not disappear in the face of human simplification. Its power to corrupt does not suspend itself before human innocence or indifference. Reality means the way things are as they are able to affect other things. The intent of the doctrines of faith is to describe realities. Great social systems and epochs of those systems are reality. The enduring relation between a man and woman in marriage is reality. If faith is an existence in the world, it cannot avoid being a response to and interpretation of reality, as inherited tradition and as present challenge. And these responses and interpretations are those of the believer himself or herself whose wisdom is not simply another's wisdom, even if it occurs in connection with the wisdom of others in the community of faith. Few would disagree with this. But because this wisdom has to do with reality, it cannot avoid the rigours and disciplines which reality evokes. This is why there is a *telos*, an impetus in faith itself to appropriate whatever is available to it to assist its responses, its interpretations and its insights. This is the deeper reason why the Christian faith's repudiation of obscurantism and its positive relation to ordered learning is not a mere accident of historical influence. Something about faith itself, the faith of the believer, creates an orientation to reality and, therefore, to ordered learning, a summary word for disciplined efforts to equip the believer to interpret reality.[4]

So far we have argued that faith involves a kind of wisdom and that wisdom itself as reality-related involves ordered learning. We have said little about what 'ordered learning' is. Generally speaking, it refers to the institutions or processes of culture which communicate to its members the products and methods of interpreting that culture's version of reality in its various dimensions. Hence, there is an ordered learning in ancient and modern Judaism, in ancient Greece, in the Middle Ages in Europe, and in the public education movements of modern times. However, since the Enlightenment, ordered learning has a more specific connotation. The Enlightenment represents a massive shift in the history of ordered learning which the church ignores at its peril. This shift is not simply from pre-modern to modern cosmologies or from an age of politically established religious faiths to an age of secularity and religious toleration. Enlightenment means a shift in the ways of knowing, enquiring, and relating cognitively to the world. According to this new cognitive posture, everything which presents itself for being understood and for enquiry is part of a larger system or process of relations and events. And cognition and understanding are responsible to go as far as evidence permits in grasping things in their relations, backgrounds, and historical and natural causalities. All contemporary sciences take this posture for granted. The posture combines both the principle of appropriate evidence and the principle of historical-natural relationality (relativity). From the viewpoint of this posture, nothing which presents itself for understanding is immune from the demand for evidence and from relationality to other things. Affected by this posture is not just scientific method in general but historical method as it would reconstruct the past, deal with ancient texts, and interpret past authorships. And all the refinements of method which have occurred since the Enlightenment presuppose this posture, including contemporary hermeneutics, social scientific analyses, and phenomenology.

The Christian church has responded and adjusted to this cognitive posture of the Enlightenment piecemeal and with continuing ambivalence. This ambivalence is manifest in the continuing conflicts between 'evangelical' and conservative groups (both Catholic and Protestant) and liberal and revisionist groups. In most schools for clergy education in mainline denominations, the methods of criticism reflecting the cognitive posture of the Enlightenment are taken for granted. Hence, several generations of clergy have been educated in methods of interpreting Scripture, church confessions, doctrines and moral issues which acknowledge the historical character and relativity of these things. Because this is the case, 'ordered learning' has now the specific connotation of the Enlightenment cognitive posture. Ordered learning in our day is not simply identical with Greek *paideia* or the catechesis of earlier Christian times. The ordered learning of clergy education takes for granted the principles of evidence and relationality throughout all the so-called theological disciplines.

This development adds a new dimension to faith's wisdom and the need of wisdom for ordered learning. The critical posture of the Enlightenment is available to the believer as something which assists the interpreting response to reality. This includes the believer's interpretation of the tradition or Christian heritage, the appraisal of its truth, and the relating of such to situations. The logic which presses faith toward wisdom and ordered learning impels that learning toward the cognitive posture of the Enlightenment. For that is what our epoch has made available to the believer in the ongoing struggle with reality.

Educated clergy, uneducated believers

We are exploring the mystery of educated clergy and uneducated believers as a structure in the life of the church. The one side of the anomaly is the presence of ordered learning throughout the church's history and the 'logic' which propels faith toward reality and thus to ordered learning. The other side of the anomaly is the church's failure to take seriously the education (ordered learning) of the believer. Why is it that the vast majority of Christian believers remain largely unexposed to Christian learning – to historical-critical studies of the bible, to the content and structure of the great doctrines, to two thousand years of classic works on the Christian life, to basic disciplines of theology, biblical languages, Christian ethics? Why do bankers, lawyers, farmers, physicians, homemakers, scientists, salespeople, managers of all sorts, people who carry out all kinds of complicated tasks in their work and home, remain at a literalist, elementary school level in their religious understanding? How is it that high school age church members move easily and quickly into the complex world of computers, foreign languages, DNA and calculus, and cannot even make a beginning in historical-critical interpretation of a single text of Scripture? How is it possible that one can attend or even teach in a Sunday school for decades and at the end of that time lack the interpretive skills of someone who has taken three or four weeks in an introductory course in bible at a university or seminary?[5]

A defensive reaction to these questions will point to the religious and Christian education movements with their sophisticated literatures, the profession of specially trained Christian educators, the thousands of devoted teachers throughout the church's Sunday schools, the carefully designed denominational curricula arriving month after month and year after year as attestations of the church's seriousness about the education of the believer. Such evidences only deepen our mystery. In the light of all *that*, how can it be that the majority of Christian believers remain theologically uneducated? This gulf between theological education as ordered learning and 'education' in the church is not a surface or trivial phenomenon, but part of the deep structures of the church's self-understanding. It involves, therefore, fundamental assumptions about faith, theology, learning and education. The question as to why this gulf persists is a historical question, but its answer does not lie simply in a 'history of church education'. Instead, we must pursue history in the sense of certain formative presuppositions which effected and now maintain this gulf between theologically educated clergy and non-theologically educated laity.

At the deepest level of all is the ambivalence the Christian movement has always had about the importance of learning, knowledge and the sciences. These things have been in the church in some way almost from the beginning. At the same time, medieval Christendom's treatment of Galileo and Bruno, the debates over geology and evolution, and the two century-long hesitancy to embrace post-Enlightenment historical methods all testify to the fact that the church, as someone has said, had to be brought kicking and screaming into the modern world. Continued debates over evolution and creationism remind us that the kicking and screaming have not ceased but may even be escalating. This ambivalence suggests that deceit, the violation of intellectual honesty, the resistance to reality, and the fear of truth are all very much with us and always will be. They manifest the dialectic of corruption and redemption which will always characterise the church militant.[6]

A second stratum which accounts for the absence of ordered learning in church education is the social structure of earlier Western societies which restricts learning to the elite classes. Here, learning is posited as a single entity to either be pursued or not pursued. In Charles Dickens' world, ordered learning showed one to be a 'gentleman' or 'gentlewoman'. In a social world where classes are relatively fixed, learning is for the few – royalty, aristocracy, clergy, physicians, lawyers. This correlation between learning and elite classes would reinforce the gulf between educated clergy and uneducated believer. It does not, however, account for the persistence of that gulf. The reason is that we live in a time which has embraced the democratisation of learning. We now assume that public education communicates rudiments of history, mathematics, literature, natural sciences. With certain exceptions, church education is offered to a population educated in these rudiments. However, the churches still offer an 'education' which fails to be ordered learning. Hence, it perpetuates the older assumption that ordered learning *with respect to matters of religion*, its texts, history, beliefs and practices, is not a possibility for the believer. We must now probe beneath these two general strata of our past historical ethos to uncover the specific formative presuppositions which have created this gulf.

What follows is an unavoidably selective attempt to uncover these formative presuppositions. Three themes illumine the mystery of this gulf: the professionalisation of 'theology', the homiletic paradigm of the way faith occurs, and the generalising of the meaning of education. All three of these presuppositions were also historical movements which found embodiment in institutions which assure their social persistence: namely, institutions of the seminary or theological school, the act of preaching performed by educated clergy, and the religious (Christian) education movement.

The professionalisation of theology

Formative in the gulf between theological education and church education is the gradual narrowing of the concept of theology and the attendant location of theology in the university.[7] For over a thousand years (until the eighteenth century), the word theology referred to a wisdom or sapiential knowledge of God. This does not mean there was utter agreement on the basis and nature of this knowledge. There were mystical versions (Pseudo-Dionysius, Bonaventure), scholastic versions (Thomas Aquinas) where this knowledge had the character of demonstrated conclusions, biblicist versions where the knowledge was a knowledge of God mediated through God's written word. All agreed, however, that theology was a kind of knowledge, a *habitus* or disposition of the believer. Viewed this way, *theologia* was a part of Christian existence as such. Even the distinction between lower and higher levels of this knowledge was a distinction offered to the believer *qua* believer. It was not a distinction between priests and laity, scholars and non-scholars. The story of how theology came to mean something else is a long and complex one. This story includes the rise of universities in Europe and the move of theology into the university as a university science. It includes a shift in Protestant schools in the seventeenth century in which theology named not a disposition or wisdom but the referent and content of that disposition, and thus became a term for doctrines, beliefs, or systems of beliefs. Once theology is located in the schools which educate clergy, it becomes an umbrella term for the cluster of sciences or disciplines which organise that education. In a final narrowing, theology moves from a general term for 'clergy sciences' because it is identified with one of them, namely systematic or doctrinal theology. Once this narrowing takes place, theology is expelled even from the clergy, the ordained leaders, and is restricted to teacher-scholars who preside over clergy education or over one of its fields. The result of this long process of narrowing is that clergy education and theology become correlative. The school of clergy education is the primary location of theology, and fields (or one of them) pursued in that school define what theology itself is, a scholarly discipline.

One can see immediately how this shapes the church's posture toward the education of the believer. Whatever education in the church is, it cannot be theological education since that is what clergy study in schools designed for their training. Church education, if it exists at all, must therefore discover some other meaning of education than education which is theological. Since the theological school as a post-college seminary is an enterprise of ordered learning appropriating (at least in its ideal sense) the best resources of learning which are available, education in the church as non-theological education must formulate itself in some other way than ordered learning. Further, because education in the church must differentiate itself from theological education, and therefore from theology, it is unable to appropriate the original meaning of theology as wisdom, discipline, and interpretation of tradition, truth and situation. It is thus unable to appropriate the ordered learning which theology as wisdom requires. Church education must carve out some niche for itself separated from wisdom and the need for ordered learning.

The homiletic paradigm of how faith occurs

The church has never questioned the importance of the 'formation' of the believer. What the gulf between theological education and church education presupposes is that ordered learning is not important for that formation. Ordered learning, then, is needed by the ordained leadership in its special role and not by believers as they exist in the world before God. This presupposes either that faith has nothing to do with wisdom and the knowledge of the tradition in its truth for the situation, or there is such a wisdom important to faith but it does not require ordered learning. Earlier I argued that faith as existence in the world before God does entail theology or wisdom. More characteristic of the church's position is the second alternative. There is a wisdom proper to faith, but it does not require education in the sense of ordered learning. In addition to the narrowed understanding of theology, a second pervasive presupposition operates to support such a view, namely the homiletic paradigm of the way faith is formed.

According to this paradigm, faith is primarily formed and nurtured in the weekly liturgical event of churchly life. According to the Protestant version, this event centres on proclamation and the sermon. Therefore, the sermonic liturgical event is the primary resource for the believers' knowledge of tradition and interpretation of situations. Central to this homiletic paradigm is the Protestant Scripture principle. The imagery, symbols, history, events and normative figure of tradition are located in and mediated by the texts of Scripture. Proclamation, then, is an act which discovers some route from text to sermon, and the corporate event of this preaching is the decisive and sufficient way the faith of the believer is formed.

Homiletic, valid and important as a moment in the church's worship, is inadequate as a comprehensive paradigm of the way the believer's existence in the world before God is effected and disciplined. In its claim to be sufficient, the homiletic paradigm subverts the very structure of the reflective wisdom of the believer. It does this by reducing the relation of the believer to the tradition or heritage of faith to a relation to texts and by its assumption that exposition of the authoritative text settles the question of truth. Further, its method of 'application' of text to life vastly simplifies and even replaces the complex tasks of interpreting and reflecting on situations. In other words, the homiletic paradigm telescopes and reduces the situation of the believer and violates the nature of faith's wisdom by repressing its elements, requirements and tasks. The reason this paradigm buttresses the gulf between theological education and church education is that it requires ordered learning for the proclaimer, the one who struggles with the texts, doctrines and the problems of interpretation and application, and withholds ordered learning from the process of faith itself. The believer's wisdom, if it is granted at all, is viewed as a passivity shaped by proclaimed and applied texts, and hence does not have the character of a disciplined reflection in constant struggle with tradition, truth and situation. As a passivity, it is released from the deliberate enquiry and thinking expected of seminary-trained clergy.

At first sight, the homiletic paradigm appears to be a hierarchical version of faith's formation. In fact, it is not. The products of the church's learning and scholarship are not in fact communicated, 'passed on' to the laity. Clergy, not laity, are sometime recipients of ongoing theological scholarship. What is it then, which *is* passed on in the sermon? Insofar as a traditional version of the authority of Scripture is dominant, with each discrete text viewed as a unit of *a priori* truth or applicability, the text must be mined for whatever *can* be applied or made relevant to the hearer. That about a text which does lend itself to application tends to be its moral content, its lesson for life, its consolatory (therapeutic) power. Hence, what is mediated to the believer tends to be the tradition of piety or morality, which, in more recent times, has taken a therapeutic turn. It should be clear why the homiletic paradigm is one of the powers of history which prevent church education from being theological education. Insofar as the transaction between believer and the sermon event is regarded as sufficient to faith's formation, ordered learning for the believer is dispensable.

The generalising of the meaning of education

The inadequacy of the homiletic paradigm has not gone unnoticed in the church. The history of education in the church since the nineteenth century describes attempts to correct and supplement that paradigm. At the same time, the corrective movements, religious education and Christian education, have presupposed and also fostered the gulf between theological and church education. Assuming that church education cannot and should not be theological education, and offering severe criticisms of catechetic-instruction education, the literatures and institutions of twentieth-century church education so expanded the very meaning and definition of education as to create a fundamental genre equivocation.[8] Desiring to correct both the homiletic paradigm's claim to be sufficient to faith's formation and the catechetical paradigm for how the tradition is taught, these movements began to treat education as a term for the total social formative process in which faith originates and is nurtured.[9]

Few would dispute the valid insight that the homiletic paradigm is an inadequate account of this process. Nor would many dispute the claim that everything the church does in its inner and outer mission has 'educating' (influencing, formative, nurturing) effects. However, once 'education' comes to mean simply that, two serious consequences occur. First, education as ordered learning is no longer under consideration as *the* meaning of education. More specifically, education in its usual and ordinary sense is suspended. This is what this article has been calling ordered learning, and it refers to self-conscious attempts, usually in a corporate setting, to transmit by means of a sequential process of disciplined didactic activity both the insights and deposits of the past and the methods and modes of thought and work which enable new insights. The elements of education in this ordinary sense are teachers, students, sequential cumulative learning, appropriate discipline.[10] Once education comes to mean a community's total formative process, virtually its sociology of knowledge, this ordinary meaning disappears and a different *genre* and phenomenon altogether is under consideration.

The second consequence of this change of genre is a new positive agenda for the literature, 'discipline' and guild of Christian educators. Once education's genre meaning is generalised, ordered learning is identified as one of many 'approaches' to or interpretations of education.[11] As an 'approach', it exists in the debates of a guild and a literature, and becomes a literary phenomenon. The absence of ordered learning in church education is hardly noticed since 'education' now means something else. The new positive agenda which this creates is a 'search for Christian education' in the sense of a total formative, socialising, existentialising process. This search explores Christian education (total formative ecclesial process) as a possible academic discipline, its relation to 'theology', the educative (formative) effects of liturgy, social action and Sunday school, and the stages of human development in relation to formative process. It should not be necessary to say that these explorations are not only legitimate but crucial. Perhaps the great contribution of the twentieth-century church education movement is just this focus on the elements of ecclesial process. However, when education itself is generalised to mean formative process, the long-held assumption that ordered learning is not for the believer is perpetuated.

There are, of course, elements in the church's institutional life which seem to have to do with ordered learning. Modern churches are unambiguously committed to buildings, educational spaces, advanced degrees, teachers, directors and curricula. Because of these elements, the churches offer what appears on the surface to be a genuine educational undertaking. However, it is, curiously, an undertaking minus the essential elements of ordered learning: subject matters with their attending methods and modes of thought, cumulative, sequential stages of learning, rigorous disciplines. Because of the absence of these things, the elements which offer an apparent education (buildings, teachers, curricula, etc.) all take on a distinctive character. Since ordered learning does not determine the agenda of the undertaking, the field of Christian education becomes defined by the twin tasks of programme administration and development psychology. Curriculum becomes a literature which is simply an event in the present and does not, like the curricula of ordered learning, start at one place in order finally to get to another place. 'Teacher' does not name someone with special training or knowledge in a subject matter, but a volunteer willing to broker the present-oriented curriculum. The content of teaching is not a subject matter with its requirements, but whatever is identified by the curricula or teacher as having general formative relevance. Since education does not mean ordered learning, there are no measures of the success or failure of ordered learning in the church. And this renders invisible the monumental educational failure of church at the level of its laity and congregations.[12]

In conclusion, if the church ever does repudiate and move beyond its inherited axiom that church education cannot be theological education, comprehensive reconstruction will be involved. Cumulative, rigorous educational process and post-Enlightenment tools of analysis and interpretation (historical, literary, social, psychological, philosophical) will have to be introduced into church education. A new population of a very different kind of church teacher will be called for. Directors of Religious Education will have to be more than administrators of educational programmes. The educator on the church staff will have to be a theologian-teacher. Anticipating that time, the church needs to assess the axiom which its educational enterprise takes for granted, the axiom that church education cannot be theological education.

Notes

1. The essential ambiguity of the word 'education' is discussed later in the essay. Because of this ambiguity, I shall use the expression 'ordered learning' as a designation of education.

2. A description of how the ecclesial community is the environment and mediator of reality in the forming and nurturing of faith can be found in part two of the author's *Ecclesial Man: a social phenomenology of faith and reality*, Philadelphia, Fortress Press, 1975.

3. The persisting corruptibility of reality especially as it creates structures of oppression is the central theme of Paulo Freire's influential writings on education. It is precisely because reality is complex and corrupt that education must always be a 'problematising' which would develop a critical consciousness. Furthermore, Freire will not settle simply for education in its generalised sense of influence and action, but explicitly calls for disciplined reflection and contemplation. Without action, education is mere verbalism. Without reflection, it is mere activism. See *Pedagogy of the Oppressed*, New York, Herder and Herder, 1972, pp. 75–76.

4. Education as the experience of such disciplined efforts accords with A N Whitehead's definition of education as the 'acquisition of the art of the utilisation of knowledge'. See *The Aims of Education and Other Essays*, New York, The Free Press, 1929, p. 4.

5. A number of students of the twentieth-century church education movement speak of its failure. Thus, 'Christian educators began to suspect that American Protestants as a whole were biblically illiterate and ethically uncommitted. If, indeed, some sixty million hours were devoted every Sunday to Christian education in the churches, much of the energy seemed to have been wasted.' Wayne R Rood, *Understanding Christian Education*, Nashville, Abingdon Press, 1970, p. 77.

6. Something like this dialectic of corruption and redemption seems indicated in John Gordon Chamberlin's explanation of the 'denigration' and 'marginality' of the education enterprise in the church. One of the powers at work in this is simply the 'subordination of the intelli-

gible content of the Christian faith'. See *Faith and Freedom: new approaches to Christian education*, Philadelphia, Westminster Press, 1965, p. 16.

7. See chapter 2 of my *Theologia: the fragmentation and unity of theological education*, Philadelphia, Fortress Press, 1983, for a fuller account of the narrowing career of 'theology'.

8. The ambiguity of education in its multiple meanings is described by Chamberlin who lists ten meanings of the term in current usage. See *ibid.*, p. 19. Chamberlin works his way through these meanings in order to avoid the generalising of education. He thus argues that education names an intentional process which selects what is important enough to be taught and which involves teachers and students.

9. The reason this is a genre mistake and an equivocation is that it identifies some valid but very general *aims* of education with the educational act or process itself. Further, the aims which are frequently set forth tend to be the desiderata not simply of the educational act in its ordinary sense, but of the total community of faith in all of its activities. Hence, 'development of life-styles in persons and groups' (John H Westerhoff III, 'Toward a definition of Christian education', in John H Westerhoff III [ed.], *A Colloquy on Christian Education*, Philadelphia, Pilgrim Press, 1972, pp. 60–70), and 'shared praxis' and a 'way of knowing' (Thomas H Groome, *Christian Religious Education*, San Francisco, Harper and Row, 1980) are surely what the community of faith hopes to happen as the total effect of its preaching, counselling, action-organisation, administration, intersubjective structures, and liturgy. The list of features of the 'educating community of faith' offered by John H Westerhoff III are clearly general features of the ecclesial community itself in its essence and desired telos, not features of ordered learning. See *Values for Tomorrow's Children*, Philadelphia, Pilgrim Press, 1973, pp. 63–64. To argue that all these things have formative (educational) effects is no doubt correct. To *define* education as that totality is to obscure the church's low commitment to ordered learning for non-clergy.

10. It would be difficult to improve on Whitehead's description of the specificity, rigour, and challenge of education (ordered learning). 'All practical teachers know that education is a patient process of the mastery of details, minute by minute, hour by hour, day by day. There is no royal road to learning through an airy path of brilliant generalisations.' See *The Aims of Education and Other Essays*, New York, The Free Press, 1929, p. 6.

11. A number of typologies of approaches to Christian education have been offered. A recent example is the book edited by Jack Seymour and Donald E Miller, *Contemporary Approaches to Christian Education*, Nashville, Abingdon Press, 1982, where five basic approaches are described. See especially Seymour's introduction. These studies are very helpful maps of current literature. There is, however, some vagueness as to exactly what the approaches have in common, that to which they are approaches. It would not help to say it is 'Christian education' since that means either a historical movement containing the variety or a term whose meaning and referent is itself not a matter of consensus. More than likely, the approaches are to the 'discipline' or field of Christian education as a literary, pedagogical undertaking. Insofar as typology assigns ordered learning to an 'approach', the genre confusion and the generalising of the meaning of education tends to be obscured. One can then debate the issues on the basis of approaches to a discipline without confronting the legitimacy of expanding education to stand for general formative influence.

12. These apparent institutional elements all come together in the Protestant Sunday school. The fact that the Sunday school movement originated in an attempt to imitate the public school and that it does have these visible elements of educational space, teachers, and curricula should not mislead us into thinking that the Sunday school is an institutionalisation of ordered learning. Insofar as these outward elements mask the absence of cumulative, sequential, rigorous learning, the Sunday school is only a pseudo-school. Hence, one can only sympathise with the thesis of John H Westerhoff III that church education should not be identified with the Sunday school. However, Westerhoff identifies the failure as being because the Sunday school is a *school*. I would identify the failure as due to the fact that it is not. John H Westerhoff III thinks of his call away from schooling and classroom instruction as a radical new way of thinking about education. That call, in my view, simply perpetuates the first commandment of Protestant church education: 'Thou shalt not engage in ordered learning.' See chapter 6, 'Down with school!' in *Values for Tomorrow's Children*, Philadelphia, Pilgrim Press, 1973, especially p. 56.

1.4 Religious education and theology

James Michael Lee

Introduction

Until the early 1970s, theology was generally regarded as comprising the macrotheoretical approach to Christian religious instruction.[1] As the macrotheory of religious instruction, theology was alleged to possess the power of explaining and predicting and verifying the entire range of religious instruction phenomena. Thus it was claimed that theology is capable of devising and testing effective teaching techniques, of explaining the conditions under which religious learning could or could not take place, of directly devising successful religion curricula, of predicting who would or would not be an effective religion teacher, and so forth. In 1971 a book was published which frontally challenged this centuries-old view of theology as the macrotheory of religious instruction. This book, *The Shape of Religious Instruction*,[2] claimed that it is social science and not theology which constitutes the only adequate and valid macrotheory for religious instruction. Since 1971 the issue of whether theology or social science is the proper macrotheory has been one of the most recurrent and most hotly debated issues in the field. It would appear that the social-science approach is gaining the upper hand over the theological approach, so much so, in fact, that a prominent advocate of the theological approach could lament that all of religious education is now beginning to take its direction from the social sciences.[3] However, the adequacy and validity of either the theological approach or the social-science approach cannot be satisfactorily resolved by appeals either to venerableness or to recent ascendancy. The adequacy and validity of any theory (and macrotheory) can only be gauged by ascertaining the degree to which it does what a theory or macrotheory is by its very nature supposed to do, namely explain and predict and verify the phenomena under its purview. This section of my article will be devoted to such an investigation. Restrictions of space permit only the sketchiest treatment of the many points I will advance.

Theology or social science

In order to satisfactorily investigate whether theology or social science is the appropriate macrotheory for religious instruction, we must always keep as the centre and as the touchstone that with which we are dealing, namely the nature and actual operation of religious instruction endeavour. The results of this kind of investigation will reveal the appropriate macrotheory for religious instruction. A theory or macrotheory is by its very essence a tentative overall explanation of the concepts, facts and laws which it treats. Consequently, a valid and adequate macrotheory must be drawn or inferred from the actual operations of religious instruction activity itself. Thus neither the relationship between religious instruction and theology nor the role of theology in religious instruction can be determined *a priori*. It is invalid both logically and ontically to assert *a priori* that just because religious instruction deals with faith, that it is therefore essentially theological. Conversely, it is invalid to assert *a priori* that just because religious instruction deals with the facilitation of learning that it is therefore essentially social-scientific. The proper and valid determination of the appropriate nature and macrotheory for religious instruction can only come from keeping central in our investigation the way in which theology and social science do indeed function in the religious instruction act. By the term 'religious instruction act' I do not mean exclusively or even primarily the classroom teaching act. A religious instruction act is that particular kind of endeavour in which religion teaching of any sort occurs. A Christian liturgy, for example, is fully as much a series of religious instruction acts as is a classroom situation. Much of the recurring confusion and fuzzy thinking gripping religious educationists and educators concerning the relationship between religious instruction and theology occurs precisely because these individuals all too often conceptualise this relationship on an *a priori* basis rather than by grounding their investigation in the way in which religious instruction and theology actually work together in the real order, namely in the religious instruction act itself.

Before embarking on our investigation, two recurrent but patently erroneous claims can be quickly dispatched to the logical rubbish heap.

The first patently erroneous claim is that both the basic nature and overarching macrotheory of religious instruction must be fundamentally theological because the aims of religious instruction, the operations of religious instruction, and macrotheorising on religious instruction all contain hidden or manifest theological presuppositions.[4] This claim is devoid of merit because it fails to recognise primary ontic and functional distinctions among realities. After all, in a world which God created and suffuses, every human activity contains certain theological presuppositions. There is a sense in which art, conversation, medicine, even football, farming, having a baby, have certain theological presuppositions. To claim that religious instruction is fundamentally theological because it has theological presuppositions is as silly and as pretentious as claiming that art, conversation, medicine, football, farming and having a baby are fundamentally theological because each of these human activities also has certain theological assumptions. If one were to take the presupposition-equals-essence position seriously, then one could make a strong case that the essence of theology is really philosophy because theological activity utilises a great many prior and influential philosophical presuppositions. After all, much theological reflection is itself based on prior and more basic philosophical tenets such as the validity of knowledge (epistemology), the canons and criteria of reasoning (logic), the fundamental nature of existence (ontology) and so forth. Furthermore, the general and specific ways in which various Christian theologies developed was a direct and linear result of the philosophical and cultural ecology in which these theologies were formed, took root and developed. The shape and thrust of western Christian theology, for example, has been decisively conditioned by the Hellenistic philosophy and culture upon which western theological categories and modes of investigation are directly built.

The second patently erroneous claim is that religious instruction is essentially a form of practical or pastoral theology because it is a type of the ecclesia's practical or pastoral work. This claim is devoid of merit because, like the first claim, it also fails to recognise primary ontic and functional distinctions among realities. There is a vast ontic difference between the theology of ecclesial practice and the practice itself. Theology is one kind of cognitive reflection on ecclesial practice; theology is not coextensive with ecclesial practice. Furthermore, there is a great deal of ecclesial practice which is not basically theological and for which an overriding theological macrotheory is therefore inadequate and invalid. For example, a particular ecclesia, as part of its pastoral work, might sponsor a parish dance, a teen-club picnic, a fund-raising event, an architectural renovation of the church building, a religious instruction programme and so on. It is flagrantly silly to assert that the nature and operations of these types of pastoral work are adequately or validly explained by theology. There may or may not be a theological dimension to, or even some theologising taking place in, a dance, a picnic, fund raising, architectural renovation, religious instruction. But to claim that these pastoral works are satisfactorily explained by theological macrotheory because they have a theological dimension and may involve some theologising is essentially the same kind of fallacy as claiming that these pastoral works can satisfactorily be explained by linguistic theory because language is a dimension of and is used in all these pastoral works. Dancing is properly explained by a theory of dance, and not by theology. Architectural renovation is properly explained by a theory of architecture, not by theology. Religious instruction is properly explained by a theory of religious instruction, and not by theology.

There are, then, two basic points which should be kept in mind when assessing the claim that religious instruction is a form of practical or pastoral theology because it is a type of the ecclesia's practical or pastoral activity. First, a dimension is not at all the same as the whole, or even the same as the basic ontic or functional nature of the whole. Each of God's creations has a theological dimension, just as each has a philosophical dimension. But the nature and workings of each of God's creations such as dance or architecture or teaching cannot be satisfactorily explained in terms of any one of its dimensions; otherwise a competent theologian would automatically be a competent dancer, a competent fund raiser, a competent architect, a competent engineer, a competent teacher and so on. Second, the use to which a reality is put does not change the basic nature of that reality. Few realities are pastoral by nature. A reality can be put to pastoral use, but this pastoral use neither fundamentally affects the basic nature of that reality nor replaces the theory which adequately explains the reality. For example, religious psychology is a branch of the discipline of psychology. When it is used in pastoral work such as in the religious counselling of terminally-ill patients or in retreats for youth, the subdiscipline of religious psychology still retains its fundamental psychological and social-scientific character.[5]

The key to an effective investigation of whether theology or social science constitutes the appropriate macrotheory for religious instruction is to attend constantly to the basic nature and fundamental functions of religious instruction itself. A macrotheory of religious instruction is adequate and valid only to the extent that it comprehensively and systematically explains, predicts and verifies the religious instruction process. But what is the religious instruction process? What does religious instruction do? Religious instruction facilitates religious learning. The validity of this assertion can be easily demonstrated by the answer to the question: 'How can we know when teaching actually has taken place?' The answer to this question, obviously, is 'when learning has occurred'. The basic nature of religious instruction is properly described in terms of the causation of desired learning outcomes. If learning outcomes have not occurred, then there has been no religious instruction, no matter how holy or how theologically erudite the religious educator is. An appropriate macrotheory for religious instruction, therefore, has to be able to comprehensively and systematically explain, predict and verify how teaching actually takes place, namely how the four major variables involved in religious instruction interact in such a way that desired learning outcomes are thereby facilitated. This is and must be the touchstone of any investigation of the appropriate macrotheory for religious instruction.

The major point made in the preceding paragraph can be further sharpened by posing two pointed questions. Does a religious educator's knowledge of and proficiency in theology directly bring about desired learning outcomes? Or, on the other hand, does a religious educator's knowledge of and proficiency in social science directly bring about desired learning outcomes? These questions can be further refined in the following comparative example. Religion teacher A understands that he and the learners are redeemed in God's grace. He is deeply aware that despite this redemption, he and the learners still suffer some of the deleterious after-effects of original sin. He knows full well that he and the learners are members of the mystical body and can cooperate with each other to further God's kingdom in religious instruction activity. This religion teacher is also proficient in theologising about these and other theological concepts involving the teacher and the learner and the instructional process. Religion teacher B, in contrast, knows the dynamics of the teaching-learning process. He understands the substantive content (religion) and the structural content (pedagogical practice) of religious instruction as these contents are related to the here-and-now religion teaching situation. This religion teacher is also proficient in social-scientifically structuring the pedagogical variables in such a way that the desired learning outcomes take place. Which of these religion teachers is the more likely to be successful as a direct consequence of his knowledge and proficiency? The answer to this question provides an important clue to the solution of the basic issue under discussion, namely the issue of whether theology or social science is the adequate macrotheory for religious instruction.

The six-component test

The correct identification of the appropriate macrotheory for religious instruction can only be satisfactorily made by rigorously analysing the basic nature and operation of religious instruction in terms of the macrotheories which purport to explain, predict and verify religious instruction phenomena. A particularly fruitful way of analysing religious instruction in operation is the category system devised by Harold William Burgess.[6] Burgess' category system analyses the workings of religious instruction in terms of six major variables which he has found to be present and indispensable in all religious instruction activity: aim, subject matter, teacher, learner, environment and evaluation. Burgess rightly maintains that the relative merits and potency of a macrotheoretical approach to religious instruction can be ascertained by testing the adequacy to which competing macrotheoretical approaches can explain, predict and verify the six variables separately and as a whole.

Aim

Advocates of the theological approach to religious instruction characteristically declare that the aim of religious instruction is to be found in theology.[7] The task of religious instruction is to act merely as a delivery system to faithfully transport theological content and processes intact from educator to learner. Every aim of religious instruction is theological: it is theological because it directly and explicitly enfleshes theological content and/or because it contains basic theological presuppositions which might be more hidden than manifest.

The social-science approach to religious instruction states that the aim of religious instruction is to be found in the learner as he interacts with his environment. The task of religious instruction is to facilitate the learner's religious development in such a way that he is optimally fulfilled as a person. Every pedagogical aim is basically social-scientific because there can be no taught-learned aim which is in any way separate from the learner's here-and-now developing self-system.

In an earlier section I treated the issue of theological presuppositions in religious instruction. Consequently I will centre my attention here on the locus (extrinsic or intrinsic) of the religious instruction aim.

By stating that the aim of religious instruction is theological, advocates of the theological approach thereby contend that the aim of religious instruction is extrinsic to the learner. But to assert that the aim of religious instruction is extrinsic to the learner is to assert that religious instruction is not first and foremost a human activity. By definition, every human activity has the person not only at the centre but also existentially involved in every speck, movement and perimeter of that process. Human learning means that the person interacts with environmental variables (including theological subject matter) in such a way that these variables, when learned, lose their autonomous ontic character and become incorporated into the individual's dynamic self-system. In order to learn, all extrinsic variables (for example, theological subject matter) must become intrinsic (learner) on the learner's own dynamic existential terms according to where he is developmentally and how he is becoming a person. For example, when a person learns the Ten Commandments, the result is not the autonomous ontic structure of the Ten Commandments somehow existing independently in his mind. Rather, what is learned are the Ten Commandments as *he* has heard them spoken or seen them written, as *he* has perceived them, as *he* has conceptualised them, as *he* has interpreted them, as *he* has incorporated them into his self-system. What has been learned, then, is not the Ten Commandments in themselves, but *his personal* acquisition of the Ten Commandments. Hence there can be no such thing as extrinsic aims where human learning is concerned.

It is precisely because the aims of religious instruction are intrinsic rather than extrinsic to the learner that the theological approach is incapable of devising proper or adequate aims for religious instruction, and why, in turn, social science possesses this capability. Social science, after all, is that confluence of disciplines which, by definition and comprehension, explains, predicts and verifies *human behaviour*. Learning is a word used to signify a certain kind of human behaviour.

No satisfactory aim of religious instruction can be erected primarily on presuppositions, hypotheses, forces or institutions outside of or extrinsic to the developing learner. This statement does not mean that the aims of religious instruction are devoid of extrinsic theologies, philosophies and ideologies of one sort or another. Rather, this statement asserts that the way in which extrinsically derived aims are incorporated into religious instruction activity in its processes or goals must be done in a manner consistent with and indeed based upon the learner's developmental self.

If religious instruction is to work, its aims must be framed in such a way that they can be taught and learned. If aims are such that they cannot be taught or learned, they are not religious instruction aims. My analysis in the preceding three paragraphs implies that theological principles and content cannot be stated as aims of religious instruction unless they are stated religiously and social-scientifically. Theological content must be cast into religious form if religious instruction is to remain *religious* instruction. Theological content must also be cast into social-scientific form if it is to be rendered teachable and learnable. The teaching-learning process is a behavioural activity governed primarily by social-scientific laws. A quick way to render religious instruction unteachable and unlearnable is to state an aim in terms of theological content.

To assert that theological aim must be fundamentally reconceptualised and restated into social-scientific aim is in no way to assert that religious instruction lacks a theological dimension. Rather, it is to assert that in the work of religious instruction, theology in one way or another takes on the processive shape and flow of the social-scientific activity of religious instruction. Perhaps an analogy will illustrate my point. Let us say that a theologian asks a sculptor to make a statue which conveys the theological aim of the evil of sin. Unless and until the sculptor radically reconceptualises this theological aim into a sculptural aim, and then operationalises this aim into specific sculpturing procedures, he will never be able to carve a statue. To carve the statue, the sculptor must always adhere to the aims and procedures of sculpting, not of theology. The statue which he finally produces is the fruit of sculptural aim, not theological aim. Further, the statue was made by the procedures of sculpture, not by the procedures of theology. The end result, the statue, was not the work of theology, but the work of sculpture. The statue possesses a theological dimension, but it itself is not theology, nor is it primarily theological in aim or execution.

Subject Matter

Advocates of the theological approach to religious instruction typically state that the substantive subject matter of religious instruction is theology in one form or another. The source and type of theological subject matter is determined on the basis of the particular brand of theology which the denominational religious education officials mandate, which the religion schoolteacher or parent prefers, and so on.

The social-science approach to religious instruction states that the substantive subject matter of religious instruction is religion, religion as it is actually taught-learned in the religious instruction act.

The theological approach maintains that the substantive subject matter of religious instruction is theology. But such an assertion is *prima facie* false. As its name and hence its definition unambiguously indicates, religious instruction is religious instruction and not theological instruction. Religion and theology have essentially distinct natures.

Another consideration intrudes itself. Because the theological approach is perforce rooted in one or another specific theology, it is fundamentally defective as a macrotheory explaining, predicting and verifying all of religious instruction. An adequate macrotheory for religious instruction must, by definition, explain, predict and verify all kinds of subject matter which are present in all kinds of religious instruction acts. This is a task which the theological approach is incapable of accomplishing because of its very nature. For example, an Evangelical Protestant advocate of the theological approach would understandably deny that the theological approach taken by a conservative neo-Tridentine Roman Catholic would be adequate or acceptable as a macrotheory explaining, predicting and verifying the selection and implementation of substantive subject matter in religious instruction. The social-science approach, on the other hand, is value-free in that it not only accommodates all sorts of diverse theological views as a dimension of subject matter, but is admirably capable of explaining, predicting and verifying the effective selection and implementation of the entire spectrum of complementary or conflicting religious subject matter.[8]

To equate substantive content with focused revelation and with the bible, as is common with many leading Evangelical Protestant religious educationists like Herbert Byrne and Lawrence Richards, strengthens rather than weakens the position developed in the previous four paragraphs. To live in and with revelation is religion, or at least a major dimension of religion. Revelation is not primarily or even essentially theology. Theology is just one way of cognitively reflecting on the nature and meaning of revelation. To live in and with the bible is religion, or at least a major dimension of religion. The bible is not primarily or essentially a piece of theology. The bible is simultaneously a religious instruction document and a history of God's religious instruction activities with human beings. Theology is just one way of cognitively reflecting on the nature and meaning of the bible.

Teacher

Advocates of the theological approach to religious instruction generally pay scant attention to the teacher. This statement holds true especially with regard to what the teacher actually does in the religious instruction act. Most proponents of the theological approach claim that effective religion teaching can be explained, predicted and verified by any one or more of the following theories: the personality theory, the witness theory, the dedication theory, the authenticity theory or the blow theory. These theories hold, respectively, that religion teaching can be explained, predicted and verified primarily or even exclusively by the educator's personality, the educator's Christian witness, the educator's dedication, the educator's authenticity or by the mysterious unfathomable action of the Holy Spirit.[9]

The social-science approach pays a great deal of attention to the teacher. The social-science approach is always concerned with laying bare those pedagogical variables in the religious instruction dynamic which have been empirically demonstrated to correlate positively with effective religion teaching.

None of the various theories of religion *teaching* advanced by the proponents of the theological approach is an adequate theory of religion teaching precisely because none of them is capable of doing what a theory must perforce do if it is to be a genuine theory, namely to comprehensively and systematically explain, predict and verify the laws and phenomena of religion *teaching* in a satisfactory manner. Each of these so-called 'theories' highlights one and only one factor which *might* be responsible for the successful facilitation of learning in a *particular* situation. But there is no available empirical research to indicate that any one of these factors, or indeed all of them combined, are in themselves sufficient to adequately explain, predict or verify how the religion teacher actually facilitates desired religious learnings.

It is not at all surprising that the advocates of the theological approach to religious instruction have proposed such fatally flawed pseudotheories of religion teaching. After all, the construction of a workable and valid theory of teaching is a matter of social-scientific competence since the pedagogical process by definition and classification falls under the domain of social-scientific fact, law and theory. Theological theory simply lacks the capability to explain, predict and verify nontheological realms of being, such as teaching, dentistry, politics, economics, loving and the like. When advocates of the theological approach to religious instruction propose one or another 'theory' to explain, predict and verify religion teaching, these persons do, in fact, unwittingly utilise the social-science approach rather than the theological approach. Since these individuals are usually untrained in and indeed are often antipathetic to social science, their incognisant attempts to devise social-scientifically-based teaching laws and procedures on the basis of theological premises typically fall flat on their faces. Theology can no more validly or effectively generate social-scientific procedures such as teaching practice than social science can validly or effectively generate theological procedures such as bible-based methods of enquiry into the existence of God.

While the theological approach looks to the nature and operation of theology as the basis for constructing a valid and workable theory of teaching, the social-science approach looks to the nature and operations of the actual here-and-now teaching-learning process as its basis for devising instructional theory. A social-science-based teaching theory, then, is derived from *descriptive* statements of the empirically demonstrated causal relationship between the religious educator's antecedent pedagogical behaviours and the learner's consequent performance behaviours. A social-science-based theory of religious instruction, then, holds that the significant variables which explain, predict and verify the process of teaching religion are those involved in the effective modification of the learner's behaviour along religious lines. A social-science-based theory of religious instruction shows how and why the four major variables present in every teaching act (teacher, learner, subject matter and environment) dynamically and continuously interact in such a fashion as to yield desired religious outcomes. Thus, in the end, a general theory of instruction becomes essentially *prescriptive* in setting forth rules concerning the most effective pedagogical procedures for facilitating desired learning outcomes.[10]

Learner

Proponents of the theological approach to religious instruction view the learner and the learning process primarily and often exclusively from the vantage point of one or another theological interpretation of the learner. Thus, when advocates of the theological approach do discuss the learner, they typically deal with him *sub specie* a responsible person who can respond in faith to those initiatives made by the Holy Spirit in the context of fellowship and the Christian community.

The social-science approach, on the other hand, views the learner and the learning process from the perspective of how, in fact, the learner actually functions as a human being and how, in fact, the learner actually learns.

It would appear that the claim of the theological approach with regard to the learner and the learning process represents the logical fallacy of *ignoratio elenchi*, namely that of avoiding the central issues of learning in general and of learning as it occurs in the religious instruction act. The central issue around which all dimensions of the religious instruction act must proceed is how the learner does indeed function religiously and how the learner does indeed learn. All interpretations of the learner and learning, be these interpretations theological or philosophical or psychological or biological, must be continuously grounded in and tightly tethered to the actual reality of human functioning. In the final analysis, a theological interpretation of the learner and the learning process does not substantially affect the ongoing psychophysiological nature and functions of the learner or the learning process. Psychophysiological facts and laws of human functioning hold true regardless of whether one interprets the learner and his learning from a Calvinistic theological stance, from a Tillichian perspective, from a neo-Tridentine position, from a Mormon viewpoint and so on. To be sure, any valid and fruitful theological interpretation of the learner and the learning process must be based on or at least be in compliance with verified facts and established laws of psychophysiological reality.[11]

The basic set of empirically verified facts and laws relating to the learner and the learning process can be summarised in one short sentence: all learning takes place according to the mode of the learner. Advocates of the theological approach tend to ignore or uneasily bypass this basic and pivotal assertion. These individuals concentrate instead on high-sounding but vague statements such as 'The person is God's masterpiece' or 'Learning takes place mysteriously because it is the Holy Spirit who prompts the person and brings learning to pass'. While sweet and pious, such statements are useless for religious instruction because they fail to address themselves to the all-important religious instruction issue of how and in what matter learning actually takes place. The fact of the matter is that the learner acquires, for example, a knowledge of the Ten Commandments (cognitive outcome), a love of the Ten Commandments (affective outcome) and an obedience to the Ten Commandments (lifestyle outcome) primarily according to the on-going laws of his own human development and not primarily to the logical structure or eternal import of the Ten Commandments themselves.

There is no empirical research evidence to suggest that a person learns religion (or even theology) in a way fundamentally different from the basic manner in which he learns any other area of reality. Consequently, the attempt by some advocates of the theological approach to exempt religious learning from the laws governing the learning process itself on the basis of appeals to the Holy Spirit's mysterious activity is an attempt utterly without foundation. Furthermore, those persons typically fail to explain why the Holy Spirit operates in religious (or even theological) learning but not in other types of human learning. (Parenthetically, one is tempted to enquire how so-called nonreligious learning takes place if the Holy Spirit is not present in these kinds of learning also. Can any reality exist or function without God's continuous and continual cooperation?)

Environment

Advocates of the theological approach to religious instruction largely ignore both the environment in which religious teaching takes place and the environmental variables outside the intentional teaching situation which dynamically interact with the learner. Most advocates of the theological approach seem to regard the learner's spiritual powers plus God's grace as constituting the key factors in religious learning, with environmental variables so negligible as to be hardly worth mentioning.

The social-science approach to religious instruction places great stress on the environment in the work of religious instruction. Based as it is on the empirical study of what actually occurs in the teaching-learning dynamic, the social-science approach contends that the environment is of tremendous importance precisely because it constitutes one of the four major interactive variables present and operative in every pedagogical situation.

There is a whole host of empirical research data which suggest that religious learning, and indeed all other kinds of human learning, are significantly affected by the structure and flow of one's interaction with the environment.[12] A valid macrotheory and usable approach to religious instruction, consequently, must utilise the all-important environmental variable as one of its central features. The social-science approach does indeed make extensive use of the environment in explaining, predicting and verifying the work of religious instruction. The omission of the environment from axial consideration by proponents of the theological approach constitutes a major and indeed fatal deficiency in the validity of this approach as a macrotheory purporting to explain, to predict and to verify the work of religious instruction.

Even a cursory look at the religious instruction act reveals how the learner is continuously and elementally interacting with environment variables such as the location in which the process is taking place, the socio-emotional climate, the other persons involved in the situation, the pedagogical materials, even with such frequently overlooked but often influential factors as temperature, light and spatial arrangement. Usually the religious educator himself is the most potent aspect of the instructional environment because it is he who structures the features of the environment (including his own activity) in such a fashion that learning is thereby facilitated. I suspect that one major reason accounting for the gross neglect of the environment by advocates of the theological approach is that they tend to concentrate their attention on theology rather than on the real-life situation in the here-and-now religious instruction act. It is difficult to imagine any approach which focuses its attention on what is really happening in the here-and-now religious instruction act failing to take the environment into account as a central, major and inextricable variable in the teaching-learning of religion.

The theological approach really does not come to grips with environmental variables by issuing vague and amorphous statements about the Holy Spirit or the faith community providing the environment for effective religious pedagogy. Unless and until the advocates of the theological approach can factually demonstrate that the Holy Spirit and/or the faith community actually do exert one or another particular specifiable environmental influence on religious instruction, their statements to this effect must remain gratuitous. Even if it were assumed or proven that the Holy Spirit and/or the faith community do indeed exert one or another particular specifiable environmental influence, little or nothing has been gained by such information which is useful for religious instruction. To be practical and useful for religious instruction, advocates of the theological approach must not simply state *that* the Holy Spirit and/or the faith community act as powerful environmental factors, but *how* these environmental forces specifically affect religion teaching and learning. It makes much more sense to assert that the Holy Spirit works according to the laws of nature, created and kept in continuous existence by the Holy Spirit, than to assert that the Holy Spirit somehow directly intervenes or withholds action in each and every pedagogical act. If this statement is true, then assertions about the Holy Spirit as the basic environmental factor mean nothing beyond what is known empirically about the specific effects which various environmental factors have on teaching and learning.

Evaluation

Supporters of the theological approach generally accord little or no integral attention to a careful or systematic evaluation of religious instruction. A great many advocates of the theological approach claim that the real effects of religious instruction are spiritual, unfathomable and mysterious gifts of the Holy Spirit, hence these effects are not able to be evaluated. Other exponents of the theological approach claim that theology itself has the broad task of evaluating religious instruction insofar as it compares what is learned in religious instruction against theological standards.

The social-science approach considers evaluation to be an integral and vital dimension of religious instruction. The social-science approach contends that evaluation is a crucial and indispensable factor in the work of religious instruction for several reasons: evaluation helps discover if the learner has indeed learned, it ascertains what he has learned and the degree to which he has learned it, it finds out how he has learned it, and it provides valuable information to both educator and learner about their respective progress in the teaching-learning dynamic.

The advocates of the theological approach end up in intellectual nihilism when they claim that religious instruction cannot be evaluated because its processes and effects are spiritual, unfathomable and mysterious gifts of the Holy Spirit. If this claim of the theological approach were true, then it would be impossible to judge anything (including even chemical or physical reactions) since all reality is a once and continuing gift of God. If the processes and effects of religious instruction cannot be known or evaluated because they are mysterious and unfathomable, then it is manifestly impossible for anyone, including advocates of the theological approach, to make any meaningful or valid statement about the actuality of the religious instruction dynamic.[13] If the processes and effects of religious instruction are mysterious and unfathomable, then there is no way for the educator to know the success or failure of any of his pedagogical procedures, or for the learner to know if he has gained anything from his participation in the religious instruction endeavour.

I find it a source of amusement that virtually all those advocates of the theological approach who claim that the processes and effects of religious instruction are mysterious and hence cannot be evaluated are the very people who most unambiguously claim that their own pet proposal for improving religious instruction is more effective than an alternate proposal or that their own favourite pedagogical procedure in religious instruction has proved effective time after time. Obviously there is a basic contradiction between claims of the mysteriousness and unfathomability of the processes and effects of religious instruction on the one hand, and claims of the superior workability and effectiveness of their own proposals and procedures on the other hand.

To claim that theology itself has the broad task of evaluating religious instruction insofar as theology compares what is learned against theological standards is to seriously beg the question on at least two counts. First of all, religious instruction is religious instruction and not theological instruction. Hence to evaluate the religious instruction act on the basis of theological standards is irrelevant in terms of religious instruction. Second, because of its nature and structure, theology simply does not possess either the means or the procedures to evaluate how and to what extent the four major variables in the religious instruction dynamic interact in such a way as to bring about learning outcomes. In the final analysis, all theology can do is to state whether some of the effects of religious instruction square with this or that theological proposition. Thus theological activity does not evaluate either the processes or the religious outcomes of the religious instruction act, but rather evaluates only the theological dimension of some of the effects of religious instruction. Perhaps an analogy will further clarify this point. Theology may legitimately evaluate the theological dimension of some of the effects of a certain dentistry procedure; however, this kind of evaluation is of a far different genre than that of theology attempting to evaluate the interactive dynamics of the dental process itself or of attempting to evaluate the dental effects of this process.

By their fruits you shall know them

One of the most important and significant tests of the adequacy and validity of a theory is its fruitfulness, namely the degree to which it gives rise to new practice. It is an astounding fact that the theological approach has not directly given rise to or elicited a single new pedagogical practice for religious instruction in the many centuries of the existence of this approach. Surely this fact is one of the most damning indictments of the theological approach. Every single advance in structural content, whether this advance be the age-old lecture/telling technique or the modern action-reflection technique, has been imported into religion teaching from other areas of instructional endeavour. Why is this so? The answer is obvious: all other areas of instruction have adopted a potent and effective macrotheory. This macrotheory, of course, is the social-science approach. Of all areas of instructional activity, only religious instruction still clings to the outmoded theological approach, and only religious instruction has failed to adopt the social-science approach. It is a sure sign of an inappropriate and sterile macrotheory when the theological approach is unable directly to give rise to any new pedagogical practice, or to adequately explain or verify or predict those pedagogical practices which are already occurring. It is utterly unimaginable for any field of endeavour to retain as its guiding and governing approach one which has consistently failed over many centuries directly to give rise to any concrete or workable practice within the field or which has consistently proven incapable of explaining or predicting or verifying the basic phenomena and laws operative in the field. Yet the utterly unimaginable holds true for much of Christian religious instruction insofar as it adheres to the theological approach. This patently preposterous state of affairs could never obtain in a respectable field of endeavour; indeed, I am unaware of any field in which such ridiculousness obtains. It is small wonder, then, that religious instruction is such a noncredible field, one brimming over with all sorts of bizarre gratuitous statements and wild, unsupported claims.

Consistency

Another major test of the adequacy and validity of a theory is the degree to which its various interlocking principles and components are consistent with one another. Lack of consistency is a sure sign of a defect in theory because when principles or components which are supposed to be interlocking and coherent are instead disjointed, the structure and operation of the theory is significantly weakened. The greater the inconsistency, the less adequate and valid the theory.

The theological macrotheory of religious instruction is woefully lacking in consistency. Thus, for example, it claims that religion teaching is a mysterious and an unfathomable activity of the Holy Spirit while simultaneously advocating one or another specific pedagogical procedure like the action-reflection technique as a particularly effective pedagogical device, or by stating that a religious educator must possess certain qualities such as holiness or theological knowledge in order to successfully facilitate desired learning outcomes.

Without a doubt, the grossest inconsistency with respect to theory occurs when the most basic principle upon which virtually all elaborations of the theory are derived stands in direct contradiction to the fundamental form and thrust of that theory. No theory or macrotheory can survive such a tremendous inconsistency for the obvious reason that an inconsistency of this magnitude means that the theory or macrotheory is worthless. Yet, amazing to say, such a shocking inconsistency is actually advocated by at least two of the proponents of the theological macrotheory of religious instruction, namely John Westerhoff and Berard Marthaler. Both of these persons consciously take socialisation as their major and overarching principle for explaining, predicting and verifying religious instruction endeavour.[14] Socialisation is first and foremost a social-science construct in nature and in theoretical elaboration. A theological approach with a social-science foundation is as self-contradictory conceptually as it is impossible existentially. By making socialisation the foundation of religious instruction, Westerhoff and Marthaler automatically, though perhaps unwittingly, abandon the theological approach and concomitantly assert that the social-science approach constitutes the adequate and valid macrotheory for religious instruction. After all, one cannot take a social-science construct as one's basic foundation and then claim that the endeavour which is built on this foundation and through which the structural/substantive process of this foundation flows is theology. If the theological macrotheory were indeed adequate and valid as the foundation of religious instruction, then Westerhoff and Marthaler would obviously use it as a foundation rather than jettisoning it and adopting a social-science foundation.

A theology of religious instruction – the proper use of theological theory in religious instruction

It is important to bear in mind that theological reflection on the religious instruction act is of a fundamentally different genre than the religious instruction act itself. Consequently, the basic theory of and competencies required for the fruitful exercise of theological reflection are fundamentally different in most respects from those required for the fruitful exercise of religious instruction. Religious instruction may utilise theological reflection in such ways as to further the work of religious instruction, but this is far different from asserting that theological reflection is the same or equivalent to the pedagogical dynamic of teaching religion.

If the theological macrotheory is indeed inadequate, invalid and inappropriate to explain/predict/verify the concepts/facts/laws of religious instruction, then what is the proper function of the theological macrotheory with respect to the religious instruction endeavour? The proper function of theological theory with respect to the religious instruction endeavour is that of a theological theory which reflects on the theological meaning of the nontheological reality called religious instruction, and not that of a theological macrotheory attempting to explain, predict and verify religious instruction concepts, facts and laws.

The theological meaning of a biological reality, for example, is *eo ipso* of a fundamentally different genre than the biological meaning of that reality. Theological theory states what this or that biological concept, fact, or law means to theology. Similarly, theological theory can only state what this or that religious instructional concept, fact, or law means to theology; theological theory cannot state what this or that religious instructional concept, fact, or law means to religious instruction.

What I have just written does not suggest or imply that theological theory lacks an authentic or valid function with respect to nontheological reality such as the biological world or the religious instruction world. Rather, what I have written teases apart the valid from the invalid functions of theology with respect to nontheological reality. The proper function of theology with respect to nontheological reality is to explore the *theological meaning* of the nature and operations of one or another reality. For example, theological theory examines the *theological ramifications* of producing a human embryo *in vitro*. And theological theory furnishes a *theological perspective* on the use of role-playing to teach the learners attitudes toward sinners. To examine the theological meaning of *in vitro* embryos and of role-playing pedagogy is, of course, far different from explaining, predicting and verifying the nature and operation of *in vitro* fertilisation or role-playing pedagogy. Rather, to theologically explore these realities is to make more clear the theological dimensions of these diverse realities, dimensions and ramifications which, while not revealing the autonomous ontic nature and operations of these realities, nonetheless do reveal their theological import.

There are instances in which theological theory gives external aid to the work of nontheological realities such as biology and religious instruction; in other instances, theological theory is of marginal or no benefit. When theological theory is of help to biology, to religious instruction and so on, then these nontheological activities can and should incorporate the fruits of theological reflection into their work *sub specie* that work. Thus the general rule is that religious instruction makes use of a theology of religious instruction only to the extent that this theology in some way furthers and advances the work of religious instruction.

Mediator: a new stage

A new stage is needed to explain how and why theology relates to religious instruction, in such a way that the integrity of religious instruction is preserved and theology plays its proper role rather than an imperialistic role. Such a stage must be capable of theoretically explaining the structure of religious instruction as the dynamic combination of substantive content and structural content in a single new ontic entity.

There is a new and higher stage which performs these explanatory tasks. I call this stage that of mediator, a conceptualisation which I first proposed in the early 1970s.[15] I am not referring to a mediator as an arbitrator between two opposing parties, or as an intercessor between a party of lesser power and one of greater power. Religious instruction is not an arbitrator between religion and theology or between pedagogy and theology. Nor does religious instruction serve as theology's intercessor or *vice versa*. The mediatorship to which I refer is mediatorship in its highest, most authentic and most effective form, namely mediatorship in which two or more realities become united in a new reality. This new reality is of such a nature that it not only unites its components but unites them in such a fashion that the components are no longer separate entities but rather are subsumed into a new reality. This new reality simultaneously, first, incorporates and retains the essential features of its original components; and second, puts the essential features of the original components into a new fused relationship with each other so that they are no longer separate but become inextricably combined in the new reality – so inextricably combined, in fact, that in this new reality the components are no longer separate and distinct ontic entities but exist in the new reality only in their united state.[16] Mediatorship means that substantive content and structural content are so united in the religious instruction act that religion no longer exists as religion *in se* but now exists under the form of religious instruction, and that instruction does not exist as instruction *in se* but now exists under the form of religious instruction.

The full and authentic kind of mediatorship which I am discussing has at least two fundamental properties: first, subsumption[17] into a new ontic reality, and second, unity. A mediator subsumes into a new reality those entities of which it is composed. A mediator is thus not the sum total of its components but rather a new entity formed by the new ontic and configurational and functional *relationship* in which these subsumed components now find themselves. The core properties of each component remain, but not in the same ontic or functional fashion as was the case when they existed as separate independent entities outside the mediational reality. In the mediational reality, the core properties of each component are altered ontically and functionally by virtue of and in the degree to which each component now substantively and structurally relates to the other(s). Each component is still recognisable. This recognisability does not inhere in the original component but rather inheres in this component as it is ontically and functionally altered in the new subsumptional reality. Thus in religious instruction, religion is still recognisable; however it is recognisable as it exists in religious instruction and not as it exists in itself. The subsumptional process creates a new unity. Whereas previously the components existed separately and autonomously, now in mediatorship they are subsumed to form a wholly new unity forged from a new ontic relationship between components. In full mediatorship, the ultimate unity is accomplished, namely the unity whereby the components unite into a new entity in which they became aspects or dimensions of a new reality. This unity brought about by subsumption is one of wholeness in which the original components are not obliterated but rather are brought into new ontic fullness and wider functional power. Because the original components are fused into a new ontic and functional reality, no one component dominates the other(s) or puts the other(s) into servitude. A dynamic equilibrium reigns. The mediator sustains its components within the ontic and functional unity of its mediatorship. Owing to its property of unity, all the efforts of the action of the mediator are efforts of the whole mediator and not the efforts solely of any one or more of its components.[18]

Religious instruction is a mediator of religion and instruction, that is, of substantive content and structural content. This mediatorship is forged through the dynamic subsumption of the distinctly separate realities of religion and instruction, a subsumption which eventuates in that new reality called religious instruction. In the mediational reality called religious instruction, the core properties of religion and instruction are altered functionally and ontically in that religion takes on the form and nature of religious instruction while instruction takes on the form and nature of religious instruction. Thus we have the united mediated entity of religious instruction rather than the mixed entities of religion and instruction.[19] As mediator, religious instruction does not stand between substantive content and structural content, but rather ontically reconciles them in the fundamental new reality called religious instruction. Religion as its exists in religious instruction is different from the way it exists in religious dance *per se* or in religious mediation *per se*. In the full mediatorship of religious instruction, religion and instruction cease to be separate entities but become aspects or dimensions of the new subsumptional reality known as religious instruction. In this new reality, neither religion nor instruction is obliterated; rather, each is brought into a new ontic fullness and functional power insofar as religion and instruction are both changed and broadened and deepened by the merger with one another. Through the ontic merging of religion and instruction in the subsumptional process there emerges the mediation stage of religious instruction. In the mediated stage of religious instruction, neither religion nor instruction are imperialistic to one another. Instead, a dynamic equilibrium reigns. This equilibrium is that of two complementary dimensions of one ontic reality rather than of two separate ontic realities thrown into a single functional grab-bag.

The place of theology in terms of the mediated entity called religious instruction is determined not by criteria external to the mediated entity (such as theological criteria *in se*), but rather by internal criteria, namely how theology fits into religious instruction on religious instruction's own distinctive ontic and functional terms as religious instruction is being enacted in the here-and-now. Since the dynamics of the here-and-now are in constant flux, so too will the role of theology be in constant flux. Hence, in some instances the place of theology in religious instruction endeavour will be considerable, at other times minimal, and so on. What I have written in this paragraph in no way suggests that theology is a handmaid to religious instruction. Rather, my analysis suggests that the proper role of theology in religious instruction is determined by the manner and degree to which it relates to religious instruction endeavour at any one particular time or phase of that endeavour. Because religious instruction is a mediated reality, theology is not incorporated into religion in the religious instruction endeavour, but rather is incorporated into the whole of the new subsumptional reality of religious instruction on religious instruction's own ontic and functional terms. In the religious instruction act, theology no longer exists as theology's theology but instead as religious instruction's theology. Because the fruits of a mediated reality come through the mediator as a whole, any theological fruits which may and do eventuate from religious instruction activity come directly from religious instruction activity and not from theology *in se*.

A mediator reconciles, brings to wholeness. In so doing, a mediator brings a 're-novation' and 're-newal' to each of the realities which are subsumed into it. Thus religious instruction as mediator brings a renewal both to religion and to instruction. This renewal constitutes a major vital force for the prophetic nature and function of religious instruction, not only to the dimensions of religion and instruction which are intrinsic to religious instruction but also for every reality which religious instruction endeavour touches.

Ontic autonomy

Step by step since the beginning of this article, the evidence has been progressively mounting and the logic has been inexorably closing in on the inescapable conclusion that religious instruction enjoys ontic autonomy. By ontic autonomy I mean that religious instruction is not subject to theology but is rather a separate and independent field. Religious instruction and theology are basically different ontic entities and operate on different levels of reality.

The ontic autonomy of religious instruction from theology stems from two fundamental and converging vectors, namely fact and theory. In terms of fact, religious instruction is ontically autonomous from theology because each is and does fundamentally different things. Religious instruction is the pedagogical activity in which religious outcomes are facilitated, while theology is the cognitive investigation of the nature and the activities of God. In terms of theory, two points are especially worthy of mention, one negative and the other positive. Negatively, theology fails the six-component test required of any theoretical base claiming to validly serve as an adequate explainer and predictor and verifier of religious instruction activity. Positively, theology's claim to *seigniory* is smashed by the mediator conceptualisation of religious instruction. As a mediator entity, religious instruction is formed by uniting structural content and substantive content in such a fashion that these two contents are no longer separate entities but rather are subsumed into a new reality. Thus theology, which usually but not necessarily is an ingredient in substantive content, disappears *qua theology* when substantive content is essentially transformed in the subsumptional process of mediation. Thus any theology which might have been present in substantive content prior to mediation, now, having been mediated, exists under the form of religious instruction. Theology as a distinct science *external* to the religious instruction act can and usually does see a *theological* significance in religious instruction endeavour. In other words, theology can ascertain what religious instruction *means for theology*. Also, theology can externally present this theological meaning to religious instruction, first, for possible reflection by religious instruction itself on what religious instruction is doing and ought to do; and second, for possible incorporation into religious instruction on religious instruction's own autonomously ontic terms.

Every ontic entity has its own ground and its own medium. Religious instruction endeavour is no exception. If a field is to be coherent and fruitful, its fundamental ground and basic medium must be congruent. The proper ground and medium of religious instruction is social science. As the ground of religious instruction, social science is that which religious instruction *works out of*. As the medium of religious instruction, social science is that which religious instruction *works through*.

The proper ground of religious instruction is social science precisely because the essential nature of religious instruction is the facilitation of desired religious outcomes. The only valid theoretical ground for adequately explaining, predicting and verifying the facilitation of these outcomes is social science. Only social science possesses the theoretical tools and capability to serve as an adequate ground for religious instruction. Theology, by definition and nature and operation, simply lacks the requisite theoretical tools and capability. The only practical ground for enabling religious instruction to successfully accomplish its task of actually facilitating desired outcomes is social science. Theology's practice *eo ipso* lies in quite different directions.

The proper medium of religious instruction is social science precisely because religious instruction in all its activity *functions* essentially along facilitational lines. Religious instruction is a process of facilitation; hence its specific medium is the bringing about of desired learning outcomes. Social science is the sole overall medium in which this special kind of activity takes place. Thus social science and only social science has the capability of empowering the effective deployment of religious instruction activity. In and through the way it functions, theology simply lacks this capability.

The assertion that social science rather than theology is the proper ground and medium of religious instruction does not mean that one imperialism (theology) is overthrown so that another imperialism may take its place. Theology is imperialistic when it attempts to exert absolute domination over an area of reality which is not properly its own. Such improper domination is what constitutes an empire, after all, as for example the Roman Empire, the British Empire, the Soviet Empire and so on. Theological imperialism consists in the absorption by theology of sectors of reality inappropriate to it, which is exactly what happens when theology tries to rule over religious instruction. Theological imperialism is the attempt to dictate the very nature and operations of areas which are foreign to it, such as 'Christian teaching methods', 'Christian learning theory', 'Christian dental techniques', 'Christian engineering theory' and the like. Social science is not imperialistic with respect to religious instruction because religious instruction genuinely belongs in what is properly social-science territory. Theology is imperialistic when it tries to impose norms and procedures from a source extrinsic to the religious instruction act itself, namely from theology. Social science is not imperialistic with regard to religious instruction because social science merely clarifies and operationalises those existential norms and procedures which underlie and flow through religious instruction activity itself. The foundation of a nonimperialistic ground and medium of religious instruction is the religious instruction act itself, especially the developmental nature of the learner and the actual functioning of the pedagogical dynamic. Religious instruction simply uses social science as ground and medium, first, in order to theoretically explain and predict and verify from its own nature what it is doing, and second, in order to practically augment the effectiveness of its operation. This is not domination: it is enlightenment and enhancement. Advocates of the theological approach to religious instruction must learn to accept the fact that each nontheological sector of reality operates according to its own essential and developmental laws, and not according to theological laws.

Notes

1. A macrotheory is an overall and global form of theory into which are inserted theories and subtheories of a lesser scope. For example, the theory of grace is a major macrotheory in theological science. The atomic theory is a major macrotheory in chemical science.
2. James Michael Lee, *The Shape of Religious Instruction*, Birmingham, Alabama, Religious Education Press, 1971.
3. John H Westerhoff III, 'Value catechesis', *New Review of Books and Religion*, 4, 1980,

p. 3. The other two areas of religious education, namely religious guidance/counselling and the administration of religious education activities, long ago rejected the theological approach as their macrotheory, and instead adopted the social-science approach. Religious instruction for years was the lone holdout. But then again, this is not surprising since religious instruction always seems to lag behind.

4. See, for example, Randolph Crump Miller, 'Continuity and contrast in the future of religious education', in James Michael Lee, *The Religious Education We Need,* Birmingham, Alabama, Religious Education Press, 1977, pp. 38–39; Randolph Crump Miller, *The Theory of Christian Education Practice*, Birmingham, Alabama, Religious Education Press, 1980, pp. 2, 153–164.

5. On this point, see James Michael Lee, 'Christian religious education and moral development', in Brenda Munsey (ed.), *Moral Development, Moral Education, and Kohlberg,* Birmingham, Alabama, Religious Education Press, 1980, p. 354.

6. Harold William Burgess, *An Invitation to Religious Education*, Birmingham, Alabama, Religious Education Press, 1975. As far as I am able to ascertain, this splendid volume is the most widely-used textbook for foundations courses in religious education in Protestant and Catholic graduate schools and seminaries in North America.

7. John H Westerhoff III states that the aim of religious instruction is theology. John H Westerhoff III, 'A discipline in crisis', *Religious Education*, 54, 1979, pp. 7–15; here pp. 10–11.

8. Some religious educationists and theologians erroneously claim that I hold social science to be value-free in the sense that it neither presupposes nor embodies certain values. Such a claim is palpably false. I specifically state in my books that value-freedom in social science means, among other things, that (1) social science is not normative with respect to religious and moral values; hence social science cannot state what ought to be religiously or morally; (2) social science of itself cannot assign moral or religious value to any reality; (3) social science can deal with a wide variety of morally and religiously value-laden areas without having to necessarily express a preference for one or another value based on the intrinsic moral and religious merits of that value. See James Michael Lee, *The Shape of Religious Instruction*, Birmingham, Alabama, Religious Education Press, 1971, pp. 143–144, 207–208.

9. For a brief discussion of these theories, see James Michael Lee, *The Flow of Religious Instruction*, Birmingham, Alabama, Religious Education Press, 1973, pp. 149–196.

10. See H Edward Everding Jr, Clarence H Snelling Jr, and Mary M Wilcox, 'Toward a theory of instruction for religious education', unpublished paper presented at the October 1976, meeting of the Association of Professors and Researchers in Religious Education.

11. In classical theological method, this is called the negative check on theology.

12. See, for example, James Michael Lee, *The Flow of Religious Instruction*, Birmingham, Alabama, Religious Education Press, 1973, pp. 65–73; Merton P Strommen (ed.), *Research on Religious Development*, New York, Hawthorn, 1971.

13. William Jacobs urges religious educators not to be 'particularly conscious of results. God alone knows them and this is quite sufficient.' William J Jacobs, 'The catechist as witness', in J T Dillon (ed.), *Catechetics Reconsidered*, Winona, Minnesota, St Mary's College Press, 1968, pp. 85–89, quote on p. 88.

14. John H Westerhoff III and Gwen Kennedy Neville, *Generation to Generation* (2nd edition), New York, Pilgrim Press, 1979.

15. Mediatorship stands as a central element in my overall theory of religious instruction. For an early formulation of my concept of mediatorship, see James Michael Lee, *The Flow of Religious Instruction*, Birmingham, Alabama, Religious Education Press, 1973, pp. 18–19.

16. It is tempting to make my position completely analogous to that which happens in a chemical compound, especially in a covalent chemical compound. A chemical compound is a pure substance with its own distinct identity. It is formed by the chemical union of its components in such a manner that the components lose their own separate identities. The constituents of a compound cannot be separated by physical means. Thus a compound differs significantly from a mixture. A mixture is a substance in which the components keep their own separate identities and are simply joined together in a conglomerate substance. The components of a mixture can be separated by physical means. Unlike an ionic compound which is formed by the loss and gain of electrons, a covalent compound is formed between like and unlike atoms because they are able to share pairs of electrons. However, I am not using a chemical compound as a perfect analogy with mediatorship for several reasons, among the most important of which is the fact that the composition of a pure chemical compound is always the same – the law of constant proportions.

17. I am using the term 'subsumption' in the sense of ontic synthesis and not in the sense in

which this term is used in formal logic or in Scottish law. Furthermore, my position is not identical to nor has ever been identical to dialectic as originally conceptualised by Georg Hegel or as subsequently used with modification by Karl Marx.

18. There is an important strand in modern Christology which uses one or another conceptualisation of mediator. The major and most seminal of the treatments of Jesus as mediator is Emil Brunner, *The Mediator* (translated by Olive Wyon), Philadelphia, Westminster Press, 1967.

19. My thesis of mediatorship and of religious instruction as a new ontic entity clearly indicates that I do not have an educational theory, as O'Hare mistakenly claims. I have a religious instruction theory, which is vastly different from having an educational theory. In contrast to O'Hare's misconception, Mary C Boys has correctly interpreted my position on this matter. See Padraic O'Hare, 'The image of theology in the educational theory of James Michael Lee', *Living Light*, 11, 1974, pp. 452–458; Mary C Boys, *Biblical Interpretation in Religious Education*, Birmingham, Alabama, Religious Education Press, pp. 231–239.

2. Theological foundations: the bible

Christian theology is, in part, an articulation, systematisation and critical interpretation of the imagery, ideas, history and religion expressed in the Christian scriptures. Christian education, therefore, is, in part, an education in this biblical material, and it frequently appeals to educational practices and insights contained within the biblical tradition itself.[1]

Walter Brueggemann,[2] an Old Testament scholar, focuses on the nature of education in ancient Israel. He describes this as a 'nurture in passion' through the telling and hearing of open-ended stories that equip and authorise people to cry, care, rage and hope. It is also an education into a tested perspective on human conduct and its outcomes ('the deed-consequence construct'), four dimensions of which are analysed here. Brueggemann's article, 'Passion and perspective: two dimensions of education in the bible' (*Theology Today*, 42, 1985, pp. 172–180), concludes with some reflections on the possible and the impossible in education in the bible.

With the second article in this section we move to the New Testament, and reflect on the lack of concern there with the question of schooling. E A Judge addresses this problem in his article 'The reaction against classical education in the New Testament', with particular reference to the way Paul rejects both the ideals of classical notions of higher education and those of the professional teacher. Paul's overthrowing of 'the value-system upon which Greek education had been built up' allows a radical new patterning of human relationships in which each may contribute to the upbuilding of the others. Judge's paper was first published in the *Journal of Christian Education*, papers 77, 1983, pp. 7–14.[3]

John Tinsley's article, 'Tell it slant', first published in *Theology Today*, 35, 1979, pp. 398–404 and *Theology*, 83, 1980, pp. 163–170, offers a particular perspective on Christian education in general. Tinsley contends that Emily Dickinson's famous phrase must be applied to Christian communication, as should a variety of appeals from other quarters for 'reticence', 'indirection' and 'obliqueness' in truth-telling. Noting

Kierkegaard's comments on 'deceit', and the use made by others of a theology of indirection, Tinsley proceeds to analyse the Jesus of the parabolic method as a 'prophet of indirect communication' and argues that 'indirection is the essence of witnessing for Christ'.

Professor Walter Brueggemann is Professor of Old Testament at Columbia Theological Seminary, Decatur, Georgia, USA. Professor E A Judge has recently retired as Vice-Chancellor and Professor of History at Macquarie University, New South Wales, Australia. The late John Tinsley was Bishop of Bristol, England, and formerly Professor of Theology at the University of Leeds, England.

Notes

1. See, for example, Mary C Boys, *Biblical Interpretation in Religious Education*, Birmingham, Alabama, Religious Education Press, 1980; William E Anderson, 'A biblical view of education', *Journal of Christian Education*, papers 77, 1983, pp. 15-30; Marianne Sawicki, 'How to teach Christ's disciples: John 1:19-37 and Matthew 11:2-15', *Lexington Theological Quarterly*, 21, 1986, pp. 14-26, and 'Educational policy and Christian origins', *Religious Education*, 85, 1990, pp. 455-477; Charles F Melchert, 'Creation and justice among the sages', *Religious Education*, 85, 1990, pp. 368-381, and 'Wisdom is vindicated by her deeds', *Religious Education*, 87, 1992, pp. 127-151. See also Charles M Wood, *The Formation of Christian Understanding: theological hermeneutics*, Valley Forge, Pennsylvania, Trinity Press International, 1993.

2. See also Walter Brueggemann, *The Creative Word: canon as a model for biblical education*, Philadelphia, Fortress, 1982.

3. See also E A Judge, 'The interaction of biblical and classical education in the fourth century', *Journal of Christian Education,* papers 77, 1983, pp. 31-37.

2.1 Passion and perspective: two dimensions of education in the bible

Walter Brueggemann

Education in passion

In 1918, Max Weber made the following statement: 'Politics is a strong slow boring of hard boards. It takes both passion and perspective. Certainly all historical experience confirms the truth – that man would not have attained the possible unless time and again he had reached out for the impossible.'[1] There are clues here for understanding important dimensions of education, biblically understood.

Education in ancient Israel is education in *a quite concrete passion*. Education consists in the older generation communicating its concrete passions to the younger generation and, hopefully, having that younger generation appropriate them with zeal and imagination.

The texts that mark the beginning point of our discussion (Exodus 12:26, 13:8, 13:4; Deuteronomy 6:20–21; Joshua 4:6, 21) are those that show the parents inculcating the young into what is foundational for the community. In one form or another, all of these texts anticipate a time to come when there will be learning readiness and the child will ask the questions of the community: What does it mean to be Israel? Why do we live the way we live and do what we do? The answer, in various castings, is to tell the story of this community, the long deep memory which started with nobodies who were surprised by transformation and became a community through the historical process (cf. Deuteronomy 10:22). This community has a distinct identity that is in considerable tension with the values and the presuppositions of the dominant community. That distinct identity is the primary subject matter of education in passion.

Education in passion, in the bible, is nurture into a distinct community that knows itself to be at odds with dominant assumptions. Torah education is an insistence on being fully covenanted Israel who has been chosen, summoned, commanded and promised. This nurture in passion is concrete and specific, as indeed passion must always be. While Torah acknowledges that 'others' are there and struggles with how Israel is to relate to and be understood in the midst of the others (cf. Genesis 12:1–3; Deuteronomy 7:6–11, 23:3–8), it is nurture in particularity that is the main focus, a nurture that produces adults who know so well who they are and what is commanded that they value and celebrate their oddity in the face of every seductive and powerful imperial alternative.

Narrative life

Israel practises nurture in passion by including its young in its narrative imagination. Education in this mode consists in telling and hearing stories that are deeply rooted in the memory and experience of this people, but which are open-ended and can be imaginatively carried in many different directions depending on need, possibility and circumstance. Israel asserts to its young that *these are the stories*. There can be no other stories. These are not negotiable. These must be embraced to be who we are. But Israel, at the same time, is enormously open to what these stories say and mean, and thus allows great *freedom in interpretation*. That is why some of the stories receive such different tellings. It is not because of redaction and editing, but because the stories are themselves acts of communal freedom.

The narrative life of Israel is a practice in *tales of buoyancy*. The narrative memory of Israel is cast as a story in which Yahweh, the invisible God and key actor in the narrative plot of Israel, is the subject of active verbs of liberation and nurture. Israel, and derivatively each person in Israel, is the object and recipient of Yahweh's liberating, nurturing work. The claim of the narrative grammar is that the crucial actions concerning Israel in the past are done for and to Israel, not by Israel (cf. Exodus 19:4; Isaiah 40:31, 46:4). The central passions evoked in Israel by these stories are amazement which leads to praise, and gratitude which leads to obedience.

But, of course, the memory of Israel is more than a tale of well-being. Israel is capable of critical self-awareness and wants its young to be self-aware of the dangerous miscarriage of these tales of buoyancy. Therefore, the tales of buoyancy are oft-times made into *tales of chagrin*. Israel has enough self-knowledge to see that the relationship is skewed, that the gift of liberated life has been perverted, that the grant of free, fertile land has been abused. What has been given can be lost. The recital is turned so that it becomes a confession of sin (cf. Deuteronomy 32:15–18; Psalm 78, 106; Nehemiah 9). It may be argued that this second version of the foundational narrative is not definitional. However, I suggest that the reality of 'suspicion' in the life of Israel is indeed crucial. This does not lead to a sense of morbidity, but it does lead to a dialectic that is at the heart of Israel's passion. Both gratitude and guilt function to keep Israel's life with God alive and open.

Practices of passion

Such nurture in passion leads to particular practices of passion in the public life of this people.

First, this passion in Israel *equips people to cry*, to feel pain, to articulate the anguish, to sense the pathos and act on it. Israel's life with Yahweh begins in a cry (Exodus 2:23–25). That cry is not a confident address to God. Indeed, it is not even addressed to God. Israel's faith does not begin with theological boldness but with social need and social rage. The cry is a desperate assertion that life in its oppressive mode has become unbearable. Such a cry is not only an act of sensitivity but also an act of enormous boldness, for it dramatically delegitimates the claims of the Egyptian empire and announces that the imperial system is dysfunctional and therefore rejected. This cry is re-enacted in Israel's credo (Deuteronomy 26:7) and in Israel's law (Exodus 22:23, 27).

Second, this passion in Israel *empowers Israel to care*. The most succinct statement of this passion is in Deuteronomy 10:19:

Love the sojourner therefore;
for you were sojourners in the land of Egypt.

Nothing in that memory is as crucial and compelling as the core affirmation that Yahweh has strangely and inexplicably identified with and intervenes for those without social value and power. This central religious affirmation becomes the driving force for Israel's public ethic. Much of its ethical tradition is borrowed from common cultural deposits, but at the decisive points Israel's ethical tradition derives from this distinctive memory, as is evident in Torah instructions.

Third, this passion in Israel *permitted rage*, a theological act whereby Israel assaults what is or appears to be Yahweh's fickleness, indifference or infidelity. Israel practises and teaches its young that it must not be excessively submissive even at the throne of God, for excessive submissiveness to God is most probably allied with excessive conformity to the social powers of the day. This is not to say that Israel refused awe, wonder, reverence, even silence at the throne, but that this is held in tension with the boldness to critique God to God's face.

The material for this posture (now largely lost in the practice of a submissive church) is found in the lament Psalms, in extreme form in the poem of Job, and remarkably in the person of Moses in his daring prayers (see Exodus 32:32, 33:12–16; Numbers 11:11–15). Such a passion for rage is, of course, a dangerous agenda for education, not easily welcomed in a settled community. Most settled communities would rather teach docility and respect for authority. To be docile, submissive and passive, to refrain from rage, is a way to maintain order and to nurture obedience, respect and conformity. But Israel's tradition is 'an-iconic' in extreme form. It understands that the holiness of God demands acute seriousness from the human side. This education nurtures Israel's young into freedom at the throne which spins off in freedom in the face of every illegitimate oppressor (cf. Daniel 3:16–18).

Fourth, this passion in Israel *authorises Israel to hope*. God will work an unextrapolated, underived newness, wrought *ex nihilo*, only out of God's power and purposes. One of the major gains of recent

Scripture study is the rediscovery of the promissory character of the biblical God. This God makes promises and sojourns with this people to watch over the promises to bring them to fulfilment. We arrive in the narrative at the irreducible self-disclosure of God who is 'on the way' with God's people. This people, conversely, is summoned to be 'on the way' with this God to a new land, a new family, a new home, a new kingdom (cf. Hebrews 11).

The capacity to hope, grounded in the very character of God, is the assertion of a critical principle. Keeping the future open to God's newness (which hope does) serves inevitably to keep the present open and under review, to preclude absolutising the present. It is that tradition which causes Torah-nurtured people to be so impatient, so problematic, so energised, so difficult to administer.

Education in perspective

Education in ancient Israel is education in *urbane and reflective perspective*. 'Perspective' is the element paired with passion in Weber's programmatic statement. Education consists in the older generation communicating its deposit of tested perspective to the younger generation and, hopefully, having that generation appropriate that perspective with respect and discipline. The wisdom teaching of Israel makes such perspective available.

In both contexts of clan and court, the instruction of the young is fundamentally consolidating and conservative. It is done by those who have been able to 'tame' life to their advantage. They have learned the secrets of economics, power, domestic life, speech, work, and all of the social operations which can enhance or endanger life. The test of such 'secrets' is that they have produced a stable, well-ordered, reasonably prosperous and secure social existence. Wisdom literature intends that the young should share this perspective in order that the well-being, prosperity and security of the community can be sustained, so that the next generation can enjoy the social advantage now in hand which should not be risked.

At the very centre of wisdom instruction is a buoyant, confident affirmation of God who presides over this orderly social process that produces well-being. It is the link between pragmatic benefit and theological affirmation that makes wisdom instruction so powerful and so convincing. Such teachers are not merely shrewd operators but they spend their time trying to discern how God presides over the creation and human life.

A number of contemporary biblical scholars have in various ways argued that the wisdom instruction reflects a class orientation. It is the voice, experience and perspective of the propertied class, that very group which takes responsibility for society, which generates security and well-being for the entire populace. In contrast to the awkwardness of the tales of passion and the sense that Israel is something of an oddity, there is no such awkwardness or sense of oddity in the wisdom perspective. The appeal is to common experience which is shared by non-Israelite tradition. Where the God of Israel is mentioned, that God is linked to and aligned with the truth that all could arrive at through reflection on experience. Education must equip the next generation of prosperous believers with a perspective on ethics and epistemology that will withstand the scrutiny of a pluralistic culture. 'Perspective' permits one to function in public places and to make sense of general human interaction without recourse to obscurantist or sectarian claims.

The deed-consequence construct

This tradition of education can be seen in the notion of deed-consequence, the studied reflection on the coherence of human conduct with social and 'natural' outcomes. This construct (identified by Koch and now commonly cited by scholars) seems to be an overarching conviction of wisdom teachers. To make sense of human experience through the deed-consequence construct is to educate the young so that they may appropriate and honour the modes of coherence and continuity practised in this community. Thus the deed-consequence construct is a way of speaking to the young about how social power, social goods and social access are distributed in this community and the criteria by which they are distributed. It is a statement of theodicy. Like every theodicy this is, in part, a *reflection of theological conviction*. There are some givens that are ordained in the world and are known to be the will of God. The young must learn these and learn to respect and honour them, for their own well-being. In part, every theodicy is, however, also a *reflection of social interest*, a statement of the kind of behaviour which this community approves and rewards and the kind of behaviour which this community disapproves and punishes. Both elements must be learned in order to succeed in the community. Wisdom instruction imparts to the young both its best theological judgement about God's will and the community's best defence of its preferred social arrangement, which is also taught as sanctioned by God.

Dimensions of nurture

Four dimensions of nurture in perspective, typified in the deed-consequence construct, may be suggested.

First, this perspective affirms that life in its many parts is *coherently interrelated*. The social process does not consist of discrete, isolated acts, each of which can be taken on its own terms. It is the self-deception of powerful people that one can mock the interrelatedness of life by being smart, quick, powerful or ruthless, so that one can commit deeds and avoid consequences. It is thus assumed that one's actions are unfettered and one may do what one pleases.

The wisdom teachers, however, teach against such a conclusion and seek to mobilise every kind of evidence available to support their teaching. The simplest examples include: pride brings disgrace (Proverbs 11:2); crookedness destroys (11:3); righteousness delivers from death (11:4); security for a stranger causes pain (11:15). These examples, in their various forms, hold to the central conviction that things hang together in a moral coherence which cannot be outflanked, mocked, or escaped.

In our social context, we are now in an amorphous way trying to discern the connections between greed and order, between selfishness and justice, between permissiveness and happiness, between oppressiveness and humaneness. This tradition of perspective affirms that there are quite concrete and specific connections which are quite reliable. Close study will lead to their discernment. They are not finally hidden.

Second, this perspective acknowledges that there is *transcendent mystery* in the midst of the interrelatedness. It is the business of kings (and all those who have a monopoly on knowledge) to try to figure out the connections (Proverbs 25:2), but the connections are beyond their control. There is a holy mystery at work in the coherence of life that cannot be penetrated or dissolved. If that is not so, life could be programmed to produce the desired results. That, of course, is the deception of all technical reason and scientific positivism.

The affirmation of the wisdom perspective is, therefore, twofold. It affirms that life's connections are discernible and every effort must be made to master those connections. There is a deep human yearning to know, and it is a proper yearning that is at the heart of nurture in perspective. But at the same time, wisdom teaching affirms the mystery and the recognition that God is not readily available and that life cannot be tightly managed. Indeed, such a tight management, were it possible, would surely lead to oppression and totalitarianism, not only political but epistemological as well. The wisdom tradition, as a whole, knows that such a reductionism is bad theology and a bad reading of experience. There are two kinds of fools: those who mock the order and pretend that it does not exist, and those who think they know too much and seek to control the order.

Third, the sapiential perspective, as expressed in Job and Ecclesiastes, not only knows but practises a *critical unmasking* of its own claims to knowledge. Education in this perspective requires the practice of critical unmasking or, in the language of Paul Ricoeur, the practice of suspicion. It is not the case, as is often suggested, that Job and Ecclesiastes reflect the disintegration of the sapiential tradition. Rather, those literatures are the on-going practice and construction of that very tradition. Proverbs by itself is inclined to know too much and to believe too much in a naive way. Job and Ecclesiastes practise the other pole of sapiential reflection, in which the settled consensus is exposed as being at variance from the facts of experience. Job and Ecclesiastes are conversations about the reality of experience in the face of formulae which have grown cold and hard.

The capacity for suspicion, unmasking and criticism is exceedingly important for the well-being of a community, though largely lacking in our own educational enterprise. It is important theologically, for without it one is unable to distinguish the true God from a variety of idols. It is important for social practice, because without it one is readily taken in by the claims of ideology and propaganda in which vested interest is only thinly disguised. The current intrusion of sectarian religion into public life in a most ideological fashion is a measure of the naïvety and gullibility of a community which believes all of the Proverbs but has never noticed the realities of Job and Ecclesiastes.

Fourth, this nurture in perspective does not, however, end in suspicion. Public life cannot finally be based on scepticism. Faith cannot be reduced simply to healthy doubt. Thus, at the end, this perspective arrives at *trustful submission and yielding*. That is, when the idols have been exposed and rejected, true wisdom ends in the fear of the Lord. One must state this carefully, as it comes only at the *end* of the process of education. If it comes earlier, it will short-circuit the suspicion, and then trustful obedience becomes the kind embodied in Job's friends and perhaps even in Proverbs. But at the end of the process, such trustful submission is offered even in Job (28:28) and Ecclesiastes (12:13). This perspective guards against an arrogant legalism and a mocking autonomy, and finally concludes that life consists in faithful obedience.

The possible and the impossible

The statement by Weber with which this article opens contains another dialectic statement I want to pursue with regard to education: 'Certainly all historical experience confirms the truth – that man would not have attained the possible unless time and again he had reached out for the impossible.' I suggest that education in the bible concerns both the possible and the impossible.

The wisdom tradition is stone cold sober about the possible. The wisdom teachers are voices of realism, shapers of policy, responsible participants in public life. They are not excessively given to flights of fantasy, wish, dream or vision. They study how human and social processes work and how they can be made to work better. They study how creation processes work and how the human creature can be allied with them. There is, for this tradition, an enormous stake in being faithful, obedient people, in being voices of realism and responsible participants in public life. The wisdom teachers are the ones who thought intensely about the distribution of goods and management of social power. Some of the wisdom teachers surely lived close to the throne, and they knew that policy issues had to be addressed. They were committed to the processes of the possible.

But such a perspective taken by itself, Weber warns, is hazardous. It may reduce policy formation to technical reason, so that options are limited to a narrow range of perceptions and interests. Weber's shrewd judgement is that it is only in reaching out for the impossible that the possible is attainable. In a thematic way, I suggest that Torah education in passion is precisely education in impossibility. That is what makes Torah such an attractive, maddening, dangerous literature. It is not excessively committed to being reasonable. Its appeal is not to common sense but to imagination that invariably violates common sense. It invites the listener not to realism but to amazement.

Torah tells tales of babies born to old women (Genesis 18:1-15), of water held back for freedom only to drown the empire (Exodus 14), of bread strangely given but not to be hoarded (Exodus 16), of water flowing from rocks (Exodus 17:1-7), of cities falling before trumpets (Joshua 6). Impossible claims pervade this narrative rendition of reality: slaves are freed, empires are brought low, poor become rich, empty become full, dead come to life, last become first. None of that could be turned directly into policy. But this narrative presentation of a counter-reality lives in the community to redescribe reality, to assault imagination, to open the horizons of what may be hoped and trusted.

When one is deeply nurtured in this tradition of impossibility and then returns stone cold sober to policy, questions of policy look very different. In Torah, the theme of impossibility occurs not only in the narrative, but also occurs in what we call 'law': protection of runaway slaves (Deuteronomy 23:15-16); cancellation of debts (15:1-6); sanctuary for murderers (19:1-10); loans without interest (23:19); limit of public beatings (25:1-3). The impossibility of narrative began to move into actual policy formation.

Both in narrative and in policy proposal, Israel's Torah playfully lives at the brink of impossibility. From this brink, Israel is invited to the perspective and shrewdness of wisdom, to think with hard-nosed realism about what is possible and what will work. But when one moves from the playground of Torah to the laboratory of wisdom, one sees the interplay between possibility and impossibility differently. One sees all old technical reason in jeopardy, all old priorities made porous, all old presuppositions kept under review.

The educated Israelite moves back and forth between passion and perspective, between impossibility and possibility, between free imagination and sober realism. It is never known ahead of time which will triumph in a particular situation. But the tradition consistently claims that the impossibilities of *passion* will eventually prevail over the more disciplined *perspective*. That is why, theologically as well as historically, the canon gives prior authority to Torah. The realism and cunning of wisdom must ultimately yield to this memory of impossibility.

Passion and perspective

The programmatic statement by Weber concerns politics, not education in the bible. What is striking is that a statement on politics can serve so well as a statement on education. The reason, of course, is that the bible is a statement about public life. In both Testaments, the dominant metaphor of kingdom is a political metaphor. Biblical education, then, concerns public life, the use of power, the management of resources and the shaping of policy. In the best, most comprehensive sense, this education is for political life. The passions of Torah education are public passions concerning freedom and justice. The perspectives of wisdom education have to do with convictions and mystery as they operate in interpersonal relations and around such public issues as sexuality, money, power and work. The passions and impossibilities of Torah are public. The perspectives and possibilities of wisdom are public.

Perhaps the primary issue in education, in relation to the bible, is to break the grip on church education which tends to be privatistic, idealistic and spiritual. The crucial question before us is whether, for the difficult decades to come, we shall have men and women in public life who have a passion for justice and a perspective of mystery, awe and amazement. Without such passion and perspective, we are left with the worst forms of pragmatism, technical reason and utilitarianism which uncritically practise self-interest of a brutal kind. Israel's alternative education insists that life in this world requires glad obedience to the coming kingdom in which the blind see, the lame walk, lepers are cleansed, the dead are raised and the poor have good news preached to them (Luke 7:22). Without this education in passionate impossibility, the blind, lame, lepers, dead and poor go unnoticed, and all the others are fated then to live in anxiety and despair until we destroy each other. Without this education in a perspective on the possible, there will be no concrete context for the impossible.

Note
1.   'Politics as vocation', in H H Gerth and C W Mills (eds), *From Max Weber: essays in sociology,* New York, Oxford University Press, 1946, p. 128.

2.2 The reaction against classical education in the New Testament

E A Judge

Introduction

In talking of 'Christian Education' one advances well beyond the framework of New Testament thought. Indeed, insofar as we are talking about schooling, we have to say that it is a matter that is not dealt with in the New Testament at all. The fact that some of the ministries in the churches, notably teaching, are described in educational terms, and that educational metaphors are sometimes used of church life, is not at all a good reason for thinking that the principles of upbuilding in Christ can be transferred to schooling in particular. The subject is available for metaphor because it is not being dealt with in itself. This only sharpens the problem of why the New Testament writers were not concerned with schooling. In other cases, such as economics, where the New Testament does not seem to face a subject in our way, we may say that it is because such questions were not conceptualised in our way at the time. But with education the opposite applies. By New Testament times the Greeks had for centuries both practised education and discussed it in essentially the same terms as we do.[1]

Classical education

Hellenistic education proceeded through primary, secondary and tertiary levels roughly corresponding to ours. Grammatical and literary studies were dominant at the lower levels, but linked with mathematics, music and physical training. Girls and boys were treated alike. But from adolescence boys were admitted to the privileged ephebic education in the gymnasium, originally intended for military training. It became a kind of public school system in the elite sense, conferring social status. From Roman times one might seek official registration in the old boys' union of 'those who were from the gymnasium', provided one's family had been in it for several generations.[2] For tertiary education one might expect to move to a major centre, to study under a famous rhetorician (a sophist), or under a philosopher. These two types of school were distinguished by two basically different curriculums, not unlike our distinction between Arts and Sciences, and they were highly critical of each other. The rhetoricians specialised in the training of a man for public life, while the philosophers concentrated upon the theoretical analysis of man and the universe.

Broadly speaking this is the pattern of education that has persisted, witness especially the tradition of the British Public School or the German Gymnasium, into our own lifetimes. Central to it has always been the study of the classical authors. Students in St Paul's day concentrated upon the same writers, and by much the same methods of grammatical analysis and literary commentary, as would a modern Classics student – Homer, the Athenian dramatists and Demosthenes; or Cicero, Horace and Vergil if they were being educated in Latin. But behind the ascendancy of these studies in nineteenth-century church schools lies a paradox. Classical literature embodies ideals profoundly in conflict with those of the bible: polytheism, for example, and an ethical stance that fostered exploitative sexual and social relations. In the early centuries the churches denounced this as poison, to which church training in the bible was the antidote. But why did it not arise as a problem in the New Testament?

New Testament context

A simple explanation would be that the churches were made up of uneducated people. This was frequently asserted against them by their critics in the next two centuries. It was taken up as a serious historical explanation in the early part of this century, when the newly found papyrus letters were held to show that the New Testament letters came from a similarly sub-literary level of culture.[3] Paul seemed to endorse this in 1 Corinthians 1: 26–29, and perhaps, it was said, could not even write himself, simply adding his signature to what he had dictated as in Colossians 4:18. But we now have a petition and a letter from Lollianos, the public grammar-school teacher from Oxyrhynchus in the mid-third century, which shows that he also preferred to dictate.[4] Indeed, not writing one's own letters was the mark of a gentleman, who could afford a secretary. Paul's low rating of the Corinthians is probably sarcastic. The commonest opinion now is that the churches were partly drawn from educated circles. It has been shown that the papyrus letters of ordinary people do not document the level of Greek seen in the New Testament. It is to be identified rather with the professional prose used by technical writers of the time. This was the contemporary Greek of educated people, though distinctly modern compared with the already ancient classical Greek of the Athenian fifth century. There was a vogue starting in Paul's day for trying to reimpose this as the standard of educated expression. By a massive effort of educational archaism it subsequently prevailed in the schools, so that the great Fathers of the Greek church in the fourth century, notably John Chrysostom, wrote in the style of 800 years before. These classicisers were well aware that Paul did not use the Attic diction now essential to the educated man. They had lost sight of the fact that Paul was writing in the form of the language current amongst educated people in his day.[5]

Nor need we attempt to say that as a Jew Paul would not have been at home with Greek.[6] Judaism, like Hellenism, passed into an archaising phase in later antiquity, so that to read the Talmud one might think there had been little cultural contact between the two. But the very existence of the New Testament, as of Philo and Josephus, shows how closely interlocked the two cultures were. Modern studies have shown that one must allow for a diversity of cultural arrangements in the Judaism of the first century.[7] Paul would have had the opportunity of a Greek education even in Gamaliel's school at Jerusalem. The Talmud means by 'Greek wisdom' specifically the formal education that was necessary to cosmopolitan life.[8] Even Bar Kokhba, the last great Jewish nationalist in the second century, found it easier to write his letters in Greek, as recent discoveries have shown.[9]

The terminology of education arises occasionally in the New Testament letters. But it is used for the discussion of other matters. Neither *paideia* (the general word for the education of children) nor *gymnasia* (the word for training), nor the cognate forms, is used with reference to the central intellectual content of education (though an instance of this occurs in Acts 7:22). In Hebrews 12:5-7 *paideia* is used of the paternal discipline which shows that God is treating us as sons. The word is in effect taken back to its root meaning, disregarding the educational sense it would normally carry in Greek. This is so even when it is applied to the actual upbringing of children as in Ephesians 6:4. Similarly in 1 Timothy 4:8 *gymnasia* is explicitly identified as physical training (which is what the word literally meant), while in 2 Peter 2:14 it is taken up pejoratively as a figure of calculated and practised acquisitiveness. A cynic might say that it was not the last time that the education has fallen out between the punishment and the sport.

On the other hand what the New Testament churches were doing could in some respects very readily have been described in educational terms. There is a considerable amount of teaching going on and great emphasis is placed on growth in understanding. But when analogies are sought for this, as in 2 Timothy 2:2-6, they are not drawn from education. Not only then do the letters not deal with the educational system as a problem for believers, but they also fail to recognise what was going on in the churches as a kind of schooling. The whole matter seems to be of no concern to them.

Nevertheless, the basic significance of education as a cultural boundary-marker is clearly registered by Paul. When he says in Romans 1:14 'I am under obligation both to Greeks and to barbarians', he refers to the classic distinction made by Greeks between those who shared their *paideia* and those who could not speak Greek at all. Similarly, when he speaks in the same sentence of 'the wise' and 'the foolish', he refers to the distinction within Greek culture between those who were highly educated and those who were not. The word *anoetos* means 'mindless'. Julian was to use it at the end of his rescript on Christian teachers for the children of Christian parents, who needed to be cured by a proper Hellenic education.

Paul and education

Yet Paul does not grapple with these problems. He simply rides over them, and supersedes the issue of educational development by taking his followers on to the infancy of a new life in Christ.[10] It is not a matter of reconstructing the existing system, but of starting a new way of life as an adult. In what may well be his earliest letter, we find Paul dwelling on the theme of the nurse who suckles the child she has not borne.[11] He is very interested in the beginnings of the new life, but otherwise his mind jumps to adulthood. Childhood is something to be left behind.[12] Those who are still there[13] are restricted in their response to others. Similarly in Hebrews, it is seen as a defect to be still learning the ABC[14] when one should oneself be a teacher of others. The reference to the 'first principles' picks up a term from elementary education, but the term 'teacher' does not come from the Greek schools so much as from Jewish tradition – a teacher of the law or the gospel as the case may be. The object of the teaching is moral discrimination.[15] Paul does, however, twice pick up a distinctively Greek technical term of schooling and apply it to the experience of the believer. In Galatians 3:24 the *paidagogos* supplies a metaphor for the law in relation to Christ. The *paidagogos* was the servant who walked the child to school, his 'custodian'. He is not the teacher. Similarly in 1 Corinthians 4:15, Paul uses the same metaphor to distinguish his own paternal relationship to his converts in Christ from that of the countless others who were only custodians. The consistently deprecatory use of educational terms is probably not a coincidence. For although Paul shows no sign of finding primary or secondary education a source of problems, there are very clear indications that he had thrown himself into a total confrontation with those who espoused the reigning values of higher education.

It is tantalisingly unclear whether Paul had had a full-scale rhetorical education at tertiary level. To a modern observer he seems a great controversialist. His letters are overwhelming in their argumentative drive. They turn the mind with insistent logic or appealing metaphor, and compel assent with pleas or reproaches. Yet we know from the fourth-century Fathers that he did not conform at all to the complex rules of classical rhetoric. Moreover, he poured scorn on the rhetoric of his rivals, who one may assume followed the standard pattern. It is my belief that he deliberately refrained from the formal techniques of persuasion because he rejected the moral position one must adopt to employ them, and that he was driven into a confrontation with those in the churches who did use them by the fact that his own followers were disturbed by his irregularity. They would have liked him to have done it properly too.[16]

For Paul it was not simply a question of style. He rejects also the substance of academic debate. Rational calculation in the Greek tradition is vitiated by idolatry.[17] The fundamental error of the Greeks over the nature of God makes their reasoning futile. The same terminology is used to condemn disputatiousness within the church at the end of the letter.[18] By 'disputes over opinions' he refers to legalistic arguments in the Jewish tradition. The Pastoral epistles criticise such a spirit of argumentation that had by then established itself in church life.[19] In 1 Corinthians 1:20 Paul challenges the three main types of tertiary scholar of his world: the rationalistic philosopher ('the wise'), the Jewish legal expert ('the scribe') and the rhetorician ('the debater').

Whereas in other respects (for example in the field of personal relations and the ministries in church) Paul is very ready to forge his own vocabulary, here he by no means concedes their terms to his opponents. Wisdom (*sophia*), reason (*logos*) and knowledge (*gnosis*) are all ideals central to his own position. He stigmatises what is invalid in the case of others by qualifying the terms with phrases such as 'of the world' or 'according to the flesh'. The error lies in exalting these ideals into self-sufficient powers. Paul disclaims any 'excessive' reliance upon speech or wisdom,[20] and pin-points 'persuasiveness'[21] as the particular excess he wishes to avoid. This is because his test of truth is that it comes from God and is demonstrated in positive human relations. The way to the treasures of wisdom and knowledge concealed in Christ is through the hearts that are 'knit together' in love.[22] Against that we find set two terms unique in the Pauline vocabulary: 'persuasiveness of speech' (2:4) and 'philosophy' (2:8) which is coupled with 'empty deceit'. Both the great divisions of Greek higher education are explicitly discounted at this point.

In asserting a new source and method of knowing about the ultimate realities of the world, and about how one should live in it, Paul is occupying the territory that belonged to higher education. He is promoting a new kind of community education for adults. This involved him in a confrontation with his own churches because they wanted him to adopt the status in life that was appropriate to a tertiary teacher.

When Paul says,[23] 'we are not, like so many, peddlers of God's word', he is criticising his rivals at Corinth for accepting professional status. They took payment for their teaching. They also had their professional credentials verified (3:1). It turns out that the Corinthians actually objected to not being able to pay Paul for his services (11:7) but that he was determined not to give in on this point, though he readily accepted support from other churches (11:9). It is a matter of status (12:14). They should depend upon him as their parent, and not the other way around. In other words, in their case (presumably because of the construction they placed upon it in distinction from the attitude adopted in other churches), he will not put himself under an obligation to them. Gifts and benefactions in the ancient world were a recognised way of establishing social patronage. One's dependents might be classified as friends, but it was a friendship that was created from above and placed the privileged recipient under commitments. To refuse such a benefaction, on the other hand, constituted a breach of friendship, and one could slip into the exhausting rituals of formal enmity. The tense and contentious atmosphere of the second letter to the Corinthians may well imply that Paul is being drawn into a confrontation of this type.[24]

That correct professional behaviour as a teacher is at stake is shown by another trail of complaints that Paul plays back to the Corinthians. His critics complain that 'his letters are weighty and strong, but his bodily presence is weak and his speech of no account'.[25] Notice the coupling of physical bearing with quality of speech. Beauty and truth support each other in the Greek ideal, and Paul's authority is discounted because he is physically unimpressive. The fact that he could write powerful letters, which they concede, ought to mean that he had the capacity to deliver himself of persuasive speech as well. One must assume that he deliberately chose to add to the handicap of a poor physique the default of not adopting the arts of rhetoric. He will not use the techniques expected of a man in his position. This is confirmed by another term he quotes from his critics. He is 'unskilled in speaking'.[26] The word *idiotes* means 'unprofessional'. It was to live across the centuries to haunt Paul's memory. In the trial of Phileas, bishop of Thmuis, under Diocletian, the governor, Culcianus, attempting to break the bishop's resistance, challenges him with the non-professionalism of Paul's style, using this very term.[27] The fact that Paul concedes this point to the 'superlative apostles'[28] proves that his rivals were performing in the church at Corinth as professional rhetoricians or sophists, and presumably being paid for it into the bargain.

The problem with Paul was that he would not compete. He refuses to class or compare himself with some of those who commend themselves.[29] We know what is referred to here from a papyrus letter written by a university student in Alexandria to his father at home in Oxyrhynchus.[30] Neilus complains of the difficulty he has had in finding decent teachers, since the cleverer one he had hoped to use had died. There was a shortage of sophists, and he had had to settle for Didymus. 'What makes me despair is that this fellow who used to be a mere provincial teacher sees fit to compete with the rest.' Paul suffered a double handicap: he would not do it properly anyway, and thus could not attempt to compete with the rest. The term for the competition in the student's letter is Paul's term *synkrisis*, 'comparison'.[31]

Self-recommendation is the point at which Paul draws the line. It may seem a conventional triviality to us living in a culture which has fully absorbed the Pauline principle. But the long paroxysm into which Paul enters over the matter reveals how fundamental and agonising a break he was making with what was expected in his day. Graeco-Roman culture set a high value on self-esteem. Not to praise oneself was to neglect one's own virtues. But Paul regards boasting as folly. Yet his argument with his competitors draws him inexorably into it ('you forced me to it'[32]) and he suddenly launches himself into a formal and long-sustained recital of his credentials.[33] It recognisably conforms to the schematic conventions of self-display as we know them from other sources. But Paul, in an appalling parody, inverts the contents of his self-eulogy, in order to boast of his weaknesses. Again we face the difficulty that this too has become a convention in our culture. But for Paul's day it is an unprecedented atrocity, which must have profoundly shocked his listeners. Why did he do it? Because he had learned from the case of Christ the paradox that weakness and humiliation put one in the position where God's power prevails.[34]

This is a revolutionary point in our cultural tradition. The value-system upon which Greek education had been built up is deliberately overthrown. Paul was not apparently concerned with the threat which classical literary studies represented to children at primary and secondary levels. But he reacted powerfully against the perversion of human relations which he saw inculcated by the ideals of higher education. It was a perversion because it enshrined the beautiful and the strong in a position of social power. In his own case he deliberately tore down the structure of privilege with which his followers wished to surround him. In its place he set out a fundamentally new pattern of human relations in which each is endowed by God with gifts to contribute to the upbuilding of the others.[35]

Notes

1. F A G Beck, *Greek Education, 450-350 BC*, London, Methuen, 1964; F A G Beck, *An Album of Greek Education*, Sydney, Cheiron Press, 1975; H I Marrou, *A History of Education in Antiquity*, London, Sheed and Ward, 1956.
2. See the applications for scrutiny of credentials published by J R Rea, *The Oxyrhynchus Papyri*, volume 46, London, Egypt Exploration Society, 1978, numbers 3276-3284.
3. G A Deissmann, *Light from the Ancient East*, London, Hodder and Stoughton, 1910; for the history of the debate in the past 25 years see E A Judge, 'The social identity of the first Christians: a question of method in religious history', *Journal of Religious History*, 11, 1980, pp. 201-217; and for discussion of some recently published papyrus documents, see E A Judge, *Rank and Status in the World of the Caesars and St Paul*, Christchurch, University of Canterbury, 1982, pp. 9-20.
4. P J Parsons, *The Oxyrhynchus Papyri*, volume 47, London, Egypt Exploration Society, 1980, no. 3366, text reproduced with discussion by E A Judge, 'A state school teacher makes a salary bid', in G H R Horsley (ed.), *New Documents Illustrating Early Christianity: a review of the Greek inscriptions and papyri published in 1976*, North Ryde, Ancient History Documentary Research Centre, 1981, pp. 72-78.
5. L Rydbeck, *Fachprosa, Vermeintliche Volkssprache und Neues Testament*, Uppsala, Universitetsbiblioteket, 1967; E A Judge, 'St Paul and classical society', *Jahrubch für Antike und Christentum*, 15, 1972, pp. 19-36; E A Judge, 'Paul's boasting in relation to contemporary professional practice', *Australian Biblical Review*, 16, 1968, pp. 37-50.
6. E A Judge, 'The conflict of educational aims in New Testament thought', *Journal of Christian Education*, 9, 1966, pp. 32-45.
7. M Hengel, *Judaism and Hellenism*, Philadelphia, Fortress Press, 1974; M Hengel, *Jews, Greeks and Barbarians*, Philadelphia, Fortress Press, 1980; S Freyne, *Galilee from Alexander the Great to Hadrian*, Notre Dame, Notre Dame University Press, 1980.

8. R J Z Werblowsky, 'Great wisdom and proficiency in Greek', in *Paganisme, Judaisme, Christianisme: influences et affrontements dans le monde antique (Melanges offerts a Marcel Simon)*, Paris, Boccard, 1978, pp. 55-60.

9. He excuses himself from using Hebrew because he 'could not make the effort', B Lifshitz, 'Papyrus grecs du desert de Juda', *Aegyptus*, 40, 1962, p. 241.

10. 1 Corinthians 3:1.

11. 1 Thessalonians 2:7-11.

12. 1 Corinthians 13:11.

13. 2 Corinthians 6:13.

14. Hebrews 5:12; 6:1.

15. Hebrews 5:14.

16. For an analysis of the Epistle to the Galatians in rhetorical terms see the *Hermeneia* commentary by H D Betz, Philadelphia, Fortress Press, 1979.

17. Romans 1:21.

18. Romans 14:1.

19. 1 Timothy 1:4; 6:3-4; 6:20.

20. 1 Corinthians 2:1.

21. 1 Corinthians 2:4.

22. Colossians 2:2.

23. 2 Corinthians 2:17.

24. See the unpublished PhD thesis of Macquarie University by P Marshall, 'Enmity and other social conventions in the relations between Paul and the Corinthians'; S C Mott, 'The power of giving and receiving: reciprocity in Hellenistic benevolence', in G F Hawthorne (ed.), *Current Issues in Biblical and Patristic Interpretation: studies in honor of Merrill C Tenney*, Grand Rapids, Eerdmans, 1975, pp. 60-72; and F W Danker, *Benefactor: epigraphic study of a Graeco-Roman and New Testament semantic field*, St Louis, Clayton, 1982.

25. 2 Corinthians 10:9-10.

26. 2 Corinthians 11:6.

27. H Musurillo, *The Acts of the Christian Martyrs*, Oxford, Oxford University Press, 1972, number 27, column 8 (based on the Bodmer papyrus); for the new Chester Beatty papyrus being edited by A Pietersma, see G H R Horsley, *New Documents Illustrating Early Christianity: a review of the Greek inscriptions and papyri published in 1977*, North Ryde, Ancient History Documentary Research Centre, 1982, number 106.

28. 2 Corinthians 11:5.

29. 2 Corinthians 10:12.

30. C H Roberts, *The Oxyrhynchus Papyri*, volume 18, London, Egypt Exploration Society, 1941, number 2190.

31. See a study of this matter by C B Forbes, 'Comparison, self-praise and irony: Paul's boasting and the conventions of Hellenistic rhetoric', *New Testament Studies*, 32, 1986, pp. 1-30.

32. 2 Corinthians 12:11.

33. 2 Corinthians 11:22-33.

34. 2 Corinthians 12:9-10.

35. This article was adapted from a tape-recorded conference address with the help of Mrs Elizabeth Gardiner and Mr I R Burnard.

2.3 'Tell it slant'

John Tinsley

Introduction

The human mind is ill at ease with ambiguity and paradox. This is especially the case with the religious mind which has a special impetus to convert all ambiguities and paradoxes into the most explicit and unequivocal assertions, while remaining blind to the half-truths it creates in the process. The slogan and the abstraction have such an immediate appeal that their distortion of the facts is not noticed. Hence the tendency, in the heady enthusiasm of evangelism, to convert the gospel into a communiqué, a divine authoritative fiat which brooks no hesitation and no scepticism.

The axis of a communiqué is *vertical,* a speaking *de haut en bas* in tones of, at best, paternalist authority. It is understandable, but regrettable, that Christian evangelists have so readily assumed that this must be the pattern for Christian communication. We have paid a heavy price for the assumption that the model for the Christian preacher (and indeed the teacher) is the Old Testament prophet with his 'Thus says the Lord'. No doubt the attraction of that model was that it seemed to give indubitable authority to the preacher or teacher. But it is possible to be authoritative without being authoritarian. Christ is an authoritative sign but a sign that can be spoken against. His gospel is not a royal decree issued from on high to subjects below. It is the 'scandal' (paradox, offence) of his gospel that its axis is *horizontal*. God amazingly treats human beings as equals, on the level, as friends (cf. John 15:14 ff.) reversing all decrees (for example, of justice) by his 'justification'. This for Paul is the essence of the 'foolishness' of God.

Tell it slant

The injunction to 'tell it slant' is an imperative for the Christian not simply or primarily in the interests of what is thought to be effective or strategically desirable in getting it across. These motives I believe are likely to damage the Christian gospel. 'Telling it slant' is more than an appropriate form of the gospel; it is its essential content, a manner incumbent upon the Christian communicator by the very nature of the gospel. The gospel is not only *what* is said, but *how* it is said. The title of this article is part of a longer quotation from Emily Dickinson:[1]

Tell all the truth but tell it slant
Success in circuit lies.

There are many other quotations I could have chosen, particularly from Auden, like:[2]

Truth in any serious sense
Like Orthodoxy, is a reticence.

It is not surprising that Auden should come immediately to mind. Like many a preacher and teacher, Auden always found himself incurably didactic, with an itch to preach and moralise. At the same time, he was convinced that direct frontal speech (so to speak) is inappropriate in our own day. The burden of my concern is that frontal speech is not only inadmissible in our day but, besides being inimical to courtesy and tact in human relations, is profoundly foreign to a Christian mission that seeks its base in the manner of Christ.

Other quotations from other poets would readily spring to mind: Shakespeare's 'by indirection find directions out', or W B Yeats on what he called 'the crooked way of life' as distinguished from 'inorganic logical straightness'. But there was a striking comment on our theme from a television review in the *Sunday Times* a few years ago.[3] It was an article by Maurice Wiggin on what he called 'television coroners' who move from crisis to crisis and deluge the viewer with 'exhortations and alarums, sensationalism and foreboding, misery and shrill tickings-off'. Wiggin then concluded:

> But I think I always knew that topicality is a drug like any other. We are creatures of our time, inescapably; but our most reliable guide to the holy and eternal *now* is not the man shouting the latest odds at his stall in the market place of personalities, but the artist – poet or priest – who stands at an individual angle to the traffic-choked highway and looks obliquely into the ravaged and aspiring heart of man.
>
> This is the voice for which we must keep an ear in tune, through the cacophony and the cries of alarm, the twittering and stentorian brass, the cackling and the pontifical explanations and prognostications, which do not drown, but amplify unbearably, the ticking of the clock.

The question of what Christian communication might mean in a post-ecclesiastical society was a major concern of the Danish philosopher Søren Kierkegaard. He is the apostle of indirect communication. The two works of Kierkegaard which are of most importance for a study of his thought about indirection are *Training in Christianity*[4] (especially the section called 'The Offence') and *The Point of View for My Work as an Author*.[5]

In *Training in Christianity*, Kierkegaard is concerned with the necessary indirection of the Incarnation as a divine incognito. If people are told that Christ is the God-man, they expect to see God plainly there for themselves. And if they don't, if all they see there looks like the reverse of God (weakness, suffering, death) they find Christ a stumbling-block and are offended.

But God is there in Christ for the recognising:[6]

> He is the God; and yet he picks his steps more carefully than if angels guided them, not to prevent his foot from stumbling against a stone, but *lest he trample human beings in the dust*, in that they are offended in him. He is the God, and yet his eye rests upon mankind with deep concern, *for the tender shoots of an individual life may be crushed as easily as a blade of grass*.

Christ cannot therefore put himself into words (at any rate directly). That constitutes the offence of Christ. But blessed are those who find no stumbling-block in him.

And because it is Christ who speaks through Christians, Christians cannot put Christ directly into words either. This is always the case, but pre-eminently so when Christendom has become what Kierkegaard called 'a prodigious illusion'. This is a condition which appears after a period of Christianisation, in what I have called a post-ecclesiastical era when, to quote Kierkegaard, 'thousands and thousands call themselves Christians as a matter of course'. This complacency, argues Kierkegaard, would only be perpetuated by direct speech. Such an illusion can never be destroyed directly; it can only be radically removed by indirect means. Hence a missionary in a Christendom situation 'will always look rather different from a missionary to the heathen'.

The method Kierkegaard advocates he calls 'deceit', and he develops what he means by deceiving as follows:[7]

> What then does it mean, 'to deceive'? It means that one does not begin *directly* with the matter one wants to communicate, but begins by accepting the other man's illusion as good money. So one does not begin thus: I am a Christian; you are not a Christian. Nor does one begin thus: It is Christianity I am proclaiming; and you are living in purely aesthetic categories. No, one begins thus: Let us talk about aesthetics.

Kierkegaard is arguing in *The Point of View* that indirection is primarily a strategy for a 'Christendom' situation. But he raises the question himself in what he says about the offence of Christ whether indirection is more than a tactical device, whether in fact it is an indissoluble part of the gospel.

Kierkegaard has influenced both poets and theologians in our time. T S Eliot and W H Auden both sought to cultivate indirection. As I mentioned earlier, Auden was always conscious of a strong didactic bent, but was also suspicious of any attempt to communicate moral truth directly. This seemed to him an insidious form of human presumption and the will to power over others. It reminded him somewhat of Fascist politics.

Auden wrote:[8]

> You cannot tell people what to do, you can only tell them parables, and that is what art really is, particular stories of particular people and experiences, from which each according to his immediate and peculiar needs may draw his conclusions.

Hence Auden's search for what he calls a 'poetic teaching', in every poem seeking to surprise, shock or woo the reader into serious self-examination; Auden taking the mickey out of serious subjects in order to create seriousness. Hence his interest in 'secondary worlds', allegory and irony.

T S Eliot was also much tempted to propaganda in the Christian cause. He came to renounce his earlier directness of manner in *The Rock*,[9] becoming increasingly disposed toward semi-allegorical forms of statement. This came about not only because of a deep concern with communication in the world of modern people 'to whom the language of Christianity is not only dead but indecipherable', but also because of the theological and moral demands of an Incarnation which because it is a genuine incarnation runs the risk of creating a situation where there is 'knowledge of words and ignorance of the Word'.

In theology, Tillich and Bonhoeffer are two of the most interesting writers who have sought a theology of indirection. For Tillich the gospel cannot simply be thrown at people, 'like a stone', as he put it. This may be an effective method of revivalist preaching in certain psychological situations, but it is not the communicative role of the church. Bonhoeffer sought indirection in the form of some hidden 'secular' way of proclaiming the gospel.

But such 'indirection' is not simply a concession to a strategy that happens now to be thought appropriate to our times. If we return to the biblical sources with this question in mind, I believe we discover more clearly than before that an essential part of the gospel is its disclosure of the divine pedagogy of indirection.

Biblical sources

For those who want everything to be grounded in some warranty of Scripture, there is no shortage of exhortations to cultivate a certain deviousness, a certain indirection. Paul characterises Christian missioners as 'deceivers yet true' (2 Corinthians 6:8), proclaiming Christ whether *in pretence* or in truth (Philippians 1:18). This truthful deception, or deceptive truth, is a theme of many a saying and parable of Christ: 'Be wise as serpents (cf. Genesis 3) and harmless as doves' (Matthew 10:16); 'Make to yourselves friends of the mammon of unrighteousness' (Luke 16:9). 'Behave wisely towards those outside your own number', says the Epistle to the Colossians, 'study how best to talk with each person you meet' (Colossians 4:5-6).

When therefore Christians are dubbed 'hypocrites' there may be more truth in it than their critics realise. They are in one important sense dissemblers, seemingly devious in their indirection. The problem facing the Christian is how to be satisfactorily lucid, and yet leave enough implication for the gospel to reverberate in and through what is said.

We see the bible pointing to a divine pedagogy of love, especially God's love of freedom. It is therefore a pedagogy which necessarily involves both 'signs' and 'stumbling blocks' (offences). The gospel is necessarily *mysterion* (mystery) and it is *krypton* (hidden). As the author of 1 Timothy puts it: 'Great beyond all question is the *mysterion* of our religion: (God) manifested in the body' (3:16).

Signs, to be signs, are necessarily ambiguous, mistakable, indirect. They cause people to stumble, especially those attached to the 'direct communication' of law and tradition. The only adequate response to these signs is not to label them once and for all as if they are over and done with, but to point to them again in a language which sounds a logical absurdity, the logical absurdity of paradox, as in 2 Corinthians 6:8–10:

> Imposters yet true
> unknown, well-known
> dying, living
> sad, happy
> poor, wealthy
> destitute, abundant.

Karl Jaspers, the German philosopher, distinguished three kinds of 'masters': first, the masters of 'general principles' (Stoics); second, the masters of 'the whole systems' (Aquinas, Hegel); and third, 'prophets of indirect communication' (Socrates).

But I believe it is also correct to speak of Jesus as a 'prophet of indirect communication'. This may sound strange to anyone who comes straight from a reading of the fourth gospel with its direct 'I am' sayings. But I believe it possible to show that the fourth gospel is not the exception which does not prove the rule but is a very sophisticated treatment of indirectness or irony, making the point over and over again that it was perfectly possible to hear and understand (at one level) what Jesus said (his *lalia*) without hearing his Word (*logos*).

In the earlier gospel tradition, Jesus is certainly indirect about himself, declining any explicit self-identification and returning the question of identity back to his questioner ('Let me ask you a question'). He is surprisingly indirect about God, even God as Father. The latter theme never comes in general teaching to crowds but only in intimate talk with disciples – or in prayer. In fact, there are hardly any *direct* statements about God in the teaching of Jesus. His awareness of God could apparently only be contained in indirect or paradoxical language. He is acutely aware of how God stands on end the traditional 'righteousness' of the Torah. All this is involved in his 'radicalisation' of the Law. Jesus seems to have been suspicious of what we would call the 'miraculous' and to have discouraged it, being much more concerned with insight and receptivity as significant ways of responding to the ordinary and familiar.

Whatever the happenings were that Jesus identified as tokens of God's activity for his time, they were not 'miracles' in the modern sense. They were not, to use a New Testament phrase, 'signs from heaven'. In fact to seek for such prodigies was for Jesus characteristic of 'an evil and adulterous generation'. No sign in the sense of a prodigious miracle was to be given to such a generation. The kingdom of God did not come with 'miracles' of the kind that people could say 'Look, here it is' or 'There it is'. The kingdom of God was in their midst. Where and how? That was for his contemporaries to decide.

It is also significant that the miraculous is never an element in that part of the teaching of Jesus where it might have come in, namely his parabolic narratives. In fact the end of the parable of Dives and Lazarus (Luke 16:31) is all of a piece with his attitude elsewhere of discouraging the idea that the truth of religious belief could be solved satisfactorily by some 'miracle' like a raising from the dead ('if they do not hear Moses and the prophets neither will they be convinced if one should rise from the dead').

And yet we should not be surprised at all at this because Jesus himself indicates why there must needs be indirection about God. The kingdom of God (God's revelation) does not come 'with observation' in a way that you can say, directly, 'It's there!' The whole problem as Jesus saw it is not *whether* there should be indirection, but *of what kind* it should be: 'How shall we liken the kingdom of God?' Hence the central significance of the parabolic method of Jesus which is not to illustrate homely truths but point to awesome mystery, often in an uncomfortable and bewildering way. Jesus' commendation of the unjust steward and the injunction to make friends with the mammon of unrighteousness is on a par in its outrageous paradox with his summons to hypocrisy in fasting (Matthew 6:16 ff.). To pretend not to be fasting when one is fasting is what the ordinary world calls hypocrisy. But Jesus calls on God for support: God sees this hypocrisy, and rewards it.

All this is a reminder that revelation is provisional. The God who reveals is greater than what is revealed. God is not exhausted even in the Incarnation. This incompleteness, hiddenness, is indicated by signs, ambiguities, parables, ironies. The believer, the one who takes the signs on trust, is one who looks to the future for completion, for consummation, who looks for the unveiling to come when the hidden things shall be made clear.

Conclusion

Origen said long ago that we should use clearly Christian ideas and perspectives but not fuss about getting them acknowledged as such. It is more important that Christian beliefs should be seen to be true than uniquely Christian. This is another way of saying that the church is most truly in communication when least self-conscious. 'Tell it straight' often has a self-consciousness about it which seriously gets in the way. And if mission becomes, as it so easily does, propaganda, it is not only a mistake, but a perversion of the gospel. Indirection is the essence of witnessing for Christ. Witnessing for Christ ought to be the most self-effacing thing one can do, but how often it has looked and sounded exhibitionist.

It may be accepted that 'tell it slant' is good strategy only in 'discourse with the Greeks' but that it's too sophisticated for the generality. But this could be a kind of élitism. Receiving the gospel is not a matter of having brains but of free personal response where imagination, thought and emotion are integrated.

Another suspicion is that the 'tell it slant' approach is bound to be vague, indecisive, uncommitted; that it would 'water down' the gospel. But on the contrary, it is direct evangelism that produces what Charles Péguy called 'abstractionism', generalisations and platitudes. It is the fixed, definite phrases ('accepting Christ as Lord and Saviour') which can be so vague and elusive. 'Indirection', as the poets show us, is a continuous demand for the concrete, the parable and the symbolic.

Notes

1. Emily Dickinson, *Complete Poems* (edited by Thomas H Johnson), London, Faber, 1970, number 1129.
2. W H Auden, *Shield of Achilles*, London, Faber, 1955, p. 46.
3. Maurice Wiggin, *Sunday Times*, 10 January, 1971.
4. Søren Kierkegaard, *Training in Christianity: and the edifying discourse which 'accompanied' it*, Princeton, New Jersey, Princeton University Press, 1967.
5. Søren Kierkegaard, *The Point of View for my Work as an Author*, London, Oxford University Press, 1939, pp. 40–41.
6. Søren Kierkegaard, *Philosophical Fragments*, Princeton, New Jersey, Princeton University Press, 1985, p. 40.
7. See note 5 above.
8. W H Auden, 'Psychology and art', in Geoffrey Grigson (ed.), *The Arts Today*, London, John Lane the Bodley Head, 1935, pp. 1–21; here pp. 18–19.
9. T S Eliot, *The Complete Poems and Plays of T S Eliot*, London, Faber and Faber, 1969.

3. Theological foundations: the church

The ecclesial community is second only to the bible in importance as a foundation of Christian theology: dogmatics,
accordingly, is always *church* dogmatics. The church, both as
the paradigmatic locus for the work of the Spirit and as the
communal embodiment of Christian faith and practice, is the
principal and essential context for Christian formation and
criticism.

Stanley Hauerwas' article, 'The gesture of a truthful story'
(*Theology Today*, 42, 1985, pp. 181–189), argues that everything the church is and does is 'religious education', for the
church *is* a form of education that is religious. Analysing first a
similar claim about Christian social ethics as the place 'where
the story of God is enacted, told, and heard',[1] Hauerwas identifies the virtues of hope and patience as those that are crucial to
learning this story properly. At best, however, the Christian
social ethic is 'but a gesture'. It is, however, God's gesture on
behalf of the world to create a space and time in which we might
have a foretaste of the Kingdom. And religious education is our
ongoing training in faithfulness through the learning of the skills
for appropriating (the 'gestures' of) God's story.

Craig Dykstra's inaugural address at Princeton, published in
The Princeton Seminary Bulletin, 6, 1985, pp. 188–200, is entitled 'No longer strangers: the church and its educational
ministry'. Dykstra also takes an ecclesiological perspective,
analysing faith as participation in the church in the redemptive
activity of God, by knowing 'what the community knows' (the
community's story, the experience of redemption, its hope and
its task) and responding through worship and everyday life. The
article concludes with an account of what growth in faith
involves and some reflections on the implications of learning to
participate in the communal practices of the Christian faith.

'Educating in the Spirit', by Carol Lakey Hess, explores the
question of how Christian education 'can look to the Holy Spirit
for its origin, starting point, and foundations', by attempting to
develop an understanding of Christian education based on an
analogy between pneumatology and anthropology, that is

between the activity of the Spirit of God and the developmental evolution of the human spirit. Christian education is defined here in terms of its ability to create environments in which we encounter liminality, and are taught security and centredness with openness and vulnerability. The context of all this is the Christian community. 'Educating in the Spirit' was first published in *Religious Education*, 86, 1991, pp. 383–398.

Professor Stanley Hauerwas is Gilbert T Rowe Professor of Theological Ethics at Duke University Divinity School, Durham, North Carolina, USA. Dr Craig R Dykstra, formerly Thomas W Synott Professor of Christian Education at Princeton Theological Seminary, is currently Vice-President (Religion) of the Lilly Endowment Inc., Indianapolis, Indiana, USA. Dr Carol Lakey Hess is Assistant Professor of Christian Education at Princeton Theological Seminary, New Jersey, USA.

Note
1.   See also Stanley Hauerwas, 'Character, narrative, and growth in the Christian life', in James Fowler and Antoine Vergote (eds), *Toward Moral and Religious Maturity*, Morriston, New Jersey, Silver Burdett, 1980; *Vision and Virtue: essays in Christian ethical reflection*, Notre Dame, Indiana, University of Notre Dame Press, 1981; *A Community of Character: toward a constructive Christian social ethic*, Notre Dame, Indiana, University of Notre Dame Press, 1981; *The Peaceable Kingdom*, Notre Dame, Indiana, University of Notre Dame Press, 1983; *Christian Existence Today: essays on church, world, and living in-between*, Durham, North Carolina, Labyrinth Press, 1988.

3.1 The gesture of a truthful story

Stanley Hauerwas

Introduction

I worry about the idea that religious education is some special activity separated from the total life of the church. When that happens, it makes it appear that what the church does in its worship is something different from what it does in its education. I would contend that everything the church is and does is 'religious education'.[1] Put more strongly, the church does not 'do' religious education at all. Rather, the church *is* a form of education that is religious. Moreover, if that is the case, then I think there is a very close relation between Christian education and social ethics, at least if how I understand social ethics is close to being right. Such an assertion is by no means clear, nor are its implications immediately apparent. I will try to unravel that claim by analysing first a similar contention about Christian social ethics, namely, that the church does not have a social ethic, but rather is a social ethic.[2]

A social ethic

The claim that the church is a social ethic is an attempt to remind us that the church is the place where the story of God is enacted, told and heard. Christian social ethics is not first of all principles or policies for social action, but rather the story of God's calling of Israel and of the life of Jesus. That story requires the formation of a corresponding community that has learned to live in ways appropriate to them. The church does not have a social ethic, but is a social ethic, then, insofar as it is a community that can clearly be distinguished from the world. For the world is not a community and has no such story, since it is based on the assumption that human beings, not God, rule history.

Therefore, the first social task of the church is to help the world know that it is the world. For without the church, the world has no means to know that it is the world. The distinction between church and the world is not a distinction between nature and grace. It is, instead, a distinction that denotes:[3]

> the basic personal postures of men, some of whom confess and others of whom do not confess that Jesus Christ is Lord. The distinction between church and the world is not something that God has imposed upon the world by prior metaphysical definition, nor is it only something which timid or pharisaical Christians have built up around themselves. It is all of that in creation that has taken the freedom not yet to believe.

The fact that the church is separated from the world is not meant to underwrite an ethic of self-righteousness on the part of the church. Both church and world remain under the judgement of the Kingdom of God. Indeed, we must remember that the church is but the earnest of the Kingdom. Those of us who attempt to live faithful to that Kingdom are acutely aware how deeply our lives remain held to and by the world. But this cannot be an excuse for acting as if there is no difference between us and the world. For if we use our sin to deny our peculiar task as Christians and as members of the church, we are unfaithful both to the Kingdom and to ourselves – and most importantly to the world itself.

Moreover, when we deny the distinctive task of the church, we implicitly deny the particularity of the narrative that makes us what we are in the first place. As Christians, we are not after all called to be morally good, but rather to be faithful to the story that we claim is truthful to the very character of reality, which is that we are creatures of a gracious God who asks nothing less of us than faithful service to God's Kingdom. In short, we are people who know who is in control. What it means to be Christian, therefore, is that we are a people who affirm that we have come to find our true destiny only by locating our lives within the story of God. The church is the lively argument, extended over centuries and occasioned by the stories of God's calling of Israel and of the life and death of Jesus Christ, to which we are invited to contribute by learning to live faithful to those stories. It is the astounding claim of Christians that through this particular man's story, we discover our true selves and thus are made part of God's very life. We become part of God's story by finding our lives within that story.

For the church to *be*, rather than to *have*, a social ethic means that it must be a community where the truth is lived and spoken. The story that forms the church is, as I have suggested, a reality-making claim that tells us the truth about the world and ourselves. Such truth is indeed hard. It means that we cannot know the truth until we have been transformed by the story. We cannot know Jesus without becoming his disciples. There is, therefore, an unavoidably self-involving character to Christian convictions. It requires that our very selves be transformed if we are to face the truth that we are sinners yet saved.

A community of such people cannot help but be a social ethic, since it must stand in sharp contrast with the world which would have us build our relations on distortions and denials. The world is where the truth is not spoken for fear such truth might destroy what fragile order and justice we have been able to achieve. But the church, which claims to be construed by a people who have no fear of the truth, must be a polity where the truth is spoken, even if such truth risks pain and threatens disorder. The church is thus a polity that takes as its constitution a story whose truth creates a people who love honestly, because they have the confidence that such love binds our lives to God's very character.

Such a community cannot help but stand in sharp contrast with the world. A people formed in the likeness of God cannot be anything less than a community of character. That is, it is a community which takes as its task the initiation of people into the story in a manner that forms and shapes their lives in a decisive and distinctive way. Put bluntly, the church is in the world to mark us. The church, therefore, aims not at autonomy but at faithfulness. We believe that it is only as we learn to be faithful that we have the ability to be free. Freedom, contrary to much contemporary thought, consists not in having *no* story, but rather comes only through being trained and acquiring the skills of a *truthful* story.

That is why the church, in contrast to many communities, knows that the only way to learn to be faithful is through initiation by a master. Most of contemporary morality, both in its philosophical and popular expression, assumes that the moral life is an achievement that is open to anyone. On such a view of the moral life, what is required is not a master but simply the ability to make well-reasoned decisions. In contrast, the church knows that the life of faithfulness is not easily acquired but involves those skills that can be learned only through apprenticeship to a master. Living morally is not simply holding the right principles; it involves nothing less than learning to desire the right things rightly. Such desiring is not so much a matter of choice as it is the slow training of our vision through learning to pay attention to the insignificant. Such attention is gained only as we have the story mediated to us by masters who have learned what the story says by learning how difficult it is to hear it. In short, the church, Christians, are the group of people capable of engendering and recognising saints.

To be able to do that is no small feat. Saints cannot exist without a community as they require, like all of us, nurturance by a people who, while often unfaithful, preserve the habits necessary to learn the story of God. Moreover, such a community must have the skills of discernment that make them capable of recognising the saints in their midst. Recognising the saints, especially while they are still alive, is no easy task either. For by their very nature, saints remind us how unfaithful we have been to the story that has formed us.

Hope and patience

To be a community capable of engendering as well as of recognising the saints requires that we be a people formed by the virtues of hope and patience. These are the virtues, the habits, crucial to learning well the story of God. To learn that story means we must desire nothing less than the accomplishment of God's rule, the Kingdom, over all nations and peoples. That rule is nothing less than the establishment of peace between ourselves and God, from which we learn how to be peaceful in ourselves and with one another. Because we have tasted this peace, because we have found how marvellous it is to have violence rooted out of our souls, is why we so desperately desire it for all. We know God's peace is not easily made one's own. But we have confidence that if we are faithful to God's Kingdom, God will use our faithfulness to realise this Kingdom for all.

But just to the extent that we have been taught to hope, we must also be patient. For God does not will that the Kingdom be accomplished through coercion or violence. In the cross, we see how the Kingdom will come into the world and we are charged to be nothing less than a cruciform people. We must, then, learn to wait as we seek to manifest to the world God's peace that comes into our lives by no other means than the power of that truth itself. Such waiting is painful indeed in a world as unjust and violent as ours. But we believe it justified, since we have been promised that God will use our waiting for the complete triumph of the Kingdom. Moreover, patience is required because at least part of what it means for the church to be, rather than to have, a social ethic involves a rethinking about what is meant by social ethics. Too often, in an effort to appear socially relevant, the church has accepted the world's agenda about what 'real' politics involves. Thus, calls for us to serve the world responsibly have too often resulted in the church simply saying to the world what the world already knows. We thereby end up trying to secure a 'justice' which is only the continuation of some people's domination of others.

In contrast, I am suggesting we must be a patient people, as well as a courageous people, who have the skills to think through the current illusions about social justice and peace. We must be the kind of community that can draw on the character of convictions that expose the sentimentalities of the world, not the least of which is the assumption that nation-states have the right to qualify our loyalty as members of the church. It takes a patient as well as courageous people to manifest that the unity of God's eschatological meal is the only true internationalism.

Such a meal:[4]

> posits and proclaims a unification of mankind whose basis is not some as yet unachieved restructuring of political sovereignties but an already achieved transformation of vision and community. That all mankind is one cannot be demonstrated empirically nor can it be brought about by political engineering. That all mankind is one must first be affirmed as a theological proclamation. Only then is the engineering and structuring which are needed to reflect it even conceivable. It could just as well be said that Christian internationalism is the true unity which the servant church must let be restored.

Nor must we forget that the most embarrassing divisions in the church are not between Catholic and Protestant, UCC and Methodist, Presbyterian and Church of Christ, liberal and conservative, but between social and economic class, race and nationalities. Such divisions give lie to the fact that we are one people rooted in the God who has called us into the Kingdom inaugurated by Jesus' life and death. Thus, the first concern of any Christian social ethic must be with the fellowship of the church. We must be a community with the patience, amid the division and hatreds of this world, to take the time to nurture friendships, to serve the neighbour and to give and receive the thousand small acts of care that ultimately are the heart blood of the Kingdom. That we must take the time to help the neighbour in need, no matter how insignificant that neighbour or his or her need is from the perspective of the world, is but a sign that we recognise that we are called not to make history come out right, but to be faithful to the kind of care we have seen revealed in God's Kingdom.

In this respect, the church as a social ethic must take its lead from those like Mother Teresa. From a perspective that would associate the church's social task with effectiveness, Mother Teresa is a deeply immoral woman. She takes the time to hold the hand of a dying leprosy victim when she could be raising money in Europe and America for the starving in India. Yet she sits there holding the hand of a dying person, doing that while surrounded by unbelievable suffering and injustice, because she knows that God will have the Kingdom come exactly by such care. And she knows she can do so because she does not seek to be like the powerful to help the poor and dying. She has learned instead that power derives from being faithful to God's Kingdom of the poor.

Gestures

This, surely, is not the word we want to hear today. We want a word that puts the church on the right side for a change, the side for political change and justice. This news I bring, therefore, seems more bad than good. If being Christian does not put us where the action is, if being Christian does not put us on the side of the progressive forces in this or any other society, then I suspect many of us would be a good deal less happy with being Christian. The claim that the church is, rather than has, a social ethic cannot help but appear to many as a dangerous withdrawal of the church back into a self-righteous pietism that ignores the social agony of the world. At best, such a Christian social ethic is but a gesture; at worst, it is a failure of Christians to face responsibly the complexity of the social problems confronting us in these troubled times.

I am ready to concede that the church, and Christian social ethics, as I have tried to depict it, is but a gesture, but I do not think that to be a damaging admission. For nothing in life is more important than gestures, as gestures embody as well as sustain the valuable and significant. Through gestures, we create and form our worlds. Through gestures, we make contact with one another and share common tasks. Through gestures, we communicate and learn from each other the limits of our world.

In this sense, the church is but God's gesture on behalf of the world to create a space and time in which we might have a foretaste of the Kingdom. It is through gestures that we learn the nature of the story that is the very content and constitution of that Kingdom. The way we learn a story, after all, is not just by hearing it. Important and significant stories must be acted out. We must be taught the gestures that help position our bodies and our souls to be able to rightly hear and then retell the story. For example, while we may be able to pray without being prostrate, I think prayer as an institution of the church could no longer be sustained without a people who have first learned to kneel. If you want to learn to pray, you had better know how to bend the body. The gesture and posture of prayer are inseparable from learning to pray. Indeed, the gestures are prayer.

Of course, some of our most important gestures are words. But we can easily overestimate their significance if we assume that words can be separated from the context of their enactment. For example, the Apostles' Creed is not simply a statement of faith that can stand independent of the context in which we affirm it. We must learn to say it in the context of worship if we are to understand how it works to rule our belief and school our faith. The Creed is not some deposit or sum of the story; rather it is a series of reminders about how best to tell the story that we find enacted through the entire liturgy.

In the same way, baptism and the eucharist stand as crucial gestures that are meant to shape us rightly to hear as well as enact the story. Through baptism and eucharist, we are initiated into God's life by our becoming part of Jesus' life, death and resurrection. These are essential gestures of the church; we cannot be the church without them. They are, in effect, essential reminders for the constitution of God's people in the world. Without them, we are constantly tempted to turn God into an ideology to supply our wants and needs rather than have our needs and wants transformed by God's capturing of our attention through the mundane life of Jesus of Nazareth.

Thus liturgy is not a motive for social action, it is not a cause to effect. Liturgy *is* social action. Through liturgy we are shaped to live rightly the story of God, to become part of that story, and are thus able to recognise and respond to the saints in our midst. Once we recognise that the church is a social ethic, an ethic that is to be sure but a gesture, then we can appreciate how every activity of the church is a means and an opportunity for faithful service to and for the world. We believe that the gesture that is the church is nothing less than the sign of God's salvation of the world.

Education

But what does all this have to do with Christian education, and in particular the claim that the church does not do religious education, but is a form of education that is religious? First of all, it reminds us that religious education has as its first task the initiation of a people into a story. Its task is not to teach us the meaning of that story, but to teach us the story. There is no point that can be known separate from the story. There is no experience that we want people to have apart from the story. There are no 'moral lessons' that we wish to inculcate other than the story. The story is the point, the story is the experience, and the story is the moral.

The task of religious education therefore involves the development of skills to help us make the story ours. Or, perhaps better, the task of religious education is to help remind us of those skills present in the church that are essential for helping us make the story ours. Such reminders may well involve psychological insights about how such skills work, but the former cannot be a substitute for the latter. The content of the story must control where and how the story is to be made our own.

Put simply, religious education is the training in those gestures through which we learn the story of God and God's will for our lives. Religious education is not, therefore, something that is done to make us Christians, or something done after we have become Christian. Rather, it is ongoing training in the skills we need in order to live faithful to the Kingdom that has been initiated in Jesus. That Kingdom is constituted by a story that one never possesses, but rather constantly challenges us to be what we are but have not yet become.

The primary task of being educated religiously, or better Christianly, is not the achievement of better understanding but faithfulness. Indeed, we can only come to understand through faithfulness as the story, and the corresponding community, which forms our life asks nothing less from us than our life. The story requires that we learn to live as a people who have been forgiven and thus can be at peace with ourselves as well as with others. We do not learn to be forgiven by intellectually admitting that we often have failed to live up to our own moral ideals, but rather by learning to depend on God as the source of life and the sustainer of our community. What we are asked to be is first and foremost a people who embody and manifest the habits of peace characteristic of a forgiven people, not just those who provide worldviews through which to make sense of the world.

We become faithful just to the extent that we learn to participate in the activities of the people of God we call the church. Therefore, it becomes our duty to be a people who submit to the discipline of the liturgy, as it is there that we are trained with the skills rightly to know the story. We are required to care for one another and to accept the care of others, for it is by learning to be cared for that we learn to care. Such duties may be no more than gestures, but they are the essential gestures that initiate us into the narrative of God's dealing with people.

Yet all this may still sound far too abstract. Therefore, let me try to provide a concrete case that I hope will draw out the implications of the position I have tried to develop. One of the tasks people concerned with religious education have taken for themselves has been the attempt to find ways to help people better understand what it means to be a Christian. This most often has naturally taken the form of encouraging greater study of Scripture and theology, the assumption being that we will be better Christians if we simply know more. While I have nothing against the study of Scripture and theology, I think our emphasis in that respect has tended to make us forget that the way we learn the story is by learning such gestures as simple as how to kneel. More troubling, such an emphasis excludes in a decisive manner a whole group of people from participation in God's Kingdom. For what do you do with the mentally handicapped?

The mentally handicapped are a reminder, a test case, for helping us understand how any account of religious education involves assumptions about the nature of Christian conviction and the church. It is certainly true that the mentally handicapped may not be able to read the story; nor are they always able to 'understand' the 'meaning' of the story; nor do they know what social implications the story may entail. But what they do know is how the story is embodied through the essential gestures of the church. They know the story through the care they receive, and they help the church understand the story that forms such care. Moreover, they learn the story through its enactment as they feel and are formed by the liturgy that places us as characters in God's grand project of the creation and redemption of the world. They know that they too have a role in God's people as they faithfully serve God through being formed by a community that is nothing less than the enactment of that story.

It is important that we guard against a possible misunderstanding that may be occasioned by the interjection of the place of the mentally handicapped in religious education. I am not suggesting that the retarded represent some bottom line or minimum that must be met for religious education. On the contrary, I am suggesting that they, and I am sure there are other equally compelling examples, offer a clue about the centre of the task of Christian education and why it is that the church as such is Christian education. For if faithfulness is our task, if it is through faithfulness that we rightly learn to hear, tell and embody the story, then the mentally handicapped are a crucial and ever present reminder that such is the case.

Nor am I suggesting that the mentally handicapped are somehow naturally ready to be formed by the story. They are no less sinners than any of the rest of us. Their desires require training no less than our desires. Faithfulness is not a natural task for the mentally handicapped or for us. We equally must be trained to face the world, as it is not as we would like it to be. In like measure, we all must learn to accept and give forgiveness; as we also must learn to be people of peace and justice.

However, there is another connection between the argument I have tried to make about the church as a social ethic, the implications of that for religious education, and the mentally handicapped. For at least part of what it means for the church to be a social ethic is that it has the time to care in an unjust world for those who do not promise to make the world better, more just, or direct the course of history. The church as God's gesture in and for the world must be the people who manifest our conviction that we do not live on the world's time but in God's time. I suspect we do that best when we show ourselves to be a people who have the time to care for one another even when some of us happen to be mentally handicapped.

It may seem extremely odd to end an article on Christian education by calling attention to the mentally handicapped. To end there seems to suggest that our intellectual skills are not as important as we would like to think. I must admit, moreover, that I am not entirely unhappy with such a conclusion, even though it is clearly exaggerated. After all, I am among those who have engaged in that most ambiguous enterprise that we identify as theology. And I believe that the church is less if it does not engender and sponsor the critical activity we call theology.

Yet, in an interesting way, that activity, and the educational institution necessary to sustain it, draws on the same presuppositions and virtues that sustain the church's commitment to having the mentally handicapped among us. For the activity of theology can only be sustained by a community that has learned to wait patiently in a world of suffering and injustice. Theology and theologians do little to make the world better. Rather, our craft involves the slow and painful steps of trying to understand better what it means to be a people formed by the story of God. Let us not forget, then, that as theologians we, no less than the mentally retarded, depend on and serve a church which provides us with the gestures necessary to being the people of God.[5]

Notes

1. The phrase 'religious education' seems to me to be misleading, if for no other reason than that the content of 'religious' is vague at best and, at worst, may involve reductionistic assumptions about positive Christian convictions. Moreover, it is by no means clear how 'religious' or 'Christian' can qualify 'education', since it is not clear whether 'education' is a coherent enough activity or idea to be able to know what difference any qualifier would make.

2. For a fuller analysis of this claim than I can offer here, see my *A Community of Character: toward a constructive Christian social ethic*, Notre Dame, University of Notre Dame Press, 1981, and *The Peaceable Kingdom: a primer in Christian ethics*, Notre Dame, University of Notre Dame Press, 1983.

3. John Howard Yoder, *The Original Revolution*, Scottdale, Pennsylvania, Herald Press, 1971, p. 116.

4. *Ibid.*, p. 130.

5. This article is a version of one that previously appeared in *Encounter*, a journal published by the Christian (Disciples of Christ) Theological Seminary in Indianapolis.

3.2 No longer strangers: the church and its educational ministry

Craig R Dykstra

Christian education and ecclesiology

In my work over the past several years, I have been concerned with the question of what it means for people to be formed in faith as Christians and how that happens. There are many aspects to this exploration, but one of the simple answers that repeatedly arises in a variety of ways has to do with the church. People are formed in faith as Christians in Christian community, and our word for that is church. My own work is taking a turn toward more explicit and systematic attention to the church, wondering what we really mean when we use that word and what the actual reality of it suggests for the church's educational ministry. One way of dealing with this issue that I am finding helpful comes through asking the following question: what difference does it make that the church does Christian education?

The usual way in which Christian educators have asked this question puts the emphasis on the words 'Christian education'. What difference does it make that the church does *Christian education*? In other words, the question is taken to be one about why the church should engage in *education*. It is assumed that we know what the church is, and the answers then given are justifications for the significance of education in and by the church and descriptions of how that is being or should be carried out. But I want to start, at least, by asking the question in a different way, by emphasising the word 'church'. What difference does it make that the *church* does Christian education? If we ask it this way, we ask not so much why the church needs Christian education, but in what way Christian education is given its distinctive shape by being in and of the church.

There are different answers to this question depending upon what one thinks the church is. And the question of what the church is, is extremely complex. The New Testament itself contains a variety of answers. The history of theological writing contains many renderings of the nature of the church. Add to all this the variety of understandings of the church in popular culture, both among church members and beyond, and you can see the difficulty. It is multiplied by the fact that there are different ecclesiologies (some explicit, most implicit) in the various theories of Christian education and in the, often hidden, 'theories-in-action' of people actively engaged in the educational work of the church.

It is obviously impossible to examine all of this diversity here, though in the long run it is instructive to do so. At this point, I want only to look at one particular text from the New Testament and develop in relation to that some directions for an understanding of the church which I think may be useful to us, both in thinking about what difference it makes that *the church* does Christian education and in carrying out that ministry.

The text is from Ephesians 2:19–22:

> So then you are no longer strangers and sojourners, but you are fellow citizens with the saints and members of the household of God, built upon the foundation of the apostles and prophets, Christ Jesus himself being the chief cornerstone, in whom the whole structure is joined together and grows into a holy temple in the Lord; in whom you also are built into it for a dwelling place of God in the Spirit.

This is in many ways an amazing text. It suggests that the 'you', whoever they are (we will get to that in a minute), have had and are having something happen to them. They have become what they were not. And they have become this through being 'built into' something that they were not a part of before. Furthermore, whatever it is they are being built into is itself growing, developing somehow, and they along with it. Finally what they, altogether, are being built into is, of all things, a dwelling place of God in the Spirit, a habitation of God where God can be known and God's presence can be apprehended; an amazing text.

The 'you' who are being referred to here are, of course, gentile Christians. If the exegetes I have read are right, the ones to whom the word is addressed are not just a small group of gentile Christians at a particular place (say, Ephesus) but all the gentile Christians. And that, of course, is what we are: gentiles, not Hebrews or Jews, but gentiles who in Jesus Christ (rather than in some other way[1]) are built into the household of God. What the author of Ephesians is taking about, of course, is the church. So, if we dare think it, this is a word to us. What it means is that, by being in the church, *we* have had and are having something done to us. *We* have become what we were not, have become built into something that we were not a part of before, and through being a part of this we are being joined together and are growing into a habitation of the Spirit.

Now this is fairly 'high church' ecclesiology, something Ephesians is well-known for. It can be read rather idealistically, as something that has little to do with the ordinary, everyday church that we are all a part of. Therefore, it is important in this context to take seriously some advice from Karl Barth. Barth says that when we talk about church, we must not fall into the trap of thinking that the church is something heavenly beyond the earthly, or something pure hidden within the fallible, or something invisible lying behind the visible. No, he says. When we do this 'we are all inclined to slip away with that in the direction of a *civitas platonica* or some sort of Cloud-cuckooland, in which the Christians are united inwardly and invisibly, while the visible church is devalued'.[2] He goes on to say that:[3]

> In the Apostles' Creed, it is not an invisible structure which is intended but a quite visible coming together, which originates with the twelve Apostles.... If the church has not this visibility, then it is not the Church.... We believe the existence of the Church, which means that we believe each particular congregation to be a congregation of Christ. Take good note, that a parson who does not believe that in this congregation of his ... Christ's congregation exists, does not believe at all in the existence of the Church. *Credo ecclesiam* means that I believe that here, at this place, in this visible assembly, the work of the Holy Spirit takes place.

With these claims, Barth catches with a simple and penetrating concreteness what is so powerful about these words in Ephesians 2:19-20. They mean that you and I, through being taken up by, through being built into, the particular congregations of which we are members, have had and are having something done to us that changes us. They mean that through this very process, we are no longer strangers and sojourners, no longer aliens separated from God's presence and God's living Spirit, no longer foreigners to God's redemptive activity in the world. Rather, we are 'fellow citizens with the saints and members of the household of God'.

All of this has very significant implications for Christian education and a number of things that Christian educators are concerned with. These can be articulated in a series of five theses. The five theses are:

a. faith is participation in the redemptive activity of God;
b. we participate in this activity by being active in the manifold relationships of the church, a community which knows that this redemptive activity is taking place and which is making itself open to it through its worship and discipleship;
c. growing in faith involves the deepening and widening of our participation in this community and its form of life;
d. we can learn to participate in this activity, and this learning requires that we be taught;
e. Christian education is the dialogical process of teaching and learning (involving activities of enquiry, interpretation, reflection and care) through which the community comes to see, grasp and participate ever more deeply in the redemptive transformation of personal and social life that God is carrying out.

Faith as participation

The first thesis has to do with what we can understand faith to be. I want to argue that faith is best understood as participation in the redemptive activity of God. To get at this, we can begin by looking back at our text. What is this 'dwelling place of God in the Spirit'? We get into trouble when we imagine this in spatial or even social-structural terms, though this is tempting to do given the 'building' imagery that is used here. Rather, we must think in dynamic, active and historical terms. The dwelling place of God in the Spirit is not a particular physical place, either earthly or heavenly, or even an institution or social group. The dwelling place, as the Scriptures as a whole testify, is where God is active. Jürgen Moltmann says:[4]

> In the Old Testament Yahweh was experienced, not as heavenly substance but as a divinely historical person, and the promise of his presence was believed in his name: 'I am who I am', 'I will be who I will be', 'I will be there' (Exodus 3:14). In the same way, in the New Testament Jesus is not remembered as a dead man belonging to the past, nor is he defined as a heavenly authority; he is believed as the subject of his own presence. It is also true of the one who has been exalted to God that 'I am who I am', 'I will be there'.

God's dwelling is wherever God is carrying out God's work of freeing human beings and the whole creation from its bondage, from its bondage to patterns of destruction in which people can find no other way to secure their existence than by manipulating, deceiving and even killing one another; from its idolisation of powers of force and control which promise peace but turn out to enslave us all in ever more subtle webs of violence; from its bondage to fear of any reality which is separate and different and thus threatening to us; in short, from the powers of sin and death which ravage our lives, our communities and our planet. God's dwelling is where God, out of God's own steadfast love, is carrying out God's redemptive work in the world for the sake of the world.

This is the dwelling that we are built into. The dwelling is a work, an activity. Furthermore, it is a work that is already going on, and always has been. Therefore, we are not to think of the church, either in its beginnings or now or in the future, as the first and only dwelling of God; as if here, in the church, now, at long last, God finally has a place to live and be. No. It is not *God* who is being built into the *church*'s dwelling, but we who, in Christ by the power of the Spirit, as the church are being built into God's dwelling. That is, in Christ by the Spirit in the church, we are being called into, led into, built into participation in the ongoing redemptive activity of God in the world. We do not take over that activity for God. We do not exhaust that activity. But being built into it does mean that we come to know of it and are called to respond to it, living our lives and carrying out our own activity in the world in a way that is so governed by God's activity that we in fact participate in it with God.

This is the fundamental connection between faith and church. Faith means to know and respond to the redemptive activity of God by participating in it, and we have been built into this in the church. When we define faith in this way, we should not lose sight of the fact that faith is a reality of multiple dimensions and cannot be exhausted by just one meaning. Just as in the case of 'church', the New Testament (indeed, in this case, the whole Scriptures) speaks about 'faith' in a great variety of ways, and theological writing, again, has had many and diverse things to say about faith. As John Cobb has put it:[5]

> Faith has meant and rightly means many things. Sometimes it means a vision of reality or a structure of existence.... Receptivity to the personal presence of Jesus is faith, as is the assuredness of the one who knows himself or herself justified. Faith in a different sense is 'the substance of things hoped for'.... In other contexts faith is used to mean faithfulness, life-affirmation, confidence, commitment, trust and ultimate concern. Indeed, an exhaustive list of meanings is impossible.

But then Cobb goes on to say something very important, and a clue to what we are after here. He says that 'a central and normative theological meaning of faith is *the appropriate, primal response to what the divine is and does*'.[6] Faith is response, and it is response to God. To put it in our terms, faith is response to the God of Abraham, Isaac and Jacob to whom we have become related in a new way as gentiles in Jesus Christ. We know that God to be the God who redeems and saves. And the appropriate, primal response to that God is thanksgiving for and participation in God's redeeming activity. Faith is participation in the redemptive activity of God.

The church as context of participation

The second thesis is that if faith is participation in the redemptive activity of God, then we participate in this activity by being active in the manifold relationships of the church, a community which knows that this redemptive activity is taking place and which is making itself open to it through its worship and discipleship. Faith knows and faith responds, and the crucial features of the church are that as a community it knows and it responds. We come into faith by participating in the faith of the faith community, by knowing in its knowing and responding as a part of its response. But what does the faith community know?

What the community knows is first of all a story, a narrative. Stanley Hauerwas says we are a 'story-formed community',[7] and that indeed is what we are. The story is a multifaceted one, made up of many particular stories, but it is nonetheless a very concrete one. It is about particular people and particular events in which they are involved. It recounts what happened, what people said and what people did in response. Furthermore, as story these events and people are rendered to us through a particular constellation of images which provide those who hear it ways of understanding what the story means, where it is going and why it is significant.[8]

This story does certain things. It does not just sit there by itself to be admired from a distance. It itself performs certain actions when told, heard and remembered. One thing the story does is *render an agent*, namely God. What this means is that through this story we begin to see that behind and in everything that happens there is an active presence to whom it is all related and in whom it all holds together. These are not just isolated events and persons who appear and do what they do by chance. There is another agency, a will, that emerges through the action of the story. Thus, this story is not just about a people who think that there is a God and that this God is doing something redemptive in history. Nor is God just one of the characters in the story. Rather, God is the agency which makes the story and who is revealed through the story. In other words, through the telling and hearing of the story, God is revealed to its contemporary hearers as a present reality.[9]

Another thing the story does is *render a world*, the kind of world that is appropriate to the God who becomes present to us through the story. What is meant here is not that we get to know something about the ancient Middle East or first-century Palestine or Rome (though we may), but that through this particular story, which is set in a variety of geographical and historical arenas, is portrayed what is really and ultimately going on in the creation as a whole. As we hear, tell, think about, interpret, use and appropriate this story, its 'world' more and more becomes our 'world'. Our thinking, believing and behaving become shaped by it, so that we come to think, believe and behave by means of it. This story's 'world' is no longer a world outside of us which we look at, but that world from which and by means of which we see at all. Furthermore, the world that is rendered is not a provincial world, the world of the church apart from the world as a whole. Rather, it is understood to be the world itself, as it is; the world seen for itself rather than refracted through vision disfigured and distorted through deceit and alienation. Hauerwas suggests that if the world rendered through this story does not help us to see the world as it is, then it should be given up. 'But the claim of the Christian is that (this) language actually envisages the world as it is.'[10]

And then, the story also acts upon us by *rendering a way of living*. It is not so much that the story presents ideals for how people should live or models of the perfect life. Rather, it marks out the kind of pilgrimage life is, the dangers it encounters, the limitations inherent in it, what sorts of things are necessary for sustaining it, the treasures that might be found there. It renders the adventure and gives clues both as to how ordinary human beings can get in on it and as to how it is they can miss it entirely.

So, the first thing the church knows is a story; and by knowing the story it finds itself in a new world, on an adventure, and in relation to the agent who initiates and sustains it all. The second thing that the church knows is the experience of redemption. What this means is not that the church knows perfect peace or perfect obedience or perfect freedom from bondage to all that enslaves and oppresses. Of course not. Nor that the church knows what perfect peace, obedience and freedom *would be like*, as if what it knows is just an ideal. For one thing, the church does not know perfection, even as an ideal. And for another, it knows more than an ideal. What the church knows is the reality of having been given peace (not perfect or complete peace but still real peace), of having been given obedience (not perfect obedience but still real obedience), of having been given freedom (again, not perfect freedom but still real freedom). What the church knows is that in its history certain structures of violence have been resisted, that certain kinds of idolatry have been seen for what they are and turned away from, that from time to time the deepest fears have been relieved and that because of that, people and groups have been able to move forward despite the odds. And it knows, too, that all of this has happened, whenever it has happened, by the power of that same Power who is rendered in its story, has happened in the same world that is revealed in the story, and takes place through the same adventure that runs through the story that it knows. What the church has experienced is the redemptive *modification* of its own alienated existence, and thereby experiences the whole world as moving by the power of God *toward* redemption.[11]

Then there are the third and fourth things that the church knows: a hope and a task. The church knows a hope. It knows that both the story and the experience of redemption are not finished, and it knows that neither of them can end without God's redemptive work somehow being completed. This is the ground of the church's hope, and it proceeds in the adventure of life on these grounds. And because the church hopes in this way, the church is both freed for and called to a task. It is precisely the task of living the adventure which its story renders, no matter the odds and on the basis of its hope. It is the task of participating in this redemptive activity of God.

The claim being made here is that the church knows all this. In making this claim, we are not saying that every (or even any one) church member knows the whole story. Nor are we saying that to the extent people do know the story they are to that same extent conscious of the rendering activity that that story is working on them. Nor are we saying that every person in the church has or is now experiencing the redemptive modification of an alienated existence, or that we all live by the hope that is given us and respond fully to the task at hand. What is being claimed is that the *church*, as a worldwide historical body which lives in many places and continues over a long period of time, knows the story and has been and continues to be so affected by it, has experienced and continues to experience redemptive transformation, has lived and continues to live in hope, and has responded and continues to respond to its task. The claim is being made for the church, not for individuals. And the claim is being made for the whole worldwide church, not just for particular individual congregations or even denominations. And finally, the claim is being made for the church as it lives in the present out from a very long past toward the future, not for the church of an isolated moment in time.

Even the church, understood in this large way, does not and has not ever done any of this perfectly or fully. It, like all the world, has lived and continues to live unredemptively, nearsightedly and half-blindedly, sinfully. But still, as Ephesians witnesses, something has happened. And what has happened is that God has begun redemptive work and has seen fit to build the church into it. The church knows that and lives in response to it.

The church responds by making itself open to God's redemptive activity through its worship and discipleship. In worship, the church gathers to give thanks to God for God's presence and for God's redemptive work. It confesses its sin, its blindness, its obstinacy, its resistance, its fear and its failure. It gathers to hear again the story, to enact the sacraments which are ordained through it, and to have rendered to it again through all this the God, the world and the life that is at its heart. It prays for itself and for the world that in many particular ways this redemptive activity of God may continue, that the church may be faithful in response to it, and that its faith may increase. And then it disperses itself into its everyday life to live in discipleship the worship that it has conducted.

Our faith as individuals (and even as particular congregations and denominations) is our participation in the redemptive activity of God by the power of the Spirit through the church. As we, as individuals, participate as part of the church (which is giving thanks, confessing, hearing, enacting, praying and going to live in discipleship), we lay ourselves open to and participate in the redemptive activity of God. The church knows, and as we participate in the church's life, we too know. The church responds, and as we participate in the church's response, we too respond.

Growing in faith

We can, to be sure, participate in this knowing and responding in and through the church in very minimal ways. We, as individuals, may know very little and respond hardly at all. We may do nothing more than 'go to church', for whatever ambiguous reasons. But even though

that is not much, it is not nothing. Just by going to church, we participate with the community at least in its gathering. Even there, there is
some slight knowing and some slight responding to the redemptive
work of God, even if we do not know that that is what we are doing.
We need not worry too much about the beginnings or their adequacy.
That is of no account. Our concern is with the growing. And this leads
us to the third thesis: growing in faith involves the deepening and
widening of our participation in the church, and in its form of life.

Growing in faith is not so much like going through stages as it is
like exploring a new country (or, perhaps, like exploring more deeply
and more extensively a country in which one has lived for a long
time), and living in the light of what one finds there. There is always
more to be seen and understood and taken in. And each step we take
opens up new realities before us while it changes each of us within.
This is a dynamic process. It does not happen just by our being there.
It happens by doing, by looking, by paying attention, by having
encounters, by our acting. Hauerwas says:[12]

> Christians are simply those people who engage and do not engage in
> certain practices because they have found them appropriate or inappro-
> priate to their way of life. The individual Christian's character is formed
> by his (or her) association with the community that embodies the
> language, rituals and moral practices from which this particular form of
> life grows. Perhaps this is why some have become Christians not so
> much by believing but by simply taking up a way of life. This is pos-
> sible because the Christian gospel is at once belief ... that involves
> behaviour and a behaviour that involves belief.

Growing in faith is not *simply* a matter of action, of course. And it
does not happen *just because* we will or intend it. But it does not
happen *without* our own willing and intending either. These are both
involved and required. Growth in faith requires that we be active, and
activity means that, in part, we do and will the action.

Growth in faith involves, then, action in which we engage together in
the context of the community of faith. It involves active engagement in
certain *practices* which are central to and constitutive of the church's
life. By engaging in these practices with others, we both lay ourselves
open to what God is doing redemptively in the world and participate in
that activity ourselves. What all these practices are can never be fully
spelled out. Some of the more significant, however, are:

a. telling the Christian story to one another;
b. interpreting together the meaning of that story for our life in the
     world;
c. worshipping God together: praising God and giving thanks for
     God's redemptive work in the world and for our lives together;
d. praying together;
e. listening and talking attentively to one another;

f. confessing to one another, and forgiving and reconciling with one another;
g. tolerating one another's failures and encouraging one another;
h. giving one another away, letting go of one another, freeing each other for the work each must do and the life each must live;
i. performing faithful acts of service and witness;
j. suffering for and with other people;
k. providing hospitality and care, not only to one another but also (perhaps especially) to strangers; and
l. criticising and resisting all those powers and patterns (both within the church and in the world as a whole) which destroy human beings and corrode human community.[13]

This list is illustrative rather than exhaustive. And considerable exposition would be necessary to demonstrate what each of these practices involves, what levels of engagement in each of them might be articulated, and why each one is crucial in the life of Christian faith. At this point, only three things of a general sort can be said about them. First, whatever the practice and whatever the level of engagement, it is crucial that people who are growing in faith actually do these things. This means that if we are to help a person to grow in faith, we must be sure to engage him or her in practices such as these in particular physical and material settings in the context of actual face-to-face interactions with us and with other people. Second, for these practices to become the *actions* of growing persons, they must increasingly become their own. That is, over time the growing person must come to understand more fully and clearly what these activities mean, take more and more initiative in beginning and carrying through with them, understand more and more why he or she is doing them, and take more and more responsibility for them. Third, we grow in faith as our participation in these practices becomes more complex, as it becomes more varied, as the various activities become more clearly related to one another, as they are carried out in broader arenas, and as we become more able to sustain and initiate these activities ourselves in relation to others.[14]

To give just one example, it is one thing to recite a prayer of confession along with a congregation. It is another thing actually to *pray* that prayer: to see those words as one's own in common with the wider community, understand what it means to say them, and say them as a prayer to God. It is still more complex to lead others in prayers that one composes or prays spontaneously while drawing simultaneously upon the scriptures, the prayer tradition of the church, the world and historical situation in which the people are praying, one's own existential situation, and one's awareness of the needs and hopes of those others whom one is leading in prayer. And when prayer of confession takes place not just in church services but also in the home, in prisons and hospitals, at work and at play, and through-out the daily events of one's life, then the praying practice of the church has become one's own deep practice, and one's own practice contributes more and more fully into the praying of the church.

Learning to participate

The move from reciting prayers to praying is one that some children make while many adults still do not. An important question is why that is. Our fourth thesis is a simple answer to this question. It is that these practices must be learned, and that this learning (often, at least) requires teaching. The reason why many adults cannot pray is that they have never learned to do it, have never been taught. And some children can pray because (even though they are less mature in other ways, cognitively and socially, for instance) they have learned how to pray; they have been taught. If we do not learn these practices, we cannot do them. And a major reason why we often do not learn them is that we have not been taught.

There are many ways to learn things, of course; and not all of them require what we call teaching. We may observe another person or a group of persons doing something and imitate them. Or, we may simply start doing something on our own and develop our own ways of and reasons for doing that. All of this is learning, and much of this kind of learning takes place in the church and in relation to its consti-tutive practices. But this is not enough. The practices of the church are of a kind that cannot be learned without the benefit of direct, intentional teaching.

There are four characteristics of the practices of the church that make this necessary. The practices of the church are first, historical, second, communal, third, difficult, and fourth, at least to some degree, countercultural. Because these practices are historical prac-tices, we cannot make them up ourselves. We must learn them from others who have learned them before us, and they from others who in turn learned them from their forebears, all the way back to their beginnings.[15] Because these practices are communal practices, we must do them with others. This requires that we know what others are doing as they do them with us; and we can only know this, really, as they tell us and explain to us what they are doing. Because these prac-tices are difficult practices and involve the integration of knowledge and skill with appropriate attitude and perspective, they require train-ing under the discipline of others who have mastered them more than we. And because they are, at least to some degree, in conflict with the practices we learn in the larger culture, we cannot expect that they will be learned apart from the purposeful guidance of people who have learned the difference between Christian faith and civil religion, between tempting forms of idolatrous life and the oftentimes painful rigour of life open to the redemptive activity of God.

Christian education for participation in redemptive activity

Christian education is that particular work which the church does to teach the historical, communal, difficult, countercultural practices of the church so that the church may learn to participate in them ever more fully and deeply. It is the dialogical process of teaching and learning through which the church comes to see, grasp and participate ever more deeply in the redemptive transformation of personal and social life that God is carrying out. This is my fifth thesis.

In 1970, D Campbell Wyckoff published an article in which, among other things, he asked what the organising principle for Christian education ought to be. He suggested several possibilities, but concluded that the most fruitful is 'the church's experience'. He said:[16]

> The church's experience includes the various aspects of its response to its call, constitution, assignment and empowerment. The church's experience is its life and work, as in personal and group experience the great concerns of the Christian faith and the Christian life are dealt with and its objective taught.... Naturally, education is not a matter of throwing people willy-nilly into experiences that are supposed to educate them. Involvement in the modes of the church's experience, its life and work, means participation in worship, study, action, stewardship, fellowship and creative expression in a cycle of orientation, engagement, reflection, reorientation, re-engagement, reflection and so on.

It is something very much like this that I, in turn, have been arguing for. The church, as a worldwide historical body, knows a story, experiences the redemptive modification of human existence, lives a hope and has a task. This is 'the church's experience'. Christian education is not itself the church's experience and the church's experience is not the same thing as Christian education. Christian education *depends upon* the church and its experience; it does not make the church or create its experience. But it does help people to see it for what it is, grasp something of its dynamics and nature, and participate in it more broadly and deeply.

There is no possibility of a Christian education where there is no church, where there is no body of believers, fellow citizens with the saints and members of the household of God being built into the redemptive work of God in Christ Jesus. But because, in Christ, a people have been called and have responded and still today are called and do respond (however imperfectly and perhaps even halfheartedly), we too may join in, participating in that life. And because of all that, we can do Christian education. We can learn from and teach one another what it means to participate in that life, how to do it, why to do it, what to do as we do it, not as strangers and sojourners alien from God's household, but as those being built into it for a dwelling place of God in the Spirit.[17]

Notes

1. See Paul Van Buren, *Discerning the Way*, New York, Seabury, 1980, for an excellent discussion of the relations between Christians and Jews and the different ways in which they are each related redemptively to God and God's work in the world.
2. Karl Barth, *Dogmatics in Outline* (translated by G T Thompson), New York, Harper and Row, 1959, p. 142.
3. *Ibid.*, pp. 142–43.
4. Jürgen Moltmann, *The Church in the Power of the Spirit* (translated by M Kohl), New York, Harper and Row, 1977, p. 122.
5. John B Cobb Jr, *Christ in a Pluralistic Age*, Philadelphia, Westminster Press, 1975, pp. 87–88.
6. *Ibid.*, p. 88.
7. Stanley Hauerwas, *A Community of Character*, Notre Dame, University of Notre Dame Press, 1981, see chapter 1.
8. Edward Farley, *Ecclesial Man*, Philadelphia, Fortress Press, 1975, p. 117.
9. See David H Kelsey, *The Uses of Scripture in Recent Theology*, Philadelphia, Fortress Press, 1975, pp. 39–50, for an excellent discussion of Barth's understanding of what the scriptures do in these terms.
10. Stanley Hauerwas, *Vision and Virtue*, Notre Dame, Fides Publications, 1974, p. 46. See also Farley on 'perceptivities', *op. cit.*, pp. 191–93, 213–15.
11. These terms are Edward Farley's. See *ibid.*, pp. 128ff.
12. Stanley Hauerwas, *Character and the Christian Life*, San Antonio, Trinity University Press, 1975, pp. 210–11.
13. The stimulus for this list, and some of the items on it, is from John H Westerhoff III, *Bringing Up Children in the Christian Faith*, Minneapolis, Winston Press, 1980, pp. 36–52.
14. An important theory of human development which has action, intrinsicity, and complexity at its core (and on which I am partly dependent here) is Urie Bronfenbrenner, *The Ecology of Human Development*, Cambridge, Massachusetts, Harvard University Press, 1979.
15. This is not to deny the fact of and the need for creativity and the contemporary, but the Spirit who acts redemptively today is the same Spirit who has worked in and through the church's whole history. In order to test the spirits and to participate in the Spirit, we must test and participate historically.
16. D Campbell Wyckoff, 'Understanding your church curriculum', *The Princeton Seminary Bulletin*, 63, 1970, pp. 82–83.
17. This paper was originally delivered as the author's inaugural address as the Thomas W Synnott Professor of Christian Education at Princeton Theological Seminary.

3.3 Educating in the Spirit

Carol Lakey Hess

Introduction

The purpose of this article is to explore and provide a suggestive response to a problem that has created confusion in Christian education theory.[1] The problem is the relationship between the Holy Spirit and Christian education, a relationship that is widely affirmed but not so widely or clearly understood. The Holy Spirit often is more of a cipher than a presence in Christian education. It has been saluted 'above', 'alongside' and 'within' the educational setting. The attempt to understand the Holy Spirit and become a part of the Spirit's work has not been carried through sufficiently in systematic theories of Christian education. Historically, we have tended to presume we know what Christian education is and then fit the Spirit into that formulation. The problem before us is not where the Holy Spirit fits into education, or how education is influenced by the Holy Spirit. It is rather how education can be according to the Spirit.

The problem is one that merits some in-depth exploration, and it is one that I spent a dissertation examining.[2] We can only scratch the surface in such a short article. However, I feel that it is important enough to begin a conversation (or several conversations) that I hope will continue. We will move through several important links in the argument, even though we will only be able to do so in a rather cursory manner. We will begin with an overview of the problem of the relationship between the Holy Spirit and Christian education. We will then move to the foundational claim that there is an analogy between the human spirit and the work of the Holy Spirit in relation to the human spirit. This analogy focuses on the dynamic of centredness, openness that is characteristic of both the developing human spirit and the work of the Holy Spirit. The analogy is woven around the interconnection of the achievements and the limits of human knowing, human securing and human suffering. Finally, we will extend this analogy to describe what Christian education patterned after the Holy Spirit might be like.

The Spirit of the gaps

The issue at stake is not where we put the Holy Spirit in Christian education or even how much participation we 'grant' the Spirit. As stated above, the matter is how Christian education can look to the

Holy Spirit for its origin, starting point and foundations.

Twenty-five years ago, Edward Farley alerted us to the pervasive problem of incoherence on the issue. Farley addressed this issue in his series of articles on the Holy Spirit and Christian education.[3] It was his contention that Christian education, beginning with the religious education movement early in the century, had conflated nurture and instruction. Education, instead of focusing on ordered learning, then became 'anything and everything God uses to fulfil his saving purposes'.[4] The most obvious problem with this formulation was its vagueness. While education had repeatedly suffered from being defined too narrowly (that is, as what happens in a classroom when students sitting at a desk memorise the information the teacher transmits), when it lost all definition it lost its intentionality. The goal of Christian education was nebulous; there was simply an implied hope that education would somehow contribute to the process of conversion or sanctification.

This understanding of Christian education carried with it an appeal to the Holy Spirit to complete a process that was begun by teachers and programmes. 'The formula seems to be, Christian education plus Holy Spirit equals salvation or sanctification.... When this is the case the Holy Spirit becomes a kind of explanation for the x-factor in salvation not covered by human efforts.'[5] The Holy Spirit here fills the gaps of education, the leftovers of human endeavour. As Iris Cully framed it, 'We teach, but the Holy Spirit brings response.'[6] There is no coherent theology to this, just an understanding that we are somehow operating 'under the guidance of the Holy Spirit' and an implicit assumption of some causal relationship between our efforts and sanctification. Yet, for all intents and purposes, the Holy Spirit is really rather 'superfluous' in these theories, insists Farley: 'The Holy Spirit is not an indispensable means to the goal for which educational processes are obviously designed.'[7]

The real predicament caused by this confusion is the unintentional marginalisation of the Holy Spirit. The Spirit is almost seen as a relief pitcher who comes in at the ninth inning to sustain a win (or perhaps even reverse a loss), but who is otherwise on the periphery. Even when the Spirit is seen to be more integral to the educational process, there is little understanding as to what this really means. Rather than being the centre of Christian education, the Spirit is simply referred to as being involved in the enlightening process that education seeks to foster. While this may produce a devotional attitude within Christian education, it can degenerate into a seal of approval that one can slap on one's means and ends, or an excuse for neglecting means and ends altogether.

In his biting critique of this understanding of the Holy Spirit and Christian education, Farley indicts most of the religious educators of the fifties and sixties. References to the Holy Spirit are sprinkled throughout the major works on Christian education during this period, and in most cases the working of the Spirit is undefined and the 'x-factor' formulation is inadvertently implied.[8] The key problem is that the Spirit is relegated to an explanation, 'namely, explaining how this human process really does contribute to salvation'.[9] The Spirit was dutifully accepted into the educational process, as either above or within it somehow, instead of the educational process being a function of who the Spirit is. Farley contends that rather than naming our endeavours after the Spirit, we need to transform what we do in light of who the Spirit is. Then 'Spirit functions not merely as an explanation of something, but the designation of a certain way of living and walking'.[10] In this way, the Spirit is not reduced to 'working supernaturally in the gaps of the instructional process'.[11]

Farley's rather abrasive articles raised a critical issue regarding Christian education theory and practice. However, Farley did not go beyond raising it; he left Christian educators with a weighty task. How do we make the reversal he calls for? How do we 'transform what we do in light of who the Spirit is'?

Before we consider how we might pattern our theory and practice of education after the Spirit, we need to press the issue even further. Farley identified the incoherence, but he did not fully recognise the source of that incoherence. He too glibly (and offensively) asserted that it was bad theory, and that is probably why these particular articles have gone unheeded.

The problem with the theories of Christian education that take recourse to the 'Spirit of the gaps' is that they have not examined the fundamental relationship between the Holy Spirit and the human spirit. Many of these theories understand very well the process of human development, and they are very sensitive to the psychological, emotional and physical aspects of human being. And many of these theories are theologically informed regarding the work of the Holy Spirit. However, they are not able to articulate the relationship between the work of the Holy Spirit and the developmental process of the human spirit. They do not understand the developing human person as *spirit*. So you have the developmental process, and you have the process of sanctification. And you have a gap in between them. And thus you have the Spirit filling in the gaps.

Analogy of the Spirit

This attempt to develop an understanding of Christian education that begins with the work of the Holy Spirit is based on more than a desire to address a theological confusion in Christian education theory (though it is partly based on that). It is more fundamentally based upon a theological anthropology. The mutually informing studies of the work of the Holy Spirit in relation to the human spirit and the developmental evolution of the human spirit point to an analogy between the two.[12] There is a likeness between the way in which the work of the Holy Spirit is described in the biblical texts and theology, and the way in which the nature of the human spirit is described in developmental theory and theological anthropology. Briefly stated, the pattern that sustains the analogy is a dialectic between centredness and openness. It is this pattern that is central to what it means to be *spirit*, and it is this pattern that describes the relationship between Holy and human spirits.

The biblical texts witness to the role of the Holy Spirit in centring the human spirit in God and opening the human spirit toward God and the world. Here we can only summarise and contend that the Spirit of God, associated with the giving of life in general, is continually witnessed to as the source of new life in terms of new knowledge and truth, a new centre that leads to openness, and a renewed ability to act and suffer in relation to others. There is a corresponding witness to the way in which the human spirit becomes limited in its ability to know (idolatrous), limited in its tendency to centre on itself or other sources of security (self-securing), and limited in its willingness to act and suffer toward change and in relation to others (passive or oppressive).[13] When the Spirit is described as being present to individuals or to the community, these people are confronted with the limits of their knowing (the reality construction that has thus far been legitimated) and of their centring (the source of security and order that has been protected) and of their acting (the absence of mercy and justice toward others).

The presence of the Spirit creates something akin to what anthropologists call liminality, a situation betwixt and between coherent states of being, or what sociologists describe as strangeness, a situation of being 'outside' of the 'given' world view.[14] And yet, crucially, the presence of the Spirit provides a source of stability in the midst of this unsettledness. Thus, the Spirit of God is simultaneously expressed as the Presence of God which confronts us with our creaturely finitude and limit and the Presence of God which makes possible the opening up of our disruptive limits. The Spirit is present at the limen of human existence, that place where the human spirit meets its limits, is shaken from its present understanding and worldview, and is plunged into the possibility of openness to revelation. The Spirit centres humanity in God, or more fully in the cross of Christ. This centring provides both the security humanity seeks and the openness that otherwise threatens that security. Thus, 'love in the Spirit' is summarised in Colossians as love and faith 'that spring forth from the hope that is stored up for you in heaven and that you have heard about in the word of truth, the gospel that has come to you'(1:5,8).

The second chapter of Acts provides us with a paradigm case that draws together the themes surrounding the Holy Spirit. The Spirit is present in the midst of a gathered group of individuals who, upon meeting with the Spirit-filled disciples, are sequentially described as devout (v. 5), confounded (v. 6), utterly amazed (v. 7), perplexed

(v. 12), questioning (v. 12) and misunderstandingly mocking (v. 13) in the first half of the account. Perhaps, to reach backward and forward into the biblical themes we are exploring, we are witness to an unfolding disorientation and reorientation in these devout ones. The writer is very careful to point out the devoutness and the religiousness of those gathered. Moreover, the writer emphasises the particularity of those gathered by distinguishing between the Galileans and the listeners (v. 7), by twice mentioning that the listeners heard 'their own native languages' (vv. 6–8), and by precisely identifying just what those languages were (vv. 9–11). In the midst of the experience of the Spirit's power, the shaken group exposes both ignorance (v. 12) and self-securing (v. 13). However, upon experiencing the Spirit in the context of the word of the gospel, 'they were cut to the heart' (v. 37). They proceed from asking 'What does this mean?' (v. 12) to 'What shall we do?' (v. 37). The result is that a community of repentance, worship, sacrament and service is formed where 'all believers were together and had everything in common' (v. 44). This narrative takes us through the restructuring of existence that is characteristic of the work of the Spirit. Those who were centred on themselves are re-centred in Christ and opened to those around them, and the recentring continues throughout the narrative of Acts. Though the presence of the Holy Spirit is experienced as an indwelling, it is not an infusion that separates human beings from the everyday reality of life. It is rather revelation in relation to life and to that which is strange in the midst of life.

This work of the Holy Spirit, traditionally described as justification and sanctification, has often been understood as a discontinuous process that ruptures the natural process of human development. While 'discontinuity' and 'rupture' are part of the reality of faith, the process of justification and sanctification is not foreign to the human spirit. A study of human development suggests that the pattern, openness through centredness, is the very motion of human life.[15] Piaget, Erikson, Fowler, Kegan and others have described the pattern of life as one that is characterised by centring, decentring and recentring.[16] The human person is seen as functioning from a coherent centre that is the basis for its knowing, its identity and its acting. It is only because of these centres of organisation that the human person can organise and make sense of the world; and it is out of these centres of organisation that intelligible communication and action flow. Thus, knowing, centring and acting are all intertwined.

And yet, in order to adapt to the world and increasingly acknowledge the 'otherness' of that which is outside of the self's centre, the self has to reconstruct and expand that which centres its knowing. As other people and other things, things that are strange, unfamiliar and outside of the coherent centre, impinge upon the world construction of the self, the self must either defend its position or give it up to a new one. In terms of cognitive development, Piaget discovered that defence (or assimilation) is often the first strategy for challenged structures. Fowler and Kegan both recognise that stabilisation usually occurs before the self has developed to maturity. But defence is not always possible, and the restructuring of life is often supported by the environment.

According to Kegan, the most determinative factor in the 'evolution' of the self is what he calls the 'holding environment'. The holding environment is the group of people (for example, family, peers) or the institution (school) that carries out the dialectical functions of holding on (affirming) and letting go (contradicting). If the holding environment is able to keep these two in balance, then the self is able to move without either fear of rejection (remains held) or anxiety over the loss (allowed to let go). Contrarily, if the holding environment holds on too tightly, movement may be arrested, or if it proceeds it may cause great anxiety and depression. If the holding environment stresses letting go and contradicting, movement may be rushed and it may be at the expense of a sense of identity and confirmation. The stressed self may become hyper-independent or it may ultimately react against movement.

Whatever the developmental history of the self, the human spirit inevitably expands to some degree in its knowing and is unavoidably de-centred at many points in its evolution. And that decentring involves a period of liminality where the human spirit leaves behind a former structure of the self and moves toward a qualitatively different structure of the self. Though the change involves an expanded capacity for functioning, it is nevertheless a loss of a former state of being and causes some pain and suffering to the disoriented self.

These thinkers have understood this to be a progressive, hierarchical process, where higher and higher levels of conflict with life challenge developmental centres and urge the human person toward more and more sophisticated and complex centres of coherence. To use the language I have presented, the understanding seems to be that the human spirit begins very self-centred and scarcely aware of and open to the reality and being of others (Piaget). However, the centres of human coherence progressively expand to include others until, at the *telos* of human development, the coherent centre is described by inter-dependence (Kegan) and inclusivity (Fowler). The dialectic between centredness and openness is the basic dynamic of the human spirit. And, if these theorists are correct in projecting the *telos* of the developmental process, the human spirit is being drawn from a state of self-centredness into a state of other-centredness. Thus, the openness into which the self-centred infant is pushed out of its ego-centricity ultimately becomes an openness which defines and gives the self its *exo*-centricity (other centredness). Thus we can say that the process and dynamic that we understand theologically to be the work of the Holy Spirit is analogous to the fundamental motion of the human spirit as described by developmental psychology.

However, analogy implies difference as well as similarity. It is arguable from the standpoint of theological anthropology that human development and progress is perhaps more spiral than incremental. While the metaphor of development is helpful in describing the way in which human capacities emerge, it is also somewhat distortive. The scales are biased toward the pattern shown in western white male development; the hierarchical image leads to an imperialism of certain ways of functioning over others; and the progressive emphasis reinforces western pride and control. However, the most serious weakness in the developmental framework is the assumption that a human being reaches its incrementally described destiny by virtue of some internal capacity or through the sponsoring of its holding environments.

There are several problems with this assumption. First, there are no holding environments that hold us as well as we need to be held and let us go as lovingly as we need to be let go. And yet, we begin as and remain insecure human beings who seek and look for centres of security that will order our lives and stabilise our spirits in the midst of threat and challenge.

Second, if it is true that we go through a process of centring and opening ourselves, it is also true that we become increasingly *more* self-centred even as we are becoming increasingly more other-centred. That is to say, development is a process that tests and tries the human ego's capacity to order and sustain itself. And, as we all know, we grow more and more capable of doing so. In fact, we reach a point at the upper end of human development (Kegan's stage of the Institutional Self; Fowler's stage of Individuative-Reflective) where the human ego is described by its capacity to order, control, define and defend itself. The 'achievement' of this stage is the capacity for ideology. However, along with this achievement comes something of an incapacity, an inability to sustain true openness. As Kegan states, 'the hallmark of the institutional balance, its self-possessiveness, is also its limit'. The ideology becomes the stabilising and securing force in life, providing an anchor for the insecure human ego. While all previous centres held similar power over the self, the institutional centre has even more force. All the adaptive capacities have matured, and the self is consciously aware of its own power to both self-control *and* other-control.

That is, just at the height of human power, knowledge and capability, the human spirit compresses rather than expands its centre of coherence. Just when the human being is capable of more consciously ordering its world, understanding others and disciplining itself, the human spirit curves in on itself and limits its potential for openness (Reinhold Niebuhr, Pannenberg). Increasingly aware of its seeming *un*limited capacities to control and secure life, and acutely conscious of the insecurity of life, the human spirit easily grasps onto that which it has created and zealously protects that source of security.[17] Overly challenged by the accumulations of decentrings, the human spirit levels off in development when it has reached the stage where it is capable of seizing control.[18] Reinhold Niebuhr, almost as if anticipating present developmental theory, provides a trenchant theological analysis of the way in which the self that is near the peak of human maturity turns its achievement of knowledge and self-transcendence into a weapon for self-securing and deceitful idolatry.

The reality of the relationship between self-centredness and sin has led many theologians to assert the radical discontinuity between the human spirit and the Holy Spirit. Some even refuse to use the term spirit in association with human beings (Barth). Contrarily, the reality of the similarity between the human spirit and the Holy Spirit has led others to so closely identify the two spirits that no distinction is made (Pannenberg). The analogy enables us to hold these two tendencies in balance; it both affirms the similarity and the relationship and acknowledges the discontinuity and the 'otherness' of the divine Spirit.

The openness and other-centredness which drew the human spirit along is not sustained in the normal process of human development. Only a centre outside the self, a centre that embraces the exigencies of human life, a centre in a crucified Lord, can uphold the motion of the human spirit (Pannenberg). The analogy holds true, but it also points beyond itself.

Education in the Spirit embraces both the similarity and the dissimilarity between the Holy Spirit and the human spirit. It takes into consideration the way in which both of these function in the educational situation. And education in the Spirit points beyond itself to that Spirit which is its source of life and meaning.

Education and human limits

The educational situation is one that carries with it the human limits that define the human spirit. The reality of human limits to knowing, self-securing and suffering action pervade the educational environment. Though education is a process that engages and hopes to open up these limits, it must be careful neither to deny these limits nor exploit their nature. On the one hand education, so often dubbed the panacea for human problems, too easily attacks these problems with the assumption that enlightenment and instruction are all that is needed to head humanity in the proper direction. That is an optimism that fails fully to recognise the complex nature of human limits and the way they influence the educational situation. On the other hand education, perfectly cognisant of the driving force of human insecurity, too readily provides answers, solutions and ideologies that the vulnerable human spirit is only too ready to grasp.

We need to be aware that education embraces human spirits who have histories, interests, worldviews, traditions and emotions that provide both the limit and the potential for a rich educational environment. And we need to confront the way in which both liminality and strangeness surround the vulnerable human spirit. We cannot assume that we have open pitchers just waiting to be filled with the proper elixir for society's ills. We need to be alert to the fact that these human spirits may nevertheless ask just for such a filling. Their history, stage in life and interests may predispose them to seek security and certainty.

We can both confess and celebrate the limitedness that is a part of our nature. We confess that our interests and perspectives limit what we can know and do know. We acknowledge that we all are invested in our worldviews. And we reflect upon the way in which our fears and insecurities prevent us from suffering change and acting for others. We celebrate that our limits make us who we are. We do not hold them tightly, and we do not claim they are everlasting. We try to keep them open without giving them up altogether.

Educating in the Spirit

Christian education can be understood as a means of grace that supports us in the midst of and even brings us into the kind of places and situations where the Spirit of God is understood to be at work.[19] Christian education can pattern itself after the work of the Spirit and provide opportunities for the opening of knowing, the recentring of life and the empowering for suffering. By providing a context that centres on the cross and grace of Christ, Christian education can support and encourage openness. The educational context can be a 'holding environment' which performs the twin functions of confirmation and contradiction (Kegan). As it acknowledges and accepts the reality of personal strangeness, it also welcomes and responds to the strangeness outside of its culture. This holding environment surrounds the learners with acceptance and simultaneously challenges them, releases them and empowers them into the world beyond itself. This kind of educational environment is one that liberates the learners to explore their life and their surroundings with honesty and openness.

We will look at Christian education in terms of the three characteristics of the Holy Spirit that we mentioned above. We spoke of the Holy Spirit in relationship to knowledge and truth, centredness in Christ, and suffering and love in this world. Education in the Spirit: first, fosters encounters with things that are 'other' and people that are 'strangers'; second, proclaims the word of our security in God and the way of the cross, becoming a means of grace for the liberating work of the Spirit in opening us to other things and other people; third, engages the learning community in acts of worship, mercy, justice and suffering for others. As these occur, a space is opened for the Spirit to move learners into greater truth, centredness and obedience.

It is no doubt true that these characteristics of something called 'educating in the Spirit' describe many of the things already done in

Christian education. What is important is that these things are all held *together*: an intentional encounter with otherness (liminality), an interpretation of life through the centrality of the cross (centredness), and an active response of mercy and justice (openness). We have historically swung back and forth between these three characteristics, most often between 'proclaiming' and 'engaging', without recognising the important dynamic between these processes. The centring and opening nature of the work of the Spirit in the life of faith calls for a centring and opening dialectic in Christian education. If we focus only on centring, we may either make personal comfort and affirmation the whole of the educational experience (that is, emotionally secure the human spirit) or make an absolutised transmissive content the substance of education (that is, intellectually secure the human spirit). This not only may lead to passivity or ideology but it may also backfire. The comfortable human spirit may become jaded and seek stimulation elsewhere, and the indoctrinated human spirit may become idolatrous and shut off intellectual enquiry. If we focus on opening, we may overly stress the insecure human spirit that requires some sense of stability. Such a plunge into repeated upheaval may either weary the human spirit or provoke it to be defensive and reactively self-protective.

Though certainly not understood to be the only locus of the Holy Spirit, this definition of Christian education is offered: *It is the particular task of Christian education to create environments in which we are brought to the 'limen' of our personal world constructions in a context where security in God is both taught and embodied and where an understanding of the cross invites both openness and vulnerability on the part of both learners and teachers*. Though we cannot really unpack this definition, we can reflect upon some of its implications.

The limen of our personal world constructions

Educating in the Spirit would affirm rather than avoid liminality. Though the sharing of knowledge is perfectly appropriate, teachers and students would not gather in order to assert their mastery of faith. Rather they would come together to pursue the adventure of struggling with, playing with and living out the particular way in which their faith is understood. There would be a recognition that the limits to knowing, the limits of self-securing and the limits to acting and suffering are part of the educational situation for all involved. A key aspect of Christian education would be listening to the voices of texts, strangers and others that have been left out of a community's confessions. Learning would come as much from the 'practical wisdom' of living faith as from systematically thinking about faith. At the heart of this would be a willingness to live with questions and a suspicion of ideological answers.

Christian education can affirm liminality by acknowledging the way in which we are all strangers in life. In fact, the community of Christ is a community of those who have recognised their alienation from power structures and ideologies; and it is a community that is intentionally inclusive of those who are strangers to itself. Instead of making conformity and uniformity the norm, the community of Christ allows that which is different and strange, both within us and outside of us, to be brought in its midst.

Security in God is both taught and embodied

Education according to the Spirit would not focus on the learner, the teacher or the subject matter as its primary point of reference. It would rather continually point to the God in Christ who manifested the divine being in and on the cross. The cross of Christ places repentance, forgiveness and resurrection at the centre of community life. It embraces conflict, disorientation and suffering as well as unity, centredness and healing. Any other centre in Christian education encourages idolatrous attitudes.

This is not only taught through words (though it is that); it is also embodied in the learning environment. Though teachers retain the role of influencing and guiding students, their role is always relativised. Teachers are learners as well: learners with limits, histories, interests and failings. This should not be hidden but allowed to become part of the learning environment. The learning environment aims to be a hospitable place (Parker Palmer) for the adventure of struggling and questioning. As a kind of 'holding environment' it allows for both affirming and contradicting. And yet it points to Christ as the source of true holding and letting go.

The importance of the word of God is upheld. However, it is important to realise that it is possible to neutralise the power of the word so that it comes as familiar and pre-interpreted. We latch onto a master theological theme and fit all biblical texts into that theme. Or we ignore those texts that we can't fit into our theology, relegating them to the 'null curriculum'. We listen to those commentators who support our theme and we do not hasten to involve voices and interpretations that would shake this reigning theology. To a lesser or greater extent this is inevitable. It is the role of Christian education to make the extent lesser by broadening the range of voices beyond the ones to which we are already immune.

Openness and vulnerability on the part of both learners and teachers

The opening of knowing is closely connected with vulnerability. Unless we are vulnerable to suffering change and to listening to and acting for others, we remain closed. If we remain closed, we cut ourselves off from the truth of God. We uphold such vulnerability by creating an environment where we can all confess our mistakes, forgive one another and acknowledge the inevitability of our need for both. We further sustain openness and vulnerability by allowing for the living out of our faith. The truth and wisdom that are associated with the Holy Spirit are in the midst of life; truth is understood in relation to conflicts, situations and earthly realities. The wisdom of God is a 'practical wisdom' in that it arises in specific situations. Though it may carry with it general principles (for example, Acts 10 and the overturning of the meaning of 'unclean') that reinterpret our faith, the principles follow from but do not precede the situation.

Educating in the Spirit means living in the Spirit. Though that includes a certain kind of environment and process in education, it also means more. It means involvement in the world, and it means reflection on how the wisdom gained from that involvement inspires and interprets our faith.

Though there is an emphasis here on mutual empowerment (rather than the holding of power over others) there is not a dissolution of the role of the teacher. The teacher still brings certain promises to the learning situation, and the teacher is still in an undeniable position of power and influence. These are affirmed and celebrated, but they are also confessed and relativised. The teacher remains teachable and the learners are treated as being learned. There is an overflow in roles and there is a sharing of the power.

The Spirit in context

It is important to keep in mind that the context for this understanding of educating in the Spirit is the *community*. This is not a method to employ on an individual basis. Here, the individual encounters that which is 'other' and 'strange' in relationship to a community that is centred in Christ and open to the world. In this way the individual encounters strangeness, and even indwells 'otherness', while maintaining bearing in a community of faith. In no way is this meant to be the basis for a communal ideology that elevates that which is strange or other to the status of absolute good.

Thus, the intended outcome of this thesis is not for individuals to go in search of 'otherness', nor is it for individuals to choose community allegiance on the basis of strangeness. Rather, the intention is that Christian communities open to and embrace strangeness and thus foster such openness (to their own strangeness as well as to others') in individuals. As individuals participate in such a community, they place themselves in the kind of situation in which we understand the Spirit of God to be at work.

Notes
1. This is a highly compressed argument based on a larger work that develops all of the present themes in greater detail. My hope is that it can generate some thinking on the issue even in this abbreviated form.
2. See Carol Lakey Hess, *Educating in the Spirit*, Princeton Theological Seminary, 1990. I am working on modifying this for publication into a book.
3. See Edward Farley, 'The strange history of Christian paideia', *Religious Education*, 60,

1965, pp. 339–346; 'Does Christian education need the Holy Spirit?', *Religious Education*, 60, 1965, pp. 427–479; '"Rigid Instruction" versus Brahman: a reply', *Religious Education*, 61, 1966, pp. 229–240.

4. Farley's section, 'The work of the Spirit in Christian education', in 'Does Christian education need the Holy Spirit?', *Religious Education*, 60, 1965, pp. 427–479; here p. 429.

5. *Ibid.*, p. 430.

6. Iris Cully, 'Instruction or nurture', *Religious Education*, 62, 1967, pp. 225–261.

7. Edward Farley, 'Does Christian education need the Holy Spirit?', *op. cit.*, p. 430.

8. See Harold Burgess, *An Invitation to Religious Education*, Birmingham, Religious Education Press, 1975, p. 118.

9. Edward Farley, 'Does Christian education need the Holy Spirit?', *op. cit.*, p. 430.

10. *Ibid.*, p. 421.

11. Now, it must be said, there is no way to avoid completely an indeterminate description of the work of the Holy Spirit. In fact, the x–factor formulation has brought an extremely important message to the fore. It has affirmed the mystery of the work of the Spirit and placed it at the centre of the relationship between teacher, student, and the bible in Christian education. This is not inherently confused. When this mystery is truly appreciated, the educational context can become the community of the Holy Spirit. However, when this mystery is only tagged on as an afterthought, the educational context can miss the opportunity to become the community of the Holy Spirit.

12. The sources that provide the background for this thesis are: the biblical texts; George Hendry, *The Holy Spirit in Christian Theology*, London, SCM, 1965; Wolfhart Pannenberg, *Anthropology in Theological Perspective*, Edinburgh, T and T Clark, 1985; Reinhold Niebuhr, *The Nature and Destiny of Man*, London, Nisbet, 1941; and Robert Kegan, *The Evolving Self*, Cambridge, Massachusetts, Harvard University Press, 1982. Again, this whole discussion is very abbreviated in this present article.

13. While we cannot speak of *the* biblical understanding of the Spirit of God, we can point to various images and themes that emerge throughout the biblical canon.

14. See Victor Turner, *The Ritual Process*, London, Routledge and Kegan Paul, 1969; and Alfred Schutz, 'The stranger', in *Collected Papers* (edited by Arvid Brodersen), The Hague, M Nijhoff, 1964, pp. 91–105.

15. Robert Kegan, *The Evolving Self*, Cambridge, Massachusetts, Harvard University Press, 1982.

16. This is also traceable to Hegel, who described this pattern on a more cosmic level.

17. See Edward Farley, *The Fragility of Knowledge: theological education in the church and the university*, Philadelphia, Fortress Press, 1988.

18. In a larger work I have argued that Kegan's stage 4 (would apply for Fowler's stage 4 as well), the stage of ideology, is the stage where this occurs – making the movement into stage 5 (inter-independence) unlikely without a religious centre.

19. See Craig Dykstra, *Growing in the Life of Christian Faith: a report approved by the 201st General Assembly*, 1989, Presbyterian Church, USA.

4. Theological approaches: postliberal theology

Christian education has been influenced by a succession of liberal (or revisionist) theologies, such as process theology,[1] which are characterised by a desire to express the Christian faith through contemporary scientific and cultural categories. In the last two decades, however, the basic assumptions of the liberal perspective have been directly attacked by an informal coalition of 'postliberal' theologians, for whom Christian identity is inseparable from the Christian community and the stories that sustain it. Postliberalism, associated with Stanley Hauerwas, Ronald Thiemann, and George Lindbeck (who popularised the title),[2] among others, has far-reaching consequences for religious educators, and has had a major impact upon theological education, in particular through the work of writers like Edward Farley and Charles Wood.[3]

Gregory C Higgins' article, 'The significance of postliberalism for religious education', was first published in *Religious Education*, 84, 1989, pp. 77–89. It identifies postliberalism as a significant conversation partner for religious educators and proceeds to survey George Lindbeck's discussion of three approaches to the study of religion: propositional, experiential-expressivist (or liberal), and cultural-linguistic (or postliberal). The majority of the article is taken up with an analysis of the corresponding teaching methodologies in religious education: the catechism approach, the experiential approach, and a postliberal approach that is faithful to the Christian narrative and construes religious understanding 'as a matter of learning the language' of a particular religion. The author concludes with a number of unresolved questions about the impact of postliberalism on Christian education.

Lucien Richard's 'Theology and belonging: Christian identity and the doing of theology' explores the notions of tradition and identity in Christianity, with particular reference to the historical and critical functions of hermeneutics. The role of the ecclesial community, as a 'pluralistic faith community', in the development of both individuality and identity is discussed in the context of the tasks facing the theologian and the student of theology. This article appeared first in *Religious Education*, 79, 1984, pp. 392–413.

Dr Gregory C Higgins teaches at the Christian Brothers Academy in Lincroft, New Jersey, USA. Dr Lucien Richard is a member of the faculty of Weston School of Theology, Cambridge, Massachusetts, USA.

Notes

1. See, for example, Randolph Crump Miller, 'Continuity and contrast in the future of religious education', in James Michael Lee (ed.), *The Religious Education We Need*, Birmingham, Alabama, Religious Education Press, 1977; Iris V Cully and Kendig Brubaker Cully (eds), *Process and Relationship*, Birmingham, Alabama, Religious Education Press, 1978; Jay McDaniel, 'The role of God in religious education', *Religious Education*, 79, 1984, pp. 414-422; and Brennan Hill, 'Alfred North Whitehead's approach to education: its value for religious education', *Religious Education*, 85, 1990, pp. 92-104.
2. See, for example, Stanley Hauerwas, *A Community of Character: toward a constructive Christian social ethic*, Notre Dame, Indiana, University of Notre Dame Press, 1981; Ronald Thiemann, *Revelation and Theology: the gospel as narrated promise*, Notre Dame, Indiana, University of Notre Dame Press, 1985; George Lindbeck, *The Nature of Doctrine: religion and theology in a postliberal age*, Philadelphia, Fortress, 1984.
3. See, for example, Edward Farley, *Ecclesial Reflection: an anatomy of theological method*, Philadelphia, Fortress, 1982; *Theologia: the fragmentation and unity of theological education*, Philadelphia, Fortress, 1983; *The Fragility of Knowledge: theological education in the church and the university*, Philadelphia, Fortress, 1988; and Charles M Wood, *The Formation of Christian Understanding*, Philadelphia, Fortress, 1981; *Vision and Discernment: an orientation in theological study*, Atlanta, Georgia, Scholars Press, 1985; *An Invitation to Theological Study*, Valley Forge, Pennsylvania, Trinity Press, 1994.

4.1 The significance of postliberalism for religious education

Gregory C Higgins

Introduction

The field of religious education remains in a state of disarray over the question of its relationship to theology. The claim put forth here is that there exists a real, though not always explicit, relationship between theology and religious education.[1] This article, in fact, stems from the concern that there exists little dialogue between religious educators and theologians. One's theological commitments do indeed have a direct bearing on how one goes about teaching in the classroom. The growing cluster of theologians who have expressed support for 'postliberalism', therefore, offers religious educators an important conversation partner in the theological community. Since postliberalism challenges the theological foundation on which much of contemporary religious education is based, this exchange can stimulate much needed discussion between theologians and religious educators. It also provides religious educators with an opportunity to rethink the theological principles which guide their teaching.

The increasing attention given to postliberalism can be attributed to the publication of George Lindbeck's *The Nature of Doctrine: religion and theology in a postliberal age* in 1984.[2] Here, Lindbeck systematically outlines an alternative theological methodology which has been pioneered in large part by Yale scholars such as Hans Frei, David Kelsey and Brevard Childs. With the publication of this important volume, Lindbeck provided both critics and supporters alike with the opportunity to evaluate this approach, which had been appearing in fragmentary ways over the past decade.

This article falls into three parts: the first outlines the three approaches to the study of religion which Lindbeck discusses (propositional, experiential-expressive and cultural-linguistic); the second relates each approach to a type of religious education; the third examines the impact postliberalism might have on teaching methodology.

Three approaches to the study of religion

The first approach outlined by Lindbeck is the most traditional. This propositional approach 'emphasises the cognitive aspects of religion and stresses the ways in which church doctrines function as informative propositions or truth claims about objective realities'.[3] Since religious statements are truth claims about the nature of reality, theology has a significant investment in metaphysics. From the early Greek apologists to contemporary theologians such as Rahner, there has been an interest in securing a foundation for theological truth-claims in metaphysics. This links faith and reason, theology and philosophy, study and prayer. Many regard this synthesis as essential to Christian theology. The God proclaimed in scripture must also, by necessity, be the First Principle spoken of by the philosophers. In addition, formulations of truth statements are not subject to change. 'For a propositionalist, if a doctrine is once true, it is always true, and if it is false, it is always false.'[4] The continuity of a religious tradition is based on the transmission of these truths from one generation to the next.

Immanuel Kant delivered the decisive challenge to the use of metaphysics for theological purposes. By restricting human cognition to knowledge of phenomena rather than noumena, Kant severed the bond between theology and metaphysics. The idea of God simply served a regulative function in the ordering of our experience by allowing us to view the world as an ordered and regulated whole. Etienne Gilson correctly concludes, 'Since God is not an object of empirical knowledge, we have no concept of him. Consequently God is no object of knowledge, and what we call natural theology is just idle talking.'[5] Post-Kantians recognised that a new basis for theological language would be needed if they were to again speak meaningfully about God. Kant had safeguarded the concept of God from the more critical movements of his day but, as Lindbeck notes, 'his reduction of God to a transcendental condition (albeit a necessary one) of morality seemed to the sensibilities of most religious people to leave religion intolerably impoverished'.[6] Friedrich Schleiermacher sought both to accept the Kantian critique and to restore 'feeling' to religion. Schleiermacher had relocated the centre of religious knowledge in the immediate self-consciousness. The task of theology was to reflect on the feeling of absolute dependence as experienced in the innermost depths of the individual. This is the second approach discussed by Lindbeck.

Lindbeck labels this approach initiated by Schleiermacher 'experiential-expressivism'. At other places he refers to it as 'revisionist' or simply 'liberal'. Those in this tradition posit the existence of a core experience of transcendence which is accessible to all persons in all cultures. The experience of this core transcendence in turn becomes objectified in different cultural forms. Religions in this model 'articulate or represent and communicate that inner experience of the divine (or, perhaps, of the "unconditioned") which is held to be common to them all'.[7] 'Thinkers of this tradition', Lindbeck writes, 'all locate ultimately significant contact with whatever is finally important to religion in the prereflective experiential depths of the self and regard the public or outer features of religion as expressive and evocative objectifications (that is, nondiscursive symbols) of internal experience.'[8]

The third approach, the one advocated by Lindbeck, is the 'cultural linguistic' (or postliberal) view of religion. In this view, 'religions are seen as comprehensive interpretive schemes, usually embodied in myths or narratives, and heavily ritualised, which structure human experience and understanding of self and world'.[9] The predominant image employed by the proponents of the cultural-linguistic model is that of a language. Like a language, a religion provides a framework through which the adherents of that religion interpret experience. Lindbeck maintains that the cultural-linguistic model provides a framework in which significant ecumenical advances can be made. He devotes the bulk of the book to questions of doctrinal development and specific questions about christology, Marian dogmas and papal infallibility. The implications of his methodology, however, extend beyond the question of doctrinal development. This article will examine the implications that the cultural-linguistic model holds for Christian religious education.

Teaching methodologies

In the field of religious education there are corresponding methodologies to each of the three approaches under examination. Each of these methods carries with it certain strengths and weaknesses.

The propositionalist approach may be best represented by a 'catechism approach' to religious education. If Christianity is a matter of identifying and assenting to orthodox beliefs, then religious education consists in the instruction and inculcation of those beliefs. The advantages offered by a catechism, of course, are numerous. A catechism provides a clear and orderly presentation of the central Christian beliefs. It begins with the most rudimentary questions and builds on that foundation as the discussion moves to more abstract questions. In this way, the student can see how various Christian beliefs are related to one another. The catechism provides a standard text so that Christians living in different regions have a common religious training. The shortcomings of the catechism approach, however, are also well known. Chief among the negative features is the assumption that Christianity is ultimately a matter of parroting back the correct response. The catechism appears too rigid, too rational, too divorced from the experiences of the students.

The experiential approach in religious education seems to be the ideal complement to this overly dogmatic catechism. This approach draws upon the theological insights of liberalism. The experiential method takes as its starting point the experiences of the students and relates those experiences to the traditional affirmations of the faith. If Christianity is ultimately a relationship of a person to his or her transcendental source (for example, one's 'ground of being'), then religious educators should elicit from the students their deepest questions about life and relate Christianity to those existential questions. The student is then not simply parroting responses to questions that he or she is not asking. The most articulate representative of the experiential approach in our century was Paul Tillich. His method of correlation relates the questions of human existence with the answers given by Christianity. 'It correlates questions and answers, situation and message, human existence and divine manifestation', writes Tillich.[10] In this way, Christian message remains existentially relevant to believers.

The experiential approach dominates the field of religious education. The reasons for its popularity are clear. It provides a methodology that directly addresses itself to the deepest questions of the students, thereby making Christianity relevant to the lives of the students. The methodology openly acknowledges that the pursuit of truth is a common human quest. By virtue of our humanity, we all have 'ultimate concerns'. No one group monopolises truth, we are all pilgrims, and we can learn from those outside our own group. Consequently, we can make use of a host of different sources in the classroom. All literature, music, newspaper stories and movies are potentially a source of understanding and enrichment since all persons must grapple with questions of human existence. Lastly, it seems religiously compelling to us to say that genuine reflection on life will reveal 'signals of transcendence'[11] which make the question of the nature and purpose of God a relevant question for all persons.

Postliberalism

Although postliberals take issue with the propositionalist approach, the main focus of their attack is against experiential-expressivism. The postliberal argument is advanced on two grounds: philosophical and strategic. In sum, Lindbeck first feels expressivism fails to recognise the formative influence of language, and second, he feels those in this tradition assume an incorrect theological posture towards the world.

The philosophical issue involved is the relationship between language and experience. In the experiential tradition, religious language is an expression of the encounter with this universal transcendence. Lindbeck challenges the premise that undergirds the experiential-expressive approach by insisting that language is prior to experience. He states clearly that 'public linguistic categories shape even preexperiential activity'.[12] By extending the influence of language to this pre-reflective experience, Lindbeck has challenged the very foundation upon which the experiential tradition rests. 'It remains true, therefore', writes Lindbeck, 'that the most easily pictured of the contrasts between a linguistic-cultural model of religion and an experiential-expressive one is that the former reverses the relation of the inner and the outer. Instead of deriving external features of a religion from inner experience, it is the inner experiences which are viewed as derivative.'[13] It is the experience which is the product of the language. Once people learn a language, 'this shapes the preexperiential physical basis of their conscious experience and activity. Thus language, it seems, shapes domains of human existence and action that are preexperiential.'[14]

The second criticism voiced by Lindbeck concerns the liberal commitment to apologetics as the best means of commending Christianity to the world. How can the church best preach to a secularised society? The liberal approach, again ably represented by Tillich, has been first to secure a common ground, through a common set of questions, language or experience, and then proceed to demonstrate the reasonableness and viability of Christianity on the basis of the common ground shared by the two parties. In this way, the church and the world share a common language. Tillich writes, 'A theological system is supposed to satisfy two basic needs: the statement of the truth of the Christian message and the interpretation of this truth for every new generation.'[15] In our age, Tillich would argue, the fulfilment of this dual requirement necessarily means that theologians enter into dialogue with those in such diverse fields as psychology, philosophy, political theory, art and the physical sciences. He continues later, 'It is the task of apologetic theology to prove that the Christian claim also has validity from the point of view of those outside the theological circle. Apologetic theology must show that trends which are immanent in all religions and cultures move towards the Christian answer.'[16] If theologians fail to address the wider culture, then they will have failed to communicate the Christian message in any meaningful way.

Lindbeck insists that this apologetic approach has been detrimental to Christianity. On a theoretical level Lindbeck, as mentioned above, insists that religions are best thought of as languages rather than expressions of transcendental experiences. In order to understand a religion, therefore, one must do so on the terms of the religion. He writes, 'In short, religions, like languages, can be understood only in their own terms, not by transposing them into an alien speech.'[17] On a practical level, Lindbeck argues that this apologetic approach has undermined the distinctiveness of Christianity. If Christianity is saying essentially the same thing as any other religion, only using different language, then it has nothing new to say to the world. Lindbeck insists, along with many other postliberals, that Christianity has something to say to the world only to the extent that it can produce communities which embody a distinctive way of life in the world. Lindbeck writes that a religion 'is likely to contribute more to the future of humanity if it preserves its own distinctiveness and integrity than if it yields to the homogenising tendencies associated with liberal experiential-expressivism'.[18] In a sympathetic review of Lindbeck's work, William Placher summarised the choice between liberalism and postliberalism well:[19]

Does one influence society most effectively by beginning with society's shared assumptions and trying to move in a new direction (revisionism) or by simply describing one's own world-view as forcefully as possible (postliberalism)? Should the moral and spiritual leadership of our society, and the future of our church, lie more with those who work within the common discourse, the established institutions (revisionism), or with those who create exemplary enclaves of speech and action (postliberalism)?

Towards a postliberal teaching methodology

If it is true that theological positions directly inform teaching methodology, then postliberalism directly challenges any methodology linked to liberalism. Lindbeck himself hints that a reconsideration of religious education is in order. He claims that 'Western culture is now at an intermediate stage ... where socialisation is ineffective, catechesis impossible and translation a tempting alternative.'[20] Although Lindbeck does not explicitly outline a postliberal theory of religious education, his work, I believe, suggests two major methodological shifts are in order.

The first shift concerns the way religious educators commend Christianity to their students. It is the postliberal claim that the liberal methodology no longer serves the best interests of the Christian community. To most Christians, says Lindbeck:[21]

> It seems essential in our day to adopt an apologetic approach that seeks to discover a foundational scheme within which religions can be evaluated, and that makes it possible to translate traditional meanings into currently intelligible terms. The postliberal resistance to the foundational enterprise is from this perspective a fatal flaw.

Lindbeck, however, suggests that a continued commitment to liberalism may instead be a 'fatal flaw'. Postliberals insist that the liberals are mistaken about how to best present Christianity to a secularised culture. As any sports enthusiast will testify, strategies must fit the needs of the given time and place. What works in one situation may prove disastrous in another. Both the postliberal and the liberal readily acknowledge the penetrating effects of secularisation within western culture but differ radically as to how to go about preaching the gospel to that secularised world. Liberals insist that an apologetic approach offers the best possibility for commending Christianity, while postliberals insist that the development of strong communities of Christian witness offers Christianity its best chance for relevance to the modern world.

Religious educators know well that the 'the secularised world' is not a purely theoretical tag tossed about by those working in ivy towers. They meet members of this secularised world each day in their classrooms. The way in which they go about presenting Christianity in the classroom unavoidably depends on whether they support the liberal or postliberal theological methodology. In a provocative article dealing with this issue, James DiGiacomo writes, 'Missionaries must not only adapt to the natives they serve; they must also be faithful to the message they have come to proclaim. How well are we doing this? Are we helping produce a generation of disciples, or just turning out a different kind of religious consumer?'[22] Have we, asks DiGiacomo, been selling cheap grace? Christian educators fear that presenting a Christianity which is not relevant to the lives of the students will further alienate the dwindling number of students who are willing to listen.

The postliberal discussion of ecclesiology and church-world relations illustrates how a postliberal methodology could alter one's approach in the classroom. Postliberals insist that the primary task of the church is to be faithful to the Christian narrative. Liberals see this as an excuse for navel-gazing quietism. Postliberals insist, however, that the church can best communicate to the world by first distinguishing itself from the world. In that way, the church has something to say to the world. Postliberals claim that liberalism has diminished the ability of Christians to see themselves as a people with a distinctive vision. Stanley Hauerwas puts it well when he states that 'the truthfulness of Christian convictions can only be tested by recognising that they involve the claim that the character of the world is such that it requires the formation of a people who are clearly differentiated from the world'.[23] In this way, Hauerwas later writes, 'the task of Christians is to be the sort of people and community that can become a real option and provide a real confrontation for others'.[24] This stance towards the culture, according to the liberal, leads only to isolation and irrelevance. On a stronger note, liberals charge that this is irresponsible since it seems to ignore the Christian mandate to advance the cause of social justice.

Liberals would insist that this postliberal approach would prove counterproductive in the classroom. First of all, it runs the very serious risk of alienating students. Second, it removes the church from the concerns of mainstream America. Third, it diminishes the ability of Christians to be significant participants in the political process. By stressing the particularity of the Christian vision, however, educators make it clear to the students that Christianity is a call to undertake a radical way of life in a world which may consider such a life foolish. The church is a body of believers who undertake a distinctive way of life. The failure of the churches themselves to make clear this distinctiveness to their congregations has contributed to the present crisis, which postliberalism seeks to remedy. As Lindbeck notes, 'When or if de-christianisation reduces Christians to a small minority, they will need for the sake of survival to form communities that strive without traditionalist rigidity to cultivate their native tongue and learn to act accordingly. Until that happens, however, catechetical methods of communicating the faith are likely to be unemployable in mainstream Christianity.'[25]

A preference for postliberalism would also result in a second shift in teaching methodology. Postliberalism undercuts the tendency to locate Christianity within the wider spectrum of general religiosity. For instance, one popular high school text states, 'This experience of a God beyond ourselves has apparently been shared by the people of every known culture in the history of humanity. Every culture has demonstrated its belief in a power or powers beyond the control of people, a God or at times multiple gods who in some way explained the world and made sense of life.'[26] Echoing the expressivist position the author continues, 'Throughout history people have struggled to find ways to express outwardly what they have experienced and come to believe about God. And this is what *religion* is all about.'[27]

In contrast to this project of locating Christianity within the sphere of universal religiosity, postliberals insist that each religion, as a language, must be appropriated on its own terms. Each religion is an all-encompassing interpretive framework with its unique criteria of intelligibility. As Lindbeck argues, 'to become religious involves becoming skilled in the language, the symbol system of a given religion. To become a Christian involves learning the story of Israel and of Jesus well enough to interpret and experience oneself and one's world in its terms.'[28] One acquires an understanding of a language through performance. This process of learning enables believers to locate their lives in the larger story of Christianity. That process is indeed a long one, but it is only through that process that believers can make sense of the language they hear and speak.

The correlative to the insistence on the particularity of each religion is the claim that religious understanding is a matter of learning the language of that religion. 'To the degree that religions are like languages and cultures, they can no more be taught by means of translation than can Chinese or French. What is said in one idiom can to some extent be conveyed in a foreign tongue, but no one learns to understand and speak Chinese by simply hearing and reading translations.'[29] Religions, like languages, lose something in the translation. It is only through performance that one comes to comprehend a language. The ability to speak a language precedes the ability to understand a language. To understand religious language one must learn the grammar and vocabulary of that community. This naturally involves a strong emphasis on Scripture and the primary theological categories (for example, creation, salvation, sin, etc.).

In terms of Christian religious education this moves Christian language and the vision resulting from the interiorisation of that language to the centre of the discussion. Rather than using human experience as an entré into a discussion of the meaningfulness of Christian language, the effort is made to demonstrate how experience itself is changed when seen by Christians. Reality is seen and described through the Christian language, rather than vice versa. Therefore, 'The cross is not to be viewed as a figurative representation of suffering nor the messianic kingdom as a symbol for hope in the future; rather, suffering should be cruciform, and the hopes for the future messianic.'[30] This undercuts the tendency among many authors writing for high school students to see all things in terms of love. For example, one finds statements to the effect that 'The totality of Jesus' message is summed up with the concept that he spoke of often, the kingdom of God which he was announcing to the world.'[31] The implication made here is that Jesus was really talking about love but used a conventional expression of the day, 'kingdom of God', to express himself. The integrity of the gospel message is endangered when this translation into categories outside the text is thoroughgoing.

Conclusion

This examination of the impact of postliberalism on religious education leaves many unresolved questions. First, does Lindbeck sufficiently develop the idea that we as believers are not only shaped by the language we have received, but in turn shape the language and vision of the church of tomorrow? He acknowledges that the relationship between religions and experiences is reciprocal,[32] but concentrates almost exclusively on the influence of religious language on experience. Christian religious education requires that both the wisdom of the past as well as the challenge of the future be communicated to the students. Second, Lindbeck does not completely dismiss apologetics but insists that it must not stand at the centre of theology.[33] Does not teaching require some element of apologetics? The acquisition of any language is a long, arduous process. In order to understand a new language, the student must first make the appropriate connections between the language that the student speaks and the language that the student is learning. In French or Spanish, students first learn to conjugate the important verb forms and begin to establish a vocabulary. In terms of Christian religious education, this process would be classified as apologetics. Postliberals would rightly charge that apologetics has come to dominate religious formation and that Christian formation tends to conclude rather than begin with apologetics, but this does not deny the truth that some apologetics is necessary. Third, if religions are 'comprehensive schemes', is not the line between education and indoctrination in danger of being crossed? Should Christian education take place in highly sectarian isolated groups? We 'speak' many languages. Science, for instance, provides an interpretive scheme through which we view reality. When hurricanes ravish coastal towns, we explain the tragedy in terms of meteorology, rather than God's wrath. In what ways, then, is postliberalism asserting the need for religious language to provide an all-encompassing interpretive framework? Finally, does postliberalism tend to ghettoise theology? Lindbeck acknowledges this danger. An emphasis on establishing Christian identity need not mean a discontinuation of efforts at mutual understanding between different groups. This list does not exhaust the practical questions; in fact, it suggests that continued dialogue is needed.

Lindbeck concludes his work with the thought, 'If a postliberal approach in its actual employment proves to be conceptually powerful and practically useful to the relevant communities, it will in time become standard.'[34] For our purposes, 'the relevant communities' are the classrooms across the nation. If postliberalism has something important to say to teachers as they go about their business of education and to students as they begin to examine Christianity in a more critical light, then for the present time postliberalism will have established itself as a viable, if not superior, theological foundation for religious education.[35]

Notes

1. For a helpful analysis of the status of the question of the relationship between theology and religious education, see Mary C Boys, 'The role of theology in religious education', *Horizons*, 11, 1, 1984, pp. 61–85. See also Norma H Thompson (ed.), *Religious Education and Theology*, Birmingham, Alabama, Religious Education Press, 1982. This issue is further clouded by the various definitions given to such central concepts as 'theology' and 'religion'.

2. George Lindbeck, *The Nature of Doctrine: religion and theology in a postliberal age*, Philadelphia, Fortress, 1984. For articles dealing with postliberalism which have appeared in popular magazines see Stanley Hauerwas and William Willimon, 'Embarrassed by God's presence', *The Christian Century*, 102, 4, 1985, pp. 98–100, as well as the readers' response to that article in *The Christian Century*, 102, 15, 1985, pp. 447–50. See also two articles by William Willimon, 'Making Christians in a secular world', *The Christian Century*, 103, 31, 1986, pp. 914–917, and 'Answering Pilate: truth and the postliberal church', *The Christian Century*, 104, 3, 1987, pp. 82–85. See also Paul Giurlanda's 'The challenge of post-liberal theology', *Commonweal*, 114, 2, 1987, pp. 40-42.

3. George Lindbeck, *op. cit.*, p. 16.

4. *Ibid.*

5. Etienne Gilson, *God and Philosophy*, New Haven, Yale University Press, 1941, p. 109.

6. George Lindbeck, *op. cit.*, p. 21.

7. *Ibid.*, p. 47.

8. *Ibid.*, p.21.

9. *Ibid.*, p. 32.

10. Paul Tillich, *Systematic Theology*, Chicago, University of Chicago Press, 1967, p. 8. For an appreciative review of the work of Tillich and Jung in addressing themselves to the spiritual climate of the modern age, see John P Dourley, 'Jung, Tillich, and aspects of the Western Christian development', *Thought*, 52, 204, 1977, pp. 18-49.

11. I borrowed this expression from Peter Berger. See his *The Heretical Imperative*, Garden City, Anchor Press, 1979.

12. George Lindbeck, *op. cit.*, p. 37.

13. *Ibid.*, p. 34.

14. *Ibid.*, p. 37.

15. Paul Tillich, *op. cit.*, p. 3.

16. *Ibid.*, p. 15.

17. George Lindbeck, *op. cit.*, p. 129.

18. *Ibid.*, p. 128.

19. William C Placher, 'Revisionist and postliberal theologies and the public character of theology', *The Thomist*, 49, 1985, p. 416. That issue of *The Thomist* contains a number of review articles on Lindbeck's work.

20. George Lindbeck, *op. cit.*, p. 133.

21. *Ibid.*, p. 129.

22. James J DiGiacomo, 'The new illiteracy: catechetics and youth', *Church*, 2 (fall), 1986, pp. 3-7; here p. 4. For an article dealing with the need to recover the distinctiveness of the

religious life in our time, see Albert Dilanni, 'Vocations and the laicization of religious life', *America*, 156, 10, 1987, pp. 207–211.

23. Stanley Hauerwas, 'The church in a divided world: the interpretative power of the Christian story', in *A Community of Character: toward a constructive Christian social ethic*, Notre Dame, University of Notre Dame Press, 1981, p. 91. This is an excellent article dealing with postliberal ecclesiology (though Hauerwas himself does not designate his work as 'postliberal' in this article).

24. *Ibid.*, p. 105.

25. George Lindbeck, *op. cit.*, pp. 133–34.

26. Thomas Zanzig, *Understanding Your Faith*, Winona, Minnesota, St Mary's Press, 1980, p. 49.

27. *Ibid.*, italics his.

28. George Lindbeck, *op. cit.*, p. 34.

29. *Ibid.*, p. 128.

30. *Ibid.*, p. 118.

31. Thomas Zanzig, *op. cit.*, p. 89.

32. See Lindbeck, p. 33, 'It is simplistic to say (as I earlier did) merely that religions produce experiences, for the causality is reciprocal.'

33. See *ibid.*, p. 129, 'Resistance to translation does not wholly exclude apologetics, but this must be of an *ad hoc* and nonfoundational variety rather than standing at the centre of theology.' Lindbeck also praises the work of Paul Tillich. 'Tillich communicated to a wide range of intellectuals a generation ago, but it is doubtful that his numerous liberal successors could match his record even if they had his talent.' See *ibid.*, p. 130.

34. *Ibid.*, p. 134.

35. I would like to thank Jamie Massa for his helpful comments and suggestions.

4.2 Theology and belonging: Christian identity and the doing of theology

Lucien Richard

Tradition

In Romans 10:13–15 Paul outlines the basic process that governs access to Christian existence: 'everyone who invokes the name of the Lord will be saved'. How could they invoke one in whom they had no faith? And how could they have faith in one they had never heard of? And how hear without someone to spread the news? And how could anyone spread the news without a commission to do so? And that is what Scripture affirms: 'How welcome are the feet of the messengers of good news!' Faith in Christ, and therefore Christian existence, is essentially ecclesial. The church is the prime recipient of the gospel. Only in connection with the church does the individual have access to the revelation of God in Jesus Christ.

Karl Rahner writes: 'If salvation history is the history of God's transcendental self-communication to man in a history which can be experienced in time and space, then it follows from this perspective too that in the Christian understanding, religion is necessarily ecclesial religion.'[1] As specifically Christian, salvation history is ecclesial. Again, Rahner writes: 'The concreteness of Jesus Christ as something which challenges me must confront me in what we call the Church.'[2] Faith in Christ is inseparable from the church. The church is essentially a mediating reality, spatial and historical. Accepting Ernest Troeltsch's important insight, David Tracy writes: 'It is the tradition of the church that *is* our central mediation to the actual Jesus, the Jesus remembered by the church; it is our present experience of that mediated Christ-event which impels our belief in Jesus Christ.'[3]

The present experience of the Christ-event is mediated through the tradition. Trust in the reality of the Christ-event as made present to us implies essentially trust in the mediation itself.[4] The tradition is an essential structure in the emergence of Christian existence and identity. Tracy writes: 'We live in the Christ-event in and by the tradition, the community, the church.'[5]

It is not accidental that one of the major theological achievements of the Second Vatican Council was its teaching on tradition. Vatican II proposed a total notion of 'tradition':[6]

> The Church in her teaching, life and worship, perpetuates and hands on to all generations all that she herself is, all that she believes. ... whose wealth is poured into the practice and life of the believing and praying

Church ... the sacred writings themselves are more profoundly understood and unceasingly made active in her; ... the Holy Spirit, through whom the living voice of the gospel resounds in the Church, and through her, in the world, leads unto all truth those who believe and makes the word of Christ dwell abundantly in them.

Tradition is not understood as the mere transmission of doctrine but as the total reality of the church. Tradition is identified with the being and faith of the church. This is a dynamic understanding of tradition. It emphasises the traditionary process.

What is handed down is 'everything which contributes to the holiness of life, and the increase in faith of the People of God'.[7] That 'everything' is essentially the apostolic tradition and this is basically identified with the Scriptures. Although originating from within the church as tradition, the Scriptures possess an absolute normative value. Karl Rahner writes:[8]

Theology is referred to scripture as its only *material*, absolutely original and (*quoad nos*) *underived* source ... Scripture ... is handed down ... as the *norma non normata* of the Church's faith, since it is the pure objectification of the permanently authoritative conviction of faith of the apostolic Church.

Yet the Scripture cannot be separated from its matrix, the church. As *Dei Verbum* affirms, the church holds Scripture as the supreme rule of faith, but in a way that the Scripture is not the 'living voice of the gospel' unless it is 'constantly actualised in the living tradition of the church. Scripture alone does not suffice because it is only in the faith life of the church that it becomes the living and present word of God.'[9]

Within that traditionary process there exists a hierarchy of interpretive roles. *Dei Verbum* affirms that 'in order to keep the gospel forever whole and alive within the Church, the apostles left bishops as their successors, "handing over their own teaching role" to them'.[10] And consequently 'the task of authentically interpreting the word of God, whether written or handed on, has been entrusted exclusively to the living teaching office of the Church, whose authority is exercised in the name of Jesus Christ'.[11]

The Christ-event is mediated through the particular historical form that the Christian church is. Thus, the church as tradition is the way for the organisation of human experience as Christian. This systematic organisation is a communal possession which provides stability and an effective way of living for the believer. As Christians, individuals are socialised and constituted by the Christian tradition. It is the Christian tradition which enables the individual to remember the past Christ-event, celebrate its actual presence and anticipate its future fulfilment. The tradition plays an integrating role by uniting past, present and future. The Christian community formed by the Christian tradition, is a community of memory, celebration and expectation.

Identity

The inherited Christian tradition forms the Christian individual's identity. Christian identity is the result of a process of socialisation. Socialisation involves the process of being inserted into a social-cultural environment which in fact produces one's self identity. That process of insertion demands the internalisation of the society's self-understanding, self-image and valuing. Thomas Groome, paraphrasing Herbert Mead, writes:[12]

> Having externalised ourselves into culture and society, and culture and society having taken on a life of their own, the empowerments and limitations of that world are now taken back into our consciousness as our own. The possibilities and parameters that our social/cultural context appears to offer become our own perception of our possibilities and parameters. In other words, the objectified culture and society created by us and our predecessors become internalised as the basis of our own self-identity.

The process of socialisation determines the process of self-interpretation. As Joseph Cahill says: 'in many instances this self-interpretation is really a misnomer since the interpretation is really done by others rather than by a genuinely autonomous or inner-directed self'.[13] In this context a new self-interpretation, a new self-image, is never simple nor easy. One of the basic problems inherent to the process of socialisation is the fact that social structures and cultural patterns tend to be conservative and to overwhelm the individual. This is well expressed in a play by Dorothy Sayers, 'The Just Vengeance'. It is about an airman who has just died and is welcomed by his own townspeople from the past:[14]

Recorder
What matters here is not so much what you did
As why you did it ... Can you recite your creed?
Airman
I believe in God ...
Chorus
(*picking him up and carrying him along with it*)
... the Father Almighty,
Maker of heaven and earth.
And in Jesus Christ ...
Airman
No! No! No! What made me start off like that?
I reacted automatically to the word 'creed' –
My personal creed is something totally different.
Recorder
What is speaking in you is the voice of the city,
The church and household of Christ, your people and country.
From whom you derive. Did you think you were unbegotten?
Unfranchised? With no community and no past?

> Out of the darkness of your unconscious memory the stones of the
> city are crying out. Go on.

The corporate belief of a community seems to provide the necessary
matrix for the emergence of personal creeds, that appear to the individual as 'something totally different'. While the possibilities and
parameters intrinsic to tradition tend to become the individual's own,
yet the individual is not ultimately determined by the socialisation
process. Change can occur; the individual can be critical and needs to
be critical of his/her cultural and social structures. While the individual Christian appropriates his/her Christian faith and identity through
the internalisation of the Christian community's self-understanding,
yet he/she is not fully determined by the ecclesial reality. The interaction between the Christian self and the ecclesial community is
dialectical and involves necessarily some tensions which can be
creative yet always conflictual.

The importance of tradition has serious consequences for our understanding of Christian faith, Christian identity and therefore Christian
theology. Faith can be defined as a remembrance of Jesus Christ, as a
mediated experience which depends upon the entering into an ecclesial
community through a process of socialisation. Faith comes to us as the
appropriation of the collective remembrance of a 'community of
memory'. And since texts are so essential to this community, faith can
be understood with Paul Ricoeur as 'the attitude of one who accepts
being interpreted at the same time that he interprets the world as the
text'.[15]

Christian faith as emerging from within the Christian community
through a process of socialisation must necessarily characterise the
process of theology. Theology has been defined in a lapidary phrase,
now classical, as *fides quaerens intellectum*, faith in search of understanding. While all three words are essential, the governing element is
faith. Depending on how one understands faith, so will one understand
what theology is. Historically, faith has been given a variety of meanings.[16] In the context of the ecclesial dimension of Christian identity,
faith is essentially and primarily ecclesial. Not that the church is the
object of faith: God is always the centre and goal of all faith. Yet
there is no Christian faith that is not mediated by the church; there is
no Christian faith that is not essentially remembrance. The theologian
as necessarily a believer is always personally situated and sociologically and historically conditioned; this qualifies his/her construing of
self and world as they relate to God and thus contributes to the character of his/her theology.

To use an ecological image, theology is conditioned by its environment. While that environment is manifold, interpersonal, social,
ecclesial, immediate and specific, it is the Christian community. The
church must be considered as the matrix of faith and of theology, the
ecclesia with its life-world altering message, a distinctive complex of

symbols and a distinctive kind of intersubjectivity. Believing is essentially belonging, and so is theology. Theology, as faith in search of understanding, is essentially a participatory form of understanding available within an ecclesial community through a lived sharing in the meaning of the determinate network of symbols. The ecclesial communities are, therefore, in Ghislain LaFont's words:[17]

> at once theological place and hermeneutical place. They are the former because if the conduct and the objectives which define a community are in conformity with the gospel in a given situation they deliver by themselves something of the evangelical message which can be read and revealed only there. They are a hermeneutical place because the objective gift of faith is never perceived except from the angle from which each of the communities, in fact, receives and lives it.

As such, within the Christian context theology is essentially an ecclesial discipline; it can only be done within a believing community.[18] As an ecclesial discipline, theology is essentially hermeneutical. It does not begin with a set of *a prioris*, either philosophical or dogmatic, nor with an unmediated experience; it begins with a collective memory lived and handed down in an ecclesial community. In an hermeneutical theology, understanding can never be the product of the individual's autobiographical reflection alone. Inherited knowledge constitutes the framework in which an individual perceives and experiences.

Hermeneutics

The importance of hermeneutics in contemporary theology has been stated in a variety of ways.[19] The hermeneutical problem is basically understood as one of getting across distances. According to Paul Ricoeur, the task of hermeneutics is to understand the meaning of a text. The object of interpretation is that meaning and the world it discloses.[20] The question of distanciation is also operative here. The fixation of the meaning of discourse in writing brings out into the open a distanciation at the heart of all discourse, between the event of saying and what is said. Interpretation and distanciation are linked and complementary. Ricoeur points out:[21]

> Distanciation is not the product of our methodology and therefore is not something added and parasitic, rather it is constitutive of the phenomenon of the text as written. At the same time, it is also the condition of interpretation. 'Distanciation' is not only what understanding must conquer, but also its condition. We are thus ready to find between objectification and interpretation a relation much less dichotomising and consequently much more complementary than that instituted by the Romantic tradition.

The object of interpretation is the meaning of discourse. 'It is to explicate the "world of the text".'[22] Ricoeur explains what he means by the 'world of the text':[23]

> It is this referential dimension which is absolutely original with fictional and poetic works which, for me, poses the most fundamental hermeneutical problem. If we can no longer define hermeneutics as the search for another person and psychological intentions which hide behind the text, and if we do not want to reduce interpretation to the identification of structures, what remains to be interpreted? My response is that to interpret is to explicate the sort of being-in-the-world unfolded in front of the text.
>
> In effect, what is to be interpreted in a text is a proposed world, a world that I might inhabit and wherein I might project my ownmost possibilities. This is what I call the world of the text, the world probably belonging to this unique text.

In Heideggerian terms, self as existent is a way of being-in-the-world.

The process of knowing, therefore, is dialogical. The knower is in conversation with the tradition to which he/she belongs. In a fruitful interpretation, there is a need for belonging.

The starting point of an hermeneutical reflection is in the interpreter's reflective belonging in his/her own tradition. In that process, self-interpretation is essential. Self-interpretation involves the attempt to understand how one has become what one is in and through the appropriation of one's own tradition. In the context of the Christian tradition, self-interpretation is interpretation as religious self and, therefore, demands a decision for the tradition.

In an article entitled 'The public character of systematic theology', David Tracy writes the following:[24]

> A defining existential characteristic of systematic theology is its insistence that the theologian as theologian is a faithful member of a particular religious tradition. Her/his major task is the re-interpretation of that tradition for the present situation. All serious re-interpretation of the tradition for the situation is called systematic theology.

Hans Gadamer has argued that it can be shown on strict philosophical grounds that belonging to a tradition is absolutely unavoidable because of the very nature of our human selves.[25] It is not possible for the subject of faith simply to be an individual. The subject of faith is not 'I' but 'we'. Placed outside of a confessing community, theology becomes what Kant called 'erudite exegesis', and at its extreme, a mere exercise in logic.

Pluralism

Because theology is essentially ecclesial, and faith is a remembrance and a belonging, the doing of theology in a pluralistic situation like the contemporary one is problematical and critical, both for the professional theologian and the students. For the professional theologian, the problem poses itself in the following way: in a pluralistic environment where the Christian tradition is marked by dissonance (which, according to J Cahill 'is the chasm between the intelligibility of symbolic structures in the world of theory and their compelling force in the world of practice'),[26] how can one stand critically and with commitment within one's own specific tradition, within one's community of consent?

One must be aware of the liberating and, for some, undermining character of modern hermeneutics in regard to the more traditional understanding of theology. Claude Geffré writes: 'Modern hermeneutics ... underscores the plurality and the divergence of meanings, the historical succession of interpretations and the difficulty which exists in surmounting the conflict among interpretations.'[27] This conflictual situation is of greater consequence within the context of an ecclesial situation where sources of interpretive authority are clearly located. An hermeneutical approach is also affected by the socialisation process; it poses clearly the problems of the relation between present faith experience and past faith-expression, between the individual believer's understanding and that of the ecclesial community's creed.

David Tracy claims that a confessional position can unite with a profound modern sense of historical reality 'without collapsing into the privateness of either Christian secularism or secularist relativism'.[28] Yet one must redress the undermining character of modern hermeneutics in regard to the proper logic of tradition and confessional theology. The historical-critical method has imposed upon the theologian the necessity to recognise the dual exigencies inherent in accepting as her or his data the true meaning of the tradition: the need to recognise the validity of the tradition and at the same time the need to recognise the inherent cultural and historical limitation. According to Tracy, 'the insistence upon the hermeneutical understanding of systematic theology is not a search for that "middle" ground beloved by moderates but an articulation of the only ground upon which any one of us stands; the grounds of real finitude and radical historicity whereby hermeneutical understanding alone can prove faithful to the reality of our actual situation'.[29] In this understanding of systematic theology, 'the systematic theologians by definition will understand themselves as radically finite and historical persons who have risked their trust in a loyalty to a particular religious tradition'.[30]

Hermeneutics both in its historical and critical functions has brought about a radical displacement of the classical *loci theologici* as expressed in Melchior Cano and which for centuries directed theology within the Catholic tradition. Cano borrowed his concept of *loci theologici* from the section of rhetoric which treats of the art of discovering the matter and arguments of a discourse. The goal was to assure the communication between the speaker and one's audience. The *loci theologici* simply stated what are the authoritative sources for the theologian: *probatur ex scriptura, ex traditione, ex ratione*. The epistemology of the *loci* is regulated and dominated by authorities. In adopting the historical-critical method in the doing of theology, an epistemological break occurred. Contemporary theologians find themselves without the classical epistemological instruments. They possess no mode of reasoning or critical tools that are simply proper to their own field. Both B Lonergan and K Rahner have pointed out the implications of hermeneutics for traditional theology.[31] The taken-for-grantedness of a tradition has been challenged by the historical-critical method and by the experience of living in modern societies. The social matrix for theologians is a pluralistic one; it is the churches, the academic community and the wider public community of social, political and cultural praxis. In this situation the question must be asked whether or not it is possible to avoid what Peter Berger has described as the 'heretical imperative'. Berger underlines the fact that the original meaning of heresy is to choose. In the context of theology that traditional meaning of the word 'heresy' presupposes the authority of religious traditions: only with regard to these authorities can one take an heretical stance. The heretic is the one who does not accept the authority of a tradition in its fullness, but picks and chooses.[32] The danger of picking and choosing is the proliferation of interpretations without foundations.

The major problem for the professional Christian theologian is a critical fidelity to a tradition perceived historically. For the students entering theology, the problem presents itself differently. Most of them are coming to theology with very little knowledge of their tradition. Their cultural context can be described as one of unqualified relativism. And yet the decision to enter into a programme of theology directly related to ministry demands an initial commitment to a tradition not thematically grasped and from within a culture that is essentially pluralistic. Sharon Parks describes the situation of the entering students in the following way:[33]

> It should be evident that persons come to theological education at differing moments in this faith journey. But it is my perception that our students typically seek theological education at the moment of emerging innerdependence and probing commitment, the moment in faith development I term 'young adult'.
>
> The one who is young adult in faith stands on the other side of both authoritarian dualism and unqualified relativism. The person is engaged in the quest for commitment and stands on the threshold of innerdependence. Critically disengaged from earlier assumptions and not yet formed in the pragmatism of later adulthood, the young adult has a unique capacity to respond to the 'ideal'. This is the developmental moment for a fresh envisioning of the world as it may become. It is here

that the heart may be captured by a vision of a new age. In this era the soul seeks the kingdom of God.

This 'young adult' faith upon entering theology is immediately challenged by the situation described above. Karl Rahner sees the situation in the following way:[34]

> The average person who comes to theology today, and this includes not only those who are preparing for the priesthood, does not feel secure in a faith which is taken for granted and is supported by a homogeneous religious milieu common to everyone. Even the young theology student possesses a faith which is under challenge and is by no means to be taken for granted, a faith which today must ever be won anew and is still in the process of being formed, and he (*sic*) need not be ashamed of this. He can readily acknowledge this situation in which he finds himself because he is living in an intellectual and spiritual situation today, or is even coming from such a situation himself, which does not allow Christianity to appear as something indisputable and to be taken for granted.

Christianity is no longer sustained by plausibility structures. This being the case for theology students, 'then the beginning of their theological studies must help them, so far as this is possible, to overcome this crisis in the situation of their faith honestly'.[35]

The 'overcoming' of this situation is no easy task. As mentioned earlier, theology is essentially ecclesial. As theologians, or as students in theology, there is an ongoing dependency on a network of belonging. The ecclesial community must be trusted; the theologians must have confidence that their tradition as lived will hold. As David Tracy writes: 'the theologian by risking faith in a particular religious tradition has the right and responsibility to be 'formed' by that tradition and community'.[36] That risk is not without conditions:[37]

> A systematic theologian's commitment and fidelity to the particular classical religious tradition should be trusted on two conditions: first, once it reaches a proper depth of personal experience in and understanding of (*fides quaerens intellectum*) that very tradition which 'carries one along'; second, once appropriate forms of expression (genre, codification, systematic exigency) have been developed to represent that tradition's basic experience and self-understanding of an appropriately public manner.

The students who are beginning theology need something else to make their risk reasonable. They need the conviction and reliability of their professors and the confirmatory value of their ecclesial environment. Sharon Parks writes about students:[38]

> When young adults come to us they seek first, trustworthy guides, and second, a community with which to make their way. Faith development

study confirms the appropriateness of these two expectations. All persons need a social context, a 'network of belonging' or a 'holding environment' in which to wrestle with and be confirmed by Being, God, the Transcendent. Having begun to reflect critically on assumed authorities, the young adult still requires and is vulnerable to the authority of those perceived as competent in matters of faith. The emerging, but still fragile, self of the young adult seeks leadership which makes sense in a relativised and suffering world. The young adult is therefore beckoned and confirmed by charismatic persons and groups who can both intellectually inform and affectively ground the task of recomposing faith.

The students' faith is essentially related to a tradition of faith. That tradition is now expressed and concretised in their school which now functions as faith community. Theological knowing arises from reflection on one's own experiences in relationship with the experiences of the community. The truth-claims of this tradition are not only 'correspondence, correlation truth' but also 'consensus' truth.

Both for the professional theologian and for the student the reality of 'belonging' is integral to the process of doing theology. The faith-community affects every aspect of the doing of theology. A faith-community must necessarily be in a developmental situation. As it matures it develops its own sense of purpose and its own vision and identity. Joseph Cahill writes:[39]

> A community is normally constituted by temperament, shared presuppositions, common modes of interpretation and understanding, and by a common meaning that unites all the members of the group. Maintenance of community depends on the protraction of common meaning, on genuine communication; it is theoretically developed, understood and integrated by some form of metacommunication.

A faith-community is essentially dynamic in structure; it is not a place but a project.[40] The maturing of the faith-community is in direct proportion to its efforts to interpret the past, the text, in the light of its own needs and insights; it is in direct proportion to its willingness to be transformed by that which it transmits. Understanding is a happening; it is not simply an accomplishment. As an event, understanding involves the correlation of theory and practice. It involves response to the 'history'. Peter Hodgson writes: 'Response and practice belong to the essence of the hermeneutical enterprise. They do not merely follow from understanding but enable it: truth is won only by engagement.'[41]

There can be no separation of action and meaning, no escape of faith to the realm of pure subjectivity and inwardness. There can be no dichotomy between subject and object, between being and consciousness. Discovery is the paradigm case of knowledge. Personal knowledge requires not an abstract, empty apprehension of the self, but an apprehension of the self in its relations with the world outside of itself. Self-consciousness is not a primary but a secondary movement. The self must first immerse itself in the world and only then, through reflection, will it be found again in its fullness. The self realises itself in its activity, in a sense losing itself in the world. It is only through knowledge of the world that anything significant is learned about the self. Human identity is not simply achieved through a process of internal discovery, but by coming to terms with an exterior context which defines the human subject and which must be internalised and overcome. Identity is achieved through a process of reconciliation and transformation of external reality.[42]

A faith-community, both in its theoretical and practical (praxis) dimensions, provides a social and dialogical context for personal religious integration. The question of personal integration and religious identity is put in a social context and achieved in relationship to others. In this encounter, some of one's horizons are negated and others affirmed. Some elements in the object's horizon recede and others come forward. Both object and subject have been called into question in terms of the answer they have given to the questionableness of existence. All knowledge that is a real understanding is linked to the self-formative process of the knowing subject. According to Palmer, 'every true hermeneutical experience is a new creation, a new disclosure of being, it stands in a firm relationship to the present and historically could not have happened before'.[43]

Here human activity is located not primarily in the realm of contemplation, in the realm of the *cogitare*, but in the realm of action, in the realm of praxis. We must penetrate the object in communion with it; we must respond to the object as though we must change, *respondeo etsi mutabor*. Indeed we are ready to listen even if we *must* change. Long writes: 'The interpreter as he moves from symbolism to rationality will find that he must make another movement back into the shadows of his ego and history for he discovers that his being is mirrored in the reality of life and history and simultaneously created by him in the moment of comprehension.'[44]

Understanding of the past and actual self-understanding are inseparable. Understanding of the past and actual self-understanding either of an individual theologian or of the magisterium are inseparable. In some way, every true hermeneutical process is a new creation. There can be no intention of imposing on the text one's own subjectivity so as to avoid one's own transformation.

Conversion arises as a real necessity of an hermeneutical approach. Bernard Lonergan remarks on the criteriological necessity of conversion:[45]

Nor may one expect the discovery of some 'objective' criterion or test or control. For that meaning of the 'objective' is mere delusion. Genuine objectivity is the fruit of authentic subjectivity. It is to be attained only by attaining authentic subjectivity. To seek and employ some alternative prop or crutch invariably leads to some measure of reductionism.

The faith-community is essential for the personal and subjective religious identity of the theologian and the student. Yet 'belonging' and 'subjectivity' are not easily harmonised. Social structures, such as a faith-community, be it a school or a diocese or a parish, 'tend to be conservative and to overwhelm the individual'.[46]

Because the past must be critically appropriated, theology as hermeneutical process must be dialectical. This dialectic involves an affirming, a refusing, and a moving beyond. Thomas Groome writes:[47]

> In a dialectical hermeneutic of any 'text' there is an activity of discerning its truth and what is to be affirmed in it, an activity of discerning the limitations in our understanding of it that are to be refused, and an attempt to move beyond it, carrying forward the truth that was there while adding to it in the new understanding.

An hermeneutical approach to theology demands one's trust in the ecclesial community but it does not, in the words of David Tracy, allow 'the familiar distortions of that faith into ecclesiolatry and traditionalism'.[48] In fact, the theologian's trust of the church as tradition should free him/her to accept the ever-present need for self-reform. As Tracy affirms:[49]

> We need the reformatory impulse present in the gospel and the entire tradition to find new ways not merely to develop, but also, when necessary, to challenge, confront, transform the tradition itself for the sake of the tradition's own fidelity to the apostolic witness to Jesus Christ and the fuller forms of expression in the Scriptures to that witness.

In order for a faith-community to allow individuality and subjectivity as well as nurturing and identity, it must be of such a nature as to permit authentic pluralism. Vatican II in its *Dignitatis Humanae* affirms:[50]

> Hence every man (*sic*) has the duty, and therefore the right, to seek the truth in matters religious, in order that he may with prudence form for himself right and true judgements of conscience, with the use of all suitable means.
>
>   Truth, however, is to be sought after in a manner proper to the dignity of the human person and his social nature. The enquiry is to be free, carried on with the aid of teaching or instruction, communication and dialogue. In the course of these, men explain to one another the truth they have discovered, or think they have discovered, in order thus to assist one another in the quest for truth. Moreover, as the truth is discovered, it is by a personal assent that men are to adhere to it.

That search for truth can only be possible in a faith-community that allows and fosters authentic dialogue. True dialogue does not invade;

it does not manipulate. For there can be no such thing as dialogical manipulation. The primary dimension of true dialogue is intersubjectivity, or intercommunication, which cannot be reduced to a simple relation between a knowing subject and a knowable object. Just as there is no such thing as an isolated human being there is also no such thing as isolated thinking.

According to Paulo Freire, 'The thinking subject cannot think alone. In the act of thinking about the object, he/she cannot think without the cooperation of another subject. There is no longer an "I think", but a "we think". It is the "we think" which establishes the "I think", and not the contrary.'[51] Dialogue is simply the co-participation of persons in the very act of thinking and speaking. In this dialogue the object is not simply the goal of the act of thinking, but the mediator of communication. Dialogue achieves a communion of horizons which leads to self-disclosure and self-understanding.

To espouse dialogue as a ruling principle entails a risk which the faith-community of all communities must be the first to be willing to run. A faith which is not personal cannot claim to be an authentic saving faith.[52]

Integration and formation of self-identity must occur in a pluralistic milieu. James and Evelyn Whitehead describe this pluralism in the following manner:[53]

> But what does a pluralistic faith community mean as community? We think it means that the community as a collectivity believes all of the Christian faith – the different beliefs that make up the richness of the Christian fabric are represented (co-existing in tension, of course) in this community. No one individual can or should be asked to sum up in himself the variety of beliefs, understandings and expressions of faith that comprise the Christian church. This is, in fact, what community means: it is the community which believes in the fullness of the revelation and expresses the fullness of the tradition. Let us take the example of the Creed. As the community confesses publicly these beliefs, it testifies that as a community it believes them. No one individual is expected to believe fully and express fully all the beliefs stated in the creed.

A 'pluralistic faith community' recognises that Christians do not live their faith-life in such a way as to have the same relation to all the elements of their faith world. Rather there is something paramount in the Christian faith-world itself, something which grounds it, unifies it, influences it and which is the primary referent of Christian faith. This is the Christ-event as revelation of God. It remains as a central task of an hermeneutical theology to point to what is essential in Christian faith. That is no easy task since the Christ-event is historical and comes to us mediated by tradition. One cannot avoid noticing how pluralistic, how diverse and conflictual have been the past and contemporary interpretations of Christianity. The Christian faith today is largely the product of and response to a series of interpretations that go back to the time of Jesus Christ.[54]

Any statement of the supposed essence of Christianity is itself an interpretation of that essence, given in terms of a particular structure of understanding.

Openness

An hermeneutical theology cannot simply be a repetition of the past interpretations. There is an ongoing need for new interpretations. That task is the risk of a creative interpretation of the past and the present in a critical yet participatory manner of both the past event and the contemporary situation. An hermeneutical theology involves two processes that are dialectically related. Paul Ricoeur characterises the first as a 'hermeneutics of retrieval'. Thomas Ogletree sees the second movement as a 'hermeneutics of hospitality'.[55] Retrieval involves a deeper engagement with the past. Yet as Ogletree writes:[56]

> To balance and limit the recollection of our own heritage, we also have need of a hermeneutic of hospitality, a readiness to welcome strange and unfamiliar meanings into our own awareness, perhaps to be shaken by them, but in no case to be left unchanged.

In an hermeneutical theology there is no one response, 'no single journey of recognition and expression of the Christ-event ... Rather each theologian finds some elective affinity between some interpretation of the questions and responses of the Christian tradition and hence of the Christ-event.'[57]

What is implied here is that Christians are invited to commitment to a relative 'essence'. This is no easy stance since it demands that an individual move beyond the explicit ideological systems and clear boundaries of identity. James Fowler describes this stance as conjunctive faith. According to Fowler:[58]

> This position implies no lack of commitment to one's own tradition. Nor does it mean a wishy-washy neutrality or mere fascination with the exotic features of alien cultures. Rather conjunctive faith's radical openness to the truth of the other systems stems precisely from its confidence in the reality mediated by its own tradition and in the awareness that that reality overspills its mediation.

The awareness of the relativity of all our own constructs and interpretations frees us from the illusion of control and enables us to appreciate more fully the truth and relativity of past interpretations. John Cobb writes: 'the more deeply we trust Christ, the more openly receptive we will be to wisdom from any source, and the more responsibly critical we will be both of our own received habits of mind and of the limitations and distortions of others'.[59]

If Christian theology is essentially ecclesial and demands a belonging on the part of the theologian, such a theology demands a decision for a specific tradition, yet with an openness willing to examine motivation and distortions inherent to the decision. The theologian enters on a journey which is not entirely his/her own, but which he has to make his/her own. The goal of an hermeneutical theology is that of appropriation. A communion of meaning between the theologian and the tradition, as lived and expressed within a specific faith-community, must emerge. This communion is similar to what Gadamer calls a 'fusion of horizons'. But such a fusion should not involve a loss of identity although it does imply a conversion, a change. In our pluralistic situation such a 'fusion of horizon' and conversion implies on the part of the theologian a willingness to join the tradition in its search for truth. This implies that the tradition is open to such a search and is able to open others to the same search. Truth is still in the making and theology as interpretation is itself also constitutive of such creativity. Here the goal is not certitude but understanding. John Dunne writes: 'To find God, I came to believe we must give over the quest of certitude for a quest of understanding.'[60] The divine mystery as revealed in and narrated by Jesus Christ is never fully specifiable in propositions. Maurice Blondel writes, tradition 'is the guardian of the initial gift insofar as this has not been entirely formulated nor even expressly understood, although it is always fully possessed and employed'.[61]

Again:[62]

> The progress of religious truth resembles flowing water which is searching for a bed. It twists and turns, encounters a thousand obstacles, flows back, rises again, breaks through and flows on again unceasingly, even making use of the reserves of energy built up in meeting all those obstacles.

Can Christian identity emerge in a context where religious truth is still in the making? Can a fragmented tradition anchor a religious identity? Religious identity as previously mentioned is formed by a religious community. Yet personal religious identity cannot simply be the case of a material identity with a specific religious community. A central thesis now emerging from various areas of study is that we are essentially story-telling human beings. I can only answer the question 'Who am I?' if I can answer the previous question, 'Of what story or stories do I find myself a part?' A story gives an individual the necessary identity. MacIntyre writes:[63]

> What the narrative concept of selfhood requires is thus twofold. On the one hand, I am what I may justifiably be taken by others to be in the course of living out a story that runs from my birth to my death; I am the subject of a history that is my own and no one else's, that has its own peculiar meaning.
> The other aspect of narrative selfhood is correlative: I am not only accountable, I am one who can always ask others for an account, who

can put others to the question. I am part of their story, as they are part of mine.

The unity and identity of a human life is the unity of a narrative quest. My identity is both historical and social. The story of my life is embedded in the story of various communities. Christians do not primarily form an argumentative and reasoning community, but a story-telling community. David Tracy writes:[64]

> There is something intrinsic in experience which demands narrative. In part, I suspect, narrative alone provides us with some fuller way to order and unify our actual lived experience with its tensions and surprises, its reversals and triumphs, its experience through memory of a past and, through anticipation and hope, of a future in the tensed unity of the ever-vanishing now of the present and its possible illusory sense of sequence. The stories persons tell disclose their character. The story each person *is* discloses a human possibility that otherwise might go unremarked. The classic stories disclose the meaning of a life lived in the grip of a classic possibility: real tension and struggle, the lived actuality of hope, tragedy, resignation, fulfilment, justice, love. The particular focus of the fundamental questions in the situation often receives far more disclosure from some classic story than from other modes of reflection: the story of how a single human being lived and faced death, as distinct from philosophical reflection upon mortality; distinct from ethical reflections upon finitude; a classic story disclosing the reality of a utopian world, as distinct from sociological reflections upon ideologies and utopias.

The power of a narrative lies exactly in its potential to produce a community of interpretation sufficient for the growth of further narrative. The narrative dimensions of the Christian conviction also underline that there is not one story but many. One important aspect of this for the church as a community of discourse is to provide a structure sufficient to accept the variety of stories. Stanley Hauerwas writes:[65]

> The crucial and necessary interaction of story and community for the formation of truthful lives is an indication that there exists no 'story of stories' from which the many stories of our existence can be analysed and evaluated. This is not to deny that a taxonomy and classification of various kinds, forms and elements of stories and narratives might prove illuminating for certain purposes. But the constructive theological task remains primary, for our concern must be to understand better both how to live appropriate to the God that we find in the narratives of Israel and Jesus and how these stories help provide the means to recognise the critically appropriate other stories that claim our lives. This task of understanding is necessary, for it is rightfully observed that we always find ourselves enmeshed in many histories, of our families, of Texas, America, Western civilization and so on, each of which is constituted by many interrelated and confusing story lines. The moral task consists in

acquiring the skills and the character sufficient to negotiate these many kinds and levels of narrative in a truthful manner.

Theology, being essentially ecclesial and therefore hermeneutical and transformative, must necessarily be concerned with narrative, for the faith commitment that lies at the heart of such a theology depends essentially on a narrative and narrators for its existence. 'How could they invoke one in whom they had no faith? And how could they have faith in one they had never heard of? And how hear without someone to spread the news?' (Romans 10:13–15). The narrative that lies at the heart of Christian theology not only gives meaning but can also bring salvation. Metz affirms this in the following way:[66]

> Christianity as a community of those who believe in Jesus Christ has, from the very beginning, not been primarily a community interpreting and arguing, but a community remembering and narrating with a practical intention, a narrative and evocative memory of the passion, death and resurrection of Jesus. The logos of the cross and resurrection has a narrative structure. Faith in the redemption of history and in the new man can, because of the history of human suffering, be translated into dangerously liberating stories, the hearer who is affected by them becoming not simply a hearer, but a doer of the word.

An ecclesial theology implies a belonging where 'praxis' is as essential as meaning and truth.

Notes

1. Karl Rahner, *Foundations of Christian Faith: an introduction to the idea of Christianity*, New York, Seabury Press, 1978, p. 323.
2. *Ibid.*, p. 344.
3. David Tracy, *The Analogical Imagination*, New York, Crossroads, 1981, p. 323.
4. *Ibid.*
5. *Ibid.*
6. *Dei Verbum*, II, 8, in W Abbott (ed.), *The Documents of Vatican II*, New York, Herder and Herder, pp. 115–116.
7. *Ibid.*
8. Karl Rahner, 'Scripture and theology', in *Theological Investigations*, volume 6, New York, Seabury Press, 1974, p. 91.
9. *Dei Verbum*, VI, 21, p. 125.
10. *Dei Verbum*, II, 7, p. 115.
11. *Dei Verbum*, II, 10, pp. 117–118.
12. Thomas H Groome, *Christian Religious Education*, San Francisco, Harper and Row, 1980, p. 112.
13. Joseph Cahill, *Mended Speech: the crisis of religious studies and theology*, New York, Crossroads, 1982, p. 154.
14. Dorothy L. Sayers, *The Just Vengeance*, London, Gollancz, 1946, p. 24.
15. Paul Ricoeur, 'Philosophy and religious language', *The Journal of Religion*, 54, 1974, pp. 71–85.
16. A Dulles, 'The meaning of faith', in John C Haughey (ed.), *The Faith That Does Justice*, New York, Paulist, 1977, pp. 10–46.
17. Ghislain Lafont, 'Monastic life and theological studies', *Monastic Studies*, 12, 1976, pp. 1–30.
18. A Dulles, *op. cit.*, writes, 'The task of theology is to conduct a methodic or systematic reflection on faith. As an ecclesial discipline, theology is done within the believing community. It endeavours to give a coherent systematisation of Christian faith, guided by the symbols and by past formulations, especially those which have normative value in the

church. According to the sacramental understanding, these formulations refer back to the experience of conversion, which continually goes on within the church. They express certain aspects of a commitment that necessarily remains, in great part, tacit or implicit.'

19. See E Schillebeeckx, *The Understanding of Faith*, New York, Seabury Press, 1972.

20. Paul Ricoeur, 'From existentialism to philosophy of language', *Philosophy Today,* 17, 1973, pp. 88–96.

21. Paul Ricoeur, 'The hermeneutical function of distanciation', *Philosophy Today,* 17, 1973, pp. 129–141; here p. 133.

22. Paul Ricoeur, 'Philosophical hermeneutics and theological hermeneutics', *Studies in Religion/Sciences Religieuses,* 5, 1975–1976, pp. 14–33; here p. 25.

23. Paul Ricoeur, 'Philosophy and religious language', *Journal of Religion,* 54, 1974, pp. 79–80.

24. David Tracy, 'The public character of systematic theology', *Theology Digest,* 26, 1978, pp. 401–411.

25. H Gadamer, *Truth and Method*, New York, Seabury Press, 1975, pp. 235–274.

26. J Cahill, *Mended Speech: the crisis of religious studies and theology*, New York, Crossroads, 1982, p. 63.

27. Claude Geffré, *A New Age in Theology*, New York, Paulist Press, 1972, p. 44.

28. David Tracy, 'The public character of systematic theology', *Theology Digest,* 26, 1978, pp. 401–411.

29. *Ibid.,* p. 407.

30. *Ibid.*

31. B Lonergan, 'Theology in a new context', in *Second Collection,* Philadelphia, Westminster Press, 1979, pp. 58–59; K Rahner, 'Reflections on methodology', *Theological Investigations,* volume 2, New York, Seabury Press, 1974, pp. 72–73.

32. One may suppose that the possibility of heresy has always existed in human communities, as one may suppose that there have always been rebels and innovators. And, surely, those who represented the authority of a tradition must always have been troubled by the possibility. Yet the social context of this phenomenon has changed radically with the coming of modernity: 'In premodern situations there is a world of religious certainty, occasionally ruptured by heretical deviations. By contrast, the modern situation is a world of religious uncertainty, occasionally staved off by more or less precarious constructions of religious affirmation.' Indeed, one could put this change even more sharply: 'For pre-modern man, heresy is a possibility – usually a rather remote one; for modern man, heresy typically becomes a necessity.' Or again, 'modernity creates a new situation in which picking and choosing becomes an imperative'. P Berger, *The Heretical Imperative*, Garden City, Doubleday, 1979, p. 30.

33. Sharon Parks, 'Contemporary challenges to issues of vocational preparation', *Theological Education*, 19, 1982, p. 99–107.

34. Karl Rahner, *Foundations of Christian Faith: an introduction to the idea of Christianity*, New York, Seabury Press, 1978, p. 5.

35. *Ibid.*

36. David Tracy, 'The necessity and insufficiency of fundamental theology', in R Latourelle and G O'Collins (eds), *Problems and Perspectives of Fundamental Theology*, New York, Paulist Press, 1982, pp. 23–36; here p. 35.

37. *Ibid.*

38. Sharon Parks, 'Contemporary challenges to issues of vocational preparation', *Theological Education,* 19, 1982, pp. 99–107.

39. J Cahill, *Mended Speech: the crisis of religious studies and theology*, New York, Crossroads, 1982, pp. 157–58.

40. Bernard Lonergan writes about community, 'A community is not just a number of men (*sic*) within a geographical frontier. It is an achievement of common meaning, and there are kinds and degrees of achievement. Common meaning is potential when there is a common field of experience, and to withdraw from that common field is to get out of touch. Common meaning is formal when there is common understanding, and one withdraws from that common understanding by misunderstanding, by incomprehension, by mutual incomprehension. Common meaning is actual inasmuch as there are common judgments, areas in which all affirm and deny in the same manner; and one withdraws from that common judgment when one disagrees, when one considers true what others hold false and false what they think true. Common meaning is realised by decisions and choices, especially by permanent dedication, in the love that makes families, in the loyalty that makes states, in the faith that makes religions. Community coheres or divides, begins or ends, just where the common field of experience, common understanding, common judgement, common

commitments begin and end. So communities are of many kinds: linguistic, religious, cultural, social, political, domestic. They vary in extent, in age, in cohesiveness, in their oppositions to one another.' See Bernard Lonergan, *Method in Theology*, London, Herder and Herder, 1972, p.79.

41. P C Hodgson, *Jesus – Word and Presence: an essay in Christology*, Philadelphia, Fortress Press, 1971, p. 39.

42. Karl Rahner writes, 'As existing in an interpersonal world, a person arrives concretely at his own self-interpretation, however much it comes from within and enters within, only within the self-interpretation of his interpersonal world, and by participating in and receiving from the tradition of the historical self–interpretation of those people who form his (*sic*) interpersonal world from out of the past and through the present into the future. A person always forms his own secular self-understanding only within a community of persons in the experience of a history which he never makes alone, in dialogue and in experience which reproduces the productive self-interpretation of other people.' See Karl Rahner, *Foundations of Christian Faith: an introduction to the idea of Christianity*, New York, Seabury Press, 1978, p. 160.

43. R E Palmer, *Hermeneutics*, Evanston, Northwestern University Press, 1969, p. 244.

44. C H Long, 'Archaism and hermeneutics', in J M Kitagawa (ed.), *The History of Religions*, Chicago, University of Chicago Press, 1967, pp. 67–87.

45. B Lonergan, *Method in Theology*, London, Herder and Herder, 1972, p. 29.

36. See note 14.

47. Thomas H Groome, *Christian Religious Education*, San Francisco, Harper and Row, 1981, p. 196.

48. David Tracy, *The Analogical Imagination*, New York, Crossroads, 1981, p. 323.

49. *Ibid.,* p. 324.

50. *Dignitatis Humanae* I, 3, in W Abbot, *op. cit.*

51. Paulo Freire, *Education for Critical Consciousness*, New York, Seabury, 1973, p. 137.

52. Karl Rahner writes, 'It is just as true to say that the formal authority of the teaching office depends upon the power of the truth of faith as proclaimed to command the allegiance of our faith as to say that the latter depends upon the former. This relationship in which either factor influences the other is distorted, however, if we rely exclusively upon the formal authority of the teaching office. It can be stated absolutely as a matter of principle that in its individual decisions and the preliminary proposals leading up to these the teaching office of the church acts best and most correctly when it allows the truth which is sustained by grace and inherent in the reality itself which it is treating of and seeking to teach to make its own impact, and allows its own formal authority most completely to be effected by giving pride of place to this truth. As we have said this is the right approach to adopt simply because the truth that the teaching office has this formal authority is in any instance supported and kept alive by faith in the fundamental truths of Christianity. Hence in the concrete exercise of its functions the teaching office must again and again re-establish its connections with these truths.' See 'The Teaching Office of the Church in the Present-day Crisis', p. 26.

53. E Whitehead, 'The parish and sacraments of adulthood: access to an educational future', *Listening*, 12, 1977, pp. 88–89. See also Karl Rahner and Karl-Heinz Weger, *Our Christian Faith: answers for the future*, New York, Crossroads, 1981, pp 124–140.

54. David Tracy writes: 'As everyone knows, the later Christian tradition from the post-New Testament period to the present is yet more radically pluralistic in its interpretations of Christianity and often mutually contradictory. The history of the conflict of Christian interpretations on any single Christian symbol – God, Christ, grace, creation, redemption, eschatology, sacrament, word, church, faith, hope, love, sin – will document this clearly enough for any interpreter still infected by the impoverishing virus of an ahistorical, word-less 'orthodoxy'. The history of the conflict of interpretations within any single church tradition clarifies the same reality. Pluralism is not an invention of our present age. Pluralism is a reality in all the traditions. The conflict of interpretations is merely a new expression for the actuality and destiny of Christian self-interpretation. An appeal for a focus upon the classics is merely one strategy for clarifying some major paths through this conflict.' See David Tracy, *The Analogical Imagination*, New York, Crossroads, 1981, p. 372.

55. Thomas Ogletree, 'The activity of interpreting in moral judgment', *Journal of Religious Ethics*, 8, 1980, pp. 1–25.

56. *Ibid.,* p. 19.

57. David Tracy, *The Analogical Imagination*, New York, Crossroads, 1981, p. 372.

58. James Fowler, *Stages of Faith*, San Francisco, Harper and Row, 1981, p. 187.

59. John Cobb, 'The religions', in P C Hodgson and R King (eds), *Christian Theology*, Philadelphia, Fortress Press, 1982, pp. 299–322.

60. John Dunne, *The Reasons of the Heart*, New York, Macmillan, 1978, p. 149.

61. M Blondel, *History and Dogmas*, New York, Holt, 1964, p. 268.

62. M Blondel, *Attente du Concile*, Paris, Plon, 1969, p. 43.

63. A MacIntyre, *After Virtue*, Notre Dame, Indiana, Notre Dame University Press, 1981, p. 202.

64. David Tracy, *The Analogical Imagination*, New York, Crossroads, 1981, p. 275.

65. S Hauerwas, 'The church in a divided world: the interpretative power of the Christian story', *Journal of Religious Ethics*, 8, 1980, pp. 55–82.

66. J B Metz, *Faith in History and Society*, New York, Seabury Press, 1980, p. 212.

5. Theological approaches: liberation theology

'Liberation theology', although closely associated with Latin America, is a generic term for a family of theologies which have developed all over the world during the last thirty years. Theologies of liberation understand theology as a form of critical reflection upon the practice of liberation – making the liberation of a specific group from social, economic, racial, or sexual marginalisation theologically fundamental. Liberation theology, which, particularly in the Latin American context, is itself indebted to educational thinking, has had a profound effect on the theory and practice of Christian education in recent years.[1] The two articles in this section investigate various aspects of this influence.

Paulo Freire has been widely influential for his work on the practice and theory of education, developed first in literacy education in Latin America.[2] In his article here he explores issues concerning 'Education, liberation and the church' with reference to his concept of 'conscientisation' (education for critical consciousness) and various misinterpretations to which it has been subject. The role of liberation theology and the responses of the churches (which cannot be politically neutral) are explored. The traditionalist approach ('unquestionably allied to the ruling classes') and its modernising alternative (which 'reforms so as to preserve the status quo') are rejected in favour of a prophetic perspective and an education that is 'an instrument of transforming action, as a political praxis at the service of permanent human liberation'. Freire's article is from *Study Encounter*, 9, 1973, pp. 1–16 (item SE/38). It was also published in *Religious Education*, 79, 1984, pp. 524–545.

Frank Marangos' article presents an overview of the principal emphases in liberation education and liberation theology, particularly as they are applied outside the third world. Christian liberation education (as 'critical reflection on Christian praxis in the light of the Word') is explored in terms of the educational hermeneutic and the concept of 'lifestyle', and liberation theology in terms of Christian discipleship and witness, Christian hope and Christian anthropology. 'Liberation theology and Christian education theory' was first published in the *Greek Orthodox Theological Review*, 29, 1984, pp. 381–392.

Dr Paulo Freire was founding director of the Centre for Studies in Education in São Paulo, Brazil and teaches at the Pontifical University there. The Revd Dr Frank Marangos is priest at St Mark's Church, Boca Raton, Florida, USA.

Notes

1. See, for example, Allen J Moore, 'Liberation and the future of Christian education', in J L Seymour and D E Miller (eds), *Contemporary Approaches to Christian education*, Nashville, Tennessee, Abingdon, 1982, chapter 5; William Bean Kennedy, 'Ideology and education: a fresh approach to religious education', *Religious Education*, 80, 1985, pp. 331–344; Daniel S Schipani, *Religious Education Encounters Liberation Theology*, Birmingham, Alabama, Religious Education Press, 1988; Allen J Moore (ed.), *Religious Education as Social Transformation*, Birmingham, Alabama, Religious Education Press, 1989.

2. Compare Paulo Freire, *Pedagogy of the Oppressed*, translated by Myra Bergman Ramos, New York, Seabury, 1972, and John L Elias, *Paulo Freire: pedagogue of liberation*, Malabar, Florida, Krieger, 1994.

5.1 Education, liberation and the church

Paulo Freire

A change of consciousness

We begin with an affirmation; though almost a truism, it clearly sets forth our position on the present subject. We cannot discuss churches, education or the role of the churches in education other than historically. Churches are not abstract entities, they are institutions involved in history. Therefore to understand their educational role we must take into consideration the concrete situation in which they exist.

The moment these statements are taken seriously, we can no longer speak of the neutrality of the churches or the neutrality of education. Such assertions of neutrality must be judged as coming either from those who have a totally naïve view of the church and history or from those who shrewdly mask a realistic understanding behind a claim of neutrality. Objectively, nevertheless, both groups fit into the same ideological perspective. When they insist on the neutrality of the church in relation to history, or to political action, they take political stands which inevitably favour the power élites against the masses. 'Washing one's hands' of the conflict between the powerful and the powerless means to side with the powerful, not to be neutral.

However, alongside the neutral attitude there are more subtle and more attractive means of serving the interests of the powerful while appearing to favour the oppressed. Here again we find the 'naïve' and the 'shrewd' walking hand in hand. I refer to what we might call 'anaesthetic' or 'aspirin' practices, expressions of a subjectivist idealism that can only lead to the preservation of the status quo. In the last analysis the basic presupposition of such action is the illusion that the hearts of men and women can be transformed while the social structures which make those hearts 'sick' are left intact and unchanged.

The illusion which thinks it possible, by means of sermons, humanitarian works and the encouragement of other-worldly values, to change people's consciousness and thereby transform the world, exists only in those we term 'naïve' (or 'moralist' as Niebuhr would have said[1]). The 'shrewd' are well aware that such action can slow down the basic process of radical change in social structures. This radical change is a precondition for the awakening of consciousness, and the process is neither automatic nor mechanical.

Although, objectively, both groups are equally ineffectual in producing liberation or the real humanisation of human beings, there is still a basic difference between them which should be underlined.

Both are caught up in the ideology of the ruling social class, but the shrewd consciously accept this ideology as their own. The naïve, in the first instance unconscious of their true position, can through their action come to take the ideology of domination for their own and, in the process, move from 'naïveness' to 'shrewdness'. They can also come to renounce their idealistic illusions altogether, forsaking their uncritical adherence to the ruling class. In committing themselves to the oppressed, they begin a new period of apprenticeship. This is not, however, to say that their commitment to the oppressed is thereby finally sealed. It will be severely tested during the course of this new apprenticeship when confronted, in a more serious and profound way than ever before, with the hazardous nature of existence. To win out in such a test is not easy.

This new apprenticeship will violently break down the elitist concept of existence which they had absorbed while being ideologised. The *sine qua non* which the apprenticeship demands is that, first of all, they really experience their own Easter, that they die as elitists so as to be resurrected on the side of the oppressed, that they be born again with the beings who were not allowed to be. Such a process implies a renunciation of myths which are dear to them: the myth of their 'superiority', of their purity of soul, of their virtues, their wisdom, the myth that they 'save the poor', the myth of the neutrality of the church, of theology, education, science, technology, the myth of their own impartiality – from which grow the other myths: of the inferiority of other people, of their spiritual and physical impurity, and the myth of the absolute ignorance of the oppressed.

This Easter, which results in the changing of consciousness, must be existentially experienced. The real Easter is not commemorative rhetoric. It is praxis; it is historical involvement. The old Easter of rhetoric is dead, with no hope of resurrection. It is only in the authenticity of historical praxis that Easter becomes the death which makes life possible. But the bourgeois world-view, basically necrophilic (death-loving) and therefore static, is unable to accept this supremely biophilic (life-loving) experience of Easter. The bourgeois mentality, which is far more than just a convenient abstraction, kills the profound historical dynamism of Easter and turns it into no more than a date on the calendar.

The lust to possess,[2] a sign of the necrophilic world-view, rejects the deeper meaning of resurrection. Why should I be interested in rebirth if I hold in my hands, as objects to be possessed, the torn body and soul of the oppressed? I can only experience rebirth at the side of the oppressed by being born again, with them, in the process of liberation. I cannot turn such a rebirth into a means of *owning* the world, since it is essentially a means of *transforming* the world.

If those who were once naïve continue their new apprenticeship, they will come to understand that consciousness is not changed by lessons, lectures and eloquent sermons but by the action of human beings on the world. Consciousness does not arbitrarily create reality, as they thought in their old naïve days of subjectivist idealism.

Conscientisation

They will also discover to what extent their idealism had confused any number of concepts, for example conscientisation, which is so badly understood, when they tried to offer magic remedies for healing the hearts of humankind without changing the social structures or, equally idealistic, when they claimed that conscientisation was a similarly magic means of reconciling the irreconcilable.

Conscientisation appeared to them then as a sort of third way which would allow them to escape miraculously from the problems of class conflict, creating through mutual understanding a world of peace and harmony between oppressor and oppressed. When both were conscientised there would be neither oppressor nor oppressed, for all would love each other as brothers and sisters, and differences would be resolved through round-table discussions, or over a good whisky ...

Basically, this idealistic vision, which works only for the oppressors, is exactly the position that Niebuhr vehemently condemned as 'moralistic', whether it be found in the religious or the secular domain.[3]

Such mythologising of conscientisation, be it in Latin America or elsewhere, be it at the hands of the shrewd or the naïve, constitutes an obstacle rather than an aid to the liberation process. It becomes, on the one hand, an obstacle because, in emptying conscientisation of its dialectical content and thus making it into a panacea, it puts it, as we have seen, at the service of the oppressors. On the other hand, it creates an obstacle because such idealistic disfiguration leads many Latin American groups, especially among youth, to fall into the opposite error of mechanical objectivism. In reacting against the alienating subjectivism which causes this distortion, they end up by denying the role of consciousness in the transformation of reality and therefore also denying the dialectical union between consciousness and the world. They no longer see the difference between such things as class consciousness and the consciousness of class needs.[4] Between the two there is a sort of dialectical gap which must be bridged. Neither subjectivism nor mechanical objectivism is able to do this.

These groups are right in affirming, as do we, that one cannot change consciousness outside of praxis. But it must be emphasised that the praxis by which consciousness is changed is not only action but action *and* reflection. Thus there is a unity between practice and theory in which both are constructed, shaped and reshaped in constant movement from practice to theory, then back to a new practice.

Theoretic praxis is what occurs when we step back from accomplished praxis (or from praxis which is being accomplished) so as to see it more clearly. Thus, theoretic praxis is only authentic when it maintains the dialectical movement between itself and that praxis which will be carried out in a particular context. These two forms of praxis are two inseparable moments of the process by which we reach critical understanding. In other words, reflection is only real when it sends us back, as Sartre insists, to the given situation in which we act.

Hence conscientisation, whether or not associated with literacy training, must be a critical attempt to reveal reality, not just alienating small-talk. It must, that is, be related to political involvement. There is no conscientisation if the result is not the conscious action of the oppressed as an exploited social class, struggling for liberation.[5] What is more, no one conscientises anyone else. The educator and the people together conscientise themselves, thanks to the dialectical movement which relates critical reflection on past action to the continuing struggle.

Education for liberation

Another dimension of the mythologising of conscientisation, whether by the shrewd or the naïve, is their attempt to convert the well-known 'education for liberation' into a purely methodological problem, considering methods as something purely neutral. This removes, or pretends to remove, all political content from education, so that the expression 'education for liberation' no longer means anything.

Actually, in so far as this type of education is reduced to methods and techniques by which students and educators look at social reality, when they do look at it, only to describe it, this education becomes as 'domesticating' as any other. Education for liberation does not merely free students from blackboards just to offer them projectors.[6] On the contrary, it is concerned, as a social praxis, with helping to free human beings from the oppression which strangles them in their objective reality. It is therefore political education, just as political as the education which claims to be neutral, although actually serving the power élite. It is thus a form of education which can only be put into practice systematically when society is radically transformed.[7] Only the 'innocent' could possibly think that the power élite would encourage a type of education which denounces them even more clearly than do all the contradictions of their power structures.[8] Such naïveness also reveals a dangerous underestimation of the capacity and audacity of the élite. Truly liberating education can only be put into practice outside the ordinary system, and even then with great cautiousness, by those who overcome their naïveness and commit themselves to authentic liberation.

A growing number of Christians in Latin America are discovering these things and finding themselves forced to take sides: either to change their naïveness into shrewdness and consciously align themselves with the ideology of domination or else to join forces with the oppressed and in full identification with them seek true liberation. We have already stated that, if they renounce their uncritical adherence to the dominant classes, their new apprenticeship with the people presents a challenge; in meeting this challenge they encounter risks formerly unknown.

During what we are calling their 'new apprenticeship', many Christians soon realise that previously when they had engaged in purely palliative action, whether social or religious (for example, fervent support of maxims such as 'The family that prays together stays together'), they were praised for their Christian virtues. They now begin to realise, however, that the family that prays together also needs a house, free employment,[9] bread, clothing, health and education for their children, that they need to express themselves and their world by creating and recreating it, that their bodies, souls and dignity must be respected if they are to stay together in more than suffering and misery. When they begin to see all this, they find their faith being called into question by those who wish to have even more political, economic and ecclesiastical power for the re-shaping of the consciousness of others.

As their new apprenticeship begins to show them more clearly the dramatic situation in which the people live and leads them to undertake action which is less 'help-oriented', they come to be seen as 'diabolic'.[10] They are denounced as serving an international demonic force which threatens 'western Christian civilization', a civilization which, in reality, has very little that is Christian about it.

Thus they discover through praxis that their 'innocent' period was not in the least impartial. But at this point many are afraid; they lose the courage to face the existential risk of historical commitment. They return to their idealistic illusions, but now as members of the 'shrewd' camp.

But they need to be able to justify their return. So they claim that the masses, who are 'uneducated and incapable', must be protected from losing their faith in God, which is 'so beautiful, so sweet and so edifying'; they must be protected from the 'subversive evil of the false Christians who praise the Chinese Cultural Revolution and admire the Cuban Revolution'. They sign up for the 'defence of the faith', when what they are really defending is their own class interests, to which that faith is subordinated.

They must then insist on the 'neutrality' of the church, whose fundamental task, they say, is to reconcile the irreconcilable through maximum social stability. Thus they castrate the prophetic dimension of the church, whose witness becomes one of fear: fear of change, fear that an unjust world will be radically transformed, fear of getting lost in an uncertain future. However, a church that refuses historical involvement is nevertheless involved in history. In fact, those who preach that the church is outside history contradict themselves in practice, because they automatically place themselves at the side of those who refuse to allow the oppressed classes to be. Afraid of this uncertainty, and anxious to avoid the risk of a future which must always be constructed and not just received, the church badly loses its way. It can no longer test itself, either through the denunciation of the unjust world or the annunciation of a more just world to be built by the historical-social praxis of the oppressed. In this situation, the church can be no more utopian, prophetic or filled with hope than are the ruling classes to which it is allied.[11] Deprived of its prophetic vision, it takes the road of formalism in bureaucratic rites where hope, detached from the future, becomes only an alienated and alienating abstraction. Instead of stimulating the pilgrim, it invites him or her to stand still. Basically, it is a church which forbids itself the Easter which it preaches. It is a church which is 'freezing to death', unable to respond to the aspirations of a troubled, utopic and biophile youth to whom one can no longer speak a medieval language, and who are not interested in discussing the sex of angels, for they are challenged by the drama of their history. Most of these young people are well aware that the basic problem of Latin America is not the 'laziness' of the people or their 'inferiority' or their lack of education. It is imperialism. And they know that this imperialism is neither abstraction nor slogan but tangible reality, an invading, destroying presence. Until this basic contradiction is overcome, Latin America cannot develop. It can only modernise.[12] For without liberation, there can be no real development of dependent societies.

A theology of liberation

Many Latin American theologians who are today becoming more and more historically involved with the oppressed, rightly speak of a political theology of liberation rather than one of modernising 'development'. These theologians can really begin to speak to the troubling questions of a generation which chooses revolutionary change rather than the reconciliation of irreconcilables. They know very well that only the oppressed, as the social class which has been forbidden to speak, can become the utopians, the prophets and the messengers of hope, provided that their future is not simply a reformed repetition of the present. Their future is the realisation of their liberation,[13] without which they cannot *be*. Only they can denounce the 'order' which crushes them, transforming that 'order' in praxis; only they can announce a new world, one which is constantly being re-created and renewed.

That is why their hope rests not in an invitation to halt the pilgrimage, an invitation offered not only by the traditionalists but also by the alienating modernisers. Their hope lies in the call 'Forward march!', not the senseless wandering of those who give up and run, but the 'Forward march' of those who hold history in their hands, who create it and re-create themselves in it. It is the 'Forward march' which they will eventually have to embark upon if they are to experience 'death' as an oppressed class and be born again to liberation.

We must stress yet again, however, that this journey cannot be made 'within' their consciousness. It must be made in history. No one can make such a journey simply in the 'inside' of his being.

But there are a growing number of people who, whether or not they still claim to be Christians, commit themselves to the liberation of the dominated classes. Their experience teaches them that being Christian doesn't necessarily imply being reactionary, just as being revolutionary doesn't always imply being demonic. Being revolutionary implies struggling against oppression and exploitation, for the liberation and freedom of the oppressed,[14] concretely and not idealistically. In their new apprenticeship they finally realise that it is not sufficient to give lip service to the idea that men and women are human beings if nothing is done objectively to help them experience what it means to be *persons*. They learn that it is not through good works (Niebuhr's phrase here was 'humanitarian') that the oppressed become incarnate as persons. They have, then, managed to overcome the first obstacles which were too much for some of their travelling companions; but that, however, is no guarantee that they will survive the harder trials that lie ahead.

At some point in the process the oppressor's violence will be directed exclusively against the working class, usually sparing committed intellectuals, since in the last analysis they belong to the same group as the ruling class; at other times, however, their violence will be indiscriminate. When this happens, many will retreat, keep quiet, or adjust to the situation; others will react by undertaking new commitments. A basic difference between those who leave and those who stay is that the latter accept, as an integral part of existence, the dramatic tension between past and future, death and life, staying and going, creating and not creating, between saying the word and mutilating silence, between hope and despair, being and non-being. It is an illusion to think that human beings can escape this dramatic tension. We have no right so to submerge ourselves in the 'dramaticity' of our own life that we lose ourselves in daily triviality.[15] In fact, if I lose myself in the details of daily life, I lose, at the same time, a vision of the dramatic meaning of my existence. I become either fatalistic or cynical. In the same way, if I try to escape from the daily demands and details to take up my life's dramatic character, but without at the same time becoming historically involved, I can have no other destiny than to fall into an empty intellectualism, equally alienating. I shall then see existence as something impossible and hopeless. I have no other chance of conquering the alienating trivialities of daily life than by way of historical praxis, which is social and not individual. It is only in so far as I accept to the full my responsibility within the play of this dramatic tension that I make myself a conscious presence in the world.

I cannot permit myself to be a mere spectator. On the contrary, I must demand my place in the process of change. So the dramatic tension between the past and the future, death and life, being and non-being, is no longer a kind of dead-end for me; I can see it for what it really is: a permanent challenge to which I must respond. And my response can be none other than my historical praxis, in other words, revolutionary praxis.

The revolution, however, does not do away with the dramatic tension of our existence. It resolves the antagonistic contradictions which make that tension even more dramatic, but precisely because it participates in that tension it is as permanent as the tension itself.

A reign of undisturbed peace is unthinkable in history. History is *becoming*; it is a human event. But rather than feeling disappointed and frightened by critical discovery of the tension in which my humanity places me, I discover in that tension the joy of being.

At the same time, dramatic tension cannot be reduced to my own existential experience. I cannot of course deny the singularity and uniqueness of my existence, but that does not make my existence, in itself, isolated from other existences, a model of absolute meaning. On the contrary, it is in the inter-subjectivity, mediated by objectivity, that my existence makes sense. 'I exist' does not come before 'we exist', but is fulfilled in it. The individualistic, bourgeois concept of existence cannot grasp the true social and historical basis of human existence. It is of the essence of humanity that men and women create their own existence, in a creative act that is always social and histori-cal even while having its specific, personal dimensions.

Existence is not despair, but risk. If I don't exist dangerously, I cannot be. But if my existence is historical, the existential risk is not a simple abstract category; it is also historical. That means that to exist is first and foremost to risk oneself, though the form and effec-tiveness of the risk will vary from person to person and from place to place. I do not assume risk in Brazil as a Swiss assumes it in Geneva, even if we are both of one political mind. Our socio-historic reality will condition the form our risk will take. To seek to universalise the form and content of existential risk is an idealistic illusion, unaccept-able to anyone who thinks dialectically.

Dialectical thinking constitutes one of the major challenges to those who follow the option we are talking about here. It is not always easy, even for those who identify with the people, to overcome a petit-bourgeois education which is individualistic and intellectual, dichotomising theory and practice, the transcendent and the mundane,[16] intellectual work and manual work. This trademark shows constantly in attitudes and behaviour patterns in which the dominated classes become mere objects of their 'impatient revolutionarism'.

The role of the churches

In trying, now, to analyse more deeply the role of the Latin American churches, especially their educational role, we must return to some of the points made above; first of all, to the fact that they cannot be politically neutral. They cannot avoid making a choice, and therefore we in turn cannot discuss the church's role abstractly or metaphysically. Their choice will condition their whole approach to education: its concepts, objectives, methods, processes and all its auxiliary effects.

This conditioning affects the theological training of the leadership of the militant church, as well as the education dispensed by the church. Even theological education and reflection are touched.

In a class society, the power élite necessarily determine what education will be, and therefore its objectives. The objectives will certainly not be opposed to their interests. As we have already said, it would be supremely naïve to imagine that the élite would in any way promote or accept an education which stimulated the oppressed to discover the *raison d'être* of the social structure. The most that could be expected is that the élite might permit talk of such education, and occasional experiments which could be immediately suppressed should the status quo be threatened.

Thus the Episcopal Conference of Latin American (CELAM) can talk about 'liberating education' in nearly all its official documents; as long as it is not put into practice, nothing serious will happen to it. At any rate, we should not be surprised (though this is not based on actual knowledge) if one day CELAM is severely restricted by the power élite, through the anti-prophetic church of which we spoke. This church, which is 'freezing to death' in the warm bosom of the bourgeoisie, can certainly not tolerate any ideas, even if only verbal, which the élite consider 'diabolic'.

Our task in considering the role of the Latin American churches in education would be simplified if we could count on coherence between church and gospel. In that case, it would be sufficient to look at the dependent condition of Latin American society (with the exception of Cuba and up to a point Chile) and set up a strategy of action for the churches. The reality, however, is different, and we cannot think in a vacuum.

It is not possible to speak objectively of the educational role of the Latin American churches as being unified and coherent. On the contrary, their roles differ, sometimes opposing each other, according to the political line, whether evident, hidden or disguised, which the different churches are living out in history. The traditionalist church, first of all, is still intensely colonialist. It is a missionary church, in the worst sense of the word, a necrophilic winner of souls, hence its taste for masochistic emphasis on sin, hell-fire and eternal damnation. The mundane, dichotomised from the transcendental, is the 'filth' in which humans have to pay for their sins. The more they suffer, the more they purify themselves, finally reaching heaven and eternal rest. Work is not, for them, the action of men and women on the world, transforming and re-creating, but rather the price that must be paid for being human.

In this traditionalist line, whether it be Protestant or Catholic, we find what the Swiss sociologist Christian Lalive calls the 'haven of the masses'.[17] This view of the world, of life, satisfies the fatalistic and frightened consciousness of the oppressed at a certain moment of their historical experience. They find in it a kind of healing for their existential fatigue. So it is that the more the masses are drowned in their culture of silence, with all the violence that this implies on the part of the oppressors, the more the masses tend to take refuge in churches which offer that sort of 'ministry'.[18] Submerged in this culture of silence, where the only voice to be heard is that of the ruling classes, they see this church as a sort of womb in which they can hide from an aggressive society. In despising this world as a world of sin, vice and impurity, they are in one sense taking their 'revenge' on their oppressors, its owners. It is as if they were saying to the bosses: 'You are powerful, but the world over which your power holds sway is an evil one and we reject it.' Forbidden as a subordinate social class to have their say, they fool themselves that the prayers for salvation they voice in their 'haven' are a genuine form of 'speaking out'.

However, none of this resolves the real problems of the oppressed. Their catharsis actually alienates them further, for it directs their anger against the world and not against the social system which is ruining the world. So, seeing the world itself as the antagonist, they attempt the impossible: to renounce the world's mediation in their pilgrimage. By doing so, they hope to reach transcendence without passing by way of the mundane; they want meta-history without experiencing history; they want salvation without knowing liberation. The pain of domination leads them to accept this historical anaesthesia in the hope that it will strengthen them to fight sin and the devil, leaving untouched all the while the real causes of their oppression. They cannot see, beyond their present situation, the 'untested feasibility', the future as a liberation project which they must create for themselves.

This traditional type of church is usually found in backward, 'closed' societies, mostly agricultural, which depend upon the export of raw materials and have only a minimal internal market; here the culture of silence is fundamental. Like the archaic social structures, the traditionalist church remains unchanged throughout the modernisation of these societies. The force of such traditionalist religion[19] is seen even in the urban centres which are being transformed under the impact of industrialisation. Only a qualitative change in the consciousness of the people can overcome the need to see the church as the 'haven of the masses'. And as we have seen, this qualitative change does not happen automatically, mechanically or 'inside' the consciousness.

Furthermore, technological modernisation does not necessarily make people more capable of critical analysis, because it too is not neutral. It is dependent on the ideology that commands it.

For all these reasons,.and for many more that would take too long to analyse, the traditionalist line is unquestionably allied to the ruling classes, whether or not it is aware of this. The role that these churches can (and do) play in the field of education is conditioned then by their view of the world, of religion, and of human beings and their 'destiny'. Their idea of education and its application cannot help being paralysing, alienating and alienated. Only those who hold this perspective naïvely, rather than shrewdly, will be able to escape from their trap through praxis, by entering into a totally different commitment to the dominated classes and so becoming truly prophetic.

The modernising church

Some churches abandon the traditionalist perspective for a new attitude. The history of Latin America shows that the new position begins to emerge when modernising elements replace the traditional structures of society. The masses of the people, previously almost completely submerged in the historical process,[20] now begin to emerge in response to industrialisation. Society also changes. New challenges are presented to the dominating classes, demanding different answers.

The imperialist interests which condition this transition become more and more aggressive. They use various means of penetration into and control over the dependent society. At a given moment the emphasis on industrialisation gives rise to a nationalist 'ideology of development' which makes a case for, among other things, a pact between the 'national bourgeoisie' and the emerging proletariat.

Latin American economists have been the first to analyse this process, followed closely by sociologists and some educators. Together they plan and put into practice the concept of social planning. At this point, the Economic Commission for Latin America (CEPAL) begins to play a decisive role, both through technical missions and through its adherence to 'development politics'. Later comes the contribution of the Latin American Institute for Economic and Social Planning (ILPES), an organ of the United Nations whose job is to educate economists for the entire continent.

Obviously, none of this happens by chance or in isolation. The process is an intrinsic part of the history which Latin American societies are living, in varying degrees of intensity. This complex movement, like the different perspectives produced in response to the so-called 'backwardness' of Latin America, is neither accidental nor the result of some caprice.

As we have seen, imperialistic economic interests, such as the need for wider markets, force the national élite (which is almost always a purely local expression of a foreign élite) to find ways to reform the archaic structures without, at the same time, frustrating their interests. For imperialism and its national allies, the important thing is that this reformist process, publicly called 'development', should not affect the basic relationship between the master society and its dependent societies. Development is acceptable, but it must not alter the state of dependence! With the exception of a few minor points which will not alter the state of the subordinate society, the political, economic and cultural decisions concerning the transformation of the dependent society will be made in the master society.

So it is that the Latin American societies, with the exception of Cuba since its revolution, and up to a point Chile, are 'modernising' rather than 'developing' in the real sense of the word. Latin America can only truly develop when the fundamental contradiction of dependence is resolved. This demands that decision-making regarding change must rest in the hands of the masses of oppressed people in the society concerned; it must be independent from a superimposed bourgeois élite.

Thus development is liberation on two levels: the whole dependent society liberating itself from imperialism, and the oppressed social classes liberating themselves from the oppressive élite. This is because real development is impossible in a class society.

The process of imperialist expansion produces new political and social situations. The process of transition in the dependent society implies the contradictory presences of both a proletariat which is being modernised and a traditional proletariat, a technico-professional petite bourgeoisie and a traditional middle class,[21] a traditional church and a modernising church, a highly baroque academic education and the technico-professional education demanded by industrialisation.

So it is that in spite of what the 'mechanists' think, the movement from one stage to another is not automatic. There are no rigid geographical frontiers between the stages; both dimensions co-exist in transition.

The proletariat of the modernisation phase lives in a new historical experience, that of transition, giving birth to a new political action style: populism. Its directors play the game of mediator between the emerging common people and the ruling classes.[22] Populism is unthinkable in a situation where the common people have not yet made their emergence. It is found in urban centres rather than in the *latifundios* where the peasant masses are still 'submerged'.

At the same time, in the historical framework which gives birth to it, populism tends towards 'do-goodism'; hence its possibilities of manipulation. The emerging masses of common people are intensely conditioned by their experience in the culture of silence.[23]

During the process of emergence they obviously have no class consciousness since their former state of immersion gave them no chance to develop it. They are, then, as ambiguous as the populism which attempts to respond to them. On the one hand they make demands. On the other, they accept the formulas of do-goodism and manipulation. That is why the traditionalist churches also survive the period of transition, even in the modernised urban centres. These churches often choose to enhance their own prestige, since after the stage of populism there may well be a new phase characterised by violent military regimes. Repression, reactivating the old life-styles of the masses (the culture of silence), forces them to take refuge in the church. As we have seen, these churches, existing side by side with those which have modernised, modernise too in certain respects, thereby becoming more efficient in their traditionalism.

We have seen that the modernisation process of the dependent society never gets translated into fundamental changes in the relationship between the dependent society and the master society, and that the emergence of the masses does not by itself constitute their critical consciousness. In the same way, it is interesting to note, the churches' pilgrimage toward modernisation never gets translated into historic involvement with the oppressed people in any real sense that leads toward that people's liberation.

Challenged by the increased efficiency of a society which is modernising its archaic structures, the modernising church improves its bureaucracy so that it can be more efficient in its social activities (its 'do-goodism') and in its pastoral activities. It replaces empirical means by technical processes. Its former 'charity centres' directed by lay persons (in the Catholic church by the Daughters of Mary) become known as 'community centres', directed by social workers. And the men and women who were previously known by their own names are today numbers on a card index.

'Mass media' (which are actually media for issuing 'communiqués' to the masses) become an irresistible attraction to the churches. But the 'modern' and modernising church can hardly be condemned for attempting to perfect its working tools; what is more serious is the political option which clearly conditions the process of modernisation. Like the traditional churches, of which they are a new version, they are not committed to the oppressed but to the power élite. That is why they defend structural reform over against the radical transformation of structures; they speak of the 'humanisation of capitalism' rather than its total suppression.

The traditionalist churches alienate the oppressed social classes by encouraging them to view the world as evil. The modernising churches alienate them in a different way: by defending the reforms that maintain the status quo. By reducing such expressions as 'humanism' and 'humanisation' to abstract categories, the modern churches empty them of any real meaning. Such phrases become mere slogans whose only contribution is to serve the reactionary forces. In truth, there is no humanisation without liberation as there is no liberation without a revolutionary transformation of the class society, for in the class society all humanisation is impossible. Liberation becomes concrete only when society is changed, not when its structures are simply modernised.

In so far as the modernising churches busy themselves with no more than peripheral changes and plead the case of neo-capitalistic measures, they will have their audience only among the 'naïve' or the 'shrewd'. The young people who are neither naïve nor shrewd but are challenged by the drama of Latin America cannot accept the invitation of the modernising churches which support conservative and reformist positions. Not only do they refuse the invitation: it provokes them into assuming attitudes which are not always valid, such as the objectivist position discussed elsewhere in this article.

The churches' conservative position, rejected by these young people, does not contradict their 'modernism', for the modernisation of which we are talking is eminently conservative, since it reforms so as to preserve the status quo. Hence the churches give the impression of 'moving' while actually they are standing still. They create the illusion of marching on while really stabilising themselves. They die because they refuse to die.

This is the kind of church which would still say to Christ today, 'Why leave, Master, if everything here is so beautiful, so good?' Their language conceals rather than reveals. It speaks of 'the poor' or of 'the underprivileged' rather than 'the oppressed'. While it sees the alienations of the ruling class and dominated class on the same level, it ignores the antagonism between them, the result of the system that created them. But, if the system alienates both groups, it alienates each in a different way. The rulers are alienated to the degree that, sacrificing their *being* for a false *having*, they are drugged with power and so stop *being*; the dominated, prevented to a certain degree from *having*, finish with so little power that *being* is impossible. Turning work into merchandise, the system creates those who buy it and those who sell it. The error of the naïve and the shrewdness of the shrewd is seen in their affirmation that such a contradiction is a purely moral question.

The ruling classes, as is the logic of the class system, prohibit the dominated class from *being*. In this process the ruling class itself ceases to *be*. The system itself keeps them from rising above the contradiction, from any movement which would end their alienation as well as that of those they dominate. The dominated alone are called to fulfil this task in history. The ruling class, as such, cannot carry it out. What they can do, within their historical limits, is to reform and to modernise the system according to the new demands which the system allows them to perceive, thus in effect maintaining that which results in the alienation of all.

Under the conditions in which the modernising churches act, their concepts of education, its objectives, its applications, all must form a coherent unity within their general political position. That is why, even though they speak of liberating education, they are conditioned by their vision of liberation as an individual activity which should take place through a change of consciousness and not through the social and historical praxis of human beings. So they end up by putting the accent on methods which can be considered neutral. Liberating education for the modernising church is finally reduced to liberating the students from blackboards, static classes and text-book curricula, and offering them projectors and other audio-visual accessories, more dynamic classes and a new technico-professional teaching.

The prophetic church

Finally, another kind of church has been taking shape in Latin America, though it is not often visible as a coherent totality. It is a church as old as Christianity itself, without being traditional; as new as Christianity, without being modernising. It is the prophetic church. Opposed and attacked by both traditional and modernising churches, as well as by the élite of the power structures, this utopian, prophetic and hope-filled movement rejects do-goodism and palliative reforms in order to commit itself to the dominated social classes and to radical social change.

In contrast with the churches considered above, it rejects all static forms of thought. It accepts becoming, in order to *be*. Because it thinks critically this prophetic church cannot think of itself as neutral. Nor does it try to hide its choice. Therefore it does not separate worldliness from transcendence or salvation from liberation. It knows that what finally counts is not the 'I am' or the 'I know'; the 'I free myself' or the 'I save myself'; nor even the 'I teach you', 'I free you', or 'I save you', but the 'we are', 'we know', 'we save ourselves'.

This prophetic line can only be understood as an expression of the dramatic and challenging situation of Latin America. It emerges when the contradictions in Latin American society become apparent. It is at this moment, too, that revolution is seen as the means of liberation for the oppressed people, and the military coup as the reactionary counter-move.

Latin America's 'prophetic' Christians may disagree among themselves, especially at the point of 'action', but they are the ones who have renounced their innocence in order to join the oppressed classes, and who remain faithful to their commitment. Protestant or Catholic – from the point of view of this prophetic position the division is of no importance – clergy or lay, they have all had to travel a hard route of experience from their idealistic visions toward a dialectical vision of reality. They have learned, not only as a result of their praxis with the people, but also from the courageous example of many young people. They now see that reality, a process and not a static fact, is full of contradictions, and that social conflicts are not metaphysical categories but rather historical expressions of the confrontation of these contradictions. Any attempt, therefore, to solve conflict without touching the contradictions which have generated it only stifles the conflict and at the same time strengthens the ruling class.

The prophetic position demands a critical analysis of the social structures in which the conflict takes place. This means that it demands of its followers a knowledge of socio-political science, since this science cannot be neutral; this demands an ideological choice.

Such prophetic perspective does not represent an escape into a world of unattainable dreams. It demands a scientific knowledge of the world as it really is. For to denounce the present reality and announce its radical transformation into another reality capable of giving birth to new men and women, implies gaining through praxis a new knowledge of reality. The dominated classes must take part in this denunciation and annunciation. It cannot be done if they are left out of the picture. The prophetic position is not petit bourgeois. It is well aware that authentic action demands a permanent process which only reaches its maximal point when the dominated class, through praxis, also becomes prophetic, utopian and full of hope, in other words, revolutionary. A society in a state of permanent revolution cannot manage without a permanent prophetic vision. Without it, society stagnates and is no longer revolutionary.[24]

In the same way, no church can be really prophetic if it remains the 'haven of the masses' or the agent of modernisation and conservation. The prophetic church is no home for the oppressed, alienating them further by empty denunciations. On the contrary, it invites them to a new Exodus. Nor is the prophetic church one which chooses modernisation and thereby does no more than stagnate. Christ was no conservative. The prophetic church, like him, must move forward constantly, forever dying and forever being reborn. In order to be, it must always be in a state of *becoming*. The prophetic church must also accept an existence which is in dramatic tension between past and future, staying and going, speaking the word and keeping silence, being and not being. There is no prophecy without risk.

This prophetic attitude, which emerges in the praxis of numerous Christians in the challenging historical situation of Latin America, is accompanied by a rich and very necessary theological reflection. The theology of so-called development gives way to the theology of liberation, a prophetic, utopian theology, full of hope. Little does it matter that this theology is not yet well systematised. Its content arises from the hopeless situation of dependent, exploited, invaded societies. It is stimulated by the need to rise above the contradictions which explain and produce that dependence. Since it is prophetic, this theology of liberation cannot attempt to reconcile the irreconcilable.

At this moment in history, theology cannot spend its time discussing 'secularisation' (which in the end is the modern form of 'sacralisation'[25]) or try to entertain us with the 'death of God' discussion which in many ways reveals an a-critical tendency of complete adaptation by the 'unidimensionalised and depoliticised person of the affluent societies' as Hugo Assmann says in an excellent book.[26]

To digress a moment from our specific subject, we should add here that this prophetic attitude towards the world and history is by no means exclusive to Latin America or other areas of the Third World. It is not an exotic attitude peculiar to 'underdevelopment', first because the original Christian position is itself prophetic, at whatever point in time and place. Only the particular content of its witness will vary, according to the precise historical circumstances. Moreover, the concept of the Third World is ideological and political, not geographic. The so-called 'First World' has within it and against it its own 'Third World'. And the Third World has its First World, represented by the ideology of domination and the power of the ruling classes. The Third World is in the last analysis the world of silence, of oppression, of dependence, of exploitation, of the violence exercised by the ruling classes on the oppressed.

Europeans and North Americans, with their technological societies, have no need to go to Latin America in order to become prophetic. They need only go to the outskirts of their big cities, without 'naïveté' or 'shrewdness', and there they will find sufficient stimulus to do some fresh thinking for themselves. They will find themselves confronted with various expressions of the Third World. They can begin to understand the concern which gives rise to the prophetic position in Latin America.

Thus it is clear that the educational role of the prophetic church in Latin America must be totally different from that of the other churches we have discussed. Education must be an instrument of transforming action, as a political praxis at the service of permanent human liberation. This, let us repeat, does not happen only in the consciousness of people, but presupposes a radical change of structures, in which process consciousness will itself be transformed.

From the prophetic point of view, it makes little difference in what specific area education happens, it will always be an effort to clarify the concrete context in which the teacher-students and student-teachers are educated and are united by their presence in action. It will always be a demythologising praxis.

Which brings us back to our opening statement: the church, education and the role of the churches in education can only be discussed historically. It is in history that humanity is called to respond to the prophetic movement in Latin America.[27]

Notes
1. Reinhold Niebuhr, *Moral Man and Immoral Society*, New York, Charles Scribner's Sons, 1960.
2. A phrase I owe to Erich Fromm, *The Heart of Man*, London, Routledge and Kegan Paul, 1965.
3. Referring to the 'moralists', Niebuhr says: 'They do not recognise that when collective power, whether in the form of imperialism or class domination, exploits weakness, it can never be dislodged unless power is raised against it ... Modern religious idealists usually follow in the wake of social scientists in advocating compromise and accommodation as the way to social justice.' Reinhold Niebuhr, *Moral Man and Immoral Society*, New York, Charles Scribner's Sons, 1960, pp. xii and xix.
4. 'For the purposes of the historian, i.e. the student of micro-history, or of history "as it happened" (and of the present "as it happens") as distinct from the general and rather abstract models of the historical transformation of societies, class and the problem of class

consciousness are inseparable. Class in the full sense only comes into existence at the historical moment when classes begin to acquire consciousness of themselves as such.' See E J Hobsbawm, 'Class consciousness in history', in Istvan Meszaros (ed.), *Aspects of History and Class Consciousness*, London, Routledge and Kegan Paul, 1972, p. 6.

5. On this, see Georg Lukacs, *Histoire et Conscience de Classe*, Paris, Les Editions de Minuit, 1960.

6. Paulo Freire, 'Cultural action: an introduction', in *Conscientization for Liberation*, Washington, CICOP, 1971.

7. See Paulo Freire, *Pedagogy of the Oppressed*, New York, Seabury, 1970.

8. A representative of a Latin American élite, answering a journalist's question during an interview, said: 'I could never permit an educational process which would awaken the potential of the masses and put me in the difficult situation of having to listen to them. It would be like asking for a rope to hang myself by.'

9. Concerning free employment as a necessary condition for human liberty, see *Fifteen Bishops Speak for the Third World*, Mexico, CIDOC, 1967, Dec. 67/35, pp. 1–11.

10. Dom Helder Câmara, the prophetic Archbishop of Olinda and Recife (Brazil), is today considered as one of these terrible 'demons'. It's always the same. The necrophiles can never stand the presence of a biophile.

11. 'From the beginning of modern times, hopes for something new from God have emigrated from the church and have been invested in revolution and rapid social change. It was most often reaction and conservatism that remained in the church. Thus the Christian church became "religious". That is, she cultivated and apotheosised tradition. Her authority was sanctioned by what had been in force always and everywhere from the earliest times.' See Jürgen Moltmann, *Religion, Revolution and the Future*, New York, Charles Scribner's Sons, 1969, pp. 5–6.

12. This theme is more fully worked out in my *Pedagogy of the Oppressed*, New York, Seabury, 1970.

13. In reality, only the oppressed can conceive a future which is radically different from their present, in so far as they gain a dominated class consciousness. The oppressors, as the ruling class, can only imagine the future as the preservation of their present – their role of oppressors. So while the future of the first rests in the revolutionary transformation of society – a condition for their own liberation – the future of the second presupposes mere social modernisation in which they can maintain their position as rulers.

14. At this point, of course, no revolutionary, Christian or non-Christian, can accept a church which innocently or shrewdly aligns itself with the ruling class, loses its utopian dimension and empties itself of prophetic mission. There is no need to denounce such a church. It denounces itself through its defence, surreptitious or not, of the ruling class.

15. Karel Kosik, *Dialéctica de lo Concreto*, Mexico, Grijalbo, 1967.

16. This term refers here to the condition of incarnation in the world.

17. See Christian Lalive, *Haven of the Masses: a study of the Pentecostal movement in Chile*, London, Lutterworth Press, 1969.

18. A sociological analysis of this fact in Latin America is essential, but it is important that the starting point of such research be social class structures and not the religious phenomenon itself.

19. See Beatriz Muniz de Souza, *A Experiéncia da Salvação: Pentecostais em São Paulo*, São Paulo, Duas Cidades, 1969.

20. Paulo Freire, *La Educación como Práctica de la Libertad*, Montevideo, Tierra Nueva. Also in French: *La Pratique de la Liberté*, Paris, Editions du Cerf.

21. See Fernando Henrique Cardoso, *Politique et Développement dans les Sociétés Dépendantes*, Paris, Editions Anthropos, 1971.

22. See Francisco Weffort, *Classes Populares e Politica (Contribução ao Estudo do Populismo)*, São Paulo, Universidade São Paulo, 1968.

23. Paulo Freire, *Cultural Action for Freedom*, Harmondsworth, Penguin, 1972.

24. A prophetic vision need not be the result of a religious position.

25. There are no societies more 'sacral' than those which are bourgeois. They react viciously to the slightest attempt to disrupt patterns which they consider universal, eternal and perfect.

26. *Opresión–Liberación: Desafio a los Cristianos*, Montevideo, Tierra Nueva, 1971.

27. Translated from the Portuguese by William Bloom, with the help of Esther Meyer, Helen Mackintosh and Helen Franco.

5.2 Liberation theology and Christian education theory

Frank Marangos

Introduction

The last decade has seen considerable development in Christian education. Gone are the days when it was invariably envisioned as an institution, a home, an educational system, a mission agency or a school for Christian living. More recently, modern educators have examined a number of approaches through which Christian education may become a focus of involvement of all groups concerned with the shaping of culture and the reshaping of society towards humane goals.

In part, today's crisis in education was produced by a rapid development of technology, by rising expectations among previously submerged and oppressed sectors of the human community, by the changing values and priorities and by the global marketplace where divine-human movements and faiths have converged. While these approaches to Christian education are not exclusive of one another, they do illustrate how our contemporary scene has, in fact, contributed to shaping a more comprehensive and coherent theory for the practice of Christian education.

While none of these approaches can be found 'pure' in the Christian education practice, I will attempt to examine the consequences of liberation theology upon Christian education theory.

Liberation, education and theology

'Education is a human activity in the cultural order.'[1] This is how education was defined in the final document of Puebla. Liberation theology, therefore, is currently proposing a new paradigm for education. The theologians of liberation have called fresh attention to the tension of future hope which they argue offers the guiding focus for our faith. This emphasis on the future is beginning to impact Christian religious education, particularly through the work of Thomas Groome. The basic issue arising out of this systematic theology is: How does the religious community live in faithfulness to its past and in openness to its present and future? This raises fundamental questions as to how God is revealed and where the authority of the religious community lies. The questions in Christian education have been closely related to this. The questions concern what to teach, how and why. Is the content of Christian education the biblical and historical experience of the community and the world or the hoped-for kingdom of God? The desire to transcend the continuity/change dualism is not new in religious education. What is novel is the process by which and in which liberation theology attempts to enable this reality.

True liberation education in the churches of North America must, therefore, begin with a critical awareness that we are part of the world problem and that our experience is totally different from that of the oppressed people with whom this approach was generated. This 'consciousness' that the vast majority of us, who see ourselves as free, are really captives of the same structures and forces that cause the poverty and oppression we wish to eliminate is an essential element for liberation education. This development of such a new Christian consciousness, which will be aware of the global context of oppression, will lead Christians in constructing new faithful lifestyles. The very presence of liberation education raises again the classical conflict between the nurturing ministry of the church and its mission and sacrificial service to the world. We must not lose sight of the fact, however, that the liberation movement and its association with education emerged primarily in the Latin American context where oppression and poverty are historical realities, not ideas to be examined and debated. However, 'If we can become aware of the social, political and economic systems that control our lives, we may then find ourselves on the same side of the struggle as those who are outcasts of those systems.'[2] Liberation, therefore, is not merely another technique for education, but the manner by which man knows God. The hermeneutics of liberation education are 'to love Yahweh ... to do justice to the poor and oppressed'.[3] In short, 'to know God is to do justice'.[4]

The Greek verb *hermeneuein*, often understood as 'translation' or 'explanation', can also be translated as 'to proclaim' or 'to speak'. The hermeneutics of liberation then have to do with an education which stresses both proclamation as well as explanation. This double character, therefore, relates it to a traditioning community and to the education which must necessarily be concerned with the community's expression and explanation of its faith. Hence, liberation education has its grounding in a dialectic ideology that reflects the actual experience of people who have never known any way of life but oppression. This is indeed the dialectical process which, for Asian theologians such as D Preman Niles, 'forms a new humanity in Christ ... not just in the modern Asian revolution but as a continuous historical process coming from the past'.[5] The Christian story, therefore, must be 'looked at from the perspective of the people'.[6] Few of us can comprehend its true nature of total oppression, much less identify with it. Hence, 'they can become our teachers rather than we theirs'.[7]

Educational theory and practice will be affected by this new direction of liberation theology. One particular aspect will be the degree beyond which individuals will be led from merely encountering the notion of liberation to a real engagement or involvement. 'Theological education', writes J Deotis Roberts, 'needs insight from the other side of town and from the underside of history. It needs to be informed by the cries of the oppressed at home and abroad.'[8] 'The God of biblical revelation is known through interhuman justice.'[9] For Gutierrez, liberation means nothing less than this: the capacity to express love. To be truly free is to live in God's love and this includes the struggle against all that hinders love. Hence, the starting point for an educational theory of liberation is its political-social rather than theological basis. 'In this participation', writes Gutierrez, 'will be heard nuances of the word of God which are imperceptible in other existential situations.'[10] What is new, therefore, in Gutierrez' understanding of praxis, the active hermeneutic of community, is in his distinction between a methodology and a methodology's frame of reference. Praxis, therefore, is the praxis of the poor. Unless we understand Gutierrez' theology in this fashion, liberation education can be co-opted into a non-threatening middle-class programme.

There is certainly a need for a more critical awareness of the meanings represented in the way the people we teach approach the world. Such critical reflection will not arise from discussions about morality but from reflection on the praxis of morality. Gutierrez believes that the church's pastoral action, which includes education, should lead to a clarification of commitment and to the identification of those who are willing to share in the Christian praxis. Christian education, according to liberation theology, cannot, therefore, be neutral. Hence, one of the most significant commitments of Puebla is encapsulated in a phrase from Document 18 (the document on which Gutierrez worked) that the church must make 'a preferential option for the poor'.[11] Liberation education must translate this phrase into a living reality. It presents, however, one of the greatest challenges the church will face in our time. It must serve to help persons be critical of their commitments and separate those who are seeking a new awareness of the gospel for the world's oppressed from those who are Christians for the convenience of belonging to a social élite.

The liberation movements may be pushing North American educational systems within the church to draw the meaning of the Christian way of life more closely to the kind of church 'ethos' that once characterised Eastern Orthodox communities in Europe. Hence, it is appropriate to quote another characteristic statement of liberation education from Puebla at this point. Education 'should contribute to the conversion of the total human being, not just the inmost individual ego of the person, but also that person's peripheral and social ego'.[12]

'Latin American dependency is not only economic and political, but also cultural.'[13] The 'key' for such a liberation process is in the words of *Populorum progressio*, a 'liberation education', which for Gutierrez appears to be the 'entering into the circle of charity which unites the three persons of the Trinity ... to love God as God loves'.[14]

In other words, 'knowing' is redefined as 'doing', a stress on the communion and brotherhood as the ultimate meaning of human life.

Political theory is an ambiguous expression. Education which nurtures an individual's experiential consciousness, his political social ethos, is an alternative approach which takes into consideration the political dimension of faith and is, indeed, aware of the most pervasive and acute problems which man encounters today. Within such an approach, Gutierrez asserts, 'men are called together as a community and not as separate individuals to participate in the life of the Trinitarian community, to enter into the circuit of love that unites the persons of the Trinity'.[15]

Liberation education might be defined as critical reflection on Christian praxis in the light of the Word. Henceforth, wisdom and rational knowledge have more explicatory ecclesial praxis as their starting point of departure and context. 'It is in reference to this praxis', insists Gutierrez, 'that an understanding of spiritual growth based on scripture should be developed and it is through this same praxis that faith encounters the problems posed by human reason.'[16]

The 'sinful situation' of the exploited and oppressed 'challenges all our practice, that is to say, it is a reproduction of the whole existing system to which the church itself belongs'.[17] This challenge, however, must not be understood as merely an interior crisis, a private or individual problem. Sin is a social historical reality which is evident in oppressive structures, the root of a situation of injustice and exploitation. 'In this anxiety and sorrow the church sees a situation of social sinfulness.'[18]

The purpose of liberation education must, therefore, include the humanisation both of individuals and the society at large. Such education must, by necessity, be an ongoing process. It cannot be confined to the years spent in formal education. It must nurture the awakening of critical consciousness and the participation in the construction of a just social order, 'to offer joyful proclamation to the poor as one of the Messianic signs of Christ's kingdom'.[19]

Liberation education, therefore, attempts to place its process within the dynamics of the historical current of humanity. 'In this current', insists Gutierrez, 'there is not only an effort to know and dominate nature ... but also a situation which both affects and is affected by this current – of misery and despoliation of the fruits of man's work ... a confrontation between social classes ... a struggle from oppressive structures.'[20] Liberation theology has made us aware of the fact that we can no longer think of sin in historical and abstract terms. Sin manifests itself in concrete political, economic and social decisions, structures and systems.

Liberation education, as we have observed, should 'contribute to the conversion of the total human being, not just the innermost individual ego ... but also that person's peripheral and social ego'.[21] As Ziegler states:[22]

> Liberation theology is calling classical theological education to radical transformation ... to accept the multidimensional implications of Christian faith. It is calling Christian believers to faithfulness articulated in justice. It does its work in the hope that 'the kingdoms of this world will become the kingdom of our Lord'.

Hence, such an educational hermeneutic 'demands a kind of double personality'[23] wherein our 'consciousness must continue to remind us of evil from which we benefit while others suffer'.[24] We cannot escape the conclusion, however, that the church, where the gospel places it unequivocally on the side of the oppressed, is usually ranged against the poor either in overt action against them, or in covert disregard of them under the banner of 'neutrality'. Our ability, therefore, to listen to these oppressed voices will challenge our complicity in such realities and demand that we repent, rethink and regroup so that we can begin to embody a gospel that equates the knowing of God with the doing of justice. 'The premises – that God speaks through the world's suffering', writes Harvey Cox, 'that salvation and liberation go together, that knowing and serving the God of justice require a corporate response – are not only all soundly biblical but have already begun to inform an emergent consensus in the world church.'[25]

Liberation theology and education

When viewed from this perspective, lifestyle is a basic issue to be addressed by liberation education. Lifestyle, however, must encompass a larger manifestation than merely the personal dimension, the patterns of beliefs, values and attitudes which can be described and characterised in the way a person chooses to live. Liberation theology creates an education which does not neglect the social and collective values and behaviour that become the shared way of life for a group of persons. Hence, 'the Christian message', writes Kim Yong Bock, 'not only brought about personal spiritual transformation of Korean Christians but also provided the language to interpret the world and history'.[26] Liberation education must confront Euro-American theology, therefore, with the necessity of recollecting the radically historical character of scripture. At every point in its development, it relates to God's action to human response in the context of particular situations. For example, 'It is a way of saying', writes Gerald Anderson concerning the Critical Asian Principle, 'that we will approach and interpret the gospel in relation to the needs and issues peculiar to the Asian situation.'[27] Scripture is indeed the record of the acts of God, who was concerned and acted for their deliverance. Referring to the dynamics of preaching, Justo and Catherine Gonzalez underscore this fact by writing, 'the more it can be shown that what is being emphasised by liberation theology is at the heart of the gospel ... the more helpful it will be to the community'.[28]

As we have seen, discipleship is a necessary component of Christian understanding. The Christian message entrusted to the church as the tradition of apostolic witness becomes meaningless unless handed over to the world as historic reality by messengers who live out its implications. 'The bond between the neighbour and God', writes Gutierrez, 'is changed, deepened and universalised by the incarnation of the Word ... Matthew 25:31–45 is a good illustration of this two-fold process.'[29] The gospel, therefore, as the proclamation of authentic existence, is also a message of hope to individuals who are persistently denied such an authenticity by the present world order.

Liberation theology places eschatological hope at the centre of Christian education. 'The primary mandate to be obeyed by respondents to God's kingdom is that we love God and our neighbour in response to God's radical love for us.'[30]

The church must return to the essential eschatological nature of her faith and of her life. No theological reflection on the world will be of any help, no theological reflection will be, may I be so bold as to say, possible unless we rediscover that reality which alone constitutes the church and is the source of her faith, of her life and therefore, of her theology. This reality is the kingdom of God. The church is in *statu viae*, in pilgrimage through 'this world', sent to it as its salvation. But the meaning of this pilgrimage, as indeed the meaning of the world itself, is given and revealed to us only when the church fulfils herself as being in *statu patriae*, truly at home at Christ's table, in his kingdom.

This precondition requires a radical rethinking of our theological enterprise. It is not enough to quote patristic sources to certify our theological position, for it is not quotations, be they scriptural or of other points of tradition, that constitute the ground of theology, but as we have observed from the liberationists, the *experience* of the church herself. All this, in the final analysis, means a return to a 'historic faith' which has no other experience than that of the kingdom, one that is constantly moving towards God's future. 'We must learn to claim our inheritance in such a way that it is a help rather than a hindrance in our march toward the future.'[31]

Schubert Ogden argues that theologies of praxis are typically not so much theology as witness, 'the rationalisation of positions already taken rather than the process or product of critical reflection on those positions'.[32] Praxis viewed as a theological enterprise, therefore, offers an opportunity for disciplined reflection on the Messianic mission of the church as it is actualised in the world. In turn, this enterprise defines Christian discipleship as the criterion which, though practical, is grounded in none other than contextual analysis. Thomas Groome's volume, *Christian Religious Education*, is a seminal work which presents a convincing case for the adoption of praxis as the norm for Christian education.

Since the decade of the fifties and despite certain achievements, the ample hopes for development have come to nothing. 'The marginalisation of the vast majority and the exploitation of the poor has increased.'[33] Likewise, Gutierrez believes that the kind of development that our own society has achieved is distorted. In his words, 'since the supporters of development did not attack the roots of evil, they failed and caused instead confusion and frustration'.[34]

The optimism of the developmental theories has clearly been observed as unable to speak adequately about or to respond to the oppressive conditions of the great majority of Third World people. In these theories salvation, for the most part, is confused with the First World or American way. These theories have unfortunately shaped the very horizon of meaning in terms of questions about ourselves, our world and our God. Development schemes in the past, for example, involved rich nations helping poor nations to get on their feet by financial grants, loans or outright gifts. Seeking to accelerate such activities, the United Nations sponsored the 'Decade of Development', but at the end the gap between rich and poor had increased. Gutierrez maintains that there is a relation wherein the rich get richer by exploiting the poor and keeping them that way. Development, in the final analysis, is tokenistic, exploitive and paternalistic. For Gutierrez, it is only within the broader framework of liberation 'that development finds its true meaning and possibilities of accomplishing something worthwhile'.[35] True freedom, true liberation, true development, which liberation education must espouse, must direct us, therefore, to the creation of a new man and a qualitatively new society. For this reason, Gutierrez and other spokespersons for the Third World have chosen to call the process by which it will overcome the oppression 'liberation' rather than 'development'. The Third World has no desires to imitate the institutions, values or lifestyles of its oppressors. It understands its liberation in terms of freedom from the social restraints imposed on them by the First World, as well as freedom to create a qualitatively new order. In Gutierrez' words, 'The liberation of our continent needs more than overcoming economic, social and political dependence.'[36] For Gutierrez, liberation means, in a deeper sense, 'to see the becoming of mankind as a process of the emancipation of man in history. It is to see man in search of a qualitatively different society ... in which man will be an artisan of his own destiny.'[37]

Liberation education, therefore, aims at nurturing 'suspicion' about the common assumptions about the problems of oppression. In so doing, it can begin to analyse the roots of the problem by using the critical tools provided by the social sciences. As we analyse the roots of the problem, however, we should also formulate and identify specific instances of how those systems and ideologies actually contribute to the problem. After we have analysed the present situation and clarified our views about its roots and our involvement in it, liberation education must reflect on the situation and our response to it in light of faith. This process is in fact what Juan Luis Segundo calls the 'hermeneutic circle' in which there are four basic moments. The final moment is 'our new way of interpreting the fountainhead of faith (that is, scripture) with the new elements at our disposal'.[38] The pain and struggle of the hermeneutical circle is, in fact, the educational process of liberation out of which theology is done.

A theology of man is germane to our understanding the nature of the teaching process of liberation education. Religious educators in the early decades of this century developed a theory of teaching which assumed that man could be educated into the good life. The kingdom of God was confused with, as George Albert Coe once put it, the 'democracy of God', a human possibility, if man could provide the proper kind of education. The God of Christian revelation, however, is a God made man. Hence, the famous comment of Barth, 'Man is the measure of all things since God became man.' 'All of this', writes Gutierrez, 'has caused the re-evaluation of the presence and the activity of man in the world, especially in relation to other men.'[39] This re-evaluation has resulted in man's realisation that his 'freedom always implies the capacity to be (his) own person ... to go on fashioning community and participation on the inseparable planes; our relationship to the world as its martyr, to other persons as brothers and sisters and to God as God's children'.[40] Hence, liberation education must provide the process through which man can obtain a consciousness which 'must remind us of evil from which we benefit while others suffer'.[41] Justo and Catherine Gonzalez are correct in asserting that our 'tendency is not a duality', but as we have observed from Puebla, 'three unsurpassable planes'.[42] The tendency to regard education, therefore, as a cure for social problems, based on the assumption that oppression and other social ills are due to individual failures, directed society to seek no further than improving the individual. By focusing on this single element, the systematic and structural roots of the problem went unnoticed. In the end, such educational reforms failed in their lofty goals because they were not accompanied by more direct and structural change. Without promoting structural change, liberation education can, at best, only change the cast of characters who occupy pre-existing numbers of positions on the top and on the bottom. Liberationists insist, therefore, that the liberation mode of education cannot be adopted to serve the current North American need for a renewal in Christian education. They believe that the question of church progress must be set aside until the future of humankind and the structures of human life are resolved. The church cannot go about its usual work of nurturing a way of approaching life that reinforces the establishment and ignores the deeper longings of those who are denied their humanity, on either one or all three 'inseparable planes'.

Liberation theology, therefore, calls into question the very understanding of theology and of its function in Christian education. How are we to understand the problems of oppression and our educational response to it in light of faith? Gustavo Gutierrez argues that we should not fall into the trap of thinking about history on two levels: the supernatural and the temporal. There is but one history. 'The God of history', writes John Mbiti, 'speaks to all people in particular ways. In Africa the traditional religions are a major source for the study of the African experience of God.'[43] Puebla likewise asserts that 'a secularism essentially separates human beings from God ... it views the construction of history as purely and exclusively (our) responsibility'.[44] Liberation education must, therefore, proclaim and reveal that Jesus Christ is 'actively present in history', setting the church 'in a radical confrontation with the secularist movement'.[45] This confrontation requires a commitment to become active in the transformation of the old order. Such transformation, according to Justo and Catherine Gonzalez, begins with oneself, by participation in the changes required by the new order. 'This thought is essential if we are to see how liberation theology can relate to our preaching and to many of our churches.'[46] People learn by acting critically toward the old order and by envisioning the new order toward which they move. Liberation education must serve to help us learn again the story of faith and to rediscover the heritage of Christians who gave all they had in order to serve the oppressed. This is one of the major tasks of liberation education which must 'help congregations develop an awareness of how they are viewed by the powerless ... to ask the question how would this biblical text be heard and applied authenti-cally by someone in a radically different political and social setting'.[47] Hence, central to a liberation approach to Christian education is teach-ing *this* gospel of 'good news'. It is here that we will discover that we are delivered from dependency on the old ways and that we are free to move into a new way of life. 'The political question is the first one that we must ask as we approach a biblical passage.'[48] Hence, the message of the gospel is viewed by its very nature as a subversive message. This is what Richard Dickinson, Dean of Christian Theological Seminary, implies when he writes that liberation educa-tion's invitation 'calls for a new reading of the Christian heritage from the underside of history'.[49] The gospel's purpose is to challenge the status quo and establish a new order in its place. The life and preach-ing of Jesus, liberationists hold, continues the political activity of God in history. Jesus announces the end of the order, the end of all hatred and exploitation, and proclaims its replacement by the creation of a qualitatively new order based on the values of love, justice, peace and freedom. Hence, liberation education in the local congregations, for example, will require a unique enabling style of leadership, committed to this concept of the gospel and to the belief that persons must and can come to a realisation of the need for change. The biblical witness, therefore, is fundamental to liberation education, an unequalled source of concepts, images and modes of liberation climaxing in the supreme revelation of God in Jesus Christ, the Liberator. Personal experience, therefore, that 'Jesus is freedom' is the task of liberation education. Only this can ultimately result in creating integrity for an educational theory of liberation all its own. Liberation education rightly calls the Christian community to identify with the crying needs of the oppressed. It will remind us that theology has a political dimension and teach us that word and deed cannot be separated, that our concern should be for social justice as well as personal holiness.

Notes

1. John Eagleson and Philip Scharper (eds), *Puebla and Beyond*, Maryknoll, New York, Orbis Books, 1979, p. 251.
2. Justo L Gonzalez and Catherine Gunsalus Gonzalez, *Liberation Preaching*, Nashville, Abingdon Press, 1980, p. 27.
3. Gustavo Gutierrez, *A Theology of Liberation*, Maryknoll, New York, Orbis Books, 1973, p. 194.
4. *Ibid.*
5. Kim Yong Bock (ed.), *Minjung Theology: people as the subjects of history,* Singapore, Commission on Theological Concerns, Christian Conference of Asia, 1981, p. 11.
6. *Ibid.*
7. Gustavo Gutierrez, *op. cit.,* p. 27.
8. J Deotis Roberts, 'Liberating theological education: can our seminaries be saved?', *The Christian Century,* 100, 1983, pp. 98 and 113–116.
9. Gustavo Gutierrez, *op. cit.,* p. 195.
10. *Ibid.*
11. John Eagleson and Philip Scharper (eds), *op. cit,* p. 127.
12. *Ibid.,* p. 252.
13. Gustavo Gutierrez, *op. cit.,* p. 109.
14. *Ibid.,* p. 198.
15. *Ibid.,* p. 110.
16. *Ibid.,* p. 14.
17. *Ibid.,* p. 175.
18. *Ibid.,* p. 174.
19. John Eagleson and Philip Scharper (eds), *op. cit.,* p. 191.
20. Gustavo Gutierrez, *op. cit.,* p. 174.
21. John Eagleson and Philip Scharper (eds), *op. cit.,* p. 252.
22. Jesse H Ziegler (ed.), 'Theological education and liberation theology: a symposium', *Theological Education,* 16, 1979, p. 21.
23. Justo L Gonzalez and Catherine Gunsalus Gonzalez, *op. cit.,* p. 27.
24. *Ibid.*
25. Jesse H Ziegler (ed.), *op. cit.,* p. 25.
26. Kim Yong Bock (ed.), *op. cit.,* p. 103.
27. Gerald H Anderson and Thomas F Stransky (eds), *Mission Trends III,* New York, Paulist Press, 1976, p. 25.
28. Justo L Gonzalez and Catherine Gunsalus Gonzalez, *op. cit.,* p. 106.
29. Gustavo Gutierrez, *op. cit.,* p. 196.
30. Thomas H Groome, *Christian Religious Education,* San Francisco, Harper and Row, 1980, pp. 49–51.
31. Justo L Gonzalez and Catherine Gunsalus Gonzalez, *op. cit.,* p. 31.
32. Schubert M Ogden, *Faith and Freedom: toward a theory of liberation,* Nashville, Abingdon Press, 1979, p. 33.
33. John Eagleson and Philip Scharper (eds), *op. cit.,* p. 279.
34. Ibid., *op. cit.,* p. 26.
35. *Ibid.,* p. 36.
36. *Ibid.,* p. 91.
37. *Ibid.,* p. 91.
38. Justo L Gonzalez and Catherine Gunsalus Gonzalez, *op. cit.,* p. 31.
39. Gustavo Gutierrez, *op. cit.,* p. 7.
40. John Eagleson and Philip Scharper (eds), *op. cit.,* p. 168.
41. Justo L Gonzalez and Catherine Gunsalus Gonzalez, *op. cit.,* p. 27.
42. *Ibid.,* p. 28.

43. John Mbiti, 'The encounter of Christian faith and African religion', *The Christian Century*, 97, 1980, p. 819.
44. John Eagleson and Philip Scharper (eds), *op. cit.*, p. 183.
45. *Ibid.*
46. Justo L Gonzalez and Catherine Gunsalus Gonzalez, *op. cit.*, p. 26.
47. *Ibid.*, p. 100.
48. *Ibid.*, p. 69.
49. Jesse H Ziegler (ed.), *op. cit.*, p. 31.

6. Theological approaches: feminist theology

Feminist theology is a species of liberation theology concerned with the liberation of women from patriarchal structures which generations of theologians have justified and legitimated. Through its distinctive styles of analysis, criticism, and reconstruction, feminist theology has significantly influenced religious education in recent years,[1] and two examples of this influence are reproduced here. It has also played a part in the theological education debate,[2] in which the methodological touchstone of 'women's experience' has been creatively qualified, and even radically questioned,[3] by feminist theologians themselves.

Mary Elizabeth Moore begins her article with a number of stories that highlight the segregation of a privatised sacred realm from the public realm of life, and the restriction of the less powerful and those 'in feminised vocations' to the former. Drawing on North American assumptions about dualistic thinking between the sacred and the public, Moore connects this with dualistic patterns of thinking about female and male in early Christianity and the way in which women's experience is relegated to the private sphere both in the biblical tradition and in a variety of cultures. Religious educators should seek the unity of sacred and public, aided by a feminist theology that recognises the destructiveness of the dualism and seeks to subvert it, while offering 'an alternative view of the world and church praxis in which the sacred and the public are held together'. 'The unity of the sacred and the public possibilities from feminist theology' was first published in *Religious Education*, 84, 1989, pp. 384–401.[4]

Mary C Grey's 'Feminist images of redemption in education' is from the *British Journal of Religious Education,* 12, 1989, pp. 20–28. In this survey of the 'new images of redemption' offered by feminist theology, Grey discusses the images of reclaiming (or recovering), of self-affirmation, of self-knowledge, and of mutual empowerment. In exploring the significance of these images for education, she outlines an educational vision in which human wholeness is fundamental.[5]

Professor Mary Elizabeth Moore is Professor of Theology and Christian Education at the School of Theology at Claremont, California, USA. Professor Mary C Grey is Professor of Contemporary Theology at LSU College of Higher Education, Southampton, England.

Notes

1. See, for example, Fern M Giltner (ed.), *Women's Issues in Religious Education*, Birmingham, Alabama, Religious Education Press, 1985; Nicola M Slee, 'Women's silence in religious education', *British Journal of Religious Education*, 12, 1989, pp. 29–37; Gloria Durka, 'Feminist spirituality: restoration and transformation', *British Journal of Religious Education*, 12, 1989, pp. 38–44, and 'The changing faces of feminism: a religious educator's view from the United States', *Panorama*, 2, 1990, pp. 54–64.

2. See The Cornwall Collective, *Your Daughters Shall Prophesy: feminist alternatives in theological education*, New York, Pilgrim Press, 1980; Carter Heyward *et al.*, 'Christian feminists speak', *Theological Education*, 20, 1983, pp. 93–103; The Mud Flower Collective, *God's Fierce Whimsy*, New York, Pilgrim Press, 1985; Rebecca Chopp, 'Emerging issues and theological education', *Theological Education*, 26, 1990, pp. 106–24.

3. See Mary McClintock Fulkerson, 'Theological education and the problem of identity', *Modern Theology*, 7, 1991, pp. 465–482, and *Changing the Subject: women's discourses and feminist theology*, Minneapolis, Minnesota, Fortress, 1994.

4. See also Mary Elizabeth Moore, *Teaching from the Heart: theology and educational method*, Minneapolis, Minnesota, Fortress, 1991.

5. See also Mary C Grey, *Redeeming the Dream: feminism, redemption and Christian tradition*, London, SPCK, 1989, and '"Sapiential Yearnings": the challenge of feminist theology to religious education', in Jeff Astley and Leslie J Francis (eds), *Christian Theology and Religious Education: connections and contradictions*, London, SPCK, 1996, pp. 78–94.

6.1 The unity of the sacred and the public possibilities from feminist theology

Mary Elizabeth Moore

Story and dilemma

A woman sits in a professional meeting discussing theological papers. She notices that her contributions to the discussion are often ignored, except for an occasional rebuke by one of the group of all-male colleagues. She assumes that her interpretation of the situation is a sign of her paranoia, and she dismisses herself as silly. The day comes for her to present her paper, and she awakes with eagerness to share this paper that represents the best of her labours. Now she will be able to communicate her ideas with wholeness and clarity. But her respondent launches the discussion with a scathing critique, not of her ideas but of her deficiencies in scholarship. After the discussion, she sits with a woman who has gone with her to hear the paper. The woman says, 'They did not even discuss your paper; they were trying to put you in your place.' Later, some of the male participants compliment her in private for her fine paper. Why was this woman's contribution not taken seriously in the public discourse?

A woman is employed by a local church to work with the youth. When she is hired, the pastor and some in the congregation express concern to her about a woman doing youth ministry, at least over a sustained period of time. The woman is unnerved by the comments but not defeated, because she has a strong sense that women need not be limited to stereotypes. She does not intend to be boxed in by those notions herself. She begins her work in youth ministry, and the church folk soon discover that she is effective, very effective. This is known more by the dynamism among the youth, however, than by any public visibility of this woman in youth ministry. In fact, she begins to realise that she is the only one on the church staff who is invisible. All others have public functions in worship and in other settings. She is visible only with the youth in the privacy of their world. She is responsible for their spiritual development, but this is a responsibility more visible when it is not performed than when it is. The public eye turns to this youth minister only when persons in the congregation perceive that she is not fulfilling her sacred task, that is, when the youth are not behaving according to plan. Why is the work of this woman hidden from the public and valued only at a personal level?

A man in theological education teaches in religious education, a feminised discipline. He teaches in an institution where other theological disciplines are highly valued and rewarded with larger salaries, more public recognition, and accolades shared within the institution. This man in religious education carries a large load, a very large load, but the salary, the public recognition, and the accolades elude him. Why do the discipline of religious education and those who teach and practise education get de-publicised?

A Christian woman in Africa is theologically trained, but she says that she could never carry leadership in the church. She says, 'They would not be able to deal with me because I would be straightforward about things in the church that I think need to be changed.' She teaches a children's Sunday school class in the private, sacred realm of church, and she limits her public leadership to the secular realm. Why do religious communities often have difficulty dealing with women in public discourse and action?

I share these stories because they really happened. Each is distant enough from me personally that they cannot be identified, but I could tell six or seven other stories similar to each one. These stories highlight a problem, namely that the sacred and public realms of life are often segregated from one another, and the less powerful people are often restricted to the privatised sacred realm for their duties and recognition. This dynamic is very often a pressure experienced by women and by men in feminised vocations.

The dilemma posed is one that challenges religious educators to look at themselves very seriously, especially since the majority of religious education practitioners are women, and the discipline itself has been seen as a woman's profession through much of this century.[1]

The focus of this article is on Christian religious education, and much of the research is based in Protestantism in the United States. The historical-cultural dynamics may well be similar in other traditions, and some attempts will be made to draw parallels. I will not be presumptuous, however, to speak for traditions that I know less well.

The avoidance of religious education studies is common among women in Protestant seminaries today, and most Protestant denominations face problems in finding people to fill the educational ministry positions in local churches. Women often resist these placements for fear they will become stereotyped and stuck in what has been seen as a woman's role in the church. Men often resist these placements for fear that they will have less status and benefits in these specialised, associate positions. Though many schools of theology have witnessed a shift in these patterns in recent years, and though many denominations are witnessing a clamour after persons who are gifted and interested in educational ministry, the dilemma remains evident. The responsibility for educating the congregation is often praised as a sacred task, but its place in the public arena of the church is almost always along the sidelines. Its theorists and practitioners are often along the sidelines as well, no matter how effective they may be or how much they may be valued personally.

The dilemma named here is one that is not likely to be reversed quickly and certainly not likely to be remedied by saying that the situation needs to change. Even women and men of courage who choose to resist the stereotypes and to value and practise religious education with excellence will not reverse the problem alone. A fundamental reconception of religious education is needed, one in which the relationship between the sacred and the public is freshly considered. Religious educators need to examine critically the sacred-public duality that keeps religious education and its practitioners in a set-apart sacred realm, with little or no direct influence on the public realm. Religious educators need also to examine the relationship between the sacred and the public in order to discover how religious education can address the sacred dimensions in the public arena and the public dimensions in the sacred arena.

The problems addressed in this article are three: first, that a duality between the sacred and the public is assumed in North American culture; second, that the duality is connected with other dualities, especially female and male; and third, that the natural result is for one side or the other to be undervalued or ignored.

The way out of these problems may actually be led by women and religious educators themselves. The basic thesis of this article is that the oppression of women is related to the sacred-public duality and that the contributions of women can contribute to a sacred-public unity. Paulo Freire argues that liberation cannot be brought about by oppressors; the oppressed must lead the struggle for their own liberation and that of the oppressors.[2] Freire's view points to the essential role of women in leading liberation struggles, especially for the liberation of women, the liberation of a feminised profession, and the liberation of religious communities from a worldview that dichotomises the sacred and the public. Religious education theory about the sacred and the public needs to be re-envisioned by feminist women and men, and religious education practice needs to bring forth new contributions from women. We need to name a new reality and live toward it.

The basic challenges in this work will be to rediscover the sacredness of all reality and the public dimensions of all that is sacred. This moves beyond calling religious educators to participate in both realms, bringing a little of each into their work; the calling is to seek and foster unity between the sacred and the public.

Problem of dualisms

We live in a culture for which dualistic thinking is taken for granted. People assume dualisms between mind and body, between the individual and community, and between personal and social responsibility. We should not be surprised, therefore, that dualistic thinking about the sacred and public spheres is all-pervasive. Such dualistic thinking has had particular impact in religious education, which has given fervent attention to matters internal to the sacred institutions of church and synagogue. Charles Foster attributed this dynamic in North American Christianity to the prevalent assumption that the social context of the Christian communities is relatively stable and secure, and that the leaders in religious education are needed primarily to maintain and extend the life of the institutions.[3] Whatever the causes, the tendency of religious educators to focus on the sacred, and usually private, realm is often done at the expense of attending to the public realm. When this takes place, the public realm is relatively secure from the critique and reforms of religious communities.

Duality between the sacred and the public

Dualistic thinking about the sacred and the public realms is so common as to be taken for granted in the United States. This has been particularly evident since the industrial revolution of the nineteenth century, during which both women and religion were marginalised to the private sphere. Susan Thistlethwaite, building on the work of Ann Douglas, drew a correspondence between the privatisation of religion and of women, neither of which made obvious contributions to industrial capitalism. This, coupled with dominant ideas about the role of women in the education of children and in exerting moral/religious influence, led to the association of women and women's virtues with religion and religious education.[4]

Another dynamic contributing to the privatisation of sacred communities in the United States may be the concern for religious freedom. Since the founding of the country, attempts to separate church and state have been sustained by public opinion, the law and the Constitution. In the interest of religious freedom, the government has sought to minimise ties between the religious and public institutions so that neither would meddle in the affairs of the other. Of course, the very fact that the language about that separation is the language of 'church and state' points to one way in which the separation has not been fully complete. The language betrays the nation's assumption that it is dealing with Christian churches and the religious freedom among them. The recognition of other religious communities and their freedoms has come rather late in our history. An analysis of civil religion in the United States reveals further that the expressed desire for religious freedom has been oriented more particularly to religious freedom among Protestant Christian churches. Roman Catholic observers have been particularly astute about the way in which the Protestant beliefs and ethos have pervaded civil religion and the institutions of the state, even while the separation of church and state was being espoused.[5]

Despite the lack of complete separation between religious institutions and the state, the value of separation and the assumption that the separation is possible have persisted in popular ideology. Interestingly, the most vocal questioning of the separation ideology has come from Protestant Christians themselves, who have in recent years seen the demise of what they call Christian (or religious) values in the public schools and who decry what they call the secular humanist tendencies of these schools. They have begun to encourage new models for the church-state relationships in public education, believing that public support of the educational institutions of various religious communities will offer a much needed alternative to the secularised public schools in the United States.[6]

This movement of recent years only serves to accent the assumed duality between the sacred and public spheres, which has been institutionalised in this country by the careful separation of church and state. Such dualistic thinking is not so easily presumed in other parts of the world. Even in other parts of North America, such as Canada, the situation is different and the radical separation between church and state is not written into law in the same radical way.

One of the most vivid examples of non-dualistic thinking about the sacred and public spheres is found in Africa. In Africa the separation of the spiritual realm from other aspects of life would be unthinkable.[7] Kenya, for example, has neither a state religion nor a complete separation between religious communities and the state. In that country, the language of partnership is used to describe the relationship between the secular state and the churches and mosques. In fact, the national motto, *harambee*, is used to describe how the various religious communities and the state need to unify or pull together for the good of everyone. In the villages, the spirit of *harambee* is invoked when a Christian church and Muslim mosque decide to work together on a project for the people of that village.

At the national level, the Kenyan government leaders have themselves been confessing Christians, and the relationship of the government with Christian churches has been more actively articulated than the relationships with other religious communities. This has been particularly true in public education.[8] Increasingly, however, the relationship of the government's public schools to the mosques has been discussed and encouraged. At present, the government's Department of Religious Education has formal ties with the Christians, Muslims and Hindus. All three religious groups work with the government in developing the syllabi and examinations in religious education. This arrangement makes it possible for school children and youth to receive religious instruction in any one of these faith traditions. The arrangement also makes it possible for the government to require religious education for all of its young people without imposing one particular set of religious beliefs.

So far, the statement about the relations between the state and religious communities may sound like a manifesto for stronger relationships. It is not. In fact, the argument is intended to illustrate the depth of dualistic thinking in the United States and the complexity of the issues. In a country like the United States, where dualistic thinking is taken for granted, certain subtle relationships between the sacred and public realms go unexamined (such as the pervasive influence of white Anglo-Saxon Protestantism). In a country such as Kenya, where the dualistic thinking is not engrained, the relationships between sacred and public realms are more visible, but no less complex. The issue of equitable treatment of different religious groups still arises.

Duality between female and male

The dualistic habits of thought may seem rather innocuous until one begins to push below the surface to recognise the interconnections among our favourite dualisms and the consequences of dualistic thinking for the distribution of power and value. In this section we will examine the dualistic patterns of thinking about female and male and particularly the way in which this dualism interplays with the sacred-public dualism.

The differential way of dealing with women and men and the restrictions of women to the private realm are well-documented in the biblical texts from which Jews and Christians build their traditions. These patterns are also quite evident in the later developments within both traditions. Similar patterns have been analysed in other religious traditions, but these will not be elaborated here. The attention here will be given to three biblical-historical cases from Jewish and Christian traditions that highlight the problem. The first will be elaborated in some detail, and the other two will be cited briefly.

Private-public and female-male patterns in early Christianity

The first case is drawn from private-public patterns of relationship in early Christianity. These have been analysed by Elisabeth Schüssler Fiorenza in connection with female-male relationships. She recognised how early Christianity inherited the Aristotelian patriarchal model of society in which the state, or public sphere, was considered more elevated in the hierarchy than the household, or private sphere. Furthermore, the public sphere was the arena for freeborn and propertied males who were heads of households. The private sphere was the arena for women, children and slaves, in that order. The early Christians lived in the tension between the patriarchal structures of the Greco-Roman world and the egalitarian currents with the Christian community itself.[9]

Out of this Aristotelian hierarchy grew a more heavily layered hierarchy in the church. In this hierarchy, the religious realm led by the clergy was seen as superior over the secular realm in which the laity lived. This pattern grew up in the Constantinian period, which saw the merging of church and state. The merging of church and state meant that the public and religious spheres were now united, and public religious leaders were at the top of the hierarchy. Within the public religious sphere many layers of hierarchy existed, with the Pope at the top, moving down to the clergy, and, finally, the nuns and sisters. The private secular sphere also had its gradations, with the laymen in the superior position, followed by their wives and mothers, by single women and, finally, by non-Christians.[10]

This analysis has been corroborated by Karen Torjesen, whose study of the Greco-Roman world of the early centuries of the Christian era indicated that women often had considerable power in the private arena but were carefully restricted in public life. She deduced this through the documents reprimanding women who had inappropriately crossed the boundaries into the public sphere.[11]

The descriptions offered by Fiorenza and Torjesen not only point to the radical separation of public and private arenas and the superior power given to the public sphere, but they point to the way in which the hierarchy of public over private fits neatly with other hierarchies: male over female, master over slave, and clergy over laity. The existence of this kind of cultural system, which increasingly became the church's system, underlines the radicalness of certain subversive elements of the biblical account.

Fiorenza accentuated the subversive elements in her feminist approach to historical reconstruction. She cited evidence that the house church in early Christianity was actually a discipleship of equals that stood over against the dominant culture. She said:[12]

> The early Christian vision of the discipleship of equals practised in the house church attracted especially slaves and women to Christianity but also caused tensions and conflicts with the dominant cultural ethos of the patriarchal household ... In fact, it was the religious ethos – of equality – that was transferred to and came in conflict with the patriarchal ethos of the household. The Christian missionary movement thus provided an alternative vision and praxis to that of the dominant society and religion.

The reconstructive work of Fiorenza has raised awareness of a liberating praxis in early Christianity that is not commonly discussed by biblical interpreters. But her work also leads to questions of why this more liberating strand is so little discussed and recognised, especially in light of the lengthy discussions throughout Christian history of the household codes urging wives to be subject to their husbands, children to their parents, and slaves to their masters (Ephesians 5:21 to 6:9). The household codes have formed the rationale for much doctrine on family and human relationships, but the house church has not been a dominant image or a primary source of doctrine.

The widow of Zarephath

The picture does not look any brighter when one looks at the trajectory of interpretation of other potentially radicalising biblical texts. One such story has been regularly explained without direct reference to the woman in the story, except as an example of how a very lowly person can be touched and used by God. This is the story of the poor widow of Zarephath who fed Elijah during the drought in the land (I Kings 17:8–16).

We know that widows in the ancient Middle East were at the bottom of the social scale in terms of social benefits, and they were severely restricted in their economic rights and social movement. Laws protected others from their potential attraction or subversion.[13] Though the laws in Israel were somewhat less restrictive than in surrounding nations, they were restrictive all the same.[14] Likewise, we know that the social situation of widows and the restrictions on them in the early Christian church were similarly restrictive and placed them near the bottom of the social hierarchical scale. In all of these contexts the widow was to stay very strictly within the private sphere.

The low social position of a widow and the even lower position of a poor and foreign widow underlines the radicality of the story of the widow of Zarephath. Strangely, most commentators emphasise that this is a story about Elijah, speaking of his power and presence with the widow that gave her the faith and ability to continue feeding him when the supply of grain and oil seemed to be at an end.[15] No mention is made of the way this woman's actions, restricted as they were to the private sphere, mediated God's gifts to Elijah and had public consequences. No mention is made of the social structures that oppressed the widow in the first place.

The woman with a haemorrhage

Another such story is the healing of the woman with the haemorrhage (Matthew 9:20–22, Mark 5:25–34, Luke 8:43–48). We know that women who were in their menstrual cycle were restricted from public interchange and religious rituals in Jewish tradition, and they were considered unclean.[16] The woman with a haemorrhage, then, was restricted to the private realm and was considered a public outcast. In fact, she was restricted from both the sacred and the public realms insofar as the sacred was itself public. She was permitted only the private sacred practices.

The outcast position of a woman during her menstrual period underlines the radical courage of this woman with an unending haemorrhage who touched Jesus' garment in order to be healed. But again, the attention of the commentators has not been drawn to the courage of the woman or the radicalness of this message for the social structures of the day. Attention has been focused instead on the care of Jesus for such a lowly one and his concern for saving and healing the unfortunate.[17]

As long as these stories of the widow of Zarephath and the woman with a haemorrhage are kept in the private sacred sphere, we can easily ignore their implications for the public sphere. The public holiness of Elijah and of Jesus are featured and also the way in which their holiness touched the private lives of two particular women. The holiness of the women themselves goes unrecognised, and the public structures that led these women to be outcast and lowly in the first place goes uncritiqued. We should not wonder why these texts have received less attention than others and why their radical public nature has been softened. The capacity of these texts to subvert the public order is great.

Valuing of public and male over sacred and female

Not only have dualisms existed between the sacred and the public, and not only have these been connected with other dualisms such as female and male, but the dualisms have contributed to patterns of devaluation and discrimination. Dualistic thinking makes it easy to value one part of a dualism over another. The two parts of the dualism are considered as so separate that they need not be considered as interrelated or mutually dependent. In this case, the public sphere is seen as relatively unaffected by what goes on in the private/sacred sphere; thus, politics and religion can easily be separated, as can a person's public and private life. Female and male are seen as such discrete categories that they can easily be set apart in different spheres of life with different roles and different valuations.

This analysis may not seem obvious to persons who have not themselves experienced these patterns of discrimination. Two examples may serve to describe the way in which these patterns can function. One comes out of the Jewish community and the other from China. The two examples are drawn from different communities in order to reflect how broad and pervasive the problems actually are.

Karen Fox described how the separation of private and public domains has perpetuated certain patterns of sexual exclusion within the Jewish community. She said, 'For 5,000 years women were involved in the private domain of Jewish life while men controlled the public arenas.'[18] She explained that women were given responsibility for home and family, but until relatively recent years, they were restricted from being counted in the prayer quorum, from witnessing, and from voting and being elected in synagogue. When the Reform Movement arose in Judaism between 1860 and 1880, it began to address the public religious responsibilities and roles of women; however, ordination did not become possible until 1973 within that Reform Movement.[19] Fox's historical description offers evidence of how easily the separation of the public and private areas, and the corresponding association of the public with males and the private with females, is based upon discriminatory restrictions on women.

The story from China is one that was shared by Pui Lan Kwok, who was told the story by a journalist:[20]

> Ah Ching is a little girl who lives in a village in China. Her parents are hard-working peasants. Ah Ching's father likes the little girl but he wants to have a son. One night when Ah Ching was asleep, she suddenly felt a heavy blanket pulling over her and she could hardly breathe. She struggled and yelled, 'Mama, Mama, help, help me!' To her amazement, she found out the one who tried to suffocate her was her father! She cried and prayed that her father would let her go and promised to be a nice girl.
>
> Ah Ching was so afraid that when the dawn broke, she escaped from the farm house and she went to seek rescue from her old grandma. When the grandma heard the story, she was so sorrowful that tears began to run down her wrinkled cheeks. The night came, grandma put Ah Ching to bed and comforted her. But at midnight grandma, summoning all her strength, suffocated Ah Ching with an old blanket with her trembling hands.

Pui Lan Kwok explains this story in terms of China's attempt to deal with overpopulation by lowering the birth rate. Since couples are restricted to having only one child, the birth of a girl means that the family's genealogy will come to an end.[21]

The story and the explanation give obvious evidence of the valuing of male over female, but on closer look, the story reveals more than that. It reveals a valuing of the public over the private and sacred as well. What is at issue is the public existence of a family's name, which supersedes the value of one person and the sacredness of life. Again, we see the pattern of the public valued over the private or sacred and of male valued over female.

Rosemary Radford Ruether described these patterns of devaluation and pointed out how dehumanising they are. She demonstrated how morality and religion have been pushed into the private sphere alongside women. Christian virtue, the institutional church and the clergy are privatised in this same process, while the public world of business and politics and power are seen as something quite separate.[22] She concluded this analysis with a recognition of the cultural impact of such patterns: 'The alienation of women culminates in the dehumanisation of society.'[23]

The ironic twist to Ruether's analysis is that the vary same patterns that serve to isolate women and religion in the private sphere also serve to place responsibility on them to solve the problems of the public sphere. While kept powerless and dependent in the public realm, women are often asked to provide remedies for public ills, such as the ecological crises. Ruether warned:[24]

Women should look with considerable suspicion upon the ecological band-aids presently being peddled by business and government to overcome the crisis of exploitive technology. The ideology which splits private morality from public business will try to put the burden of ecological morality on the private sector. To compensate for the follies of the system, the individual consumers will be asked to tighten their belts; the system itself will not be challenged to change. Changes in the consumption patterns of the home can only be tokenism, since ecological immorality belongs to the patterns of production and social exploitation that is systemic.

The problem of privatisation, then, is exacerbated by the extra burdens that are placed on those individuals and institutions that are privatised.

The consequences of all of these patterns for religious education are probably obvious. This is a field that is mostly peopled by women, and it is part of the life of the privatised religious institutions. Thus, it is subject to devaluation in more than one way. Susan Thistlethwaite pointed out that the openness of the religious education field to women and its association with feminine virtues, such as maternal nurture, places religious education in 'double jeopardy'.[25] She concluded, 'Religious education is the wife of the church.'[26]

When one puts that picture in the cultural context where religion itself is marginalised into the private realm, one sees a rather bleak vista. The issue is the powerlessness and ineffectiveness of the private sacred sphere, and also the powerlessness and ineffectiveness of religious education, when it is the private sphere within the private sphere. Religious education too often becomes the margin of the margins.

The road ahead

The picture I have drawn is indeed bleak, and some attention to the road ahead is necessary for hope and perhaps even for survival. The promise in the title of this article is that feminist theology may offer some hope for the unity of the sacred and the public. So where is the hope?

I suggest that the feminist analysis itself offers some hope. It points to the artificiality and oppressiveness of dualisms between the sacred and the public and between female and male. It points to the possibility that the sacred and public can be seen in unity. This is not a new idea, however, waiting to be discovered by feminists. Jack Seymour, Robert O'Gorman and Charles Foster trace this kind of thinking to George Albert Coe and William Clayton Bower, both of whom believed that 'religion is intrinsic to the social process'.[27] In their own work, these three modern authors projected a relationship between the church and the education of the public based on an inherent relationship between religion and public life.

What is contributed from feminist theology to this discussion? The feminist offering is this: an analysis of the human and ecological destruction caused by the dualisms (signs of disaster), an awareness of strands of tradition that subvert the reigning dualisms (signs of hope), an interpretation of some of the obstacles to unity (signs of warning), and an alternative view of the world and church praxis in which the sacred and the public are held together in unity (signs of possibility). Fundamental to this feminist view are the ideas that all reality is sacred and that everything sacred has public dimensions.

The feminist view put forth here does point to the road ahead. The road is filled with challenges for religious educators who would seek the unity of sacred and public. Some of these challenges are offered here in conclusion, but the list is only a beginning. It is really an invitation for others to join in the process of naming the role of religious education in unifying the sacred and the public. The challenges for religious education are as follows.

First, name the potential destructiveness of the sacred-public dualism. This article is not merely concerned with two spheres of life that would be nice to hold together. The sacred and public dimensions of life can actually be destructive when separated. The first challenge, then, is to reject the false notion that the privatisation of religion is healthy for society. Such privatisation hampers any attempts by religious communities to address questions of value in the public sphere. It further hampers any critique of the religious community's private sacred life. This is dangerous, because the sacred community's lifestyle may well be reinforcing patriarchal and restrictive patterns in public life.

One specific way of naming the danger of dualisms is to recognise that sexist language is not simply a private matter; in fact, it affects public attitudes toward women. The reform of language, then, can potentially lead to a more inclusive worldview and a more inclusive relationship between women and men.

Another way of naming the dualisms as dangerous is to recognise the public influence of sacred doctrine. Doctrines of God, for example, often become patterns for human relationships. The image of Christ as the head of the church became Paul's metaphor for the husband-wife relationship in Ephesians 5:23–24: 'For the husband is the head of the wife as Christ is the head of the church ... As the church is subject to Christ, so let wives also be subject in everything to their husbands.' Just as reforming language can potentially transform male-female relationships, reforming doctrine can potentially transform the way we value and relate to the world. The failure to critique language and doctrine can lead to public life that is destructive.

Second, recognise the subverting tendencies within the religious tradition itself. Stories from the Jewish and Christian traditions, such as the widow of Zarephath and the healing of the woman with a haemorrhage, suggest the value of women in God's eyes. Certainly these women were valued more in these stories of encounter with God and Jesus than they were in the social order of their day. Furthermore, the widow of Zarephath reminds us of how private acts of feeding can have public meaning and consequences. The healing of the woman with a haemorrhage reminds us of how often the public rejection and exclusion of a person was superseded by Jesus's actions toward that person.

We have already discussed the subversive nature of the house church in early Christianity. The analysis of Elisabeth Schüssler Fiorenza reveals how the house church threatened to subvert the patriarchal public order. By remembering this subversive movement, we can discover a bold critique of our present public order, as well as a vision and hope for reform.

Third, recognise the obstacles that move against the unifying of sacred and public. Persons find it difficult to introduce virtues and insight from the sacred realm into the public. The efforts of religious communities to influence public policy are often seen as naïve, or they are ignored altogether. Simple recognition of the obstacles in sacred-public discourse is helpful in overcoming them.

One vivid effort to overcome the private-public split is Julia Ward Howe's Mother's Day Proclamation, delivered in Boston in 1870. The occasion was the first Mother's Day, when mothers gathered to protest war. Howe said:[28]

> Arise, then, women of this day! Arise all women who have hearts, whether your baptism be that of water or of tears! Say firmly, 'We will not have great questions decided by irrelevant agencies; our husbands shall not come to us, reeking with carnage, for caresses and applause. Our sons shall not be taken from us to unlearn all that we have been able to teach them of charity, mercy and patience.'

Julia Ward Howe's words were her own attempt to overcome obstacles and to enter private sacred virtues into the public sphere where decisions were being made regarding war and peace. The very fact that Mother's Day has been relegated into the private sacred realm speaks of how persistent the obstacles can be. Howe's story is silenced.

Fourth, offer an alternative view of the world and church praxis in which the sacred and public are held together in unity. This task has two dimensions. One is to seek the holy in public life, or to reverence the sacredness of all creation. Concretely, this means that we seek God in all places, we respect God's creation, and we seek to respond to God's call in everything we do. The theme named here as feminist is also a major theme in the proposals of Seymour, O'Gorman and Foster. They speak of sacramental imagination as a way by which we name the mystery of the holy.[29] The sacramental imagination could certainly be fed by feminist theologising on the sacredness of creation.

The second way to offer an alternative view is to reform our sacred communities so that they model for the whole public a new way of being in the world. Underlying such reforms would be the assumption that everything sacred has public influence. The challenge, of course, is to critique and reform our church praxis, as well as to allow ourselves to be critiqued and transformed by those subversive, sacred traditions that are so easy to ignore.

These and other challenges are left with religious educators to work out in practice. No community is better suited to address the sacred-public split than one that has been so affected by it, one that has often been on the margin of the margins.

Notes

1. The increasing numbers of women in the profession of religious education and the corresponding rise of patterns of discrimination and devaluation are described in Dorothy Jean Furnish, *DRE/DCE: History of a Profession*, Nashville, Christian Educators' Fellowship, 1976, pp. 39–41; David W Danner and Clarisse Croteau-Chonka, 'A data-based picture: women in parish education', *Religious Education, 76*, 1981, pp. 369–381; and Susan Thistlethwaite, 'The feminization of American religious education', *Religious Education, 76*, 1981, pp. 391–398.

2. Paulo Freire, *Pedagogy of the Oppressed*, New York, Seabury, 1970, pp. 39–42.

3. Charles Foster, *Teaching in the Community of Faith*, Nashville, Abingdon Press, 1982, pp. 10–11.

4. Susan Thistlethwaite, *op. cit.*, pp. 392–394.

5. One helpful analysis of this is found in Jack L Seymour, Robert T O'Gorman and Charles R Foster, *The Church in the Education of the Public*, Nashville, Abingdon Press, 1984, pp. 18–19. These authors describe the Roman Catholic approach to the dilemma as one of educating a public within the public. See particularly, pp. 19 and 67–93.

6. See, for example, Gordon Spykman, Rockne McCarthy, Donald Oppenwall and Walfred Peterson, *Society, State and Schools*, Grand Rapids, Michigan, Eerdmans, 1981.

7. The unity of sacred and secular is an oft-repeated theme. John Pobee noted that Africa is a characteristically religious continent, though highly pluralistic in religious forms. See John S Pobee, *Religion in a Pluralistic Society*, Leiden, E J Brill, 1976, p. vii. Geoffrey Parrinder described this phenomenon in terms of spirits, or powers. In African thought, all powers (divine and human and natural) are understood to be interrelated. For this reason, an easy separation of material and spiritual, secular and sacred, is not possible. See Geoffrey Parrinder, *Religion in Africa*, Harmondsworth, Penguin, 1969, p. 47; see also pp. 26–27. A similar theme of religion's permeating all of life is found in David B Barrett, George K Mambo, Janice McLaughlin and Malcolm J McVeigh (eds), *Kenya Churches Handbook: the development of Kenyan Christianity 1498–1973*, Kisumu, Kenya, Evangel Publishing House, 1973, pp. 291–292.

8. Cooperative work between Christian churches and the state is particularly evident in the areas of education, medicine, social work and rural development. One clear description of the *harambee* relationship between church and state is found in Bishop Rafael Ndingi, 'Church and state in Kenya', in *Kenya Churches Handbook*, pp. 43–48. A discussion of the particular relationship between church and state in education is found in Thomas Farelly, 'Religious education in the schools', in *Kenya Churches Handbook*, pp. 49–58. Farrelly cited the Kenya Education Commission Report of 1964 and The Education Act of 1968 which outlined the churches' continuing role in 'sponsoring' schools and providing religious education. In these documents, the rights of parents to have children excused for religious observances and instruction was guaranteed, and the difference between the kinds of religious education offered by church and mosque and that offered in the public schools was delineated.

9. These are recurring themes for Fiorenza. See particularly Elisabeth Schüssler Fiorenza, *In Memory of Her*, New York, Crossroads, 1983, pp. 91–92, 245–279; Elizabeth Schüssler Fiorenza, *Bread Not Stone*, Boston, Beacon Press, 1984, pp. 70–83.

10. Elizabeth Schüssler Fiorenza developed these ideas in an unpublished lecture, delivered in a seminar on Feminist Issues in Biblical Theology, Immaculate Heart College, Los Angeles, August 3, 1984.

11. Karen Torjesen, *When Women were Priests: women's leadership in the early church and the scandal of their subordination in the rise of Christianity*, San Francisco, Harper, 1993.

12. Elizabeth Schüssler Fiorenza, *In Memory of Her*, New York, Crossroads, 1983, p. 251.

13. One example of severe suspicion and restriction of widows is found in the *Babylonian Talmud*. Widows were told they should not rear dogs for fear that their heathen male neighbours would frequent their houses and use the dogs immorally when the woman was not at home. Likewise, widows were told not to house students for fear that the widow might tempt the student out of his modesty. See Isidore Epstein (ed.), 'Abodad Zarah', *The Babylonian Talmud*, London, The Soncino Press, 1935, volume 29, p. 114.

14. The Jewish Law provided for some protection and maintenance of the widow, but also for limits on her ownership and movement. Sigal has noted, for example, that the husband's estate was to be used to sustain his widow, but that the rights to inherit and to be free from dependence on her children were not hers. In Jerusalem and Galilee the children inherited and the widow was maintained. See Phillip Sigal, 'Elements of male chauvinism in classical Halakhah', *Judaism*, 24, 1975, pp. 226–244; here pp. 229–230.

15. The emphasis is placed on Elijah's words and acts by Simon J DeVries, *Word Biblical Commentary*, Waco, Word Publishers, 1985, pp. 216–217. Simon J DeVries deals with the text primarily as a prophet–authorisation narrative demonstrating Elijah's power (see p. 207). Other commentators also focus on Elijah rather than the widow. See also Burke Long, *I Kings With an Introduction to Historical Literature*, Grand Rapids, Michigan, Eerdmans, 1984, pp. 181–182; Edith Deen, *All of the Women of the Bible*, New York, Harper and Row, 1955, p. 134; Edith Deen, *The Bible's Legacy for Womanhood*, Garden City, Doubleday, 1969. Deen understood the widow to be instructed and empowered by Elijah's teaching.

16. See, for example, Leviticus 15:19–31. The fact that the woman was ritually unclean is particularly noted by some of the early twentieth century gospel commentators: Allan Menzies, *The Earliest Gospel*, New York, MacMillan, 1901, p. 125; G Campbell Morgan, *The Gospel According to Mark*, New York, Fleming H Revell, 1927, p. 124.

17. Emphasis is often placed on Jesus' sensitivity and compassion. See, for example, G Campbell Morgan, *The Gospel According to Mark*, New York, Fleming H Revell, 1927, pp. 124–130; A E J Rawlinson, *St Mark*, London, Methuen, 1942, pp. 67–69. One commonly used commentary emphasises both Jesus' compassion and the woman's faith, but raises some questions about the faith that suspiciously borders on magic or delayed action. See George A Buttrick, *The Interpreter's Bible*, Nashville, Abingdon Press, 1951, volume 7, pp. 357–358, 720–722; *Ibid.* (1952), volume 8, pp. 161–162.

18. Karen L Fox, 'Whither woman rabbis?', *Religious Education*, 76, 1981, p. 361.

19. *Ibid.*, pp. 336–362.

20. Pui Lan Kwok, 'God weeps with our pain', *East Asia Journal of Theology*, 2, 1984, pp. 228–232; here p. 228.

21. *Ibid.*

22. Rosemary Radford Ruether, *New Woman New Earth*, New York, Seabury Press, 1975, pp. 22–23; see also 196–204.

23. *Ibid.*, p. 23.

24. *Ibid.*, p. 200.

25. Susan Thistlethwaite, *op. cit.*, p. 397; see also pp. 392–396.

26. *Ibid.*, p. 397.

27. Jack L Seymour, Robert T O'Gorman and Charles R Foster, *The Church in the Education of the Public*, Nashville, Abingdon Press, 1984, p. 115.

28. Julia Ward Howe, 'Mother's day proclamation', reprinted by the Commission on the Status and Role of Women, United Methodist Church, 1870.

29. Jack L Seymour, Robert T O'Gorman and Charles R Foster, *The Church in the Education of the Public*, Nashville, Abingdon Press, 1984, pp. 125–153.

6.2 Feminist images of redemption in education

Mary C Grey

Prologue

The theme of this special issue first prompts the historical question as to the extent to which women have been and are included within the whole educational enterprise. Seeking for images of women excluded from the educational scene, I do not have far to look: my own aunts from the north of England were excluded by poverty from secondary education. So I appreciated this as a prominent theme in the work of women novelists, women's struggle for access to education. I felt the contrast between my own good fortune and that of George Eliot's Maggie Tulliver, prevented from going to school, absorbing crumbs of learning from the books of the unappreciative Tom.[1] I believed passionately in Virginia Woolf's re-creation of Shakespeare's sister, similarly dependent on the learning of the fortunate bard, and mourned her undeserved fate.[2]

Yet the struggle for women to enter the academy is far from over: Chaim Potok, the Jewish novelist, in his latest novel *Davita's Harp*,[3] describes a young Jewish girl's successful courageous gesture in reciting *Kaddish* in the synagogue for her dead father, a practice strictly reserved for men, but also her unsuccessful attempt to win a coveted academic prize, which she justly merited: it could not be awarded to her by her Yeshiva Academy simply because she was a girl. But the story of women and education is not simply one of struggles for inclusion and equal rights. The feminist contribution is first and foremost about re-setting the terms of the discussion itself. Alice Walker shows this in a moving essay, 'A writer because of, not in spite of, her children', which tells the story of a Nigerian novelist, Buchi Emeta, and her book *Second Class Citizen*.[4] What she admires about this woman, whose struggle for education makes her doubly an outsider, from her own family, and from the British people she meets, is that she regards her children not as *distractions* but as *contributions* to her work:[5]

> Since this novel is written to the adults her children will become, it is okay with her if the distractions and joys they represent in her life become part of it .... In this way she integrates the profession of writer into the cultural concept of mother/worker she retains from Ibo society. Just as the African mother has traditionally planted crops, pounded maize and done her washing with her baby strapped to her back, so Adah can write a novel with her children in the same room.

It is with this double notion of exclusion, of being an Outsider, and of re-setting the boundaries of the discussion that I begin this study of feminist images of redemption in education. I do so with the conviction that 'redemption' evokes a very positive dimension in terms of human integrity, a dimension which reaches out across the boundaries of culture and religion, lifting areas of failure and brokenness into realms of achievement, celebration and hope.

Redemption as reclaiming

With the word 'redemption' I argue that there is a spiritual vision of education to be reclaimed. Yet the concept of *redemption* in a secular British society has largely lost the central focus which it derived historically from both the Jewish and Christian religion. Again, in a multi-cultural, multi-faith society we can no longer be characterised by the Christian term, the 'Easter People', even if Christian liturgical renewal rightly stresses bringing back Easter as its central sacramental focus. Yet I believe that contemporary feminist theology is offering new images of redemption at a time when the educational scene is unarguably under strain.

The first image is that of reclaiming, of recovering. What needs recovering, above all, is this lost vision for education. Teachers today perceive themselves at the mercy of conflicting demands, while pupils feel disenchanted with what they see as dwindling job possibilities and a curriculum shrinking to meet both government demands and market forces. Education as an holistic process has, in many cases, been lost sight of or never encountered. Even if, historically speaking, models of education have broken free from either predominantly monastic or military models, with the creative experiments of Maria Montessori, Rudolph Steiner and others, with some exceptions, such creativity has often been extinguished through lack of resources or siphoned off into the private sector.

Second, the activity of reclaiming means recovering the educational process as an activity spanning the whole life-cycle, not merely to be reserved for school years. So the question of access to education is clearly crucial, not only for women after the child-rearing years: the experience of poor Third World communities highlights the relationship between education and taking responsibility for community problems. It has long been recognised that girls ought to be educated because of the influence they can exert over growing children, with the mother of King Alfred the Great a shining example given in Britain! But what is rapidly coming to the fore in places like Nicaragua and El Salvador, for example, is the role which women are playing as agents of social change. For this process education is vital. In Britain the education departments of CAFOD and Christian Aid are commendably trying to support these efforts in their educational programmes. This in turn throws into relief the need to reclaim a variety of *spaces* for education. While many schools are suffering unjustly from sub-standard premises and shortage of the simplest of facilities, like a piece of chalk, feminist groups, in reclaiming a variety of living spaces for education (such as kitchens), are pointing out that education is far wider than the academy. Adah, Buchi Emeta's heroine, could write with her children playing in the room. Emily Brontë, perhaps the most mystical of nineteenth century poets, could compose her poems while baking bread, her arms deep in flour.

Third, we reclaim education as a process to which *women* have contributed. This means recovering the contribution of women, like Octavia Hill,[6] to educational processes through the centuries. Within faith-communities, for example, this means painstakingly piecing together the picture of how women have participated in the process of handing on the faith: it means highlighting the leadership roles exhibited by Jewish women in the Scriptures, as well as their great contribution to Jewish learning in history; it means valuing the ministerial and catechetical roles of Christian martyrs like Perpetua in second century Carthage, the educational roles of the great Saxon Abbesses like Hilda of Whitby, as well as the more recent founding of the great teaching orders of women, originally for the education of poor girls. But this is only to speak of the great; there are also the innumerable untold stories of women in poor communities who have kept alive the love of learning, kindled the spark of creativity in their children, when their own lives were crushed by back-breaking physical work.

So the task means assessing realistically the contribution of women to the development of the teaching of science, history and languages. This will mean recognising the contribution women have always made as primary educators of their children's linguistic development, values and world-picture. It means the recovering and remembering of the wisdom of the 'raging stoic grandmothers', [7] that handing-on of wisdom from mother to daughter which is never given recognition as being of educational value. And if there are gaps and silences, it means discovering what has happened to the lost contribution of women, the areas where there are no contributions, and mourning their absence and the structures which are responsible.[8]

But most of all, it is about reclaiming, through feminist thinking, that spiritual vision of the wholeness of the human person for which the educational process aims. Feminist theory refuses to split the human personality through dualistic divisions, to separate, in a damaging way, matter and spirit, mind and body, stimulating the one (mind) and either tolerating or despising the other (body). Having been for centuries identified by theology with the body, and therefore with nature, the weaker sex, intellectually inferior, it is understandable that women's entry into education has largely meant striving for intellectual achievement alone, rejecting identification with bodily qualities, yet not challenging the limitations of former educational presuppositions.

Feminist thinking attempts to reclaim despised female sexuality, to redeem bodiliness as a positive dimension in the educational process. To do so we have to reclaim a sense of connectedness with these bodily processes and a sense of embodiment in the environment as redeeming strength, what Mary Daly calls 'elemental energy',[9] before there can be any movement forward.

In order to do this, the prerequisite is a positive sense of self.

Redemption as self-affirmation

Of all the images of redemption offered here, this probably strikes the deepest chord. Every teacher recognises the significance of positive self-image in the learning process. Nor would it be claimed that women alone suffer from low or negative self-image: numerous children from minority ethnic groups find their language, religion and culture unrecognised at school, despite the efforts of a small number of gifted teachers to implement multi-cultural and multi-racial policies. How are they to develop a sense of self-worth in the face of the dominant culture? As well as this, the extreme competitive ethic in many schools will inevitably inflict a negative self-image on those who cannot measure up to its academic rigours. In addition, it is lamentable that bullying still continues in some schools: where this prevails, in verbal or physical intimidation in classroom or playground, positive self-images are literally beaten out of developing pupils.

Because women have suffered throughout history from low self-image, due not only to experience in schools but also to family relationships and employment situations, the feminist cry 'self-development is better than self-sacrifice'[10] is a particularly crucial one for the educational process. Numerous feminist writings document this struggle for a positive sense of self-worth from an existential situation of no-self or self-loathing. Virginia Woolf speaks of the discovery of '"moments of being" embedded in many more elements of non-being'.[11] In religious terms I see this as the discovery and affirmation of oneself as God's good creation, in the midst of the debased forms of femaleness which surround us. Feminist writers reveal that this cannot happen without an actual redemptive process. Doris Lessing, in her five volume saga *The Children of Violence*,[12] charts the journey to self-realisation of Martha Quest, whose life had consisted of passive 'drifting' or irresponsibility, of being 'acted upon' and never making a 'connected' decision. At the end of a long and painful process, which comes to a climax in the fifth novel *The Four-gated City*, she expresses the insight that self-realisation can never be reached without coming to grips with the depths of one's own fears and 'inner demons':[13]

Where? But where? How? Who? No, but where, Where? ... Then

silence and the birth of a repetition. Where? Here. Here, where else, you poor fool, where else has it been ever ...?

But at the same time this revelation comes with the insight that self-becoming, the beginning of a sense of integrity, comes with a recognition that the evil which she has projected on to the exterior world is actually part of herself:[14]

> I am what the human race is. I am 'The Germans are the mirror and catalyst of Europe': also 'dirty Hun', 'Filthy Nazi'.

That self-realisation is accompanied by a sense of corporate involvement in human tragedy has significant implications for ethical responsibility.

Another example is the protagonist of Margaret Attwood's novel *Surfacing*: her self-image was so distorted that even her memory of events was blocked and falsified. After the painful redemptive process of climbing back to self-affirmation, she cries: 'This above all – to choose not to be victim.'[15]

This renunciation of the victim situation I see as crucial to the redemptive process. *Self-realisation, rejection of the victim situation* and *assumption of responsibility* are thus three core images of the redemptive journey.

Redemption as self-knowledge

For education, the aspect of self-affirmation which is of direct significance is that of self-knowledge. Self-knowledge has been frequently linked with spiritual vision. It is no coincidence that the figure of the woman mystic is being reclaimed as a source of power for women. The cultural meaning of the role of the woman mystic and teacher has enormous variations within Sufism, Hinduism, Buddhism, Sikhism, Judaism and Christianity,[16] and present investigation is uncovering the lives of women mystics both as source of empowerment for contemporary women, as well as inspiration to the development of a particular feminist mysticism.[17]

Catherine of Siena, the Italian mystic and reformer, and Teresa of Avila, the Spanish mystic, foundress of the Carmelite sisters, both stressed the importance of self-knowledge. Teresa of Avila wrote:[18]

> At the same time the matter of self-knowledge must never be neglected. No soul on this road is such a giant that it does not need to become a child at the breast again. ... And self-knowledge with regard to sin is the bread which must be eaten with food of every kind ... without this bread we could not eat our food at all.

Mary Ward, seventeenth century foundress of the first order of Christian religious sisters devoted to the education of poor girls, saw that it was difficult for women to come to self-definition, because of the effects of male definitions on the development of women.[19] She simply tells her sisters to pay no attention to them:

> You may know them by the fruits of their counsels. For what can this profit you, to tell you that you are but women, weak and able to do nothing, and that fervour will decay?

Here is a seventeenth century formulation of the educational psychological insight that pupils conform to what is expected of them and in many cases, grossly under-achieve. Hence Mary Ward warns that learning can corrupt knowledge, that women must 'unlearn' certain things, and look beyond the minds of men to the mind of God.

But what kind of knowing can be termed 'redemptive knowing'? Here I search for an epistemological method which harmonises with the theological categories of both redemption and creation. It is redemptive and healing for an abused child or adult to reclaim a lost sense of personal wholeness; it is at the same time creative to make dynamic those healing ways of knowing which remain operative for a life-time.

Again feminist thinking offers insight: Nelle Morton, a feminist theologian who recently died, has made famous in her theology the metaphor of 'hearing' as a redemptive tool in education. Morton claimed that hearing is ontologically prior to speech. It was hearing, listening, she said, which evoked the great creative word at the beginning of time. In her moving autobiographical work *The Journey is Home*,[20] she describes listening to a woman in a conscious-raising group who is telling her painful life-story. The woman:[21]

> seemed to suffer almost physically in the act of narration. Suddenly the woman narrowed her eyes and said to the group: 'I have a strange feeling you heard me before I started. You heard me to my own story.'

From this event, in which a woman knew herself 'heard all the way', Morton first received a totally new understanding of hearing and speaking.

But suppose this metaphor of being 'heard to speech' was not only relevant to situations of brokenness which called out for healing; suppose it characterised a holistic way of knowing, a wholeness which refused the divisions of cognitive and affective knowing. This is exactly what the authors of *Womens' Ways of Knowing*[22] suggest. They appeal to educational processes to help the person to disentangle 'received knowledge', which is handed-on from others, and then to assist the bringing-to-birth of the person's own voice, or way of knowing. How is he or she to know how and when to trust the inner voice of intuition, or the voice of reason; to move from separate knowing to what the writers name as 'connected knowing'? 'Connected knowing', far from being a passive form of knowledge, the knowledge of facts, will develop procedures for gaining access to other people's knowledge. These will depend on a capacity for empathy (p. 113) and for forbearance (p. 117). 'Connected knowers ... want to embrace the self in some ultimate sense of the whole' (p. 137).

In integrating the voices of reason, intuition and conflicting world-views, 'connected knowers' are able to construct reality, say the writers, and open 'mind and heart to embrace the world' (p. 141). What is redemptive here is both the process and what results from the process: for 'connected knowers' the knower and the known are held together in relationship. Hence self-knowledge, far from being a narcissistic focus on self, or merely a tool to assist the traumatised, could actually be the key to that authentic wisdom which links the person to 'reality' and transcends traditional dualisms of 'being' and 'doing'. Hence education is much more about empowering people to take responsibility for their choices and life-situations than about passing on quantities of information.

So what is the redemptive role of the teacher in fostering the process of coming to self-knowledge, to 'connected knowing'? The image of the teacher as 'midwife' is an inspiring one.[23] Here the teacher, instead of putting knowledge into a pupil's head (the so-called 'banking' model of teaching), evokes or draws out the evolving process of the birth of ideas. The emphasis is always on the end-achievement of the process, the 'baby', as belonging to the pupil, not the teacher. (A celebrated example would be the relationship between Helen Keller and her teacher, Annie Sullivan.) So the dynamics of the process are that of mutual empowerment. Whether the slow, painful birth of an idea springs from areas of science, languages or the humanities, the achievement in human terms is never divorced from either affective or intellectual processes.

Midwife teachers 'assist in the emergence of consciousness' (p. 218). They are concerned to preserve the vulnerable child. For this a distinctive way of thinking is demanded, which has been developed by Sara Ruddick as 'maternal thinking'.[24] Based on what she sees as the characteristics of mothers' relationships with children, Ruddick describes maternal thinking as:[25]

> a response to growth (and acceptance of change) along with a sort of learning that recognises change, development and the uniqueness of particular individuals and situations; resilient good humour and cheerfulness even in the face of conflict, the fragility of life, and the dangers inherent in the process of physical and mental growth.

Maternal thinking emphasises *attentive love*, responsive to the reality of the child, and *humility*, seen as selfless respect for reality. Applying maternal thinking to the midwife teacher means that the teacher will be the enabler of the creativity of the pupil. The teacher will be the nurturer of the birth of the achievement. This model of learning sees teacher and pupil as equally involved in the creative process; it has burst the bonds of education as merely oriented to *self*-achievement. So this model is 'redeeming' in its efforts to heal the old subject-object split inherited from Descartes: it moves us from a focus restricted to *self*-knowledge, *self*-affirmation to yet another feminist image of redemption.

Redemption as mutual empowerment

The process of arriving at the necessary self-knowledge and affirmation for living a responsible life can never be achieved by the individual in isolation, for we inhabit a universe which consists at its most basic level not of separate units, but of myriad interconnections. On every level of the educational process we depend on these levels of interconnection and the way in which they may operate positively or negatively in the life of the growing child.

On the most basic level of all, the environmental context is the setting for educational development. Yet until recently education has had an ambivalent relationship with the environment. 'Nature' entered the curriculum in the Primary school through awareness of seasons, ('new life' in spring, changing leaves in autumn), together with learning to care for baby animals, and a certain amount of interest in the plight of the seals and disappearing species. In the secondary curriculum Health and Sex Education have had an ambiguous effect in consciousness-raising about the environment. The study of biology, too, has an inbuilt ambiguity concerning animal rights. Currently, ecology programmes such as 'Watch' are inspiring a much more broad-based approach.

Feminist thinking invites a radical approach. So many aspects determine whether the environment is a nurturing or a positively damaging context. Is it actually safe, or a place of fear? Is it visually stultifying or stimulating? Feminist theology's emphasis on persons being *embodied* focuses on the qualitative possibilities of the learning space and perceptiveness as to physical well-being.

Feminist thought also demands a re-thinking of the kind of model of psychosexual development which has so far inspired education, asking if it sufficiently discerns gender, personal and social differences. While it seems that a young person must develop in a linear way, step by step, with achievable, testable goals, it is also true that a cyclical pattern is being enacted. At the same time there is a spiralling development occurring, by which we experience the same processes, physical, sexual or psychological, over and over again, but *in a different manner*. The complexity of these developmental processes is one of the reasons why a spirituality of education is necessary, which I believe can be rightly named as a 'spirituality of mutual empowerment'.

As regards the social and political environment of the school, its role within the community must be explored as well as the quality of inter-relating with parents and carers of pupils. It makes an enormous difference whether the learning process is contextualised in a rural or spacious setting or an over-crowded inner-city, where open spaces are unavailable.

In terms of the group environment, an individual pupil learns in the connectedness of the group, class or set: the relational pattern is clearly crucial, particularly as to whether or not this operates through-out the entire school or educational institute on purely competitive terms. Scott Peck, the American psychiatrist, in his book *The Different Drum*,[26] describes the difference which this can make to a child, when the relational scene fosters development. In this passage he has just transferred from Exeter Academy (USA), where he was very unhappy, to a small Quaker school ('Friends'):[27]

> Friends was the opposite of Exeter: it was a day school whereas Exeter was a boarding-school; it was small, whereas Exeter was large ... it was coeducational whereas Exeter was all-male at the time; it was 'liberal' whereas Exeter was purely traditional; and it had something of a sense of community whereas Exeter had none. I felt I had come home ... I began to thrive: intellectually, sexually, physically, psychologically, spiritually. But this thriving was no more conscious than that of a parched, drooping plant, responding to the gift of rain ... . Perhaps for the first time in my life I was free to be me.

What Scott Peck is groping to articulate, I believe to be the mutuality which is a vital part of the educative process. It is vital because it empowers through the basic fact of connectedness. The midwife teacher empowers through a nurturing or empathic involvement in the bringing-to-birth of projects or ideas; but the child learns (= is empowered) through what can be described as epiphanies of connection. These are the moments of deep insight when a realisation is attained, an idea which illuminates previous confusion. There is connection, and with it new energy and *pleasure*: too little is *eros* discussed in educational contexts.

When a pupil makes the connections between coffee-growing in Brazil and prices in the local supermarket, between the images and experiences of war-poets and current decisions on arms-spending, between industrialisation, inner-city poverty and patterns of employment, links are made which enable the transcendence of individual separatism. But only on a basis of redemption as mutuality or deep connectedness will these links be made between interpersonal becoming and communal well-being. As the American feminist writer, Carter Heyward, so movingly wrote:[28]

> We see broken bodyselves crying to be healed; separated people yearning for relation; suffering humanity raging for justice; nations,

strangers, friends, spouses, lovers, children, sisters, brothers, with us, we begin to remember ourselves, compelled by a power in relation that is relentless in its determination to break through the boundaries and boxes that separate us. We are driven to speak the word that spills over among us:

'Without our touching, there is no God.'

'Without our relation, there is no God.' ...

For in the beginning is the relation, and in the relation is the power that creates the world through us, and with us, and by us, you and I, and we, and none of us alone.

Accepting the truth of relationality as underlying existence and claiming this as power for development, means mutual empowerment in ever-deepening levels of mutuality. But as long as the capitalist, separatist model prevails in society, will mutuality seem merely a soft option, accused of lacking intellectual rigour?

Epilogue: seeking the other side of silence

Hence redemption in education means all these things: refusal of the victim situation, recovery of self-image, the process of coming to self-knowledge and the discovery of deepening layers of connectedness. But it will be an ongoing story: redemption is also reclaiming, the reclaiming of those despised areas of self, of memories and forgotten experiences of wholeness. It is also the reclaiming of the stories which have never yet been told, the stories of the determined women who nurtured the creative spark in their children; it will reclaim images and symbols from sexist and exploitive connotations, and above all, redemption will be reclaiming the silences beyond the boundaries of language and culture barriers, at the same time being creative in pushing to the telling of new stories. It is at the same time inseparable from justice-making, as it refuses sexist structures within the educational system and challenges the concepts which continue to uphold them.

Thus 'redemption' for education strikes a deeper chord than political education, education for peace and liberation, although it will include all three. For it focuses on the total well-being and becoming of the human person in the many layers of connectedness with the environment and the global scene. Redemption as mutuality challenges even when human brokenness and finitude prevail, and calls for just relation to be established as part of an ongoing process. Thus it appeals across religious and cultural boundaries as a central, educational notion:[29]

With you I begin to realise that the sun can rise again, the rivers can flow again, the fires can burn again. With you I begin to see that the hungry can eat again, the children can play again, the women can rage and stand again. It is not a matter of what 'ought' to be. It is a power that drives toward justice and makes it. Makes the sun blaze, the rivers roar, the fires rage. And the revolution is won again. And you and I are pushed by a power both terrifying and comforting.

And, as Gandhi said, we have to begin with our children.

Notes
1. George Eliot (Mary Ann Evans), *The Mill on the Floss*, London and Edinburgh, William Blackwood and Sons, 1860.
2. Virginia Woolf, *A Room of One's Own*, Harmondsworth, Penguin, 1945, pp. 111–112.
3. Chaim Potok, *Davita's Harp*, New York, Fawcett Crest, 1985.
4. Alice Walker, 'A writer because of, not in spite of, her children', in *In Search of Our Mother's Gardens*, London, The Women's Press, 1983, pp. 66–70.
5. *Ibid.*, p. 69.
6. Octavia Hill (1838–1912), who, before she became involved in housing and eventually one of the founders of the National Trust, worked for the education of poor women as secretary of the classes for women at the Working Men's College.
7. The phrase of the poet Adrienne Rich, from 'Natural Resources', in *The Dream of a Common Language*, New York, W and W Norton, 1978.
8. Maria Harris, in *Women and Teaching*, New York, Paulist Press, 1988, describes the phases of the educational process as Remembering, Ritual Mourning, Artistry and Birthing.
9. Mary Daly, *Pure Lust: elemental feminist philosophy*, Boston, Beacon, 1984.
10. This was already exclaimed in the nineteenth century by Elizabeth Cady Stanton, author of the *Women's Bible Project*, New York, 1898.
11. Virginia Woolf, *Moments of Being: unpublished autobiographical writings* (edited by Jeanne Schulkind), London, Chatto and Windus, 1976, p. 70.
12. Doris Lessing, *The Children of Violence*, consists of *Martha Quest* (1952), *A Proper Marriage* (1954), *A Ripple from the Storm* (1958), *Landlocked* (1962), *The Four-gated City* (1972) – all published by Grafton Paperbacks.
13. Doris Lessing, *The Four-gated City*, *op. cit.*, p. 591.
14. *Ibid.*, pp. 538–539.
15. Margaret Attwood, *Surfacing*, London, Virago, 1973, p. 191.
16. An outstanding authority on mystical women in Islam is Annemarie Schimmel, 'Women in mystical Islam', *Womens' Studies International Forum*, 5, pp. 145–151.
17. For feminism and mysticism see Mary E Giles (ed.), *The Feminist Mystic*, New York, Crossroads, 1985.
18. Teresa of Avila, *A Life*, from *The Complete Works of Saint Teresa of Jesus* (edited and translated by E Allison Peers, from the critical edition of P Silversio), London, Sheed and Ward, 1946.
19. Quoted from Joan Chittister, *Winds of Change: women challenge the church*, London, Sheed and Ward, 1986, p. 79.
20. Nelle Morton, *The Journey is Home*, Boston, Beacon, 1985.
21. From 'Beloved image', in Nelle Morton, *The Journey is Home*, Boston, Beacon, 1985, p. 127.
22. Mary Field Belenky, Blythe McVicker Clinchy, Nancy Rule Golberger, Jill Mattuck Tarule (eds), *Womens' Ways of Knowing*, New York, Basic Books, 1986.
23. See *Ibid.*, p. 127.
24. Sara Ruddick, 'Maternal thinking', *Feminist Studies*, 6, 1980, pp. 342–367.
25. Cited by Jean Grimshaw, *Feminist Philosophers*, London, Wheatsheaf Books, 1986, chapter 7.
26. Scott Peck, *The Different Drum*, London, Rider and Co, 1987.
27. *Ibid.*, pp. 30–31.
28. Carter Heyward, *The Redemption of God: a theology of mutual relation*, Lanham, University Press of America, 1982, pp. 171–172.
29. *Ibid.*, p. 162.

7. Spiritual formation and the worshipping community

The primary aim of Christian education, in any given context, is often said to be not so much to transmit Christian beliefs as to foster the characteristic values, attitudes, and dispositions of the Christian life. As such, it is concerned with 'spiritual formation'. The cognitive and affective dimensions of faith are, in fact, interdependent, as the three articles in this section – which argue that spiritual formation is essentially a function of the church as a community of worship – demonstrate.

John A Berntsen's account of the relationship between 'Christian affections and the catechumenate' (first published in the journal *Worship*, 52, 1978, pp. 194-210) defines catechesis as 'the shaping of religious emotions and affections in the context of teaching doctrine'. Drawing on recent work on the philosophy of emotion, Berntsen contends that we cannot drive a wedge between emotion/experience and belief/doctrine. Since emotions have a 'logic', form and determinacy that relate to their accompanying thoughts, beliefs and objects, religious teachings may properly be said to be 'held in the mode of the emotions'. The author illustrates the centrality of this approach to teaching doctrine for the pedagogy of the fourth century catechists.

Jeff Astley quotes from Berntsen in his account of 'The role of worship in Christian learning'. He argues that worship, although it has no ulterior (even educational) purpose, produces a profound effect through its power to express religious attitudes and emotions and evoke them in others.[1] It may also evoke more objective religious experiences. Drawing on Donald Evans' analysis of 'attitude virtues', Astley contends that these implicit spiritual attitudes are best formed – along with the more cognitive dimensions of Christian truth – in and by worship. This article first appeared in *Religious Education*, 79, 1984, pp. 243–251.

The final article in this section is Craig Dykstra's analysis of the formative power of the congregation, which develops the claim that although the congregation is 'caught up in powerful patterns of sin and alienation', of mutual self-destruction through self-securing, it also 'mediates redemptive power'. Both the destructive patterns and the redemptive power operate primarily at the pre-reflective level. It is in worship, Dykstra argues, that the patterns of mutual self-destruction become redemptively transformed through the generation of freedom. Christian education is here described as 'the church's attempt to help its people see and grasp the inner character and hidden nature of its own experience'. 'The formative power of the congregation' is from *Religious Education*, 82, 1987, pp. 530–546.[2]

The Revd Dr John A Berntsen is the pastor of Trinity Lutheran Church, Perkasie, Pennsylvania, USA. The Revd Dr Jeff Astley is Director of the North of England Institute for Christian Education, and Honorary Lecturer in Theology and Education in the University of Durham, England. Dr Craig R Dykstra, formerly Thomas W Synott Professor of Christian Education at Princeton Theological Seminary, is currently Vice-President (Religion) of the Lilly Endowment Inc., Indianapolis, Indiana, USA.

Notes
1. See also Jeff Astley, 'Christian worship and the hidden curriculum of Christian learning', in Jeff Astley and David Day (eds.), *The Contours of Christian Education*, Great Wakering, McCrimmons, 1992, chapter 10.
2. Compare Joseph C Hough and Barbara Wheeler (eds), *Beyond Clericalism: the congregation as a focus for theological education*, Atlanta, Georgia, Scholars Press, 1988.

7.1 Christian affections and the catechumenate

John A Berntsen

Introduction

Catechesis is the shaping of religious emotions and affections in the context of teaching doctrine. Recent discussion by liturgists, theologians and historians confirms this. Historians in particular have testified to the intensity of religious experience undergone by candidates for baptism in the late fourth century. There was, we are told, a 'systematic play upon the emotions' of the catechumen.[1] The rites of the paschal season were calculated to leave 'a deep and lasting impression on the candidate's emotions'.[2] All agree, in other words, *that* religious experience is part of Christian formation. *How* this is so and what conclusions we may draw from it, however, seem to me more questionable. Specifically, does our desire to emphasise religious experience in initiation force us, as many casually assume, to play upon contrasts like that between experience and doctrine? Are such contrasts legitimate and, if so, in what sense does our commitment to an experiential catechesis bind us to them?

The thesis of this article is that the way religious emotions and affections fit in with catechesis both confirms and runs counter to the view of many contemporary liturgists. It confirms it insofar as it attests that the shaping of the affections, and to that extent religious experience, is indeed part of coming to faith. It runs counter to it by showing that religious affections themselves have implications for belief, teaching and doctrine. No logical or theological wedge should therefore be driven between emotion and belief, or between experience and doctrine.

To see this last point, we need conceptual clarity on the nature of religious affections and historical testimony. My discussion is accordingly divided into the following parts. First, I shall sketch the view of many liturgists on the importance of religious experience in initiation. Within that context I shall focus upon religious affections in particular and, with the help of some contemporary philosophical work on emotions, try to clarify their relationship with belief, teaching and doctrine. Second, I shall turn to an historical witness by showing how the shaping of religious affections was part of the catechetical strategy of Cyril of Jerusalem, John Chrysostom and Theodore of Mopsuestia. Third, I shall recapitulate and, in a highly compressed form, draw some pastoral and theological conclusions. Among other things, I shall argue that it is precisely by our attention to religious affections in initiation that a major *theological* theme is sounded. The theme is that of nature and grace or, alternatively, creation and covenant.

I wish to clarify two final matters before we begin. This article deals with the topic of religious experience, but it does so by focusing upon religious affections. I am not simply equating the latter with the former. I shall assume in what follows that all religious affections are instances of religious experience, but not all religious experience is an instance of emotion or affection. The concept of religious experience is broader and more generic than that of religious affectivity. I am dealing with the latter as simply one way of talking about the former.

The second matter has to do with the troublesome modifier 'religious' which is part of the expression 'religious emotions and affections'.[3] In the following pages, I shall make no attempt to define what it is that makes an emotion religious as opposed to anything else. I shall shamelessly avoid the issue, not because it is unimportant, but because it calls for the kind of treatment beyond the scope of this article. Based upon what I shall say in the first two parts of the article, however, the matter can in principle be discussed.

On being affected

I want to contrast how I understand the role of the affections in catechesis with a widely accepted view on the importance of religious experience in initiation.

I can generalise by saying that the arguments which buttress the widely accepted view often depend upon a sharp contrast between experience and doctrine. There is an abiding temptation, we are told, to confuse catechesis with education and the latter with didactic procedures such as giving information. When we postulate catechesis as the learning of a set of beliefs, however, no real engagement is required between individuals and the faith community. We need rather an experiential catechesis in which we can judge *in practice* whether people can pray and share a life together. Indeed, initiation into the paschal mystery is 'first of all an event and an experience, and only secondly a doctrine'.[4] Just what 'experience' is supposed to include is not always clear. References are made to such things as community process, dialogue and common prayer. But it remains, or so it seems, that the concept of experience often gets its sense from a polemical contrast with doctrine or dogma.

The contrast between experience and doctrine is then basic to this view. It is not, however, one-dimensional. Bound up with it are other contrasts which may be taken separately or regarded as dimensions of each other. It is common, for instance, to insist that coming to faith is not intellectual assent to a body of propositions but living in a community of shared faith. As one writer has put it, 'It is not enough for the "I believe in God" to be a formula known by heart; the faith which the creed expresses has to become the "form" of a life lived.'[5] The accent here is decidedly sociological or, more accurately, social-psychological. Related to this is a further contrast, one between religious education and conversion. Here the stress is upon the therapeutic character of initiation as against any instructional ends. 'Catechesis is not about doctrinal or ecclesiastical data, but about conversion.'[6]

One thing that strikes us about these contrasts is that, whether understood separately or as dimensions of some fundamental contrast, they circle back upon each other and make a similar point. We are at times led to believe, though it must be said that the authors who draw the contrasts do not always or finally intend it, that our commitment to the importance of religious experience in initiation carries with it an anti-dogmatic and anti-institutional force. The abuses to which past church practice have led are clearly the target. To uphold the integrity of persons and how they develop religiously, such contrasts are drawn. But can't these contrasts become misleading when hardened into theoretical distinctions? It can begin to look as if our concern for experience, mystery and awe in initiation entails hypotheses about the difference between emotion and belief, education and conversion, or the experiential and the doctrinal. Not all say this explicitly, but many seem to proceed as if we must choose between something like *instruction* and true religious *formation*.[7]

How does it stand with the religious affections? I said their role in initiation should tell us something, but not everything, about the kind of inferences we may draw from our commitment to an experiential catechesis. We first need conceptual clarity, however, on the nature of emotions and affections themselves. For this I shall turn to some recent work in the analytic philosophy of mind.

Out of Ludwig Wittgenstein's later philosophy, or at least within an atmosphere created by it, a whole literature on the nature of emotions has grown.[8] I cannot detail here all the issues this literature has taken up. I wish, however, to advert to those of its conclusions which have to do with our topic. In particular, I shall trade on the claim that the concept of an emotion cannot be elucidated without recourse to concepts other than behavioural and psychological ones. This simply means that emotions get their determinacy from, and thus must be understood in conjunction with, the thoughts, beliefs and objects that accompany them. Such thoughts, beliefs and objects are part of any complete description of an emotion or affection. Consequently we should not contrast emotion and thought, reason and passion or, ultimately, religious experience and doctrine. They are not opposed but entail each other.

One of the most important points recent philosophical discussion of emotions has made is that we can speak of the 'logic' of an emotion.[9] To say that emotions have a logic will seem incredible to some. Not only is it generally assumed that emotions, passions and feelings are one thing while thoughts, reasons and beliefs are another; distinctions are often made between these for polemical purposes. Either emotions are held in contempt as subjective, irrational and idiosyncratic, or reason and thought are said to be at one remove from life's vital centre. This view of the matter, however, will not do. One cannot claim that the absence of emotion makes an act rational any more than one can say the presence of reason makes it unemotional. The right contrasts are between *kinds* of cognitive-affective human acts.[10]

Emotions have a logic. This means further that they have conceptual determinacy. They are not, that is, wholly intelligible apart from the thoughts, reasons, beliefs and knowledge that go along with them. Being affected by something presupposes having in some fashion perceived, remembered, believed or known it.[11] It is not that, say, the religious person's 'fear of the Lord' just *is* a belief or thought about the divine; but such affective regard for the religious object presupposes who or what the divine is believed, described and thought to be. The appraisal of the divine articulated by a religious teaching, whether it is explicit or not, is part of any complete description of the emotion involved. Emotion and thought are not different floors of a building but connecting rooms in the same suite.

That emotions have a logic can also be seen in the explanatory power our use of emotion language has.[12] When you say what a person desires, fears, holds in contempt, and so forth, by implication you tell what governs much of his or her behaviour. Someone might remark, for instance, 'Schwartz is a hateful person.' This works not only as a description of Schwartz but tells us *why* he lashes out at others and habitually kicks his dog. Our use of the vocabulary of the emotions and affections, in other words, has explanatory power. It gives a kind of *reason* for the actions a person undertakes.

Emotions and affections then have a logic, and this in the several senses I have mentioned. I must add to this point, however, a second. Many emotions and affections, though to be sure not all, have objects. To be affected but not about, at or for anything would be odd. The father does not simply rejoice, but rejoices *over* the prodigal or *upon* the occasion of the latter's return. The Jew praying the synagogue liturgy does not simply hope, but hopes *for* the rebuilding of Jerusalem and the gathering of the exiles.

The concept of the object of an emotion is, one must admit, notoriously slippery. One could argue, for example, that the notion is too vague to be of any use. The only suggestion I would make is that the old scholastic idea of the formal object (*formalis ratio objecti*) of a human act goes some way toward clarifying what is meant by the object of an emotion. The formal object of a human act or faculty, thought Aquinas, must be distinguished from an object considered materially. Whereas the faculty of sight, for instance, can have a host of material objects (horses, rocks, trees, bodies and so on), its formal object is the class of things *as being*, say, coloured. The *a priori* 'light' under which singular objects are grasped, in other words, tells us what the formal object of a human act is. This distinction helps clear up some of the ambiguity surrounding the concept of the object of an emotion or affection. What the object of an emotion is admits of distinctions, distinctions which can be specified in a given situation. The proposition *that* he is about to suffer pain and injury, for example, can be the object of the matador's fear no less than the charging bull itself; and the concept of the object of an emotion is none the worse for it.

The claim that many emotions have objects is especially important when it comes to religious emotions. Not only does it help us make sense of biblical ideas like the fear of the Lord; it also shows us that religious affections have different *kinds* of objects. There may simply be awe in the presence of the divine. But a religious emotion may also take an object which can only be characterised as 'descriptive', such as a story, a teaching, a belief or a doctrine.[13] This is the sense of 'object' that interests us here. It is significant, for example, that awe figured more prominently among Christian religious sentiments when, toward the end of the Arian controversy, Christ's divinity was emphasised and it was laid down that Jesus was 'consubstantial with the Father'. Religious teachings can, in other words, be held in the mode of the emotions. Neither the one nor the other is the worse for this wedding.

What then should we say about the commitment to an experiential catechesis? Does its maintenance require the sharp contrasts liturgists often draw? What I have said above about emotions and affections has, I think, different implications. The first one is that thought, reason, belief and knowledge do not occupy a domain hypothetically cut off from religious affectivity. In a given situation they are part of any complete description of the latter. Precisely by our focus on religious experience in catechesis, therefore, we shall also find ourselves speaking, however formally or informally, of religious beliefs, teachings and doctrines. If contrasts are in order, they will be those between different kinds (implying qualitative grading) of religious emotions, affections and experience.

Second, I said that the explanatory power of emotion language shows how emotions can be adduced as a reason for human actions. In this light the refashioning of a person's affections would imply a change in the behaviour and entire life of that person. Religiously something like conversion would be involved. Because of the relationship between belief and affection, however, this would not imply that teaching and doctrine would then become secondary concerns.

Third, the religious affections take objects of various kinds. Among these are descriptive objects like stories, teachings and credos. Attention to such supposedly conceptual things is not in itself incompatible with a commitment to the importance of religious experience in initiation. Religious stories, teachings and doctrines may in fact call forth and specify the life of the affections in a rich and determinate way.

Affections and the catechumenate

It is time now to turn to an historical witness. Though I have reached several conclusions about the relationship between affections and belief, it is important to find out what these have to do with any catechetical strategy as actually practised. I shall take my lead from the catechetical lectures of Cyril of Jerusalem, John Chrysostom and Theodore of Mopsuestia.[14] The patristic writers of course did not hold the same theories about emotion as modern thinkers. The way religious affections and experience fit in with their pastoral activity, however, does connect up with some of the conclusions I drew earlier. First, the shaping of the affections was a fundamental intention of their catechetical strategy. Far from showing they had no vital interest in teaching and doctrine, however, this attests precisely to their concern for the conditions under which teaching and doctrine were received. Second, more than anything else about a candidate's affective state, the early catechists were concerned with its quality. Though they certainly recognised a difference between such things as emotion and thought or intellectual assent and experience, they did not oppose them. They wanted to know what *kind* of dispositions and affections you had, not how these differed from your thoughts and beliefs.

As to the first point, one proof that the life of the affections figured in the early catechist's pastoral thinking was their concern for 'the heart'.[15] Cyril of Jerusalem was particularly exercised by the question of a candidate's sincerity and intentions. One way this comes out is in his fascination with the figure of Simon Magus, whom Cyril regards as a paradigm of hypocrisy. Simon approached the baptismal waters and was dipped in the font but, Cyril charges, 'he was not enlightened (*ephōtisthē*). While he plunged his body in the water, his heart (*kardian*) was not enlightened by the Spirit.'[16] It is significant that this concern for the disposition of the heart is tied to the classic concept of baptism as illumination. Illumination of course implies the imparting of a revealed system of knowledge. Because of its focus on the heart, however, it is clear that such divine pedagogy is intellectual, moral *and* affective. God himself is, moreover, constantly described as one who 'knows your hearts'[17] or is 'investigating your heart'.[18] Cyril can thus caution his listeners that 'if ... not your heart but only your lips proclaim your assent, well, it is the "reader of hearts" (*kardiognōstēs*) who is your judge'.[19] Examples like this could be multiplied. Each shows Cyril's care for the shape of his hearer's dispositions and affections.

A more specific instance of the way the disposition of the heart figured in Cyril's pastoral thinking was his concern for a catechumen's 'resolve'. The term 'resolve' (*proairesis*) and its variants appears throughout the lenten lectures and is Cyril's most frequent designation for the strength of purpose expected of a candidate. Commenting on the ceremonies surrounding their admission into candidacy, for example, Cyril says this to his listeners at the beginning of the *Procatechesis*:[20]

> You have walked in procession with the tapers of brides in your hands and the desire (*epithymia*) of heavenly citizenship in your hearts; with a holy resolve (*prothesis*) also, and the confident hope which that brings in its train. ... Yes, God is generous and kind; nevertheless God requires in every man a resolve (*proairesin*) that is true. ... It is the sincerity of your resolution that makes you 'called'. It is of no use your body being here if your thoughts and heart (*dianoian*) are elsewhere.

From this passage it appears that by resolve Cyril means the motives and inclinations of his hearers, the purity of their intentions. The concept goes beyond moral and volitional connotations, however, to include affective and dispositional ones as well. Resolve is but another way of specifying the desire (*epithymia*) of the heart for heavenly citizenship; and along with it, remarks Cyril, comes a 'confident hope'.

The shape of the affections is a pastoral concern for Chrysostom as well. At the very outset of his baptismal instructions, he declares the paschal season to be 'a time of joy and gladness of spirit'.[21] Like Cyril, Chrysostom focuses his attention on the heart. Those admitted into the catechumenate are urged to 'prove with your whole heart (*dianoia*) that you are through with your past'.[22] Peculiar to Chrysostom is how this disposition of the heart is often spoken of in terms of human effort: 'In view of the great honour God bestows, you should dispose your hearts well and be willing to contribute your fair share (*ta par heautōn eisenenkein*).'[23] The phrase 'contribute your fair share' is a favourite of Chrysostom's and is found frequently in his writings. Though a moralising air surrounds this way of speaking, for Chrysostom it has affective and emotional reaches as well. Using the example of Saint Paul, for instance, he claims that after baptism the apostle 'contributed his fair share'; this, he specifies, was 'his zeal (*zēlon*), his ardour (*prothymian*), his noble spirit, his seething desire (*ton pothon ton zeonta*)'.[24]

We can agree then that the life of the affections was of fundamental importance to the early catechists. Theirs was not, however, an interest in religious experience *simpliciter*. This is clear especially in Cyril of Jerusalem's lectures. He exhorts the catechumens to 'prepare your heart (*kardian*) for the reception of teaching (*didaskalias*) and the fellowship in the holy mysteries (*hagiōn mystēriōn*)'.[25] The theme of the heart's alliance with religious teaching is sounded with the utmost economy here. Cyril's emphasis on the shape of the affections should be regarded as a function of the demand for the conditions under which the Christian teachings will be rightly received and understood.

Two other passages in Cyril give a more detailed witness to this point. The first depends upon the use of simile and comes when the catechumens are urged to faithfulness in their attendance of the catechetical lectures. The paschal season, remarks Cyril, is like a season of planting and the prebaptismal instructions themselves the implements with which we prepare the earth. What is the nature of the ground that is being prepared? Cyril answers this by implication when he passes on to say that his hearers must 'grasp by experience (*peira*) the sublimity of the doctrines'.[26]

The second passage that points to the connection Cyril sees between experience and doctrine involves an elaborate wordplay. Contrasting their understanding of the Christian message at the start of their training and now as they are about to be baptised, he says this to his listeners:[27]

> You used to be called a catechumen (*katēchoumenos*), when the truth was being dinned into (*periēchoumenos*) you from without: hearing about the Christian hope without understanding it; hearing about the mysteries (*mystēria*) without having a spiritual perception of them; hearing the Scriptures but not sounding their depths. No longer in your ears now but in your heart is that ringing (*enēchē tēn dianoian*); for the indwelling Spirit henceforth makes your soul the house of God.

The wordplay in this passage depends upon the derivation of 'catechumen' and its variants from *ēchē*, 'a ringing sound'. *Katēchō* then means 'sound in the ears', 'teach orally' and finally, 'instruct in the elements of Christianity'. We should note the term 'mysteries' as well. Not only does it stand for the sacramental rites, as in the Latin Church; but in Cyril it also covers the doctrine of the Trinity and the Creed. Particular weight is thus given to the ensuing proclamation, 'No longer in your ears now but in your heart is that ringing.' What rings in the heart are quite obviously the Christian teachings and doctrines. For Cyril, therefore, the affective and the instructional require each other.

Our first point is then that the life of the affections was of prime importance for the early catechists. However, any account of how they played upon religious experience in initiation would be inadequate if it left out how doctrine and experience are tied to each other. The whole point of their centring on the heart and its disposition was to call attention to the way the Christian teachings were to be held by persons.

We have alluded to our second point several times already. The early catechists were more interested in the quality of human dispositions and affections than anything else about them. Since they were convinced that, far from compromising it, the Christian teachings called forth religious experience in a rich and determinate way, the real question was what *kind* of experience you had. Cyril of Jerusalem touches upon this when he remarks to his catechumens that even if their resolve is half-formed at the point of giving in their names for baptism, they have forty days for repentance. During this time there is opportunity in plenty 'for undressing, for laundrywork, for dressing again and returning'.[28] 'If the fashion of your soul was avarice', urges Cyril, 'put on another fashion.'[29]

John Chrysostom is perhaps the best witness to this point. Not only is his celebrated evocation of the fear and awe surrounding the sacramental rites worth remembering; but his preoccupation with the 'passions' of baptismal candidates is even more pertinent to our theme. Chrysostom never tired of exhorting his listeners to cleanse and purify their passions. When we read what he says about this, however, we must not imagine he is after some neutral state of the self. Rather, the curbing of the passions was for him but a prelude to the development of, really, new passions.

This last point comes out in the very first of Chrysostom's baptismal instructions. After their enrolment, John speaks at length to the catechumens about the importance of preparation for baptism. A vital part of this preparation, he says, is cleansing the passions. This does not, however, imply an unaffected self. In place of the dark passions, we must put on joy, peace, patience, kindness and goodness. It is these new affections which, formed 'by constantly chanting the lessons of piety',[30] are the mark of purity of mind. Moreover, though we must make our souls comely, this is brought about by 'zeal'.[31]

The concept of zeal (*spoudē*) is important throughout Chrysostom's baptismal instructions; and we must always understand what he says about the passions in conjunction with it. We find this above all in the second of the postbaptismal lectures. Chief among the threats to the preservation of the newly received baptismal gift are the 'deadly passions' which darken our reason and cause a loss of understanding. When in the grip of such passions, warns John, one's judgement and powers of discernment are just about destroyed: 'I exhort you, let us flee, then, both the drunkenness which comes from wine and the eclipse of reason which comes to us from our disordered passions (*tōn pathōn tōn atopōn*).'[32] It is easy to misunderstand Chrysostom here. Though he certainly counsels purifying the passions, he is not after a kind of *stasis* of the self. The sign of being cleansed of the passions is precisely the catechumens' 'zeal' and 'ardour'. The candidates are urged to 'have great zeal for virtue'[33] they must 'show abundant zeal' since Christ has nourished them with his blood;[34] the neophyte must 'show great zeal' in his or her prayers and confessions in the assembly';[35] and while vessels measure the water from natural springs, 'the water from the spiritual fountains (the tombs of the martyrs) is measured by our understanding';[36] such understanding, Chrysostom specifies, is 'our fervent desire (*hē zeousa prothymia*)'.[37] These passages, and more that could be cited, show two things. First, though Chrysostom was convinced that coming to faith demanded a life of reason and understanding, this by no means implied the absence of religious fervour and emotion. Such fervour and emotion were in fact one sign of religious understanding and a reasoned existence. Second, one reason Chrysostom was able to maintain this balance in his pastoral thinking was that he was above all interested in what *kind* of affections a catechumen had. Though he called for passionlessness like his philosophical contemporaries, he was after a new and different passion, a zeal marking gracious affections.

Theodore of Mopsuestia is a witness to our second point as well. To understand what he says about the affections, however, requires some background. The stress in Theodore's baptismal lectures is upon the initiate's being refashioned in nature from mortal, corruptible, mutable and passible to immortal, incorruptible, immutable and impassible. Theodore characteristically explicates this with the image of citizenship. Being refashioned in nature is like a person's passing from a status of outcast to one of enfranchisement in a new and great city. The purpose of the catechumenate is to verse believers in the rights and requisites of their new citizenship. The anthropology implicit in this view rests upon Theodore's christology of *homo assumptus* and his doctrine of the two ages.[38] God's act in Christ was, for Theodore, that act whereby God the Word 'assumed a man from us'[39] who would keep the commandments and remain free from sin. By his death and resurrection, the *homo assumptus* became forever immortal and incorruptible in nature and 'received close union with the divine nature'.[40] In baptism believers are united with the *homo assumptus* and so, eschatologically, the benefits of his incorruptibility and immutability accrue to them. Theodore also taught that the cosmos and humankind were subject to two ages or *katastases*. Man's refashioning from mutability to immutability is thus connected with being subject to two dispensations and, in virtue of this, the visible representative of the cosmos.

We must understand the place of the affections in Theodore's pastoral thinking against this background. From the emphasis he places on the self's becoming immutable and impassible, one might expect that he would have no time for religious emotion or affection. But this is not so. To be sure, the divine nature 'willed at the beginning and made us passible and changeable, and at the end will make us impassible and unchangeable'.[41] But this passage from mutable and passible to immutable and impassible must not be represented as an anaesthetisation of the self. Theodore makes this clear in what he says about the role of the Trinity in baptism. It is the triune being of God that refashions human nature and is the source of the benefits conferred at baptism:[42]

> it is by them that our renewal is accomplished, by them the second birth is granted to us, by them we are refashioned into immortal, incorruptible, impassible and immutable men, and by them we cast away the old servitude ... and delight in eternal and ineffable benefits.

The passage to impassibility and immutability here does not imply the voiding of emotion or affection but demands the religious self's *delectatio*, its delight. Theodore says repeatedly that it is from the Trinity 'that we expect to receive the delight in all good things';[43] and it forms 'the one cause from which we expect the delight in the benefits which are looked for in baptism'.[44] Though it is common to say that Antiochene spirituality was characterised by a sense of awe, reverence and fear, these references to delight and its kind have as much, if not more, claim to our attention. Theodore often emphasises that candidates come to the church for baptism 'because of our deliverance from tribulations and our delight in good things';[45] and though it is the awe-inspiring sacrament of the font that grants us a share in future benefits, this subserves that 'We expect to delight in these benefits.'[46]

The witness of Theodore then must be placed beside that of Cyril and Chrysostom. Though he emphasised the radical (and eschatological) refashioning of human nature, this did not mean religious emotion and affection dropped out of consideration. The change from mutable and passible to immutable and impassible implied the transfer, and not the elimination, of the neophyte's affections.

This brief look at the place of the affections in the catechumenate of the late fourth century has had a restricted purpose. I have attempted to establish but two points. First, while they framed no theories about the matter, the early catechists showed in their pastoral activity that the Christian teachings demanded the life of the affections. Their concern for the latter, however, did not represent the commitment to an experiential catechesis *as against*, say, an instructional one. The disposition of the heart was of such importance, not as a surrogate for the church's teachings but precisely in virtue of the place those teachings must find in the life of the newly baptised. The fear, remorse, zeal and joy of the paschal season were marks of religious understanding. Second, though such distinctions were not foreign to them, the early catechists were less interested in the difference between emotion and thought or reason and passion than in distinctions within the domain of religious experience itself. Though they could call for passionlessness like their philosophical contemporaries, they were far from interested in an unaffected self. Not *whether* you were affected but *how* you were affected was the issue. In this sense the catechetical writers were kinspeople of the Augustine who distinguished between two loves and, in a different time and setting, the Jonathan Edwards who sought to delimit the true and false affections.

Affections, creation and covenant

I began this article by saying that liturgists often back their commitment to an experiential catechesis by sharply contrasting emotion and thought, education and conversion, or experience and doctrine. I hope that it has become clearer now why, though they cannot be eliminated completely, these distinctions are not the necessary, nor even sufficient, conditions for upholding the importance of religious experience in initiation. Our obligation is not just to show how experience and doctrine differ but also how they are bound up with each other. In a sense the matter goes beyond even this. The pedagogy of the early church was not exactly experiential nor yet doctrinal and instructional. It was a unity of teaching and experience which, taken as a whole, was understood to be at the behest of the paschal mystery itself. *Thus, it is not catechesis and baptism which must become experiential: experience itself must become baptismal and paschal.* Creation, in the guise of experience, is not the internal basis of the covenant; the covenant, as Karl Barth thought, is the internal basis of creation.

These last remarks invite a question. If neither religious experience *nor* teaching command our view but are themselves seen as a function of that which is baptismal, this latter notion seems almost empty of content. It becomes so highly *theological* that it either absorbs everything around it or, on the other hand, is adventitious. Not only do acute conceptual and logical problems arise; we verge on the perennial topic of nature and grace. The question is whether to lament or, rather, to work with this fact.

The claim that catechesis ought to concern itself with the kind and quality of religious affections rather than how they differ from beliefs is a bridge to our theological theme. If the early catechists were interested in the difference between disordered passions and gracious affections, this emotion and that, or one grade of experience and another, one can ask questions such as the following. How far are an initiate's own affections simply made over and given a different shape in catechesis? Are the passions and desires of the old life simply curbed or are they, in a subtler way, outstripped in the very act of being fulfilled? Under the impress of the Christian story and its concepts, are the affections not only shaped but in some instances *constituted* in persons as new endowments? How should we deal with the play of continuity and discontinuity in which, as a larger pattern, all these questions seem to be involved?

If answers are what we are after, these questions must be begged, at least here. The possibility and the manner of their being raised, however, are themselves important. The way the shaping of the affections involves a question of continuity and discontinuity suggests that it is within the catechetical setting that problems surrounding nature and grace and theological anthropology must be addressed. Of course traditional sacramental theology with its talk of the 'means of grace' has not neglected baptism. But it is not often appreciated that the catechumenate as a whole, and within it, the way religious affections are shaped, is a setting for this theological theme. Insofar as we ask what is implied by the refashioning and constituting of religious affections in catechesis, we ask about the relationship between nature and grace, creation and covenant. It is not my place to try to answer such a question here. I simply want to establish that what I have said about religious affections claims our attention theologically and claims it in this way.

Though I cannot give a detailed answer as to how our discussion of the affections might help address the problem of nature and grace, I can at least say the following. If grasping the Christian teachings and message in any sense entails the shape of the affections, then we cannot represent grace, as traditional theology sometimes did, as being totally beyond the region of consciousness. The kind of 'extrinsicism' which makes of grace a superstructure imposed upon human nature is ruled out. As Karl Rahner has remarked, the action of grace cannot be merely an entitative, transconscious elevation of human acts.[47] On the other hand, because in the catechumenate the affections are truly refashioned, made over and constituted, that action of grace cannot simply be identified with an internal dynamism resident in persons. It is of course a mistake to represent grace as a 'something' at all. It is the divine itself, giving itself to the creature. It is the free action of a love which is only 'at the disposal' of persons as they are 'at the disposal' of the divine love.[48] Part of the sense of such being 'at the disposal', as the early catechists knew so well, is found in the role of the affections in initiation.

Finally, we must recognise that even the theme of nature and grace does not exhaust the implications of the place of the affections in initiation. The refashioning of the affections, their making over from the passions of a former life to gracious affections, gives a new sense to 'rite of passage' itself. Even the problem of nature and grace must then be seen as a matter of dying and rising. It too is finally a paschal question and must be so addressed.

Notes

1. Edward Yarnold, 'Baptism and the pagan mysteries in the fourth century', *Heythrop Journal*, 13, 1972, pp. 247-267.
2. *Ibid.*, p. 259.
3. The careful reader will notice another problem this expression contains: the use one for another of terms like 'emotions' and 'affections'. I shall at times speak of emotions, affections and dispositions. I have no special purpose in this diversity of expression. Though the terms have different nuances, I shall use now one, now another as if they are synonymous for religious affectivity.
4. Ralph A Keifer, 'Christian initiation: the state of the question', in *Made, Not Born: new perspectives on Christian initiation and the catechumenate*, Notre Dame, University of Notre Dame Press, 1976, p. 149.
5. Charles Paliard, 'The place of catechesis in the catechumenate', in Johannes Wagner (ed.), *Adult Baptism and the Catechumenate*, New York, *Concilium*, 22, 1967, p. 91.
6. Aidan Kavanagh, 'Initiation: baptism and confirmation', *Worship*, 46, 1972, pp. 262-276.
7. For a good discussion of this, see F Coudreau, 'Introduction to the pedagogy of faith', in Gerard Stephen Sloyan (ed.), *Shaping the Christian Message: essays in religious education*, New York, Macmillan, 1958, pp. 135-152.
8. The literature is large and in recent years has become rather scholastic in its refinements. Among the more general treatments, see in particular William Alston, 'Feelings', *Philosophical Review*, 78, 1969, pp. 3-34; Errol Bedford, 'Emotions', in D Gustafson (ed.), *Essays in Philosophical Psychology*, London, Macmillan, 1967, pp. 77-98; O H Green, 'Emotions and belief', in N Rescher (ed.), *Studies in the Philosophy of Mind*,

Oxford, Blackwell, 1972, pp. 24–40; Anthony Kenny, *Action Emotion and Will*, London, Routledge, 1963; G D Marshall, 'On being affected', *Mind*, 77, 1968, pp. 243–259; Gareth Matthews, 'Bodily motions and religious feelings', *Canadian Journal of Philosophy*, 1, 1971, pp. 75–86; R S Peters, 'Reason and passion', in *The Proper Study: Royal Institute of Philosophy Lectures*, 4, 1971, pp. 132–152; George Pitcher, 'Emotion', *Mind*, 64, 1956, pp. 326–346; Gilbert Ryle, 'Feelings', *Philosophical Quarterly*, 1, 1951, pp. 193–205; Irving Thalberg, 'Emotion and thought', *American Philosophical Quarterly*, 1, 1964, pp. 45–55; and B A O Williams, 'Pleasure and belief', *Proceedings of the Aristotelean Society,* supplement, 33, 1959, pp. 57–72.

9.   Robert Solomon, 'The logic of emotion', *Noûs*, 11, 1977, pp. 41–49.

10. R S Peters, 'Reason and passion', in *The Proper Study: Royal Institute of Philosophy Lectures*, 4, 1971, pp. 132–152; here p. 147.

11. G D Marshall, 'On being affected', *Mind*, 77, 1968, pp. 243–259; here pp. 249–252.

12. Errol Bedford, 'Emotions', in D Gustafson (ed.), *Essays in Philosophical Psychology*, London, Macmillan, 1967, pp. 77–98; here p. 96.

13. I owe this point to discussions, in various contexts, with Don E Saliers of Emory University and Paul Holmer of Yale University.

14. Though I am taking our three authors as a unitary witness, I should not overlook differences between them. Thus, though Cyril's writings are often counted among the witnesses to liturgies of the Antiochene type, his own thought bears the marks of the Alexandrine theological tradition. See A A Stephenson, 'St Cyril of Jerusalem and the Alexandrine Heritage', *Theological Studies*, 15, 1954, pp. 573–593.

15. For patristic thinkers 'the heart' had a broader meaning than it does today. *Kardia* designates the seat of the affections and the will, the mind as visible and illumined by God, the source of moral acts, and the place of the divine presence and grace. *Dianoia* in turn implies understanding, insight, the affections, and the disposition of the heart and mind. Such richness of meaning makes the way the catechists associate religious teachings with the heart that much more suggestive.

16. Cyril of Jerusalem, *Procatechesis*, 2, in *The Works of Saint Cyril of Jerusalem* (translated by Leo P McCauley and Anthony A Stephenson), Washington, Catholic University Press, 1969, p. 71 (*Fathers of the Church*, volume 61).

17. *Procatechesis*, 17, *op. cit.*; see *Fathers of the Church*, volume 61, p. 84.

18. *Procatechesis*, 2, *op. cit.*; see *Fathers of the Church*, volume 61, p. 71.

19. *Procatechesis*, 8, *op. cit.*; see *Fathers of the Church*, volume 61, p. 77.

20. *Procatechesis*, 1, *op. cit.*; see *Fathers of the Church*, volume 61, p. 70.

21. John Chrysostom, *Baptismal Catechesis* I, 1, in *St John Chrysostom: baptismal instructions* (translated by Paul Harkins), Westminster Press, Maryland, Newman Press, 1963, p. 23 (*Ancient Christian Writers*, volume 31).

22. *Baptismal Catechesis* I, 18, *op. cit.*; see *Ancient Christian Writers*, volume 31, p. 30.

23. *Baptismal Catechesis* II, 1, *op. cit.*; see *Ancient Christian Writers*, volume 31, p. 43.

24. *Baptismal Catechesis* V, 19, *op. cit.*; see *Ancient Christian Writers*, volume 31, p. 88.

25. *Procatechesis*, 16, *op. cit.*; see *Fathers of the Church*, volume 61, p. 83.

26. *Procatechesis*, 12, *op. cit.*; see *Fathers of the Church*, volume 61, p. 80.

27. *Procatechesis*, 6, *op. cit.*; see *Fathers of the Church*, volume 61, p. 75.

28. *Procatechesis*, 4, *op. cit.*; see *Fathers of the Church*, volume 61, p. 73.

29. *Ibid.*

30. *Baptismal Catechesis* I, 33, *op. cit.; see Ancient Christian Writers*, volume 31, p. 36.

31. *Baptismal Catechesis* I, 34, *op. cit.*; see *Ancient Christian Writers*, volume 31, p. 36.

32. *Baptismal Catechesis* V, 6, *op. cit.*; see *Ancient Christian Writers*, volume 31, p. 82.

33. *Baptismal Catechesis* I, 46, *op. cit.*; see *Ancient Christian Writers*, volume 31, p. 41.

34. *Baptismal Catechesis* III, 20, *op. cit.*; see *Ancient Christian Writers*, volume 31, p. 62.

35. *Baptismal Catechesis* VIII, 17, *op. cit.*; see *Ancient Christian Writers*, volume 31, p. 126.

36. *Baptismal Catechesis* VII, 11, *op. cit.*; see *Ancient Christian Writers*, volume 31, p. 108.

37. *Ibid.*

38. Timothy A Curtin, *The Baptismal Liturgy of Theodore of Mopsuestia,* Ann Arbor, University Microfilms, 1972.

39. Theodore of Mopsuestia, *Catechetical Homily* XII, in *Commentary of Theodore of Mopsuestia on the Lord's Prayer and on the Sacraments of Baptism and the Eucharist* (translated by A Mingana), Cambridge, W Heffer, 1933, p. 22 (*Woodbrooke Studies*, volume 6).

40. *Ibid.*

41. *Catechetical Homily* XIV, *op. cit.; see Woodbrooke Studies,* volume 6, p. 59.

42. *Catechetical Homily* XIV, *òp. cit.*; see *Woodbrooke Studies*, volume 6, p. 60.

43. *Ibid.*

44. *Catechetical Homily* XIV, *op. cit.;* see *Woodbrooke Studies,* volume 6, p. 61.

45. *Catechetical Homily* XII, *op. cit.*; see *Woodbrooke Studies*, volume 6, p. 30.

46. *Catechetical Homily* XIV, *op. cit.*; see *Woodbrooke Studies*, volume 6, p. 53.

47. Karl Rahner, 'Nature and grace', in *Theological Investigations* IV (translated by K Smyth), Baltimore, Helicon Press, 1966, p. 167.

48. *Ibid.,* p. 177.

7.2 The role of worship in Christian learning

Jeff Astley

Introduction

The claim is often made that the worship of the church should be a central focus of concern for the Christian educator. Historically, catechumens received their Christian education both as a preparation for (the catechumenate), and as a reflection on (the *mystagogia*), the liturgical act of Christian initiation. Thereafter they continued to learn the Christian story and its implications in the heart of the worshipping community, paradigmatically through bible readings and preaching in the Liturgy of the Word at the eucharist. Today the centrality of these acts of worship to the concerns of Christian catechesis is being rediscovered by many Christian denominations, as is the importance of the educational task of integrating such worship with the more everyday λειτουργια, the work of the people of God. As the National Catechetical Directory for Catholics of the United States expressed it, catechesis:[1]

> prepares people for full and active participation in liturgy (by helping them understand its nature, rituals and symbols) and at the same time flows from liturgy, in as much as, reflecting upon the community's experiences of worship, it seeks to relate them to daily life and to growth in faith.

Much of this Christian learning occurs through explicit, deliberate, systematic and sustained activities which lead to the development of a knowledge and understanding of Christian beliefs. As such it may be described as 'Christian education'. But the context and complement of all these activities is the implicit catechesis that takes place within the worship of the church. This latter process, deriving as it does from ritual (words) and ceremonial (acts) of worship, is hardly an intentional activity and certainly not a systematic one. However it does result in a change in a person as a consequence of conscious experience. We may say, therefore, that it produces 'learning', even if it is not itself 'education'.[2] I shall argue in this article that what is thus learned in Christian worship is a range of emotions, experiences and attitudes that lie at the heart of Christian spirituality.

The nature of worship

A word should be said at the outset about the pointlessness of worship. Worship is not *for* anything; it has no ulterior point or purpose, least of all an educational one. Religious people do not worship in order to do or become anything else, to teach or to learn. Worship is an end in itself.

As such it has close affinities with play, indeed it has been claimed that 'worship can be seen as the explicitly religious form of play'.[3] For play is a non goal-directed activity. As children we need to play in order to mature and to learn, but we do not enter into play with either intention.

It is often claimed that a distinction should be made between worship and meditation. Thus Ninian Smart distinguishes between, on the one hand, the religious phenomenon of meditation-contemplation-mysticism which leads to a union of the believer and Reality/God, a union that transcends the subject-object distinction; and, on the other hand, the concept of worship which is essentially relational and implies an object.[4] This is a useful distinction in the general phenomenology of religions, but I would contend that Christian worship can contain some elements of meditation-mysticism and I shall assume this wider view of worship in the account that follows. It is useful to note at this point that both worship and meditation have a powerful effect in leading to a loss of self-centredness, although in 'worship-proper' there is no loss of individuality. Thus Evelyn Underhill writes:[5]

> we are called to worship because this is the only safe, humble and creaturely way in which men can be led to acknowledge and receive the influence of an objective Reality. ... Worship, then, is an avenue which leads the creature out from his inveterate self-occupation to a knowledge of God, and ultimately to that union with God which is the beatitude of the soul; though we are never to enter on it for this, or any other reason which is tainted by self-regard.

Smart attempts an account of the nature of worship which is worth quoting at some length:[6]

> worship is relational; it typically involves ritual; this ritual expresses the superiority of the Focus; it also sustains or is part of the power of the Focus; the experience which worship tries to express is the numinous, and the object of worship is thus perceived as awe-inspiring; worship involves praise, but addressed direct to the Focus; this Focus transcends, however, the manifestations. All this implies the personalised character of the Focus.

On this view, worship is an activity which *expresses* certain religious attitudes, affections and experiences and tends to *evoke* them. In their worship, Christians express Christian attitudes and emotions. Such expressions serve to reinforce those attitudes and emotions in the worshippers and to evoke them in others, as well as supplying other people with (secondhand) expressions of what it means to be Christian. In so far as worship expresses religious experience, other people learn *about* a Christian's religious experience from his/her worship. In so far as worship sustains, deepens and evokes religious experience, it helps the worshippers and others to learn *from* their religious experiences about the nature of religious reality.

Such an account of worship will lead us to construe the language of worship as performing non-cognitive, rather than cognitive, functions. That is to say, the language used in worship does not directly assert facts or provide descriptions. 'Holy, holy, holy, Lord God of hosts; heaven and earth are full of your glory' does not serve as a description of God, but as an expression of praise to him. 'We worship thee, we acknowledge thee to be the Lord' does not describe a state of the worshippers, but expresses their worship. Similarly, 'Thy kingdom come, thy will be done' is a request or prayer, not a description of a state of affairs.

Uses of language of this nature were described by the Oxford philosopher J L Austin as 'performatives', words, phrases or sentences which *do* things (other than making statements); speech-acts that make requests or promises or warnings.[7] In his later thinking Austin saw all language as a speech-act.[8] He argued that in any and every *locution* (or locutionary act) of saying something, I perform an *illocution* (or illocutionary act) of making a request, a promise or a statement, issuing a command, expressing an attitude, etc. The type of illocution I perform is determined by the logic or conventional form of the locution. Austin noted a number of different types of illocutions, including 'verdictives' (evaluative judgements), 'exercitives' (commands, requests, etc.), 'commissives' (promises and expressions of intention) and 'behabitives' (expressions of attitudes and social behaviour). Very many locutions during acts of worship are the media for such illocutions, for example, marriage vows, religious oaths, prayerful requests, and expressions of religious attitudes of trust, conviction, promise, awe, gratitude, longing, guilt and forgiveness.

In addition to the illocution, Austin also distinguished the *perlocution* (or perlocutionary act) which is what I do by (not 'in') saying something. This is the actual effect of the request, command, expression, promise, etc. I may issue my speech-act and it may succeed in 'persuading' someone, or it may only 'frighten' or 'embarrass' them. In situations of worship, speech-acts are apparently focused on God and one's theology may allow one to think of God as being affected by them in one way or another (being 'pleased' or 'persuaded'; 'entering a covenant with us', etc.). But such a 'vertical' effect is outside the scope of this discussion. There is a more tangible 'horizontal' effect, however, in their perlocutionary effect on fellow worshippers and, in a reinforcing way, back onto the language user himself/herself. It is this perlocutionary effect of the language of worship that I have described as evoking, sustaining and deepening religious attitudes and religious experiences. We should note that the study of such perlocutionary effects requires an empirical psychology of religion rather than an armchair theological or liturgical account of the nature of the language of worship.

The nature of religious attitudes

To be religious is to have certain religious attitudes and to express them in certain patterns of behaviour. Religious people probably have such attitudes because they have learned them. They have developed them as a result of certain experiences, including their experiences of other people. As Austin Farrer puts it:[9] 'How did religion get into our heads? It was taught to us, was it not?'

Such basic attitudes, which give rise both to beliefs and worship in religion and to beliefs and conduct in ethics, have been surveyed by the Canadian philosopher Donald Evans who designates them 'attitude-virtues'.[10] He describes them as pervasive stances for living, or 'modes of being in the world'. They are existential categories as well as dispositions to act in certain ways, and they constitute the 'style' or 'timbre' of a person's personality. The attitude-virtues are the main constituents of human fulfilment when victorious over the corresponding 'attitude-vices'. They represent what 'ought to be' and are therefore intrinsically valuable states of the personality. Evans regards certain of these attitude-virtues as bearing metaphysical and religious implications, for example, 'basic trust' implies a really existent focus for such trust. The attitudes are 'pervasive' both internally and externally, in that they influence all of a person and all a person's situations. They are 'unifying' in that they unify all a person's being and all of his/her experiences and environments.

The eight attitude-virtues discerned by Evans are listed and briefly described below, with the corresponding attitude-vice noted in brackets. Evans describes attitude 1 (basic trust) as the most fundamental and notes that attitudes 6, 7 and 8 together constitute 'love', the supreme goal of human life, for which attitudes 1 through 5 are prerequisites.

1. Basic Trust (opposite: basic distrust)
   an attitude of cosmic trust-readiness or confidence incorporating 'assurance', 'receptivity', 'fidelity', 'hope' and 'passion'; Evans' account of this fundamental attitude-virtue draws on the work of Peter Berger, Erik Erikson and Sam Keen;
2. Humility (opposite: pride/self-humiliation)
   the realistic acceptance and exercise of our own powers and freedom;
3. Self-acceptance (opposite: self-rejection)

the acceptance of oneself and the rejection of pervasive guilt about oneself;
4. Responsibility (opposite: irresponsibility)
    the conscientiousness and competence of a trustworthy person;
5. Self-commitment (opposite: alienated dissipation of self)
    the integration of personality and 'being true to oneself';
6. Friendliness (opposite: self-isolation)
    the willingness to enter an I-Thou relationship of love;
7. Concern (opposite: self-indulgence)
    the willingness to help others pastorally or prophetically;
8. Contemplation (opposite: self-preoccupation and self-consciousness)

> The stance of a person who profoundly appreciates the reality and uniqueness of each particular in the universe, including himself. It is fostered by various forms of meditation which discipline his attention, cleanse his vision and open his heart. Gradually he is liberated from the self-preoccupation and self-consciousness which distort and subjectivise our usual perception of reality. He also becomes aware of a still centre within himself which somehow participates in a reality which is ultimate, and from this vantage point he can see that all things similarly participate.[11]

This last attitude-virtue incorporates 'detachment', 'attention', 'celebration' and 'peace'.

It is clear that such attitudes incorporate certain human affections, although they are not 'merely emotions'. It is further evident that religious worship is one of the contexts in which many of these spiritual attitudes are nurtured. This is especially true of trust, humility, self-acceptance, concern and contemplation. Much of Christian liturgy, hymnody and liturgical preaching serves to express and evoke these attitude-virtues.

Religious experience and worship

The phrase 'religious experience', like the word 'experience', is ambiguous. It may refer to 'subjective' feeling-states of acceptance, worth, justification, grace, election, guidance, etc. (cf. 'I feel elated/depressed'; 'I experience elation/depression'). On the other hand, the phrase may denote an 'objective' experience of a religious reality: in the Christian case, an experience of God/the risen Christ/the Holy Spirit (cf. 'I feel the table'; 'I experience the light'). These 'experiences of' lead to feeling-states, of course; God is not just experienced neutrally but in awe and joy.

Much of what has been said above about religious attitudes and emotions may be taken as an account of subjective 'religious experiences'. But a further word is needed about putative objective experiences of God. For many would claim that worship does not only develop religious feeling-states but also evokes experiences of God. And it is the latter objective experiences which give rise to the subjective ones.

At the heart of worship, it is said, is a numinous sense of the presence of the holy God. The numen is experienced 'outside oneself', 'over against' the worshipper.[12] Some may be willing to supplement this account with elements of mystical experience, for I have suggested that Christian worship may on occasions lead to this form of religious experience also. Here God is known in 'the journey inwards', in ultimate union with the worshipper's own deepest being.

Whatever account of objective religious experience is accepted, the point is that worship may serve to prepare for, allow and evoke such experiences of God. It may put people in the place, psychologically and epistemologically, where God can be 'seen' and 'heard'.[13] That would be learning-through-experience with a vengeance.

Christian education and the emotions

Catechesis has been defined by John Berntsen as 'the shaping of religious emotions and affections in the context of teaching doctrine'.[14] Berntsen draws on contemporary writings in philosophy to argue that we cannot drive a wedge between emotion/experience and belief/doctrine. All human acts are cognitive-affective; merely affective or merely cognitive acts do not exist. Furthermore, emotions have a 'logic': a grammar, form and determinacy which derive from, and must be understood in conjunction with, the accompanying thoughts, beliefs and objects of the emotion. It is possible, therefore, for religious teachings to 'be held in the mode of the emotions'.[15] Berntsen goes on to argue that it was this way of teaching doctrine that was central to the pedagogy of the catechists of the fourth century. He writes:[16]

> the early catechists showed in their pastoral activity that the Christian teachings demanded the life of the affections. Their concern for the latter, however, did not represent the commitment to an experiential catechesis *as against*, say, an instructional one. The disposition of the heart was of such importance not as a surrogate for the church's teachings but precisely in virtue of the place those teachings must find in the life of the newly baptised. The fear, remorse, zeal and joy of the paschal season were marks of religious understanding.

One may note, then, that even the more explicit educational processes that take place before, during and after worship go along with these more implicit shapings of religious affections and attitudes. The former are verbal, cognitive, often analytical and critical 'left lobe' ('western lobe') activities. The latter are intuitive, aesthetic, imaginative and non-verbal 'right lobe' ('eastern lobe') activities.[17]

The point is that the good health of Christian education is dependent upon the operation of both lobes of the brain, so that Christian truth is learned both affectively and cognitively. It is when reason and emotion are divorced that religion most rapidly loses its sense and its power for people. Religion is a cognitive-affective activity.

Such an account might go at least some way towards meeting the point of those who claim that religions do not function by providing a metaphysical explanation of reality, but a practical, salvific spirituality.[18] A less radical position would be that the doctrines and the explanations of religion must always be embedded in the spirituality, and can never be separated from it. God is not hypothesised as a theoretical explanation to satisfy our cold curiosity at the existence of the cosmos. Rather he is known (through a glass darkly and only with a passionate leap of reason) in a warm, affective way as the revealer of his own truth and the only ultimate satisfaction for our desperate human needs and desires. Christian educators should be acutely aware that this is the fundamental nature of the Christian religion and of the ways in which it is learned.

Conclusion

The teaching of Christian doctrine and the formation of Christian attitudes must take place together. Neither process can take place authentically without the other. And it is the contention of this article that Christian worship is the paradigm situation for that joint activity. In the explicit catechesis of liturgy the Christian story, always the basic format for Christian doctrine, is proclaimed in the context of affective, experiential worship so that it can be felt and experienced. There salvation is preached and people feel it; God speaks and we hear God for ourselves. And there, too, through the implicit catechesis of liturgy, we come to learn the Christian mode of being in the world as our attitudes, emotions and experiences are formed through the symbolic power of ritual and ceremonial. There it is that we become fully Christian.[19]

Notes
 1. *Sharing the Light of Faith*, Washington, US Catholic Conference, 1973, p. 66.
 2. P H Hirst and R S Peters, *The Logic of Education*, London, Routledge and Kegan Paul, 1970, chapter 5. See also John H Westerhoff III, *Who Are We? the quest for a Christian education*, Birmingham, Alabama, Religious Education Press, 1978, p. 266.
 3. G Wainwright, *Doxology*, London, Epworth, 1980, p. 26.
 4. Ninian Smart, *The Concept of Worship*, London, Macmillan, 1972, pp. 24f.
 5. Evelyn Underhill, *Worship*, London, Nisbet, 1936, pp. 17f.
 6. Ninian Smart, *The Concept of Worship*, London, Macmillan, 1972, p. 51.
 7. J L Austin, *Philosophical Papers*, Oxford, Oxford University Press, 1970, pp. 98ff., 233ff.
 8. J L Austin, *How to Do Things with Words*, Oxford, Oxford University Press, 1962.
 9. Austin Farrer, *Faith and Speculation*, London, A and C Black, 1967, p. 3.
10. Donald Evans, *Struggle and Fulfillment*, London, Collins, 1979. See also Donald Evans, *Faith, Authenticity and Morality*, Edinburgh, Handsel Press, 1980.
11. Donald Evans, *Struggle and Fulfillment*, London, Collins, 1979, p. 7.

12. Rudolf Otto, *The Idea of the Holy*, London, Oxford University Press, 1925.
13. For the use of such visual and auditory analogies in different accounts of revelation, see my 'Revelation revisited', *Theology*, 83, 1980, pp. 339–346.
14. J A Berntsen, 'Christian affections and the catechumenate', *Worship*, 52, 1978, p. 194.
15. *Ibid.*, p. 200.
16. *Ibid.*, p. 208.
17. See, for example, G Durka and J M Smith, *Aesthetic Dimensions of Religious Education*, New York, Paulist Press, 1979.
18. See, for example, Don Cupitt, *Taking Leave of God*, London, SCM, 1980; Don Cupitt, *The World to Come*, London, SCM, 1982; Patrick Burke, *The Fragile Universe*, London, Macmillan, 1979; D Z Phillips, *The Concept of Prayer*, London, Routledge and Kegan Paul, 1965, *Religion Without Explanation*, Oxford, Blackwell, 1976; and W Cantwell Smith, 'A human view of truth', in John Hick (ed.), *Truth and Dialogue*, London, Sheldon, 1974, pp. 20–44.
19. In an earlier discussion of this article, Fr Kevin Nichols suggested that John Wilson's model of 'educating the emotions' might be appropriated for use in an account of Christian worship. However, Wilson's discussion in *Education in Religion and the Emotions*, London, Heinemann, 1971, seems to depend very much on discussion techniques which help people identify and understand emotions, and to discern appropriate targets for them. Certainly we need help to do this, especially in turning our emotions away from inappropriate (because penultimate and created) focal points. But it seems to me that in the context of true worship appropriate targeting is almost guaranteed. It is when worship has gone astray that catechesis needs to engage in such remedial activity outside of the context of worship.

7.3 The formative power of the congregation

Craig R Dykstra

Introduction

The faith community has formative power in the lives of people. It can nurture their faith and give shape to the quality and character of their spirits. Faith is formed, developed and owned in the context of communities of faith. Spirituality deepens in community rather than individualistic isolation. The beliefs, values, attitudes, stories, rituals and moral practices of one's faith community are the human forces most powerful in shaping a person's spiritual journey.

There seems to be general consensus on this matter among religious educators at the present time.[1] Within this consensus, however, there also seems to be some uneasiness. The formative power of communities of faith is crucial, it is agreed. But we worry, first, whether these communities are powerful enough and, second, whether the power they have is used for good rather than for evil. There are so many socialising and enculturating forces working in people's lives in our contemporary, highly mobile and pluralistic culture that the formative power of faith communities, especially congregations, seems rather weak in comparison. Furthermore, congregations are not always all that faithful. More often than not, and in many ways, they seem more a reflection of the wider culture's values (and, too often, some of its worst) than something that is really 'radical' or 'counter-cultural'.

Formation and critical reflection

These are extremely difficult problems for those of us who count on the faith and spirit forming powers of religious communities. Answers to them are difficult to come by. One answer seems to be that if we could be more faithful as faith communities, we would indeed be more radical and counter-cultural. Christians and Jews are participants in quite radical, counter-cultural faiths. Closer knowledge of and adherence to that tradition, rather than the kind of superficial civil religiosity that pervades most of our present corporate life, would generate more radical faith. This is a good answer, but how do we get from here to there?

A prevalent answer to that question is one articulated by Thomas Groome: 'our religious education must promote a critical reflective activity in the midst of our socialising if our faith is truly to be our own and for the sake of the ongoing reform and faithfulness of the whole community'.[2] This is also a very good answer, an indispensable one, in fact. But it begs still another question: where does the capacity for critical reflection come from? Groome's answer to this last question is not entirely clear to me. He seems to suggest that critical reflection is possible for all people given the appropriate developmental capacities and that it emerges in dialogue with others when we think and talk together about our 'present action' in relation to the tradition's 'story' and 'vision'.

This is probably true, *if* we are free to reflect critically on our present lives. But whether we are, in fact, really free to do this is not evident. Reflecting critically on our present lives is dangerous business. There is much at stake, namely, our present lives. In order to be free to reflect critically on our present lives, we must be willing to allow our lives to be changed, in a sense to be given up. We ought not to be too optimistic about people's freedom to do this. Anyone who has tried to get people in a congregation to reflect critically, really critically, on their *own* lives, their own patterns of present action, probably is not very optimistic.

The problems, then, are not easily solved. Perhaps a way to a solution requires another look at the fabric of life of faith communities, one which looks realistically at its limits and at what resources it may have for engendering the freedom we need in order to become what we are not. In an attempt to do something like this, I want to focus on the limits and power of the Christian congregation. What is said here may or may not have implications for other religious faiths and other forms of community life.

Sin and transformation

The exploration begins with and is structured by two basic claims. The first is that a basic reality of congregational life is that we are engaged in socially acceptable (indeed, socially celebrated) patterns of mutual self-destruction. The second claim is that, in and through congregational life, these patterns are at the same time being redemptively modified, transformed. Congregations are profoundly caught up in powerful patterns of sin and alienation. This we must admit. But despite, and even within the context, its embeddedness in these patterns, the congregation mediates redemptive power. Precisely in the midst of its sinfulness, rather than apart from it, the congregation has power to mediate the gospel in such a way that the 'speaking' of it can re-structure and transform human personal and social life.

To see how this is so, it is helpful to begin with a story. This is a story of an upper-middle-class church member, his family and a few of his friends. It reveals, I believe, certain important dynamics going on in the daily lives of many people in our culture and in many of our churches and synagogues.[3]

Carl Phillips walked back to his car after leaving Mary Matthews' house. His mind was reeling with the jarring awareness that he might have been able to prevent the death of Mary's husband and his friend, Tom Matthews. ... As soon as he learned of Tom's suicide, Carl had gone immediately to the Matthews home.

As Carl drove slowly home he recalled his conversation with Mary. Carl thought he had known Tom Matthews pretty well but now was aware that he actually knew very little about him. Mary had confided that in the past few months Tom had had an increasing problem with alcohol, that he was frequently depressed, and was basically unable to accept being 'phased out' of his executive position in a large New York firm six weeks ago. Carl repeated to himself what he had told Mary, 'If I'd only known. ...'

Carl Phillips was also being 'phased out' of his managerial position in a New York advertising concern quite similar to Tom Matthews'. ... At first Carl had fought for his job, appealing to personal friends higher up the executive 'ladder'. He had an impressive record ... but (it soon became clear that) he would be one of six men to go ....

Carl had not told his wife Marilyn that he was losing his job until three weeks ago. ... Carl wondered again why he had waited so long to tell her. ... 'I guess it was ... my male ego. I've been conditioned from childhood that the father is the head of the household and the provider of the family.'

When Carl reached home he found Marilyn in the kitchen. ... Carl told Marilyn what he had learned about Tom Matthews and put to her the nagging question in the back of his mind. 'Marilyn, to what extent does my Christian responsibility demand that I share my own defeats with other people, especially if this kind of openness could give someone else the courage to share their burdens as well?'

Marilyn responded slowly but firmly. 'If you're thinking about telling the world about being fired, that's nothing but masochism. You feel guilty about not having known about Tom Matthews. Maybe you *could* have helped him, but it's too late now. You would only be punishing yourself and your family by flaunting your failure. ... Look, we live in a very status-conscious community and I don't want to have to deal with anyone else's pity.'

Carl admitted that Marilyn hit some pretty raw nerves with that 'status conscious' comment. ... From the viewpoint of those 'upstanding taxpaying citizens' in his economic bracket, 'people on unemployment compensation are shiftless "bums" waiting in line for a handout'. Perhaps most problematic of all, could he really accept and face what he saw as personal failure to the extent that he could admit this to his friends?

But Carl also responded to what he saw as the 'other side of the coin' as he argued with both himself and his wife. 'Marilyn, Tom's suicide has painfully forced me to recognise the tremendous unspoken needs of people around us. I've talked before about the little "pigeon-holes" we put ourselves into and the crying need to break out of this pattern. We look to different kinds of programmes in the church to do this for us, but we're not really willing to *risk* ourselves to get to know each other. I want to be honest with myself and with other people about where I am, but I don't know what that means for you or the boys *or* me.'

Tom Matthews, Carl Phillips, both their wives and families, their business colleagues, their local community and probably the congregations of which they are members live under the power of a pattern of mutual self-destruction. This particular pattern is called by social psychologists, the achievement-oriented life-style.[4] The achievement-oriented life-style is a style of life which has as its centre the *compulsion* to succeed or achieve in whatever social world one lives. A person whose style of life is structured by the achievement motive is one whose self image depends upon 'making it' in one way or another. Who one is, one's identity, depends upon *earning* the affection of others through the value of what one produces or does. This compulsion to achieve affects, almost to the point of determining, one's behaviour, attitudes, values and fundamental beliefs. This is because a life-style is, according to James E Loder, 'centrally a matter of personal, social and cultural integration based on a formal pattern which pervades and interrelates the registers of behaviour, shaping and directing a personality through scores of varied activities and extremities'.[5]

The achievement motive is socially mediated and socially expressed. It has its roots in early childhood (as Carl Phillips poignantly recognised), and is reinforced at every level of the American cultural system. There is nothing that people need and want more than to be loved and found worthy, just for who they are. But in most American early childhood training, affection (the concrete sign of love) is not given unconditionally. Affection is used as a manipulative device. It is withheld until the child performs well; or at least it is bestowed with most intensity and enthusiasm when the child has done something that makes the parents proud. This same pattern continues, and indeed is intensified, in the school situation. In school, the ones who develop a sense of self-worth are those who produce. They get the grades or other social rewards. They get the affection of their teachers. They get the acclamation of their classmates. And the more people succeed, the more they reap the benefits of the social system. There are rewards for those who achieve. Those who do not achieve have no real place in the social matrix. There is obvious evidence for this in our treatment of the mentally retarded, the 'uneducated', the physically blemished and the economically disaffected. Furthermore, this whole system of social priorities is sacralised by the language patterns, symbols, images and rituals which define our culture. Thus, the achievement motive is a socially acceptable, indeed socially celebrated, pattern of social interaction. Who, really, argues with success, especially when that success is earned?

But it is a pattern of mutual self-destruction. The achievement-oriented society and culture gives birth to persons who do indeed produce and are purposeful. But they also tend to manipulate others for their own purposes and suffer from debilitating internal stress. Why? Because becoming an achiever costs something. One pays the price by repressing the need to be loved unconditionally. 'The central tendency of achievement-orientation is repressive of a deep human cry for assurance of ascriptive (not achieved) worth. The outcome is aggression, tension, domineering control and cruelty.'[6] This repression is self-destructive and destructive of others. It is self-destructive, not only because it produces ulcers (or ultimately, as in Tom Matthews' case, suicide), but more fundamentally because it locks the door to the one thing on which human life most fundamentally depends: unconditional love.

In the achievement-oriented life-style, people become utterly, deeply, existentially convinced that they cannot be loved just as they are, with all their failures, inadequacies and finitude. We are driven to earning love. But earned love is not what gives us life; only unearned love does that, because only unearned love is fully love. So, by being compelled to earn love, we forfeit the possibility of receiving what we most truly and basically need. It is mutually destructive, not only because aggression and cruelty (however subtle) tends to maim those toward whom it is directed, but also because those who cannot receive ascriptive love cannot give it either.

We have here, then, a pattern of socially acceptable mutual self-destruction. One crucial fact of the matter is that this pattern pervades the church. Achievement as a compulsion is fostered, accepted and even celebrated in the church as much as anywhere. 'Model churches' are successful, achieving churches. Persons who are honoured in churches are persons who are purposeful, productive and accomplished, persons who excel and achieve in and out of the church. Concrete evidence for the pervasiveness of the achievement-oriented life-style in congregations is the obvious sympathy we all feel for Marilyn Phillips' response to her husband's thoughts about opening himself up to others in their congregation. To do so would be very risky. Why? Because both Carl and Marilyn *know* that to do so would be to rupture the achievement-oriented norms, values and expectations of the community. It would be 'flaunting failure' rather than 'being one's self'. To do this would create pain and conflict, and might very likely lead to the rejection of the Phillips by their friends.

Here we have, then, a painful reality of congregational life. In congregations and as congregations *we* are engaged in socially acceptable patterns of mutual self-destruction. And the achievement pattern is only one of them. Authoritarian, racist, sexist, imperialistic and other oppressive patterns are among the many self-destructive life-styles that pervade our culture and our churches. Furthermore, it is not just that we *behave* in achievement-oriented, authoritarian, racist, sexist or imperialistic ways. These fundamental patterns are institutionalised, passed on from generation to generation, and become the patterns of personality within which individuals are virtually compelled to act, feel, think and even imagine.

Patterns and limitations

The compulsive and pervasive nature of these patterns of mutual self-destruction is what limits our freedom so in relation to them. Critical reflection upon them is difficult to attain. Part of the reason for this is that they operate largely at a pre-reflective level. As Edward Farley points out in another (but correlative) context, it is 'too close to see because we "see" by means of it, that is through a consciousness already modified by it'.[7] Bringing them to consciousness may elicit recognition. When the patterns are identified and articulated, people may say, 'It's true. I hadn't thought about it before, but at the same time I knew it all along.' But this does little to rob them of their power. Consciousness of the patterns in our own lives, their contradictions and their diabolical results does not make us any less captive to them or free from them. Indeed, even our consciousness of the patterns may be co-opted by them. The achievement of critically reflective discernment may simply reinforce our dependence on our intellectual powers as our source of self-worth, make us compulsively critically reflective, and leave us unable to do anything more than strive further to be more critically acute than the next person. Critical reflection is not the primary *source* of freedom from these patterns of mutual self-destruction; it is, rather, a fruit of that freedom.

Furthermore, the mere presence of the story, vision and language of the faith is no guarantee that these powerful patterns will be overcome. The patterns easily survive in congregational life, no matter how much that life may be filled with talk about sin, crucifixion, the love of God or the grace of the Lord Jesus Christ. The pattern in the achievement-oriented congregation, for example, is to learn to manipulate this language well. The achiever is one who will strive to be articulate about sin, convincing in an analysis of the centrality of the crucifixion in contemporary theology, effective in proclamation, purposeful and disciplined in the work of the church, all in order to earn respect and love in the congregational context. The achiever will use the language and live in the context of the congregation in a particular way. 'The achiever will take only "appropriate" risks and probably therefore only "successful" ... risks, learn the "winning" answers, interpret them to justify his (*sic*) style, and assume, perhaps not erroneously, that the church is celebrating his way of life.'[8]

Self-securing

The patterns which I have been describing are a manifestation of one basic kind of response to the human situation.[9] We human beings are human beings, in part, just because we recognise our own non-necessity.[10] That is, we recognise that we might not be. Death is the paradigm evidence of this; and only human beings live anticipating death. We know that our existence, the fact *that* we are, is not necessary. But we also know that *who* we are is not necessary. Through different decisions and circumstances we might be very different from who we are. And the future leaves open the possibility that we will become different in the future. The result of this is a fundamental insecurity. Human life recognises that it is surrounded by *chaos*. The creation stories in Genesis bear witness to this. (In the creation stories, God does not destroy chaos; God pushes it back and separates the creation from it.)

This recognition that we are surrounded by chaos is accompanied, however, by a correlative refusal. Human being, as such, refuses chaos as the ultimate framework of human endeavour.[11] This refusal may take two basic forms, however: what Farley calls 'self-securing'[12] on the one hand, and faith on the other. Self-securing is primarily typified by the attempt to refuse chaos by one's own powers. Faith is primarily typified by the trust and knowledge that God alone can refuse chaos, and that God has done and continues always to do so.

The self is a very fragile thing. It is threatened on all sides. How is it to be established and secured? How can we know for sure that we are something, something good and valuable and worthy of being around, in spite of the fact of our physical and personal non-necessity? We can know that we are only if we are *noticed*. If no one notices that we are here, our lives, our very selves, are in jeopardy. It is in being noticed by others that children come to know that they exist in the first place. If children are not noticed, if their presence is not felt by others, their being is not secured and the formation of a sense of self is impossible. The need to be established and sustained can only be met by the development of a sense that one is profoundly and permanently noticed by another. To learn from one's parents when one is very young that one is accepted, valuable and indispensable in the world is to learn that one *is*.

But note what happens when this certainty is not forthcoming or begins to break down. In this case, we begin to *make* people notice us. We begin to use people as mirrors in which to see ourselves reflected. We begin to manipulate others into responding to us, and in our own terms. This can have many different kinds of effects. It can make us so hungry for power that we begin to destroy others in the process of trying to get it. It can make us engage in all kinds of activities that we think will get us what we think we need in order to be somebody. I would say, in fact, that every personal and social evil has its roots in our need to manipulate the world into paying attention to us.

And when the world does not respond, because it, too, is engaged in its own self-securing, our attempts to make it respond become continuously more desperate. This dynamic, I am arguing, is at the root of the achievement-oriented life-style and all other self-destructive patterns of social existence. And when our desperate attempts to make the world take notice do not work (in the context of our present discussion, when achievement fails to bring love), we increasingly look for ways to anaesthetise ourselves (through alcohol, prejudice, vain-glory or, *in extremis*, suicide) against the knowledge that we are not being noticed in the way we want or need to be.

This dynamic operates in all of us to one degree or another. Another word for it is sin. Our sin is overcome, the dynamic is broken, only insofar as we are profoundly and permanently noticed in love. One of God's greatest blessings is the love and attention we receive from other people, especially love and attention which we somehow sense is not self-seeking. But because we are all sinners, none of us can be the source of permanent establishment and sustenance for another. We all grow up, and the existence that was secured for us in childhood by our parents always breaks down. We find out that our parents are not perfect, omnipotent and eternal. They fail us, on the one hand, and they die, on the other. More disastrously, so does everyone else.

That is why our release from sin (and correlatively, from all of the pattern of mutual self-destruction in which we are embedded) depends upon God and faith in God. Unless there is this reality which does in fact establish and sustain us, secure us in existence, notice us in love, permanently and utterly, and unless, through faith, somehow deep within our being we *know* that, we have no choice but to continue desperately to secure our own selves.

The redemptive power of worship

Now we are at the point where we may speak of the redemptive power of the congregation. Our second claim is that these mutually destructive patterns are being redemptively transformed and that in this lies the power of the congregation to mediate the gospel. Since the patterns which destroy us lie at the pre-reflective level, and since the roots of these patterns lie in the desperate attempts at self-securing that characterise our historical existence, the redemptive power of the congregation must be a transformation of self-securing and must somehow be mediated at a pre-reflective level.

It is not enough for the congregation to speak religious phrases. Nor is it enough for it simply to try more ardently to become a community of mutual love. Because the patterns of mutual self-destruction operate at a pre-reflective level, mere speech has no effect. And because the life of the congregation continues to be self-destructive, it cannot, under its own power, become a community of mutual love. Even to make the attempt is to continue to strive toward self-securing.

It might seem, then, that the congregation has no redemptive power and there is nothing the congregation can do. But this is not the case. What the congregation can do is, first, acknowledge its participation in patterns of mutual self-destruction (in theological language, this is called confession), second, articulate its incapacity to secure itself (this is called repentance), and third, recognise, proclaim and celebrate the establishing and sustaining power which belongs to God alone (this we call proclamation and prayer). In brief, the congregation may worship. Worship is the core of congregational life and provides the paradigm for its peculiar form of life. In worship, the congregation is a congregation. Through worship, patterns of mutual self-destruction become redemptively transformed.

Worship, in this context, is not simply cultic ritual (though as ritual, worship teaches the congregation who they are). Worship is rather a style of life which may pervade the whole of a congregation's existence, even while it continues in sin. Look again carefully at the example with which we began. What Carl Phillips is yearning to do in sharing his defeats with other people is to worship. His yearning to be honest with himself and with others is a yearning to worship (to confess, to repent and to proclaim and pray) in spirit and in truth. He is yearning to come before God as he is. And he knows that the only way to come before God as he is, is to come before God with others as they are. Furthermore, he suspects that the others with whom he might come are yearning to worship in the same way. He suspects this because the testimonies and stories of the faith tradition of which he is a part (he speaks of his Christian responsibility) tell him that this is true.

Thus, right in the middle of the self-securing and mutually destructive form of social life of the status-conscious, achievement-oriented congregation of which Carl Phillips, and many of us, are a part, there is worship and the yearning to worship in spirit and in truth. And here lies the power of the congregation to mediate the gospel. For in a pre-reflective way, the worship that goes on from week to week, corrupted as it is, continues to break up self-securing self-destructive patterns. This provides the fulcrum by which our mutually self-destructive social life may be and is being transformed for our redemption. It is worship, more than critical reflection, that is the context of our freedom. Insofar as (and as long as) the congregation worships, the congregation remains the church. And insofar as the congregation's whole life increasingly takes on the form of worship, to that extent the congregation increasingly more powerfully and influentially bears redemptive power.

Worship may seem an odd place to locate the source of the freedom that is required for the ongoing transformation of personal and corporate life. And, of course, it is not always. Worship may degenerate into idolatry. Worship is what we once called 'divine worship' only insofar as it is worship of God, the God whose nature and living presence the faith community's story and vision (to use Groome's terms) render. Furthermore, worship as communal style of life is worship only insofar as all its common expectations and processes of socialisation (for both good and ill) are governed by and continually altered by apprehensions of and dealings with God. Unless this underlies all of its practices, structures and patterns of mutual human relationship (constructive or destructive), life in the community of faith is nothing more than participation in still another sociological group, no different in any essential way from participation in a profession, a club or a social movement. In such cases, the ultimate reality becomes the community *itself* with its beliefs, practices, values and ways of seeing. Then, idolatry reigns.

What makes a community a worshipping community is the fact that, as Farley points out, its 'social structures and individual behaviours and attitudes are at best vehicles for whatever realities faith apprehends but are not the realities themselves'.[13] Farley goes on to describe the way in which this conviction lies at the heart of Christian faith:[14]

Historical study of the origin, development, events, personages and 'essence' of Christianity reveals a prevailing consensus that faith is directed to realities which are not unreducible to the images, experience or behaviours of this historical religion. Even if we grant the 'doxological' dimension in the language about God in this historical faith, the praise of God is not praise of praise. It is not intended as praise of a community engendered symbol or image. When an early church father or reformer criticised an opponent's Christology, a state of affairs was intended which pertained to Jesus himself, not simply the literary, psychological or sociological features of the opponent or the tradition. There is no question that the historical faith in its very 'essence' testifies to realities which transcend its own determinacy, representations and theology.

The loss of God as a known, believed and present *reality*, transcendent to the community, is the loss of faith itself. Without God as the ultimate referent of all of a faith community's activities, distorted and corrupted as they may often be, faith simply reduces to the human construction of reality through social means. Socialisation becomes nothing more than the incorporation of persons into a social group and its ways, and mutual human relationships lack any meaning that transcends personal and social immediacy. What, in faith, had been only means have become the end or *telos* itself.

In faith, however, patterns of mutual expectation and socialisation are not ultimate. They are means by which the community as a whole and individuals in it come to know and live appropriately in response to God. Because the community and its ways are never ultimate, they are always open to change on the basis of deeper understandings of God and relationship to God. It is continually susceptible to judgement and renewal from its source and ground, because its source and ground is not itself.[15] This is why recognition of the need for confession of sin and repentance is more fundamental to the church's experience than any claims it might make for its own moral goodness.

When this is the case in the life of a congregation, the freedom that emerges is quite stunning. A marvellous example is reflected in a story Harvey Cox tells about a Sunday morning in his own little congregation in Cambridge, Massachusetts.[16] Cox begins his story by saying that one Sunday, 'the minister of the small Baptist church I belong to did a very nice thing. During the pastoral prayer, along with remembering the sick and the shut-ins, he also asked the Lord to bestow a special blessing on our informer.' The 'informer', it turns out, is a person who has infiltrated the life of the congregation and is informing the FBI of its activities. Whimsically, Cox notes their surprise at the government's need for an undercover agent.

> There isn't anything very confidential about our church. The title of the sermons, such as 'Begin the faith journey today', are displayed on the bulletin board outside. The newsletter carries more information than most of our members want to know. The bulletins the ushers hand you on Sunday tell you whose birthdays and anniversaries are coming up and whose memory is invoked by the flowers on the communion table.
>
> What surprised us most was that the FBI thought it would be hard to worm information out of us. Many people think our church's problem is just the opposite. Since we are Baptists and therefore maybe a little on the zealous side, we are more often accused of telling people too much. Indeed, some of our members feel that the last place they would tell somebody a secret would be at church, not because somebody might spill the beans but because in all probability people already know.

Cox goes on to tell of the various kinds of things that go on in his rather active, but not atypical congregation: Sunday school, morning worship, coffee hour, adult discussion groups, choir rehearsals, bible studies, committee meetings, prayer circles, potluck suppers and so on. Apparently, what has the government upset is that one of the church committees helps a Salvadoran refugee whom the congregation had brought to Cambridge and whose children are still down there.

The presence of the informer has the congregation a bit worried, but not too much. It is something of a nuisance and a few people have become wary of strangers. But Cox says:

> Still, in the meantime, I am glad our preacher asked the Lord to grant a special blessing to the informer. In fact, we all secretly hope our infiltrator does not get tired and quit. If he stays around long enough, he'll learn that when we say our church is a 'sanctuary', we don't mean just for Salvadoran refugees. Churches are sanctuaries for homeless, lost and confused people of all kinds, including secret agents. They, too, are welcome to come and pray, listen to the gospel reading and belt out 'Beulah Land' with us. Who knows, they might even end up getting saved. It wouldn't be the first time.

In the context of a worshipping congregation, a remarkable freedom obtains. One senses it not so much in any acuteness of critical analysis (though one does not doubt that this can be done if it is needed); rather, the freedom comes through in the lightness of touch, the humour that proves that nothing, neither external threat nor internal order, is taken with ultimate seriousness, precisely because nothing else *is* ultimate but the God whom they worship. It may not look much like freedom. But, in praying for the sick and the shut-in, in all the open conversation at the coffee hours, the adult discussion groups and the potluck suppers about things that matter in people's lives (and some things that don't), in the goings on at the choir rehearsals, the bible studies, the prayer circles, the committee meetings and, above all, in the high if somewhat comic drama of the worship service where God's presence is invoked, where the word of God is read aloud, where the good news is preached, where God is praised in voices lifted up in song, where people come from east and west and north and south to sit at table with the risen Christ, and where, who knows, from time to time a few even end up getting saved . . . in all this there is considerable freedom.

There is freedom from compulsive self-securing. There is freedom from the patterned, pre-reflective forces that generate mutual self-destruction. The worshipping people are never utterly or perfectly free, of course. The self-securing is redemptively *modified*, not eliminated. The mutual self-destruction is ameliorated in some ways, though never completely. Still, there is a point of leverage and some movement, maybe even enough to enable the people to open their arms to strangers, both Salvadoran refugees and FBI informers.

Christian education and understanding

This point of leverage is crucial for education in the congregational context. It is all we need. In my view Christian education, at least, is dependent upon the church; it does not create the church in the first place. It depends upon it already being there. If there are congregations where there is absolutely no movement toward confession, repentance, proclamation and prayer and no one who has experienced to any degree or any way some release from the mutually self-destructive dynamics of personal and social life that comes by God's grace, then, in that congregation, there is no possibility of Christian education. For Christian education is the church's attempt to *understand its own experience*. When a congregation has absolutely no experience as a church, there is nothing, Christianly speaking, for it to understand.

Although a congregation may have little experience as a confessing, repenting, proclaiming and praying community, however, it is rare for one to have none. At the very least, most congregations still have a liturgy which has been passed on to it through the tradition that still goes through the motions of confessing, repenting, proclaiming and praying. It is a place to start. Also, most congregations are in one way or another connected to the larger Christian community where these activities are going on. This is another place to start.

Let us look at this notion of Christian education as the church's attempt to understand its own experience. When I use the word understand, I mean more than 'know a good deal about ...' (though I very definitely want to include that). 'Understanding', however, includes more. It includes having been initiated into the experience one understands. It also includes an intellectual and emotional appreciation for what one understands. But most of all, understanding means to be able to 'see and grasp the inner character and hidden nature of things'[17] in one's experience; one has insight into its reality and meaning. Thus, Christian education is the church's attempt to help its people see and grasp the inner character and hidden nature of its own experience as a confessing, repenting, proclaiming, praying community in response to God's gracious, redeeming activity in the world.

The prerequisites of Christian education, understood in this way, are some minimal experience of confession, repentance, prayer and proclamation. The effect of Christian education will be the deepening and broadening of the church's experience as those who come more and more to understand it also take more and more responsibility for it. But the process itself is at once an investigative process which guides people in the exploration of this experience, a critical process which jars people out of the patterns of thinking, feeling, valuing and behaving that make it difficult for them to participate in this experience, a hermeneutical process which aids people in the interpretation of this experience, and a caring process which invites people continually more deeply into this experience in freedom. Through investigation, criticism, interpretation and care, Christian education helps the Christian community see and grasp the inner character and hidden nature of the mutual self-destruction and redemption that goes on in its own experience in order that, in its whole ministry, it may participate less and less in its own destructive patterns and those of the broader society and may more and more be open to the redemptive activity of God.

Notes

1. If there is such a consensus, John H Westerhoff III has undoubtedly had considerable influence in bringing it about. The themes of this consensus that I have articulated have been central to virtually all of his work.
2. Thomas H Groome, *Christian Religious Education*, San Francisco, Harper and Row, 1980, p. 108.
3. The story is a case reported in Robert and Alice Evans and Louis and Carolyn Weeks, *Casebook for Christian Living*, Atlanta, John Knox, 1977, pp. 66–68. The case is a write-up of an actual incident, though the names are fictional.
4. I am depending, in my discussion of this life-style pattern, on James E Loder, 'The fashioning of power: a Christian perspective on the life-style phenomenon', in A J McKelway and E David Willis (eds), *The Context of Contemporary Theology*, Atlanta, John Knox, 1974, pp. 187–205. Loder uses the phrase, 'socially acceptable patterns of self-destruction', which I modify here. See p. 187.
5. *Ibid.*, p.187.
6. *Ibid.*, p. 191.
7. Edward Farley, *Ecclesial Man*, Philadelphia, Fortress Press, 1975, p. 141.
8. James E Loder, *op. cit.*, p. 192.
9. See Edward Farley, *op. cit.*, chapter 6, for a phenomenological description of this situation.

10. *Ibid.*, pp. 132–33.
11. *Ibid.*, p. 133.
12. *Ibid.*, p. 143.
13. *Ibid.*, p. 15.
14. *Ibid.*, pp. 15–16.
15. The criticisms of socialisation theory in religious education, including Groome's, have been made largely on the grounds that socialisation necessarily implies domestication and the preservation of the status quo. This seems to me to involve too simplistic a reading of socialisation theory. I believe there is more dialectic built into the position of John H Westerhoff III than is usually recognised, though he is not, to my mind, adequately clear or forceful about this. In any case, a more fundamental problem than any perceived lack of dialectic between the faith community and the larger world or between the community and its members is the problem of what Farley calls 'reality loss' (the loss of a believable sense of the reality of God as a foundation for the community's life). Advances can be made over both 'socialisation' and 'critical dialectical hermeneutical' theory only by confronting this issue directly. This is a project yet to be undertaken.
16. The story appeared in an editorial, 'The spy in the pew', *The New York Times,* March 3, 1986, p. A15.
17. Raymond Holley, *Religious Understanding and Religious Education*, London, Routledge and Kegan Paul, 1978, p. 75.

8. Spiritual formation and ministerial education

The relation of spiritual formation to theological education, especially in the case of the education of Christian ministers, is a problematic one. Disputed issues include the theological and educational status of the theme of spiritual formation, the relation between spiritual formation and other aspects of ministerial education, and the form that spiritual formation might take within a programme of studies. One particularly difficult question concerns the relation between the general spiritual formation of all Christians and the special spiritual formation of their future ministers.

James E Loder's article, 'Transformation in Christian education', originally published in *The Princeton Seminary Bulletin*, 3, 1980, pp. 11–25 and in *Religious Education*, 76, 1981, pp. 204–221, serves as a theoretical prologue to the debate. Loder identifies 'transformation' as 'one theme in which the major disciplines foundational to Christian education may be integrated', which makes it particularly significant for constructing a systematic foundation for Christian education. Yet the theme of transformation is not specifically theological, but part of a depth structure of human experience which is constant although its 'expressions' differ according to the subject-matter in question.[1] In the theological context, transformation itself is transformed, as the Spirit 'transforms the origin and destiny of the transformational work of the human personality'. Finally, Loder sketches the five learning tasks which correspond to the stages of the transformational pattern, and the dangers to which each of these is subject.

George A Lindbeck's influential account of postliberal theology[2] was referred to earlier (see article 4.1 and the *Overview*). In this article, he compares spiritual formation to acquiring linguistic competence, suggesting that the patterns of the bible function as 'grammatical paradigms' for the Christian community. A special spiritual formation for ministers is, therefore, undesirable because of the danger of 'clerical elitism', and yet may have become necessary in the present context. But theology and spirituality have been separated for so long that the integration of spiritual formation into programmes of ministerial education seems especially problematic. There are grounds for optimism, however, in the dissolution of the foundationalist assumptions of modernity, which made theology depend upon other disciplines for its scholarly status; if spiritual formation is given its due in theological accounts of the Christian religion, theological education is much more likely to give spiritual formation the attention it deserves. Lindbeck's 'Spiritual formation and theological education' is reprinted from *Theological Education*, 24, supplement 1, 1988, pp. 10–32.

Charles M Wood shares Lindbeck's conviction that theological education and spiritual formation are part of the Christian education which belongs to the Christian community as a whole, but also agrees that there is something distinctive about ministerial education. In 'Theological education and education for church leadership', he sets out a series of 'key distinctions' which, he suggests, are necessary for thinking coherently about the theory and practice of theological education. Wood argues that the three interdependent components of Christian education are 'education in Christian faith', 'education in Christian life', and 'education for ministry', and that education for church leadership, although specifically related to the third, requires 'a particular intensification and development' of all three components. As such, it involves theological education, and 'the aim of *theological* education is not to form Christians, but to form the habit of critical reflection on one's formation'. The article concludes with an account of the relation between 'practical theology' and 'pastoral theology' in education for church leadership. It was first published in *Quarterly Review*, 10, 1990, pp. 65–81, and is reprinted in Charles M Wood, *An Invitation to Theological Study*, Valley Forge, Pennsylvania, Trinity Press International, 1994.

Professor James E Loder is Mary D Synnott Professor of the Philosophy of Christian Education at Princeton Theological Seminary, Princeton, New Jersey, USA. Professor George A Lindbeck is Pitkin Professor of Historical Theology at Yale University Divinity School, New Haven, Connecticut, USA. Professor Charles M Wood is Lehman Professor of Christian Doctrine at Perkins School of Theology, Southern Methodist University, Dallas, Texas, USA.

Notes
1. See also James E Loder, *The Transforming Moment: understanding convictional experiences*, San Francisco, Harper and Row, 1981.
2. George A Lindbeck, *The Nature of Doctrine: religion and theology in a postliberal age*, Philadelphia, Fortress, 1984.

8.1 Transformation in Christian education

James E Loder

The interdisciplinary problem

It is with Dr Wyckoff's view of the field of Christian education that I wish to begin, since his more than any other's is the most adequate overall organisation of this sprawling complex phenomenon, 'Christian education'. It is he above all others who makes it clear that without *theory*, self-consciously constructed, making the bridge between foundational disciplines (which includes the conventional theological disciplines as well as the human sciences) and the major educational questions (which include such basic matters as educational objective, scope of what is to be taught, how it is to be taught, where, when and by whom) – without good theory, 'than which there is nothing more practical', we will fall into a kind of mindless pragmatism, drawing from this or that discipline at random, or no discipline at all, to answer whatever educational demand seems most pressing. However, it is precisely in the construction of theory, which attempts to bridge between the foundational disciplines on the one hand and educational questions on the other, that we have a major unresolved issue which I want to explore here. Namely, what basis for integration can be found for correlating the foundational disciplines among themselves such that they can inform educational concerns without generating contradiction and hopeless confusion in the answers they provide for educational practice?

This it seems to me is a prior question, not something that will emerge as the practice of Christian education goes on. In fact, as it goes on without addressing this question it tends to entrench itself in its derivative role as servant of current educational fads. There is a general problem which in my view is the prevailing obstacle to further systematic development of the field. C Ellis Nelson, another prominent theorist in this field, once asked the key question: 'Is Christian education something particular?' I would answer, 'Yes, institutionally, pragmatically and historically, but in terms of any systematic integrity, currently the answer must be, No.' This is the problem we must address.

Method

The proposal I have for interdisciplinary method is derived from other contexts, particularly interdisciplinary seminars in the human sciences. Incidentally, by human sciences, I do not mean those that aim toward human engineering, but those disciplines that strive to describe and interpret (without manipulating) culture, where the basic units are symbol and value; society, where the basic units are the group and the social organisation of groups; personality, where the basic unit is the human personality, its structure, dynamics and part-processes. At one such interdisciplinary meeting of these human sciences, Claude Levi-Strauss, the French social anthropologist, together with others called attention to the 'uninvited guest' at every interdisciplinary discussion; namely, 'the human mind'.[1] Levi-Strauss had reference here to what for several years Piaget has been developing under the more specific notion of 'genetic epistemology'.[2] That is to say, there are certain generic structures embedded in raw, that is, uninterpreted, human experience that give shape to language and thought, to self-understanding, to the ordering of personal, interpersonal and intergroup relationships, to the formation of hierarchies of value and symbol systems, including the disciplines we use to study these phenomena. What these figures and others, such as John Dewey, Polanyi and Parsons have done in their respective ways is to suggest, if not legitimate, by theory and research a thematising of the human sciences. By inferring from observable behaviour that certain elementary structures or patterned processes underlie and give shape to our general experience, they assert that whether one analyses culture, society or personality these patterns will inevitably appear, although in different manifest form depending upon which order of reality is in question. For instance, John Dewey's theme or key-patterned process was 'transaction' which he found operative in all orders of reality from organic life to the highest levels of enquiry and social organisation. Polanyi's theme was 'personal knowledge' which was grounded in the organisation of body and brain, and it extends to the formation of modern culture. Parsons' theme was 'socialisation' according to four pattern variables which structure an isomorphic relationship among organic life, personality, society and culture.

What I will propose in more modest terms in the following paragraphs is such a thematisation for not all, but certain of the foundation disciplines most germane to Christian education. I propose that it will integrate appropriate theoretical reflections not only upon the human sciences but also upon the conventional theological disciplines as they together attempt to address the educational concerns of the church. In my conclusion, I will try to show in some specific ways that such a thematisation may make considerable difference in how one conceives of education in a theological context.

The theme of transformation

The basic theme of this article, then, is transformation because this is one theme in which the major disciplines foundational to Christian education may be integrated. Moreover this theme is central to these disciplines, so their coming together in transformation is not treating any one of them in a peripheral way; accordingly, the integration I am suggesting is not a tangential matter for any. Thus my hypothesis is that the theme of transformation provides a major step in constructing a systematic, *inter*disciplinary (as opposed to a *multi*disciplinary) foundation for Christian education.

To develop this theme, I propose to divide it into its underlying structure and its surface manifestations. By analogy to language, I propose to call the underlying structure 'the grammar of transformation' and its surface manifestation 'the expressions' which are generated or given coherent meaning by that underlying structure or grammar. By talking about a grammar of transformation, I do *not* have reference to Noam Chomsky's transformational grammar. That is, I do not want to account for grammar by means of transformations. Rather, I want to account for transformation by using 'grammar' as a metaphorical description of a pervasive and persistent structure of meaning which, in fact, is inferred from sequential realities.

As such a structure, transformation is synchronic. That is, it has an inherent 'logic' that maintains a consistent patterning of relations among basic elements. Thus, the basic units of any particular order of reality (that is, the psyche and its subparts, if one is talking psychology, value and symbol, if one is talking about culture, or groups and their interaction if one is talking sociologically, or the relationship between God and any one or all of these forms of human organisation, if one is talking theologically) are patterned for transformation in a recognisable fashion regardless of which order of reality is being discussed. The regularity of this patterned process, involving basic parts in a systematic interrelatedness (as described by appropriate disciplines), will be called the 'grammar' of transformation.

Although the grammar of transformation as a structure is ahistorical, its generative capacity produces a great variety of expressions which are diachronic or historical in nature, ranging from personal history to the broader expressions of social and cultural transformation. As linguistic grammar through semantics is generative of an infinite variety of meaningful sentences, so transformational grammar through the basic units of the order of reality under consideration is generative of a great variety of manifest sequential, historical expressions. These expressions are simultaneously, utterly new *and* coherently linked with past conditions and meanings. Thus transformation consistently weaves continuity and discontinuity into a coherent pattern of meaning.

Summarily, then, the theme of transformation taken as a whole is a deep structure of experience that generates a multiplicity of personal, social and cultural expressions. Accordingly it appears in virtually all of the major disciplines foundational to Christian education. Thus, in interdisciplinary work, identification of the *structure* will enable us to trace the analogy of transformation from one order to the next, but *expressions* of the structure will remain unique to the order of reality being considered.

A paradigm case

In order to fill out the discussion of the *grammar* of transformation a bit more fully, I will take a paradigm case of its *expression*, which is used both by Lonergan and Koestler,[3] namely, the instance of Archimedes' discovery of the first principles of hydrostatics. You will recall that King Hiero the tyrant of Syracuse had had a crown fashioned by a goldsmith of doubtful character. He wanted to know from Archimedes whether or not any baser metals had been added to the gold. Archimedes knew the weight per unit volume, but he could not determine the volume of such a complicated ornament. Confronted with the problem he was apparently baffled at first, but one day while getting into his bath he watched the water level rising from one smudge on the basin to the next as his body sank into immersion. Then it occurred to him in a flash that the volume of water displaced was equal to the volume of the immersed parts of his body. This sudden bisociation between the complicated figure of his body in the water *and* his problem with the crown released such tremendous energy and enthusiasm that he jumped out of the bath and ran naked through the streets of Syracuse shouting 'eureka'. Fortunately he could account for himself afterward by developing the principles of hydrostatics and proving them in an empirical test. Thus, a particular *expression* of transformational grammar made history.

The grammar of this sequence which intertwines novelty and continuity consists of five steps: first, a conflict borne with persistence; second, interlude and scanning; third, insight felt with intuitive force; fourth, release and redirection of the psychic energy bound up with the original conflict; and fifth, interpretation which tests the insight for *coherence* with the terms of the conflict and for *correspondence* with the public context of the original conflict. This particular episode is an expression of transformation that proceeds sequentially through the steps following an underlying pattern which in itself as structure is synchronic. The pattern is present all at once as a latent structure of meaning capable of constructing a coherent relationship among novel mental connections, or 'bisociations' as Koestler calls them, and the given terms of the original conflict situation.

The sense of the coherence of the structure consists in this: once the conflict is entered and energy invested in it, the psyche seeks resolution and is deeply reluctant to give up the conflict until a resolution is found. When no insight is forthcoming this may give rise to 'negative insight', that is, one has the wrong problem or a misleading conflict. Then, the conflict may be dismissed or redefined and the process begun again. The coherence of these steps, like the coherence of a sentence, has a built-in expectation of completion. We all have, as Frank Kermode said of narrative, 'a sense of ending', and that is because of the underlying grammar.

The second aspect of the grammar or wholeness of this sequence is that one may enter the sequence consciously or intentionally at any point in the structure, but still be drawn to complete the whole. I have suggested with Archimedes how one enters at the point of an initial conflict. However, there are often times when we have answers before we know what the questions are. Lest you think that this is sloppiness, it was Einstein's procedure for discovery. He knew intuitively that there was something wrong with the Newtonian world view and that he had the answer somewhere in himself when he first read Newton's *Principia Mathematica*. If one enters the process in the middle, transformational grammar would call for one to work backward into the latent conflict resolved by the insight, and forward again into interpretation.

One may also enter on either side of the middle step (insight) of the grammar. Sometimes one finds he or she is working on a latent conflict, scanning for an orientation to a problem that has not yet been articulated, and the expected solution has not yet come forth. Such persons are 'the seekers' or 'the wonderers' who sense an as-yet-undisclosed beginning and ending to a process in which they find themselves already immersed.

One may also enter on either side of the insight with a sense of new energy ready to reinvest. One might wake from a dream in which insight and resolution occurred, but upon awakening the dream is nearly forgotten and one merely feels good, like celebrating. The grammar of transformation calls for a working back through to the source of the resolution, recovery of the dream, if possible, and a grasp of what latent conflict has been resolved and how. It also calls for working forward into an interpretation of the sequence and a validation of the insight.

The final thing to note about the pattern of transformation is that *mediation* is required for the elements of the original conflict to come together in a new way. In Archimedes' case, the insight erupting from the creative unconscious mediated the elements of the conflict for the construction of new meaning. The substance of the mediation is based on 'bisociation' or 'habitually unrelated frames of reference coming together to form an unexpected meaning', such as taking a bath and measuring the purity of a gold crown. Thus, the creative unconscious, which produces a complex bisociation between the bath and the gold problem, brings about a spontaneous antithesis-in-synthesis and so constructs new meaning. This is the source and substance of the discontinuity in transformation and the locus of what is fundamentally new in relation to the overall sequence.

Transformation in human sciences

It can be shown that this grammar has an organic base in orthogenesis, that is, the tendency of organic development to continue in a straight line regardless of environmental influence. However, it first appears in a complete psychological form in the stage-transition process of human development.[4] It seems to be the internal organisation of the process by which the personality makes its way from lower to higher levels of complexity and complexity management, and at the same time maintains integrity and continuity within itself. As a process implicit in development, it operates with unreflected or non-intentional regularity during the earliest, highly formative years of life, giving rise to intellectual and linguistic competence as well as maturation of the ego in object relations. The wider significance of this transformational pattern becomes evident when it is appropriated by conscious intention and transposed to different orders of experience. For instance, the use of narrative forms (folktale, parable, myths) to construct patterns of world coherence and personal identity are common transpositions of the pattern (via symbol and metaphor) in fictional or imaginary time.[5]

It is this process transposed into an intentional effort to deal with experienced conflicts, for which there is no known, satisfactory, prescribed frame of reference, that gives rise to the creative process, a sequence worked out in real time. This was exemplified in Archimedes' case, but the creative process is not confined to the work of genius. It is a process we may all employ to bring new insight into an undefined, conflicted situation. In fact, it *is* the process we will use if the conflict situation is to become an occasion for new insight and the heightening of consciousness, or 'conscientisation' as Paulo Freire would say. The creative process, then, may be seen as development made intentional and intelligible.

It is also the process by which standard stages and patterns of development themselves are transformed. In Carl Jung's description of individuation,[6] and Erikson's description of young man Luther,[7] the standard developmental sequence of stages is itself transformed in what may be called a transformation of the ego. Here the logic of transformational grammar is preserved, but it is transposed from that which acts upon development from within as the steps of the stage-transition process to that which acts *upon* development from outside as archetype (Jung) or Spirit of God (Luther).

In personal development one finds transformational grammar overturning and then renewing patterns of adaptation; it is also the case in the social and cultural contexts. Since this is currently an emerging aspect of my thesis, I will cite just a few examples: social anthropologist Anthony Wallace's studies of revitalisation movements,[8] and political scientist Manfred Halpern's[9] analysis of social and political change are just two for whom transformation is the key process on a widespread social and political scale. These theorists find that certain major social movements exhibit a complex series of surface interactions, but over a period of time the logic of transformational grammar seeks to emerge as the infrastructure of social and political reorganisation.

There are others for whom transformation is reinterpreted in light of other processes such as socialisation in a tension-reduction, pattern-maintenance system. One such figure would be Talcott Parsons[10] who reinterpreted the transformational dialectics of Karl Marx as a strategy for radical social change that is ultimately subject to the pervasive power of the pattern variables in socialisation. Marxists and other transformationalists, of course, make the reverse emphasis. Others might be cited, but this should suffice to suggest the location, power and pervasiveness of the theme of transformation in social and political thinking. Even though I cannot here make any assessment of its significance, transformation is certainly not a peripheral matter at the level of social organisation, but one that requires careful systematic study and analysis both in relation to the structure and the particulars of a given social context.

In similar manner, let me just suggest that at a cultural level, where symbol systems function to preserve the core values of a given social order, transformational grammar is a significant and sometimes dominant force. It is essential to the systematic structure and educational application of Larry Kohlberg's work on the development of moral judgement.[11] Also, though it may not be as pervasive as Claude Levi-Strauss thinks, his monumental work on mythology and the formation of culture is an elaborate demonstration that cultural forms may well be guided by transformational grammar.[12] Here one also thinks of Robert Bellah's work on 'symbolic realism'.[13] As already indicated, parable, narrative and myth may all depend upon the operation of a transformational grammar. They may either embody an explicit expression of transformation and/or call forth new experience as a transformation of the old.[14]

I do not, by mentioning a few key figures and positions, expect to establish a full-blown thesis, but rather to suggest the fecundity and integrative potential of transformation as a theme running through those human sciences which are most germane to the foundations of Christian education. No systematic understanding of Christian education can avoid it and, as we will see, in a theological context it becomes a matter of primary importance. In fact, it is the theological understanding of how we can learn faith that thrusts transformation as a general theme into the foreground. Thus, we now move from created to uncreated forms of grace.

The theological context: transformation transformed

The appearance of transformational grammar in its theological context takes us directly to the heart of education as a Christian reality, and simultaneously gives that grammar its ultimate form, the form by which we must finally come to understand and interpret all penultimate forms. If the teacher of Truth is the Holy Spirit, and it is by his Spirit that Christ is bestowed and faith is created, then we must take special note of the person and pattern of *Spiritus Creator*. The creator Spirit, it is suggested by Luther, is characterised by a 'grammar' of its own.[15] If Regin Prenter's study of Luther, *Spiritus Creator*,[16] is correct, grammar begins as the Spirit of Christ makes the gospel meaningful for us, that is to say it begins in inner conflict. To have the gospel come to us with meaning is to be thrown into a conflict of immense proportions. The Spirit of Holiness makes us sinners, the enlightenment makes us blind; the dimension of the holy calls into play the threats of evil, annihilation and damnation. The self, its community and its world are exposed as alienated from each other and within themselves.

This is the intention of the Spirit in Luther, to convict through conflict and then to overcome that conflict through the word of the gospel. Thus Luther himself is moved by that Spirit from the just God who condemns to the just God who justifies by faith. Between the mortification and the vivification, the death and the new life, is anguish and longing, a struggle of immense proportions, far beyond the dimensions scanned in an ordinary growth process and certainly beyond those dimensions scanned by the creative scientist or artist in the throes of productivity. In this 'eros is crucified', the human spirit is exposed in its brokenness and restored only as the gift of that same sovereign Spirit. The destiny of this regenerative work is a sanctifying unity with Christ in worship and in his ongoing redemption of the world.

In this highly condensed illustrative account, it is possible to see transformation transformed. The grammar of transformation remains constant, but *Spiritus Creator* radically transforms the origin and destiny of the transformational work of the human personality. In the human personality transformation begins and ends with the development of the personality's adaptational capacities or, in simple terms, begins and ends with the human ego. But in the theological context it is a pattern that begins with Christ's initiative borne in upon the personality by his Spirit and brought through conflict into faith and worship, of which theology is an integral part. A similar kind of argument could be made for social and cultural transformations undergoing transformation by the Spirit of Christ.[17] Thus does double transformation in the theological context bring expression to Christ's word in, according to, and beyond the life and the times of his people.

As in the paradigm case, the aspect of continuity in the theological context is all important. The intention of Christ's Spirit toward us cannot be broken without our falling into an existentialist's narcissistic love of struggle, an enthusiast's repressive denial of it or a rationalistic obsession with interpretation, to suggest just three possible distortions. From the origin to the destiny of the Spirit's work, from the inner to the outer aspects of human participation in that Spirit, continuity is to be maintained for the sake of the integrity of the Spirit's act of creation.

When transformational grammar is operative in the creation of faith, the crucial feature of novelty is the new creation, the jolt into awareness whereby one awakens, as Barth put it, to the on-going transformational activity of Christ's Spirit in the world. This awakening Barth himself describes with dramatic bisociative language:[18]

> the jolt by which man is wakened and at which he wakens ... is not the work of one of the creaturely factors, co-efficients and agencies which are there at work and can be seen, but of the will and act of God who uses these factors and himself makes the co-efficients and agencies for this purpose, setting them in motion as such in the meaning and direction which he has appointed. We are thus forced to say that this awakening is both wholly creaturely and wholly divine. Yet the initial shock comes from God.

What is 'wholly creaturely and wholly divine' represents the extreme in 'habitually unrelated frames of reference coming together to form a meaningful unity' (Koestler), especially when one considers the impassable gulf of sin which would otherwise eternally separate all that is creaturely from the divine creator. Thus, the intertwining of ultimate continuity with ultimate discontinuity according to the pattern of transformation makes this which we call conversion, or the awakening into sanctification, or being shocked into *metanoia*, a personal instance of the word of God under the agency and initiative of God.

Let us be clear that the transformational activity of Christ's Spirit in the church and the world reflects the same grammar personally expressed in conversion, but transposed and extended to the redemption of all creation. Conversion is not conversion out of but *into* the transformation of *all* things. Thus, as Arthur Darby Nock has pointed out in his classic study of conversion,[19] the threat that Christianity posed to Rome was vastly greater than, say, Mithraism or any other sort of cultic conversion since one could, so to say, be a Mithraist on the side. In the theological context when transformation is transformed, one cannot be a Christian on the side. That is to say, neither on the private nor on the public side alone, but only through a comprehensive style of life. Thus we have in conversion an instance of uncreated grace, which marks the transformations already embedded in personality, society and culture as created grace. These may be taken in faith as pedagogical analogues for participation in the ultimate reality of the Transformer of all things. We must say more about this in the following section on education.

In H R Niebuhr's classic study, *Christ and Culture*,[20] the fifth type, 'Christ the transformer of culture', suggests the long standing significance of the transformational theme in the history of the church and its theological self-understanding. From predominantly Johannine and secondarily Pauline biblical sources, this view extends historically up to the present through Augustine, Calvin, F D Maurice (a nineteenth-century British theologian) and, more recently, Professor Willis' inaugural earlier this year establishes a direction also in line with this approach. By mentioning this historical and typological continuity, I do not wish to pigeonhole what anyone may be saying. Niebuhr points out that with the exception of Maurice, no one fits the type perfectly. Rather by way of this typology, I simply wish to indicate where the transformational theme converges with the traditions of the church. Using this typology (one of five) is also a convenient way to acknowledge the fact that this is not the only way to think about these matters.

Now we must examine how the transformational thematisation of the foundational disciplines of Christian education might affect how we perceive the practice of Christian education.

Education in a theological context

Transposing the transformational theme into a theologically oriented educational context means that the theme becomes, not an ideology or archetype, but a model. The model indicates that between the two aspects of this inherently interdisciplinary field, 'Christian' stands not in a modifying but in a transformational relationship to 'education'. So in conclusion, I will illustrate briefly two ways this may take more concrete form. The first concerns what is called the 'guiding principle'; the second concerns 'learning tasks'.

The guiding principle

The guiding principle articulates, in a way that is both theologically and behaviourally sound, the nature of the essential reality with respect to which all the various subdivisions and aspects of Christian education are to be defined, directed and evaluated. As we know, what questions one can ask and what action one can take depends greatly on how and what one can perceive. The guiding principle tells one in the field how to perceive him or herself in relation to the fundamental reality that is at stake.

I have said that the whole enterprise may be systematically related to transformation as an integrative theme. Its internal structure, the manifold expressions generated by it, and its own ultimate transformation by the Spirit of Christ are all implied when I propose that the guiding principle and way of perceiving the entire enterprise, is 'transformation in both its penultimate and its ultimate forms'. The value of this particular formulation is that it includes other candidates for the position, such as 'the bible', 'Jesus Christ' or 'Christ's redeeming activity in the world',[21] but to speak of the transformational activity of Christ's Spirit makes explicit connections between those theological concerns which most directly bear upon education and those understandings of the human sciences which are most relevant to the reconstruction of human life in the modern world.

Lest this be left without more specific implications, I will draw a few concrete conclusions for the learning tasks of the church, parochial school or seminary as guided by the theme of transformation. My hope is that with the guiding principle of transformation, intentional efforts at Christian education on a personal or institutional level may be less likely to rend the whole cloth of theological learning.

The learning tasks

Rethinking the learning tasks under the guidance of transformation takes its primary directive from the five separate steps of the transformational pattern and from the implicit drive toward continuity among them. We have said that one may consciously and intentionally enter that transformational pattern at any of the five points, but if we are to be guided by the logic of transformational grammar, entrance at any one point implies and presses toward participation in all five. However, movement toward such closure among these learning tasks may be influenced by any number of factors, and the particular types of learning may be arrested or perverted. Christian learning tasks, then, are intentionally fostered forms of learning by which one comes to participate in the ongoing transformational Spirit of Christ. Accordingly these tasks overcome some of their potential inhibitions and perversities when they are seen and practised in a transformational relationship to each other.

I will briefly specify five types of learning, both in their positive form and in their most common perversion. 'Types' of course are subject to further breakdown and specifications, but these types will nevertheless serve to make transformation more educationally concrete. I will not take the five steps in the order given above, but in the order in which they represent how we most commonly think of and practise Christian education.

The first type of learning is *learning interpretation and responsible action*. I put it this way because interpretation and action should be seen as mutually informing. In the paradigm case, it was all important that Archimedes could account for himself in theory and verification, that is, interpretation and responsible action. This is the fifth step in the sequence generated by transformation, but the most common point of intentional entrance into the practice of education. It seems that we tend to begin at the end. It is this task with which we most commonly associate education. Who does not ask his or her child 'What did you learn?' and 'What did you learn to do?', assuming this is the point of all education? In more sophisticated terms this task is associated with the best sense of the term 'professional', one who professes and practises in accordance with the knowledge he or she professes. We are most familiar with this task so I will not say more about the positive aspect.

However, a common educational perversity is close at hand; that is, interpretation easily becomes *not* an activity that reaches back into the history of the intense struggles and redeeming insights that give rise to the knowledge one professes, an especially serious omission when theological content is at stake. Instead interpretation slips into becoming the *answer*. Similarly the learner's action becomes *imitative* and not a personal engagement that generates further insight *vis-à-vis* the demanding claims of the content Christianity teaches. One becomes a 'good' learner, learning how to study but never how to generate his or her own thought, and one becomes a 'good' practitioner but without thinking. In essence, the perversity is that interpretation is reduced to answers, albeit 'good' ones, and practice is reduced to imitation and following 'good' advice, with the result that professional*ism* emerges in the wake of stagnant ideas and empty jargon. Instead, learning interpretation in correlation with responsible action is staying alive and responsive to the transforming Spirit of God who continually gives rise to biblical, theological and historical meaning in the very midst of current human action.

The second type of learning most common to us starts at the opening end of the sequence of transformation; namely, with conflict. This is learning to *face and embrace appropriate conflict with perseverance*. This is a complex matter; diagnosing critical conflicts with care requires considerable sensitivity, as Paulo Freire and the advocates of praxis make plain. Care is as important as perseverance; one cannot create what he or she does not care about and persist in. Difficult as this is, it is what is required especially in relation to the social issues of oppression and justice and to more clinically oriented educational experiences.

The perversity which lies embedded in this type of learning, if it should get separated from the guiding principle of transformation, is that learners become narcissistically preoccupied with the *human* struggle, and conflict fails to heighten consciousness of *God*'s action in the world. This occurs because it is not clarified from the outset that the ultimate and decisive conflict is not 'my suffering', 'their suffering' or 'our suffering'. Rather, what is God doing in this world, 'the humanising environment of good and evil' (as Paul Lehmann would call it), to create a people who are truly human according to the humanity of Christ? That is the conflict to face and embrace with perseverance because in its many particular forms which always engage human suffering, that is the conflict that initiates transformation as Christ's living answer.

The third in the order of learning tasks familiar to us and inherent in the sequence of transformation is *learning to celebrate*. Although 'learning' and 'celebration' may sound to some like a contradiction of terms (since some associate celebration with what you do after learning is done), that is precisely the perversion of celebration and calls us to the importance of rethinking celebration according to the grammar of transformation. In the paradigm case, Archimedes does not celebrate disorder but the discovery of the hidden order of things. Celebration in transformation is not an isolated outburst; it is not a temporary self-indulgence in random selection of instinct gratification, but the repeated awakening to and profound appreciation of the fundamental but hidden order of all things undergoing transformation into the glory of God. In this particular learning task there is an important corollary; namely, one tends to learn what one celebrates or whatever generates energy and enthusiasm. Hence, *what* order or *whose* order one celebrates is the all-important consideration since that is the order which will be learned and driven deeper into the learner with every repetition. In cryptic terms, you become what you celebrate.

The fourth type of learning task I will call *contemplative wondering*. This leads one to enter the transformational sequence at the point of interlude and scanning. Here the learner is encouraged and supported in a state of expectant searching; he or she is immersed in the exploration of connections and combinations of meanings for which both the basic problem and the redeeming conflict may still be obscure. He or she has only a strong hunch, or rather I should say, the hunch has him or her. It is like following an inner voice or carrying on an internal dialogue with the unseen teacher as Augustine and Calvin suggested.[22] Most of us visible teachers have a great deal of trouble with learners who do not know exactly what they want to learn but at the same time put us in competition with an unseen voice they trust implicitly.

However, Carl Rogers for one has been especially instructive in showing us that a context of persons who supply the freedom to learn,[23] supporting and refocusing that inner guidance, rather than supplying answers or interpretation, is a vital part of the overall process of learning anything. Most especially this is true of spiritual matters. It is obviously a crucial part of transformational learning because without scanning, or in broader terms, without legitimation and support for contemplative wondering, insights will be proportionately shallow and governed by expediency rather than satisfying the deeper longings behind contemplative wondering. One may learn the language and thought of Karl Barth (or anyone's favourite theologian) even to the point of knowing what he might say next, but without acquiring the capacity for contemplative wonder one will never come to an intuition of the Source that gave rise to Barth's language and thought in the first place. So this is the deeper longing to be learned and supported: contemplative wonder that moves toward ever more comprehensive or universally valid understandings of that inner leading into the reality of the Transformer of all things.

The perversity of this is, of course, subjectivism and the dark love of 'inscape'. However, it should be noted that the chronic fear of subjectivism or self-absorption is as antithetical to transformation as its opposite. The first perverts contemplative wonder by self-indulgence, the second by denial.

The fifth, the form of learning I believe we understand least, is perhaps most crucial to the transformational process: namely, learning from convictional experiences or from insights that reach the proportions of convictional significance. Those numinous experiences which have overwhelming convicting force often seem to be threatening aberrations from the ordinary course of life because they are the bearers of the discontinuity of grace, yet they have a profound significance upon the lives of those who have them. Some studies show that 75 per cent of Presbyterian clergy, UPUSA, have had experiences of sudden spiritual awakening; 45 to 47 per cent of Presbyterian laity[24] have had such experiences; and about 40 per cent of the American population.[25] Now, it is not that everyone must be induced into having an experience, nor is that we should worship convicting experiences, nor should we gather into groups for which the membership ticket is having had an experience or being able to have one on a weekly basis. These are some of the perversities of how such experiences teach. When such experiences do their educational job, they serve a prophetic role; symbolically and substantively they preserve the sense of the reality of 'uncreated grace', and make the decisive break with the human order and the human spirit. They declare that grace is God's alone to give and so move one through the dialectic of transformation into the worship and glorification of him, the supreme end of the transforming work of Christ's Spirit. As such they are signs of the presence and power of the kingdom of God and they belong not to the convicted person but to God's people. They expose, however momentarily and partially, the nature of the reality into which all of life is being integrated.

Each of the five types of learning needs the others to complete the overall theme of transformation as the guiding principle of intentional Christian education. However, no one person will be equally competent in all, but all together in the body of Christ under his unifying intention, constitute the learning community of faith that exhibits the transforming life of Christ in and for the world.

Of course, much more needs to be said about answering the educational questions which were mentioned at the outset, but this may at least suggest the direction of the vision of Christian education that begins to emerge when the theme of transformation takes a more systematic role in structuring of the field.

'Therefore every scribe who has been trained for the kingdom of heaven is like a householder who brings out of his treasure what is new and what is old' (Matthew 13:52).[26]

Notes

1. C Levi-Strauss, *Structural Anthropology*, New York, Doubleday Anchor, 1967, p. 70.
2. J Piaget, *The Principles of Genetic Epistemology*, New York, Basic Books, 1972.
3. B Lonergan, *Insight*, New York, Philosophical Library, 1970, pp. 3f; and Arthur Koestler, *The Act of Creation*, New York, Dell, 1969, pp. 105f.
4. An instance connecting stage–transition to orthogenesis is Peter Wolff's monograph, *The Developmental Psychologies of Jean Piaget and Psychoanalysis*, New York, International Universities Press, 1970 (in the series *Psychological Issues*, volume 2, number 1, monograph 5).
5. E Maranda and P Maranda, *Structural Models in Folklore and Transformational Essays*, The Hague, Mouton, 1971, especially pp. 83f; J Fowler, *et al.*, *Life Maps*, Texas, Word Books, 1978.
6. C G Jung, *The Structure and Dynamics of the Psyche*, in the *Collected Works*, volume 8, Princeton, Princeton University Press, 1969; or *The Portable Jung*, New York, Viking, 1971, especially chapters 1, 2, 6, 9.
7. Erik Erikson, *Young Man Luther*, New York, W W Norton, 1962.
8. A Wallace, 'Revitalization movements', in W Lessa and E Vogt (eds), *Reader in Comparative Religion*, New York, Harper and Row, 1972, pp. 421–429.
9. See among his other papers, Manfred Halpern's 'Transformation and the source of the fundamentally new', a paper prepared for the American Political Science Association, 1974.
10. See T Parsons' analysis and interpretation of Marxism in *Sociological Theory and Modern Society*, New York, Free Press, 1967, chapter 4.
11. L Kohlberg, *Collected Papers on Moral Development and Moral Education*, published privately, Spring, 1973, chapter 13.
12. C Levi-Strauss, *Structural Anthropology;* and *Mythologiques* I, II, III, Paris, 1964, of which volume, I, *The Raw and the Cooked*, New York, Harper and Row, 1969, is the first to be translated into English.
13. R Bellah, 'Christianity and symbolic realism', *Journal for the Scientific Study of Religion*, 9, 1970, pp. 89–115; see also R Bellah, *Beyond Belief*, New York, Harper and Row, 1970.
14. For instance, not all folk tales are transformational in their plot structure, but as symbol systems they may call for a transformation of some aspect of the experiential order in which they arise.
15. *D Martin Luthers Werke: Kritische Gesamtausgabe*, Weimar 1883, volume 32, part 2, pp. 104–105.
16. Regin Prenter, *Spiritus Creator*, Philadelphia, Muhlenberg Press, 1953, especially pp. 184ff.
17. Paul Lehmann's work in both his major volumes, *Ethics in a Christian Context*, London, SCM, 1963, and *The Transfiguration of Politics*, London, SCM, 1975, gives indications of the direction suggested here.
18. K Barth, *Church Dogmatics*, volume 4, part 2, Edinburgh, T and T Clark, 1956, pp. 557f.
19. A D Nock, *Conversion*, London, Oxford University Press, 1952.
20. H R Niebuhr, *Christ and Culture*, New York, Harper and Row, 1951.
21. D C Wyckoff, *The Gospel and Christian Education*, Philadelphia, Westminster Press, 1959, pp. 87f.
22. J Calvin, *Institutes of the Christian Religion*, III, I, 4, Philadelphia, Westminster Press, 1960, volume 2, pp. 541–42.
23. C Rogers, *Freedom to Learn*, Columbus, Charles E Merrill, 1969.
24. *Presbyterian Panel*, March 1978 Questionnaire, Research Division of the Support Agency, United Presbyterian Church in the USA.
25. A Greeley, *Sociology of the Paranormal*, Beverly Hills, Sage, 1975.
26. This article is adapted from an inaugural address.

8.2 Spiritual formation and theological education

George Lindbeck

Introduction

This article is an attempt to think through the relation of spiritual formation to preparation for ministry. It is not a research paper, and I have not surveyed the literature for items to suggest as preparatory readings.[1] After the section 'An introductory parable', I deal with 'Spiritual formation' (in relation to ministry), 'Theological education' (in relation to spiritual formation) and 'Future prospects'. My overall theses are summarised in the penultimate paragraph. I have left them to the end because, although there is no harm in reading them first, they grow out of the paper and are not conclusions which I set out to prove.

An introductory parable

One major section of the quadrangle constructed close to sixty years ago to house Yale Divinity School was a well-equipped gymnasium. Wellington's observation that the British Empire was won on the playing fields of Eton was in those days still a commonplace, and it was not known that the YMCA ideology of muscular Christianity would shortly fade. By the 1960s, however, the gymnasium had come to seem a sinful extravagance, and it has now been taken over by the Institute of Sacred Music and by an extension of the library. The largest space, the basketball court, has been transformed into 'The Great Hall' for artistic and occasional liturgical and audio-visual academic performances. I could not help wondering as I worked on this article if perhaps sixty years from now it will be 'The Great Hall' for spiritual formation and meditation.

This bit of history can serve as a parable to the perils of prediction and of the complexity of the conditions for change in educational institutions. It is worth reminding ourselves of some of those conditions in order to put the present enquiry into perspective.

First, there must be a perceived need. The need may be sublime or ridiculous: it may be for black or women's studies, or for spiritual, or for physical, formation. But there must be something or other which is perceived as a need.

Second, the need must be felt by a group which influences institutional policy. Prospective students are such a group. If there is no gym, they may succumb to the lure of the big city and go to New

York, to Union (probably the major competitor of Yale in the 1920s). Congregations can also influence policy. If enough of them develop an enduring preference for muscular or spiritual ministers, they will get them. Teachers, administrators and governing boards also play a role, but perhaps not as independent or decisive a one as in the past. What they want, in our market-oriented society, tends more and more to be what they think the customers, the students and churches, desire.

A third requirement is for financing, for donors. Gymnasiums and spiritual formation programmes do not come into existence without money. Money, furthermore, flows towards fashionable causes, and the course of fashion is meandering. Sometimes rightist enthusiasms are mobilised by this or that cause, and sometimes leftist ones. Sometimes (though rarely in our day) fads develop which resist political classification. The point is that apart from a *Zeitgeist* which loosens purse strings, a desired development is not likely to occur or persist.

Fourth, there must be persuasive legitimations. These may be genuinely theological, but not always. *Ad hoc* arguments sometimes win the day: for example, young men need and like exercise and a philanthropist is available. Sometimes rationalisations triumph: religion is represented as a bastion of the American way of life in order to increase the cash flow. Rationalisations and *ad hoc* arguments tend to collapse when challenged, and with them the causes they promote. Rationales are required which relate the proposed change to the fundamental purposes of theological education and which show its practicability. Both normative desirability and practical feasibility must be exhibited. Those who minister to God's people (so the argument would go) should be spiritually and physically fit and, this is crucial, the seminary is a (or the) proper place for the requisite training to take place. Such training will enhance rather than detract from the theological ('academic') and pastoral ('practical') components of the professional ministerial education which is the seminary's proper business. Normative arguments, however, are not enough. What is clearly desirable may in some contexts be so disruptive of other values that instituting it may be more trouble than it is worth. That is why the United States has not yet shifted to the metric system, and why Britons have so long resisted driving on the right rather than the left.

In such situations, it is often the over-all theology, ideology or culture which is decisive. One-worlders, for example, are more likely to favour the change over to the metric system than are isolationists, and gymnasiums for divinity schools seem less odd to sports-minded English-speaking peoples than to Continentals or traditional Chinese or Indians. Views on the desirability or feasibility of integrating spiritual formation into ministerial education may depend in part on the total vision both of religion and of the contemporary situation.

It is over-all vision with which this article is concerned, but I have tried to keep in mind the other factors. This makes my argument conditional: if such and such is the case, then such and such can or should happen in the light of the understanding of spirituality, theology and theological education which is here presented. Conditionality, however, is tedious, and my sentences are for the most part declarative. Readers are asked to remember the parable of the gymnasium and make their own corrections of the apodictic tone.

Spiritual formation

Looked at non-theologically, spiritual formation may be described as the deep and personally committed appropriation of a comprehensive and coherent outlook on life and the world. From this perspective, those who are maturely humanistic or maturely Marxist, for example, are in their own way spiritually well-formed. The spiritually mature are not simply socialised into behaving under standard conditions as is expected of members of their group, but they have to a significant degree developed the capacities and dispositions to think, feel and act in accordance with their world view no matter what the circumstances. They have, in Aristotelian language, the habits or virtues distinctively emphasised by the encompassing vision which is theirs. In the Christian case, these are traditionally named faith, hope and love, but other religions when internalised may involve quite a different set of virtues.[2]

Spiritual formation involves, but is not the same as, conversion or personal commitment: the newly and ardently converted, for example, may be poorly formed. Further, there is a kind of conversion which might be described as the refocusing of an already deeply internalised religion (consider Wesley at Aldersgate), or falls from sanctity may occur and be followed by repentance or reconversion (consider Peter at Jesus' trial and again at Antioch), or there may even be conversions, however rare, from one maturely held religion to another. It needs also to be recalled that spiritual maturity is different from the psychological and moral varieties. Neurotics can be saints. Indeed, they seem more numerous than non-neurotics among the canonised, perhaps because the triumphs of grace in the psychologically abnormal are more spectacular. Similarly, the spiritually mature are sometimes inferior to the immature (or the pagans) in the cardinal moral virtues of prudence, justice (or fairness), courage and temperance, despite their eminence in the theological virtues of faith, hope and love. Selflessness is not always combined with good sense.

Spiritualities vary greatly in type as well as intensity, not only between but also within religious traditions. The dispositions and capacities for speech, feeling and action which are distinctive of Christianity, for example, both shape and are deeply shaped by differences in culture, personal history and genetic constitution. Think of Monica and of her son, Augustine, of Teresa of Avila and Luther, of Bonhoeffer and Teresa of Calcutta. All are immensely different, and yet all are exemplary instances of Christian spirituality. (For those who do not agree with these examples, there are plenty of others which can be cited to make the same point.)

In a religion of the book, such as Christianity, the ultimate even if not the proximate criteria for identifying the spiritually mature are biblical. The most influential models are likely to be contemporary, but only if they are seen as not contradicting scriptural norms. Holy writ is not to be parroted, but rather its patterns function as grammatical paradigms. Just as the rule exemplified by *amo, amas, amat* is not followed when one repeats the same words, but only when one inflects other first-conjugation verbs in accordance with it, so also with the scriptural guidelines.

Thus, to extend the analogy, it is scriptural grammar rather than vocabulary which is decisive for determining what is Christian. Feminist spiritualities, for example, may adhere to the rule of love to God and neighbour while expunging patriarchal images and language; while, on the other hand, apartheid spiritualities, most of us would say, are grammatically anti-Christian even when they are insistently biblical in vocabulary. The grammar of sacred texts, not least that of the bible when read in its canonical unity, is generative just as is the grammar of natural languages. Innumerable unanticipatable sentences and spiritualities can be formed in accordance with it even while it also excludes other sentences, and attitudes and actions, as ungrammatical, as unbiblical. (Not that grammatical sense is sufficient for truth or rightness, but it is necessary. Grammatically unbiblical apartheid, so the argument goes, simply cannot be authentically Christian, while grammatically biblical feminism, like any genuine orthodoxy, can be, even if it not always is, christianly deployed.)

When one thinks, as is suggested by the analogy we are using, of spiritual formation as similar to acquiring linguistic competence, then it is evident this can happen in many ways. The training may be informal or formal, communal or individual, public or private, inside or outside schools. There are those for whom quite literally *laborare est orare*, and others for whom meditative and devotional practices are essential. Some best find their own way, while others are helped by organised, methodical programmes.

Organised training programmes, to speak next of them, increase in importance to the degree informal procedures fail. We rely on schooling to teach us a language when we do not live in communities where it is spoken well. The church as a whole was such a community in the first centuries, and later, when the masses were only superficially christianised, monasteries played a similar role. It was perhaps only with the rise of Third Order movements in the late middle ages that spiritual formation began to become an organised enterprise distinct from life and worship in community, and it was not until the Jesuits and their *Spiritual Exercises* that there developed methodical training programmes designed to form individuals capable of maintaining a high spirituality even when isolated for long periods from supportive companions. The needs of secular Catholic clergy living alone in parishes were similar, though less extreme, than those of Jesuit missionaries among pagans and heretics, and spiritual formation programmes with objectives not unlike those of the Jesuits became a normal part of post-Tridentine seminary life.

In Protestantism, special programmes of spiritual formation have been slow to develop. Those dissatisfied with the low spirituality of the comprehensive churches have withdrawn into sectarian enclaves, formed *ecclesiolae in ecclesiam*, or engaged in do-it-yourself spiritual training. Theological education continued to take place in the medieval fashion in universities and colleges where no special provisions were made for the spiritual formation of ministerial candidates other than those available to all students, and the same held true when ministerial training was by apprenticeship. Nor was the pattern broken when Protestant churches began establishing separate seminaries in the first part of the last century. Fledgling ministers were expected to develop spiritually by the same means as other Christians. Clerical spirituality tended to be like that of devout layfold (consider, for example, the importance of family devotions) in contrast to the Catholic situation where lay spirituality was largely modelled after what developed in religious orders.

Nor was the Protestant pattern wholly inefficacious. My impressions, for what they are worth, is that when I entered Yale Divinity School in the 40s, my fellow students could generally be counted on to have been well-socialised in distinctively Christian beliefs and practices, to be familiar with biblical content even when they were from Quaker or Unitarian churches to an extent which is now exceptional even from those of fundamentalist background (and is rivalled among contemporary students most often by blacks), and to have had some exposure, often, to be sure, unsuccessful, to devotional disciplines including individual bible reading and prayer. They had, in short, the beginnings of a spiritual formation. Many now complain it did not last, but it seems likely it would have proved less fragile if it had been nurtured throughout their lives in the more supportive social settings which were characteristic of their parents' day. I am not saying, be it noted, that students were theologically more conservative in the 1940s (at Yale, they were not), but that on both the theological left and theological right, some degree of spiritual formation was present.

If common testimony and my own observations are to be trusted, the situation has changed dramatically. A much larger proportion of seminary students than in the past view themselves as religious seekers rather than adherents, lack (by their own admission) commitment to the ministry, are in need of elementary catechesis, have little (sometimes no) prior socialisation in distinctively Christian beliefs and practices (which, to be sure, in view of the present dysfunctional character of many traditional forms is not altogether a disadvantage), and have no experience with regular devotional exercises of any kind; or, if they have had such experience, this is often with practices more often associated with Eastern than Western religions.

Yet while ministerial candidates have less spiritual formation than before, the need seems to be greater. Fewer parishioners have internalised a coherent and comprehensive religious outlook, and this lack of parishioner support makes personal spiritual maturity more necessary in order to bear ministerial burdens throughout a lifetime of often thankless work. Thus as religious formation (and even socialisation) declines, the need escalates.

If this is right, the growing clamour for religious formation is not a superficial fad of fashion but has, as a Marxist might say, infrastructurally deep sources. As is often the case, the need as actually experienced does not correspond to the objective situation. The spiritual formation which most contemporary students desire is not the internalisation of a comprehensive and coherent religious outlook and correlated practices such as a communal tradition provides. They rather think in terms of discovering or eclectically constructing their own individual vision and corresponding form of life. For reasons which are widely discussed (*Habits of the Heart* by Robert Bellah[3] and associates is a good example), it is doubtful that even religious geniuses proceed in this fashion. The biblical prophets, not least him whom the apostolic writings announce as the final one, were deeply immersed in their own tradition. Jesus was a spiritually mature Jew, and only because of this, humanly speaking, a religiously creative individual.

Yet it is the needs which are actually experienced which must be dealt with, and this involves taking individualistic spiritual questing seriously. These quests are not always unsuccessful. At the core of many persons' socially-formed identities are traces of a coherent world view, a responsible religious tradition. Uncovering and recovering this heritage is nothing less than life from death for some people. This can be true even when the traditional and cultural roots of what is rediscovered are not recognised. Therapeutic self-discovery may be important to spiritual formation, even if by itself insufficient.

It was Henri Nouwen during his years at Yale Divinity School who best illustrated for me the possibility of combining spiritual therapy and formation.[4] He lured students by therapeutic tactics to discover in the depths of their beings the need for distinctively Christian devotional disciplines. There was little in these disciplines of which the desert Fathers or Loyola or the Puritans would have disapproved, and much would have seemed boringly traditional in the 1940s; but in the 1970s, they were experienced as refreshingly counter-cultural. This, to be sure, had its disadvantages. Those counter-cultural enthusiasts for Nouwen who never broke through to an appreciation of the historic heritage have, it seems to me, tended to retain only the individualistically therapeutic side of his teaching. They may meditate, but they do not go to church, and they are inclined to treat the bible and the Bhagavad Gita as interchangeable.

It should be added that something like spiritual therapy can have a place, not only in initial but also in later stages of formation. Difficulties become insuperable only when the therapeutic approach is taken as normative, when a model of what might be called 'exfoliation' replaces 'formation'. When this happens, the spiritual life is seen as one of discovering and creatively expressing a pre-given individual identity, and no attention is paid to that internalisation of a communal religious tradition which is the condition for fruitful spiritual self-expression or exfoliation, for authentic individuality and genuine creativity. When the development of spiritual selfhood is well advanced, the process of self-discovery can be an integral part of maturation, but not before. Meister Eckhart's search for the spark within or the Quaker turn towards the inner light did not take place without formation.

Before concluding this section, however, we must note that special spiritual formation for ministers may be a *pis aller*. It would be better if it were not needed. It carries with it the peril of increasing the gap between clergy and laity, and this is true no matter what the style of spirituality, whether therapeutic, liberationist or traditional. A kind of clerical spiritual élitism has been fostered in the past by special programmes, as especially the Catholic experience makes evident, and it is not clear that the strenuously egalitarian anti-hierarchalism of much contemporary spirituality solves the problem. When advanced by clergy, the claim 'We are just like everyone else' can divide pastors from congregations just as surely as clerical pretensions and communication-blocking lifestyles have often done in the past. It is best if pastor and flock are formed by basically the same means of grace and devotional disciplines. Yet when the general spiritual level is low (which, it needs to be remembered, is different from, though not unrelated to, questions of moral and psychological health) this can be disastrous. As should be clear by now, I know of no reason to challenge the common opinion that spiritual maturity is increasingly difficult, and special formation for ministers, the *disciplina arcana* of which Bonhoeffer speaks[5], is needed.

The question remains, however, whether such formation should be a programmatic part of seminary life. Can it be integrated in mutually supportive ways with the main business of the seminary, with theological education; or is it unrelated (as was the gymnasium at Yale Divinity School); or perhaps even harmfully competitive? In order to deal with such questions, we need to discuss the nature of theology and theological education, and it is to this that we now turn.

Theological education

The kind of theology with which we are concerned, the kind which lays claim to being an academic and scholarly (or, as the Germans would say, 'scientific') enterprise, is second-order reflection on *what* a religion is. Its subject matter is the primary, first-order activities of *how* to speak, feel, think and act religiously. It is pursued on behalf of the communities which adhere to the religion and therefore, in contrast to religious studies, has a normatively critical aspect. It is concerned, in other words, with publicly articulating, defending and assessing normative descriptions of how the religious communities and individuals should believe and practise in various circumstances. Because circumstances change, so also do religious traditions and, even more, the theologies which seek to describe, explain, correct and defend them. Yet, to return to the linguistic metaphor, the vocabulary of belief and practice can alter even while the grammar (cf. 'doctrine') of a religion remains much the same. Thus theological descriptions can be highly critical of what exists (for example, patriarchalism or fundamentalism or historic attitudes towards war) without contradicting basic continuity and identity. For this to happen, however, the descriptions need to be developed from within and for the sake of the communal tradition. The primary concern must be for faithfulness to intrinsic rather than extraneous evaluative criteria, to 'the biblical witness' rather than 'the modern minds', for example. (This, to be sure, does not exclude attention to external criteria, though the appropriate form and degree of that attention is sharply debated between, for example, foundationalists and non-foundationalists).

The interrelationships of theology and spirituality vary greatly because of the diversity of genetic, personal and cultural factors by which both theology and spirituality are influenced. It is possible, however, to risk a double generalisation. Competence in the first-order practice and the second-order normative description of a religion are partly independent skills, but in so far as they are interdependent, the relationship is asymmetrical: learning to practise is helped far less by learning to describe, than *vice versa*. To be sure, there are cases in which spiritual practice seems to have been enhanced by theological skill (for example, the ontological argument was a contemplative breakthrough for Anselm), but this is rare. In contrast to this, although good theology is possible without spiritual maturity (or even belief), it is generally better, other things being equal, when it is done by the spiritually mature, by those who are skilled in the practice of the faith. This is not a situation peculiar to religion. Much the same relationship obtains between other first- and second-order enterprises: science and philosophy of science, literature and literary criticism, language use and grammatical studies. Supreme masters of a tongue, such as Homer, need know nothing about grammar, but grammarians are helped by skill in using the language they study.

What we have just described is active theological ability, but there is also a kind of passive competence in which the saintly excel. The spiritually mature may have only the most meagre ability to articulate and describe their patterns of belief and practice, but they can recognise misdescriptions. They may have no talent in assessing differences between the second-order accounts which theologians formulate, but they can sense 'connaturally', as Aquinas put it, when the usages authorised by these accounts violate the deep grammar of the faith. Corporately and in the long run, those who have internalised a communal tradition are the final judges of its theology. What they reject is falsified. Here again, there is a similar relation between second-order description and first-order practice in other areas. When grammarians or philosophers of science propose usages which make no sense to the linguistically or scientifically competent and creative, it is the grammarians and the philosophers whom we say are wrong.

It would be misleading to suggest, however, that first order practitioners are always judges and never judged by second-order reflection. Many who claim to be scientifically skilled (ranging from astrologers to those who fabricate evidence) are excluded from the ranks by general consent among scientists, and it is those engaged in reflection, the philosophers of science, who attempt to articulate the criteria for this exclusion. Similarly, theologians both articulate and help shape a communal consensus on who are or are not spiritually mature representatives of the religious tradition in question. Theology and spirituality, description and practice, are reciprocally or dialectically tested by each other, but in this interaction, it is the theologians who have the more active but preliminary role, and the spiritually mature who have the more passive but decisive one.

For the first Christian millennium, theology and spirituality were not programmatically distinguished. Beginning with St Paul, those rated theologically competent were also regarded as spiritually mature, but not always *vice versa*. Theological writers were on the whole a sub-set of the spiritual ones (although, it should be added, some of their treatises, especially the polemical ones, are as useless for spiritual formation as is most contemporary academic theology).

Methodical and institutional differentiation began to develop in the West only with the rise of scholasticism and the universities. In the East, the separation never fully took place. The Orthodox were in less need of it. Unlike Latin, Greek remained a vernacular, and literacy, liturgy, mores and social order were not disrupted by barbarian invasions to the same extent as in the West. There was more unbroken tradition and spirituality on which to rely, and thus less room for the development of a distinct second-order controlling and critical theological enterprise.

Such an enterprise seemed necessary in the West in order to compensate for the low spiritual estate of the superficially christianised masses. Yet for centuries only a small portion of the clergy were theologically trained. Even those who went to university generally stopped with liberal arts or, if they went on, took other degrees such as those in canon law. Theology was the business of a small corps of specialists whose job was to advise others, including the leaders of state as well as of the church, regarding what was or was not acceptably Christian. Preachers were expected to have some knowledge of theology, and were often university trained, but the great majority of priests rarely or never preached.

It was not until the sixteenth century that the notion took hold that all ordained ministers should receive at least some theological education. Not only the Reformation emphasis on the word and on preaching contributed to this, but also the exigencies of interconfessional controversy. This helps explain why theological education for all clergy became a Catholic as well as Protestant ideal. One difference, however, was that the Protestants continued to educate theologically in universities wherever they could, while the Catholics, anticipating the Protestants by 250 years, generally established separate seminaries (as the Council of Trent had decreed). The combination of scriptural and university emphases made Protestantism resemble rabbinic Judaism in its equation of communal leadership with religious learning. Both Catholic and Protestant theology, however, were also shaped by a concern for apologetics far greater than in most rabbinic Judaism (at least after Maimonides). The dechristianisation of the high culture of the West (which began with the Renaissance and was intensified by rationalism, the Enlightenment, and the development of modern science) made it important, especially in the educated classes, that ministers be intellectually persuasive interpreters and defenders of the faith, not only against heretics but also against those indifferent or hostile to all historically particular (or, as was said in those days, 'revealed') religions. So strong was the emphasis on theological learning that 'theologians' became the name in some places (especially the continent) for all ministerial students.

Thus, the gap between theology and spirituality widened. It was, to be sure, already large in the late middle ages, but there had been for a time a *rapprochement* under the influence of the humanistic Renaissance emphasis on rhetoric reinforced by the piety of the Protestant and Catholic reforms. Increasingly, however, the ideals of intellectual objectivity characteristic of late scholasticism were revived, reinforced and transformed by rationalism, Enlightenment and scientism. Believers, even when they struggled against these developments, often came to resemble their opponents: fundamentalist notions of truth as objectivity, for example, are often scientistic in their extremism. Non-fundamentalists were also affected. The normative dimension of theological description tended to be neglected, or when it was attended to, the chief concern was often with external rather than intrinsic criteria of evaluation: the preoccupation was with making religion intelligible and meaningful by the standards of the dechristianised high culture rather than with faithfulness as judged by internal norms. Even self-involvement and existential commitment can be studied in order to exhibit the deficiencies of scientism without reference to normative questions of how to be rightly or wrongly self-involved and committed in the actual communal and individual practice of a religion. Spirituality has tended to be banished from theological education even as an object of study. Further, when it has been studied, this has often been in a fashion similar to the kind of literary criticism which focuses on facts about writers and writings and evaluates them by the alien standards of, for example, political relevance or psychoanalytic insight without concern for the enhancement of specifically literary appreciation and skill. Given the prevailing understanding of science and of scholarship, it is hard to see how it could be otherwise. Even personally devout theological educators fail to relate their teaching and research to spirituality.

The practical, pastoral or clinical side of the curriculum tends to be equally remote from personal appropriation and internalisation. The ministerial skills needed in a society such as ours are those of salesmanship (which preaching often becomes), administration, therapy and (rather peripherally except in liturgical traditions) masters of ceremonies. These abilities have their place but, as in the case of competence in academic studies, they are only extraneously related to the spiritual life. They seem neither to enhance nor be enhanced by spiritual formation.

There is a further problem which needs to be mentioned and which is perhaps inevitable when all ministers (rather than only a minority as in the middle ages) are given theological educations. Relatively few people have much aptitude or interest in second-order reflective activity. They may acquire abundant information about what others have thought, but have no talent for thinking theologically themselves. Theological education for all clergy thus has a tendency to focus on the impartation of information and the development of preferences among the available theological options. There is no decisive difference between *laissez faire* liberalism and rigid conservatism in this respect: the liberals leave choices to the students and the conservatives indoctrinate, but theological competence is not necessarily involved in either case. Other professions, as it happens, have similar problems: medical students, for example, may absorb masses of scientific knowledge without learning to think scientifically. Indeed, this difficulty is also common in education in the pure sciences. Neophytes must assimilate what others have learned and become proficient in routine skills in order, at a more advanced stage, to make personal contributions to the progress of a communal intellectual enterprise; but, as John Ziman among others has pointed out,[6] many who shine in the first phase, fail miserably in the second, while some who get through the assimilative stage only with difficulty, succeed brilliantly, if they persist, in the second. The difficulty in professional education, at least in theology, is that few have the opportunity or the incentive to go on to the second stage, the stage of actually doing science or scholarship or theology. That is left to Ph D programmes in the graduate schools.

Whether this will continue to work in the case of theology is, however, doubtful. In our pluralistic society, graduate programmes are increasingly oriented to religious studies, and the internally normative and critical aspects of theological description is neglected. Insofar as evaluation of religious traditions does occur, it tends to be from the outside in terms of external criteria rather than from the inside by internal ones. Students may become adept at assessing papalism, biblicism or patriarchalism, for example, but by alien norms rather than by those ingredient in the historic heritages. They may study theologians skilled in constructive and internally normative reflection, Rahner, Barth, Tillich, the Niebuhr brothers, to cite recent examples, but are not enabled or disposed to do as they did in ways appropriate to changed circumstances. It is as if the emphasis were more and more on producing experts in linguistics or comparative literature who focus on features common to all languages and literatures, and less and less on Arabists, Germanists or Americanists with their detailed acquaintance with the particularities of specific traditions. If this is what is happening, then specifically theological education will suffer on the MDiv as well as PhD level. Seminary teachers are trained in the graduate schools.

This trend away from theology towards religious studies is related to increased interest in certain kinds of spiritual formation. If Hindu and Buddhist texts as well as biblical ones are part of the curriculum, for example, the possibility of both enriching borrowings (as the early Christians borrowed from the Greeks) or therapeutic eclecticism (also abundantly anticipated by, for example, gnosticism in the first centuries) is enhanced. This, however, does not make spiritual formation any easier to integrate into the curriculum. The very *raison d'être* of religious studies in a pluralistic society, viz. neutrality, makes them resistant to programmatic concern for the formation of mature Buddhists or Muslims or Jews or Christians. Academically respectable graduate schools avoid such training like poison. They leave it, usually disdainfully, to gurus, ashrams, monasteries and yeshivas.

The conclusion of this section is that the difficulties of special spiritual ministerial formation within the seminary are increasing. There is a growing gap between it, on the one hand, and the academic and pastoral skill aspects of the curriculum, on the other. Yet the need is so great, as we saw earlier, that it may be necessary to emphasise formation far more than in the past; and this despite the danger that it will be as peripheral as was the gymnasium at Yale Divinity School.

What, however, of the prospects for the future? Can the difficulties decrease and the dangers diminish? Is there anything that can be done to change the situation? These are the themes of the last section.

Future prospects

The future is only minimally controllable. If changes come in the relation of spiritual formation to the rest of the curriculum, they will not to any great extent be the product of deliberate planning. It is the theological disciplines themselves which must alter for intrinsic scholarly and academic reasons rather than to serve ulterior purposes. This is a first point which must be emphasised.

This means, among other things, that theology will not change in enduringly significant ways without new developments in cognate areas of scholarship. Ours is a society which values academic credentials and respectability. Only ghettoised religious communities can afford to educate their leaders in traditional yeshivas or their Christian counterparts. Our seminaries must conform to the general standards of what passes for responsible education or they will lose students and faculty.

It is a part of any discussion of future possibilities, therefore, to try to discern shifts in the wider intellectual climate. There is, as it happens, general agreement that a major shift is taking place in the very notion of science, though no unanimity on how to describe it.

According to one characterisation, a scientific or scholarly enterprise is now increasingly seen as a research programme (or network of such programmes) carried on by a community of investigators who reach agreements on what is affirmable or not affirmable through rhetorical processes of social interaction as well as through formalisable logical and experimental procedures. They work in and out of fiduciary frameworks (Polanyi) or webs of belief (Quine) or language games and forms of life (Wittgenstein) which are untestable, unverifiable and incapable of being fully articulated. These frameworks themselves shape the standards by means of which observation, testing and verification take place. The structures of reason and experience which the Enlightenment thought of as universal and unchanging (and, in the case of Kant, *a priori*) are now seen as the products of historically conditioned communal activities and habits. The attempt to distinguish neatly and once and for all between their necessary and contingent, their *a priori* and *a posteriori*, features is futile.

In this context, the normal initial attitude of investigators is that of unquestioning acceptance of earlier results of the research programme, that is, the accumulated wisdom of the past. To question everything is paralysis. It is irrational to doubt what the community believes, whether the quarks of the physicist or the gods of Olympus, unless there are specific reasons for doing so such as the emergence of anomalous data or the discovery of inconsistencies with other things which are believed. It is intellectually irresponsible (rather than responsible as post-Cartesian modernity would say) to doubt a belief simply because it is unverified or, as far as is now known, unverifiable. Indeed, the attempt to verify in the strict sense is logically absurd, and only falsification is possible. Truth is justified belief, and a belief is justified to the extent that it is integral to the research programme (which, however intellectual it may be, is itself *praxis*) and there is nothing which tells against it.

On this view, it is not a misfortune but a necessity that what counts as rationality, truth and falsity varies from discipline to discipline. There may be universal standards (after all, all human beings do have something in common), but they are, in Charles Peirce's sense of the term, 'vague ideas' which lack normative power apart from field-specific determinations.[7] Thus even the law of non-contradiction is vague because the frameworks for identifying what are to count as contradictions are enquiry-and-community relative.

Yet this outlook is not in the least relativistic in the sense of *laissez faire*. The demands for scholarly rigour do not diminish. Different games involve different rules, but there are rules. There must be agreed-upon procedures for specifying what are anomalies and inconsistencies, for allowing particular beliefs to be questioned but not all together, and for determining when falsification occurs.

These features of scientific work are to some degree characteristic of every open-ended process of communal consensus-building in which the procedures for decision-making are internal to the enquiry (that is, 'rules of the game') rather than external (for example, bribing the players or changing the rules to ensure a given outcome). Normative reflection on a religion has at times been such an enterprise. The communal tradition of rabbinic learning has had this character, and so also, to some extent, did much patristic thought, or aspects of medieval scholasticism, or the theological consensus-building in the Reformed and, to a lesser extent, Lutheran traditions before Westminster (1649) and the Formula of Concord (1580). It is no longer possible, however, to play these particular versions of the theological game with ghettoisation, and no new versions of comparable communal significance have developed. None of the contemporary mainline traditions has sufficient procedural agreement to constitute a consensus-building community of open-ended enquiry. Catholics are stronger on community and consensus, and Protestants on open-ended enquiry, but what both lack are theology-specific criteria which effectively link consensus and open-endedness, tradition and creativity.

Instead, the procedures of academically respectable theology tend to be either adaptations of purportedly universal and increasingly discredited Enlightenment standards or else borrowings from new developments in non-theological disciplines. The tendency, for example, is to appeal to some general hermeneutics developed in a non-theological context and then apply this regionally to the bible. Few mainstream scholars think it possible to work from within scripture-specific traditions of, for example, midrashic or narrative-typological interpretation and adapt and develop these to meet contemporary exigencies. For many, to cite an example at random, structuralism has more *eclat*.

It is too early to say if this will change; but to the degree that it does, theology will cease to depend for its scholarly status on other disciplines. It will become in its own right a community, or group of communities, of consensual and open-ended enquiry into how best normatively to describe Christianity.

To the extent that this happens, it will have consequences for spiritual formation within seminaries. There will be greater scholarly attention to spirituality. This need not mean that courses on spirituality will bulk large in the curriculum. While it is true that spiritual maturity is important to the church and therefore also of interest to any theology which understands itself as a normatively descriptive enterprise in the service of the church, this does not necessarily imply that the spirituality should be a major object of study. The people of God is a mixed company composed of the mature and immature, of the faithful and the unfaithful, called to witness as a corporate whole to the one who has chosen it, to the God of Israel and of Jesus. As the Hebrew scriptures in particular make clear, that witness is not simply a function of the spiritual maturity or of the faithfulness of its members. God uses his people despite themselves to testify to his purposes among the nations, to his judgement and his mercy, even when their spirituality is gravely distorted or superficial. It is God and God's will for the world, not spirituality, which is central to biblical religion and to its theological self-descriptions. (That, at any rate, is what will be said by those who picture religions, as this article does, chiefly as shapers rather than expressions of the spirituality of their practitioners).

Yet spirituality is procedurally, even if not descriptively, central. As was suggested by the earlier comments about reception and about falsification, it is the spiritually mature who are the testers, the experimentalists, within religious communities. They have what Aquinas calls connatural knowledge, the religious equivalent of linguistic competence, which gives them a sense of what is unacceptable and infelicitous in practice even when they can themselves formulate no rules and spin no theories. Theology needs them in order to be scientific in its own right rather than parasitic on other disciplines.

This stress on spirituality is, needless to say, related to the current emphasis on *praxis*, but there is also a difference. For this article, the kind of practice which primarily counts is not political but spiritual, that is, the formation of communities and individuals who have coherently and comprehensively internalised the faith. When *praxis* in the sense of action on behalf of, for example liberation, peace and justice does not contribute to or express such formation, it is questionable. For one thing, such action is unlikely to persist when political fashions change.

Methodical attention to spiritual practice as part of the assessment procedures for theological description seems already to be increasing.

In my own university, it is in one way illustrated by Paul Holmer's work in philosophical theology[8] (which emphasises the Wittgensteinian theme that language games can be understood only in relation to forms of life and *vice versa*), and in another way by Wayne Meeks' contention that New Testament texts need to be interpreted in terms of their concrete social and ethical (and by implication, spiritual) functions in their original settings.[9] In both cases, though more overtly in the first, theological description is closely linked to spirituality. (Such spiritual assessments, it might be helpful to note, may at times have results similar to political evaluations. A preferential option for the poor, for example, may be taken as part of the normative description of Christianity on the grounds that it is integral to Christian maturity, but it may also be favoured for Marxist reasons. The way in which the option is exercised, needless to say, will at times differ in the two cases.)

A friend of mine, at one time a monk, says that years of historical-critical scripture scholarship and teaching have made it difficult for him to read the bible for edification, not because of intellectual problems, but because of the loss of taste and aptitude. His plight is reminiscent of Darwin's complaint that a life-time of science had made him lose his youthful capacity to enjoy poetry. The parallel, however, is not complete: attention to the devotional uses of sacred writings can be an integral part of their scholarly interpretation whereas poetic enjoyment is methodologically, though not necessarily personally, extraneous to the scientific investigation of biological evolution. If my friend had learned a different kind of biblical scholarship in which attention to implications for the practice of the faith in past and present is methodologically part of the interpretive process, retention of the capacity for spiritually formative reading, while not guaranteed, would presumably have been much easier.[10]

Similarly, if new understandings of science enable attention to spirituality to become part of the testing procedures of theological disciplines in general, spiritual practice and formation would be favoured. A climate would develop which would encourage students to use the means of grace which are general among Christians. Perhaps special programmes would not be necessary; and if so, so much the better. The dangers of clerical élitism and separatism which we earlier mentioned would be lessened. On the other hand, if spiritual formation were programmatic, the theological portion of the curriculum could provide more support and better guidance than at present. Whatever the details, it is not impossible that changes in the culturally-established intellectual outlook will lessen the separation between spirituality and theology with advantages to both.

This, however, cannot be counted on, and we must await the future to see whether these possibilities will be actualised. In the meantime, the conclusions of this paper can be summarised in four points. First, special ministerial spiritual formation should be avoided whenever possible because of the dangers of clerical élitism (even 'we are anti-élitists' can function as a divisive boast). Second, in the present situation when both socialisation into and personally-committed inter-nalisation of communal traditions is weak, it may nevertheless be desirable for spiritual formation to be a programmatic part of semi-nary life. Third, this is difficult. Theology and spirituality have for long been so thoroughly separated that spiritual formation, like the gymnasium of the parable, is in danger of being an orphan, an erratic block, within the seminary. Fourth, changes in the regnant view of science, of both *Natur und Geisteswissenschaften*, give some hope for the future. To the degree attention to spiritual maturity is methodolog-ically incorporated into the normative descriptions of a religion, the actual processes of theological education will encourage interest in spiritual formation rather than indifference or opposition as at present.

A final endnote may be useful. The description of spirituality and theology which I have outlined is basically non-theological. It does not depend on specifically biblical or Christian considerations, and could for the most part have been written by an unbeliever. Yet it is only candid to admit that the non-theological perspectives I have utilised were chosen because they fit my own theological commitments. I have been attracted by Geertz's understanding of religion and Peirce's view of enquiry because these seem to me consistent with that catholic version of Reformation theology which is my own. Ultimately, there-fore, my warrants for being culturally-linguistic in theory of religion and a bit of a pragmatist in my understanding of theological enquiry would have to be drawn from scripture and tradition. That, however, would be a task for another day. In the meantime, to repeat, it is a basically non-theological view of the relation of spiritual formation to theological education which I have sketched.

Notes

1. Background for what I say about theology and theological education can be found in my *The Nature of Doctrine: religion and theology in a postliberal age*, Philadelphia, Fortress, 1984, and in *University Divinity Schools* (a report I wrote in 1976 for the Rockefeller Foundation, and printed by them but never reprinted). I have been helped by and strongly recommend Edward Farley, *Theologia*, Philadelphia, Fortress Press, 1983, and Charles M Wood, *Vision and Discernment*, Atlanta, Scholar's Press, 1985, but their contribution to this paper is more indirect than direct. In reference to spiritual formation, I have relied on what I have garnered over the years from reading and teaching about the history of theol-ogy and the church, and from my experiences as a theologian and educator chiefly at Yale. On the current psychosocial and cultural scene, my own perceptions are congruent with those of Robert Bellah and his associates in the widely-read *Habits of the Heart*, New York, Harper and Row, 1985.
2. Religions are conceived in the present discussion as codes which function in the social construction of reality to give comprehensive meaning and order to human experience whether cognitive, emotive or behavioural. Some authors who have influenced my thinking on religion are Clifford Geertz (especially several of the essays in his *The Interpretation of Cultures*, New York, Basic Books, 1973), William Christian, *Meaning and Truth in Religion*, Princeton, Princeton University Press, 1964, and *Doctrines of Religious Communities*, New Haven, Yale University Press, 1987, and Peter Berger, *The Sacred Canopy*, New York, Doubleday, 1967.
3. Robert Bellah *et al.*, *Habits of the Heart*, New York, Harper and Row, 1985.
4. Henri Nouwen's career has been a varied one, and my impression is that his role for other

groups in other contexts has not always been similar to the one I here describe. His writings, while not inconsistent with his *modus operandi* at Yale, are not the main source on which I draw.

5. I am thinking here of what he himself considered the quasi-monastic (*klüsterlich*) disciplines which he introduced in the seminary of the Confessing Church in Finkenwalde from 1935-39, and which are described in his *Life Together*, New York, Harper and Row, 1954.

6. John Ziman, *Public Knowledge: the social dimension of science,* Cambridge, Cambridge University Press, 1967, pp. 69ff.

7. For a discussion of Peirce on vagueness with reference to its effects on, among other things, the logic of non-contradiction, see the paper by Mihai Nadin in Eugene Freeman (ed.), *The Relevance of Charles Peirce*, La Salle, Illinois, Monist Library of Philosophy, 1983, pp. 154–166.

8. Paul Holmer's essay, 'Wittgenstein and theology', in D M High (ed.), *New Essays in Religious Language*, New York, Oxford University Press, 1969, pp. 25-35, had programmatic importance for a widespread development which has led to works such as Fergus Kerr, *Theology after Wittgenstein*, Oxford, Basil Blackwell, 1986.

9. Wayne A Meeks, *The First Urban Christians*, New Haven, Yale University Press, 1983, and *The Moral World of the First Christians*, Philadelphia, Westminster Press, 1986.

10. This is not the place to ask what kind of scriptural and theological scholarship can best do this. My own proposals, which owe much to Hans Frei and David Kelsey, are outlined in the last chapter of *The Nature of Doctrine* (see note 1 above), but there are also other possibilities.

8.3 Theological education and education for church leadership

Charles M Wood

Introduction

The conviction motivating this article is that a source of chronic difficulty in the current wide-ranging discussion of the organisation and aims of theological study (especially when the discussion touches on the subject of practical theology) is a failure adequately to discriminate among several of the elements involved. When two or more things are not properly distinguished, they cannot be properly related. What usually happens instead is that one somehow absorbs the others, so that their own reality can only emerge from time to time as an anomaly or a disruption. This pattern of absorption and disruption has been played out repeatedly both in theoretical proposals for the reform of theological study and in curricular practice.

My aim here is not to justify this underlying conviction through a critical review of the literature, but rather to undertake a more constructive exploration of some key distinctions which, it seems to me, are essential both to coherent discussion of the issues and to a coherent vision of the structures and aims of theological study. To make these distinctions I have had to sketch out at the relevant points a few elements of a theological, or at least quasi-theological, account of ministry. I hope that these points are phrased with enough generality as to be accessible and useful to people whose full theology of ministry might be quite different from my own.

Writing of the late medieval philosophers with their concern for careful conceptual distinctions and their patience for detail, David Burrell has remarked: 'The quest for coherence led to discrimination.'[1] Although what is offered here is not exactly an exercise in 'philosophical grammar' on the medieval model, it does have the same objective: to help us avoid false generalisations, and to see and make appropriate connections.

Key distinctions

Let us begin with the distinction between *ministry* and *church leadership* – a distinction commonly affirmed in principle and ignored in practice – and, as a sort of corollary, the distinction between education for ministry and education for church leadership.

Church leadership is one sort of ministry, but it is not the whole; education for church leadership is one sort of education for ministry,

but is not the whole. Ministry (that is, service) is the gift and responsibility of all Christians. Indeed, it is the gift and responsibility of all
human beings to render service to one another, to other creatures, and
thus to God. A properly theological account of ministry would, I
think, begin with the ministry of God, that is, with the service God
renders, and would place the ministry of creatures (including, but not
limited to, that of human beings and of Christians) into that context,
as a participation in God's ministry. For the present purpose, we must
defer the development of this fuller account, and concentrate on a few
points regarding the ministry of Christians.

Christians are, without exception, human beings. As such, they are
to participate in the service which human creatures are called and
enabled to render to fellow-creatures (human and otherwise) and to
God. We might call this their human vocation. Christians normally
testify that their capacity to understand and fulfil this service has been
decisively affected by their own encounter with the Christian tradition, and with God through that tradition (whether primarily by the
preached word, the sacraments, the caring of a community, or some
other particular means). In one way or another, they have been led to
grasp for themselves the story of the universal loss or corruption of
the human vocation, of its fulfilment in Jesus Christ, and of the
promise of its restoration in themselves and in others, a promise
whose realisation they may experience, however partially or fitfully,
in their own present existence, and for whose completion they hope.
Through their participation in Christianity, they are being restored to
the human vocation of ministry. Christians need not deny (though
some do) that non-Christians may also be given the grace to recover
the human vocation, in order to affirm that it is through the Christian
faith that they themselves have been given it, and to wish to share that
possibility with others.

This brings us to the distinctive aspect of the ministry of Christians,
namely, their ministry *as* Christians: the service they are called and
enabled to render, not simply as human beings, but in their capacity as
Christians. We might call this the *Christian* vocation, to distinguish it
from the larger human vocation which Christians share with all
others. This distinctively Christian ministry is essentially a ministry of
witness or testimony (*marturia*). It is the ministry of enabling others
to receive, understand and appropriate the Christian tradition as a
means of grace for their own lives, and to join in turn in its witnessing work. Like ministry in general, this is always to be understood as
a participation in the ministry of God. The human enabling of others
is itself enabled by God.

This Christian ministry has many parts. It is in some ways corporate, and in some ways individual; it is at times 'official', that is,
explicitly commissioned and sanctioned by the community, and at
times unofficial. There are special ministries undertaken by some on
behalf of all, and there is the general ministry in which all share

simply by participating in the common life of the Christian community. Christian ministry is both explicit and implicit, direct and indirect. For most Christians, it is a ministry carried on along with, and, to a great extent, through, the other activities which occupy us most of the time (making a living, caring for a family, friendships, political action and so forth), which are at the same time the vehicles through which we exercise our human vocation more or less effectively. For some, the Christian vocation is more nearly and directly a full-time occupation, whether church-commissioned and church-supported or otherwise.

The ministry of church leadership has a similar variety to it. It can be part- or full-time, official or unofficial, 'lay' or 'professional', individual or corporate. (Actually, each of these distinctions is problematic, particularly when interpreted as a disjunction. They must be handled with care.) Its common task in all its forms is 'to equip the saints for the work of ministry, for building up the body of Christ' (Ephesians 4:12): to enable the church to be the church, to guide Christians, individually and corporately, in the exercise of their vocation. At its most basic and comprehensive, this leadership is shared by every Christian in the service one renders to another, grounded in the grace which is given to each 'according to the measure of Christ's gift' (Ephesians 4:7). In a more particular and limited sense, church leadership is entrusted (in principle, at least) to those whose gifts and opportunities are most appropriate for the specific tasks involved: teaching, nurture, administration, community-building, judgement, guidance and so forth. While recognising the common 'leadership of all believers' and the great variety of more particular forms of leadership, I will concentrate from this point onward on those kinds of leadership which are ecclesially commissioned, typically full-time and normally exercised in relation to a congregation or local Christian community.

Education for such leadership is a form of education for ministry, and is best understood within that context even though it has some distinctive features. Education for ministry, in turn, is one aspect of the broader enterprise of Christian education, understood as that whole complex of educational activities by means of which persons are received into the Christian community and are prepared, not just initially, but continually, for responsible participation in that community. Not only the more focused and deliberate occasions of teaching and learning in the church – church-school classes, study groups, and so on – but also the educational aspect of the community's ritual and sacramental life, of its care for its members in crises, and of all of its other activities, belongs to Christian education thus comprehensively understood.

Within that enterprise, three distinct (though certainly closely related) components may be identified. There is, first, that educational activity through which we attain our knowledge of the Christian tradition and of our own particular ecclesial tradition: the doctrines, events, institutions, persons and so forth which make the tradition what it is. From this we gather our own sense of what the Christian faith is all about. We could call this 'education in Christian faith'. Second, there is what might be called 'education in Christian life'. This is the lifelong process of coming to understand ourselves and our world in ways appropriate to the Christian message, with its key life-shaping concepts: ways of learning to trust in God and to be loyal to God, to acquire the attitudes, dispositions, perceptions and so forth which are appropriate to such trust and loyalty, and thus to take on a certain kind of human and Christian identity. The third component we can designate 'education for ministry', so long as we recognise that each of the other two is in its own way also education for ministry. The specific contribution of this third aspect is to equip us with the particular competencies we need in order to play our part in the Christian community's ongoing life of witness and service.

These three components are closely interdependent, and the order in which they have just been mentioned should not be taken to imply some inherent logical or pedagogical ordering of them. Understanding the Christian faith requires training in Christian life, and vice versa; and neither is possible apart from some initiation into the practice of Christian witness, both corporate and individual.[2] Nor is the third a possibility without the other two. Receiving the Christian witness and being formed by it; understanding that witness and one's own place in it, so as to affirm it for oneself; and coming to bear witness, to share the community's distinctive ministry, are all three ongoing, interwoven elements of Christian existence.

Although the three are inseparable, it is within the third, education for ministry, that we may more specifically locate education for church leadership. As we shall see, education for church leadership requires a particular intensification of all three aspects of Christian education. This is because church leadership itself demands certain sorts of spiritual maturity and certain ways of understanding the Christian faith, as well as certain capacities for the exercise of leadership, which are not required of all Christians. But since all of these special requirements are ordered to preparation for the ministry of leadership, it is in relation to that aim that they are best understood.

Of course, church leadership is one of many sorts of ministry for which some particular educational preparation is required. Acknowledging that ministry and church leadership are not synonymous terms, and then referring exclusively to education for church leadership as education for ministry or ministerial education, is one way of negating in practice what one affirms in principle. Anyone who undertakes a course of study so as to be better equipped to serve God and fellow-creature is engaged in education for ministry, and a relatively small proportion of that education goes on in schools of theology.

Some dangers in labels

Education for church leadership is frequently referred to as 'theological education', an equation which carries dangers as well as values. While the two enterprises are associated, they should not be merely equated. The distinction and relation between theological education and education for church leadership deserves some careful exploration.

Theological education, in the most strict and proper sense, is the process through which persons acquire an aptitude for theology. An aptitude for Christian theology is a capacity and disposition to engage in critical reflection upon the Christian witness (which means, upon what is conveyed by everything that Christians are, say and do as Christians, singly and together), aimed at testing the adequacy of that witness in terms of its own claims to validity.[3] The three ingredients of the claim to validity which any act of Christian witness at least implicitly makes, as I understand it, are first, the claim to be authentically Christian, that is, to represent faithfully the gospel of Jesus Christ; second, the claim to be meaningful and true; and third, the claim to be fitting, or appropriate to the context.[4] Theological reflection can take the form of a critical examination of some actual sample of Christian witness, something said or done by Christians in their capacity as Christians, to see to what extent this act of witness lives up to its own intentions to be authentic, true and fitting to the situation. Or it can take the more constructive (though no less critical) form of asking what valid witness would amount to under a given set of circumstances.

Some aptitude for Christian theology is requisite to Christian life itself. This does not mean that every Christian must be a theological scholar, nor even that she or he must be cognisant of what theological scholars are up to. It only means that every Christian, under normal circumstances, inevitably is called to make judgements as to what constitutes valid Christian witness, accepting or rejecting certain alternatives. Such judgements are involved from fairly early on in each person's Christian education, as well as in the ordinary course of Christian existence. It is for this reason that one element of Christian education, touching on all three principal components of that enterprise, is theological education. In the course of making those judgements as to the nature of Christian faith, life and practice which are involved in coming to be a Christian, people learn, from those who teach them in these matters, how to make judgements. Depending on how they are taught, they learn to judge well or poorly, reluctantly or willingly, haphazardly or with deliberation. They acquire some sort of theological aptitude, which plays an important role in determining the sort of Christian identity they take on, the way they understand the faith, and the quality of the witness they bear. A Christian community has no choice as to whether theological education, for all its members, will be an element of its educational work; it only has a choice as to the kind of theological education it will be.

The role of theological education in education for church leadership is especially crucial, since it has a large part in determining the quality of judgement of those responsible for the nurture and guidance of the rest of the community. The greater the scope of leadership, the more serious this becomes. It is altogether appropriate, then, that those institutions responsible for the most rigorous and intensive preparation of church leaders be known as theological schools. It is far more important, however, that these institutions actually *be* theological schools, and that the education they provide aspiring church leaders be, from start to finish, genuine theological education.

Three components of Christian education

The theological education of church leaders, like that of other Christians, must give attention to all three of those components of Christian education which were outlined earlier: education in Christian faith, education in Christian life and education for Christian ministry.

I said earlier that education for church leadership requires a particular intensification and development of these three components. The way in which this is so must not be misunderstood. So far as education in Christian life is concerned, we should not think that church leadership demands a higher Christian proficiency than other forms of ministry. It is a mistake to assume that anyone who shows signs of seriousness and promise in the Christian life should automatically be steered toward preparation for church leadership, for there are other kinds of ministry at least as demanding of spiritual maturity and all that it involves. There are, however, certain aspects of spiritual maturity, certain dispositions and traits of character, which are particularly (though not exclusively) pertinent to certain forms of church leadership.

For example, pastors and those in similar positions of leadership need to know themselves well. Leadership in general is full of temptations. Further, the professional roles occupied by such church leaders in our society give ample opportunity for various kinds of abuse. Self-deception, as well as the deception of others, is an easy and attractive feature of religious leadership. Misuse of time and resources, manipulation of others by means of one's professional knowledge and power, and other forms of malfeasance are not only possible, but are often subtly encouraged by the social arrangements in which church leaders find themselves and the psychological dynamics of the situation. Persons preparing for such work must know their own hearts in this regard; they must be well acquainted with their own strengths and weaknesses when faced by such challenges, and with the opportunities which both the strengths and the weaknesses afford for genuine and effective service.[5]

Church leaders are also typically called upon to know the hearts of others. If they are to provide leadership to congregations and individuals under all sorts of conditions, they must understand human behaviour in health and adversity. This requires some degree of psychological, anthropological and sociological understanding, as well as a theological grasp of the human condition before God. It also requires insight and penetration, receptivity and generosity, and a multitude of other personal qualities which rest finally upon one's self-knowledge and on the character of one's spiritual life. In these and other ways, the responsibilities of church leadership call for some special attention to the quality of the Christian existence of those being prepared for it.

Similar points can be made concerning the particular needs of church leaders in the other two component areas of Christian education. So far as their education in the Christian faith is concerned, to the extent that church leaders are responsible for guiding the church in its preservation and extension of the Christian tradition, their education must involve their acquiring not only a more extensive factual knowledge of that tradition than that ordinarily expected of other Christians, but also an understanding of how the tradition works, and a sure ability to distinguish authentic tradition, that which mediates the genuine gospel, from its counterfeits. It is not necessary that they have the erudition of professional historians of Christianity, but it is necessary that they have an ability to work with the tradition as it bears upon their responsibilities of leadership (for example, teaching the faith to others, answering questions about what Christian belief involves, sharing in the task of formulating and explicating the community's doctrines, or equipping people to discern what is going on when they are confronted with competing claims about the faith).

With regard to education in the task of leadership, it is clear that pastoral leadership, for example, requires a number of identifiable abilities in such areas as administration, counselling, preaching, group leadership and teaching. Basic competence in the functions pertaining to one's own role and its expectations is essential: one must know how to conduct a meeting, deliver a sermon, plan a service of worship and so forth, and part of one's education for leadership is acquiring and continuing to strengthen those specific capabilities. But there is an aspect of the competence of leadership whose presence or absence in a person, though not so visible as the quality of her or his skill in a particular area of functioning, is ultimately far more important. This is the capacity for critical reflection on what one is doing as a leader, through each and all of the activities and roles that one's leadership involves: the capacity to transcend the obvious demands and expectations of one's office, and to think about the direction and effect of what one is doing in relation to the mission of the church in the situation. An aptitude for that sort of reflection will not compensate for the lack of basic skills in the practice of one's ministry. It is not, by itself, sufficient qualification for church leadership. But no amount of technical virtuosity as preacher, counsellor, and so on, will make up for the absence or immaturity of that judgement on which genuine leadership, as distinguished from the competent fulfilment of certain role expectations, depends.

This brief account of the ways in which education for church leadership must address each of the three component areas of Christian education may begin to make clearer why it must involve theological education at every point. Essentially, what this account indicates is that church leadership requires a well-developed aptitude for theological self-criticism; for theological understanding of the Christian faith; and for theological criticism of one's performance in leadership. The theological education of church leaders, then, must address all three of these. It can only do so adequately if all three are explicitly brought under scrutiny in some way in the course of one's theological study.

It must be kept in mind that the aim of *theological* education as such is not to form Christians, but to form the habit of critical reflection on one's formation. It is not to mediate the content of the Christian tradition, but to equip one for theological reflection on the Christian tradition. It is not to train in leadership skills, but to cultivate an aptitude for reflection on the quality of one's own and others' leadership as an instrument of the church's witness. The service of theology to witness, and hence of theological education to Christian education, is best conceived as an indirect one: it is the service performed by reflection upon a practice, rather than by the practice itself. This is a genuine and even an indispensable service. But whenever the distinction between theology and witness or between theological education and Christian education is forgotten or denied, as it frequently seems to be, that unique service is lost.[6]

Distinct as these educational processes are, in the education of church leaders they cannot be separated. Learning to reflect theologically on one's formation not only presupposes that formation is going on, but is a part of one's formation. Learning to reflect theologically on leadership must be ingredient in the process of acquiring the specific abilities for leadership, or it is not likely to become second nature to the leader, as it should. And the process of understanding and appropriating the Christian tradition already involves the making of theological judgements and the gaining of some sort of competence in that enterprise. Theological education of the sort that theological schools conduct is not a separate stage of education to be entered upon only after one has already acquired the other requisites for church leadership. One might think of the theological school as the medium or the context within which one's development in these three areas is given some important nourishment and brought to a new level of maturity precisely through theological study. Certainly, one's Christian education (including one's education for ministry) normally begins long before one enters a school of theology, and continues long after one leaves. The distinctive contribution of the school of theology to education for church leadership is to strengthen the theological aspect of that education, across its entire range.

Differences among theological schools

In carrying out their responsibility for the theological education of church leaders, theological schools differ considerably among themselves with regard both to their explicit intentions and to their actual accomplishments. Some of the differences are matters of principle: for instance, commitment to a particular ecclesiology or a particular understanding of ministry will lead a school to a certain set of objectives and decisions which will set it apart from schools grasped by different commitments. Other differences are the results of historical or social factors. A school will do well to reflect from time to time upon both its explicit aims and those other factors in its situation which are shaping its work.

As a stimulus to such reflection, let me risk some impressionistic generalisations about one group of schools which, despite various differences of academic and ecclesiastical affiliation, share a common legacy: those institutions founded and largely maintained by what until recently we have called the main-line Protestant denominations in the United States. These schools generally seem to do a better job of teaching students to reflect on the Christian tradition than of teaching them to reflect on their own Christian existence or to reflect on the quality of their leadership. This is not to say that the schools spend more time on education in Christian faith than they do on education in Christian life or on education for ministry; the proportion of time given to each varies a great deal from place to place or tradition to tradition. It is rather to say that the schools are better at teaching students to deal *theologically* with the content of the tradition than with either their own lives or their vocation as church leaders. Such education as goes on in these latter two areas is relatively less theological in character, as a rule. With regard to Christian spirituality or formation, it is more likely to consist in a straightforward extension of basic Christian education (often of a remedial sort); and in the area of education for ministry, it is more likely to concentrate on conveying a basic functional competence in the role. My impression is that the calls which such schools frequently hear that they should give more attention to spiritual formation or to the cultivation of students' professional competence for ministry are rarely cries for more theological attention to these areas, but rather for more basic 'first-order' education in Christian life and in meeting the needs of congregations.

At the same time, in the area in which these schools do relatively well at theological (as distinguished from Christian) education, they generally do a better job at teaching students to pursue the questions of the authenticity and of the meaningfulness and truth of Christian witness than to pursue the question of its fittingness to its context. Courses in bible and history may encourage students to think about the origins and transmission of the Christian tradition, its continuity and its transformation through time, and raise (at least implicitly) the theological question of the authenticity of contemporary witness. Courses in systematic theology tend to pursue this question, sometimes in conjunction with the more philosophically-oriented question of meaning and truth. Indeed, the task of systematic theology is often formulated as that of mediating the demands of authenticity or faithfulness to what has been received, and of meaningfulness or credibility in the contemporary world. Courses in what is sometimes called 'practical theology' (the fourth division of the conventional fourfold curriculum in addition to biblical, historical and systematic studies) are for the most part courses aimed at teaching the various more or less discrete competencies required of pastors and other church leaders, and their teachers tend to identify themselves with the specific disciplines concerned (homiletics, pastoral care, education, and so on) rather than with practical theology as such.

Accounting for the emergence and maintenance of such a state of affairs in modern theological education is a task for social historians. Rather than attempt any such interpretation, I want to concentrate on a conceptual problem which, while it is not solely responsible for the tendencies just identified, seems to me to have done a great deal to encourage them. The problem has to do with the use of the term 'practical theology' to designate two distinct sorts of enquiry and instruction, each legitimate and necessary in its own right. The failure to distinguish properly between them has sometimes led to a sort of competition between them for the title, which has not served the real interests of either. I would not want to claim that the multitude of uses of the term 'practical theology' can finally be reduced to these two. My claim is rather that if these two were appropriately distinguished and recognised as legitimate and complementary enterprises rather than as rival understandings of one task, it would do something to reduce the current confusion which tends to weaken both.

One contender is that dimension of theological study whose particular responsibility is to pursue the question as to the fittingness of Christian witness to its context. The other contender is that sort of theological study whose subject-matter is church leadership, typically, pastoral leadership. The first is distinguished by the particular aspect of the validity-question which it pursues; the second, by the particular subject-matter it investigates.

One reason it has proven difficult to keep these two distinct is that each of them involves the other. Theological reflection on the fittingness of Christian witness to its context includes (but is not limited to) reflection on the role of church leadership, of the institutions, activities, and so forth, through which leadership is exercised, in enabling (or preventing) that witness to be fitting to its context. Theological reflection on church leadership – that is, on the ways in which the structures, activities, and so forth, of leadership work to further or hinder valid Christian witness – includes (but is not limited to) reflection on the fittingness of that leadership to its context. If, as sometimes happens, the church is identified with its leadership, and Christian witness reduced to the activity of church leaders, the distinction between these two intersecting enquiries becomes that much more difficult to see.

In my own constructive account of the organisation of theological study, I have reserved the name of practical theology for the first of these contending enterprises.[7] It is one of the three primary theological disciplines, each of which corresponds to one of the three constitutive dimensions of Christian theology. (In this account, the question of the Christian authenticity of the witness belongs to historical theology, and the question of its meaningfulness and truth to philosophical theology.)

When it has not been called practical theology, a name which has sometimes been assigned to the second of these enterprises is pastoral theology. Pastoral theology has often been conceived and taught in such a way as to combine theological reflection on church leadership (specifically, on the office and duties of the pastor) with theological reflection on the personhood of the leader (that is, on the pastor's own life and Christian self-understanding, particularly in relation to the responsibilities of leadership). Thus, it deals (from a theological standpoint) with both the 'education in Christian life' and the 'education for ministry' of the candidate for church leadership, and has gone some way toward addressing the lack of attention to these two areas in the typical theological curriculum. There is much to be said for this approach, so long as it is not seen as an *alternative* to practical theology (as I have used the term above), but rather as a sort of concentration of theological attention upon the theme of church leadership and upon the education of the leader. Both practical theology and pastoral theology (if we are to use these names for them) have a place in education for church leadership: the former as a necessary component of theological education as such, and the latter as a means of acquiring the aptitude for theological self-examination which is necessary to genuine leadership.

There are some difficulties, however, with the name of 'pastoral theology' for the second of these pursuits. In conventional Protestant usage, pastoral theology is concerned with 'the pastoral office and its function', that is, with the role and activity of the pastor in the congregation. Unless all church leadership is somehow to be assimilated to the pastoral office, the term has some obvious limitations as a designation for the theological examination of church leadership. Its use may also give some privileged weight to the concept or image of 'shepherd' as a key to the understanding of church leadership, a privilege which may or may not be theologically warranted.[8] At the same time, in Roman Catholic usage, and increasingly in Protestant usage as well, 'pastoral theology' has come to refer not to that discipline which deals with the office and function of the pastor, but rather to that which deals with the pastoral activity of the church as a whole, as well as with the pastoral activity of its leaders. It concerns itself with the care which the church provides to people, and its scope may be considerably broader than was previously thought: extending to the church's care for non-members as well as members, and to a care which is exercised through social and political action as well as on the individual level.

It is not clear, then, that 'pastoral theology' is the best term to use for the theological examination of church leadership. Perhaps a better term, enabling a better grasp of what this study involves, will emerge. What is crucial, in my judgement, is that the two enquiries I have here described be clearly distinguished, and that both of them be affirmed as properly belonging to theological education for church leadership.

Notes

1. David B Burrell, *Aquinas: God and action*, Notre Dame, University of Notre Dame Press, 1979, p. 4.
2. I do not mean to imply that only Christians can understand the Christian faith. However, an understanding of the Christian faith or of any other religious tradition does seem to require a kind of conceptual equipment which is normally achieved through personal participation in it. The task confronting the person who wishes to understand a faith other than her own is to 'entertain' that faith sufficiently to acquire the relevant concepts, through whatever sort of involvement is both necessary and appropriate. This is less difficult in some cases than in others, for a variety of reasons, but it is probably never easy.
3. There are other forms of theology and of theological education than Christian. To what extent, if at all, what I say about the Christian versions would be true of other traditions (for example, Jewish theology and theological education) is best left to members of those other traditions to judge. For more on the general understanding of Christian theology and theological education represented here, see Charles M Wood, *Vision and Discernment: an orientation in theological study*, Atlanta, Scholars Press, 1985.
4. Regarding the moral aspect of Christian witness (its injunctions, recommendations, etc. concerning human conduct), one might substitute 'right' for 'true' in the second category – depending on how one construes the logic of moral claims. There is a highly illuminating treatment of the possible relations between claims to authenticity and truth or rightness in religious traditions in William A Christian Sr, *Doctrines of Religious Communities: a philosophical study*, New Haven, Yale University Press, 1987.
5. I am indebted to my colleague Professor Joseph L Allen for his reflections on this theme in a recent convocation address at Perkins School of Theology.
6. Rudolf Bultmann's critique of what he called 'pious theology' in his introductory lectures on theological study makes this point very well, as has Schubert M Ogden in various places. See Rudolf Bultmann, *Theologische Enzyklopadie* (edited by Eberhard Jüngel and Klaus W Müller), Tübingen, J C B Mohr (Paul Siebeck), 1984, pp. 163–167; Schubert M Ogden, 'Christian theology and theological education', in Don Browning *et al.* (eds), *The Education of the Practical Theologian*, Atlanta, Scholars Press, 1989, pp. 21–35.
7. See Charles M Wood, *Vision and Discernment*, *op. cit.*, pp. 46–49, 95.
8. Thomas C Oden, *Pastoral Theology: essentials of ministry*, San Francisco, Harper and Row, 1983, exemplifies both of these problematic features. Pastoral theology is concerned with 'the systematic definition of the pastoral office and its function' (p. x), and 'shepherding' is the 'pivotal analogy' (pp. 49–63). Since these are matters of deliberate decision for Oden, his book provides a good contemporary indication of what is gained and lost thereby.

9. The theological education debate

The most intensive discussion of theological education in recent times began in the United States in the early 1980s, as the Divinity Schools of the 'mainline' Protestant churches re-examined the education they were providing from a self-consciously *theological* point of view. The last major debate over Protestant theological education, a generation earlier,[1] was soon eclipsed by 'the theological education debate' (as it came to be known) and the extensive literature associated with it. Initiated by Edward Farley's account of the fragmentation of theology into a collection of disciplines, and his call for the recovery of a sense of theology as *theologia*, the 'habit of wisdom', the debate generated a number of significant books,[2] as well as a continuing discussion in the pages of *Theological Education*, from which the four articles here are reprinted. As they demonstrate, the theological education debate is not just about the Divinity Schools, or the Protestant churches, or even the United States, but has consequences for Christian education everywhere.

Francis Schüssler Fiorenza's article, 'Thinking theologically about theological education', was originally published in *Theological Education*, 24, supplement 2, 1988, pp. 89–119.[3] Arguably the finest short introduction to the debate in the 1980s, it is an exploration of three approaches to the theological analysis of theological education, each of which has a different point of departure. For the first, it is 'the nature of theology' itself; for the second, it is the 'identity and mission of the church'; and for the third, it is the 'distinctive nature of ministry'. Arguing that each approach has its limitations, as well as its advantages, and that a comprehensive approach to theological education is required, Fiorenza aims 'to clarify both the possibilities and limits of theological reflection on theological education'.

Charles M Wood, like Edward Farley, exemplifies the first of the three approaches discussed by Fiorenza. In 'Theological inquiry and theological education', he argues that the aim of the educational use of theological enquiry is not the formation of judgements, 'but the formation of judgement' – of the 'vision' and 'discernment' which the practice of theology demands.

Three alternative models of theological education – as spiritual formation, as transmittal of tradition, and as professional education for ministry – are considered and criticised by Wood, as he sets out his interpretation of theological education as 'an education in theological enquiry'. 'Theological inquiry and theological education' was first published in *Theological Education*, 21, 1985, pp. 73–93, and reprinted in his *Vision and Discernment: an orientation in theological study*, Atlanta, Georgia, Scholars Press, 1985, pp. 79–95.[4]

In stressing the need to understand the entire curriculum 'as really and truly a theological curriculum', Wood is appealing for the recovery of a sense of unity in theological education. On the other hand, Rebecca S Chopp, in 'Emerging issues and theological education', reprinted from *Theological Education*, 26, 1990, pp. 106–124, emphasises the need for diversity – 'the production of discourses of multiplicity and multiple discourses'. She argues that theological education has been caught in 'the ambiguous gap' between the modern construction of knowledge and religion, and that it must, in the future, attend to 'new forms of discourses and new forms of community which encourage multiple and diverse ways of human flourishing'. The transformation of theological education she proposes is, in part, a transformation of Charles Wood's interpretation of theology, and of theological education, in the light of the theologies of liberation.

There are close connections between many of the contributions to the theological education debate and postliberal approaches to ethics and theology that emphasise the relations between narrative, community, and personal identity. David Tracy's article notes these connections, but then goes back beyond the Aristotelian tradition – which is often invoked in this context – to the origins of Western education, and in particular to the writings of Plato. It is his contention that in the dialectical and mythical richness of Plato's work we can find a 'drama of the soul' which prevents 'education for character' from collapsing into individualism. Theological education, therefore, can and should recover 'the Christian soul as the subject-in-process of the Christian identity'. David Tracy's 'Can virtue be taught? Education, character and the soul' first appeared in *Theological Education*, 24, supplement 1, 1988, pp. 33–52.

Professor Francis Schüssler Fiorenza is Charles Chauncey Stillman Professor of Roman Catholic Theological Studies at Harvard University, Cambridge, Massachusetts, USA.

Professor Charles M Wood is Lehman Professor of Christian Doctrine at Perkins School of Theology, Southern Methodist University, Dallas, Texas, USA. Professor Rebecca S Chopp teaches at the Candler School of Theology at Emory University, Atlanta, Georgia, USA. Professor David Tracy is Andrew Thomas Greeley and Grace McNichols Greeley Professor of Catholic Studies at the University of Chicago Divinity School, Chicago, Illinois, USA.

Notes

1. H Richard Niebuhr, *The Purpose of the Church and its Ministry*, New York, Harper and Row, 1956; H Richard Niebuhr, Daniel Day Williams and James M Gustafson, *The Advancement of Theological Education*, New York, Harper and Row, 1957.

2. See Edward Farley, *Theologia: the fragmentation and unity of theological education*, Philadelphia, Fortress, 1983, and *The Fragility of Knowledge: theological education in the church and the university*, Philadephia, Fortress, 1988; Joseph C Hough and John B Cobb, *Christian Identity and Theological Education*, Chico, California, Scholars Press, 1985; Charles M Wood, *Vision and Discernment: an orientation in theological study*, Atlanta, Georgia, Scholars Press, 1985; The Mud Flower Collective, *God's Fierce Whimsy: Christian feminism and theological education*, New York, Pilgrim Press, 1985; Max L Stackhouse, *Apologia: contextualization, globalization, and mission in theological education*, Grand Rapids, Michigan, William B Eerdmans, 1988; David H Kelsey, *To Understand God Truly: what's theological about a theological school*, Louisville, Kentucky, Westminster/John Knox, 1992, and *Between Athens and Berlin: the theological education debate*, Grand Rapids, Michigan, William B Eerdmans, 1993. For other references, see the overview, note 9.

3. See also Francis Schüssler Fiorenza, 'Foundational theology and theological education', *Theological Education*, 20, 1984, pp. 107–124, and 'Theology and practice: theological education as a reconstructive, hermeneutical, and practical task', *Theological Education*, 23, supplement, 1987, pp. 113–141.

4. See also Charles M Wood, 'Theological education and education for church leadership', *Quarterly Review*, 10, 1990, pp. 65–81, reprinted in his *An Invitation to Theological Study*, Valley Forge, Pennsylvania, Trinity Press, 1994, chapter 2 and above as article 8.3, and '"Spiritual formation" and "theological education"', *Religious Education*, 86, 1991, pp. 550–561.

9.1 Thinking theologically about theological education

Francis Schüssler Fiorenza

Introduction

The analysis of theological education as a theological problem is a difficult subject. One can approach theological education in many different ways, sociologically, economically, pedagogically, or professionally. But how does one approach theological education theologically? What constitutes a theological analysis of theological education? How does pluralism, especially the pluralism of theological, religious and moral criteria affect such an analysis of theological education? How does one think theologically about theological education? Theologians are more accustomed to thinking theologically about God, Christ, the church or Scripture than about theological education.

Therefore, this article will explore diverse theological approaches to theological education. It examines how these diverse approaches view theological education as a theological problem. Each of these approaches does not represent a single direction, but can in turn be subdivided into different avenues. The first approach moves from an analysis of theological enquiry or the nature of theology to the nature and reform of theological education. The second approach takes the church's identity and mission as the starting-point for its theological analysis of theological education. A third approach places a theological vision of ministry or a professional conception of ministry at the centre of its analysis of theological education.

A final section will argue that each of the three approaches, though valuable, is by itself necessarily limited. Each has built-in limitations as well as advantages. An adequate theological approach to theological education needs to be comprehensive. This article aims through its descriptive analysis of the variety of approaches to clarify both the possibilities and the limits of theological reflection on theological education. In a second, more systematic article, I have explored the relevance of contemporary hermeneutical theory for theological education.[1]

The nature of theology

One can approach theological education from the nature of theology. What constitutes good theology, its criteria and norms, should affect theological education. Theological education is an education in theological enquiry. Therefore, this approach starts out from the nature of theological enquiry. If theology is in a poor state, then theological education will be in a poor state. If theology is in need of reform, then theological education will be in need of reform. The crucial issue for theological education is: what constitutes good theology? The following will survey four contemporary attempts to show the relevance for theological education of four distinct answers to this question.

The experience of theology and theological encyclopedia

More than any other publication, Edward Farley's *Theologia* has sharpened the critical level of reflection on the nature of theological education as a theological problem.[2] The starting-point is neither the nature of ministry nor the mission of the church, but theology. Pluralism as a problem of theological education is the pluralism of theology. It is primarily the splintering of theology, traditionally understood as the virtue of wisdom, into specialised academic disciplines. These disciplines lack a coherent unity except for the functional unity of service to the church. This functional unity, Farley argues, does not suffice to overcome the modern splintering of theology into diverse disciplines.

His analysis of theological encyclopedia shows that their organisation of theological disciplines into a fourfold pattern has decisively contributed to the fragmentation of theology.[3] To restore the unity of theology, it is necessary to go beyond the functional unity of service to the church and to ground the unity of theology in the very nature of the theological task itself. In Farley's own words, 'the main thesis is that a significant reform of theological education which addresses its deepest problems must find a way to recover *theologia*. Without that recovery, theological education will continue to perpetuate its enslavement to specialties, its lack of subject matter and criteria, its functionalist and technological orientation.'[4]

The reform of theology is the condition for the reform of theological education. Therefore, a new understanding of theological enquiry in relation to the problem of pluralism leads to a reform of theological education.[5] Farley secures the unity of theological understanding in the face of the pluralism of theological disciplines insofar as he understands theology as the explication of the pre-reflective dispositions of faith itself. This faith exists in three distinct social matrices (believer, church leadership and scholarly enquiry) as distinctive modes of understanding. Theological encyclopedia have neglected the other two matrices. They gave theology a merely functional unity. They neglected to explicate its unity in the pre-reflective habit of faith.

Farley criticises Schleiermacher's reduction of theological understanding to its ecclesial function.[6] Nevertheless, his own proposal brilliantly reformulates Schleiermacher's interrelation of theology and religious experience. Theological understanding entails a fourfold dialectic. It does not start out from the authority of revelation. Instead it begins with the contemporary experience of faith in all its matrices and explicates this faith experience. With this emphasis upon the contemporary experience of faith in all its matrices, Farley explicates a vision of theological enquiry common to traditional liberal theologies as well as to contemporary liberation theologies. Whereas the former starts with contemporary experience as an anthropological universal, the latter starts with the contemporary experience of previously oppressed and excluded groups.[7]

The emphasis upon the experience of faith in all its matrices points to the dialectic of theological understanding of both criticising the tradition and displaying the enduring value of its *mythos*. Theological understanding therefore entails not only a hermeneutics of suspicion of the present situation, but it also displays 'that dialectic of understanding which is evoked by faith's attempt to exist faithfully in its situations'.[8] Such a dialectic overcomes the separation among theological disciplines and between theology and faith.

The emphasis on theological understanding as the virtuous habit of wisdom and the refusal to reduce theological understanding to the matrix of church leadership represents a significant attempt to overcome the pluralism within theology as affecting a split theology and life. The major question is: how does one obtain the habit of wisdom? For the medieval theologian, theology was wisdom because it treated of God as highest, first and final cause. Thomas Aquinas distinguishes two types of wisdom: one as the habit of virtue, inclination and gift of the Holy Spirit; the other based on knowledge and the prudent judgement acquired through study. Theological understanding belonged to the latter.[9]

Schleiermacher's functional approach, more neutrally called the 'ecclesial paradigm' rather than the 'clerical paradigm', fits the motivation of many students entering divinity schools and has the merit of acknowledging a certain methodological independence.[10] The methods used by historians of early Christianity in theological faculties are the same methods used by historians in state universities. For Schleiermacher, the difference was in terms of function and essence rather than method.[11] When one seeks to ground this difference not in function, but in a habit, then the question becomes: How does the habit of *theologia* relate to the autonomous methods of diverse disciplines, both theoretical and practical? Such a question of course relates primarily to the habit of theological enquiry. Insofar as theological education often involves the professional education of church leadership, a further question is whether the habit of *theologia* suffices or whether theological education entails training in other 'habits' or 'virtues' necessary for church leadership.

Theological education and faith

The Program of Priestly Formation (1982) by the Roman Catholic bishops in the United States represents another and quite different approach to theological education from the nature of theology.[12] The *Program* seeks to apply to the United States Vatican II's 'Decree on the training of priests' and the 'Decree on the pastoral office of bishops in the Church' as well as the *Ratio Fundamentalis Institutionis Sacerdotis* and other documents of the Roman Congregation for Catholic Education.[13]

Committee documents often bring together diverse opinions and emphases without completely integrating them. This difficulty affects my classification of the document. Much within the document focuses on priestly ministry, character and exigencies. Yet I have classified the document as an approach to the reform of theological education from the perspective of theology rather than from ministry for a couple of reasons. First, the document often treats the preparation for ministry under the rubric of personal and spiritual development.[14] It relegates preparation primarily to the guidance of a spiritual director and to the specific life of prayer and discipline within the seminary residence. Secondly, the principles of curriculum reform are primarily based upon theology, not ministry, spiritual formation or professional development.[15] In addition, the document expresses the conviction that when theology is properly and adequately taught, it leads to the personal formation of the theological student.

In basing principles of the reform of theological education upon the renewal of theology, the *Program* develops a conception of theology that is at the opposite theological pole from Farley's conception. Theology is a response in faith and in obedience to the authority of divine revelation as taught by an authoritative ecclesial magisterium. Theology is not so much explication of the pre-reflective faith experience in all its social matrices as the explication of a particular church's teaching.

Since this conception centres theology in the church's teaching of divine revelation, it seeks to reform theological education by focusing theological education on the fostering of faith in this teaching. The document therefore emphasises personal faith in revelation. Such a faith provides even the link between theological education and personal formation. The spiritual formation of a seminarian's faith and the theological defence of faith provides at one and the same time the basis of good theology.

Theology is both related and distinct from faith. As related to faith, theological education is concerned with the increase and development of personal faith. In this way theological study furthers personal spiritual formation and should affect the seminarian's whole life.[16] Where the *Program*, however, distinguishes faith and theology, it downplays theology in relation to faith. The document points out that it is necessary for students not only to recognise the relation between faith and theology, but also their distinction. Theology is the human reflection and expression of God's truth throughout Christian history and tradition, whereas faith is primarily ordered to the divine revelation.[17]

The word of God should be the focal and unifying point of theological education. 'In preparation for their ministry of service to the Word of God, seminarians should understand and appreciate God's message as it is proclaimed in sacred Scripture and reflected in the living tradition of the church.'[18] Whereas Farley's approach made the pre-reflective faith experience in all its contemporary social matrices the source of the unity of theological education, the *Program* makes the scriptures as reflected in the church's tradition the unifying principle of theological education. Consequently 'that what is learned of Scripture will truly inspire other studies'.[19] Systematic theology, pastoral studies, homiletics and religious education are all related to the study of Scripture. Nevertheless, although the *Program* makes God's word the focal point of theological education, the actual curriculum still maintains the traditional allotment. It allots more courses to dogmatics than to the study of Scripture (thirty-six for dogmatics; eighteen for Scripture).[20]

Revelation provides the unity in the face of the pluralism of theological disciplines. The document minimalises pluralism insofar as the document describes pluralism in terms of the plurality of theologies that have existed from early Christianity, through the Middle Ages, up to the present and to Vatican II. Nevertheless, not pluralism but unity is the goal. 'Theology should be presented as a genuine wisdom whose unity is established on the Word of God who is one, on the gospel of Christ which is one, and on the Catholic Church which is one.'[21]

The document alludes to the pluralism of theological disciplines, but it resolves it. The pluralism of different criteria of theology is not seen as a problem. Instead the centrality of divine revelation and its authoritative interpretation by the magisterium of the Roman Catholic Church provides the solution. Consequently, genuine pluralism, doubt and conflict of theological opinion does not exist. In this respect the document represents a traditional Roman Catholic position. Its attempt to link theological education and personal formation is grounded in theology, but much more in the object of theology (a specific version of truth) than in the habit of theology and theological enquiry. It is this aspect that the next position seeks to explicate.

Formation and theological enquiry

In *Vision and Discernment*, Charles Wood also attempts to base the reform of theological education upon the task of theological enquiry.[22] His proposal is similar to the bishops' proposal in two ways: first, he wants to link theological education with personal formation; second, his conception of theology is much more directly based upon revelation, as mediated through Christian testimony and witness. He emphasises that theology is not simply imparting a traditional set of doctrines nor is it simply imparting a set of skills, but it is the development of virtue and character. In this respect he reaffirms the traditional Aristotelian conception of virtue and character, influential in traditional Roman Catholic theology and in its official documents upon theological education and the formation of ministerial students. Wood, however, develops in an exemplary manner what the above document asserts but leaves unexplicated, namely, the relationship between theological enquiry and personal formation.

Wood argues that theological education basically continues and deepens the ordinary process of Christian nurture. It brings the resources of the Christian tradition as well as other resources to bear upon one's own self-understanding. Such a theological education cannot be reduced simply to the acquisition of knowledge or the acquisition of ministerial skills. It involves the development of critical judgement. This judgement is implied in the acquisition of the tradition and in the acquisition of skill. Education for church leadership depends upon the formation of such critical judgement. Consequently there can be no education in church leadership without theological education. Because theological education is an education in theological enquiry it involves the formation of the person.

Wood explicates the relevance of theological enquiry for theological education by developing Schubert Ogden's conception of the criteria of good theology. According to Ogden, good theology rests on diverse criteria that respond to diverse questions. There is the criterion of whether the theology is Christian. This criterion demands a correlation between theology and Christian witness. In addition there is the criterion of appropriateness to contemporary experience. Whereas the first criterion is developed within historical theology, the second is developed within practical theology. Systematic theology raises questions of the truth of the Christian witness. Consequently historical theology is much more than the study of the history of witness, practical theology is much more than the study of practice, and systematic theology is much more than the study of logic. These three dimensions are distinct, but they are intertwined.

The exercise and appropriation of these three dimensions involves the acquisition of the habit of theological enquiry. The development of this habit should form the basis of education for church leadership. Such church leadership is not simply the acquisition of ministerial skills, but involves judgements about the content of Christian witness and its appropriateness to its context.

The major strength of this proposal is also its weakness. What Wood admirably demonstrates is that critical enquiry cannot be simply identified with the acquisition of knowledge or technical competency, but involves formation in critical discernment and judgement. The goal of theological education is definitely the development of this habit of discernment. The question however concerns the relation between theological enquiry as critical enquiry and theological education as ministerial education. Whereas theological enquiry is central to the exercise of ministry, there are many elements of ministerial praxis that are not covered by the requisite discernments of critical enquiry. The habit of critical enquiry and the habit of ministerial practice entail many distinct elements so that the latter cannot be reduced to the former.

Issues of ministerial practice often involve issues where the nature, truth and appropriateness of Christian witness are not at stake. When one has formed a good theologian, one has not necessarily formed a good preacher, counsellor, consoler, or even pastor. Obviously, formation in the latter skills entails some formation in the skills of theological enquiry. In the last result, there is a distinctive element in the practice of Christian ministry that is not identical with the practice of good theology.

This distinctiveness of Christian praxis is especially emphasised in conceptions of theology that give much more importance to praxis as determinative of Christian identity. In such a conception more would be at stake in practical theology than the appropriateness of Christian witness.

Theological education and anthropology

As our fourth and final example of a theological approach to theological education, I have selected Karl Rahner's essays on the reform of theological education. Rahner wrote *Zur Reform des Theologiestudiums* in response to the German Roman Catholic bishops' application of Vatican II's 'Decree on the training of priests' to the German situation with proposals not unlike those of the American bishops.[23] Rahner argues that theology has in modern times undergone an epochal change leading to the malaise of theology. This malaise is twofold. It lacks unity as a discipline and its disciplinary or scientific character has fallen into disrepute.

The modern division of theology into a multiplicity of disciplines results from 'thousands of historical accidents' and represents a division that is neither organic nor logical. This division has brought about an 'extremely illogical' arrangement of studies.[24] For example, one studies liturgy before sacramental theology or one studies church history before one studies a theological treatment of the church or the function of church history within theology. Likewise, one studies ethics and dogmatics as separate disciplines having nothing to do with one another. The required curriculum insufficiently attends to world religions or to ecumenical studies.

Rahner argues that the malaise of theology as a discipline relates to the radical precariousness of Christian faith today. One can no longer assume as a matter of course the faith of seminarians. Seminarians often enter into theological studies doubting and questioning the Christian faith. If theological educators are to take seriously this situation, they should deal with the precariousness of faith. This precariousness challenges the order and content of theological studies. In Rahner's opinion, the episcopal document does not meet this challenge.[25]

Rahner's alternative proposal entails a revision of the curriculum and of theological method. Theological education is divided into a basic course and into a more specialised course. The basic course relates Christian revelation to human self-understanding. It represents an existential and transcendental reformulation of traditional fundamental theology insofar as the theological justification of revelation is transformed into a course of studies relating the basic truths of Christian faith to modern self understanding. Rahner's *Foundations of the Christian Faith* exemplifies his conception of such a course.[26] Along with this basic course, theological education should offer courses relating the Christian faith to the world religions, atheism and the understanding of humanity in modern literature, art and society.

Rahner has a second set of courses following the basic course. These courses, including biblical and historical theology, are so organised that they explore the relation of their disciplines to anthropological and existential questions. Systematic theology deals with salvation history, christology, anthropology and ecclesiology. The doctrine of God comes at the end as the recapitulation of all systematic theology. Besides the biblical, historical and systematic theological disciplines, Rahner argues for the inclusion of courses on psychology, anthropology and natural science. He proposes as a discipline a theology of practice that should explore moral aspects, religious experience, preaching, liturgy, sacraments, pastoral elements, and their relations to the church in the modern world. These courses should be combined with courses in missiology, catechetics, pastoral guidance, media and economics.[27]

Rahner's proposal for theological education contains several elements including an introductory course of studies that provides a unified vision of Christianity and takes seriously the challenges of faith experienced by contemporary students. Later courses build upon this introductory course of studies by relating traditional theological disciplines to anthropological questions and to current disciplines dealing with human culture and practice. Although he describes the traditional theological courses in the traditional terms of biblical, historical, systematic and practical, he relates them so explicitly to anthropology that he modifies their traditional agenda and disciplinary isolation. Norbert Lohfink, a New Testament scholar, criticises Rahner's programme for he fears that Rahner's proposal endangered the autonomy of scriptures within the curriculum.[28]

Rahner's proposal occupies a middle ground. He moves Roman Catholic theology away from an objective reliance on revelation as the source of authority. He develops a concept of theology that explicates the existential and anthropological conditions of belief in revelation. It does not so much uncover pre-reflective faith that Schleiermacher and

Farley take as their starting-points but explicates the anthropological conditions for the reception and understanding of revelation.[29]

Rahner seeks to reform and to unify theological education by a basic introductory course of fundamental theology and by anthropological orientation to the whole course of studies. Rahner seeks to reform theological education through a reform of theology. Therefore his proposal deals primarily with the credibility and unity of theology. This proposal does not have the professional training of seminarians for specific ministerial tasks at its centre.

In conclusion, these four approaches to theological education concentrate on the nature of theology.[30] That concentration leads them to a similar diagnosis. The pluralism facing theological education is a pluralism affecting the unity of theology itself. The division of the individual theological disciplines has led to the divorce of theology from life. A reform of theology itself will overcome the fragmentation of theological education and the divorce of theological education from life. These four attempts have the same diagnosis and the same goal: the unity of theology and the unity between life and theology. Yet because their theological visions differ, their reform proposals differ. Farley secures this unity through a conception of theology as the explication of a pre-reflective faith as it exists in diverse social matrices. The bishops' *Program* secures this unity by focusing theology and theological education upon divine revelation as taught by the church's official magisterium. Wood concentrates on the interpretation and practice of Christian witness. Rahner secures this unity through a reorganisation of theological studies that seeks to show the existential and anthropological credibility of God's revelation. One starting point, the nature of theology, but four different proposals for theological education!

Identity and mission of the church

Another approach starts out from the purpose, goal and identity of the church in order to arrive at a conception of theological education. The church's identity and purpose determines theological education, the nature of ministry and of theology. Two approaches, written thirty years apart, provide the paradigms illustrating the advantages and limits of this approach to theological education.

Theocentric identity

H Richard Niebuhr first asks: what purpose and goal does the church have? This purpose and goal should provide guidance for the reform of theological education.[31] The differences between Niebuhr and Farley are important. Farley proposes a dialectic of theological understanding and seeks to remove theology from the confines of the clerical paradigm. Niebuhr has argued that only when theological activity focuses on the idea and purpose of the church does it become a genuine and authentic theology. Obviously 'clerical paradigm' and 'church' are not identical. Niebuhr would also argue against any absolutising of a clerical paradigm. Nevertheless, the two approaches differ in their basic theological option and have quite different presuppositions and consequences.

Niebuhr's diagnosis of the malaise of theological education is multiplicity, pluralism and indefiniteness. The illness of theological education is a lack of purpose. This lack underlies the split among the various disciplines. Not specialisation, but lack of purpose is the cause of the fragmentation of theological education. This lack of purpose has resulted in the haphazard addition of new disciplines to the curriculum. The same lack of purpose has led to the flourishing debates about theological education, between liberals and conservatives, between those favouring content and those advocating more practice in the curriculum.[32]

What Niebuhr paradigmatically claims for bible studies applies to all disciplines, traditional and contemporary. 'If bible study has become a speciality or series of specialities today,' he argues, 'the reason is not to be sought simply in the development among teachers of theology, but rather in the loss of a controlling idea in theological education, an idea able to give unity to many partial enquiries. Similar reflections apply to the other traditional disciplines of the theological schools.'[33] How then does one obtain this 'controlling idea'? For Niebuhr, it is the purpose of the church that provides the controlling idea for theological education, and for theology itself.

First, theological education: using Aristotle's four causes Niebuhr equates almost to the point of identification the church and the theological school. Both have the same material cause: same membership; both have the same form; both have the same purpose: the increase of the love of God and love of neighbour. Both have the same efficient cause which he interprets in terms of motivation to implant by acceptance of God the love of God and the love of neighbour.[34]

The love of God and love of neighbour gives each the same, but differentiated, final cause. The theological school as the centre of the church's intellectual activity articulates the purpose of the church by exercising the intellectual love of God and neighbour. It serves the church by bringing reflection to bear on worship, preaching, teaching and pastoral care. A theological school should in its theological reflections articulate the ultimate purpose of the church. This ultimate purpose is a purpose that should not be confused with proximate goals.[35]

Second, theology: the idea of the church is the central reason not only for theological education but also for theology itself and for two reasons. Theology as an intellectual discipline abstracts. One will become committed to these abstractions and will absolutise them unless one grounds intellectual study in the idea of the church as the love of God and love of neighbour. Second, through personal participation in the life of the church one grasps the distinction between an oration and a sermon, a speech and a homily. Participatory experience in an ecclesial community is the condition of awareness of what constitutes a sermon or homily.[36]

The ultimate purpose of the church provides the key for understanding theological education and theology. The same purpose also guides Niebuhr's conception of ministry and his idea of the minister as pastoral director. His explication of this ultimate purpose displays his neo-Orthodox vision of the transcendence of God.[37] He emphasises the transcendence of God over against any attempts to absolutise religion, culture, the world, the institutional denomination and even Christology. Niebuhr's theology consistently elaborates the church's ultimate purpose as a transcendent ultimacy in relation to theology, theological education and ministry.[38]

Such an emphasis on transcendence makes this vision stronger in its critical negations than in its positive affirmations. The controlling idea of love of God and love of neighbour is in some respects a formal principle to which no one can object. Niebuhr makes it concrete in his opposition to any form of absolutising. By describing a theological school as the locus of collegial conversation and dialogue, he implies that concrete applications should flow out of that process of dialogue.

In the face of today's pluralism of method and theological criteria, it seems as though Niebuhr does not have any doubts about the problem of ascertaining Christian identity or the purpose of the church.[39] His conception places the controlling idea of the church at the centre of theological education and is taken as a matter of course for the development of his conception. The problem of the meaning of Christian identity comes more to the fore in the next proposal.

Christian inclusiveness

Thirty years later, Joseph Hough and John Cobb develop Niebuhr's basic approach.[40] They not only make the church's purpose the central idea of their conception of theological education, but they also take over several of his key categories: the distinction between internal and external history, the notion of story, and a specific view of theory-practice relation. Their basic thesis is: 'if the theological school is to be a school for professional leadership, the understanding of what it is to be a Christian community in the world will be the aim of its research and pedagogy. And it is this theological understanding that will form the basis for its curriculum and the criterion for its practice.'[41]

They specify this understanding in two steps. First they define Christian identity within a world historical horizon. Then they analyse images of the Christian community. The result: a vision of Christian identity that I shall call 'Christian inclusiveness'. One compares their vision with Niebuhr's. Niebuhr's analysis of the purpose of the church underscores the belief in the transcendence of God as critical of all absolutisations. Hough-Cobb propose an understanding of Christian identity as inclusive and as embracing new historical, social and religious elements within Christian identity.[42]

The implications for theological education and theological ministry are significant. By 'world-historical' horizon, they mean that any particular or local religious community must take as its horizon the comprehensive historical and global context. The church should understand itself within the history of life on this planet. In developing this theme, Hough-Cobb use Niebuhr's categories (internal history and Christian story) and relate them to the process of world history, in the present context of the modern European Enlightenment with its individualism and its dualism.[43] As a result they profile Christian identity over and against the Enlightenment's mechanistic dualism and individualism. The Christian story stresses community and inclusion over against individualism and dualism.

Instead of one master image, they give us eleven images of the church, because no one image is complete. Each image reflects perspectives of the church's memory of Jesus Christ.[44] An examination of these images shows that images of inclusion predominate: the church is a caring community, inclusive of physical, economic, recreational and emotional needs; a church for the world emphasises the importance of including the whole world, 'the salvation of other living creatures, of soil and water and air' (p. 57); a church for the poor learns from the poor and risks itself to proclaim good news to them; a church for all people is a church inclusive of other races; a church for women is inclusive of women; and the church as integrator is inclusive by including ecology and the natural sciences within its concern, hence offering a holistic vision.

Other images do not stress the notion of inclusiveness directly but only indirectly: a church of repentance emphasises repentance over the Christian exclusion of the poor, the world of nature, Jews, blacks and women; a church of worship underscores the importance of worshipping God as creator and redeemer of an interdependent world of nature and an inclusive attitude toward nature.[45]

Hough and Cobb's understanding of Christian identity primarily in terms of the movement of the Christian story toward inclusiveness shows itself in their theoretical conception of theological education and in their practical suggestions for curriculum reform. They emphasise three major elements of internal history: it should be critical, inclusive and move toward universality. One could state that the last two (inclusive and universal) provide the basis for the first (critical). The failure to be inclusive (the neglect of women, blacks, ethnic minorities) requires that one critique one's internal history for its distortions and failure in regard to inclusiveness.[46]

Failure at inclusiveness leads to a hermeneutics of suspicion of internal history. Likewise with universalism, the failure to include the story of Jesus and of other religions has led to distortions of Christian identity so that the move toward universality leads toward a critique of internal history. In short, failures at inclusiveness and universalism are the basis for the critique of internal history. This inclusiveness provides the direction for the revision of the theological curriculum. One must so structure a theological curriculum that it defines Christian identity within the global historical perspective and moves toward an inclusiveness and universality.[47]

The approach to theological education from the perspective of purpose and function of the church is in many ways comprehensive in that it takes into account the nature of theology and the nature of ministry. It could be open to Farley's charge of representing a 'clerical paradigm'. Yet Niebuhr's theocentricism and Hough-Cobb's inclusiveness counter this charge.[48] Interesting is a comparison between the concrete suggestions for the curriculum in the Hough-Cobb volume with the bishops' *Program* or Rahner. Rahner's approach from theology stresses courses that raise the issue of the credibility of Christianity. The bishops stress the content of belief. The Hough-Cobb volume underscores the courses dealing with the church's global mission. In short, the focus on the purpose of the church produces a curriculum that is more action and service oriented where the focus on theology is more ordered to the intelligibility and credibility of the content of faith.[49]

The Hough-Cobb volume raises a central question that it does not fully explore or answer. In discussing the conflict between Christian belief and revolutionary necessities, they note: 'For example, the love of enemies is problematical because revolutionary energies are often better mobilised by hate. Reconciliation, a notion at the heart of Christian faith, seems premature to those who are swamped by injustice.'[50] This observation raises the question of how one ascertains Christian identity in relation to contemporary practice.

Niebuhr's theocentric focus on God prevents both the idolising of all religious institutions and the overemphasising of Christology. Hough-Cobb focus more on Jesus and the Jesus story. Nevertheless they avoid the danger of a too narrow focus on the story of Jesus insofar as they make internal history more inclusive, universalise it, and use it to critique distortions of internal history. Their account explores the possibilities of inclusion. It does not explore the critiques of internal history or the Christian story that stem from contemporary experience and practice, to which liberation theologians and expecially feminist theologians appeal.[51]

The question is whether the mission and identity of the church can be adequately dealt with through the dual categories of internal/external history. Issues about the mission of the church and Christian identity point back to fundamental questions of theological method and criteria. Their proposals represent a brilliant reformulation of another side of Schleiermacher's conception of theology, the significance of making the essence of Christianity and of Christian identity normative for the determination of Christian faith and ministry.

Distinctive nature of ministry

A third approach to theological education is through a basic conception of ministry. Such an approach can follow two very distinct paths. One follows a theological vision of ministry. The other follows a more sociological, practical and professional vision of ministry. Each starts out from the specificity of ministry as the basis of theological education. Yet each has a very different view of ministry, and therefore offers a distinctive vision of theological education.

Theological vision of ministry

Whenever a specific theological conception of ministry dominates, one tends to define the specificity of ministry in relation to the personal character of the minister rather than to required professional skills. Such a theological conception predominates in those denominations, for example, Roman Catholicism or Anglicanism, that have a very sacramental conception of ministry as priesthood.

Just recently, for example, Westerhoff has insisted on the careful distinction between professions and ministers. In referring to clergy, he argues that their status as clergy 'lies not in the fact that they are professionals like any other professionals, but that they are *extraordinary* persons. A professional minister may be best defined as someone who has acquired a body of knowledge and developed particular skills; an ordained priest is best defined as a sacramental person.'[52] Referring to John Macquarries' essay on 'Priestly character', he argues that ministry is not primarily the fulfilling of roles, tasks or functions.[53] These do not need a distinctive ministry and an ordained priest. Instead, priestly character is at the heart of the priesthood. Urban T Holmes argues a similar theological position when he claims that a priest is first of all a spiritual person. This priestly 'being' has priority over knowledge, skills, functions and role.[54]

This distinction between ministerial functions and priestly character is the basis of Holmes' view of theological education. 'The function of the seminary is above all the formation of priestly character and then secondarily ministerial knowledge and skills.'[55] Westerhoff argues that the major weakness of contemporary theological education is the emphasis upon knowledge and skills rather than upon the spiritual development of the priest and the formation of priestly character.

Such an approach differs in its consequences from those views making theology or the purpose of the church determinative of theological education. The first two do not underscore the distinctiveness or apartness of the minister from the lay person. Instead they emphasise a commonality of faith, theology and purpose. They stress that faith and theological enquiry exist in a diversity of social matrices. Seminarians share the questions and doubts of all contemporary Christians. Or Christians should have as their goal the fundamental goals of their churches. However, in making the distinctiveness of ministry the starting-point, this approach underscores the fact that theological education has a unique goal: it forms a distinctive person and it moulds a person into a special 'priestly character'.[56] I have quoted Episcopalian theologians to illustrate this approach. However, these opinions also reflect the traditional Roman Catholic view of the priesthood that emphasises an 'indelible character' or a difference from laity not only in degree, but in essence, an affirmation present even in Vatican II.[57] Many criticisms of contemporary practice within seminaries flow from this viewpoint. The Marshall Committee visited Roman Catholic seminaries with the mandate of examining whether the distinctiveness of priestly character was the object of theological education.

Such a theological approach to ministry rests upon the validity of its vision of priesthood or ministry. Westerhoff's conception underscores the 'apartness' of the priest and contrasts the function of that apartness to professionalisation. 'The priest is set apart by God and the community to be an active instrument for God's illumination of our human consciousness, the mystagogue who leads us to hidden truths of the secrets of God. A ministerial priesthood is not best understood as a profession. Similarly, we need to question whether we can adequately prepare persons for ordination in the same way as we train other professions.'[58]

A theologian influenced, for example, by Martin Luther's emphasis on the priesthood of the faithful in his early writings (in distinction to his later emphasis on office) would not underscore the 'apartness' of the minister and would therefore draw different implications for theological education. For example, Martin Marty writes, 'Protestantism makes much of its doctrine of the priesthood of all believers. It professes belief in the central place of the church's laity and seeks to stimulate lay expression. But in a technical society Protestantism is also aware of the urgency of sustaining a large and well-qualified corps of professional "priests".'[59] Moreover, any theologian taking the previous approach, the mission and purpose of the church, would probably locate ministry in the wider context of the mission of every Christian within the total mission of the church. Nevertheless, it is to Westerhoff's credit that he explicitly explains his vision of ministry as distinctive and draws out its consequences for theological education.

Professional model of ministry

Another avenue of this basic approach moves toward a professional image of ministry. James Glasse in *Profession: Ministry* offers a classic example of this professional conception.[60] He counters attempts to make theological reflection or the theological specialties the starting point for an understanding of ministry and theological education for ministry. Such an approach integrates the students into the work of professors and into the life of the academy more than it initiates them into the work of the church and its practice. The result leads to a dichotomy between the preparation and training of seminarians and their life and work in the parishes and communities of their churches.

Glasse describes a profession in terms of five characteristics: first, a specific area of knowledge; second, expertise in a cluster of skills; third, service through a specific social institution; fourth, accepted standards of competence and ethics; and fifth, specific values of purposes of the profession and social institution for society. One can place the profession of ministry on a grid along with doctor, lawyer and teacher just as one can locate the institution of church alongside hospital, court and school.[61]

This approach to theological education has several important consequences. Professor Owen Thomas has formulated them well. First, he points out that this view entails a very specific educational option 'for the professional school as over against the graduate school model for the seminary'.[62] Second, 'if the purpose of a seminary is preparation for various kinds of Christian ministry, then what goes on in a seminary will depend upon the nature of this ministry and its varieties'.[63] Of course, the important question is how one determines the nature of this ministry. One should not simply take as a standard the present *de facto* exercise of ministry. Instead one should develop norms and ideals for ministries that the churches need. To do so, it is necessary to develop criteria and this task is one of theological method.[64]

The approach to theological education from a conception of ministry has also influenced the specific development of pastoral theology and the case-study method approach to theological education. For example, Seward Hiltner defines the specificity of pastoral theology as 'an operation-centred or function-centred branch of theology rather than, what we shall call for lack of a better name, a logic-centred branch of theology'.[65] Such a conception does not view pastoral theology as an applied discipline or skill that takes its principles from elsewhere and then applies them. Instead the reflection on pastoral ministry (called shepherding, but usually illustrated with examples from therapeutic ministry) gives rise to genuine theological insights and contributions.[66] The use of case-studies represents another example of a similar approach to theological education.[67]

In this view, the pluralism of theological education is neither the diversity of theological disciplines nor the diverse global tasks of the church, but rather the diverse experiences of the practice of pastoral ministry. These diverse experiences generate diverse theological conceptions. Besides the pluralism of diverse experiences, there remains the dualism between theory and practice in the distinction between operation-centred and logic-centred branches of theology. Hiltner's intention, however, is to overcome the dualism between theory and practice through a pastoral theology that reflects on practice. In this regard the term 'reflective practitioner' could be applied to Hiltner's conception.[68]

This conception raises an important theoretical issue. Whereas pastoral theology overcomes the pluralism of theory and practice, by moving from practice to theory, the other disciplines of theological education remain logic-centred. Logic-centred branches of theology remain distinct from operation-centred branches. The practice of ministry does not seem to reflect back and affect the logic of the logic-centred branch of theology. This issue is central to much recent hermeneutical theory. It raises the relation between theory and practice, an issue that the section on hermeneutics will discuss.

The effect that the professional approach has had on theological education illustrates this issue. It has influenced the addition of many specialised courses to the curriculum: psychology, sociology, counselling, management, etc.[69] However, these courses have been added more where they intersect with the practice of ministry than with the theoretical framework of theological disciplines. The implication of sociology and psychology for the logic-centred disciplines is thereby given insufficient attention.

In conclusion, many recent developments in theological education have come from the professionalisation of ministry. This professionalisation has enabled one to break down various components of ministry, ministerial practice and ministerial reflection and subject them to supervisory analysis, as the Charles Fielding study on the professionalisation of theological education has shown.[70] Moreover, this approach has led to further clarity in assessing readiness for ministry in terms of specific characteristics, some of which stem from a theological view of ministry; others, from a professional view.

Assessing the diverse approaches

The three theological approaches to theological education are interrelated. How one specifies the nature of theology affects the specification of Christian identity and vice versa. How one specifies the purpose of the church has implications for specifying not only Christian ministry, but also the nature of theology. Nevertheless one cannot simply draw implications from one to the other. For example, Schleiermacher, the father of liberal theology because of his appeal to the religious dimension of experience and to the cultural despisers of religion, is also an advocate of the 'clerical paradigm', defining the nature of theology in relation to its service to the church. Another reason for attending to the distinctiveness of each approach is that each approach considered either ideally or contextually has a specific set of advantages and disadvantages.

Ideally considered

The theological approaches are distinct. Each brings with it a particular *focus or perspective* that narrows its view of theological education. The approach from the perspective of *the nature of theology* often takes as its problem the modern fragmentation of the theological disciplines. It views this modern fragmentation to be the result of a theological idea of the organisation of theology, for example, theological encyclopedia and the fourfold division. Its reform proposals therefore tend to imply that a new idea of theology as unified, as related to faith, as a habit of theological enquiry, or as related to existential anthropology, will overcome the problem of the fragmentation of theology and theological education from life and practice.

The current status of theology is indeed a problem of theological education. Yet not all the problems of theological education stem from the problems of theology. Many arise from the particular tasks, specific constituencies, specific institutional settings of theological education. These problems may overlap but they are distinct from issues about what constitutes good theology. It does not resolve the problem to argue that the task of theology is to communicate not only a certain amount of knowledge, but also to transmit a certain set of skills and habits.

What are these skills and habits? They are usually the skills and habits of theological enquiry, research, exploration and understanding. These skills are in part significant skills for priests and ministers. Yet insofar as ministry involves many more skills than these and entails the combination of these skills with other sets of skills, the approach to theological education from the perspective of theological enquiry fails to grasp the concrete dimensions of theological education. Its greatest weakness is that it analyses the theory of theological enquiry without considering the specific purposes and practices of theological education.

The approach from the perspective of *the mission and purpose of the church* takes into account that theological education is intrinsically related to Christian identity and the purpose of the church. It thereby gives a specific focus to the task of theological education. It takes seriously the fact that the problem is not about the nature of an intellectual discipline or set of disciplines. It acknowledges the extent to which much of the discipline of theology has emerged from a particular historical identity and purpose. It acknowledges that theological education within divinity schools is concerned with the work, mission and purpose of the church.

In relating the task of theological education to the ecclesial institution, it can make 'ecclesial existence' the object of theological education. Yet by concentrating upon the church's purpose this approach avoids this danger, so well described by Niebuhr as the identification of the church with a particular denomination. Instead it orders theological education and the church to broader issues and global problems, as the Hough-Cobb volume does in an exemplary fashion.

Since these broader problems relate to the church's purpose and identity, the question is: how do they affect the interpretation of Christian identity? This question is one of the relation between theory and practice; it touches upon the norms and criteria of theology. In addition, the focus upon the church's purpose in relation to contemporary societal needs and problems can neglect the challenges to the church that come from the theoretical disciplines dealing with the origin and nature of the church's religious traditions.

The third approach from *specific conceptions of ministry* entails further specification. Theological education communicates specific knowledge and skills, specific abilities and qualifications. A training in theological enquiry unrelated to these specific skills and qualities has failed to be a professional education for ministry. A skilled technician without character or virtues is as lamentable as a virtuous minister with character but without any skills.

Theological education serves the purpose of the church in a very specific manner. By emphasising either the character or the skills of the professional minister, it has the advantage of pointing to the very concrete function of theological education.[71] Its danger, of course, is that it could neglect issues of broader concern: the purpose of the church or the complexities of theology. What Farley has labelled the 'clerical paradigm' appropriately fits this third rather than the second approach. In its best form it specifies the theory-pattern relation as the theological reflection upon pastoral experience and ministerial practice. Thereby pastoral theological analysis confines itself to reflecting upon the practice of ministry. Experiences, practices and societal issues outside of the practice of ministry do not become the objectives of reflection with this conception of pastoral theology.

Contextually considered

Besides the advantages and disadvantages of each approach, considered abstractly as an ideal type, one can raise additional issues about each approach as existing within concrete and specific contexts. Perhaps each perspective is usually developed in relation to a specific context. Theology as an academic discipline is often defined by the context of the university and by the dialogue with other academic disciplines. Just as developments in Islamic philosophy and universities as well as developments in the liberal arts had an enormous impact upon the development of medieval conceptions of theology, so too do modern universities and their academic disciplines have an impact upon theology. Theology in a university context wrestles with its intellectual, disciplinary and credibility status. It tends to neglect the practical and institutional function of theology. The opposite is true of theology within the context of an isolated seminary or theological school. The challenges from practice, function, identity and ministry often take precedence over the intellectual challenges of theological disciplines in their interaction with other contemporary disciplines or identity.[72]

An example illustrates this point. A New Testament scholar pursuing the challenge of her scholarship might very well ask: To what extent does the interpretation of the gospel miracles of Jesus need to take into account the Greco-Roman tradition of the miracles of wonder-workers or magicians? One needs to discuss the comparison between Appollinarius of Tyana and Jesus. In the divinity school context the scholar is often bombarded with the questions: How can I preach the gospel stories? How do I deal with a cancer patient, still not accepting the imminency of death and hoping for a miraculous cure? Practical rather than intellectual problems are at stake. Or the concrete context of the divinity school might be that good theology is 'orthodox theology' so that the criteria of good exegesis becomes the affirmation of orthodox beliefs about miracles or some tenet taken to be central to a credal statement or some hypothesis of the early Christian testimony.

When the church's purpose or identity is the goal of theological education, then in some concrete contexts this goal becomes a specific denominational goal. The purpose of theological education is to produce a good Methodist, Lutheran or Catholic, etc. The goal is the establishing of ecclesial boundaries; identity becomes denominational identity, faith becomes fidelity to magisterial pronouncements or congregational policy statements.

In the approach focusing on ministry, the greatest danger in concrete contexts is the 'clerical paradigm'. Then theological education becomes sharply removed from other forms of theological education, for example, university education, religious studies, education for interested adults. In addition, the concrete parochial expectations of ministers and the *de facto* wishes of church leadership become normative rather than those criteria demanded by good theology or by the purpose of the church. One theological school was recently reminded that it should see its purpose more as training ministers to fulfil what the church and parishes felt they needed than by educating the ministers to tell the church or the parishes what they (the parishes and churches) should do. A ministry professionalised to satisfying parochial expectations can become a ministry trained to be non-prophetic.

The reflections on each approach, considered ideally and contextually, highlight imperatives for thinking theologically about theological education. First, one should not examine theological education exclusively from a single perspective: be it theology, church or ministry. Instead one should keep in mind that no matter what advantages each approach has, it still presents only a limited perspective on theological education. Second, each approach raises the problem of the relationship between theory and practice. Theological education involves theoretical ideals, criteria and constraints. But it also relates these to the practice of the church and ministry within our modern world. Theological education is therefore, crucially concerned with the relationship between theory and practice. Any adequate theological analysis of theological education must take into account the complexities of the theory-practice relationship. In another article, I examined contemporary hermeneutical   ussions on the relation between theory and practice, the complementarity between explanation and understanding, and the intertwinement between interpretation and truth-claims in order to draw out the implications for theological education.[73]

Notes

1. See Francis Schüssler Fiorenza, 'Theory and practice: theological education as a reconstructive, hermeneutical, and practical task', *Theological Education*, 23, Supplement, 1987, pp. 113-141.

2. Edward Farley, *Theologia: the fragmentation and unity of theological education*, Philadelphia, Fortress Press, 1983. See also his 'The reform of theological education as a theological task', *Theological Education*, 17, 1981, pp. 93-117, 'Phenomenology and pastoral care', *Pastoral Psychology*, 26, 1977, pp. 95-112, and 'Theology and practice outside the clerical paradigm', in Don S Browning (ed.), *Practical Theology: the emerging field in theology, church, and world*, San Francisco, Harper and Row, 1983, pp. 21-41.

3. Edward Farley, *Theologia: the fragmentation and unity of theological education, op. cit.*, pp. 49-72. See also Robert Wood Lynn, 'Notes toward a history: theological encyclopedia and the evolution of Protestant seminary curriculum, 1808-1868', *Theological Education*, 17, 1981, pp. 118-144.

4. Edward Farley, *Theologia: the fragmentation and unity of theological education, op. cit.*, p. 156.

5. In addition to the pluralism of disciplines within theological schools, Farley has also argued against the dualism between religious and theological studies. See 'The place of theology in the study of religions', *Religious Studies and Theology*, 5, 1985, pp. 9-29.

6. Edward Farley, *Theologia: the fragmentation and unity of theological education, op. cit.*, pp. 73-98.

7. My survey does not cover the important contribution of a feminist conception of theology to theological education, since an earlier contribution of Professor Margaret Miles specifically addresses that contribution. Feminist theology often appeals to feminist experience as the matrix of theology that has been overlooked and even repressed, within the theological tradition. In this respect it shares the standpoint of Farley's emphasis upon the diverse contemporary social matrices. Yet it stands in contrast with Farley's phenomenological analysis of universal or transcendental structures of human experience. See for example, The Mud Flower Collective, *God's Fierce Whimsy: Christian feminism and theological education*, New York, Pilgrim Press, 1985, and the earlier volume, The Cornwall Collective, *Your Daughters Shall Prophesy: feminist alternatives in theological education*, New York, Pilgrim Press, 1980.

8. Edward Farley, *Theologia: the fragmentation and unity of theological education, op. cit.*, p. 169. Farley's suggestions for theological education should be interpreted in the context of his appropriation of phenomenology for the development of systematic theology. See *Ecclesial Reflection: an anatomy of theological method*, Philadelphia, Fortress Press, 1982.

9. In the *Summa Theologica* I, 6 Thomas defines *sacra doctrina* as a wisdom because it treats of God as the highest cause. In I, 6 and 3 he distinguishes between wisdom as a virtuous habit and wisdom as knowledge of divine things. Theology belongs to the latter. Ever since Robert Kilwardby, it was customary to consider both theology and metaphysics as wisdom

because they were sciences of the cause of all causes. See Charles Lohr, 'Theologie als Wissenschaft im fruhen 13. Jahrhundert', *Internationale Katholische Zeitschrift*, 10, 1981, pp. 316–330, and Ulrich Köpf, *Die Anfänge der theologischen Wissenschaftstheorie im 13. Jahrhundert*, Tübingen, J C B Mohr, 1974.

10. Schleiermacher's conception allows the methodic independence of the disciplines; his formula of combination of 'ecclesial interest and scientific spirit' should be interpreted in the context of the tradition of the 'inner vocation' as an essential condition of a theologian or a pastor. See Dietrich Rossler, '*Vocatio interna*: Zur Vorgeschichte des Schleiermacherschen Bildes vom Kirchenfursten', *Verifikationen. Festschrift für Gerhard Ebeling*, Edited by Eberhard Jüngel, et. al., Tübingen, J C B Mohr, 1982, pp. 207–217.

11. Friedrich Schleiermacher, *Brief Outline on the Study of Theology*, Atlanta, John Knox Press, 1980, pp. 1–30.

12. *The Program of Priestly Formation*, Washington, DC, National Conference of Catholic Bishops, 1982.

13. See *Norms for Priestly Formation: a compendium of official documents on training candidates for the priesthood*, Washington, DC, National Conference of Catholic Bishops, 1982.

14. *The Program of Priestly Formation*, op. cit., pp. 27–35 and pp. 90–104.

15. *The Program of Priestly Formation*, op. cit., pp. 36–40.

16. *The Program of Priestly Formation*, op. cit., #114.

17. *The Program of Priestly Formation*, op. cit., #118.

18. *The Program of Priestly Formation*, op. cit., #134.

19. *The Program of Priestly Formation*, op. cit., #148.

20. *The Program of Priestly Formation*, op. cit., pp. 147–152.

21. *The Program of Priestly Formation*, op. cit., p. 125.

22. *An Orientation in Theological Study*, Atlanta, Scholars Press, 1985.

23. *Zur Reform des Theologiestudiums*, Quaestiones Disputatae 41, Freiburg, Herder, 1969. This book expands his earlier essay 'Zur Neuordnung der theologischen Studien', *Stimmen der Zeit*, 181, 1968, pp. 1–21.

24. *Zur Reform des Theologiestudiums*, op. cit., p. 20.

25. *Zur Reform des Theologiestudiums*, op. cit., pp. 17–34. For other criticisms, Anton Antweiler, 'Vorschläge zu einer Neuordnung der Studienpläne', *Theologie ünd Glaube*, 52, 1962, pp. 407–425, and 'Nochmals: die Studienpläne', 54, 1964, pp. 101–115; Hans Geisser, 'Kontroverse un einen Reformplan des katholischen Theologienstudiums', *Theologica Practica*, 4, 1969, pp. 65–72.

26. Karl Rahner, *Foundations of the Christian Faith*, New York, Crossword, 1978.

27. *Zur Reform des Theologiestudiums*, op. cit., pp. 48–50.

28. Norbert Lohfink, 'Text und Thema: Anmerkungen zum absolutheitsanspruch der systematik bei der reform der theologischen studien', *Stimmen der Zeit*, 181, 1968, pp. 120–126. See Rahner's response, 'Die exegese im theologiestudiums: Eine antwort an N Lohfink', *Stimmen der Zeit*, 181, 1968, pp. 196–201.

29. See Karl Rahner, *Hearers of the Word*, New York, Herder and Herder, 1969.

30. For other proposals, see Wilhelm Hermann and Gerhard Lautner, *Theologiestudiums. Entwurf eines Reform*, Munich, 1965; Wilhelm Hahn and Hans Wolf, 'Reform des theologiestudiums', *Monatschrift für Pratischer Theologie*, 41, 1952, pp. 129–144; H E Hess and H Todt, *Reform der Theologischen Ausbildung*, Stuttgart, 1968.

31. H Richard Niebuhr, *The Purpose of the Church and its Ministry: reflections on the aims of theological education*, New York, Harper, 1956. This study is complemented by the analysis of H Richard Niebuhr, Daniel Day Williams and James M Gustafson, *The Advancement of Theological Education*, New York, Harper, 1957.

32. *Ibid.*

33. H Richard Niebuhr, *The Purpose of the Church and its Ministry: reflections on the aims of theological education*, op. cit., p. 97.

34. *Ibid.*, pp. 107–108.

35. *Ibid.*, pp. 114–116.

36. *The Program of Priestly Formation*, op. cit., pp. 126–129.

37. See C David Grant, *God, the Center of Value: value theory in the theology of H Richard Niebuhr*, Fort Worth, Texas Christian University, 1984, and Donald E Fadner, *The Responsible God: a study of the Christian philosophy of H Richard Niebuhr*, Chico, Scholars Press, 1975.

38. See also *Radical Monotheism and Western Culture*, New York, Harper, 1943, especially the essays on 'Theology and faith' and 'Theology and the university'. See James W Fowler, *To See the Kingdom: the theological vision of H Richard Niebuhr*, Nashville, Abingdon Press, 1974.

39. H Richard Niebuhr, *The Purpose of the Church and its Ministry: reflections on the aims of theological education, op. cit.*, pp. 17–39.
40. Joseph C Hough and John B Cobb, *Christian Identity and Theological Education*, Chico, Scholars Press, 1985.
41. *Ibid.*, p. 19.
42. *Ibid.*, pp. 49–76.
43. *Ibid.*, pp. 19–48. For the distinction between internal and external history, see H Richard Niebuhr, *The Meaning of Revelation*, New York, Macmillan, 1941, pp. 32–66.
44. Joseph C Hough and John B Cobb, *Christian Identity and Theological Education, op. cit.*, pp. 49–67.
45. *Ibid.*, pp. 67–76.
46. *Ibid.*, pp. 47–48.
47. *Ibid.*, pp. 128–131.
48. *The Purpose of the Church and its Ministry: reflections on the aims of theological education, op. cit.*, pp. 39–47; see also Joseph C Hough and John B Cobb, *Christian Identity and Theological Education*, Chico, Scholars Press, 1985, pp. 27–31 and pp. 43–47.
49. Comparison of the curriculum suggested by Karl Rahner with that of Joseph Hough and John Cobb indicates that the former is much more concerned with the credibility of faith, whereas the latter is much more concerned with the church's tasks of service.
50. Joseph C Hough and John B Cobb, *Christian Identity and Theological Education, op. cit.*, p. 38.
51. For an analysis of the epistemological implications of feminist theology, see Sharon D Welch's appropriation of Foucault's work, *Communities of Resistance: a feminist theology of liberation*, Maryknoll, New York, Orbis Books, 1985.
52. John H Westerhoff III, 'Theological education and models for ministry', *Saint Luke's Journal of Theology*, 25, 1982, pp. 153–169; here p. 163.
53. In R Tertwiliger and Urban T Holmes, *To Be a Priest*, New York, Seabury, 1975, p. 147. See also R C Moberly, *Ministerial Priesthood*, London, John Murray, 1897, 2nd ed. 1910.
54. Urban T Holmes, 'The strangeness of the seminary', *Anglican Theological Review*, Supplementary Series, 6, 1976, pp. 135–149. See also *The Future Shape of Ministry*, New York, Seabury, 1971, and *Priest in Community*, New York, Seabury, 1978.
55. John H Westerhoff III, 'Theological education and models for ministry', *op. cit.*, p. 163.
56. While John H Westerhoff III acknowledges the significance of certifying competence and skill, such an approach does not focus on the most fundamental aim of theological education. See 'Theological education and models for ministry', *op. cit.*, p. 165.
57. Vatican II's Constitution, *Lumen Gentium*, #10. See the exposition of Archbishop Daniel Pilarczyk, 'State of priesthood in a changing church', *National Catholic Reporter*, 22, 1, 1986, pp. 14–15.
58. John H Westerhoff III, 'Theological education and models for ministry', *op. cit.*, p. 165.
59. Martin Marty, 'Seminary enrollments 1962', *The Christian Century*, 79, 1962, pp. 1360–1362.
60. James Glasse, *Profession: ministry*, Nashville, Abingdon Press, 1968. See also Charles William Stewart, *Person and Profession: career development in ministry*, Nashville, Abingdon Press, 1974, Wolfram Fischer, *Pfaffer auf Probe: identität und legitimation von vikaren*, Stuttgart, Kohlhammer, 1977, Stewart Ransom, A Bryman and B Hinings, *Clergy, Ministers, and Priests*, London, Routledge and Kegan Paul, 1977.
61. *Profession: ministry, op. cit.*, pp. 31–56 for his use of this grid.
62. Owen Thomas, 'Some issues in theological education', *Theological Education*, 5, 1969, pp. 346–356; here p. 347.
63. *Ibid.*, p. 348.
64. *Ibid.*, p. 348, 'A normative factor is involved in the need to project what ministries *should* be performed in church and in the next fifty years.'
65. Seward Hiltner, *Preface to Pastoral Theology*, Nashville, Abingdon Press, 1958, p. 20.
66. See Seward Hiltner, *The Christian Shepherd*, Nashville, Abingdon Press, 1959, and *Theological Dynamics*, Nashville, Abingdon Press, 1972.
67. The case-study approach was introduced into legal education by Christopher C Langdell at Harvard University in the 1880s. It was then taken over by the Harvard School of Business Administration. Last and not least it became used in theological education as a device for teaching students to apply theory in practice.
68. Donald A Schön, *The Reflective Practitioner: how professionals think in action*, New York, Harper, 1983.
69. The addition of such courses was championed early by W R Harper, 'Shall the theological curriculum be modified, and how?', *American Journal of Theology*, 3, 1899, pp. 45–66.

See also the responses by George Harris (Andover), Augustus Sirong (Rochester), Charles Elliott (Harvard), Charles Hall (Union Theological Seminary), and Charles J Little (Garrett), *ibid.*, pp. 324–343.

70. Charles Fielding, *Education for Ministry*, Dayton, Ohio, American Association of Theological Schools, 1966. Originally published as *Theological Education*, 3, 1966, pp. 1–258.

71. See Steven G Mackie, 'Patterns of ministry and the purpose of a theological school', *Theological Education*, 2, 1965, pp. 82–88.

72. On the dangers of sectarianism and loss of intellectual academic leadership, see Leon Pacala, 'Reflections on the state of theological education in the 1980s', *Theological Education*, 17, 1981, pp. 9–44.

73 See note 1.

9.2 Theological inquiry and theological education

Charles M Wood

Vision, discernment and theological education

While the terms 'vision' and 'discernment' may be used primarily to designate intellectual *activities* characteristic of theological enquiry, the terms may also be used in two other important senses. They can designate the *capacities* for those activities, and they can designate their *products*. Thus we may speak of vision as a personal quality which a person might possess or strive for, meaning by 'vision' the capacity to envision; or we may speak of someone's vision of the Christian faith, meaning the general understanding of it which he or she has attained and might articulate for us in a summary account, or perhaps in a multivolume written 'systematic theology'. We may praise someone's discernment, meaning his or her capacity for insight into particular situations, or we may refer to the discernment which someone has of a particular situation, meaning the actual appraisal of it which that person has made.

In their range of senses, these two terms resemble the more general term 'judgement', of which vision and discernment are both types: 'judgement' can refer to the activity of judging, to the capacity to judge, or to the outcome. In the same way, the term 'theology' can designate the activity of theological enquiry (its primary sense), the theological capacity or *habitus* (the so-called subjective sense), or the results of theological enquiry, for example, theological judgements or proposals (the so-called objective sense).

In its own way the theological *habitus* is also a product of theological enquiry; that is, the capacity and disposition for theology is developed through active participation in it, just as many other abilities and aptitudes are gained and strengthened through exercise. Theological education is essentially just such a participation in theological enquiry, ordered to the acquisition of that complex set of intellectual and personal qualities which go to make up what we might still call the theological *habitus*.

Keeping in mind these two different sorts of products of theological enquiry, the 'objective' and the 'subjective', we might then distinguish between two uses of theological enquiry. Let us call one its *normal* use, and the other its *educational* use. Its normal use is the attainment of considered judgements concerning Christian witness. One normally engages in theological reflection in order to answer a question concerning that witness. It may be a broad question, for example, as to what the substance of the Christian witness really is, or it may be a much narrower question, for example, as to how that witness might be most appropriately enacted in a particular instance. As a rule, such judgements, both the broader and the narrower variety, have implications for action. Christians ordinarily engage in theological reflection for the sake of their own Christian practice; their reflection has a deliberative character.

The educational use of theological enquiry also involves the making of theological judgements, and also has a practical intention; but its more proper aim is not the formation of judgements, but the formation of judgement. Its impact upon Christian practice is indirect. It informs practice by equipping the practitioner not with ready-made deliberative judgements but rather with the capacity to make them. The educational use of theological enquiry then is subordinate to its normal use: it is a 'practice' whose purpose is to develop an aptitude for the practice of enquiry.

These two uses are not mutually exclusive, of course. As with any enterprise in which increased competence is gained with experience, so in theology one's education continues as one pursues the enquiry, even when education is no longer one's primary intention. Likewise the theological judgements one makes in the course of attaining a basic theological competence, while they are not the primary aim at that stage, are still significant judgements which may have profound bearing on one's understanding of the Christian faith, one's practice of Christian witness, and one's conduct of theological enquiry from that point onward. Generally speaking, involvement in theological enquiry always yields both 'objective' and 'subjective' results. Still there are times when a person's focus will be primarily on the attainment or sharpening of theological abilities, and times when it will be primarily on finding answers to theological questions.

Identifying the first sort of focus with the 'educational' use of theological enquiry may seem an arbitrary restriction, since there is no denying that finding answers to theological questions (here, the 'normal' use) has often been regarded as the main purpose of theological education, or at least of the theological part of what we conventionally call 'theological education'. On this view, one studies theology in seminary in order to figure things out, to arrive at a set of judgements about the substance of the Christian witness which one may then use as a foundation (a 'theoretical' foundation, perhaps) for one's subsequent practice of ministry. No doubt some attention must be given to the question of how such judgements are to be made, but the 'how' is of less immediate concern than the 'what'. The important thing is to emerge with 'a theology', that is, with an objective understanding of the content of the Christian faith which can serve as the basis for one's preaching, teaching, counselling, etc. From this angle professional theologians, for example, one's teachers in seminary, may seem unduly preoccupied with the 'how', and unhelpfully insistent on raising questions of method, rather than concentrating on the matter at hand. Their insistence that it is their function to help one learn *how* to think rather than *what* to think may look like evasion; and their refusal to regard preachability as the criterion of good theology may come across as a poor defence for their unwillingness or inability to make their work practically relevant.

Teachers as well as students have sometimes operated on the implicit assumption that the principal aim of theological education is to furnish students with a body of objective knowledge. When 'covering the material' is the major objective of a course, or when examinations are designed primarily to test students' familiarity with the material 'covered', or when a curriculum is shaped by a similar motivation to expose students to everything they are likely to need to know about in the course of their future employment, one may reasonably suspect that such an assumption is at work. Students can hardly be faulted for coming to share it, or at least for recognising it and coming to terms with it as a fact of academic life. (The students may also be unable to find much correlation between the mastery of objective knowledge which is expected of them in various courses and the competences they need to acquire for their future employment, and may therefore conclude that theological education is largely a meaningless exercise, a trial to endure on the way to ministry which has little to contribute to preparation for that ministry except perhaps a schooling in patience and the endurance of frustration.)

This prevalent working assumption concerning the aim of theological education is a powerful half-truth. It is not simply mistaken, because certainly one of the proper, desired results of a theological education is an enhanced understanding (in the objective sense) of the Christian witness: a vision, however tentative, of its nature, coherence and implications, a grasp of general principles relevant to Christian practice, a set of reflective judgements on various significant questions. We would normally and rightly regard a person who emerged from a course of theological training with no such understanding as miseducated. It is highly unlikely that a person could develop competence in theological enquiry without forming some theological judgements along the way. One learns to make judgements chiefly by making judgements, and then examining their grounds and implications, reflecting on one's performance, and trying again. Those judgements are admittedly provisional and heuristic, especially at the earlier stages of one's involvement in the practice; but to attempt to suspend judgement altogether is to abstain from participation in the process through which judgement is learned.

It is, however, a mistake to regard the formation of such judgements as the *principal* aim of theological education. Judgements are instead both the means and the by-product of the achievement of that principal aim, that is, the formation of judgement. Their close association with that aim helps to account for the common tendency to mistake them for it, that is, to think that the acquisition of 'a theology' (in the objective sense) is the goal and criterion of a theological education. While the possession of a set of theological judgements *may* indicate theological competence, it is not by itself an altogether reliable index, since there are many ways of coming to possess opinions other than through a process of careful, critical reflection. One's theology may be inherited, or accepted on the authority of one's teachers, or collected at random. The pressure of academic or ecclesiastical expectations may force a premature closure to judgements without the reflection which they rightly need, and even without any clear sense of the problem to which a given judgement is supposedly a solution. Judgements adopted under these conditions often lack suppleness and vitality. Since they have been acquired at second-hand rather than formed for oneself, their possessor is apt to have little feeling for the degree of firmness or tentativeness with which they should be held, and may be poorly equipped to engage in that ongoing reappraisal of one's judgements which is one mark of intelligent conduct. And to the extent that they have been prompted more by external pressures than by one's own live interest in the questions to which these are answers, these judgements are likely to have only a ceremonial function. They can be trotted out when an opinion is solicited, but they do not belong to one's own actual deliberations. Thus one might (even sincerely) profess a firm adherence to the doctrines of the Trinity and the Incarnation, after a cursory inspection, without those doctrines ever coming to function as working judgements in one's thought and conduct. It is not the mere possession of 'a theology' that is the measure of a theological education; it is rather one's ability to form, revise and employ theological judgements that counts. Vision and discernment are exhibited in practice.

So far, the thesis that theological education is essentially an engagement in theological enquiry for the purpose of developing and strengthening the capacity for that enquiry has simply been asserted. It has some initial plausibility, to be sure. If theology is properly an activity, then learning theology must, one would suppose, mean learning to engage in that activity, and not, for example, simply becoming acquainted with what its practitioners have done or said. Just as learning tennis means learning to play tennis, and learning architecture means achieving the competence to be an architect, so learning an enquiry such as philosophy or theology means learning to conduct the enquiry, or becoming a competent enquirer. And in most such instances, the principal way to learn is to practise in a context in which the necessary resources are made available, training in the pertinent skills offered, constructive criticism of one's attempts to provide, and so forth.

But theological education has not always been so understood. There are three other prominent understandings of the enterprise which might be regarded as alternatives to this one. Each has a substantial history and contemporary presence, and each has a plausible claim to the title. Two of them, the older two, are associated with what the present account has treated as the two secondary senses of the term 'theology', the subjective and the objective; the third, more modern alternative is associated with the post-Schleiermacherian fate of the term. That is, theological education may be seen as a process of 'spiritual formation' (to choose one popular designation for this enterprise); it may be regarded as the transmittal of tradition, the teaching and learning of doctrine; or it may be viewed as a course of professional training for the tasks of church leadership. In the first case, the focus is upon the subjectivity of the learner. In the second, it is upon the objective content being learned. In the third, it is upon the functions of ministry. The understanding of theological education which this article seeks to commend might best be developed and defended by considering its relationship to each of these alternatives.

Theological education as spiritual formation

Theological education has sometimes been understood to consist essentially in a process of spiritual formation. What the future priests and pastors who are its recipients need most, in this view, is not objective knowledge of the Christian tradition, nor professional skill in the performance of the tasks of leadership, though the relative importance of both of these need not be denied, but rather a thorough self-knowledge and self-possession as Christians. Church leaders need not be 'saints', but they need to be persons who truly understand themselves in the light of the gospel, and who are able to nurture a similar self-understanding in others. It is a clear awareness and appropriation of one's own Christian identity, the bringing of one's own life under the judgement and grace of God, which is the fundamental requisite for church leadership. Theological education, then, is essentially a continuation and deepening of the ordinary process of Christian nurture or spiritual formation, in which the resources of the tradition (and perhaps other resources as well, for example, from contemporary psychology) are brought to bear first upon one's own self-understanding and then, supplemented by more explicitly functional or professional training, upon the task of helping others to appropriate the gospel.

This view of theological education as personal formation is common to both 'catholic' and 'evangelical' traditions, though the idiom, the understanding of the process, and the means may vary considerably. It has liberal versions, heavily informed in theory and technique by current secular psychologies and philosophies, as well as conservative versions in which the traditional means of grace and the traditional vocabularies and practices of spiritual direction are employed without too much attention (at least of a positive kind) to other resources. To some representatives of both the liberal and the conservative versions, the understanding of theology and of theological education advocated in this article may appear to be quite wide of the mark. From some conservative standpoints Christian formation and critical enquiry are simply irreconcilable enterprises, and a theological education taking the form of a training in critical enquiry would be destructive of the very cause it professes to serve. From other standpoints within the same basic orientation the relationship between Christian formation and critical enquiry may be seen as one of mutual irrelevance, if not mutual hostility.

Opposition is frequently assumed between critical thinking and the state of mind appropriate to faith. Faith is said to come through submission to the revealed word of God, which in turn involves an acknowledgement of the weakness and deceitfulness of our own understanding. True theological understanding, the theological *habitus* or the *intellectus fidei*, is a divine gift, not a human achievement; it requires a 'conversion of the intellect', in which our ordinary ways of thinking are transformed under the impact of a new knowledge of divine things. The insistence of John Gerhard and others that the theological *habitus* is a special gift of God was linked to a recognition that human beings in their present fallen state are not naturally inclined to genuine knowledge of God. A disposition for that knowledge has to be created, and contrary inclinations subdued. 'All right knowledge of God', wrote John Calvin, 'is born of obedience.'[1]

Given this situation, critical reflection upon theological matters might well appear to be contrary to the spirit of humility and receptivity which is necessary for any genuine acquaintance with God's word and will. The conviction that faith and critical enquiry are essentially opposed is often rooted in an identification of critical thought with prideful self-assertion. Intellectual humility in this view entails the surrender of one's independent judgement; unquestioning acceptance is the intellectual form of a proper self-denial. Some writers in this tradition have advocated not merely a conversion, but a sacrifice of the intellect as a condition for the reception of divine truth.[2] But one need not think of critical enquiry as intrinsically sinful in order to doubt its theological worth. The point can be made more positively by stressing not the natural corruption of the human mind but rather the necessity of faith to understanding: a critical attitude is inappropriate for the purpose of Christian formation, in this view, because it involves a suspension of commitment, a detached, objective approach, rather than the 'engaged' stance necessary to a knowledge of God. Critical distance may be called for in other areas of life; but in theology at least understanding follows commitment. Anselm's *Proslogium* is frequently cited in this connection: 'For I do not seek to understand that I may believe, but I believe in order to understand. For this also I believe, that unless I believed, I should not understand.'[3] The route to theological understanding, it is said, is not criticism but faith.

Concerning this alleged opposition between faith and critical enquiry, two things must be said. First, it is clear that theological understanding requires personal engagement. This is nothing unique to theology. Understanding in any field presupposes a mastery of the concepts involved, and, if one does not already possess the relevant concepts, this generally requires some appropriate form of training or experience. One must not assume a competence to interpret or to judge whatever one encounters; that competence must first be gained. One must be willing to allow oneself to be affected by that which one wishes to understand: to have one's capacities extended, one's vision enlarged, one's ways of experiencing the world challenged or enriched. If, for example, I want to understand what someone has said about the work of a certain composer, I must know something about music and about its interpretation. Otherwise, although the comments may appear to me to have some sense, I will not be in a position to understand them. ('Mendelssohn is, I suppose, the most untragic of composers', wrote Wittgenstein.[4] If I know more or less what tragedy is, I can make something of that judgement, even if I know nothing of Mendelssohn or of music. But what might it mean to call *music* tragic or untragic? How is a composer 'untragic'? I will not understand Wittgenstein's remark until I see how it expresses a musical judgement; and for that, I will need some understanding of music.)

Theology is not unique in demanding personal involvement of its learners. But such involvement is especially crucial here because so many of the concepts used in Christian witness, 'creation', 'sin', 'grace', 'hope' and so forth, are what we might call *existential* concepts, that is, concepts which are instruments for self-understanding. This may not be *all* that these concepts are. That is, their meaning may not be exhausted by their relevance to the illumination or transformation of selfhood. But whatever else they may also be, they are 'self-involving' in that a grasp of them requires (or, perhaps better, amounts to) a certain capacity to understand *oneself* by them.[5] This is why theological enquiry and theological education may rightly be seen to involve something along the lines of 'spiritual formation', whatever one's intention. Some such process of conceptual development is not antithetical to critical theological enquiry, but is in fact a condition for it, since one may not properly criticise what one does not understand.[6]

Unfortunately, however, it is also the case that one may not always recognise one's lack of understanding. I may *think* I am qualified to interpret and criticise Wittgenstein's comments about Mendelssohn, or Paul's statements about the death and resurrection of Jesus Christ, simply because I am able to connect some meaning with their words and make some sense of what they say. This leads to the second thing to be said. Not only does critical theological enquiry require 'formation', that is, the acquisition of Christian concepts; this 'formation', if it is to be responsible, also requires critical reflection. One must test one's understanding: Have I, for example, really understood what Paul understands Christ's death to mean? I might simply take someone's word for it or trust my own hunches. But if I do, I will be in a poor position to justify any claims I may want to advance concerning the rightness of my understanding. And without raising some other self-critical questions, I will be similarly ill-prepared to vouch for its validity in other pertinent respects, or likewise for the validity of any witness I may offer on the basis of that understanding. Critical enquiry, far from being a manifestation of rebellious pride, is itself in this use an act of obedience.

There is a crucial distinction to be noted between questioning God's word and asking whether something really *is* God's word; between denying or resisting what one knows to be the truth, and asking whether something is in fact true; and between refusing to act responsibly and deliberating upon a responsible course of action. The familiar association of a critical spirit with impiety or immorality is made easier by a blurring of these distinctions. Admittedly, raising critical questions can be a way of evading commitment by postponing a decision indefinitely. One can ask questions from the wrong motives, and subvert the true spirit and aims of enquiry as much by a seeming interest in it as by an open hostility to it. But such abuse does not negate, but rather only underscores, the importance of a right use of enquiry in the service of one's commitment. Christian theological enquiry properly undertaken is normally an exercise in self-criticism: Is what we propose to proclaim *really* the Christian witness? Is what I want to believe and assert really worthy of belief? Is this contemplated act a fitting witness in this situation, or is the church merely performing an exercise here without attending to the circumstances? It is through participation in such self-critical enquiry, in all the requisite dimensions and phases, that one is truly 'formed' in that understanding of faith which constitutes the theological *habitus*.

Theological 'formation', then, is something quite different from mere indoctrination or habituation. The theological *habitus* sought is not a 'habit' in the popular modern sense, that is, thoughtless, repetitive behaviour. Being reflective is not a habit in that sense. If we heard someone described as 'habitually self-critical', we would no doubt think of that person as having an unreflective and probably unhealthy tendency to self-denigration. Genuine self-criticism, or critical thinking generally, of the sort we have associated with the theological task is hardly a matter of habit. It is rather a matter of bringing to conscious scrutiny behaviour which might otherwise be governed by habit, or convention, or unconscious motives, or various other factors.

The old concept of *habitus* is considerably broader than our current 'habit', however. It combines a sense of 'capacity' with a sense of 'disposition', as the treatment of wisdom as a *habitus* readily illustrates. Being wise takes more than a yearning to be wise, or a firm resolution to act wisely; a *capacity* for intelligent decision and action is also required. At the same time that capacity alone does not make one wise, for one may have the capacity and fail to exercise it. We would not say of a person (except in jest) 'He's very wise, he just never acts like it.' 'Being wise' entails exhibiting that wisdom fairly consistently in one's conduct; it is a matter of disposition or tendency as well as of ability. Perhaps 'aptitude', with its combination of 'ability' and 'inclination', comes closer now to conveying the sense of *habitus* than does 'habit'. But it may not yet go far enough.

Being reflective or being critical is more like a 'character-trait' than a skill. John Passmore has observed: 'To call a person "critical" is to characterise him, to describe his nature, in a sense in which to describe him, simply, as "capable of analysing certain kinds of fallacy" is not to describe his nature.'[7] Certainly being critical *involves* skills and abilities of various sorts; it even involves habits (for example, the habit of following certain routine investigative procedures, once it has been established that these are or may be the pertinent procedures, without having to reconsider each step; or at a more elementary stage, the habits associated with reading and writing a language). But there is also the matter of disposition. 'Being critical' qualifies the self; it is a determinant of the sort of person one is. Conversely the sort of person one is helps to determine the extent to which one is likely to become critical or reflective. To put it another way: learning to be critical involves a kind of self-formation or self-transformation.

The particular ways of being critical which constitute theological aptitude, that is, the capacity and disposition to make theological judgements, depend in part upon the acquisition of certain skills, techniques and the like in each of the relevant disciplines. But they cannot be reduced to matters of technique or routine. This is partly because the necessary competence in each dimension or phase of the enquiry requires the acquisition of what Passmore calls 'open capacities', in which complete mastery is out of the question because the enquiry continues to develop in ways which cannot always be anticipated and which call for imagination and inventiveness.[8] And it is partly because learning to exercise these capacities, learning theological judgement, learning to discern and to envision, is indeed a kind of personal formation. Iris Murdoch, in describing the capacity she calls 'attention', remarks: 'It is a *task* to come to see the world as it is.'[9] The task to which she refers is a moral one. It involves recognising and overcoming 'the tissue of self-aggrandising and consoling wishes and dreams which prevents one from seeing what is outside one'.[10] It demands patience, humility and compassion. There are, of course, various ways of describing this task and its requirements. The traditional language of 'spiritual formation' provides some resources. As we become increasingly aware of the social and historical dimensions of our ordinary self-deception, such instruments as the so-called 'critical theory' of post-Marxist philosophers such as Jürgen Habermas and Karl-Otto Apel, with its analysis of ideology and its prescriptions for emancipation, are likely to supply other, complementary, resources, or at least to provoke more reflection concerning those dimensions.[11] In any case it is clear that theological education can be properly regarded as 'formation', so long as certain long-standing misconceptions concerning the relation of 'formation' and critical enquiry are removed, and so long as it is remembered that the formation sought is precisely the formation of the *critical* aptitude of theological judgement. There is no reason not to regard such an aptitude as a divinely-bestowed *habitus*, and to describe the path to it as a path of prayer, meditation and testing, and to associate it closely with that attitude of honest and obedient self-recognition and openness to the truth which the tradition calls 'repentance'. In fact, there is good reason to do so: namely, to counteract the frequently resurgent false and dangerous characterisation of faith and critical enquiry as warring forces, one of which must ultimately vanquish the other.

Theological education as transmittal of tradition

Concerning the second alternative depiction of theological education mentioned above, that is, theological education as the faithful transmission of tradition, some of the relevant points have already been made earlier in discussing the role of 'objective' theology, or theological judgements, in the process of learning theological judgement. It was observed then that theological education involves the making of judgements, that is, the consideration, criticism and appropriation (or rejection) of representative samples of Christian tradition, and the acquisition of one's own provisional yet significant understanding of the content of the Christian faith. There can be no theological education which is not, in some sense, an encounter with tradition. As with the first alternative, however, there are ways of understanding this process which would bring it into collision with the enterprise of critical enquiry. This second potentially problematic relationship needs attention.

Theological education as a matter of handing on the tradition seems particularly important to some 'confessional' branches of the church, where the maintenance of sound doctrine is regarded as the key to faithful and vigorous Christian existence. Some of these branches may not even have what they would identify as a confession, nor would they necessarily think of themselves as having a high regard for 'tradition' as such. They may describe themselves instead as 'simple, bible-believing Christians'. But when asked what being a simple bible-believing Christian amounts to, they may well respond with a remarkably clear and well-defined *regula fidei*, an account of the content of the faith which they consider indispensable in substance if not in form. Other branches, more explicitly traditional and confessional, may be more straightforwardly concerned for the preservation of a particular denominational heritage and identity (not simply for itself alone, but for the good of the whole church).[12] In any case, the mastery of the doctrinal substance of the Christian witness is seen as the indispensable centre of education for church leadership. This may be exhibited in an emphasis on biblical studies of an expository sort, or on dogmatics, or perhaps on the history of doctrine, or on some combination of the three. The pastor or other church leader whom this education is intended to equip is supposed to be 'one who knows', one who knows the bible or knows the doctrine, and who is an authoritative teacher or preacher largely by virtue of this knowledge.

Even apart from such strands of the Christian tradition in which objective tradition figures so prominently in the design of theological education and in the understanding of church leadership, there is scarcely a strand in which it is not given some attention. (And even where it is dominant, it is rarely in sole command. Concerns for 'formation' and for professional competence are also usually apparent, in some measure.) In any setting, the question is likely to be raised of the form this 'traditioning' should responsibly take, in the context of theological education. That question might best be formulated as a question of the role of *doctrine* in theological education.

'Doctrine' in this usage refers to what the church teaches. Applied broadly, it covers everything which might be regarded as 'church teaching', from the decisions of ecumenical councils to the contents of all of last Sunday's sermons and church school lessons. Here we are concerned with a stricter usage, in which 'doctrine' refers only to what a particular church body formally and officially sets out and authorises as a normative statement of, or guide to, the Christian witness. (What constitutes 'formal', 'official' and 'authoritative' teaching varies, of course, from church body to church body. For some, there are reasonably explicit identifying marks; in others, the very notion of authoritative church teaching is problematic, so that the criteria for whatever functions as such are more difficult to determine.) Doctrines in this stricter sense, though they normally take the form of statements of Christian witness, are not intended to function directly *as* witness so much as to function as *guides* to witness, as standards or principles by which those who have responsibility for the conduct of witness can be directed. They are analogous to the rules of grammar, or to grammatical paradigms, in that, although there are few situations in which a direct recitation of the rules or paradigms is called for, a genuine grasp of them will enable one to speak correctly in a great variety of situations.[13]

Theology, understood as a critical enquiry into the validity of Christian witness, often focuses upon doctrines. This centring of attention upon what the church formally teaches has had some unfortunate consequences, in that it has usually meant the relative theological neglect of what the church *does*, and especially of what might be called the ordinary witnessing activity of the church in both word and deed, as distinguished from doctrinal formulations. Theologians as a rule have been much more adept at analysing, criticising and reforming doctrines than at reflecting critically upon the actual performance of witness. The theological preoccupation with doctrine is understandable, given the role doctrine is supposed to have in the direction of witness. Perhaps the problem has not been so much the fact as the nature of this concentration: theology has typically been concerned with the *content*, to the neglect of the *function*, of doctrine. If so, the solution is not to shift the focus from doctrine to some other area, but rather to broaden the focus so as to bring into view the way doctrine actually serves (or fails to serve or might better serve) as an instrument for the regulation of the church's existence. That is, it is the *practical* dimension of theological reflection upon doctrine which most needs strengthening. And if practical theology is conceived, not as a phase of theology which follows systematic theology (where the concentration on doctrine is most pronounced) and deals with the application of its results, but rather, as this article advocates, as a coordinate dimension of that single enquiry which is Christian theology, and indeed as a constituent part of systematic theology, it may become easier to take its distinctive question as to the functional aptness of doctrines seriously. This is not to say that theology can legitimately restrict its attention to doctrine, leaving the actual practice of witness aside; it is to suggest rather that theological reflection upon the practice of witness will be considerably enhanced if the practical dimension is already engaged at the doctrinal level.

In any case the encounter with doctrine plays a key role in theological education. It is largely through those paradigms or principles of Christian witness known as 'doctrines' that the student has access to the substance of the Christian tradition, that is, to the heritage of earlier judgements and proposals as to what constitutes valid witness, and is able to reflect upon it. But how exactly does that process of critical reflection comport with the enterprise of transmitting 'sound doctrine' which some regard as the principal business of theological education, and which few would regard as an insignificant or dispensable element in preparation for church leadership? One might, of course, view tradition and criticism as antithetical, just as one might so view criticism and 'formation'. On such a view, critical enquiry requires an emancipation from tradition: it means the freedom to make one's own judgements, rather than to accept what has been handed down. Education as 'tradition' is then as incompatible with the spirit and intentions of critical enquiry as education is as 'formation'.

As in the previous case, however, this opposition may be seen to be false. Certainly it is possible to describe, and even to attempt, the traditioning process in such a way as to rule out the possibility of critical engagement with what is received. It then becomes a matter of memorisation and drill, ultimately of 'habit', in the popular sense. But clearly such an approach, though intended to preserve the tradition from critical erosion, is finally destructive of it. It does not preserve a living tradition, because those who are its recipients have renounced the very activities which can keep a tradition alive, namely, those exercises of judgement and imagination by which it can be cleansed and renewed and fitted to new circumstances. Traditions like persons stand in need of repentance; and theological enquiry, when it is a genuine, serious effort, can and should be an instrument of self-criticism for the tradition as well as for the individual. As church theology, it is the church's own self-examination with respect to the adequacy of its attempts to bear the Christian witness. In this enquiry church doctrines, those principles by which the church intends its ordinary activities to be guided, are themselves interrogated as to their adequacy as guides.

It is through such an interrogation of doctrine, as distinguished from a passive reception of it, that persons come to that mastery of the doctrinal heritage on which the continuity of a living tradition depends. For example, only by understanding how the doctrine of the Trinity represents normative Christian witness concerning the reality of God (assuming that it does) will one be enabled to respond intelligently to proposals for its revision, reconception or replacement. Only by being able to distinguish what is essential to that doctrine from what belongs merely to the circumstances of its formulation is one in a position to adapt it to new circumstances. Only by seeing what makes it still a fitting principle for the conduct of Christian witness in one's own situation will one be able to make apt use of it. Or (to abandon those assumptions for the moment and to entertain their rivals), only if one is able to distinguish normative Christian witness concerning God from the doctrine of the Trinity will one be free to consider alternatives which may have a greater claim to validity in any or every respect. In any case it is through critical reflection on the doctrinal heritage that we are able to make it our own and to make ourselves its responsible bearers. An understanding of theological education as an education in critical enquiry is therefore not a rival to an understanding of it as the appropriation of tradition. It is clearly in tension with some more or less self-destructive versions of the latter understanding; but it is just as clearly the key to a more genuine, if more radical, realisation of its aims.

Theological education as professional education for ministry

As for the third alternative mentioned above, the view of theological education as essentially professional education for the tasks of ministry, its relationship to the understanding proposed here is formally different from the previous two relationships considered. In each of those cases, we found that each of the understandings being compared implied the other: an education in theological enquiry is, in some sense, 'formation', and 'formation' involves learning to be critical; an education in theological enquiry implies the appropriation of tradition, and any adequate appropriation of tradition involves the use of theological judgement. In this third instance, however, the relationship is not one of mutual implication. Its character might be briefly stated thus: 'theological education' is not necessarily professional education for ministry, but the heart of proper professional education for ministry *is* theological education, meaning by 'theological education' an education in theological enquiry. One may properly seek and obtain a theological education without any intention of preparing for church leadership of any sort; but one may not properly prepare for church leadership without acquiring theological competence.

The first half of this proposition might be readily granted by anyone who has not simply identified theological education with professional training for ministry, regarding the former term as merely a quaint holdover from the days when such training did somehow centrally involve something called 'theology'. That is, if there still is a coherent enquiry by that name, if it is not just a collective term for the group of studies, whatever they may be, which go to make up ministerial education, then presumably it makes sense to call training in that enquiry 'theological education', even though that might not be the ordinary usage of the term. It is the second half of the proposition which requires more explication and defence, at least in the typical American Protestant seminary setting where 'theology' appears to occupy a relatively small segment of the curriculum, and to be one of its more problematic components when one thinks in terms of its relationship to the whole. How can education in theological enquiry be the key to training for church leadership?

Theological education is the cultivation of theological judgement. It is the acquisition of the *habitus* for those activities named 'vision' and 'discernment': activities such as the imaginative grasp of the Christian witness in its unity, the assessment of one's own distinctive situation as a context for witness, and the testing of actual or potential efforts to convey the gospel. The dynamic and developing character of these activities was stressed in that account. Vision and discernment are not merely routine performances. They require intelligence, sensitivity, imagination and a readiness to deal with the unforeseen.

It is precisely this *habitus* which is the primary and indispensable qualification for church leadership, if 'church leadership' itself means anything more than the routine performance of established functions. Recall Edward Farley's observation on this score: 'The more the external tasks themselves are focused on as the one and only *telos* of theological education, the less the minister becomes qualified to carry them out.'[14] This is because the tasks of ministry require a judgement which transcends technical mastery. Schleiermacher recognised this clearly when he made the 'technical' aspect of theological study dependent upon those disciplines which, in his view, are more pertinent to the development of such judgement, that is, his philosophical and historical theology, in which one learns to grasp and to compare the essential character and the actual present reality of Christianity as a basis for deliberation upon what is to be done.

But how is such judgement to be formed in the context of the present typical curriculum, and how is its formation related to the more strictly professional aspects of education for ministry? It would help to begin by expanding our view of the place of 'theology' in the theological curriculum. This does not mean increasing the number of courses required in systematic theology or enhancing their prestige somehow. It means understanding the entire curriculum as really and truly a theological curriculum, that is, as a body of resources ordered to the cultivation in students of an aptitude for theological enquiry. This has implications for the way individual areas and courses are organised and taught: although not every course need be explicitly theological in character, the relationship to theological enquiry of what is learned in each course should be made clear. A course in logic, or Mexican-American history, or the sociology of religion, may have an important role to play in a theological curriculum, or in a particular student's programme of studies, if it furnishes concepts, skills or data which bear upon the cultivation of theological judgement in a manner appropriate to the situation and aims of the school or of the student. Courses in biblical languages, in church history, and in other traditional curricular areas may be similarly 'non-theological' in themselves, and yet serve a theological purpose. It should not be imagined, however, that no part of the curriculum outside the realm of systematic theology need be explicitly theological. Each dimension of theological enquiry demands abilities which can best be developed through concentrated attention to its distinctive problems and methods, and it is highly unfortunate if theology is left to the so-called theologians, that is, the systematicians, their colleagues having renounced any theological responsibility. Even under the best of conditions students must largely fashion their own theological education out of the available material, supplying their own connections and filling the gaps their instructors inevitably leave. But there are curricular arrangements which positively discourage such personal integration. There is a place for repentance in the life of the theological school; and this is one, but by no means the only, point at which some sustained self-examination is surely in order.

One final point needs to be made in connection with the relationship of theological education to professional education for ministry. The conventional equation of practical theology with pastoral theology does a disservice to both. It identifies Christian practice with pastoral practice, and it makes pastoral theology a one-dimensional enterprise in which the treatment of pastoral practice readily turns into a discussion of technique. There is a place for professional training for pastoral ministry, or for other forms of church leadership, within the theological curriculum. But that place is not exclusively within practical theology, nor is it in a sort of non-theological appendix to the curriculum. The specifically professional elements of education for ministry are not simply matters of technique to be tacked on where convenient. They are rather best seen as *specifications* of the broader theological enquiry. That is, here (in relation, for instance, to one's understanding of the pastoral office as a whole, or to the task of preaching, or of administration) the enquiry into what constitutes valid Christian witness is made specific: what makes (or could make) this office, this sermon, this act, an embodiment of genuine witness? Seeking answers to such questions is an engagement in systematic theological reflection, not in its practical dimension alone. It requires a consideration of the pertinent skills and techniques. Indeed when the questions are asked, as would normally be the case, in the context of one's own quest for professional identity and ability, the enquiry calls for some degree of mastery of those skills and techniques. But it also transcends the technical, calling for an exercise of theological judgement. How the study of pastoral theology, thus understood (or its counterparts for other forms of church leadership) might best be addressed in a curricular design can only be determined in conjunction with a consideration of a host of other practical issues, whose character is likely to vary considerably from one situation to another.

Notes

1. John Calvin, *Institutes of the Christian Religion*, I, VI, 2 (translated by Ford Lewis Battles in *Library of Christian Classics*, volume 20), Philadelphia, Westminster Press, 1960, volume 1, p. 72. On the relation of understanding, practice, and commitment, see Charles M Wood, 'The knowledge born of obedience', *Anglican Theological Review*, 61, 1979, pp. 331–340.
2. According to the seventeenth-century Lutheran dogmatician Abraham Calov, for example, 'it is incumbent upon us to accept the Word of God even if our mind cannot comprehend it at all, even if in our minds we are persuaded that it is false'. See Robert D Preus, *The Theology of Post-Reformation Lutheranism: a study of theological prolegomena*, St Louis, Concordia Publishing House, 1970, pp. 320–21, where this quotation from Calov appears.
3. *Proslogium*, chapter 1, in *St Anselm: Proslogium; Monologium; An Appendix in Behalf of the Fool by Gaunilon; and Cur Deus Homo* (translated by Sidney Norton Deane), La Salle, Illinois, Open Court Publishing Company, 1958, p. 7.
4. Ludwig Wittgenstein, *Culture and Value* (edited by G H von Wright and translated by Peter Winch), Chicago, University of Chicago Press, 1980, p. 1.
5. For further development of this point, see Charles M Wood, *The Formation of Christian Understanding: an essay in theological hermeneutics*, Philadelphia, Westminster Press, 1981, chapter 2.
6. This is not to say, however, that one must become a Christian in order to understand Christian witness. It is not inconceivable that one could come to learn the sense of Christian witness, and yet refrain from commitment to it. The burden of argument is upon anyone who would dispute a non-Christian's understanding of Christianity simply on the grounds that he or she is not a Christian.
7. John Passmore, *The Philosophy of Teaching*, Cambridge, Massachusetts, Harvard University Press, 1980, p. 168.
8. *Ibid.*, pp. 40–45.
9. Iris Murdoch, *The Sovereignty of Good*, New York, Schocken Books, 1971, p. 91.
10. *Ibid.*, p. 59.
11. See, for example, Jürgen Habermas, *The Theory of Communicative Action*, volume 1: *Reason and the Rationalization of Society* (translated by Thomas McCarthy), Boston, Beacon Press, 1984; Karl-Otto Apel, *Toward a Transformation of Philosophy* (translated by Glyn Adey and David Frisby), London, Routledge and Kegan Paul, 1980.
12. See, for example, the introduction to Carl Braaten and Robert W Jenson (eds), *Christian*

Dogmatics, volume 1, Philadelphia, Fortress Press, 1984, pp. xviii–xix.

13. For a highly original and important treatment of doctrines as rules, see George A Lindbeck, *The Nature of Doctrine: religion and theology in a postliberal age*, Philadelphia, Fortress Press, 1984.

14. Edward Farley, *Theologia: the fragmentation and unity of theological education*, Philadelphia, Fortress Press, 1983, p. 128.

9.3 Emerging issues and theological education

Rebecca S Chopp

Introduction

Much of the material written on the present and future situation of theological education addresses the question of the self-identity of theological education given the present structure of theological disciplines.[1] I want to ask a different question for theological faculties to wrestle with in the future, the question of what theological education contributes through its dual loci in institutions of religion and knowledge. My question is a decidedly pragmatic way of asking about the aims and purpose of theological education.[2]

To answer this question I want to analyse the context of theological education in relation to the modern structures of religion (church) and knowledge (university). The fundamental argument of this paper is twofold: first, that theological education has been caught in the ambiguous gap between the modern ordering of knowledge and religion, and second, that theological education needs, in the future, to attend to the production of heterogeneous discourses, and the corresponding development of images and resources for substantive community that is nurturing of human flourishing. In sum, I want to suggest that all of the work that we do, work defined best as the production of discourses – talking, writing, lecturing, preaching – needs to break away from its troubled loyalty to modern rules of knowledge and religion and concentrate its energies on the needs, in our situation, of learning to aid human flourishing through the production of discourses of multiplicity and multiple discourses.

My argument develops in three parts. First, I analyse the modern ordering of knowledge and religion, an ordering which also occurs in the division between what it is to be a man and what it is to be a woman, and the division between the public and the private. I suggest how theological education has had to live in the gap between knowledge and religion, contained through social myths about how knowledge and religion, public and private, men and women are ordered together to form the whole and through which comes the progressive realisation of the whole. The first section also suggests the kind of resistance theology has played in this ordering, and the breakdown of the ordering with the secular loss of belief in the social myths of progress and the whole.

The second section turns to the possibilities in the present situation for theology continuing and expanding its resistance to the ordering of knowledge in modernity. Theology must retrieve the works of modern theologians who found ways to press the ambiguities in the ordering, but it must do so, first, by examining modern theology's loyalty to the dominant order. The loyalty is most keenly felt in forms of assumptions that though marginal persons, women and persons of colour, may be let into the position of 'knower', they do not bring anything that could be called 'knowledge' from their marginal positions. In contrast, I argue that the presence of marginalised persons in the midst of theological education provides the possibility for expanding forms of discourse. Yet, we can do this in theological education only by attending to what constitutes community, for discourse and the forms of discourse are always dependent on forms of community. The greatest emerging issues for theological faculties, then, are the dual needs of new forms of discourses and new forms of community which encourage multiple and diverse ways of human flourishing.

Finally, the third section discusses the transformation of theological understanding implied in my contextualisation of theological education. Building upon Charles Wood's notion of theology as critical reflection into the validity of Christian witness, three areas must today be reconstructed: first, critical must come to include the political struggles of the day; second, the prospective activity of theological enquiry, in our context, must be taken to be an anticipatory-utopian critique; and third, vision and discernment must be redefined to mean the art of forming new discourses and practices in relation to discernment as the ability to hear and to speak of difference and specificity. In relation to education, I argue for an intentional expansion of the role of rhetoric and poetics in education.

The form and deformation of modern knowledge and religion

Since Edward Farley entitled the introduction to his *Theologia*, 'The travail of theological study', a crisis in theological education has been readily assumed by most other authors writing on this topic.[3] This crisis, as authors point out in various ways, has a great deal to do with the nature and form of theological discourse, such that if we understood what theology was really about, the crisis would be resolvable. I want to look with a somewhat different lens on the crisis, a lens with a wide-angle, in order to suggest that the crisis in our understanding of theology has also to do with the very forms of religion and knowledge in modernity, that is, how religion and knowledge are defined, structured and assigned sets of values. In sum, I want to suggest that the fragmentation of theological education is related to the way religion (which, in modernity, is primarily represented as Christianity) and knowledge are constructed.

The modern construction of Christianity and knowledge is characterised by, on the one hand, the acceptance of a particular kind of individualism, where the individual is the contact point and origin of labour and value, and, on the other hand, the modern division of the public and private, where public interests are channelled through the market place and private interests, such as religion, art and tradition, are left as optional choices for the individual. In the public, the citizen of modernity is the labourer, the master of history, while in the private, the individual is the consumer of cultural values such as art, religion, tradition and family. Knowledge in the public realm becomes formed through a scientific, instrumentalist view while in the private realm, faith is transcendentalised or existentialised, as prior to or outside of the conditions of knowledge. Faith, whether it be in the theological formulations of Barth and Schleiermacher or the religious piety of believers in New York and Kansas, is assumed to be largely prelinguistic, or other than linguistic, prior to or outside of action and knowledge. It may be brought to consciousness and thematised, for instance one may talk about her or his personal relationship to Jesus, but the true and real knowledge of God lies prior to any such talk, and all such talk is at best an inadequate way of expressing faith.

What is interesting about this construction is that it inscribes Christianity into a modern knowledge while at the same time allowing Christianity to transgress, silently, without words that can be heard, the confines of knowledge by pointing to a 'something more' or 'something other' that is outside of, or underneath, or at the limits of knowledge. Yet though modern Christianity pointed to this 'something more', theological reflection was engraved within the rules of modern knowledge, and thus required to decentre and devalue pluralistic forms of rationality for the sake of focusing on what Paul Tillich would call theology as technical reason. Theological education had to make illegitimate certain forms of knowledge such as liturgical and mystical knowledge and prohibit certain groups not occupying the dominant anthropological position, such as blacks and women, from offering discourses of knowledge. The illegitimisation of certain forms of knowledge can be rendered in a straightforward fashion: forms such as liturgy and mysticism are outside the rules of modern knowledge. Any such religious practice may be understood as expressions of private faith experiences but they cannot be considered as forms of knowledge.

The latter criticism, that modern theological education also served to prohibit knowledge of certain groups of persons, requires a bit more analysis, for such an enquiry can lead us to uncover the relations between power, interest and knowledge. The subject position of many, usually filled by white, working men, represented the values of knowledge and the power of the realm. Indeed, 'man' was the constitutive knower and citizen, and knowledge and citizenship were 'manly' affairs. The very value-laden definition of knowledge as objective, rational and logical was the same definition of man, the citizen, indeed the values of 'man' himself. Furthermore, this relationship of man, knowledge and the public derived its identity from what it was not: woman, religious, the private. As the identity of knowledge depends upon it not being religious, man depended upon not being woman, and the public depended upon not being the private. What is important to see in this patriarchal codification of knowledge is the structural relation of subjectivity, politics and knowledge that formed a unity of man, knowledge and the public through a kind of dualistic dependency on women, religion and the private. In all of this, to use a phrase of Deborah Cameron's, 'men can be men, only if women are unambiguously women'.[4]

This patriarchal codification of knowledge created all sorts of problems for theology and Christianity. For if knowledge was located in the public realm, in the subject position of white men, Christianity was located in the private realm, in the subject position symbolised by women. Thus Christianity had to shape its essence in the rules of the private, the subject position of women and its knowledge in the terms of the rules of the public, the subject position of men. The problem for theological knowledge was that man/woman, knowledge/religion, the public/private was related through a kind of dependent dualism, in which the identity of the first term depended upon the other, but also upon not being the other. We could thus expand the Cameron quotation concerning men being men only if women are unambiguously women, by saying knowledge can be knowledge only if religion is unambiguously religion, and the public can be the public only if the private is unambiguously the private. Supposedly there was a separation, a gap, between men and women, knowledge and religion, the public and private but in reality the gap was a very ambiguous, tenuous relation, for men depended upon women for procreation, nurture, caretaking, and knowledge depended upon religion for motivation, aesthetics, care for the part of existence not rational and objective, and the public depended upon the private for sustenance of that which they said they were not. Theological knowledge often danced at the edges of this ambiguity, trying hard to maintain loyalties to the modern rules, but also pointing to a kind of knowledge which, if examined, pushed at the subject position of women and men, the private and the public.[5]

Friedrich Schleiermacher's *Christmas Eve: A Dialogue on the Incarnation* is one of the best representations of the modern figuration of religious experience and knowledge, perhaps because the text renders problematic the modern figurations of knowledge, religious experience, men and women.[6] In this text, women obey the modern ordering that places them closer than men to religion or, more accurately, there is less distance in women between religion and expression than there is in men. Women speak in terms of stories, or in what Schleiermacher would call the rhetorical mode, while men speak in terms of philosophical propositions, in Schleiermacher's sense, the descriptively didactic mode. If, for Schleiermacher, women have an advantage by being closer to the unity of experience and expression, men enjoy the public role of being in the subject position that is most able to reflect on religious experience and expression with detail and precision. But Schleiermacher seems to worry with this 'rule' that faith is to women as knowledge is to men, suggesting in the early part of the dialogues that divisions of women and men are not eternally fixed. Indeed, Schleiermacher renders problematic any rigorous division between men and women, knowledge and faith by figuring the unity of religious experience and expression in the shape of first a child, Sophie, and then a quite childlike man, Josef, both of whom express their religiosity by singing, Schleiermacher's poetic mode, rather than by speaking. As one commentator has recently put it, 'There is no question that the *Christmas Eve Dialogue* seems to favour simple, childlike experience over abstract theological reflection, or that, at least in this text, women appear more suited to the former, while men are inclined to the latter.'[7] Schleiermacher adheres to the modern formulation of religion and knowledge, of women and men, but he does so in the context of calling into question the eternal divisions of men and women, refiguring knowledge or the ability to do abstract reflection on a sliding scale rather than through separate spheres, and allowing a man to represent the return to the origin of all reflection, a position usually represented by women.[8] Schleiermacher does not explicitly criticise the modern formulation of men and knowledge, women and religion, but he renders it problematic and available for questioning.

Yet today Schleiermacher's problematic seems almost a commonplace crisis as we deal constantly with competing subjects and their discourses, and competing claims as to what constitutes knowledge. The rules as to what constitutes and who controls the dominant position in the court of reason are no longer as clear as when Schleiermacher tried to render them somewhat problematic. On the one hand, the narrow definition of knowledge is breaking apart due to factors including the philosophical critiques of knowledge, the technological transformation of knowledge, the renewed interest in the relation between knowledge and ethics in public policy, military and scientific research and in the public and private educational systems. On the other hand, the multiplicity of subjects, the diversity of language games, the pluralism of discourses means increasingly that the subjects of knowledge are not one, but plural.[9]

Besides the explosion of knowledge and the awareness of multiple discourses of knowledge, there is another main difference between our day and Schleiermacher's: the loss of belief in major myths of modernity.[10] The myths were the fundamental myths of meaning, the narrative orderings that supported the definitions and practices of modernity. For our analysis we can consider two: one, the myths of the whole, that all the parts fit together, and second, the myth of progress, that the spirit or the true meaning will be realised in history. The narrative of the whole allows for the ordering of parts and hierarchies, while the myth of the origin allows for correct meanings and proper explanations. Schleiermacher could rest with his problematic because of these two myths which made him believe that the difference between men and women, knowledge and religion served the interests of the state which is related to the realisation of freedom and progress in history.[11] These myths, that all fits together into an ordered whole, and that there is or will be a correct realisation of meaning in history, no longer function to guide the politics of the state, to provide meaning for men and women, public and private, to secure the West's status as big brother of the world.

But the problem must be sharpened even further, beyond the crisis of a secular loss of belief. For the problem of the relations among the myths, rules and roles in modernity is how they have constituted a universal rule of judgement that has functioned to oppress and repress other discourses and subjects. The recent work of Jean-Francois Lyotard brings this issue into sharpest focus and, I think, expresses the current crisis of politics, language and subjectivity. Lyotard analyses the problem of a universal rule of judgement which forces all other discourses to define themselves in its terms, terms which do not count as legitimate the concerns of other discourses. Lyotard has coined the term 'the differend' as the case where 'the plaintiff is divested of the means to argue and becomes for that reason a victim' and again, 'a case of differend between two parties takes place when the "regulation" of the conflict that opposes them is done in the idiom of one of the parties while the wrong suffered by the other is not signified in that idiom'.[12] The problem with modernity, with its belief in the great narratives, with its rules of knowledge, power and interests, with its roles of the public and private, men and women, with its definition of knowledge, is that it allowed only one idiom, the patriarchal codification of knowledge, for the adjudication of all claims, and thus ruled out of court the claims and voices of all others. Indeed the present crisis is deeply intertwined with the problems of how not to adjudicate through one discourse or idiom as the universal rule of judgement but how to explode the differences, how to hear other voices, how to learn to live with multiple discourses and multiple ways of being human. It is thus the question of a pluralism which cannot be adjudicated through twin myths of the whole and of progress, but a pluralism in which we must learn to live and flourish. This is the crisis facing us; it is the issue of our meaning, our flourishing, our survival. It has many different expressions: can we know through liturgy, can we hear the meaning of other religions, can we learn to do economic trading with the Japanese, the Brazilians, the Chinese without forcing them to agree to our story of wholeness and identity, can we find ways for men and women to live together where public and private are not sex-segregated, can we find ways for Afro-Americans, whites and Hispanics in public education and church education to learn history through the use of multiple interpretations of historical events, do we know of God as an ultimate giver of openness to pluralism or the closure and ordering of multiplicity?

I want to call this the need to learn to live and flourish with heterogeneous discourses. This is a very awkward and clumsy term. The very thought, that there is no universal rule of judgement, no one final discourse to settle all claims, is quite troubling to us all, even the most post-modern among us! We want to cling, despite all the eloquent pleas from the anti-foundationists, to a belief that we can all talk in the same voice, or at least find an unambiguous form of rationality to adjudicate all our diverse claims. So, perhaps it is best to keep with the awkwardness of the phrase 'the need for heterogeneous discourses' since the very awkwardness reminds us that our task is to find new ways of speaking and living with differences and multiplicities.

This does not mean that we are left forever in our tight little language games, for language itself has a certain openness, an ability to connect, to change, to transform. If we give up the ability of language to gain the true essence of a thing, we can gain the rhetorical function of language to work toward communication, agreement, transformation. To live with heterogeneous discourses, which is today the crisis for both politics and subjectivity, requires that we find ways for discourses to be open, for communities to nurture differences and solidarity, for each of us to learn that the 'other' has neither to be exactly like us or exactly the opposite of us.

New forms of discourse and new forms of community

When facing the crisis of heterogeneous discourses, theology has a role to play in both its locus as a form of 'marginal' knowledge in modernity and in its site as already containing a pluralism of knowledge. Let me consider each in turn.

Certainly theology, as discourses of knowledge in Christianity, holds a marginal status in the modern academy and in knowledge in general. Nowhere is this so self-evident as in theological education and the academy. Religion is the one area that the well-educated person doesn't have to know anything about, presumedly because there isn't anything really to 'know'. Indeed, in some of my favourite theorists, theology is presented as something akin to numerology, superstition and magical thinking. One of my favourite thinkers, an expert in semiotics, art history, Marxist theory, literary theory and psychoanalytic theory, seems to think that when she can label something as theological, she has proved it as false or not to be taken seriously. A basic reason for the marginality of theology is the definition of knowledge, and its relation to interests and power of dominant subject groups. Yet inside theology we have laboured intensely to point out the something more or the something other at the limits of modern knowledge. Take, for instance, Schubert Ogden's essay 'The reality of God', and Paul Tillich's section on reason and revelation in his *Systematic Theology,* volume I.[13] In very different ways, both texts point out that at the limits, or in the very possibility of modern discourses of knowledge, is a drive and a need for a larger view of knowledge.

One way to pursue our theological analysis of the need for heterogeneous discourses, is to form our analysis of discourses of knowledge: to pay attention to the plurality of discourses in Christianity, to pursue the something more of the theological critique of modern knowledge and modern culture, to be open to multiple discourses within Christian witness.

Much of the material in recent years on theological education hints, and sometimes is quite explicit, about the limits of modern knowledge. Farley's concern for *habitus,* Wood's development of vision and discernment, Hough and Cobb's notion of the reflective practitioner, all can be read as trying to push at the definitions of knowledge. We must unconnect theological explorations of multiple discourses from any metanarrative of the ordered whole or the realisation of an original meaning outside of any historical constitution. Finally, we must rethink the work in theological education thus far in light of an imaginative construal of practices such as liturgy, prayer and the arts. Can we find ways to live with the different ways of knowing in Christian witness not ordering around a centred whole or unpacking to one true meaning but around the possibilities for performative practice in community? We, in theology, are particularly well located for analysing and criticising closure of knowledge, the ordering of pluralism, the hierarchy of difference in discourse, and we have resources to begin exploring ways of living, speaking, enjoying, flourishing amongst heterogeneous discourses.

Yet if we have much to offer the world in terms of living community with heterogeneous discourses, we also have much to solve in terms of our own problems with prohibiting discourses of certain subjects. If the first set of problems, the acceptance of heterogeneous discourses, has to do with unconnecting our selves from the myths of modernity, the second has to do with resisting the power-knowledge-interests relations of modernity that have so inscribed modern theological education. The place I see this most painfully is the prohibition in theological education for those occupying the subject positions of the 'others' of modernity, persons such as women, blacks, Hispanics, Asians, to multiply the discourses and to expand the parameters of knowledge. It is an irony, isn't it? As much as theology has found ways to criticise the boundaries of knowledge in modernity, it has found ways to instigate the boundaries within its own practices. Theological education, by and large, has tried to address this problem by letting 'others' in, by giving them elective courses, by including occasional lectures or books or voices in foundational courses. But theological education has failed to see the problematic hinted at by

Schleiermacher: religion, knowledge, women, men cannot be ordered or contained within the discourse of modern knowledge. What women threaten, in theological education, is the very definition and legitimatisation of knowledge, and its complex relations to dominant ordering of politics and subjectivity. The presence of women and other marginalised groups provides a position from which to resist the dominant relations amongst power, knowledge and material interests in modernity. Such de-centred positions also provide spaces in which to discover and create new ways, forms and idioms of knowledge.

What is before us is no easy task, for to learn to live with openness and heterogeneous discourses, with specificity and difference without the assumption that we are all the same underneath or there is a whole we can all fit into requires more than just finding new ways of speaking of difference and specificity. For discourses, as I have already pointed out, are dependent upon and bound to community, and the question of finding new discourses of human flourishing is closely related to finding new forms of community. The quest to discover and create new forms of community, ones which live on and nourish the heterogeneity of discourses, may be the greatest political struggle of all. Models of community based on the myths of true meaning, where if we all talk long enough we will agree with the ones in power, or on the myths of the whole where difference is hierarchically ordered, models of community based on rules and roles where certain subject positions legitimise certain powers, will simply no longer serve the needs of the world.

The quest for new forms of community in relation to the flourishing of heterogeneous discourses, is a moral, a cognitive and a personal problem. It is a moral problem, for in the present world economy we must learn to live in community in which our culture is no longer the big brother or even the major actor. It is a cognitive problem because our modern theories of knowledge are based on models of community which do not easily yield to diversity and difference on a local, let alone a worldwide scale. It is a personal problem, for subjectivity in our culture is closely tied to belonging to a homogeneous community, and to excluding others in order to secure our identity. These problems are our emerging issues in world, church and theological education: the problems of how we can discover and create new forms of human flourishing. Indeed, one of the most urgent emerging issues is to form theological education in relation to the church in the world. The last powerful expression of this is found in H Richard Niebuhr's *The Purpose of the Church and Its Ministry*.[14]

The value of Niebuhr's *The Purpose of the Church and Its Ministry* is not in terms of his own material reading or images, but in showing us how necessary the process of giving a theological account of church and world is for any discussion of theological education. When Niebuhr goes about suggesting what theological education should be, he enters a process of describing the church and its ministry in the present situation. Out of this described context, Niebuhr proposes the definition of the church as the subjective pole of the objective rule of God and develops his notion that the purpose of the church is to increase the love of God and neighbour. The theological account begins in a description of the situation, moves to a signifying or valuing of terms, and goes on to offer a substantive purpose for the church in the world, then allows Niebuhr to develop his discussion of the aims of theological education around a certain web of meaning, a set of values, a substantive interpretation of what the church and theological education ought to be about.

The greatest temptation we face in theological education is to ignore what Niebuhr's book teaches us: the necessity of a theological analysis of our situation, and of a theological construct of what the church ought to be. To follow Niebuhr's process, it seems to me, is to make theology in our situation provide networks of meaning for the possibility of community.

Let me identify how one such construct of the church in the world might be developed. Beginning at Niebuhr's point of giving an interpretation of the church in the world, we might say: the church is the visible sign of God's invisible grace. Two terms need special elaboration: as sign the church has a basic signifying function, establishing discourses and practices to make possible the realisation of grace; and grace, for which we can use Johann Baptist Metz's term, is the way of living differently, understanding from the material analysis developed thus far that living differently means developing forms of community which nurture heterogeneous discourses.[15] The church's role is to constitute the community of the faithful and to model such community in and for the world. Theological education thus serves the church and world by preparing persons to live in and signify to the world the possibility of such community.

Theological warrants from doctrines such as creation, offering a new interpretation of the relation amongst chaos, creativity and difference, and ecclesiology, would support this construct. The values, or terms of signification, would be those of openness, difference and transformation, symbolised not only in creation and ecclesiology but also in the cross and resurrection as well as what Jürgen Moltmann calls the history of the Trinity.[16]

The future of theology and education

What I have argued for, thus far, is a certain contextualisation of theological discourse, that is, an understanding of its form and function in the broad social reality of which it is a part. My argument has some suggestions for how theology and education might be construed in the present context, given again that we concede to my pragmatic question of what theological education can do in the present situation. Let me spell out how I understand the implications of my argument, first in terms of the shape of theology and second, in terms of the shape of education. My argument finds its most comfortable locus in the notion of theology as critical reflection into the validity of Christian witness as elaborated in Charles Wood's *Vision and Discernment*.[17] As I understand Wood's argument, theology is the process of critical enquiry, by which he means reflective awareness and judgement, into the validity of Christian witness, that is, how any particular witness is valid as Christian witness. Like Wood, I want to contend that the issue at stake is how in a historical period, a present reality or an idea for the future is figured, formed and judged as Christian witness. Theology includes, as Wood points out, both a subjective side, a *habitus*, and an objective side, the articulation of faith, but is itself an activity, a process of reflection and judgement on the nature of Christian witness. Given Wood's definition, I want to elaborate three basic points concerning theology in light of my argument.

First, I will explain what 'critical' entails in light of my argument thus far. As Wood notes, the term means many things: a way of being, a style of reflection, particular techniques. But it does so within the present situation: that is, what counts as the best skills and abilities, the most fitting disposition is determined within a particular situation. Critical carries the dual sense of understanding the conditions for the possibility of such particularities but also the criticism of the limits of such particularities. This second sense of critical, what Marx defined in terms of the self-clarification of the struggles and wishes of the age, needs to play a prominent role in our deliberations.[18] If you will allow me to blend in this notion of Marx's into Wood's definition, I can underscore the political reality of what we understand to be critical enquiry. Our very standards of what counts and doesn't count must be related to the needs and interests of the day. If, as I have contended, the struggles and wishes of our situation have to do with issues of pluralism of heterogeneous discourses and the need for new forms of community, then to be critical, such wishes and struggles must provide the context for emerging issues in theological education. Theology, in the future, will not only consider its own past and present, but the past, present and future of the church and world in which it lives and to which it tries to speak.

Second, Wood states that theology is concerned with prospective activity, with the future, in Wood's own words:[19]

> Theology has continually influenced the Christian tradition as the positive proposals issuing from theological reflection have been incorporated into every part of the church's life: creed, liturgy, law, pastoral practice, social action, institutional reform and the rest. As critical reflection upon the church's activity, theology is as much concerned with its prospective activity as with its history.

Given a situation in which norms are stable and secure, critical enquiry into the future would be largely a building or corrective enterprise, overseeing that all things develop as planned. In a situation in which there is a crisis of norms and values, prospective activity takes on what Seyla Benhabib has called an anticipatory-utopian critique.[20] Theology, in the future, may be an activity that teaches us to envision the future differently, to dream and have visions, as much as to understand the past and maintain the present.

If it is true that theology, at least in the near future, will need to emphasise its prospective orientation, we must alter Wood's definitions of both vision and discernment. Wood argues that theology contains both vision and discernment, the viewing of the whole and the parts. Such a visualisation is, unfortunately, too easily linked with the myth of the whole, too easily tempted to forestall prospective activity for the activity of maintaining the status quo. There is another way to interpret vision and discernment, one which I find far more compelling for emerging issues in theological education. Vision can also mean to see anew, to imagine, the anticipatory-utopian ability to make abductive judgements, while discernment can mean to see the differences, to distinguish, to appreciate specificity. I suggest we shift the notion of vision to that of the ability to make abductive judgements, to find new idioms to express the difference, to say what may be the case, while discernment is the ability to hear the particular, the specific, to understand within the specific terms of particular discourses. Theology includes both vision and discernment, the art of forming new discourses and practices in relation to discernment as the ability to hear and speak of difference and specificity.

If theology, in my argument, is nudged toward the critical formation of new discourses to address the needs and wishes of the age, the shape of education also undergoes certain changes. Let me suggest two issues for education in relation to my argument. First of all education must include rhetorical readings of past and present forms of Christianity, seeking to understand the relation of discursive practices to the material conditions in which they functioned. This includes what a historian of religion has recently called teaching Christianity as a religion, trying to understand how particular Christian beliefs, rituals, institutions, practices are formed in and related to specific cultural conditions.[21] To teach Christianity rhetorically means such things as to focus on how the bible has functioned as a cultural document, how gender relations have, in different contexts and in specific ways, influenced values, how black church traditions cannot be understood as merely alternative to the great tradition.

Second, my argument implies a distinct turn to not only rhetoric in education but to poetics in education. My argument requires a reinvigoration of the imagination in theological education, and especially the encouragement of aesthetical forms and images that can fund our work and culture.[22] It is not the case that imagination and aesthetics have been completely absent in theological education, though they have been privatised or sentimentalised in many of the practices of theological education. Today when we face the crises of values, knowledge and power, what is required, at least in part, is a new aesthetic funding, a way of knowing that will be productive of new forms of human flourishing. This will include images and discourses of community, new visions of what it is to be human, new terms for relationships, history, freedom, God, new notions of desire and knowledge. Education, for the future, must emphasise the ability to envision, to produce the aesthetic images and metaphors that fund knowledge, values, community.

In conclusion, I have been arguing that emerging issues for theological faculties should be formulated through a certain theology of culture. If this be so, then Paul Tillich might well be called on for his testimony to the continual need for such a theology of culture. In an essay on church education, Tillich maintained that education always contains three aims: the technical, the inducting, the humanistic. The technical provides tools and techniques, the inducting brings persons into the guild, the humanistic develops human potentialities. Throughout its history, Tillich believed, Christian tradition struggled with how these aims were realised and related in particular situations. Tillich's own view led him to believe that in his situation, the nature and relation of the inducting and humanistic aims were in great conflict, as Christian education wrestled with the modern world view and traditional symbols and myths. While we have not yet settled the questions that troubled Tillich's day, our situation presses another set upon us, a set that calls the form of each aim into question as well as the relations between these aims. And yet Tillich's final words in his essay, 'A theology of education', still hold promise for our deliberations on emerging issues for theological faculties.[23]

> The problem of the church school is more than the problem of a particular educational aim. It is the problem of the relation of Christianity and culture generally and Christianity and education especially. The problem is infinite and must be solved again in every generation. Within this frame, the church school is like a small laboratory in which the large questions of church and world can be studied and brought to a preliminary solution, a solution which could become an inestimable contribution to the solution of the larger problem.

To enlarge our sphere of enquiry, to give a theological account, to make theology and education critical and creative in terms of the future, is not only to solve our problems in a preliminary way, but to speak and thus contribute to the larger problems of church and world.

Notes

1. By self-identity I mean the attempt to define and solve the problems of theological education within the context of its own terms without looking at theological education within the broader constructs of knowledge and religion, or the broader structures of the public and the private.
2. For different illustrations of what I mean by pragmatic question, see David Kelsey, *The*

Uses of Scripture in Recent Theology, Philadelphia, Fortress Press, 1975; Francis Schüssler Fiorenza, *Foundational Theology: Jesus and the church*, New York, Crossroad, 1984; and Rebecca S Chopp, *The Power to Speak: feminism, language, God*, New York, Crossroad, 1989.

3. Edward Farley, *Theologia: the fragmentation and unity of theological education*, Philadelphia, Fortress Press, 1983. See also, Joseph C Hough and John B Cobb, *Christian Identity and Theological Education*, Chico, Scholars Press, 1985; Max L Stackhouse, *Apologia: contextualization, globalization, and mission in theological education*, Grand Rapids, Eerdmans, 1988.

4. Deborah Cameron, *Feminism and Linguistic Theory*, London, Macmillan, 1985, pp. 155–156.

5. For an interesting reading about the attempt to cover up ambiguity in modernity see Donald N Levine, *The Flight From Ambiguity: essays in social and cultural theory*, Chicago, University of Chicago Press, 1985.

6. Friedrich Schleiermacher, *Christmas Eve: a dialogue on the incarnation* (translated by Terrence N Tice), Richmond, John Knox, 1967.

7. Dawn De Vries, 'Schleiermacher's *Christmas Eve* dialogue: bourgeois ideology or feminist theology?', *The Journal of Religion*, 69, 1989, pp. 169–183; here p. 179.

8. This has been talked about in terms of the divided loyalties of modern theology. See Van A Harvey's excellent rendition of the contradictory position of the modern theologian in his *The Historian and the Believer: the morality of historical knowledge and Christian belief*, Philadelphia, Westminster Press, 1966.

9. There are many descriptions of our present 'postmodern' condition. The analysis in this essay is most indebted to: Jean-Francois Lyotard, *The Postmodern Condition: a report on knowledge* (translated by Geoff Bennington and Brian Massumi with a foreword by Frederic Jameson), Minneapolis, University of Minnesota Press, 1984; Walter Ong, *Interface of the Word: studies in the evolution of consciousness and culture*, Ithaca, Cornell University Press, 1977; Wayne Booth, *Critical Understanding: the powers and limits of plurality*, Chicago, University of Chicago Press, 1979; David Tracy, *Plurality and Ambiguity: hermeneutics, religion, hope*, San Francisco, Harper and Row, 1987.

10. Jean-Francois Lyotard, *The Postmodern Condition*, op. cit.

11. *Ibid.*, pp. 32–33.

12. Jean Francois Lyotard, *The Differend: phrases in dispute* (translated by Georges Van Den Abbeele), Minneapolis, University of Minnesota Press, 1988, p. 9.

13. Schubert M Ogden, *The Reality of God and Other Essays*, New York, Harper and Row, 1963, pp. 25–37 and Paul Tillich, *Systematic Theology*, volume 1, Chicago, University of Chicago Press, 1951, pp. 71–159.

14. H Richard Niebuhr, *The Purpose of the Church and its Ministry: reflections on the aims of theological education* (in collaboration with Daniel Day Williams and James M Gustafson), New York, Harper and Row, 1956.

15. Johann Baptist Metz, *The Emergent Church: the future of Christianity in a postbourgeois world* (translated by Peter Mann), New York, Crossroad, 1981, pp. 60–62.

16. Jürgen Moltmann, *The Trinity and the Kingdom of God* (translated by Margaret Kohl), New York, Harper and Row, 1981, and Rebecca S Chopp, *The Power to Speak: feminism, language, God*, New York, Crossroad, 1989.

17. Charles M Wood, *Vision and Discernment: an orientation in theological study*, Atlanta, Scholars Press, 1985.

18. Karl Marx, 'Letter to A Ruge, September 1843', in *Karl Marx: early writings* (translated by Rodney Livingstone and Gregor Benton), New York, Vintage Books, 1975, p. 209.

19. Charles M Wood, *Vision and Discernment, op. cit.*, p. 23.

20. Seyla Benhabib, 'The generalized and the concrete other: the Kohlberg-Gilligan controversy and feminist theory', in Seyla Benhabib and Drucila Cornell (eds), *Feminism as Critique*, Minneapolis, University of Minnesota Press, 1987, p. 80.

21. This suggestion comes from Frank Reynolds in his presentation 'Religious imagination and the cultivation of Christian worlds or the minister as Christian bricoleur' at a conference on Joseph Hough and John Cobb's *Christian Identity and Theological Education* held at The University of Chicago Divinity School, October 8–11, 1987. I am also indebted to Vincent Wimbush and Mark Kline Taylor for similar suggestions.

22. For an extended argument concerning the need for poetics or aesthetics to fund the language of politics, see Fred Dallmayr, *Language and Politics: why does language matter to political philosophy?*, Notre Dame, University of Notre Dame Press, 1984. In terms of the role of aesthetics and education see John Dewey, *Art and Experience*, New York, Capricorn Books, 1934, and 'Experience, nature and art', in John Dewey, Albert C

Barnes, L Buermeyer, M Mullen and V de Mazia, *Art and Education*, Merion, Pennsylvania, The Barnes Foundation Press, 1967, pp. 22–31. For aesthetics as a way of knowing see Hans-Georg Gadamer, *Truth and Method*, New York, Seabury, 1975.

23. Paul Tillich, 'A theology of education', in Robert C Kimball (ed.), *Theology of Culture*, London, Oxford University Press, 1959, pp. 156–157.

9.4 Can virtue be taught? Education, character and the soul

David Tracy

The origins of western education

However difficult the questions of character and theological education in our period, it may still be helpful at times to distance ourselves from them by returning to the origins of both education and character for western culture itself. This may seem a luxury if not a distraction from the perplexities of the present. And yet, it is not. In fact, our present difficulties have been well illuminated by several works of recent years: especially by Edward Farley's study of the material unity of *theologia* as an intellectual and moral habit (as virtue); by the several proposals for practical theology as the most demanding and most needed form of theology for our moment; by the illuminating studies of the role of narratives for community and personal identity in the works of Hans Frei, Alisdair MacIntyre, George Lindbeck and others; and by the clear and promising programmatic study of *Christian Identity and Theological Education* by Joseph C Hough Jr and John B Cobb Jr.[1] The last-named work, in my judgement, nicely summarises the three most needed elements for a solution: first, the need to rethink theological education in relationship to sustained reflection on the 'whole Christian story' of God's acting in the world creatively and redemptively; second, the need to rethink that story in 'the global context' thus demanding, implicitly, a 'critical correlation' model for the mode of enquiry that is theology; third, the need to propose new models of 'practical theology' and the minister as 'practical theologian' in order to reformulate not only the theological curriculum but the nature of theological education itself.

In a context where works of such high calibre and promise already exist, it makes good sense to focus on the further question of education and character. The more I reflected on this question, the more it seemed to me fruitful to return to reflection on the origins of western education itself: the Athens of Socrates, the great tragedians, and Plato. For here one may find not only the origins of the problems of education and character formation in our culture but also a cultural and political situation uncannily like our own. The intellectual situation of Socrates was parlous: the great threat of the sophists, for Socrates-Plato, was as much moral and religious as it was intellectual. For the sophists (especially Protagoras) claimed that virtue could be taught, but taught not as a *praxis* but as a *techne*, a technique of success in any particular community the sophist happened upon. Even the great moral exemplars of Greek culture (Homer, Hesiod and the great tragedians, in sum, 'the poets') could not function in such a corrupt situation, as transformative of character towards virtue and the good. Moreover, as such analysts as Thucydides (and, by implication, Plato himself) make clear, the earlier heroic age was in shambles as a result of the degradation of political life in an Athens turned into an imperialist power. The political disaster of Sicily, as much as the moral disaster of the treatment of Melos, and the intellectual disaster of Plato's own failed educational experiments in Sicily, united to expose a situation where education must be rethought *if* both character and virtue and intellectual enquiry were to transform the community and not merely technically inform or merely entertain it. Contemporary social scientific analyses of ancient Athens, moreover, have correctly increased our sense of the full extent of the moral and intellectual dilemmas faced by those first educators of virtue: the economic reality of a slave-population; the systemic distortion of the role (more accurately, non-role) of women in that society; the understanding of the 'others' as 'barbaric'.

As liberation, political and feminist theologies have persuasively argued, a Christian theologian should already be alert to these latter distortions in all their systemic and, yes, sinful actuality. As all classical theology (as *theologia*) can also note, the cultural, intellectual, moral and religious systemic distortions of sophistic beliefs and political imperialism render a new model of education for character (a *paideia* in Werner Jaeger's sense) crucial. It is exactly this need, I believe, which gave birth to the western notions of liberal education, both the oral practice of Socrates and the written dialogues of Plato, as well as his founding of the first 'academy'.

I have argued elsewhere that our own 'post-modern age' is best characterised as one of increasing plurality and a heightened sense of the radical ambiguity of all our traditions. All the 'grand narratives', including the Christian narrative, are far more plural, even heterogeneous, than we realised. I have also argued against dropping a concern with 'character' altogether and contenting ourselves with Bakhtin-like or Derrida-like notions of our history as a multi-voiced text. And yet I admit to a certain hesitation here. On the one hand, the notion of character can function to introduce the notion of 'personal identity' too soon by assuming, too easily, that our communal narratives are more like the 'grand narratives' of the great nineteenth century realists and less like the modernist 'epiphanic' narratives of Woolf, Proust and Joyce, or even the anti-coherence heterogeneous post-modern experiments in anti-narrative of Borges, Nabokov or Marquez. The word 'character' and its communal and narrative demands is, I believe, at once eminently retrievable in its classic senses from Aristotle through Jane Austen. At the very same time, 'character', if not also subjected to suspicion, can too easily align itself with precisely the problem most of us now admit to be *the* problem of our culture: that distinctive form of 'individualism' so well portrayed by Bellah *et al.*[2] and so well characterised as the central temptation of the European and North American churches and seminaries by Cobb and Hough.

For those reasons I have, in these reflections, returned to another largely forgotten word to try to understand our dilemma better: the word 'soul' (or *psuchē*). It is this word which is at the heart of the enterprise of enquiry, dialogue and education for Socrates and Plato. It is this reality of soul, transformed by Paul into a new Christian anthropology and transformed in myriad new ways by Christian educators from Clement and Origen and Augustine through Bernard, Thomas Aquinas, Eckhart, Teresa of Avila and John of the Cross which seems to me more promising for reflection on education and character. The historical-theological category of 'soul', to be sure, needs its own suspicions (especially on soul-body relationships). But thanks to such post-modern thinkers as Julia Kristeva and others (especially feminists), the category 'soul' has a better chance, I believe, of freeing us from the individualism which plagues us. Thereby, reflection on education and the soul may also free us for the notion of 'a subject-in-process' which theological education as both identifiably Christian and genuinely open to our present global context may well need. Why that may be so is a longer story than the one I attempt here. For the moment, it seems imperative to return to this western journey of education as a training of the soul in Socrates and Plato. For there, I have come to believe, is where education as we know it at its best was first conceived and there is where the unbreakable link between education, properly conceived, and character (reconceived as a training of the soul) was first forged.

Education and the soul in Socrates-Plato

Dialectic, dialogue and myth

The first candidate for education in Plato is dialectic. But what is that? Indeed, I agree with David Smigelskis that rather than trying to define a specific set of characteristics that we can then name 'dialectic' in Plato, it is better to begin with a very general definition, viz. dialectics is any mode of reflective enquiry on a fundamental issue. Dialectics, on this reading, is not another 'speciality'; it is, rather, a mode of enquiry that functions in every specialised form of enquiry.

This general description can be further specified in several ways. First, any mode of enquiry (whether in mathematics, in ethics or in theology) that begins from some assumption and then enquires into the grounds for that assumption (rather than simply the consequences of that assumption) is dialectical. There is no specific subject-matter for dialectics in Plato (here the difference from Aristotle is startling);

there is only the mode of enquiry which, as reflective, demands a constant examining of all our assumptions, opinions, beliefs.

There are, therefore, dialectical scientists (now named 'philosophers of science') and non-dialectical scientists. There are dialectical understandings of piety (*Euthyphro*), justice (*Republic*), love (*Symposium* and *Phaedrus*), courage (*Laches*) and all the other virtues, beliefs and practices, as well as non-dialectical understandings. There are dialectical understandings of the Good, the Forms, the Beautiful, and non-dialectical ones. There are dialectical understandings of the traditional myths, gods, rites and beliefs, and non-dialectical ones. To repeat, any mode of enquiry that involves a sustained and rigorous reflective analysis of the basic assumptions of any given belief or practice is dialectical. Any that does not, is not.

But what 'signs' can we find to indicate whether a particular mode of enquiry is or is not dialectical? A modern thinker (or, for that matter, an ancient or medieval Aristotelian) would be likely to suggest 'argument' (in both its formal and substantive modes) in modern theories and methods as the principal 'sign' of reflective thought. Yet what is interesting in Plato is that he does not make this characteristically Aristotelian-modern move.

To be sure, the demand for argument is present in Plato throughout his work: both the formal demands for internal consistency of concepts and, above all, the formal and substantive demands for self-consistency in the enquirer (negatively self-contradiction). The latter demand is most prominent in Plato's use of the dialogue form itself to communicate indirectly with the reader the direct demands of face-to-face conversation; viz. the *elenchus* method of enquiry characteristic of Plato's Socrates.

It is not what a particular person says that determines whether she or he is dialectical. It is only what persons mean by what they say and whether they can give reasons for that meaning that is the sign of the dialectical. And that functions best (for Plato) through that sustained and rigorous mode of question and answer which is the main thrust of the 'early' and 'middle' dialogues in which Socrates is the main dramatic figure.

In the early 'aporetic' dialogues, the open-endedness occasioned by the *aporia*s functions well to indicate three central Platonic presuppositions for all enquiry and all education: the fact that the question prevails over the answer in all true enquiry; the fact that true enquiry always provokes further enquiry; the fact that true enquiry, like true education, is always directed to the horizons – the interests, experience and character – of the actual enquirers. The sophists, for Plato, give speeches; Socrates engages in conversation. Even in the great 'middle' dialogues, especially the *Republic*, where more 'constructive' results are presented, the open-endedness of the dialogue form reasserts itself to forbid dogmatism and to assure further enquiry. The loss of the dialogue in modern thought is a loss, I believe, not merely of the unexampled artistry of that form as exemplifying genuine enquiry in Plato, Cicero, Augustine, Berkeley and Hume. It is also a loss of one crucial way to remind all genuine enquirers that the formal treatise or essay comprised of written arguments may be less faithful to the substantive and self-revelatory demands of all face-to-face encounters.

The *elenchus*, as the cross-examination of the enquirer in face-to-face conversation, is, for Plato-Socrates, the manifestation of whether one means what one says and can give reasons defending that meaning. In more explicit terms, the *elenchus* reveals whether or not *logos* is present in the enquirer's soul. It is always the 'soul' of the enquirer, as we shall see below, that is ultimately at stake in all dialectical enquiry. In genre terms, a dialogue can exemplify this substantive existential struggle better than a formal treatise can. In terms of enquiry, the 'dramatic' character of any face-to-face dialogue allows for both a wider range of probing enquiry and a greater manifestation to all participants of the state of their character, the presence or absence of 'logos' in their souls, their commitment or lack of such for the 'examined life', and the relationship between the formal and substantive elements in all their arguments.

I have defended elsewhere the claim that the more encompassing term 'conversation' rather than 'argument' should be the principal example of enquiry demanding analysis by all contemporary enquirers, including those proponents of 'communication-theory' like Habermas and Apel who sometimes seem to narrow too quickly the demands of 'rational communication' to the sole demands of the 'better argument'. Arguments are a necessary moment in any properly dialectical conversation. But the dialogue form is more comprehensive as a revelation of the state of the 'soul' (or, alternatively, of the existential self-understanding) of the dialectical enquirer as a subject-in-process of education. I wish we possessed more than the fragments we presently do of Aristotle's lost dialogues. I am thankful that we do possess Plato's, for there one can find dialectical enquiry in all its complexity, ambiguity, open-endedness and sometimes confusion. I do not regret the loss, if they ever existed, of the 'unwritten doctrines' of Plato, for I believe that his dialogues function better than a formal treatise as an indirect communication of a life of genuinely dialectical enquiry.

To describe the *elenchus* method as *the* sign of dialectical enquiry in Plato is not to disparage the other signs also there: including the later signs for strict argument which Aristotle, with finer logical skills and his extraordinary clarifying genius, later refined. In Plato himself, one can find the procedures of generalisation, definition and division in his early and middle dialogues and the same both used and reflected upon in his later, relatively non-dialogical dialogues, like the *Sophist*, the *Theaetetus* and, above all, the *Parmenides*.

It is notorious that Plato, however much he praises dialectic and the philosophic life, nowhere actually defines dialectic with the precision he brings to bear on all his other fundamental questions. Even in the famous section on 'dialectic' in Book VII of the *Republic*, the reader is made to understand the importance of dialectic, even, it can be said, to feel its import through Plato's artistically wondrous and philosophically dialectical way of relating his parable of the cave, his simile of light, and his image of the 'divided line'. But even here, we are not given a definition of dialectic analogous to the definition of justice.

This, to be sure, is a puzzle, but one worth dwelling upon. For if all dialectic is reflective enquiry on fundamental issues, if dialectic shows its reflectiveness by addressing assumptions and grounds for any practice or belief, if dialectic functions best in person-to-person sustained cross-examination via the *elenchus* method and second-best in written dialogues which exemplify not only the arguments but the interests and characters of the enquirers (the *logos* in their souls or its absence), if even attempts at definition, generalisation and division are genuine but not the sole exemplifications of all dialectical enquiry, then it follows that explicit arguments are also important but not the sole exemplifications of dialectical enquiry. Another exemplification (and one to which such communication-theorists as Habermas and Apel would do well to give further reflection via Plato) is one that no theologian can avoid: the question of myth. Is myth ever an exemplification of dialectics? If so, how? If not, why not? This central issue, which has haunted contemporary theology like a guilty romance, haunted Plato as well, especially whenever he turned dialectical enquiry to the most fundamental question of all: the nature of the whole as that whole can be understood by the dialectical thinker attempting to educate her or his 'soul'.

The dialogue form, to repeat, seems uniquely qualified to manifest dialectic-in-action in written form. This is the case, not merely through the artistry which is clearly Plato's. Indeed, whether Plato's model of dialogue is fashioned principally on the model of the mime or the drama is a moot point. In either case, Plato's discovery of this form allows him to show the true drama he observed in Socrates: the drama of the philosophic soul in conflict with others and, often, with the other in itself.

On this reading, therefore, it is a matter of philosophical and educational and not merely artistic import for Plato to have fashioned the dialogue form. For dialogue not only nicely exemplifies the question-and-answer method of face-to-face Socratic cross-examination. Dialogue also exemplifies dialectic-at-work in the *elenchus* method and in such refinements of that mode of enquiry as arguments on definition, generalisation and division. Dialogue is also a form capable of revealing the souls of the characters in the enquiry. In more familiar contemporary terms, dialogue is geared to reveal the existential self-understanding of the enquirers or, more exactly, the emergence of a subject-in-process, a soul. It is this latter search that is at the heart of

Plato's entire work and that makes him so clearly a contemporary of all those late twentieth-century enquirers concerned to continue the tradition of dialectical reason in Plato's sense as well as in Aristotle's clarified modes of argument. In dialogue one can show enquiry at work while also relating that enquiry directly to our primordial existential self-understanding: of the self as intrinsically relational; related to itself, to society, nature and the whole.

The drama of the soul

Plato's principal word for such existential self-understanding is *psuchē* or soul. Amidst all the scholarly debates on Plato's understanding in different contexts in different dialogues on 'soul', this much, I believe, is clear: besides its other functions (for example on self-movement) the term 'soul' is a direct analogue of what a modern like Bultmann or Ogden means by existential self-understanding or a post-modern like Kristeva means by 'subject-in-process'. To be sure, like Ogden (or in their distinct ways, Voegelin and Lonergan), Plato's interest in this existential self-understanding is deeply informed by his belief in the differentiation of consciousness that occurs to a philosophic soul engaged in dialectical enquiry. For Plato, as his famous attack on the mimetic 'poets' shows, once the philosophic drama of the soul occurs (as it did, for him, in Socrates), then even 'dear Homer' and the great tragedians (even Aeschylus to whom he otherwise seems so similar) become inadequate as accounts of our 'souls'.

The emergence of Socrates, the emergence of dialectical enquiry, has transformed the soul from its internal conflicts so well portrayed by the 'poets', especially the great tragedians, Aeschylus and Sophocles. To understand 'soul' properly, we must replace their mimesis of those conflicts with the new drama of the soul, the mimesis of the idea in the emergence of Socrates. But before one assumes that this is proof of the 'rationalism' so often charged to the Greek Socratic Enlightenment one needs to reflect further on the drama of the 'soul' in the Platonic dialogues.

The most convincing case for the charge of rationalism could be made if one examined only the *Phaedo* where the *rational* character of the soul is sternly portrayed. But even there the figure of Socrates, the presence of myth, and the open-ended nature of the enquiry-in-dialogue form is far more complex than this familiar reading suggests. But the matter of the 'soul' for Plato is complicated by several factors in other dialogues: for example, the tripartite 'division' of the soul into rational, spirited and appetitive 'parts' in the *Republic* and the *Phaedrus* and, above all, the microcosm-macrocosm analogue that dominates Plato's dialogues in the *Republic* (soul and polis) and the *Timaeus* (soul and cosmos).

The tripartite view of the soul can be read as a challenge to any purely rationalist understanding of the 'soul'. For it is one thing to claim (as Plato clearly does) that the 'rational' is the spark of the divine in the human and, once differentiated as philosophic reason employing dialectics, the rational part of the soul should justly rule the other parts which cause the inner conflicts of the soul. It is quite another matter to claim, as traditional rationalists do, that conscious reason alone is sufficient for existential self-understanding. This latter position, however familiar to many readings of western notions of enlightenment and however devastating in its effects upon modern individualism, is not Plato's.

Reason is the great hope; but only a reason that can faithfully (that is, dialectically) acknowledge its own possibilities, complexities and limits. However unsettled some forms of Platonism may be by the discovery of the reality of the unconscious in Freud and Lacan, by the 'dialectic of enlightenment' of Adorno and Horkheimer, or by the fragile character of 'reason' in post-modern thought, these discoveries, on my reading, complicate but hardly devastate Plato's own account of the soul.

Reason acknowledges its own possibilities by engaging in genuinely dialectical enquiry. This surely, as our prior section urged, is at the heart of the Platonic corpus, early, middle and late, and at the heart of all the Platonic successors in western educational theory, from Aristotle on argument to modern communication theorists. But reason, as dialectical reason, can and must, as rational, also acknowledge its own limits. This is the case not so much because reason, although the 'ruling element' in the soul, is only one of three elements. This is the case, rather, because reason-in-the-soul is the spark of the divine in the human: the way in which reason can recognise both its extraordinary possibilities and its own finite, limited status. Thereby can the soul be led to acknowledge all genuine manifestations of the whole and of the divine including those not arrived at by strictly dialectical procedures. For example, before dialectical enquiry, as the use of myth in some of the early dialogues indicates, myth is a dubious aid to the soul. In the midst of dialectical enquiry, however (here the several uses of myth in the *Republic* and the *Phaedrus* are exemplary), myth is a genuine aid to the soul.

The central clue here remains Plato's much disputed reading of art and myth. There can be no doubt that Plato is the great demythologiser of the traditional myths (even the Olympian gods) and the poets (from Hesiod through the great tragedians). For Plato, in Socrates the differentiation of dialectical reason has occurred and the drama of the philosophic soul must dialectically challenge the anthropomorphism of the traditional myths of the gods and the heroes and the mimetic disclosure of the inner conflicts of the pre-philosophic soul and the pre-Socratic polis of the great tragedians. Neither Homer, nor the traditional myths in Hesiod, nor the great characters and actions of the tragedians, can 'give a rational account', a dialectical account, of themselves.

The poets for Plato can only mimetically describe the confusions of the soul in the individual and the polis while also 'projecting' this confusion on their anthropomorphic portraits of the gods. To be sure, the traditional myths and the 'poets' contain great truths worth retrieving. But, for Plato, we must demythologise them whenever we find ourselves in a situation of political decadence (which Plato clearly considers the Athens of his day or even the earlier Periclean period) or in a situation of intellectual decadence where even the great *peithō* or persuasion theme of Aeschylus can become a travesty of true persuasion (viz. persuasion-without-enquiry into the truth of things) of the new rhetorical persuaders, the sophists.

There can be little doubt that Plato, like every dialectical theologian, does not hesitate to demythologise when either the situation (Athenian political and intellectual decadence) or the tradition (anthropomorphic portraits of the Olympian gods acting as badly as decadent humans, blasphemous portrayals of the gods demanding bribes, materialistic accounts of the whole and the divine) demands it. Plato needed to write his famous 'Dear Homer' passage as much as any dialectical Christian theologian today needs to write her or his 'Dear Paul' passage for authentic theological enquiry. But to see Plato as only the great rational demythologiser of traditional myth and art is, I believe, seriously to misunderstand him.

It is not only the case that Plato is a great remythologiser, although that is indeed true, as his apparently original creation of such great myths as the Myth of Er in the *Republic* and the myths of creation and Atlantis in the *Timaeus* and the *Critias* shows. It is, rather, that Plato is also the great rational-dialectical defender of the truth of both myth and art.

The dialectical soul, that is, the truly educated soul, unlike other souls, finds it necessary to give a rational account of itself. As that account proceeds, the soul, for Plato (here the descent-ascent theme throughout the *Republic* seems paradigmatic), finds itself 'pulled' to a depth both grounding and beyond itself which it cannot account for dialectically but can and must acknowledge through its own dialectical experience.

In modern language, authentic 'existence' demands the acknowledgement of 'transcendence' and recognises that transcendence in the 'traces' or 'ciphers' of transcendence of the great myths. That experience of a depth where the soul somehow 'participates' in or 'imitates' the whole and the divine can come in several ways: through reflection on *eros* as a divine gift (as in the *Symposium* and the *Phaedrus*): through reflection on *thanatos* as providing the clue to the truth of the philosophic life (as in the *Phaedo* or the Myth of Er in the *Republic*); through the manifestations of new works of art disclosive of the soul and its kinship with the whole (as in the mimesis of the philosophic soul which is the central drama of the dialogue form); or through new, 'true' myths which disclose the soul as participating in or imitating the cosmos itself (as in the great philosophy of myth in the *Timaeus* wherein cosmos and soul can only be understood together).

True enquiry (dialectics), as true persuasion, is driven by the divine power of eros that manifests the soul's participation in the divine and the whole. Enquiry and persuasion without love are as helpless for Plato as eros without true enquiry, and true persuasion is inevitably decadent. That the philosophic life is the erotic life par excellence is, for Plato, the central clue not only to the eros which drives every soul in myriad forms. It is also the central clue to that mode of enquiry and persuasion which drives the philosophic soul to its own depth where it recognises that it participates in the whole and the divine through all its eros from physical passion to the 'divine madness' which is a gift of the gods to the poets and seers, the *daimōn* which drove Socrates to his calling, and the faithful, eros-driven enquiry of the dialecticians.

The dialectical soul, thus impelled by love and differentiated by true reason, eventually finds itself compelled to acknowledge the truth of myth and art. Even without the backing of Plato's controversial interpretation of *anamnēsis*, this position can be warranted on Platonic grounds. The warrant is this: in the great myths and the great works of art, the soul discovers itself by discovering, acknowledging its own participation in and imitation of the whole and the divine. At the same time, the cosmos and the divine are the central clue to the psyche. Whether Plato invented or discovered the great myth of creation of the *Timaeus* remains a moot point. But that Plato accords some truth status to that myth seems incontrovertible. One can either dismiss the myth of the creation in the *Timaeus* as the strange fantasy of an old and disillusioned philosopher or accord it the kind of truth Plato did: the truth of any great myth or any great work of art that manifests the truth of the intrinsic kinship of soul and cosmos. This truth the dialectician was already led to acknowledge in her or his enquiry upon love and persuasion. This truth the dialectician turned dialectical mythologiser and artist can now acknowledge anew by recounting the myth as a 'likely story'; its likeliness is not in its details but in its central insight: the kinship of soul and cosmos.

Dialectics can acknowledge even when it cannot dialectically ground this ultimate truth. Dialectics can turn to the traditional myths and poets and retrieve this truth from their confused (because anthropomorphic and not philosophically differentiated) mimetic accounts. Dialectics can lead the enquirer to find persuasive any 'likely account' of what dialectical enquiry rationally acknowledges but never grounds: the reality of the divine, the reality of cosmos and soul, as jointly participating in the divine. A dialectician who is also a great artist (here Plato is alone) may also risk the development of a work of art (a dialogue) that can portray the new myth in the context of genuinely dialectical enquiry: the myth of Er in the *Republic*, the myth of creation in the *Timaeus*, the myth of Atlantis in the *Critias*.

Plato, I believe, continues to persuade because there is a whole in his texts which we later 'footnotes' can only glimpse: a commitment to that singular differentiation of consciousness that is western philosophic reason; a rendering of the Socratic oral performance of cross-examination into the written texts of the dialogues; the refinement, within the encompassing genre of the dialogue, of the need for argument, for *elenchus*, for definition, generalisation, division, and subdivision, even, potentially, for those refinements of argument and its conditions of possibility elaborated by Aristotle in one way and by Toulmin, Habermas and Ogden in modern terms; the insistence on the need for theological enquiry on the fundamental question of the whole and our existential relationship to that whole as a mode of enquiry demanded by dialectical reason itself; the ability to provide an artistic-philosophic rendering of existential self-consciousness in its full complexity from rational differentiation to its acknowledgement of the eros driving all true enquiry; the defence of the truth of art and myth as evoking commitment without romanticism and with an insistence on much necessary demythologising, provoked by all true enquiry.

The educational conclusion is sound: commitment and action not open to enquiry is blind; enquiry not open to commitment and action is empty. Enquiry and action, like education and the soul, rise or fall together.

The Timaeus

The *Timaeus* remains, I believe, not only the most influential text in the history of Christian theology but the clearest example of one of Plato's many uses of myth. More exactly, 'myth' is no longer only the work of the poets and sophists who functioned prior to the emergence of dialectical enquiry, as it often is in the 'aporetic' early dialogues (for example, the use of myth by Protagoras in the *Protagoras*). Moreover, myth, for the *Timaeus*, is not only in the middle or at the end of dialogues when dialectical thinking has already begun (for example, in the *Republic*). Rather, in the *Timaeus*, myth pervades the dialogue as a whole so that one could almost name this relatively non-dialogical dialogue by the genre 'myth' rather than dialogue.

And yet such a 'naming' would not be accurate either, despite the delight that later Christian neo-Platonists found in this great myth of creation which seemed to them so resonant with the Hebraic-Christian myth of a Creator-God in Genesis. Rather the *Timaeus* remains a dialogue, however atypical, insofar as here myth and dialectic, dialectic and myth, interpenetrate throughout the whole text-as-Platonic-dialogue. Even in the main body of the text, where Timaeus is almost the sole speaker and the other interlocutors listen but do not question in the familiar Socratic way, the dialectical character of the whole reading of the myth assures that we find here not merely a formal treatise nor a pure myth, but an odd form of dialogue where myth and dialectics seem always-already together to assure the movement of enquiry. This is especially the case in the great 'new start' of the entire enquiry of Part II (47E–49A) where the errant cause or necessity (*anankē*) enters to complicate the portrait and where reason (*nous*) must learn to persuade (*peithō*) necessity to bring about order. On the one hand, this new theme, as Cornford observes, is resonant to the great *peithō* theme of the conclusion of the *Critias*. On the other hand, the introduction of this new and dialectically necessary component of 'necessity' is a dialectical advance in the enquiry (similar moves occur in the mythic-dialectical notion of the 'receptacle' and the more strictly dialectical but mythically contextualised notions of the 'same' and the 'different'). Above all, the great persuasion theme recalls not only the extraordinary poetic-mythic vision of Aeschylus but the crucial Platonic dialectical theme of 'true persuasion' in the *Gorgias* and the *Phaedrus*.

I believe that such a curious but ingenious interpretation of myth and dialectic pervades the whole text of the *Timaeus* to the point where familiar debates on whether Plato's cosmology is 'myth' or 'science' seem beside the point for understanding the kind of educated enquiry into the cosmos which the *Timaeus* is. Only a full treatment of the whole text, with this model in mind, could verify my hypothesis. For the moment, the examples in the text cited above may serve to provoke reflection on the plausibility or implausibility of the hypothesis.

Some further evidence, however, is clearly needed. I will, therefore, end by citing some examples from the very beginning of the *Timaeus* where this curious genre is formed, a dialogue that is at once mythical and dialectical all the way through.

First, the characters of the dialogue do not bear the lively portraits of their principal character's traits which the early dialogues have accustomed the reader to. And yet they do seem mythically resonant: Socrates merely summarises a part of the *Republic* and, uncharacteristically, wishes now simply to listen; Timaeus of Locri (probably a fictional invention) does recall the Pythagoreans whose combination of mathematics and something like a mystery-cult does lend itself to the kind of dialectical mythic discourse which shall be his in the dialogue; Critias clearly recalls the ancient aristocracy of Athens which will free him both to remember Solon's Egyptian tale and prepare him to tell the story of Atlantis and Athens; Hermocrates (an historical figure) may serve as a warning to the Athenians, as the general who will one day (in the time of the dialogue) crush the Athenians in their most humiliating defeat at Syracuse – he reveals, by his mere presence, a warning to the *hubris* of contemporary Athens.

Second, in 17C–19A: Socrates' 'summary' of the discourse of the *Republic* is notorious for all it leaves out from that great dialogue. My own reading of why this is so is less speculative than most commentators: to begin with, Socrates has already given the discourse 'yesterday' and finds no need to repeat its dialectical subtleties here: he is here to listen, not to speak further; in addition, the mere recall of the discourse can remind the reader that dialectics is necessary for a proper understanding of any myth, including the highly dialectical myth of Timaeus which shall encompass the whole text.

Third, in 19B–20B: Socrates' request, the city Socrates has earlier described in a city of the idea. How could it function in reality, especially the reality of war? For that one needs to turn not to philosophers like Socrates (much less to the 'poets' and 'sophists') but to philosopher-statesmen like Timaeus, Critias, and Hermocrates.

Fourth, in 20C–27B: the initial responses of first Hermocrates, and then Critias to Socrates' request seem initially strange: Critias, as a result of an effort of (Platonic?) recollection of a story he heard in his youth (25E–26C) tells the Egyptian tale of Solon. This amazing myth, of an Athens which once was great and indeed seems to be the Athens in actuality of Socrates' city-in-idea, functions well to recall two salient facts about the *Timaeus* as a whole: first, dialectics resulting in the city of the idea, and myth (disguised as history) can work together to train the soul; second, the true epic, greater even than Homer's, would be the epic of that polis, the epic of the idea which could show how in the past, the city of the idea actually existed. A true art, one formed by the philosophic soul, could write that epic. Socrates (ironically?) cannot. But, as the great dialectician, he can listen and learn without the kind of further questioning which he ordinarily felt obliged to give to all the earlier pre-philosophic 'poets'. He can, more precisely, on one condition: that the poet-mythologiser is also a philosopher-dialectician who, in this sense, can do Socrates' new work for him: produce an epic of this idea which unites cosmos, soul and polis in a dialectical-mythical tale. In the persons of Timaeus and Critias (and presumably in Hermocrates) Socrates finds these dialectical tellers of tales to whom he can listen and be silent without the fear that he is hearing 'only' myth or 'only' a dialectics which will disclose the idea but not the idea-in-action.

Fifth, in 27C–29D: in Timaeus Socrates has finally found his teller of tales, a mythologiser, to whom he can listen. It is important, I believe, to see how Timaeus first engages in dialectical enquiry of a very Socratic-Platonic sort (on knowledge and opinion, on being and becoming) *before* he sets forth his mythical-dialectical creation narrative. It is almost as if the last books of Augustine's *Confessions* were required reading for all Christians about to read the book of Genesis! Timaeus, we are shown, is indeed a fine dialectician, for he knows (29D) that to tell the story of the cosmos we can only hope for a likely story: likely, because like the *eikōn*, the incarnation in becoming of the idea, which the cosmos is. Dialectics can lead us to glimpse the idea. Only a *likely* story can lead us further: to render the idea (of cosmos, of polis, of soul) actual in the state of incarnate becoming modelled in the ideas which we are and where we discover ourselves to be in kinship with the cosmos. At that point, the likely story can begin.

It is, I think, a good beginning to a good mythical-dialectical creation story. Such a curious combination of myth and dialectic in mutually critical correlation is an odd genre, to be sure: it is sometimes called theology.

In a sense, the community of enquiry in the West lives through the power of the great Socratic ideal for true education, classically expressed in the saying, 'The unreflective life is not worth living.' All communities of commitment and faith add to that classic Socratic ideal of the western community of enquiry the equally important thought: 'and the unlived life is not worth reflecting upon'.

This addition is, of course, no minor one. For all thought, I repeat, exists ultimately for the sake of action and commitment. It is true that mere action without thought is blind. It is equally true that all thought not ultimately directed to action, concern, commitment is empty.

Theological education and the subject-in-process

Of all the educational institutions, the ministry programme schools of theology are those singular institutions where action and thought, academy and church, faith and reason, the community of enquiry and the community of commitment and faith are most explicitly and systematically brought together. For any one who enters a seminary enters primarily with the goal of action, the goal of the practice of ministry in and for the community of the church and people. One enters to be educated, in the hope of finding a community that unites both thought and action to help us to find our way to both the 'reflective life' suggested by Socrates and the 'lived life' proclaimed by Jesus.

As Plato taught us, a life of enquiry has its own demands, the demands of what Bernard Lonergan nicely calls the pure, detached, disinterested, unrestricted desire to know. But there is a further insight which the community of faith has to teach. For the eros of enquiry, as Augustine reminded the Platonists of his day, is itself driven by our commitments, our faiths, our loves. To know the truth of Augustine's great insight, *amor meus, pondus meum*, is to know what ultimately drives the life of reflection in a community of enquiry rooted in a community of commitment and faith: our ideals, our hopes, our loves.

For the community of faith, the church, is that community where despite its faults, even sins, God's word is yet preached, God's story of redemption and creation is yet reflected upon and appropriated by the 'souls' of all Christians who have joined themselves to that multivoiced narrative, God's sacraments are made present anew, God's people attempt to live out in action and commitment a life of faith working through love and justice in a global context. In the community of faith each person individually and the whole people as a community attempt, now well, now poorly, to make God's own story, the story of God's pure unbounded love for all creation disclosed in the story of the people of Israel and that Jesus who is the Christ, become their story as well.

The life of the mind cannot live alone. As Aristotle insisted, only gods and beasts can do that. Rather, to think is to converse with the classics; to converse with the classics is to join the community of enquiry of the living and the dead. It is to recognise that we too can and must become part of that conversation. In truth, we are that conversation.

Nor does the life of faith live alone. We live that life because past communities of faith passed it on to us. Christians know the decisive narrative of Jesus Christ because our tradition has seen fit to pass along, to hand over this healing, transforming, gracious possibility to us. As my historical colleague Martin Marty has written, 'Christianity is always one generation away from extinction.' We too must recognise that what conversation is to the life of the mind, solidarity is to the life of action.

The Christian community of faith is a tradition which has lived by shared disclosive and transformative meanings for almost two thousand years. Christians find that those shared meanings have expressed themselves through the centuries in an explosively pluralistic way as each generation attempted to think and live them as its own. And in retrieving that reality each generation added some new classic possibility, some new insight, some new retrieval or suspicion and often retrieval of forgotten, even repressed memories of this extraordinary story through suspicion, witness, way of life.

As we experience more deeply the pluralism of our Christian community, we are likely in the future to turn yet more fully to those who are the privileged ones of the ancient prophets and of Jesus Christ, the poor, the oppressed, the marginalised, the forgotten ones. They are the ones whose present and future voice the Christian gospel calls us to hear. This truth of the Christian faith seems to me more powerfully realised in the modern seminary than in the seminary of my day. And their voice, if listened to, can become our voice as well.

Some have suggested, with a sense of resignation, perhaps even quiet despair, that even the future is not what it used to be. Yet the truth is, it never was. For at the heart of the Christian revolution of consciousness is the insistence that the future cannot be a mere *telos*, a working out of what already is. The future, for the Christian gospel, is *adventum*, that which is to come, the new, the unexpected, judgement and threat, gift and promise from God and God's disclosure in history and nature.

A theological education, grounded in continuous searching of the Christian classics, especially the bible, open to the demands of enquiry become the demands of retrieval, critique and suspicion, can become again a school for the training of the soul. That is how theological education began. That is how, I believe, it needs to see itself again. Otherwise even our noble contemporary attempts to teach 'values' and 'character-formation' may become trapped again in a mere individualism. To rethink theological education in our increasingly pluralistic and ambiguous global context is to rethink as well, not the 'individualist' model of the purely autonomous self of Enlightenment modernity, not even, primarily, the classic notions of identity-formation through character of Aristotle and his successors. It is also to retrieve, critically, suspiciously even at times, but really, the Christian soul as the subject-in-process of the Christian identity.

Notes
1. Joseph C Hough and John B Cobb, *Christian Identity and Theological Education*, Chico, California, Scholars Press, 1985.
2. Robert Bellah *et al.*, *Habits of the Heart*, Berkeley, California, University of California Press, 1985.

10. Theology, education and the university

The conviction that theological education is central to the educational work of the seminary or Divinity School is not in itself controversial, in spite of continuing disagreements about its nature and objectives. The place of theological education in the university as such, however, has been strongly challenged for many years. One influential school of thought has maintained that there is a place in the university for Religious Studies but not for Theology, partly on the basis that the former is said to be characterised by a 'scientific', 'objective', and 'neutral' methodology which the latter is deemed to lack, but which is considered normative for responsible intellectual enquiry. In Britain, where there are departments of Theology, of Religious Studies, and of Theology *and* Religious Studies, discussions of the place of theological education in the university reflect the fact of its historic presence; [1] but in the United States, the point of departure for such discussions is the fact of its historic absence, given that university departments of Religion are ultimately the product of the constitutional separation of church and state. The articles in this section, which question the institutional marginalisation of theological reflection, presuppose the special challenges of the American context. [2]

Stephen Toulmin, in 'Theology in the context of the university', first published in *Theological Education*, 26, 1990, pp. 51–65, observes that the question about the place of theology in the university is an institutional and an intellectual question at the same time. Sketching the history of the relationships between theology and the university, he argues that theology allied itself too closely to the foundationalism of Descartes and his successors. But with the fall of foundationalism, in our own time, it is possible to return to 'a *practical* conception of theology'; and because 'the central, distinctive concern of theology is precisely with the *interrelatedness* of things', theology should have a unique contribution to make to the 'transdisciplinary dialogue' of the university today.

Edward Farley identifies and criticises the 'technomania' of the modern university in general, and argues, from his conception of 'the educated person', that what it requires is 'a new hermeneutical self-consciousness'. Religion, in particular, being 'culturally specific and concrete', 'a distinctive dimension of human experience', and involved with issues of 'truth and reality', is such that its study requires the use of the hermeneutical principles of 'concreteness', 'experientiality', and 'reality' – and analogous principles are, in fact, essential to any kind of serious study. Without such principles, religious studies and theological studies alike are distorted. The conclusion, therefore, is that the aims of religious studies itself, and of the study of any one particular religion, can only be realised with the aid of a theological hermeneutic of religion. Farley's 'The place of theology in the study of religion' is from *Religious Studies and Theology*, 5, 1985, pp. 9–29.

'Theology: university and church. Is a synergism possible?', by Claude Welch, first appeared in *Philosophy and Theology*, 3, 1988, pp. 5–23. Welch believes that the interests of the university, especially in relation to the study of religion, and the interests of the church, in its theological enquiry, can and do coincide to such an extent that it is possible to talk of 'synergism'. The question of the relation of Christianity to other religions, Welch argues, is the paradigm case of this possibility, since the major contributors to this debate are, and must be, both historians of religion *and* theologians. In one critical area, therefore, there is a synergistic relation between the university and the church, which, Welch hopes, will be replicated elsewhere.

Professor Stephen E Toulmin is currently based in the Center for Multiethnic and Transnational Studies at the University of Southern California, Los Angeles, USA. Professor Edward Farley is Professor of Theology at the Divinity School, Vanderbilt University, Nashville, Tennessee, USA. Professor Claude Welch was formerly Professor of Historical Theology at the Graduate Theological Union, Berkeley, California, USA.

Notes

1. See, for example, Donald Mackinnon, 'Theology as a discipline of a modern university', in Teodor Shanin (ed.), *The Rules of the Game*, London, Tavistock, 1972; Stephen W Sykes, 'Theological study: the nineteenth century and after', in Brian Hebblethwaite and Stewart Sutherland (eds.), *The Philosophical Frontiers of Christian Theology*, Cambridge, Cambridge University Press, 1982, and 'The study of theology in university and school', in James Barnett (ed.), *Theology at 16+*, London, Epworth, 1984; Stewart Sutherland, 'Studying religion and believing religion', in Gijsbert van den Brink, Luco J van den Brom, and Marcel Sarot (eds.), *Christian Faith and Philosophical Theology: essays in honour of Vincent Brümmer*, Kampen, The Netherlands, Kok Pharos, 1992.
2. Compare Daniel W Hardy, 'Theology and the cultural reduction of religion', in Jeff Astley and Leslie J Francis (eds.), *Christian Theology and Religious Education: connections and contradictions*, London, SPCK, 1996, chapter 2.

10.1 Theology in the context of the university

Stephen Toulmin

The institutional and intellectual questions

The question 'What place does theology have in universities today?' can be addressed from two different directions. On the one hand, we can treat it as an *institutional* question: 'What are the relations between university departments or schools of theology, and the other schools or departments alongside which they work? Has theology, for instance, a place in undergraduate colleges of Arts and Sciences?' In many North American universities, the subject is taught on the undergraduate level, in most cases only as an elective subject, and usually under a pseudonym like 'Religious Studies'; at Northwestern, for example, the College of Arts and Sciences has a department of History and Literature of Religion. Alternatively, is the proper location of Departments of Theology in the graduate school? To the extent that philosophical theology, comparative religion and the like provide fields for original research on an advanced level, they have a place in graduate training. Or is the central place of theology a professional one, associated with the training of priests and ministers? In that case, the subject would pre-eminently be taught as Law and Medicine are taught, within the framework of a professional school.

Questions about the academic locus of theology may also have an *intellectual* sense. Instead of asking about the administration or organisation of university institutions, we can ask about the standing of theology, as a field for research and debate alongside, even overlapping, the fields of philosophy, anthropology, biology or whatever. How far can theology look other contemporary disciplines in the eye? How do its central intellectual concerns compare and/or connect with those of more established disciplines in the academic world, in either the sciences or the humanities? About this, the spectrum of possible views ranges from a grandiose extreme, of seeing theology as a foundational discipline, in which all other subjects should be grounded, to the more cynical extreme, of seeing theology as a 'pseudo subject' or 'non subject', and theological doctrines as disguised matters of personal preference.

At first sight, these institutional and intellectual aspects are quite distinct, and even separate. Yet that appearance is misleading. The task of deciding whether an organisational niche exists in universities for the study of theology, and if so, what, can hardly be tackled without at the same time, addressing the question of the intellectual standing of the subject. To the extent that we regard theology as that body of doctrines (or 'dogmas') that are the intellectual foundation and/or justification for a particular kind of religious life and practice, we make the subject a *theoretical* field of study, which is seen as conceptually prior to, and more basic than, pastoral theology, for the same reasons that biology is conceptually prior to, and more basic than, medicine. Conversely, to the extent that we treat theology, first and foremost, as a *practical* (though not exclusively *pastoral*) discipline, we make it harder to separate the intellectual critique of doctrines from issues of liturgy or stewardship, counselling or homiletics. That being so, attitudes to the *bona fides* and seriousness of theological concepts and issues are discussed alongside, and in conjunction with, administrative issues. Those to whom the life and practice of religion are the context for all truly theological issues will be readier to choose a 'professional school' model of organisation; those to whom doctrine is 'foundational' will give theology a narrower and more 'academic' niche in university organisation.

These generalisations may be either a commentary on the present state of affairs, or else a wider, historical commentary on the changing patterns of academic organisations to be found in different cultures and historical periods. Looking at the varied academic roles that theology has played at different times and places is a useful prelude to restating the issues confronting North American theological schools at present. Let me begin with an historical overview, and defer the more practical questions for theologians in the context of different kinds of colleges and universities. Focusing first on matters of history, we may set up some broad temporal subdivisions, marking periods during which such matters were dealt with differently.

Either way we slice it, institutionally or intellectually, we should notice some striking historical transitions. In the first centuries AD, both the intellectual and the institutional standing of Christianity were transformed by its 'establishment' in the Eastern Roman Empire, thanks to the alliance of the Patriarch Athanasius and the Emperor Constantine, and the doctrinal decisions of the Council of Nicaea. Thirteen centuries later, there was an equal discontinuity after the Protestant Reformation and the Council of Trent. Institutionally and intellectually, theology thus had a very different place in European universities from 1150 to 1550 from what it had in the 300 years from the 1650s to the 1950s. And, if there is a special uncertainty about its place today, that is because in our own generation we have seen many of the seventeenth century's innovations being once again called in question.

The rise and fall of foundationalism

In the pre-Reformation period, from Hildebrand to Erasmus, there was a standard pattern to European universities by which Divinity stood among the customary 'faculties' of the university alongside Medicine and Jurisprudence. Philosophy embraced the fundamental arts and sciences that formed the *trivium* and *quadrivium* of general education; but these were seen as preparation for professional training in the three parallel professions of Law, Physick and the Church. (That division of learning is embodied architecturally in the Old Schools at the University of Oxford, where the entrance to each traditional 'school' stands on one or another of the interior walls of the Quadrangle.)

Institutionally, from the twelfth to the sixteenth century, the theological learning required for entry into the church thus existed alongside and on the same footing as the medical and legal learning required for entry into the other two chief professions. So conceived, theology was a *practical* discipline; its content was independent of (and in many ways antedated) the theoretical arts and sciences. Since the universities of Europe were initially 'schools' for training lawyers, doctors and priests, they were the repositories for the best scholarship in Theology, as well as in Law and Physick, but were not yet committed to the intellectual primacy of a 'systematic' theology as a foundational *theory*, distinct and separate from practical or pastoral theology. Rather, the more that the medieval schools, following Thomas Aquinas, organised different fields of study along lines derived from Aristotle, the more committed they became to interpreting practical disciplines as fields for *phronēsis* (or 'prudence') rather than for the *epistēmē* (or 'theoretical grasp') of astronomy and geometry. To this day, indeed, the most serious misreadings of Aquinas come from seeing him, as a philosophical theologian, as committed to a theoretical, rather than pastoral view of the subject; whereas he was, in actual fact, as much a master of the rhetoric of Cicero and Quintilian as he was of the logical analyses of the Platonists.

Up to the time of the Council of Trent, then, intellectual debates in the universities in the middle ages and the Renaissance were conducted against the background of a general cultural consensus. The intellectual culture of western Europe embodied a shared understanding of Christian belief, a liturgy which was largely taken over from traditional Judaism, and a repertory of theological concepts, many of which could be discussed on an equal basis with Islamic scholars, too. When Aquinas writes of the central concepts of moral and general theology as accessible to thinkers from any creed or culture, via the *ratio naturalis*, this is not some kind of European parochialism, still less cultural imperialism. It reflects the fact that, for medieval scholars, pre-Christian and non-Christian writers, such as Aristotle and Cicero, made fundamental contributions to ethics, politics and theology, which were incorporable into Christian doctrine with rational confidence.

After the late sixteenth century, this changed. The politico-theological confrontation between Counter Reformation Catholics and dogmatic Protestants broke down the earlier theological consensus. No longer could one maintain the scholarly agreement between theologians from different religious communities that maintained the rational confidence of previous centuries. With the mid-seventeenth century, questions of *doctrine*, which were earlier open to intellectual speculation and debate, were transformed into matters of *dogma*, to be settled authoritatively by church authority, and ceased to be open to questioning or speculation. (Thus, the intellectually imaginative tradition of *Summas* gave way to the magisterial production of pedestrian *Manuals*.) Meanwhile, in the universities, the rise of philosophical rationalism after René Descartes offered an alternative but quite separate path to Philosophy, which only now set aside its Aristotelian heritage of rhetoric and practical philosophy and committed itself to logico-analytical methods modelled on those of geometry.

The resulting 'New Philosophy' defined the intellectual background against which arose systems of political ideas, from Thomas Hobbes and John Locke to Jean-Jacques Rousseau and Thomas Jefferson, which were later appealed to, in both the French Republic and the United States of America, as justifying a separation of church and state. So from the late eighteenth century on, educated Europeans and North Americans found it impossible to treat Theology as on a par with the secular disciplines of Law and Medicine. On their view of religion, there could be no effective consensus in theology as there still was in jurisprudence and medicine. After 1800, these differences became even more marked. The increasing confidence of the physical sciences seemed to undermine the claims of theology ever more radically; and in the early twentieth century this process culminated in the emergence of a secular positivism, many of whose proponents used the very word 'theological' as a synonym for 'empty' or 'meaningless'.

As the 1980s come to an end, the striking feature for our purposes is a new ability to challenge the whole development of modern theology and philosophy, from late seventeenth century rationalism to early twentieth century positivism. Like Ludwig Wittgenstein and Martin Heidegger (as Richard Rorty reminds us) John Dewey has critically questioned the intellectual heritage of philosophical rationalism, and opened a road by which we can move back toward both a more *practical* vision of Philosophy, and a more *pastoral* programme for Theology. The sense of stratospheric despair that many readers carry away from the absolute idealism of F H Bradley and the systematic theology of Karl Barth has turned out, on this view, to be only a natural sense of loss, in reaction to this recognition that the more grandiose theoretical ambitions of the seventeenth century were misconceived in the first place. If the critical position of these major philosophers is well founded, it opens up the chance for theological issues (at any rate, theological issues of certain kinds) moving closer to the centre of the academic debate within the universities of the future.

Throughout the three centuries beginning with the end of the Thirty Years War in 1648, accordingly, the academic culture of the European and North American university took for granted a *secular* ideal of learning derived finally from the theologically neutral rationalism of Descartes' *Discourse on Method*. Viewed against this background, theological issues were increasingly seen as divisive and particularistic: rooted in matters over which the church disagreed, rather than on any shared consensus, let alone on a *ratio naturalis*. Unless the death of Cartesianism declared by many leading philosophers during the last fifty or sixty years proves greatly exaggerated, this fact will thus have potentially major implications for theology, also. It undermines the whole 'foundationalist' programme, which required philosophy to build up a decontextualised and neutral framework of *logic and theory*, in favour of a research programme concentrated on matters of *narrative and practice*. If the varied academic disciplines in the contemporary university share any common grounding, therefore, it can no longer be found, either in the self-evident, 'clear and distinct', ideas of Cartesian rationalism, or in the more modest, but still *a priori* assumptions of Lockean empiricism. Instead, that grounding can be brought to light only by constructing the overall narrative of conceptual history (what some German philosophers today call *Begriffsgeschichte*) from which their common experiential origins can be discovered.

The intellectual situation in theology can be compared with that in ethics, where Alasdair MacIntyre's arguments, notably in *After Virtue*,[1] have put the historically developing traditions of moral thought back in the centre of the picture. It is no accident that MacIntyre and I should be moving in parallel directions. When we first met back in the 1950s, we compared the courses we were currently teaching, on the philosophy of religion and the philosophy of science respectively; and the contents of the two courses proved to be the same. Both of us saw the same central issues as forming the intellectual warp on which the fabric of western thought had been woven, whether the ideas in question were labelled as 'scientific' or 'religious'; and the level of generality and depth at which these issues arose made it hard to classify them as being 'philosophical' rather than 'theological' or *vice versa*.

Both our courses were organised around the historical evolution of these historically crucial issues. Nor were they confined to the ways in which such issues arise in the Christian world: they also extended back to classical, pre-Christian Greece, and across the line dividing Judaism from Christianity. Above all, we concentrated on giving a satisfactory account of the different *phases* in the history of western philosophy: classical and patristic (Hellenistic) thought, a medieval period which revived classical ideas, the early modern period of the Renaissance and scientific revolution, and the 200 years of mature natural science and post-Kantian ('critical') philosophy. Only with this basic narrative of western cultural history in mind could one give a proper account of the central issues that have arisen, and still arise, in either science or religion. That same narrative is still (in my view) the groundwork of liberal learning and, in its reconstruction, theology can contribute much material, both in parallel with and overlapping the results obtained in other academic fields.

Nor is the current shift in philosophical method, away from abstract theory and toward concrete narrative, all that recent: it is foreshadowed, for example, in Collingwood's discussion of absolute presuppositions in his *An Essay on Metaphysics*[2] and *The Idea of Nature*.[3] As Collingwood saw matters, there is no way to give a formal, universal analysis of 'causality', for example, that is relevant to *all* stages in their historical development; rather the changing patterns of thought about 'causality' need to be documented in historical terms, so as to bring to light the genealogical links among our varied 'causal' concepts, and the pragmatic considerations that have led to their differentiation.

It is clear in retrospect that Collingwood recognised some basic points that most professional historians of science did not yet understand. From the 1930s to the 1960s, research on the intellectual development of the natural sciences was mainly written by historians who were influenced, either by the antiphilosophical stance of George Sarton, or by the positivism of the contemporary philosophy of science, or by both. Even Jürgen Habermas' argument connecting 'knowledge' and 'human interests' assumed that we can know, in universal terms, what legitimate 'human interests' the sciences can serve; and *theological* interests were not included among them. Yet, if we look back from the present to the controversy between Leibniz and Newton to be seen in the Leibniz-Clarke correspondence, or at the widespread acceptance of Newtonian ideas between 1690 and 1750, it is clear that what was at stake for educated Europeans was as much the chance of reconstructing an intellectually defensible theodicy as it was anything in the bailiwick of twentieth century physical theory.

In pursuing this historical agenda, we should not ignore the varied strands of European thought, even within its underlying warp. Popular rhetoric today uses the catch phrase, 'the Judeo-Christian tradition'; but, for philosophical theologians as for historians of modern science, it is less urgent to underline the continuity of Judaism and Christianity than it is to study the ways in which, in patristic times, Christianity distinguished itself from the varied forms of Judaism, and established among later Christian thinkers a body of theological doctrines of which no exact counterpart exists in historic Judaism.

From the start, Christian pastoral teaching was *cosmopolitan* in its aims: its audience was 'neither Jew nor Gentile, neither bond nor free'. If Judaism was the religion of a particular people and place, the claims of Christianity were directed at people in all lands, at all times from the days of Jesus on. These *universalistic* claims appealed to pre-existing interests in the Hellenism of the eastern Mediterranean, and the debate about the legitimation of Christian practice was thus in new intellectual directions. As a result, Christian Theology entered an ambiguous alliance with Greek philosophy, and ever since the ideas and doctrines of Christianity have been exposed to theoretical critique from philosophers *for internal reasons*; this has only occasionally been true of Judaism, in the case of a few thinkers like Maimonides, who imported issues of philosophical theory into the debate *from outside*.

This contrast between the modes of discussion typical of religious debate in the (practical) Jewish rabbinical and (theoretical) Christian traditions came to a head most strikingly after the Reformation, notably with the theologico-political confrontations provoked by the Council of Trent. Arguably, pre-Reformation Christian theology shared much with medieval rabbinics; the case analyses undertaken by moral theologians within Christian ethics were basically similar to those used by rabbis in framing their own *response* on the basis of the Torah. Even in Aquinas, there is much that is best understood by placing it back in the rhetorical, not the analytical tradition in philosophy.

After 1620, however, the loss of an earlier consensus about the basic world picture, the horrors of the Thirty Years War, and the failure of communication between Protestant and Catholic theologians, were an occasion to look for neutral, rational – or 'logical' – methods of thought and analysis, open to reflective thinkers from any background. This was the source of philosophical rationalism; and, in the renewal of European society and culture after 1648, the history of theology became tightly, if not fatally, bound up with the fate of that rationalism. In medieval Europe, there was room for many coexisting viewpoints or traditions of Christian thought and practice; from the seventeenth century, by contrast, the ruling ambition was to 'prove' the central ideas and theses of theology 'irrefutably'. Hence, the transformation of Catholic doctrine into dogma; hence, also, Leibniz's appeal to the Principle of Sufficient Reason as a criterion for establishing an unchallenged core of ecumenical beliefs.

This conversion of theology from an adventurous speculative task, as in the *Summas*, into an authoritarian system of centrally validated teachings, as in the *Manuals*, has always appealed to the conservatives. (As Evelyn Waugh said in a letter to a friend, written from Jerusalem: 'For me, of course, Christianity *begins with* the Counter Reformation.') The change has also, less happily, tied theology's destiny too closely to that of philosophical rationalism. All that is problematic in Descartes' programme for a 'foundationalist' epistemology, notably, its exclusively *theoretical* aims, has thus become problematic for theology, in which the experiential roots of doctrine in human practice are obscured by an imperious demand for 'proofs'. Almost alone, the Society of Friends has objected to this change, and given the doctrinal aspects of Christianity (*epistēmē/theōria*) second place to the demands of Christian life and practice (*phronēsis/praxis*).

Subsequent challenges to Cartesianism, from Immanuel Kant in the late eighteenth century to Dewey or Rorty in our own day, have undermined the intellectual programme of post-Reformation theology and the personal self confidence of theologians alike. Schleiermacher's hermeneutics was an intelligible extension of Kant's critical programme for philosophy; so the twentieth century theological debate has focused overmuch on establishing the 'very possibility' of a rationally defensible religious belief. (Recall Kant's question, whether any rational enterprise is *überhaupt möglich*, 'possible in the first place' or 'in principle'.) For those who are still mired in the Cartesian tradition, the seemingly 'rational' status of the sciences makes religion problematic, not *vice versa*; and, as a result, Hans Küng lectures on 'Science and the problem of God',[4] not (as we might expect from a believer) on 'God and the problem of Science'.

Theology in transdisciplinary dialogue

What, then, is new in our present situation? At its heart (I argue) is the return to a *practical* conception of theology which had been central to historic Christianity, at least up to the time of the Council of Trent. From this point of view, theological issues cannot be defined in abstract, decontextualised terms; the issues of theology arise, and its concepts are meaningful, only when related to the 'forms of religious life' within which they have a point, and which they presuppose. In this, of course, they are no different from the issues and concepts of mathematics and natural science, let alone in contrast to those ideas. As Wittgenstein used to insist, collectively intelligible concepts of any kind can acquire shared meanings, only to the extent that they are used and understood by people who operate within *Lebensformen*, or 'forms of life', which are themselves sufficiently shared; the word 'innings' is understood by baseball cognoscenti in ways that are only marginally intelligible to fans and players of cricket, and *vice versa*. We can effectively understand the theological principles of Hasidic Judaism, Islamic Sufism or Quakerism, accordingly, only if we recognise how the practice of these varieties of Judaism, Islam and Christianity is distinctive; just as we can master the quantum mechanical idea of complementarity only by recognising how, in actual practice, the physics of Werner Heisenberg and Nils Bohr differs from all earlier physics.

So construed the term 'theology' cannot be read as the name of a separate discipline which exists alongside, and on a similar basis to, other academic disciplines. That would be to make it the product of some prior abstraction by which 'theological' issues were *distinguished* and *separated* from those of systematic botany or French literature. Rather, issues of theology exist, and arise, *at the base of* all abstract academic disciplines equally. Just as problems in the physical theory of relativity can be discussed *philosophically* – note the adverbial form – so, too, problems in ecology and psychoanalysis can be discussed *theologically*: that is, with an eye to their implications for religious life and experience.

This approach to contemporary theology dovetails nicely with some views that Richard Mouw cited from Martha Nussbaum: for example, what she says about the importance of setting aside the rationalist commitment 'to an "ascent" from the perception of particulars to the intellectual grasp of universals' in favour of a commitment to 'a respect for particularity and complexity'. Such a move away from the universal and toward the particular is what we can expect of any shift from an abstract and theoretical conception of theology, as one self contained academic discipline among others, to a deeper concern with concrete, specific details of human experience in the realm of the religious life.

This shift is no ground for 'theoretical despair'; still less does it imply 'nihilism'. Readers nostalgic for Cartesian foundationalism may greet its abandonment with a sense of loss, and rationalise it by talking of Absurdity. But rationalism relied from the start on a misconceived, quasi-Euclidean model of academic disciplines, and in setting it aside in the late twentieth century, we do not *lose* anything. Rather, we acknowledge that, in this respect, seventeenth century 'foundationalism' (both philosophical and theological) led into a *cul de sac* from which we are lucky to escape.

The price that seventeenth century rationalists paid for Certainty was that they turned their backs on the 'particularity and complexity' of human life, not just in the religious field but more generally. If a recognition of human finitude calls for a fresh modesty and humility from future theologians, they are not alone: to quote Richard Mouw again.

> (If) we affectively appropriate these (novel) attitudes, we can display the kind of patience that is capable of tolerating complexities and living with seemingly unconnected particularities, without giving in to despair or cynicism.

Only one comment needs adding. By this step, we join hands with the humanists of the late Renaissance, from Erasmus up to Montaigne, all of whom understood the inevitability of complexity and uncertainty, and were not tempted into the 'dead end' of rationalism.

At this point, we can return to the institutional and organisational issues we began with. The administrative structure of the university today, at least in the United States, is a tribute to the enduring power of rationalism. Most departments are still organised and identified by a commitment to the interests of some individual discipline, conceived of as not merely *distinct*, but also separate, from other parallel disciplines; the central concern of academics is to explore the ramifications of those separate inherited disciplines. As we approach the year 2000, we increasingly recognise the *limitations* of that conception. On more and more levels, any exclusive preoccupation with the ramifications of separate disciplines appears pointless and partial. In particular, if we explore the underlying presuppositions of different disciplines, and the assumptions involved in separating them, we are increasingly led into a *transdisciplinary* dialogue, of a kind to which theology has a distinctive contribution to make.

As I argued elsewhere, the practical ideas embodied in the ecology *movement*, in contrast to the biological *science* of 'ecology' have an inescapably theological colour and significance. In particular, decisions about 'environmental impact' and the like involve judgements of relative priority in the overall scheme of things: weighing the interests of human beings against those of redwood trees, smallpox viruses, snail darters and natural beauties. Many people, it is true, evaluate these choices in utilitarian terms, balancing their prospective benefits for present and future human beings. But such utilitarian calculations are inherently limited: it is no longer self-evident today that the aims and interests of human beings, whether now or in the remote future, can wholly outweigh those of other creatures with which we share this planet.

As Christopher Stone argues, such vulnerable creatures as redwood trees can be said to have legitimate 'interests' and deserve, in principle, to have 'standing' in the judicial and political arenas. Human beings may feel sober confidence that their own affairs have a serious importance, from a cosmological viewpoint; but they are not entitled to assume that their own interests are of exclusive cosmological importance. So the challenge remains, of developing a theological point of view from which to view in proper proportion the relative significance of *human* concerns as compared with those of the rest of nature. For those who speak of the natural world as God's creation, the theological status of these issues is clear enough; but, even for those people who do not explicitly attribute the Scheme of Things to its divine creator, these judgements have a kind of comprehensiveness that makes them nonetheless 'theological'.

Secondly, enduring questions arise about the idea of human nature, and its implications for the social sciences. On this second level it is sad, even embarrassing, to find theologians accepting the jargon and dicta of current sociology or anthropology as binding on their own discussions. For many of the methodological problems that afflict the human sciences today spring from their out-of-date commitment to the older rationalist picture of distinct and separable scientific disciplines. Far from current anthropology and sociology having an authority superior to that of theology, indeed, the human sciences themselves still have something to learn from reflecting on their own assumptions about the nature of human agency, and the responsibility of human beings for what they 'make of themselves'.

For the purpose of practice, not least in pastoral counselling, the affective unity of the human personality (at least, in its unfragmented, non-schizophrenic state) is, surely, a primary datum; so understood, the social, cultural and other characteristics of the human individual are so many abstract features, when considered in isolation from that unity. Rather than leave questions about 'personality disorders' and their care to the discordant diversity of psychiatrists, psychoanalysts, cultural anthropologists and ethnomethodologists alone, the challenge arises of bringing older theological concepts to bear on the understanding of our current mental afflictions. Ideas like 'grace', 'humility', 'conscience' and 'wilful ignorance' refer to *experiential* realities, on which the work of psychiatrists, cultural anthropologists and radical behaviourists may throw light, but can never displace.

If theologians take seriously the *integrating* issues which overlap the concerns of, for example, human scientists or environmentalists, they must be ready to sit down with colleagues from all relevant disciplines, with confidence that they can discuss such issues *as equals*. No discipline has a monopoly on these issues; in the nature of the case, indeed, they do not belong to any *single* discipline. Rather, novel forums are needed, where people from different backgrounds can discuss 'the best that has been thought and said' about these matters in *any* field.

One thing is true in the case both of cosmological questions about the Scheme of Things, and of confessional questions about conscience, the unity of personality, and human finitude: the central, distinctive concern of theology is precisely with the *interrelatedness* of things that, for 350 years, the academy has preferred to keep *separate*. Those years, however, were dominated by a rationalism that we have now put behind us. Recent writers on moral practice are reviving older arguments about the Just War, or the ethics of usury, for the light they throw on current questions about nuclear weapons and third world debt. In other parts of theology, too, our conceptual inheritance from earlier times, especially before the fatal confrontation between radical Protestants and Counter Reformation Catholics, can still guide our understanding of the current problems of humanity, both in the orders of society and culture, and in the renewed engagement of humanity with nature.

Postscript

Let me end on a more idiosyncratic note, with a personal response to one of the issues raised at the New Harmony meeting. The light of our conceptual inheritance will remain available, only while its *content* is preserved and kept bright; and this has implications for *how* theology is taught in the contemporary university. Up to the seventeenth century we saw Divinity had a place in European universities alongside Law and Medicine; the central concepts of Divinity were taught alongside those of Physick and Jurisprudence. To this day, the crucial strength of Anglo-American law schools is, indeed, the straightforward and lucid exposition they provide of the central concepts of civil and criminal law, real property, tort and contract, commercial transactions and the rest. Only a sound and lucid introduction to those concepts puts us in a position to claim either a proper grounding in Law or the preparation needed to research in legal anthropology or the sociology of law.

I was therefore disturbed by what Ronald Thiemann said at New Harmony: *viz.*, that the vigorous debates within the Harvard Law School about 'critical legal theory' *and the like*, mean that the standard courses on, for example, tort and contract can no longer be taught in this straightforward and lucid manner, which, he implied, is now *out-of-date*. Rather (on his account) Law is now taught at Harvard as a branch of social science, in which the practice of law is always modulated by a sense of its social and cultural relativity. To put it more exactly: if I believed that Harvard no longer gives straightforward and lucid courses on the central ideas of Anglo-American legal concepts and practice, I *would be* disturbed. And I would also be worried if theologians took on trust Thiemann's corollary: that the central ideas of theology, too, must now be taught with an eye to their social variability and cultural relativity.

If theology returns to a tradition of *practice* rather than of *theory*, we can take better heart. For what Aristotle says of ethics is then true of theology too. We know for sure from practical experience, he says, *that* chicken is good to eat; only subsequently can we ask *why*, in point of theory, on what conditions and in what respects, this is the case. In the same way, without a sound grasp of the *practical* force of terms like 'negligence' and 'strict liability', we cannot even *pose* the cross-cultural and cross-jurisdictional questions of the social sciences: for example, 'Why do English courts not accept the notion of "strict liability"?' or 'Why did the early medieval Teutonic tribes ignore issues of knowledge and negligence in assessing damages for personal injury?'

Similarly, in theology: only a sound grasp of the traditional ideas of 'grace' and 'conscience' allows us to frame meaningful questions about the theological variations among the styles of religious life and practice in different societies and cultures. So, in this field, something of lasting value may be achieved, if cultural anthropologists pay as much attention to things a sound, historically informed teacher of systematic theology can explain, as is at present the case *vice versa*. The central place that theology has played in the history of western philosophy and science makes a sound, historically informed account of the traditions of religious thought and practice in western Europe and North America as central as ever to the mission of the university today.

Notes
1.   Alasdair MacIntyre, *After Virtue: a study in moral theory*, London, Duckworth, 1981.
2.   R G Collingwood, *An Essay on Metaphysics*, Oxford, Oxford University Press, 1940.
3.   R G Collingwood, *The Idea of Nature*, Oxford, Oxford University Press, 1945.
4.   Hans Küng, 'Science and the problem of God', lecture delivered at Harvard University, 12 November, 1980.

10.2 The place of theology in the study of religion

Edward Farley

Introduction

Our topic is the place of theology in the teaching of religion in colleges and universities. The issue has been on the scene since World War II.[1] What keeps it before us? I must confess a certain confusion and vagueness about what happened in the past decade in departments and programmes of religious studies across the country.[2] I do not possess firm data as to the criteria operative in faculty building, the presuppositions which inform the way the study of religion is parcelled into areas of expertise, and the general direction of change. Something about the present situation permits or invites an enquiry about theology. Here I can only surmise that a rather pervasive anomaly in religious studies is responsible for the persistence of this issue. The anomaly is a conflict or tension between certain requisites created in the origin of religious studies in this country and the character of the resources for faculty. The creation of departments of religion in colleges occurred primarily after the First World War and most of the departments in state universities originated after the Second World War.[3] These programmes either replaced an existing school of religion staffed by local clergy or filled a vacuum. In Europe, especially Germany, the faculty of theology was an integral part of the modern university of the 18th century Enlightenment, and while certain theoretical issues eventually were raised about the propriety of 'theology' in the university, the possibility of religion as an area of serious scholarship was never really questioned.[4] In the USA, however, religious studies originated in a milieu of religious pluralism which eschewed state support for any specific religious tradition. Hence, to gain its credentials in the academic community, it was imperative that religious studies purge itself of any religious parochialism and disengage itself from the prevailing expression of religion in this country, Christianity.

The other side of the anomaly is that the departments and programmes of religious studies are heavily staffed with scholars educated in graduate programmes whose legacy and specialities of scholarship are oriented to western Christianity. The organisation of areas of religious scholarship perpetuates the European theological encyclopedia of the faculty of theology.[5] One result of this anomaly is the continuing failure to propose a unifying subject matter of religious studies and a coherent rationale for divisions of labour. Another result is what might be called the conventional way of formulating the relation between theology and religious studies.

According to the conventional formulation, religious studies names an inclusive programme or department which explores and teaches religion according to the canons of university scholarship.[6] Given these canons, no single religious faith can claim primacy or priority, and religion itself must be interpreted without special pleading and under universal scholarly criteria. Theology, on the other hand, presupposes a specific religious community as its setting, a community which in the past has hindered and even persecuted university sciences. In addition, the almost exclusive educational institution of theology is the professional school for clergy education. Further, the grounds of validity and verification of theology are not universalistic but esoteric, private and authoritarian. The code words for this apparent incompatibility of religious studies and theology are objectivity and neutrality. Some of the literature of the 1950s and 1960s drew the lines this way and then argued that the university in its commitment to the autonomy of reason needed the radical monotheism of the Christian vision.[7]

It seems clear that the conventional view offers us only a pseudo-problem. There are no historical grounds, theoretically or historically, for refusing to teach specific historical religions, for instance Buddhism or Judaism. Religious studies has done that all along. Hence, the legitimacy of teaching any specific religious faith is not in question. Nor are there grounds, theoretically or historically, for affirming an incompatibility between advocacy and scholarship. No university would tolerate teachers of the 19th-century novel, of experimental psychology, of Marxist political science who are utterly neutral toward and utterly disengaged from their subject matter, who see it as having no importance, as making no reality claims. The university assumes that the teacher-scholar is engaged with, affected by and enthusiastic about the subject. For this reason not many modern universities would see D T Suzuki as unqualified to teach Buddhism because he is a Buddhist, or Karl Rahner unqualified to teach Christianity because he was a Catholic priest. Accordingly, there never have been stated valid grounds for the excommunication of Christian studies from religious studies or of scholar-theologians who happen to be in some sense Christian believers. This is why the problem of theology and religious studies cast as two incompatibles is a pseudo-problem. Both advocacy and historical specificity are well-entrenched principles of university teaching.[8]

The conventional way of formulating the problem of relating theology and religious studies is part of our history. Given the recent prevalence of neo-orthodox theologies, and the need to obtain academic credentials for the study of religion, it does not surprise us. At the same time the controlling element in this conventional view is the politics of religious studies, the conditions to be met to obtain entrance into the university. Accordingly, I have expounded the conventional view of the problem only to lay it to rest and to proceed to another and much broader foundation.

This broader view approaches the problem of the place of theology in religious studies primarily as a problem of what it means to teach religion in the university. If that can only be determined, the contribution, irrelevance or compatibility of 'theology' to religious studies may become apparent. Since the teaching of religion in the university depends in part on one's analysis of the aims, trends and problems of the modern university, the route of the analysis will develop as follows. Beginning with a brief depiction of current university education, it then considers the nature of religion itself, and the nature of theology, especially in relation to its frequent caricatures. On these grounds it proceeds to the teaching of religion in the university and, finally, to the role of theology in the teaching of religion.

Technomania and the academy

I shall not use the hackneyed term, crisis, to describe the present situation of higher education. If the term is usable at all, it might describe the *need* for a crisis in higher education. Crisis at least suggests impending and possibly redemptive change. The larger society may or may not be in a crisis. It does seem to be on the threshold of a cultural dark age, the result of a trap modern society has set for itself.[9] The villains are frequently nominated: the international nation-state system; the consumer culture as correlate of the modern multi-national corporation; world population growth out of control. Whatever the culprit, powerful and pervasive historical forces have generated not only new technologies on which most societies now depend, but a new technological mentality. In the past, culture watchers have complained of the dominance of scientific paradigms and their impoverishing effect on education and culture. But the technological mentality must be distinguished from science. If science reflects passion for knowledge, the desire to understand, the technological mentality is the opposite of science, since its thrust is toward the ordering of corporate life. The result is that reality comes to mean data, and data means quantified information pertinent to the ordering (controlling, recording, defending, storing, organising, interpreting) of corporate life. Such is the society and age to which the university must justify its existence and from which draw its support.

Anyone who has to do with the modern university knows that its basic degree programme may not have yielded an educated person. Observations of this sort have been around for a long time. The university is described as a multiversity without unity or overall aim. Or it is said to divide into two cultures of science and humanities with little relation between them. (Three cultures might be more accurate if athletics is included.) If it is the case that an educated person is only rarely the product of the modern university, this may have something to do with the way it reflects the general societal identification of reality with data. The technological mind-set is widespread in the university, not in the sense that its faculty members think of themselves as technicians, but rather that their model for 'scholarship' is a discipline or science whose credentials and criteria are quantifiability and objectification. Thus we have data-oriented research and teaching setting criteria of scholarship for the social sciences, and establishing subtle paradigms of interpretation in history, philosophy, literature and so forth. I do not want to exaggerate this point, to so belabour it that the university is depicted as possessing a single milieu. It simply appears to be the case that educated persons are only rarely the product of the university's basic degree programme and the main reason appears to be the dominance of the technological mind-set as a paradigm of scholarship and teaching.

What do we mean by an 'educated person'? I can only offer some brief suggestions as to what it might mean, what a modern version of Greek *paideia* might be. Consider the following five marks. First, an educated person is sufficiently exposed to a plurality of experiences and modes of interpretation as to be self-conscious in his or her responses, decisions and policies. Second, this self-consciousness has a critical dimension. It is a self-consciousness about evidence, and what constitutes the establishment of a claim, the grounding of a tradition or policy. Third, this criticism reflects the capacity to look behind things and beneath things, to respond not just to surfaces and face values. Looking beneath is characteristic of the Freudian hermeneutical revolution as applied to the individual and the Marxist hermeneutic as applied to the corporate. Fourth, the educated person is self-conscious in his or her general existence in society, in the exercise of discerned obligation. In other words the person knows enough about the workings of local and larger societies to interpret critically issues of social praxis. Fifth, the educated person is sufficiently introduced to the heritage of cultural accomplishments (in literature, music, arts, etc.) as to enjoy aesthetic dimensions of experience beyond those which are commercially and faddishly orchestrated. This is the hedonistic, aesthetic dimension of education. In other words the total impact of the various types of knowledge and modes of thinking which occur in university education has experiential, pluralistic, hermeneutical, critical, rational, political and aesthetic dimensions. The educated person is thus shaped a certain way, and this shaping is not simply the production of capacities of technical functioning but the evoking of ways of existing in and interpreting reality. I realise the tentativeness of such a list. I offer it only to illustrate a serious point, that education in its most genuine sense has to do with capacities of responding to and interpreting the complexities, the various dimensions of reality. The university's current drift toward a data-oriented mind-set and its failure to educate can be turned about only by a new hermeneutical self-consciousness. That is to say, the university needs broader, more flexible paradigms of interpretation if it is to be an occasion and environment of genuine education.

Dimensions of religiousness

Since our exploration concerns religious studies and theology, the frequently posed question of the nature of religion is unavoidable. There are those who would set to rest both that question and the term, religion.[10] Sympathetic as I am to that view, I fear that the loss of a unifying term, religion, would simply turn the whole discussion over to the data-oriented mind-set and the view that 'religion' may not exist but data about religious behaviour does. The value of Wilfred Cantwell Smith's warning is its criticism of religion as a kind of reified historical entity behind other reified historical entities like Christianity or Judaism. The issue posed here is the genre question. What *sort* of *thing* is religion? It seems apparent, first of all, that religion is not a region or entity but an aspect of human, historical and personal processes, events and relations. The grasp of this aspect calls for a complex and flexible posture of interpretation which includes, among other things, philosophical scrutiny of the strangeness of the human being and its experience of the world, as well as a probing of the complex strata of human language. One of the better succinct definitions of religion occurs in an essay of the late Arthur McGill. According to him religion is 'the human response to those superior powers from which man (*sic*) sees himself and his communities deriving life and death'.[11] This definition has several advantages. First, it articulates the sense in which religion poses the issue of the nature of the most comprehensive context of human existence without specifying that context theistically. Second, the concept of human response leaves room for both personal, individual and social or corporate dimensions of response. Thus, Wilfred Cantwell Smith's proposal to replace 'religion' with the two themes of personal religiousness and corporate tradition may indicate two dimensions of this human response.

My own reformulation of the definition would go something like this. The personal-individual aspect of religion (of religiousness) originates in the strange way in which the human being is self-conscious about its own deepest problem and situatedness. The human being exists in the world not in the mode of utter unreflective contentment, indifference or instinctuality but in self-conscious anxiety about the meaning of its experience and destiny. Its most fundamental strivings or desires (for knowledge, meaning, security, happiness, contentment) strive past or through its worldly environment and thus occur on an infinite horizon.[12] When the human being responds to what it contrues that infinite horizon to be (God, Atman, nature, being, sacred powers), this anthropological structure generates religiousness or piety. The institutional-corporate aspect of religion originates concomitantly with the personal-individual aspect since the construal of the nature of the infinite horizon always occurs in connection with language, symbols, myths, processes of traditioning which preserve these things, rituals which enact them, and so forth. If we are in any way close to characterising religion here, we can conclude that religion does pose a real issue, that is to say, an issue of truth and reality. This issue is simply the character of whatever constitutes, empowers, orders, founds or even assaults the comprehensive environment (world) of the human being.

On the basis of this outrageously brief analysis I see three aspects or dimensions of religion which are so constitutive and pervasive that to ignore any one of them would be to distort seriously the interpretation of religion. The first aspect is that about which religion itself is serious, which grounds its seriousness, namely its concern with truth and reality. This is the issue of the nature of the ultimate horizon of human existence. We can call it the issue or aspect of transcendence. The second aspect is religion as a possibility and actuality of human experience. Religion expresses a distinctive way in which the human being is a human being, copes with a dangerous environment, and strives for the meaning of things. Presupposed here are certain ways that the human being is temporal and spatial, linguistic and intersubjective. Expressed here are ways the human being experiences itself as problematic, vulnerable, dangerous and evil. These things name what could be called the anthropological dimension of religion. Because of this anthropological dimension religiousness concerns not only the human being's most comprehensive environment but also its deepest and most comprehensive problematic.[13] The third aspect is the corporate and the institutional. This is the social and cultural sedimentation of (religious) experience which creates continuity over time and enables religion to take the form of complex historical movements. Here we are dealing with religion as a social continuity, a traditioning, an institutionality.

These three aspects or dimensions presuppose, of course, a genre decision and definition of religion. They also indicate three requisites or criteria for any adequate study of religion. In sum they say that religion poses a distinctive truth or reality issue, is a distinctive dimension of human experience, and is culturally specific and concrete. This dimensional complexity is what opens religion to a variety of methods in the social sciences and humanities. This same complexity also poses a subject matter for a focused exploration whose results would remain hidden if the study of religion occurred only in a variety of separate sciences. Because of its dimensional distribution, this subject matter is not identical with simply the phenomenal, historical manifestation of religion in texts, corporate activities, artifacts and the like. For part of that subject matter is that which makes the text important, certain claimed insights into or about a human being in its being toward its most comprehensive horizon and in its deepest problematic.

Theology: toward a working definition

What is theology? The question has been so often posed that one hesitates to raise it on risk of boring the audience to death. Yet, this article is about theology, so a detour around the question is not possible. Like most terms with long history and multiple usage, theology calls forth both caricatures and ambiguities. According to the caricatures theology is the systematic rendition of Scripture, a Christian gnosis whose units are doctrines, a precritical apologetic for beliefs established by church authority, the content of an established system of beliefs, or a now discredited 'metaphysical' mode of objectifying thought. The more serious problem is posed by the ambiguities because these ambiguities are ambiguities of *genre*, ambiguities concerning the kind of thing theology is. The term itself, as is well known, is pre-Christian, occurring in Plato and Aristotle, but it was quickly co-opted by the Christian community as a term for the knowledge or understanding of God and the things of God which attended redemption and revelation. With the rise of the universities in Europe it began to take on connotations of a discipline, that is, knowledge which had a self-conscious basis in demonstration, knowledge made aware of itself by awareness of the ground of the knowledge. With the rise of the modern university in 18th-century Europe, this one knowledge and discipline began to disperse. The Enlightenment produced a number of quasi-independent sciences in the theological faculty (bible, church history, moral theology, dogmatics). Once this happened, the term theology becomes a cluster term for a faculty, a set of disciplines, dogmatic theology.[14] In addition to these usages within the Christian community the term is sometimes expanded to mean any reflective interpretive enterprise of a specific religious faith, in which case there is Hindu theology, Jewish theology and so forth.

Given these historical shifts of meaning, what 'theology' are we attempting to relate to religious studies? In my view the expansion of the meaning of theology to include interpretive undertakings occurring in the major religious faiths is more or less a permanent historical occurrence. It may be the case that in earlier times theology named a distinctively Christian enterprise. Now, however, it appears that all major world religions have a self-consciousness which prompts some of their representatives both to criticise and sift their tradition and to articulate it apologetically in relation to modernity. This expansion prevents us from identifying theology with the self-conscious reflection of any one religion, but it does not, as yet, say what it is.

The only thing I can do at this time is to say what I think theology is in the hope of striking some familiar chords. I begin with a definition. *Theology is the reflectively procured insight and understanding which encounter with a specific religious faith and are evoked by it.*[15] Note the elements of the definition. First, it presupposes the historically incarnated or determinate character of religious faith. Religion occurs in the concreteness of history and culture. Even if there is an understanding evoked by considering major historical religious faiths in their relation to each other, it does not seem to have a theological character. Second, understanding is the sort of thing theology itself is. Accordingly, theology is primarily an understanding and only secondarily a science or discipline. Although I do not want to repudiate the possibility of theology as a scholarly discipline, I see that as one of several levels or forms which understanding might take. This being the case, theological understanding can and does occur in human beings who reflectively encounter a specific religious faith. Hence, it is not restricted to the professional leadership of that faith (the ministeriate, the priesthood, the rabbinate) nor to the academic leadership. Even if each of these groups has a distinctive type of theological responsibility, it has no monopolistic possession of theological understanding. Third, theology occurs in reflective mode. It is not simply the spontaneous insightfulness which may be generated by participation in or encounter with a specific faith. Theological understanding is *considered* understanding. It occurs to some degree as self-conscious understanding and hence has a deliberative, purposive character. The theologically disposed person does what is appropriate to the specificity of the religious faith in order to gain insight. Let me repeat that the understanding in question is directed to the three-fold complexity of the religious faith, not simply to its phenomenal facticity of manifestness.

Finally, that which evokes the understanding is encounter with that faith. I put it this way to avoid making belief-ful participation in the community of faith the prerequisite of theological understanding. It is probably the case that most theological understanding does in fact occur on those conditions. But it seems to me that the issue itself is something of a trap. To ask whether theological understanding is available to the so-called nonbeliever is to pose an unanswerable question. On what grounds does one human being tell another he or she is incapable of understanding or insight? If it is neither possible nor desirable to describe conditions and list credentials for understanding the metaphysical poets, or Goethe's *Faust*, why would we attempt to require such for the reflective understanding of the Tao te Ching or The Letter to the Romans? It is probably the case that there are different types of understanding evoked by Buddhist, Jewish, Islamic and Christian faith. Acknowledging that does not appear to entail the limitation of theological understanding to belief-ful cultic participation.

Hermeneutical principles in the study of religion

What does it mean to teach religion in the university? My exploration of this theme will portray an ideality, not an actuality. At the level of actuality, no clear and coherent answer to the question has obtained widespread consensus. 'Religious Studies', we remind ourselves, does not name a solution to this question. It is a substitute expression for 'department of religion', and therefore names a programme of studies, not a discipline, science or even philosophy of the teaching of religion. Because it does name a department or programme, it implies some unity of approach, perhaps even a subject matter, hence religious studies is distinguished from the 'study of religion' which is distributed among the various sciences of the university.[16] Accordingly, it calls for some way to justify this unified pedagogy and area of scholarship. The existence of a programme or department of religious studies raises the issue of a subject matter correlative to a department or faculty which would be distorted by distribution among various disciplines.

Having in mind the definition of religion treated previously, I venture that the subject matter of religious studies is religion. Named here is not an entity or a field of entities, but an aspect of human experience which has specific, historical and cultural expressions. Religion as religiousness is the individual human being's response to what it discerns to be the most comprehensive powers of its environment. Religion as historical tradition is the corporate and symbolic expression of that discernment rendered into forms of repetition, transmission, institution. If this is what religion is, what does it mean to teach it and investigate it?

I begin with what appears to be self-evident. To teach and study religion in the university is to apply the canons of universal scholarship to religion. 'Canons of universal scholarship' sounds innocent enough, but we recall that the university has no innoculation which immunises it against powerful and prevailing cultural tendencies to reduce reality to data, to the technological mind-set. Hence, 'canons of scholarship' can refer to a very specific paradigm of knowledge, enquiry and method. We are all familiar with the outrageous distortions that any field can perpetrate under the name of scholarship. Scholarship, science, *Wissenschaftlichkeit*, do validly describe the university's aim in the study of religion. But any appropriation of that aim must be critical of inappropriate paradigms and insistent that it is religion itself which is being studied.[17] If religion does constitute a claim about reality, presupposes and shapes human experience, and is perpetually embodied into social forms, the scholarly study of religion will involve a struggle with those dimensions. It needs to be, in other words, scholarship attended by a strong hermeneutical self-consciousness.[18] What then would be some of the features of a hermeneutic of religion?

Since the object or subject matter of a study determines method, and not vice versa, the hermeneutical principles for the study of religion are subject to the nature of religion itself.[19] I have described religion as making a reality claim concerning the widest context of experience, as presupposing and shaping human experience in distinctive ways, and as socially and historically concrete. These features found three hermeneutical principles for the study and teaching of religion: principles of concreteness, experientiality and reality.

The principle of concreteness protects the historical integrity of religion. It serves as a caution sign against subjecting one religion to the canons of another and against translating religion into 'religion in general' or into some wider genus (morality, aesthetics, primitive science, etc.). The actuality of religion is a historical and social actuality and this invariably includes particular origins, traditions, modes of social duration, myths, primary symbols, ritual activities and institutions. Grasping a specific religious faith sets further distinctive hermeneutical requirements to which the student of religion must attend.

Second, the principle of experientiality requires the student to attend to the distinctive way religion presupposes and illumines human being-in-the-world. Does religion, for instance, presuppose the distinctive way in which human beings exist in an imperilling world in the mode of anxiety? Does it assume human temporality and the orientation to the future? Does it not only presuppose these things but does it reshape them, affect them in some way? Is the fundamental way a religion construes the most comprehensive environment of the human being closely connected to a paradigm of the human problem, a paradigm of suffering or moral evil or finite ignorance? Is there a distinctive kind of experiencing or intentionality called forth by sacred power? All these questions address the experiential dimension and call for the kinds of enquiry which can illumine it: psychological, ontological, existential, intersubjective. Furthermore, if this dimension is totally passed over, religion itself remains hidden. Its historical concreteness of symbols, rituals, institutions and the like become external data.

Third, the principle of reality asks the student of religion to take religion's own claims seriously. I previously argued that religion's claims tend to find their unity in the issue of the most comprehensive environment or powers before which human life is conducted. The anthropological correlate of this is the human problem in its most comprehensive, most pervasive, most radical sense: the human problem as suffering, evil, *hubris* or illusion. This correlation between a comprehensive version of the human problem and the ultimate environment of that problem poses reality questions. This reality issue does not go away, as traditional positivism assumes, with modern scientific paradigms of reality and knowledge. It simply exposes those paradigms in their quasi-religious character, insofar as the paradigms pretend to be themselves the exhaustive account of the most comprehensive problem and environment of the human being.

There are subjects which find their way into teaching and study not because of their intrinsic worth or reality claims but because they are simply part of history and culture. Psychologists and sociologists may study the flat earth society, not because of its cosmology, but because it is an unusual, marginal and eccentric cultural curiosity. Without the reality principle, religion (or a specific religion) becomes just this, a cultural curiosity. We study it because, like phrenology, astrology and heavy metal music, it is part of human culture. But the claims religion makes, the issues it poses, are not of the same order as the claims of these examples, that is, relatively straightforward empirical claims which can and should be qualified, tested, revised and displaced. Since religion has to do with the issue of whatever is the most comprehensive setting of (human) life and being in correlation with the most comprehensive version of the human problem, that issue does not disappear or reappear with new empirical discoveries. As an issue it has, of course, a history, and the varying importance of the issue in culture also has a history. Further, any expression of that issue is revisable and open to criticism. Nonetheless, the issues posed by religions attend the human way of experiencing the world. Hence to reduce them to a cultural curiosity is to miss the phenomenon itself. Accordingly, without this hermeneutical principle the study of religion tends to become data-oriented scholarship, distribution among a plurality of sciences, or some reductionistic theory indifferent to religion's own self-manifestation.

These hermeneutical principles do not constitute a specific method, one, for instance, designed to interpret religious texts. They describe what might be called the hermeneutical posture which religion evokes. The advantage of such a formulation is that it does not require the study of religion to arrive at some sort of consensus about a religion behind the religions as the condition of a focused programme of studies. Except as an identifiable aspect of human existence, a way of responding to a mysterious and imperilling environment, there is no such religion. Religious studies does not depend on a consensus about general religion to ground its scholarship or provide it with a subject matter. This situation is not unique in the university. No general theoretical consensus pertaining to human psyche, behaviour, sociality, aesthetics or economics, grounds the enterprises of psychology, sociology, philosophy and the like.

Another clarification: the hermeneutical posture called forth by religion is not an exception in the university, but is an instance of a posture needed by almost every area in the university. Some counterpart to the principles of concreteness, experientiality and reality is important for any subject of serious study. The principle of concreteness seems to have a firm place in the university since the rigour of scholarship tends to be defined as proper methodological attention to detail, evidence, argument and assumption. Such is the legacy of the post-Renaissance and Enlightenment historical consciousness. Yet something is clearly missing if study and teaching stop here. Sophocles' *Antigone*, the vision of things in the religious art of the Italian Renaissance, the French Revolution, the hermeneutical revolutions of both Marx and Freud, and the 17th century metaphysical poets all proffer claims of a sort. Serious response to any of these things is not response to a mere curiosity. To reduce them to curiosities, to suspend the reality question, can only trivialise them. Not only do they release their own kinds of claims upon us, they involve dimensions and depths of human experience. They pose issues of the character of aesthetic experience, historical knowledge and moral decision. It is just these dimensions of science and education which are threatened by the data-oriented, technological mind-set. The point, however, is that when religious studies is fulfilling its scholarly and pedagogical responsibility under the guidance of its hermeneutical principles, it is furthering, not compromising, analogous principles important to a modern university.

The common plight of religious studies and theological studies

According to the conventional formulation of the relation between theology and religious studies, what produces the 'problem' in the relation is theology's subjection to a specific religion. In contrast, religious studies is presumed to be relatively unproblematic. Its credentials are established and its aims are clear. The problem then is to see whether or not theology is an essential violation of these aims. Assumed here are the health and clarity of the university's condition, the embodiment of this health and clarity in religious studies, and the incompatibility of theology with both. The major problem with this conventional formulation is that it obscures the way in which general trends in western culture and in the university have created problems for both religious studies and theology. If there is a structural incompatibility, it is not between religious studies and theology, but between the hermeneutical principles both of them require and the data-oriented methodological commitments and disciplinary loyalties of the university. Earlier on I described the technological mind-set of contemporary western society. Symptoms of this mind-set in the university are the failure of the university to formulate education as a *paideia*, an ideal of the educated person, and the trivialisation and obscuring of subject matters because of technical, expository focus on discrete units of cognition (texts, events, causes, trends, etc.). In other words, the object of knowledge is assumed to be the phenomenal or surface entities which mediate data or are translatable into data.

One effect of this is the primacy and dominance of methodologically defined 'scholarly disciplines' or sciences. The discipline is defined by its methodology and the methodology controls and restricts teaching and enquiry. The primary commitment is, therefore, to the method (and the discipline) so that the object of knowledge cannot then set its own requirements for what is appropriate to understanding it. Given such primacy of method and discipline, the teacher and student tend to restrict their relation to the subject matter to technical, phenomenal exposition and thus are prevented from participation in the claim it makes on them and from really being affected by it. This is the general milieu in which both religious studies and theological studies must justify themselves and make their way.

Theology began to be affected in this direction in the time of the first so-called modern university of Europe. The gains were obvious. Various aspects of corporate religious life (history, texts, events, etc.) could be studied in discrete, critical disciplines which were not subject to institutional or textual authorities. These gains were accompanied by certain losses. One of the losses was theology itself, in the sense of a knowledge or understanding evoked by the claims set by texts and symbols. Theology becomes largely a matter of a professional school, an education pertinent to the priestly or ministerial leadership of churches. In clergy schools, theology is distributed into disciplines, each with its method, literature and guild loyalty. Existing primarily in independent disciplines, theological studies reflect the problem of higher education in general. The primacy of method and the independent discipline removes the obligation to teach religion or theology as reflectively procured understanding which encounter with a specific religious faith and are evoked by it. What is taught are the external units (language, texts, etc.) which scholarship can deal with, plus methodologies defining that scholarship. When these clergy-school disciplines do find their way into the university, their responsibility is neither religion nor theology but the mediation of the graduate school specialities: American religion, western Christian thought, early Christian literature, Old Testament.

It would be misleading to say that religious studies underwent the same historical development. The reason is that while theology (theological understanding) existed to undergo dispersal into disciplines, there never was 'religion' in the sense of some discrete type of understanding which then became dispersed. We have here, then, not, as with theological studies, a paradigm shift in the meaning of religious studies, a shift from religion to religions. Instead, religious studies was formed from the beginning as a programme of studies by appropriating the dispersion of graduate school specialities of Christian studies plus world religions. Present here is not an ostensible subject but a search for a subject. Because of the dominance of methods and disciplines, the search has not been directed toward religion, an aspect of human existence, but toward formally similar structures which generate comparative and typological undertakings. As with theological studies, the onset of religious studies has included important gains, for instance, widespread scholarly expertise in specific world religions. And, like theological studies, religious studies participate in the general poverty of interpretation so widespread in the university. To gain its credentials, religious studies has had to assure a suspicious university community that it is capable of objective scholarly work, that is, data-oriented styles and methods which suspend the hermeneutical principles of experientiality and reality.

In sum, theological studies and religious studies reflect the university's general eschewal of *paideia* and interpretation. This means that they both tend to give primacy to the discipline and make the requirements of the subject secondary. They both pass over the subject by means of a cluster of dispersed scholarly enterprises. The specific disciplines within them tend to bypass language and interpretive categories which might obscure the boundaries of the discipline or compromise the loyalty to the method. Thus they contribute to the general resistance to a hermeneutic of experience and reality which in turn limits the meaning of scholarship to expounding and rehabilitating the unit of scholarly knowledge. Religious studies and theology, therefore, misread the situation when they identify each other as incompatibles. Such a reading obscures the larger forces which are preventing both of them from exploring what religion itself sets as reality claims and the dimensions of experience.

Religious studies: aims, disciplines and postures

We cannot take up our final question, the place of theology and theological studies in religious studies, apart from a more specific consideration of what religious studies itself is. Two principles pertinent to this issue have emerged in the argument. The negative one is that there is no religion behind the religions. This means that there is neither an actuality nor ideality which is an entity, an essence, a universal structure, an archetype, that is, the referent of the term, religion. If this is the case, there is no object of religious scholarship and teaching in any of these senses. The positive principle is a hermeneutical one and was set forth in the three themes of concreteness, experientiality and reality/truth. If there is, in fact, no 'religion' behind the religions, what is it that offers itself for study? Certainly specific historical religions invite study and understanding and this would include both historical discernment of what constitutes them and consideration of what about them poses a claim. These specific historical religions manifest certain aspects of postures of human existence and also certain formal, structural similarities; both the postures and the similarities offer themselves for exploration.

We are thus provided a clue as to the *aims* of religious studies. They would be, first, to explore and teach specific historical religions both at the level of knowledge about them and the level of encounter with the claims they set, the insights they proffer. Second, religious studies would explore and teach the structural similarities of historical religions. Finally, they would attempt to illumine religiousness itself, religion as an aspect of human existence.

If religion is in fact the sort of object suggested here and if it does set these general aims in the teaching and study of religion, then certain hermeneutical postures are indicated. I am not talking about a specific hermeneutic theory but rather about the general principles of concreteness, reality and experientiality. All three together protect the integrity, distinctiveness and seriousness of religion.

I am in no position to suggest how religious studies might in fact embody fields of expertise. Given the aims and hermeneutical principles of religious studies, one thing seems inevitable. Because religiousness exists embodied in specific cultural and historical forms, religious studies inevitably involves scholarly and critical study of specific religious faiths, attempting to do full justice to each one's integrity and uniqueness. We would expect, then, that fields of expertise in religious studies will continue to include scholarly specialities along the lines of major religious faiths. Specialities which coincide with major faiths are, as we know, easily corrptible. Three ways in which scholarly specialities can be pursued so as to undercut the aims of religious studies are especially prominent.

First, the speciality can adopt the trappings of scholarship and at the same time effect an advocacy which is uncritical, unhistorical or obscurantist. The scholarship is a thin veneer for an unhistorical absolutising of the specific religious tradition. Presumably this is a rare but not unknown occurrence in modern universities.

Second, the scholarship of a specific historical religion becomes itself so fragmented into independent disciplines that the individual teacher loses connection with the over-all historical phenomenon.[20]

Third, the scholarly discipline and its method are embraced minus the requisite hermeneutical principles needed by the university and the field of study. Here, the teacher loses the ability to use his or her scholarship to explore and test that which makes the whole undertaking important, the reality claims constituted by the religious faith. Hence, every scholar-teacher has some obligation to teach religion so that its concreteness is honoured, its experiential dimension uncovered, and its reality claims, its potential insights, tested. Thus, any teacher of religion needs both tools which enable scholarly expertise and tools that are pertinent to a hermeneutic oriented to understanding. Without both sets of tools, religion will be taught not as a dimension of human existence but as a collection of relatively independent clusters of historical data.

The contribution of a theological hermeneutic

We turn, finally, to the question of the role of theology in the study of religion which occurs in the university. According to the conventional formulation of the problem, theology's base in an actual religious community disqualifies its objectivity and its capacity to advance the critical and scholarly aims of the university. This article has attempted another formulation of the problem, the steps of which are as follows. First, insofar as the present condition and climate of the university is that of data-oriented scholarship, the 'canons of university scholarship' are not normative but themselves require correction and supplementation. Second, religion remains an elusive subject matter, easily reducible to data and structures, until the dimension of experience which enlivens it is clarified. This dimension of experience (religiousness) is the human response to whatever is judged to be the widest environment which disposes human life. Third, although religion itself exists in specific historical manifestations, certain general hermeneutical principles are requisite to the study of religion. Fourth, 'theology' names an 'understanding' which reflective encounter evokes of a specific religious faith. It can also describe the self-conscious enquiries which a specific religious faith sponsors about itself and from its own perspective. Fifth, the study of religion and theological studies share the common problem of confusion about their subject matter. This common problem is the result of the compromise or elimination of the hermeneutical principles needed by each one due to certain paradigms of modern scholarship. These five items push us to reformulate the problem of theology and the study of religion. *Given these five considerations, how can religion be studied and taught in such a way that its dimensional complexity (religiousness, historical concreteness, reality) is brought to light, and what place, if any, does theology have in these religious studies?*

What this reformulation has done is to shift the ground from the so-called antithesis of theology and the study of religion to the hermeneutical problem common to both and which, in different fashions, attends most of the enterprises of the university at large. It is at the point of a more adequate hermeneutic of religion that the question of the subject matter of the study of religion and the relation of theological studies to such can be clarified.

This article has proposed in tentative fashion some requisites for such a hermeneutic. The proposal arose from a description of religion as including dimensions of truth concern, experience (religiousness) and historical concreteness. This implies that the subject matter of the study of religion is religiousness as it is embodied in concrete historical forms which constitute claims as to the character of the widest horizon of human experience and problem. Apart from the presence of these dimensions, the study of religion becomes the study of a cultural curiosity, or a study of historical data and structures, or the study of some general thing existing above history and culture. Given these requisites for a hermeneutic of religion, a scholarly study of religion, appropriate to the aims of the university, will include studies of specific religious communities which engage the claim of these faiths to truth and reality and which attempt to uncover their experiential and human dimension (religiousness).

These hermeneutical principles for the study of religion help illuminate the aims of programmes of religious studies in the university. The most general aim of religious studies is the critical or scholarly presentation of religion, a presentation that involves both investigation and teaching. However, because of the various dimensions of religion, this general aim contains specific aims. Hence, religious studies would aim at presentations of the pluralism of historical religions, hence, of specific religious faiths. If these specific religious faiths are considered seriously and not assumed to be mere curiosities, their presentation will include their claims to truth and reality as well as their experiential dimension, the religiousness which they embody. The presentation of specific religions through historical and 'phenomenological' comparative studies may also describe an aim of religious studies. If it does, its justification would be its contribution to the illumination of religion and religiousness. When we consider the presentation of religion pedagogically, there again appears to be one general aim. It is to so present religion in its various dimensions so that 'understanding' is evoked. This understanding would include historical information about specific religions, insights evoked by their claims to reality and truth, and the manifestation of religiousness posed by the religious faiths.

We take up now the question toward which this article has moved. What is the place of theology in the study of religion and the programme of religious studies? We recall that theology in its primary sense refers to the reflective effort of a specific religious community to understand itself so as to correct itself and fulfil its aims, under criteria proper to that community. In this sense there are Christian, Jewish, Buddhist, Hindu and Islamic theologies. We note that this reflective effort can occur in ways which compromise or ignore critical modes of thought and also in ways which incorporate the critical mentality.

'Christian studies'

The question of the place of theology in the study of religion reminds us that present-day programmes of religious studies already display the influence of (Christian) theology. The university scholarship of Europe from the 12th century, through the continental Enlightenment, to the present day has produced a number of specific scholarly undertakings ('sciences') which have to do with the interpretation of the Christian religion. These disciplines, mostly of a historical character, have in recent times carried out their work under general and rigorous canons of historical scholarship: thus, biblical studies, church history, historical theology, etc. Although these disciplines reflect a past and present tie with the self-interest and agendas of the Christian religion, they tend not to allow that tie to replace or determine the evidences and proper criteria for scholarly work. This tie with the Christian religion is manifest in the way they appear in and structure the curriculum and pedagogy of schools, especially the schools for the training of clergy. In spite of this tie, these disciplines tend to be selectively independent of each other, and as such, frequently appear in programmes of religious studies under rubrics of the history of western Christianity, ethics and biblical studies. Thus, this residue of the history of studies pertaining to Christianity finds its way into the modern university. This is to say 'Christian studies', in the sense of a cluster of relatively independent fields of scholarship pertaining to the Christian religion, has some presence now in the university.

'Theological studies'

It appears clear that 'Christian studies' do not express an approach or perspective that is theological in character. The theological study of a religious faith is not simply a cluster of independent, historical-critical investigations whose only unity is a historical subject matter. Such a cluster, 'Christian studies', is in fact the historical aftermath of the loss of theology. The conventional approach to theology and religious studies assumes that the introduction of a theological perspective is, in an *a priori* sense, a compromise of the rigour and critical nature of historical scholarship. Such a view identifies theology with precritical modes of interpretation. What in fact happens when the theological perspective is introduced? When theology or a theological approach unifies a set of studies of a specific religious community, there is (as in Christian studies) a historical presentation of that community. This presentation occurs from a perspective of seriousness about the community's reality claims, and about its experiential, human dimension. It does not seem evident that such seriousness is in some *a priori* sense a compromise of general canons of university scholarship. On the contrary there appears to be some coincidence between the hermeneutics of a specific religious faith represented by this seriousness and the hermeneutics required by the study of religion.

The suggestion here is that both religious studies as a cluster of independent historical studies and Christian studies (or Jewish, Buddhist, etc.) as a cluster of independent disciplines, are inadequate to their subject matter as enterprises of both scholarship and pedagogy. Both call for a hermeneutic of religion in which the specificity of religious communities is honoured, their claims to reality are reviewed, and the experiential dimension is explored. Such a hermeneutic is what gives Christian studies their theological character, and such a hermeneutic is what enables the study of religion to recover its subject matter.

The problem of advocacy

Argued so far is that an adequate general hermeneutic of the study of religion is similar to the hermeneutic of specific religions represented by theological study. To the degree that this is the case, theological study and a theological perspective may help to realise the aims of religious studies and to unify the dispersed disciplines of Christian studies. Does this entail a recommendation for departments of religious studies to staff themselves with Christian, Jewish, Buddhist, etc. theologians? The question itself should be avoided. Any policy about staffing a university department or science is unfortunate if it makes that question a question of constituencies. A policy which identifies adherents or nonadherents to specific religions invites the university to either exclude scholar-teachers on the grounds that they are adherents or on the grounds that they are not.

This issue is, however, still before us insofar as the conventional view which posits an antithesis between theology and the study of religion assumes that adherents or participants of a religious faith are disqualified from true scholarship by the *kind* of advocacy they will inevitably pursue. I assume, in putting the question this way, that advocacy is an established principle in the university in the sense of convictions about the importance and relevance of the subject matter, and seriousness to, and openness about, its claim upon the student. There appears to be nothing about the hermeneutical principles of theological study which compromises such advocacy. Nor does there appear to be any reason why a participant in a specific religion necessarily engages in types of advocacy inappropriate to the university. It is also crystal clear that there are adherents of religious faiths (as well as nonadherents) who teach and enquire in ways which do compromise the advocacy and objectivity proper to the university. Hence, there are instances, even in state supported universities, where adherents of a specific religion press the 'one true religion' onto the structure of the department of religious studies. At the same time, violations of the university's principle of advocacy are well known. In such cases the discipline or subject matter is taught from some single, 'true' worldview, or paradigm of knowledge and reality, a paradigm which is presented to the student as virtually a creed. The point being made here is that the violation of the general canons of the university (openness, critical temper, principles of evidence) and the improper exercise of advocacy is a larger problem than one posed by the study of religion, and there is nothing intrinsic about either the hermeneutics of theological study or participation in a religious community which necessitates such violation.

I conclude then that there is a place in the study of religion for: first, the study of specific religious faiths; second, the engagement with those faiths at the point of their reality claims and their experiential dimensions (of theological hermeneutics); and third, there is nothing about these tasks which either requires or disqualifies scholars who happen also to be participants in a specific religious faith.

Notes
1. The 1950s and 1960s marked two decades of fairly frequent publications on the teaching of religion in higher education. This literature includes occasional symposia in which an essay would be included on systematic theology. Thus D D Williams, 'Systematic theology', in *Religion in the State University*, New Haven, Connecticut, Society for Religion in Higher Education, 1965. In addition are several essays or chapters addressing explicitly the problem of theology in higher education. Alexander Miller, *Faith and Learning*, Westport, Connecticut, Greenwood, 1960, pp. 110ff; W G Pollard, 'The recovery of a theological perspective in a scientific age', in J J Pelikan *et al.* (eds), *Religion and the University*, Toronto, University of Toronto, 1964; Paul Ramsey, 'Theological studies in college and seminary', *Theology Today*, 17, 1961, pp. 466–484; Julian Hartt, *Theology and the Church in the University*, Philadelphia, Westminster Press, 1969, chapter 4; and Arthur McGill, 'The ambiguous position of Christian theology', in Paul Ramsey and John F Wilson (eds), *The Study of Religion in Colleges and Universities*, Princeton, New Jersey, Princeton University Press, 1970, pp. 105–138.
2. The post-World War II literature included a number of surveys and studies of the situation. One of the first was Merrimon Cuninggim, *The College Seeks Religion*, New Haven, Connecticut, Yale University Press, 1947, based on a 1941 dissertation at Yale. The two studies by Robert Michaelsen are well known. *The Study of Religion in American Universities: ten case studies with special reference to state universities*, New Haven, Connecticut, Society for Religion in Higher Education, 1965, and *The Scholarly Study of Religion in College and University*, New Haven, Connecticut, Society for Religion in Higher Education, 1964. Another study is M D McLean and H H Kimber (eds), *Teaching of Religion in State Universities*, Ann Arbor, Michigan, University of Michigan Press, 1960.
3. While no full history of the teaching of religion in higher education in the USA has been written, there are several helpful works. See Cuninggim, *op. cit.* A general history beginning with classical antiquity is Jan de Vries, *The Study of Religion: a historical approach*, New York, Harcourt, Brace, and World, 1967. In addition see the essay by T W Merriman, in Amos Wilder (ed.), *Liberal Learning and Religion*, New York, Harper and Row, 1951. A very helpful, bibliographically oriented historical survey of the post-World War II period is the annotated bibliography in the back of Paul Ramsey and John F Wilson, *op. cit.* Wilson's introduction to the volume is one of the most helpful brief surveys of the period.
4. The social and cultural background of the strongly entrenched faculty of theology in the German universities is the territorial division of the country along religious lines and the tradition of the state supporting the three major institutions which presumably contribute to the welfare and order of the society: law, medicine and religion. Hence, the theology faculty exists alongside law and medicine as one of the three higher faculties, higher in the sense of presupposing and building on the faculty of philosophy or basic arts and sciences. In America, the tradition of religious pluralism and the disestablishment of religion prevented state support for clergy education, hence nothing equivalent to the theology faculty arose in the colleges or universities.
5. Speciality fields of theology, ethics, bible (Old Testament, New Testament), American church history, historical theology, religion and psychology, attest either directly or indirectly to the Christian encyclopedic organisation of disciplines. The standard encyclopedic structure is the four-fold classification of disciplines into bible, church history, theology and practical theology. The graduate schools retain a refinement of this, sometimes minus practical theology, and with additions from other religions.
6. It is important not to identify religious studies, a term for a programme of studies, with history of religions, a term for a certain method and perhaps discipline in the programme of religious studies. Given this distinction, the problem of relating theology to religious studies is a different problem from relating theology to the history of religions.
7. H Richard Niebuhr wrote an essay in this tone. 'Theology in the university', published originally in 1955 and reprinted in *Radical Monotheism and Western Culture*, New York, Harper Torchbooks, 1960. The focus was on what a university would look like if it was shaped under radical monotheism, thus a theological portrait of the university. Similar criticisms of the university's uncritical embodiment of autonomous reason are found in the McGill essay *(op. cit.)* and in Miller's *Faith and Learning*.
8. The major essays on religious studies and theology written after 1970 have tended to be presidential addresses at the American Academy of Religion's annual meeting. Two relatively recent addresses are offered by Christian theologians and neither of them works within the conventional formulation of the problem. Both Schubert Ogden and Paul Wiebe

stress the continuity between the aims of theology and religious studies. Obviously, the present article follows in that tradition. See Schubert Ogden, 'Theology and religious studies', *The Journal of the American Academy of Religion*, 46, 1978, pp. 3–17; and Paul Wiebe, 'The place of theology within religious studies', in A Carr and N Piediscalzi (eds), *The Academic Study of Religion*, Chico, California, Scholars Press, 1975.

9. The larger cultural background of the problem of teaching religion in the university is the central focus of William Pollard's essay, 'The recovery of a theological perspective in a scientific age', in J J Pelikan *et. al.* (eds), *op. cit.* Pollard, a physicist-theologian, sees science as setting the dominant styles of thought and he argues that this results in the loss of a whole range of reality attended to by earlier eras. What I am calling the technological or data-oriented mind-set is not so much the effect of science on modern society as a consumerism coupled with the nation-state system. In other words, the *telos* of data orientation is not so much knowledge, driven by the passion for knowledge, but is the satisfaction and maintenance of a consumer oriented economic system which has a strong nationalistic and military component.

10. See Wilfred Cantwell Smith, *The Meaning and End of Religion*, New York, Macmillan, 1962, chapter 2.

11. Arthur McGill, 'The ambiguous position of Christian theology', *op. cit.*, p. 106.

12. This formulation of religion or religiousness is close to David Tracy's language of limit-experiences. See *The Analogical Imagination*, New York, Crossroad, 1981, pp. 156ff. Limit-experiences are primarily a negative formulation of what I have expressed here in positive mode, that is in the language of striving, eros, desire. Both approaches presuppose that what we are talking about is a dimension of human existence and that it becomes specific and socially embodied with the *referent* of the eros or limit-experience as interpreted or designated. Louis Dupré cites Johannes B Lotz' definition of the religious act 'in which man knows not a particular object but the transcendental horizon of the world of objects, that is, the background of transcendent Being which is not clearly perceived in the ordinary cognitive act', *The Other Dimension: a search for the meaning of religious attitudes*, New York, Doubleday, 1972, p. 36.

13. There is clearly correlation between a specific historical religion's version of the widest environment or power and the deepest problematic of human being. If Atman-Brahman names the ultimate power in Hinduism, the fate or trap of *samsara* names its version of the deepest problematic.

14. I have attempted a historical account of the paradigm shifts of the meaning of theology, especially as it occurs in university settings, in *Theologia: the fragmentation and unity of theological education*, Philadelphia, Fortress Press, 1983, chapters 2 through 5.

15. This definition is more in accord with the older meaning of theology which dominated the Middle Ages and into the 17th century. In that older view, theology names a *habitus* or disposition of the mind which has the character of wisdom or understanding. I see something like this as the primary meaning of theology. That being the case, theology as a science, a discipline, a pedagogy, a programme of studies, may be retained but as secondary meanings and modalities of the primary one.

16. The distinction between 'religious studies' and the 'study of religion' is a standard one, although it occurs in a number of different expressions. Schubert Ogden makes the distinction in the terms used above. See 'Theology and religious studies', *The Journal of the American Academy of Religion*, 46, 1978, pp. 3–17. Robert Michaelsen distinguishes between direct and indirect approaches to religion. Indirect approaches refer to the study of religion in disciplines whose primary subject matter is something else: psychology, sociology, philosophy, etc. Frank Reynolds distinguishes approaches to religion in which religion is studied as an aspect of some other dimension of human experience (thus, psychology, sociology, etc.) and in which religion is studied as itself a 'dimension of human life'. See 'Maps, models, and boundaries', *Criterion*, 20, 1981, pp. 26–31.

17. A similar point is made by Louis Dupré in his critique of what he calls the objective fallacy. He argues that the acknowledgement that religion is a *fact* does not imply that the method of studying it is simply objective method. Suggested here is that religion is a dimension of human existence and this makes it a strange sort of fact requiring methods able to bring that dimension into view. See *The Other Dimension: a search for the meaning of religious attitudes*, New York, Doubleday, 1972, chapter 2.

18. The term, hermeneutic, which occurs frequently in this article, is being used in a very broad sense. Its strictest and probably most proper meaning is that of a theory of interpretation which is oriented primarily to written discourse, to texts. I am using the term to refer to a theory of interpretation itself. Hermeneutic self-consciousness would be the self-consciousness about the requirements of what is to be studied, understood, known.

19. For the primacy of subject over method and a strong criticism of the fetishism of method, see Wilfred Cantwell Smith's essay, 'Methodology and the study of religion: some misgivings', in Robert D Baird (ed.), *Methodological Issues in Religious Studies*, Chico, California, New Horizons Press, 1975, pp. 1–30.
20. Given the splintering of Christian theological disciplines since the 18th century, we should not be surprised by the existence of scholars of Christian studies who are so narrowly specialised that they are unable to interpret Christianity itself; thus a modern philosophical movement but not the bible, Old Testament but not any major theme of Christian tradition, early Christian gnosticism but not the larger corpus of early Christian literature, moral agency but not theology. In contrast it seems characteristic of Jewish scholars to be able to be interpreters of Judaism whatever their specialties.

10.3 Theology: university and church. Is a synergism possible?

Claude Welch

Introduction

My focus is on the question: 'Can there be or should there be in our contemporary American culture a symbiotic relationship of university and church theology?'

That is an intriguing question on which to reflect, for it embraces a couple of ambiguities, providing ample chance to raise questions for discussion. Are we thinking of church theology and the modern university in general, or of 'church theology' and 'university theology' (or study of religion)? Both are possibilities, even though they may well intersect. Mainly, I shall want to orient my remarks to the former question, though it may also turn out that we have to talk of university theology.

The other ambiguity, equally interesting, resides in the term 'symbiotic' which can have either positive or negative connotations. Strictly speaking, in the biological world symbiosis means a relationship of two or more different organisms in a close association that may be but is not necessarily of benefit to each. In common parlance, I think the term symbiotic tends to carry a negative freight. And surely it is possible, if one is concerned primarily with description of the current state of affairs, to characterise the relation of the university to church theology in the language of tension or even conflict. But the question also is, can there be anything better? And the other possibility, if one is to talk about what should be, is also genuine. Yet if we move in this direction we might want to substitute for symbiotic the word 'synergistic', which in biological terms refers to an action of two or more substances, organs or organisms to achieve an effect of which each is individually incapable. That, frankly, is the possibility I should like to explore, hence the subtitle for this article of 'Is synergism possible?' I shall want to suggest that at least in one important area, the university in its enquiry in general and in its concern with religion in particular, and the church in its theological enquiry, can and should be mutually fructifying. To this end, I shall say something about the university, about the study of religion, and about theology.

Some threats to theology

Before we come to those matters, however, we need to do a bit of ground clearing with respect to the state of the church and theology in contemporary US culture, so that my biases can be made clear at the outset.

First, I have to express my conviction that the theological enterprise is currently gravely threatened, and not mainly by the continuing marginalisation of religion in American culture, but especially by tendencies within the religious community. For one thing, there has been the renewed tide of reaction in both Catholic and Protestant circles, even to the point where the great ecumenical question is no longer the problem of ecclesiastical divisions, or of recognising and expressing unity among the churches, but theological and social divisions that cut across denominational or Catholic/Protestant lines. The great divide is the gulf between so-called liberal and conservative, or more properly put, between those who accept the historical critical method and those who do not. (Some, of course, would want also to speak of the division between the privileged and the oppressed, or between the political and economic liberals and conservatives.) I do not see that this kind of gulf in Protestantism has been closed at all by the recent tragicomedies in the televangelist world. Nor do I judge that the crisis of authority in Roman Catholicism is being overcome, certainly not by media-hyped papal junkets to all parts of the world. Both Catholic and Protestant communities are in danger of slipping (or running) back into a defensive posture or fortress mentality like that of a Pius IX or a Princeton orthodoxy in the nineteenth century, only this time often with the added dimension of an aggressive association of theological fundamentalism with political and economic conservatism.

Parallel to that sort of threat, or perhaps a function of it, is the move toward ecclesiastisation (as well as professionalisation) of theological faculties. One thinks of the frightening implications of canon 812 of the 1983 Code of Canon Law, with its requirement of a special canonical mission or mandate for all teachers of theological disciplines in any (Catholic) institute of higher studies, or the recent Vatican investigation of Catholic theological schools. The suspension of Charles Curran is only the most dramatic illustration of the problem as it relates to academic freedom in the university. The question has to be raised whether, on such lines, a Catholic university can be a real university at all.

I cannot here explore in general the idea of a Catholic university (or any 'Christian' school) or the question of the rights of ecclesiastical bodies to prescribe or circumscribe the kind of theologising that may be permitted within institutions so denominated. That would prevent us from getting to the specific point I want to make. But I must state my theological conviction that any Christian theology in the university or in the church must be free theology, and that this freedom derives from the very nature of the act of faith, which cannot be compelled, but requires the freedom of dissent within the church. The freedom to which the university is committed and the freedom of faith, I believe, mutually support each other. To this we may perhaps return.

But let us remind ourselves that the problem of ecclesiastisation and denominational control is no less a question for Protestants than for Catholics. Witness the explosion at Concordia Seminary and the emergence of Seminex among the Missouri Synod Lutherans. Witness the continuing struggles for control of the seminary boards among the Southern Baptists, with a view to the ensuring of a 'right' theological stance of the faculty. Witness even the attempts at the national Methodist level to develop a parallel accreditation procedure for schools at which Methodist seminarians study. These are only some of the indications of a pervasive ecclesiasticising kind of threat to theology.

A third sort of threat to the theological enterprise is more internal to recent theological attitudes and trends. I have in mind especially what I see as a centripetal tendency toward a Christomonistic, or Christo-ecclesiastico-monistic kind of theology. One might call it a Jesus-ology, or in H R Niebuhr's phrase a unitarianism of the second person of the Trinity. Some will naturally think of a Karl Barth in this connection. But I have in mind a much broader, non-Barthian, tendency and mood, a Christian inward-turning and inward-looking. This is harder to document except at great length, but I sense it among many of my colleagues, both Protestant and Catholic, in the Graduate Theological Union and elsewhere. One can see signs of such a Christo- or Jesus-monism in such widely disparate theologies as the 'radical theology' of the sixties and the liberation theologies of the seventies and the eighties. And I note this as a danger because it runs precisely counter to the positive direction that I want shortly to urge.

Now I would suggest that all three of these threats, though perhaps in differing ways, represent a failure to reflect the historical consciousness that is essential to responsible enquiry in our world. And this requires me now to comment briefly in general about the demands of the modern university and its canons of enquiry, about the proper hermeneutics of the study of religion in the university, and about the business of theology.

Canons of enquiry

Without pretending to any full scale analysis of what the modern university is or ought to be, or assuming that the 'modern' university is an absolute norm for the future, I propose that among the essential characteristics of the university are certain norms of 'universal scholarship', universal in the sense that we must all be bound by them. These include the canons of common and public enquiry and criticism, canons of openness and critical temper with respect to all claims to knowledge and truth, and principles of evidence. Granted that distortions of those canons regularly occur in the scholarship that goes on in the university, lapses into dogmatism, false scientisms under the banner of *Wissenschaft*, both outright and unconscious dishonesties, corruptions by personal and class interests, and the like. The hermeneutic of suspicion, from Marx, Nietzsche and Freud, has helped us to recognise those distortions. But the norms of freedom, critical temper and openness, which have come to us from the Renaissance and the Enlightenment, remain indispensable for enquiry in the university. And these have been intensified by the rise of the modern historical consciousness, which began to flourish in the nineteenth century and of which the hermeneutic of suspicion is now an essential ingredient.

Such canons require certain principles for any study of religion or theology in the university. For example, the historical integrity of religious phenomena must not be compromised: no particular religion can be subjected to the canons of another (or translated into some 'religion in general'). The study of religion must attend particularly to the experiential dimension: the psychological, the existential and the intersubjective, that is, the peculiar way religion expresses human being-in-the-world. And any religion's own claims for truth must be taken seriously.

Comparable principles, of course, are needed in almost every area of university scholarship, at least in the social and the human sciences. Questions of truth and value cannot be avoided. Yet these elements of the posture of scholarship are distinctively illuminated by religious studies, by the study of religion with its reality claims and its experiential dimensions.

This is at once to say that the supposed antithesis between religious studies and theological studies is quite false. The study of religion cannot avoid theological kinds of questions, without being reduced to the examination of a kind of cultural curiosity. (Without living religions, religious studies has no *raison d'être*, any more than political science would have a point if there were no living politics.) And both religious studies and theological studies have to stand in opposition to the merely technological, data-oriented and presumably value-free or 'objective' mind-set that too often dominates the idea of enquiry in the university.

What is distinctive about theology, I take it, is that it presupposes an encounter with a particular religious language and culture. Often it has been argued that theology is a peculiarly Christian activity. But I think it is now rightly recognised that the word can be appropriately applied to self-conscious reflective-interpretive activity in any religious community. As such, it is not at all the exclusive prerogative of a professional class of 'theologians' but an enterprise of insight and understanding that is available to all, provided it is reflective and considered understanding. Nor does theology, I believe, require 'believing' membership in the community of faith, so that theological understanding would be unavailable to the so-called unbeliever. For I do not see how we can set limits to the possibility of insight or understanding on the part of other persons. What is required is genuine encounter with the particular community of faith, out of which articulation of reflective understanding can arise. This community of faith is the context or frame of reference for insight and criticism.

And that raises again the question whether all good religious study does not become in important respects theological study, and whether (as argued by Lindbeck, 1984) theology does not need to learn from the cultural and linguistic approaches of religious studies. So also the further question, which I shall not pursue in general terms, whether or how theology in the university is different from theology in the divinity school or seminary.

A possibility of synergism

All that I have said thus far is preliminary, or context, for the particular point that I want to argue in the remainder of this article. This point, most simply put, is that in the question of the relation of Christianity to other religions, the interests of the university, as expressed especially in its studies of religion, and the interests of theology in the church, are coming to a remarkable coincidence, so that we can indeed speak not of a merely symbiotic relation, but of a synergistic relation.

It is of course obvious that 'religious studies' in the university have a heavy investment in comparative studies of religious traditions, histories, theologies, symbols, personalities, ethics, rites, etc. That is as it should be, in accord with the canons of scholarship in the university. And the past century and a half have brought us a vast accumulation of knowledge and even understanding of the 'varieties of religious experience'. The process continues.

What may not be so evident is the extent to which the problem of religious or 'world-view' pluralism has now moved to the centre of the stage for theology in the church, both Catholic and Protestant, so that the prime question is one of a theology of religions, which greatly overlaps with, though it is not the same as, the study of the 'history of religions' or 'comparative religions'.

This movement has been a long time in coming. An appreciation of the value and inner integrity of other religious traditions really began to emerge in the early nineteenth century, with a new kind of recognition of Christianity as one faith among others and the beginnings of the modern study of comparative religious history. Partly as a result of the missionary movement, both Hinduism and Buddhism experienced a renaissance in the nineteenth century, and the World Parliament of Religions, held in Chicago in 1893 in conjunction with the Columbian Exposition, stimulated the introduction of Buddhism and Hinduism into the West. As a consequence of all this, many religious thinkers (chiefly Protestants) were prepared to qualify the traditional claim to the exclusive truth of Christianity, understanding that the Christian religion is truly part of general religious history. Mostly, however, such interpreters wanted still to maintain that among all the religions, Christianity is the 'highest' or 'final' revelation, and they often understood this as the culmination of an evolutionary process in human religious understanding.

These thrusts of interpretation were generally stalled, or sidetracked, by the emergence of the post-World War I dialectical theology or neo-orthodoxy. For such thinkers as Brunner and Barth all emphasis had to be laid on the uniqueness of Christian faith, on the once-for-allness of the revelation and reconciliation in Christ, on the utter Christocentrism of Christianity (even to the point, in the early Barth, of insisting that the encounter with God in Christ is not a religion but a critique of all religion).

With the fading of the Barthian dominance, however, the second half of the present century has seen a powerful resurgence of the question of Christianity and other religions. This has been forced by many factors. The awareness of other traditions has been acutely sharpened by world events, including the Second World War, the establishment of the State of Israel, the Korean and Vietnam wars, the struggles in the Middle East and the emergence of a virulent Islamic fundamentalism, and the flood of Asian refugees into the countries of the West. With the new recognition of other cultures, 'inculturation' has become the slogan of all missionary work. And despite the fractious and divided character of the world, some sense of a common human community has begun to grow. Wilfred Cantwell Smith believes it even possible to speak of the emergence of a 'corporate self-consciousness, critical, comprehensive, and global', which means that 'the truth of all of us is part of the truth of each of us' (Smith, 1981, pp. 78–79).

The scholarly study of the world's religions has grown explosively (and not only of the great living religions, but also of primal religion, archaic religions, minor religions and quasi-religious worldviews such as Marxism). This has led both to new appreciation of the diversity within every religion and to recognition of the important periods of historical interactions among the great traditions, for example, of Judaism, Islam and Christianity in the medieval West, and of Christianity and Asian religions in connection with the nineteenth century missionary movement. Scholars have pointed to common symbols and mythic patterns among the traditions and to specific stories, ideas and practices that have circulated in different religious contexts and forms (Smith, 1981, pp. 7–11).

The twentieth century has also seen the emergence of 'new religions' in Japan and of a powerful Islamic fundamentalism. Various Buddhist traditions have been active in seeking to plant themselves in the West. And many of the so-called new religious movements that began to flourish in the United States have been mixtures of eastern and western motifs. And should one not also recall the emergence of distinctively new forms within Christianity, for example, in Korea and Japan, in Africa and in Latin America?

Finally, it is symbolic of the new mood that Ernst Troeltsch has become again a centre of intensive study and influence. It was Troeltsch at the end of the nineteenth century who offered a powerful argument for real religious pluralism and relativism, in which the religious experience of, for example, Buddhists had to be recognised as just as valid for them as Christian experience was for Christians (Troeltsch, 1923).

All these factors have profoundly affected the Protestant and Catholic theological interprise. Symptomatic of the depth of reconsideration required is the publication by Paul Tillich, after his trip to Japan, of the small book entitled *Christianity and the Encounter of the World Religions* (1963), in which he argued strongly for Christian self-criticism in light of the encounter and for dialogue instead of conversion. Shortly before his death, Tillich asserted in a lecture of 1965 that he would like to rewrite his entire *Systematic Theology* 'oriented toward, and in dialogue with, the whole history of religions' (Brauer, 1966, pp. 31, 91).

We must leave aside here the question of the relation of Christianity and Judaism. That is a special case for Christian self-understanding. Apart from this, we can distinguish several theological positions and attitudes toward interreligious encounter.

One position is that of Christian absolutism or exclusivism. This is generally the traditional view, namely, that the revelation/salvation in Jesus Christ is alone valid. All other religious claims, while there may be elements of truth and salvific power in them, are fundamentally wrong or even pernicious. This view empowered the older missionary attitude, in which the goal was to convert the 'heathen', including Jews and Muslims. It is a church-centred view, classically expressed in the slogan, *extra ecclesiam nulla salus*. And this exclusivism is still powerful in Christian circles. On the Protestant side, it is the dominant view among fundamentalists and the new evangelicals. While many of the new evangelicals would be hesitant about consigning to hell every person who had never heard of Christ, widespread support has been given to the 'Frankfurt Declaration' of 1970: that salvation is possible only through participation in faith in the sacrificial crucifixion of Jesus Christ, which occurred once and for all and for all mankind; that the non-Christian religions are not in fact ways of salvation similar to belief in Christ; and that the idea of a 'give-and-take dialogue' must be rejected in favour of proclamation that aims at conversion. And this uncompromising position was reaffirmed at a large gathering of evangelicals at the International Congress of World Evangelisation, held in Lausanne in 1974.

The Christian absolutist position, however, has in recent years been brought under heavy theological attack from a variety of directions. All these new views recognise some kind of relativity in all religious claims (though not an unqualified or indifferent relativism) and they focus on the meaning of 'salvation' as authentic present human life and fulfilment more than as some 'future state'. Christian imperialism of the old sort is rejected and mutual learning is sought. With a heightened appreciation of other traditions, both common elements and real differences are identified.

One form of the attack on Christian absolutism is a revival of the view, common in the nineteenth century, that all religions are finally the same. I do not mean here the vulgar popular idea that differences are simply irrelevant, all religions being equally valid ways to salvation, but much more sophisticated ways of saying that at bottom all religions have something in common, a fundamental religious experience which is articulated in varying ways. Some of these rely on the influential argument of Rudolph Otto that religion roots finally in the sense of the 'numinous' (a view rooted in Schleiermacher). Others emphasise the psychological commonality (for example, along the lines of Jung's archetypes). Or, in Eliade's language, stress is laid on similarities of 'hierophanies'. Still another way of putting the sameness, which has deep roots in eastern thought, is in the idea of the 'perennial philosophy', a term popularised some years ago by Aldous Huxley (Huxley, 1945). Variations on this theme have been put forward by several interpreters of Hinduism (Ananda Coomeraswamy and René Guenon) and of Islam (Seyyed Hossein Nasr) and in the recent writings of the Protestant Huston Smith (Smith, 1976, 1982). Fundamental to the perennial philosophy is the idea that the core of all religion lies in the mystical or esoteric experience of the ultimate unity or 'nonduality' of God and the self. Mystical experience is judged to be the well-spring of religion and is basically the same in all religions. The differences arise at the secondary or exoteric level of belief and practice and are to be understood as functions of historical and cultural contexts.

A quite different way of pointing to sameness in the religions, impressive and subtle in its argumentation, may be seen in the series of works by the distinguished historian and philosopher of religion, Wilfred Cantwell Smith, which has culminated in *Towards a World Theology: faith and the comparative history of religion* (Smith, 1981). To be sure, Smith expressly rejects the idea that all religions are the same, or even that one religion is the same. Also, he has vigorously rejected the notion of an essence of religion, arguing in *The Meaning and End of Religion* (Smith, 1963) that even the word 'religion' should be abandoned.

Instead of the undifferentiated and blanket term religion, Smith proposes that we speak of 'faith' and 'cumulative tradition'. Faith is an adjectival quality of a person's living, an 'inner religious experience of involvement of a particular person; the impingement on him of the transcendent, putative or real'. Cumulative tradition is 'the entire mass of overt objective data that constitute the historical deposit, as it were, of the past religious life of the community in question: temples, scriptures, theological systems, dance patterns, legal and other social institutions, conventions, moral codes, myths, and so on; anything that can be and is transmitted from one person, one generation, to another, and that an historian can observe' (Smith, 1963, p. 141).

With respect to the cumulative traditions, Smith's work has been remarkably fruitful in identifying ways in which the traditions have in fact historically interacted with each other, so that their histories can only be understood in terms of each other 'as strands in a still more complex whole'. 'The unity or coherence of humankind's religious history' is both an 'empirical fact' and a 'theological truth', and we now see indeed a world process of religious convergence (Smith, 1981, pp. 3, 6, 44).

But faith, understood not as a fixed something but as an existential quality or psychological act or spiritual state of personal being, does seem to be the same for Smith in all the traditions (and Smith's descriptions seem regularly to draw on Christian ideas of faith). The contents of faith may take myriad forms, to be sure, but the human activity which the term 'faith' denotes is a reality common to all 'religions'. And Smith also appears to hold that there is a commonality in the reference of faith to some transcendent level of reality. Thus in the end it seems fair to view Smith as a representative of the claim that despite all the differences in their histories, there is a sameness in the religions. And on the basis of this commonality, as well as their historical interactions, and especially the growing convergence, Smith can urge that we pass beyond 'dialogue' to 'colloquy'.

A second major departure from the Christian absolutist view, which has been winning wide adherence among both Protestants and Catholics, has been called 'inclusivist' (for example, by such interpreters as John Hick, Alan Race and Paul Knitter). Here one can speak of a shift from the church-centredness of the exclusivists to a new sort of Christ-centredness.

On the Catholic side, some see this view as a legitimate extension of the pronouncements of Vatican II. Without abandoning the dictum that there is no salvation outside the church, and while maintaining that the true Church of Christ subsists in the visible institution of the Roman Catholic Church, the Council did move beyond earlier efforts to open the door to participation of non-Christians in God's universal salvific love, efforts that were found in such notions as 'baptism by desire' or 'implicit faith', through which individual nonbelievers could be said to belong to the 'soul' of the church or to be imperfectly or 'tendentially' members of the church. In the 'Declaration on the Relationship of the Church to Non-Christian Religions', Vatican II could speak appreciatively of the strivings of other religions as such and could recognise that they 'often reflect a ray of that Truth which enlightens all men' and that Hinduism, Buddhism and Islam do contain what is true and holy. Thus prudent and loving dialogue should be encouraged. Yet the Council remained ambiguous on the question of how effective the truth and grace in other religions are for salvation, since Christ's Catholic Church is the all-embracing means of salvation, where alone the fullness of the means of salvation can be found. And in the decree on missionary activity, the Council treats dialogue as a means to conversion.

A much clearer and bolder Catholic expression of the inclusivist view is found in Karl Rahner's theology of religions. Starting from the basic Christian assertion that God desires to save all humankind, and the corollary that God will act on this desire, Rahner presses to the idea that human existence is constituted by openness to infinite mystery and is infused by grace. Thus revelation is universally a part of human existence, and the experience of God is inherently salvific. It follows that grace cannot be excluded from other religions and that non-Christian religions can be 'a positive means of gaining the right relationship to God and thus for the attaining of salvation, a means which is therefore positively included in God's plan of salvation'. As Christianity understands salvation to be worked out in community, so Hindus and Buddhists work out their salvation in their religions. This is not, for Rahner, a denial of the Christian claim that the event of Jesus Christ is the final cause of all saving grace, that is, the goal and norm of the entire process of universal grace. So Rahner was led to the idea of 'anonymous Christianity', a hidden reality of grace and truth outside the visible church, which is grasped in a clearer, purer, more reflective and explicit way in Christianity.

It may be argued, of course, that this idea rests on an epistemological limitation, an aspect of the relativity of points of view: from a Christian standpoint one may say that the Buddhist is an anonymous Christian, yet the Buddhist could similarly say that the Christian is an anonymous Buddhist (Rahner, 1966).

A somewhat comparable view was expressed in Hans Küng's early idea of the 'ordinary' way of salvation in the world religions and the 'extraordinary' way in Christianity. This view of Küng seems to allow for a permanent validity in the non-Christian religions but at the same time to assert that Christianity is the essential 'critical catalyst' for other faiths, the full realisation of the revelation they possess.

What is at work in this sort of 'inclusivism' is a commitment to the centrality of Christ as the final definition of truth and salvation, but without the church-centredness that holds all salvific action to be mediated through visible connection with Christianity. The truth and grace that are genuinely found in other religions, and that make real dialogue possible, are thus (for Christians) included in Christ.

Such a view is not far from that of several influential Protestant interpreters. Knitter even calls this the 'mainline' Protestant position, and sees it in the affirmations of people like Paul Althaus and Emil Brunner of a general or universal revelation in humanity, an 'original revelation' or 'creation revelation' which comes to expression in other religions. Whether these Protestant expressions really represent the sort of inclusivism I have in mind here, is not as clear to me as it apparently is to Knitter. But at a minimum, there is for such thinkers a positive connection with the apprehensions of other religions, a preparation or point of contact for the gospel of Christ, which remains of course the final norm for interpretation.

A more clear cut expression of inclusivism I find in Wolfhart Pannenberg, who puts the matter in terms of the historical and future-oriented character of human existence. Full revelation can come only at the end of history, yet the history of religions is 'the history of the appearing of the divine mystery which is presupposed in the structure of human existence'. Respect for the immediacy of the other religions to the divine mystery is required of us. Pannenberg thus eschews the description of non-Christian religions simply through Christian glasses, while at the same time holding that in Jesus the coming reign of God is known by anticipation and that Jesus' pointing away from himself to God and his self-sacrifice of his individual existence for the sake of his mission 'is a decisive condition for the infinite God becoming revealed through him'. Christians can thus learn from other religions and assimilate their truth, though in the end it is the Christian understanding of the God of the future which provides the norm (Pannenberg, 1971).

In the work of M M Thomas, of the Church of South India, the language is closer to that of the Catholic inclusivists, particularly to that of Karl Rahner's anonymous Christianity. For Thomas, it is only in Christ that human self-centredness and self-justification can be overcome. But the Christ who is the one saviour is a cosmic Christ, whose work is not restricted to the church but is to be found in all history, including especially the history of Hindus and Buddhists. Christ both relativises and affirms all religions, including Christianity, and cannot therefore be confined to one religion. This is not to say that all religions are equally manifestations of the truth, but if Christianity has in Christ the universal ultimate truth, we are to seek in dialogue with other religions their positive response of faith in the cosmic Christ (Thomas, 1969, 1980).

A final important example of the inclusivist perspective, though one that may also go beyond it, is the process theologian John B Cobb Jr. In *Christ in a Pluralistic Age* (Cobb, 1975), he developed a position intended to incorporate both the spirit of mutual recognition and the essential Christian commitment to Christ as 'truly supremely important'. All beliefs and attitudes are relative, not in the unqualified sense that any notion is as good as any other, but in the true sense that every view is historically and culturally conditioned. How then to accept the integrity and achievements of another religious tradition (for example,

Buddhism in particular) and maintain the centrality of Christ? Cobb's way of solving the problem was to interpret the idea of Christ as the power of creative transformation, which is apprehended through Jesus but is not bound to any particular religious system. Christ is the Logos and the Logos is literally incarnate in Jesus. But Christ is not simply a name for Jesus. Christ is the creative transformation which, in Whiteheadian language, transcends all particular instances but is present in all in varying ways and degrees. Thus Christ, for Christians, is 'the Way that excludes no Ways' (Cobb, 1975, p. 22).

In *Beyond Dialogue: toward a mutual transformation of Christianity and Buddhism* (1982), Cobb seems to go further. 'Beyond dialogue' means not only abandonment of all Christian absolutism but conversation in which each partner is truly open to learning from the other and therefore to being transformed by the other. Convictions are not absent but are subjected to the light of criticism and radical questioning, and for Christians this includes the ideas of Christ and of divine transcendence. Cobb is chiefly concerned with the mutual criticism and transformation of Mahayana Buddhism and of Christianity. Both see themselves as universal traditions, yet both must be recognised as constantly changing movements. Thus 'a Christianity which has been transformed by the incorporation of the Buddhist insight into the nature of reality (for example, Nirvana) will be a very different Christianity from any we now know. A Buddhism that has incorporated Jesus Christ (for example, Amida is Christ) will be a very different Buddhism from any we now know.' Christians will not abandon Christ and Buddhists will not abandon Emptiness. Differences will not be obliterated, but 'the lines that now sharply divide us will increasingly blur' (Cobb, 1982, p. 52).

In *Beyond Dialogue* Cobb verges toward a third major line of critique of Christian absolutism. This we may see as a still more pluralistic view of dialogue among the religions (or as some have suggested, a 'theocentric' view in contrast to 'Christo-centric' and 'inclusivist'). In the inclusivist approach, dialogue is theologically essential because of the recognition of full, authentic human life in others' religions, yet ways are found to attribute this authenticity and salvific power to the work of Christ, who remains unique and normative. In the more pluralistic approach, on the other hand, the claim for the finality of Christ is recognised as precisely the obstacle to mutual appreciation and understanding. This claim has thus to be suspended or, to put it another way, Christology becomes an open question.

From this perspective we have doubtless the strongest rejection of Christian imperialism. And we may see forerunners of such an attitude in Ernst Troeltsch and especially in the 'confessional' approach of H R Niebuhr, for which any claim of the Christian religion to universal empire or sovereignty is utterly incompatible with the sovereignty of God and the real meaning of revelation (Niebuhr, 1941, pp. 38–42).

The English theologian John Hick (of Birmingham and Claremont) is a well-known representative of this pluralistic view (see Hick, 1980, 1984). Arguing that the universe of faiths centres on God rather than any religion, he has proposed that each of the world religions has served as a means of revelation and (following Karl Jaspers' suggestion of an 'axial period' in human history, beginning about 900 or 800 BC) that independent 'seminal moments of religious experience' occurred in each of the four centres of civilization: in Greece (Pythagoras, Socrates and Plato), in the Middle East (the Hebrew prophets and Zoroaster), in India (the *Upanishads* and the *Bhagavad Gita*), and in China (Confucius and the *Tao Te Ching*). In each of these cultures and their subsequent histories one is to see the divine Spirit at work. With this emphasis, Hick incorporates the theme of 'sameness' in the religions. In each of the great traditions we see a distinction between the Real in itself (or his or her self) and the Real as humanly experienced, that is, between a higher Reality and a human relation to the Real. And by shifting from a Christianity-centred or Christ-centred model for viewing the universe of faiths to a God-centred model, we can see the great religions as 'different human responses to the one divine Reality, embodying different perceptions (for example, the concepts of ultimate reality as personal or as impersonal) which have been formed in different historical and cultural circumstances'.

In Christianity, then, Hick argues for thorough reconsideration of the idea of Christ as uniquely the incarnation of God. That idea, properly speaking in terms of our understanding of religious language, is mythological, or poetic imagery. This reconsideration does not require Christians to abandon the reverence for Jesus as the one through whom they have found an effective and saving contact with God. But it does require giving up the negative conclusion that there are no other saving contacts and experiences. Whether it can be established from historical evidence that Christ is the final or supreme disclosure is an open question. And the goal of conversation among religions, or a 'world ecumenism', is not a single world religion but mutual enrichment and a 'mutually interactive system' based on common humanity, common ethical ideals and the search for transformation (salvation/liberation) by a higher spiritual reality.

With Hick in such a generally pluralistic view we may associate the names of the Anglicans Ninian Smart (1981) and Alan Race (1983), Catholic thinkers Raimundo Panikkar (1978, 1981) and Paul Knitter (1985), Stanley J Samartha from the Church of South India (1982), and perhaps the German theologian Jürgen Moltmann (1982). From the Catholic side also, the work of Hans Küng, *Christianity and the World Religions* (1986), shows a partial openness to this more radically pluralistic view. He speaks of a 'global ecumenical consciousness', which will include the community of the great religions, and he seeks a way beyond absolutism and relativism, rejecting a standpoint of superiority that rates one's own religion as *a priori* better. Thus real dialogue aims at 'mutual critical enlightenment, stimulation, penetration and enrichment of the various religious traditions'. Yet Küng is not ready to surrender the normative definitive role of Christology, for that he thinks would alienate him from his faith community.

Ninian Smart, of Lancaster and Santa Barbara, is a better illustration. He writes mainly from the standpoint of a historian of religions. In his Gifford Lectures, *Beyond Ideology* (1981), he argues for a real 'plurality of patterns of basic religious experience', and proposes to speak of 'worldviews' so as to be able to take account of secular ideologies such as Marxism, nationalism and scientism. While dealing with a broad range of worldviews, he focuses particularly on the Christian and Buddhist types of religious experience. Noting the subtle internal complexity of these great traditions (for example, five distinct forms of Christianity), he suggests that Christianity and Buddhism have different dynamics in their alternate ways of representing the transcendent. There are real divergences, so that world views are not reducible to one another. Yet there are also convergences of experience, so that one can speak of Christianity and Buddhism as in important ways mirror images of each other, and of a genuine complementarity of eastern and western views and of religious and secular ideologies generally.

Raimundo Panikkar writes from the unique position of a Roman Catholic priest who was born of a Spanish Catholic mother and an Indian Hindu father and who grew up in both traditions. While continuing to affirm the 'universal Christ' as 'a living symbol for the totality of reality: human, divine, cosmic', and for a dynamic 'non-dualistic' yet 'non-monistic' unity of God, humanity and the world, he has come to reject any exclusive identification of Christ with Jesus or any single historical embodiment. Christians believe that Jesus is the Christ, but this Christ can go by many historical names, as many as there are authentic forms of religiousness. No historical form can be the full and final expression. Thus what is needed is 'dialogical dialogue' in which the partner is considered as another human subject whose convictions can be understood only by somehow sharing them. And so Panikkar can speak of a 'double belonging'. 'I "left" as a Christian; I "found" myself a Hindu; and I "return" as a Buddhist, without having ceased to be a Christian' (see Panikkar, 1978, pp. 1–23, and 1981).

In Jürgen Moltmann, the relativisation of the Christian claim is perhaps less clear than in Hick and Smart, but he too is adamant in rejecting any Christian absolutism and will let the plurality of religions remain. It is just because of the suffering of God in Christ, which is for the reconciliation of the whole world and from which no one is excluded, that Christians must be open and vulnerable in dialogue with other religions. And because Christianity's particular vocation is to prepare the messianic era among the nations (the theology of hope), 'the dialogue with the world religions is part of the wider framework of the liberation of the whole creation for the coming kingdom'. Thus Christianity can come to be a Buddhist, a Hindu, a Muslim, an animist, a Confucian and a Shintoist Christianity. And all religions can be 'charismatically absorbed and changed in the power of the Spirit, not by being Christianised or ecclesiasticised but by being given a messianic direction toward the kingdom' (Moltmann, 1980, pp. 208–09).

It is evident from these brief sketches that the lines of distinction between the various attacks on Christian absolutism are often blurred. Panikkar is at points close to Huston Smith. Hick's vision of a 'mutually interactive system' is not far from Wilfred Cantwell Smith's idea of convergence in the great traditions, or Smart's notion of complementarity. Nearly all of the views are future oriented and look for mutual transformation. And the distinction of Protestant/Catholic is hardly important.

It is equally evident that we see here a major theological shift under way, perhaps what Hick calls a 'Copernican revolution' in Christian theology (or another 'axial period'). For all these ways of dealing with the plurality of religions, it is no longer possible to do Christian theology except in dialogue with other traditions. Just as Catholicism and Protestantism need each other, so Christianity needs the other great traditions in a way not hitherto realised.

If this be so, then in at least one critical area, which I find to be the most interesting area of theological enquiry, we can indeed speak not of a symbiosis but of a synergism of church theology and university studies. Are the thinkers we have been looking at theologians or historians of religion? They are both and must be both. Their work as theologians is necessarily informed by their role as comparativists or historians of religion, subject to all the canons of university enquiry. And their scholarly study of religion is and has to be informed by the theological question of truth and reality and by the relation to their particular community of faith so that they can speak of a theology of religions.

Can such a synergism perhaps be extended throughout the relations of theology in church and university?

Note

1. For much of the material in the latter portion of this article, I have drawn heavily on sections that I have written for the second, revised edition of J Dillenberger and C Welch, *Protestant Christianity*, New York, Macmillan, 1988, and in turn on my *Protestant Thought in the Nineteenth Century*, volume 2 (1870–1914), New Haven, Yale University Press, 1985.

References

Brauer, Jerald C (ed.) (1966) *The Future of Religions*, New York, Harper and Row.
Cobb, John B, Jr (1975) *Christ in a Pluralistic Age*, Philadelphia, Westminster Press.
Cobb, John B, Jr (1982) *Beyond Dialogue: toward a mutual transformation of Christianity and Buddhism*, Philadelphia, Westminster Press.
Hick, John (1973) *God and the Universe of Faiths*, New York, St Martin's Press.
Hick, John (1980) *God Has Many Names*, London, Macmillan.
Hick, John (1984) 'Religious pluralism', in Frank Whaling (ed.), *The World's Religious*

Traditions, Edinburgh, T and T Clark, pp. 147–164.

Huxley, Aldous (1945) *The Perennial Philosophy,* New York, Harper and Brothers.

Knitter, Paul (1985) *No Other Name?,* Maryknoll, New York, Orbis.

Küng, Hans (1976) *On Being a Christian,* New York, Doubleday.

Küng, Hans (1986) *Christianity and the World Religions,* New York, Doubleday.

Lindbeck, George A (1984) *The Nature of Doctrine,* Philadelphia, Westminster Press.

Moltmann, Jürgen (1980) 'Christianity and the world religions', in J Hick and B Hebblethwaite (eds), *Christianity and Other Religions,* London, Collins, pp. 191-211.

Niebuhr, H Richard (1941) *The Meaning of Revelation,* New York, Macmillan.

Panikkar, Raimundo (1978) *The Intrareligious Dialogue,* New York, Paulist Press.

Panikkar, Raimundo (1981) *The Unknown Christ of Hinduism,* Maryknoll, New York, Orbis.

Pannenberg, Wolfhart (1971) *Basic Questions in Theology,* volume 2, Philadelphia, Fortress Press.

Race, Alan (1983) *Christianity and Religious Pluralism: patterns in the Christian theology of religions,* Maryknoll, New York, Orbis.

Rahner, Karl (1966) 'Christianity and the non-Christian religions', in *Theological Investigations,* London, Darton, Longman and Todd, volume 5, pp. 115-134.

Samartha, Stanley J (1982) *Courage for Dialogue: ecumenical issues in inter-religious relationships,* Maryknoll, New York, Orbis.

Smart, Ninian (1981) *Beyond Ideology,* San Francisco, Harper and Row.

Smith, Huston (1976) *Forgotten Truth: the primordial tradition,* New York, Harper and Row.

Smith, Huston (1982) *Beyond the Post-Modern Mind,* New York, Crossroad.

Smith, Wilfred C (1963) *The Meaning and End of Religion: a new approach to the religious traditions of mankind,* New York, Macmillan.

Smith, Wilfred C (1981) *Towards a World Theology: faith and the comparative history of religion,* Philadelphia, Westminster Press.

Thomas, M M (1969) *The Acknowledged Christ of the Indian Renaissance,* London, SCM.

Thomas, M M (1980) 'Modern man and the new humanity in Christ', in E P Nacpil and D J Elwood (eds), *The Human and the Holy: Asian perspectives in Christian theology,* Maryknoll, New York, Orbis, pp. 313-336.

Tillich, Paul (1963) *Christianity and the Encounter of the World Religions,* New York, Columbia University Press.

Troeltsch, Ernst (1923) *Christian Thought: its history and application,* London, University of London Press.

Select bibliography of articles on theology and Christian education

* indicates that the piece is reprinted (in whole or part) in this volume.

Amalorpavadass, D S (1972) 'Catechesis as a pastoral task of the church: the nature, the aim and the process of catechesis', *Lumen Vitae*, 17, pp. 259–280.

Andersen, William E (1983) 'A biblical view of education', *Journal of Christian Education*, 77, pp. 15–30.

Astley, Jeff (1981) 'The idea of God, the reality of God, and religious education', *Theology*, 84, 698, pp. 115–120.

Astley, Jeff (1984) 'The role of worship in Christian learning', *Religious Education*, 79, 2, pp. 243–251.*

Astley, Jeff (1987) 'On learning religion: some theological issues in Christian education', *The Modern Churchman*, 29, 2, pp. 26–34.*

Astley, Jeff (1992) 'Will the real Christianity please stand up?', *British Journal of Religious Education*, 15, 1, pp. 4–12.

Ban, Joseph D (1986) 'Christological foundations of theological education', *Ministerial Formation*, 34, pp. 12–24.

Berntsen, John A (1978) 'Christian affections and the catechumenate', *Worship*, 52, pp. 194–210.*

Bosch, David (1992) 'The nature of theological education', *Theologia Evangelica*, 25, pp. 8–23.

Boys, Mary C (1990) 'The tradition as teacher: repairing the world', *Religious Education*, 85, 3, pp. 346–355.

Braaten, Carl E (1982) 'The contextual factor in theological education', *Dialog*, 21, pp. 169–174.

Brueggemann, Walter (1985) 'Passion and perspective: two dimensions of education in the Bible', *Theology Today*, 42, 2, pp. 172–180.*

Capaldi, Gerard I (1983) 'Christian faith and religious education: a perspective from the theology of liberation', *British Journal of Religious Education*, 6, 1, pp. 31–40.

Chopp, Rebecca S (1990) 'Emerging issues and theological education', *Theological Education*, 26, pp. 106–124.*

Conrad, Robert L (1986) 'A hermeneutic for Christian education', *Religious Education*, 81, 3, pp. 392–400.

Craigie, Peter C (1986) 'Some biblical perspectives on education in the faith', *Touchstone*, 4, 2, pp. 9–16.

Cram, Ronald H (1992) 'Christian education in theological education', *Religious Education*, 87, 3, pp. 331–336.

Dulles, Avery (1992) 'Tradition and creativity in theology', *First Things*, 27, pp. 20–27.

Durka, Gloria (1989) 'Feminist spirituality: restoration and transformation', *British Journal of Religious Education*, 12, 1, pp. 38–44.

Durka, Gloria (1990) 'The changing faces of feminism: a religious educator's view from the United States', *Panorama*, 2, 2, pp. 54–64.

Dykstra, Craig R (1985) 'No longer strangers: the church and its educational ministry', *The Princeton Seminary Bulletin*, 6, 3, pp. 188–200.*

Dykstra, Craig (1987) 'The formative power of the congregation', *Religious Education*, 82, 4, pp. 530–546.*

Dyson, Anthony O (1977) 'The church's educational institutions: some theological considerations', *Theology*, 80, 676, pp. 273–279.

Farley, Edward (1965) 'The strange history of Christian paideia', *Religious Education*, 60, pp. 339–346.

Farley, Edward (1965) 'The work of the Spirit in Christian education', *Religious Education*, 60, 6, pp. 427–436, 479.

Farley, Edward (1981) 'The reform of theological education as a theological task', *Theological Education*, 17, pp. 93–117.

Farley, Edward (1985) 'Can church education be theological education?', *Theology Today*, 42, 2, pp. 158–171.*

Farley, Edward (1985) 'The place of theology in the study of religion', *Religious Studies and Theology*, 5, 3, pp. 9–29.*

Fiorenza, Francis Schüssler (1984) 'Foundational theology and theological education', *Theological Education*, 20, pp. 107–124.

Fiorenza, Francis Schüssler (1987) 'Theology and practice: theological education as a reconstructive, hermeneutical, and practical task', *Theological Education*, 23, supplement, pp. 113–141.

Fiorenza, Francis Schüssler (1988) 'Thinking theologically about theological education', *Theological Education*, 24, supplement 2, pp. 89–119.*

Fowler, James W (1982) 'The RCIA and Christian religious education', *Worship*, 56, pp. 336–343.

Fowler, James W (1985) 'Practical theology and theological education: some models and questions', *Theology Today*, 42, 1, pp. 43–58.

Freire, Paulo (1973) 'Education, liberation and the church', *Study Encounter*, 9, 1, pp. 1–16 (item SE/38 – also published in *Religious Education*, 79, 4, 1984, pp. 524–545).*

Fulkerson, Mary McClintock (1991) 'Theological education and the problem of identity', *Modern Theology*, 7, 5, pp. 465–482.

Grey, Mary C (1989) 'Feminist images of redemption in education', *British Journal of Religious Education*, 12, 1, pp. 20–28.*

Groome, Thomas H (1981) 'Conversion, nurture and educators', *Religious Education*, 76, 5, pp. 482–496.

Groome, Thomas H (1988) 'The spirituality of the religious educator', *Religious Education*, 83, 1, pp. 9–20.

Harris, Maria (1983) 'The imagery of religious education', *Religious Education*, 78, 3, pp. 363–375.

Harris, Maria (1988) 'Art and religious education: a conversation', *Religious Education*, 83, 3, pp. 453–473.

Hauerwas, Stanley (1985) 'The family as a school for character', *Religious Education*, 80, 2, pp. 272–285.

Hauerwas, Stanley (1985) 'The gesture of a truthful story', *Theology Today*, 42, 2, pp. 181–189.*

Hess, Carol Lakey (1991) 'Educating in the Spirit', *Religious Education*, 86, 3, pp. 383–398.*

Hester, David C (1992) 'Christian education in a theological curriculum', *Religious Education*, 87, 3, pp. 337–350.

Heyward, Carter *et al.* (1983) 'Christian feminists speak', *Theological Education*, 20, pp. 93–103.

Heywood, David (1988) 'Christian education as enculturation: the life of the community and its place in Christian education in the work of John H Westerhoff III', *British Journal of Religious Education*, 10, 2, pp. 65–71.

Higgins, Gregory C (1989) 'The significance of postliberalism for religious education', *Religious Education*, 84, 1, pp. 77–89.*

Hill, Brennan (1990) 'Alfred North Whitehead's approach to education: its value for religious education', *Religious Education*, 85, 1, pp. 92–104.

Hough, Joseph C (1984) 'The education of practical theologians', *Theological Education*, 20, pp. 55–84.

Huebner, Dwayne (1986) 'Christian growth in faith', *Religious Education*, 81, 4, pp. 511–521.

Huebner, Dwayne (1987) 'Religious education: practicing the presence of God', *Religious Education*, 82, 4, pp. 569–577.

Hull, John M (1977) 'What is theology of education?', *Scottish Journal of Theology*, 30, 1, pp. 3–29.

Hull, John M (1981) 'Christian nurture and critical openness', *Scottish Journal of Theology*, 34, 1, pp. 17–37.

Jones, Alan W (1979) 'Christian formation and the moral quest (from tadpoles to toads; from Adam to Christ)', *Anglican Theological Review*, 61, 1, pp. 63–86 (responses: pp. 87–105).

Judge, E A (1983) 'The reaction against classical education in the New Testament', *Journal of Christian Education*, 77, pp. 7–14.*

Judge, E A (1983) 'The interaction of biblical and classical education in the fourth century', *Journal of Christian Education*, 77, pp. 31–37.

Kelsey, David H (1985) 'Reflections on Convocation '84: issues in theological education',

Theological Education, 21, pp. 116-131.

Kennedy, William Bean (1985) 'Ideology and education: a fresh approach for religious education', *Religious Education*, 80, 3, pp. 331-344.

Lee, James Michael (1982) 'The authentic source of religious instruction', in Norma H Thompson (ed.) *Religious Education and Theology*, Birmingham, Alabama, Religious Education Press, pp. 100-197.*

Leech, Christopher W J (1989) 'Intentional Christian community and education', *Journal of Christian Education*, 94, pp. 33-39.

Liégé, André (1962) 'The ministry of the word: from kerygma to catechesis', *Lumen Vitae*, 17, pp. 21-36.

Lindbeck, George (1988) 'Spiritual formation and theological education', *Theological Education*, 24, supplement 1, pp. 10-32.*

Loder, James E (1980) 'Transformation in Christian education', *The Princeton Seminary Bulletin*, 3, 1, pp. 11-25 (also published in *Religious Education*, 76, 2, 1981, pp. 204-221).*

Lombaerts, Herman (1984) 'Religious education today and the catechism', *Mount Oliver Review*, 1, 1, pp. 3-15.

Lombaerts, Herman (1990) 'An international perspective on catechetics, with special emphasis on Europe and Latin America', *Living Light*, 26, pp. 304-323.

Marangos, Frank (1984) 'Liberation theology and Christian education theory', *Greek Orthodox Theological Review*, 29, pp. 381-392.*

McDaniel, Jay (1984) 'The role of God in religious education', *Religious Education*, 79, 3, pp. 414-422.

Melchert, Charles F (1990) 'Creation and justice among the sages', *Religious Education*, 85, 3, pp. 368-381.

Melchert, Charles F (1992) 'Wisdom is vindicated by her deeds', *Religious Education*, 87, 1, pp. 127-151.

Miles, Margaret R (1987) 'Hermeneutics of generosity and suspicion: pluralism and theological education', *Theological Education*, 23, supplement, pp. 34-52.

Miller, Randolph Crump (1953) 'Christian education as a theological discipline and method', *Religious Education*, 47, 6, pp. 409-414.

Miller, Randolph Crump (1977) 'Theology and the future of religious education', *Religious Education*, 72, 1, pp. 46-60.

Moore, Allen J (1983) 'Pastoral teaching: a revisionist view', *Quarterly Review*, 3, 3, pp. 63-76.

Moore, Allen J (1987) 'A social theory of religious education', *Religious Education*, 82, 3, pp. 415-425.

Moore, Mary Elizabeth (1989) 'The unity of the sacred and the public possibilities from feminist theology', *Religious Education*, 84, 3, pp. 384-401.*

Nipkow, Karl Ernst (1978) 'Theological and educational concepts: problems of integration and differentiation', *British Journal of Religious Education*, 1, 1, pp. 3-13.*

Pazmiño, Robert W (1992) 'A comprehensive vision for conversion in Christian education', *Religious Education*, 87, 1, pp. 87-101.

Ramsey, Ian T (1965) 'Discernment, commitment, and cosmic disclosure', *Religious Education*, 60, 1, pp. 10-14.

Richard, Lucien (1984) 'Theology and belonging: Christian identity and the doing of theology', *Religious Education*, 79, 3, pp. 392-413.*

Sawicki, Marianne (1986) 'How to teach Christ's disciples: John 1:19-37 and Matthew 11:2-15', *Lexington Theological Quarterly*, 21, pp. 14-26.

Sawicki, Marianne (1990) 'Educational policy and Christian origins', *Religious Education*, 85, 3, pp. 455-477.

Sawicki, Marianne (1991) 'Teaching as a gift of peace', *Theology Today*, 47, 4, pp. 377-387.

Schoonenberg, Piet (1970) 'Revelation and experience', *Lumen Vitae*, 25, pp. 551-560.

Seymour, Jack L (1979) 'Contemporary approaches to Christian education', *The Chicago Theological Seminary Register*, 69, 2, pp. 1-10.*

Slee, Nicola (1989) 'Women's silence in religious education', *British Journal of Religious Education*, 12, 1, pp. 29-37.

Stannus, M H (1972) 'Knowledge of God: the paradox of Christian education', *Educational Philosophy and Theory*, 4, pp. 29-46.

Stockton, Ian (1983) 'Children, church and kingdom', *Scottish Journal of Theology*, 36, 1, pp. 87-97.

Thatcher, Adrian (1983) 'Learning to become persons: a theological approach to educational aims', *Scottish Journal of Theology*, 36, 4, pp. 521-533.

Thistlethwaite, Susan Brooks (1981) 'A handing over of Christ to the people of God', *Education for Social Justice*, 9, pp. 25–30.

Tinsley, John (1980) 'Tell it slant', *Theology*, 83, 693, pp. 163–170.*

Toulmin, Stephen (1990) 'Theology in the context of the university', *Theological Education*, 26, pp. 51–65.*

Tracy, David (1988) 'Can virtue be taught? Education, character, and the soul', *Theological Education*, 24, supplement 1, pp. 33–52.*

van Buren, Paul M (1965) 'Christian education *post mortem dei*', *Religious Education*, 60, 1, pp. 4–10 (responses by Ian Ramsey, Paul Holmer, David Steward, Gordon D Kaufman, and others: pp. 10–48).

Wagner, Mervyn A (1990) 'Christian education as making disciples', *Lutheran Theological Journal*, 24, pp. 69–80.

Welch, Claude (1988) 'Theology: university and church. Is a synergism possible?', *Philosophy and Theology*, 3, 1, pp. 5–23.*

Westerhoff, John H, III (1978) 'Christian education as a theological discipline', *St Luke's Journal of Theology*, 21, 4, pp. 280–288.

Wood, Charles M (1979) 'The knowledge born of obedience', *Anglican Theological Review*, 61, pp. 331–340.

Wood, Charles M (1985) 'Theological inquiry and theological education', *Theological Education*, 21, pp. 73–93 (reprinted in Charles M Wood, *Vision and Discernment: an orientation in theological study*, Atlanta, Georgia, Scholars Press, 1985, pp. 79–95).*

Wood, Charles M (1990) 'Theological education and education for church leadership', *Quarterly Review*, 10, 2, pp. 65–81 (reprinted in Charles M Wood, *An Invitation to Theological Study*, Valley Forge, Pennsylvania, Trinity Press, 1994, ch. 2).*

Wood, Charles M (1991) '"Spiritual formation" and "theological education"', *Religious Education*, 86, 4, pp. 550–561.

Acknowledgements

The publisher and editors would like to acknowledge the following permissions to reproduce copyright material. All possible attempts have been made to contact copyright holders and to acknowledge their copyright correctly. We are grateful to: *British Journal of Religious Education*, for K E Nipkow, 'Theological and educational concepts: problems of integration and differentiation', 1, 3-13, 1978, for M C Grey, 'Feminist images of redemption in education', 12, 20-28, 1989; *Chicago Theological Seminary Register*, for J L Seymour, 'Contemporary approaches to Christian education', 69, 1-10, 1979; *Greek Orthodox Theological Review*, for F Marangos, 'Liberation theology and Christian education theory', 29, 381-392, 1984; *Journal of Christian Education*, for E A Judge, 'The reaction against classical education in the New Testament', 77, 7-14, 1983; *Philosophy and Theology*, for C Welch, 'Theology: university and church. Is a synergism possible?', 3, 5-23, 1988; *The Princeton Seminary Bulletin*, for J E Loder, 'Transformation in Christian education', 3, 11-25, 1980, for C R Dykstra, 'No longer strangers: the church and its educational ministry', 6, 188-200, 1985; *Quarterly Review*, for C M Wood, 'Theological education and education for church leadership', 10, 65-81, 1990 (this article was reprinted as chapter two in C M Wood, *An Invitation to Theological Study*, Valley Forge, Pennsylvania, Trinity Press International, 1994); *Religious Education*, for J Astley, 'The role of worship in Christian learning', 79, 243-251, 1984, for L Richard, 'Theology and belonging: Christian identity and the doing of theology', 79, 392-413, 1984, for C R Dykstra, 'The formative power of the congregation', 82, 530-546, 1987, for G C Higgins, 'The significance of postliberalism for religious education', 84, 77-89, 1989, for M E Moore, 'The unity of the sacred and the public possibilities from feminist theology', 84, 384-401, 1989, for C L Hess, 'Educating in the Spirit', 86, 383-398, 1991 (*Religious Education* is published by the Religious Education Association, 409 Prospect Street, New Haven, CT 06511-2177, USA, membership information available upon request); *Religious Studies and Theology*, for E Farley, 'The place of theology in the study of religion', 5, 9-29, 1985; *Study Encounter*, for P Freire, 'Education, liberation and the church', 9, 1, 1-16, 1973 (© 1973 WCC Publications, World Council of Churches, Geneva, Switzerland); *Theological Education*, for C M Wood, 'Theological inquiry and theological education', 21, 73-93, 1985 (this article was reprinted as chapter five in C M Wood, *Vision and Discernment: an orientation in theological study*, Atlanta, Georgia, Scholars Press, 1985), for G Lindbeck, 'Spiritual formation and theological education', 24, Supplement 1, 10-32, 1988, for D Tracy, 'Can virtue be taught? Education, character and the soul', 24, Supplement 1, 33-52, 1988, for F S Fiorenza, 'Thinking theologically about theological education', 24, Supplement 2, 89-119, 1988, for S Toulmin, 'Theology in the context of the university', 26, 51-65, 1990, for R S Chopp, 'Emerging issues and theological education', 26, 106-124, 1990; *Theology*, for J Tinsley, 'Tell it slant', 83, 163-170, 1980 (*Theology* is published by SPCK); *Theology Today*, for E Farley, 'Can church education be theological education?', 42, 158-171, 1985, for W Brueggemann, 'Passion and perspective: two dimensions of education in the bible', 42, 172-180, 1985, for S Hauerwas, 'The gesture of a truthful story', 42, 181-189, 1985; *Worship*, for J A Berntsen, 'Christian affections and the catechumenate', 52, 194-210, 1978; Religious Education Press, for J M Lee, 'Religious education and theology', abbreviated from 'The authentic source of religious instruction', in N Thompson (ed.), *Religious Education and Theology*, Birmingham, Alabama, Religious Education Press, 100-197, 1982.

Index of subjects

process 133–4
professionalisation of 39–40
see also Postliberalism in theology;
   Liberation theology; Feminist
   theology
THEORY OF CHRISTIAN
   EDUCATION XII, 1–68, 270
   consistency of 59–60
   fruitfulness of 58–9
Torah 73, 78–9
Tradition 146–65, 301, 351–4, 388
   cumulative 435–6
Transcendence 328, 382
Transformation 253–6, 270–84
Transmission xv, 147, 351–4
Trust 247

UNDERSTANDING 348
   in religion 263–4, 348
   theological 412–3
Universal religiosity 142, 419, 435–6
University 359, 391–443
   theological education in xi, xvi–xviii,
      391–443
Upbringing, religious *see* Formation,

Christian/religious; Nurture,
   Christian/religious

Variety of religions 432–42
Virtue(s) 287, 374–89 *see also*
   Attitude–virtues
Vision 342–6
Vulnerability 129–30

Web of belief 297
Widow of Zarephath 208, 213
Wisdom 31–7, 74–9, 130
Woman with haemorrhage 208–9, 213
World historical horizon 328–9
Worldview 103 *see also* Ideology
WORSHIP 245–7, 259–63
   and Christian education 40, 113,
      227–65
   and religious language 246–7
   evoking religious experience/belief
      227–65
   redemptive power of 259–63

Zeal 237–8

Index of names